MY FAVORITE THING IS MONSTERS

BOOK TWO

EMIL FERRIS

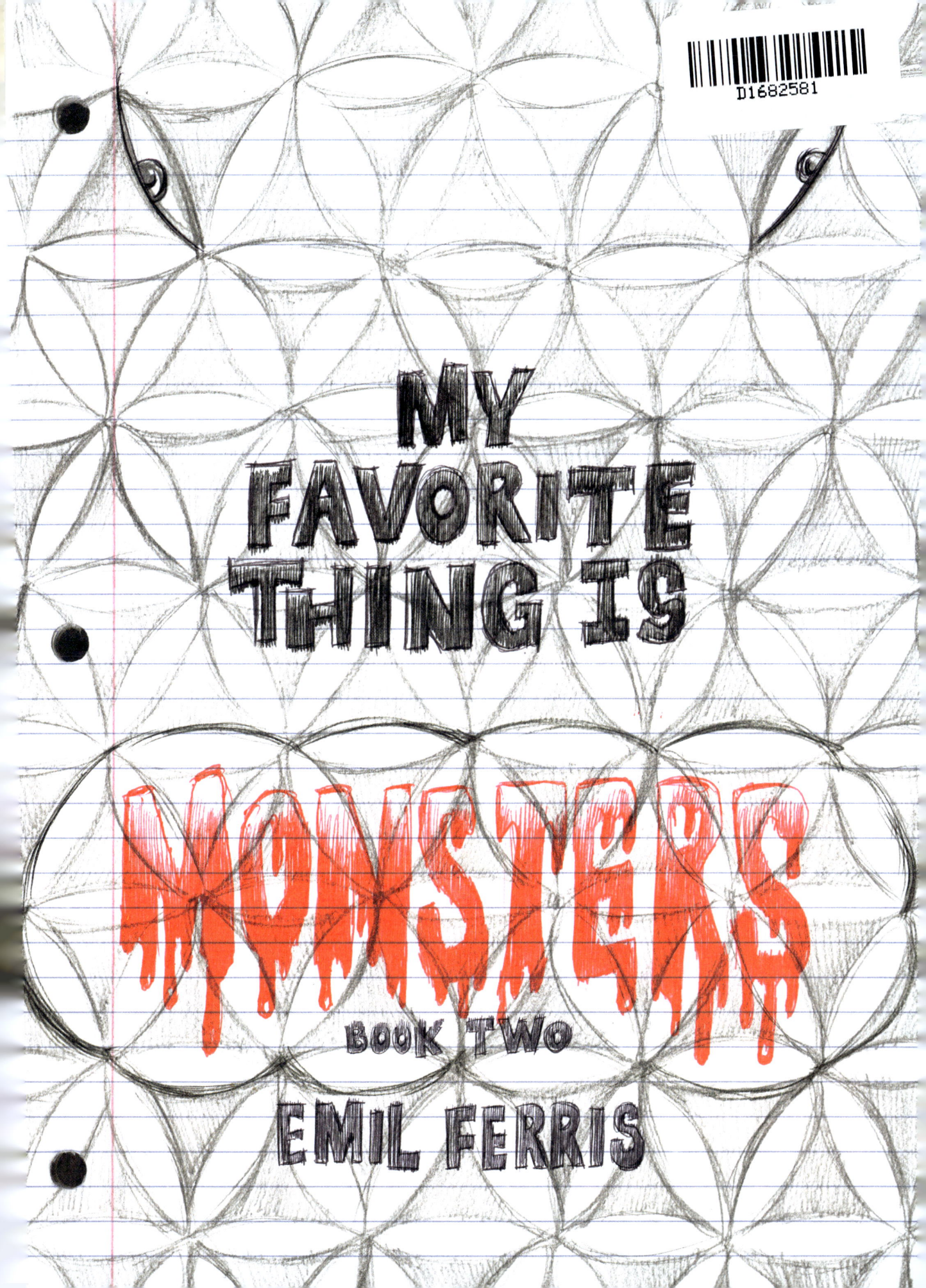

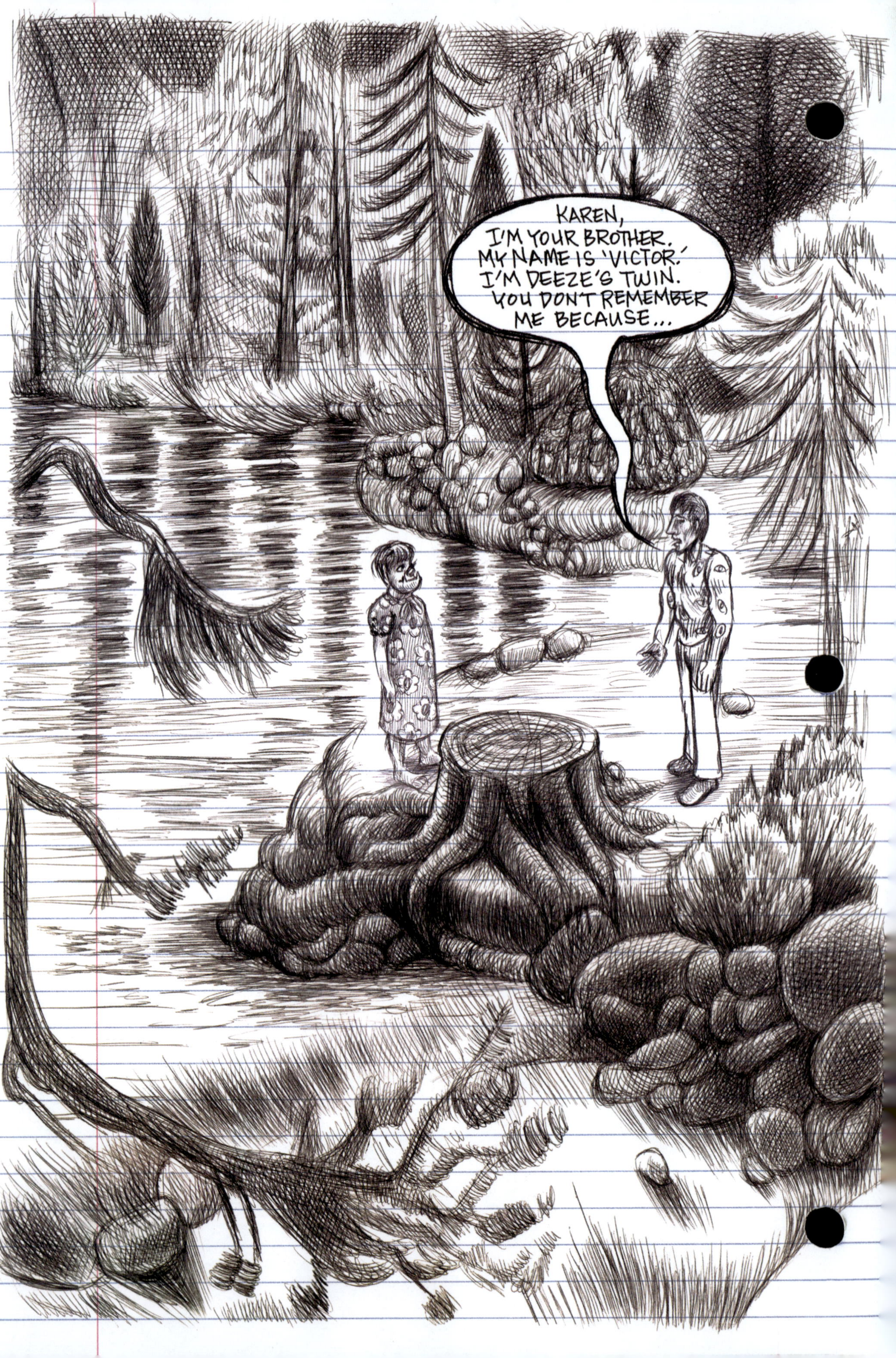
KAREN, I'M YOUR BROTHER. MY NAME IS 'VICTOR.' I'M DEEZE'S TWIN. YOU DON'T REMEMBER ME BECAUSE...

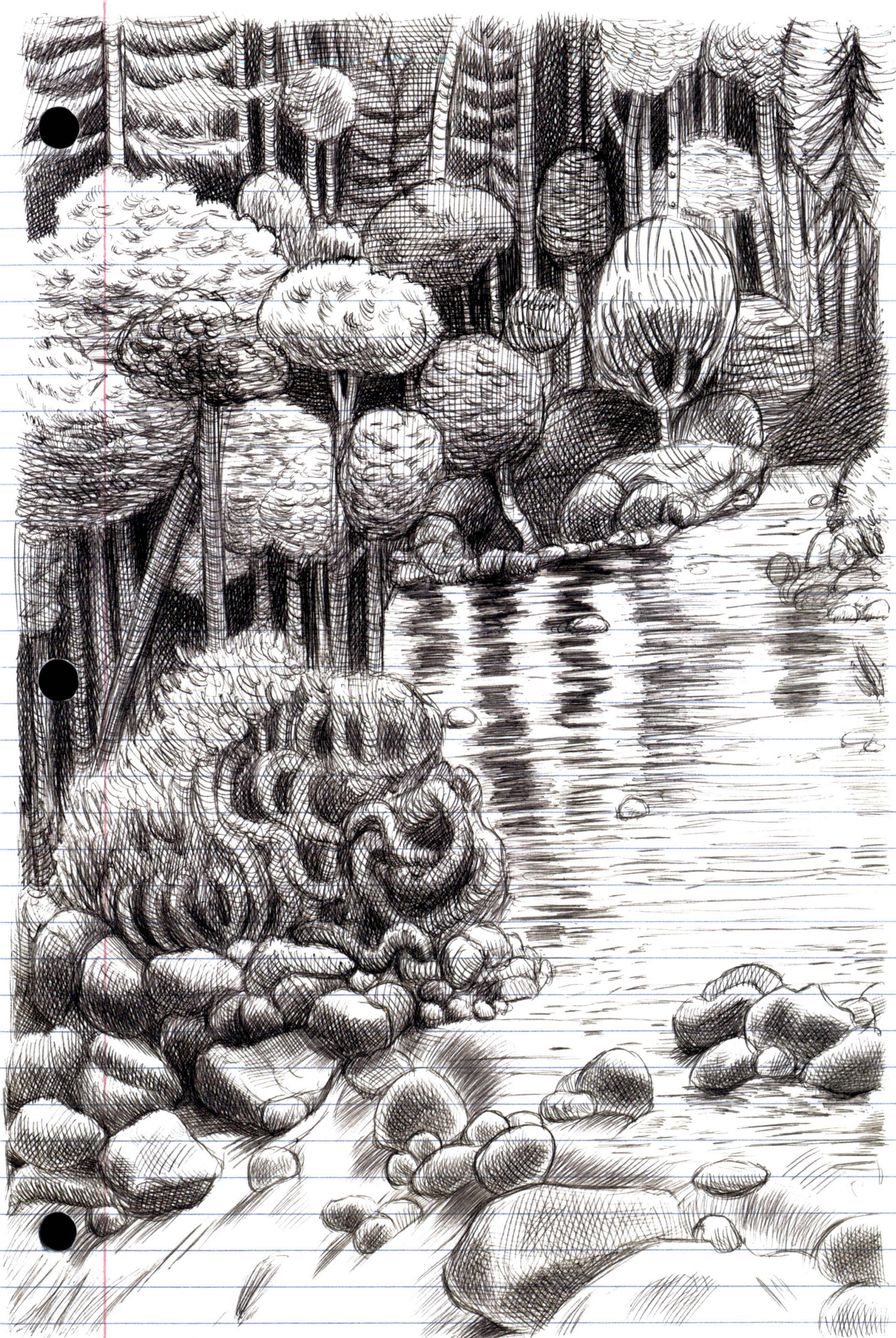

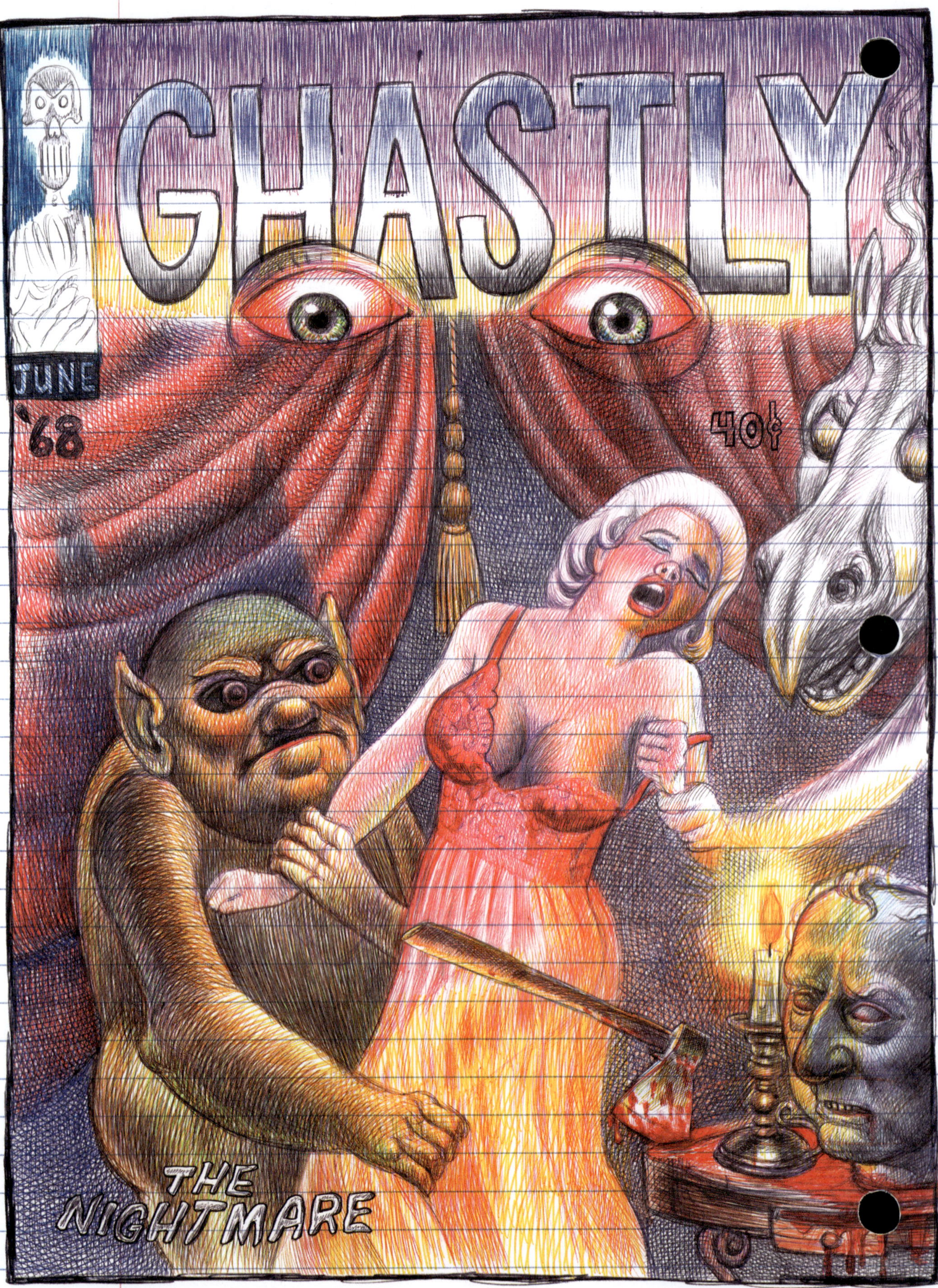
GHASTLY
JUNE
'68
40¢
THE NIGHTMARE

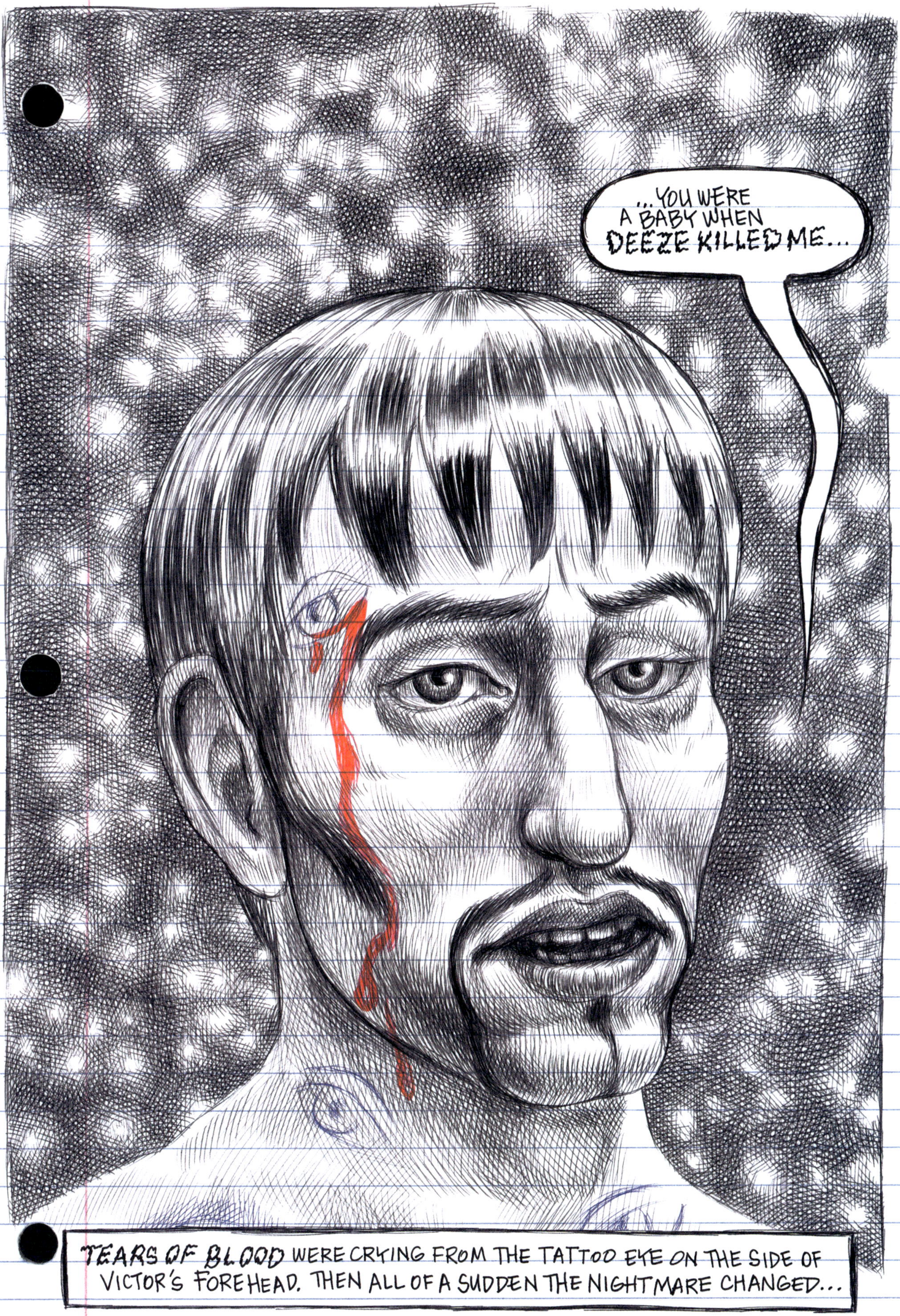
...YOU WERE A BABY WHEN DEEZE KILLED ME...
TEARS OF BLOOD WERE CRYING FROM THE TATTOO EYE ON THE SIDE OF VICTOR'S FOREHEAD. THEN ALL OF A SUDDEN THE NIGHTMARE CHANGED...

...AND I WAS SCARED AND RUNNING FROM *SOMEBODY OR SOMETHING* I COULDN'T SEE.

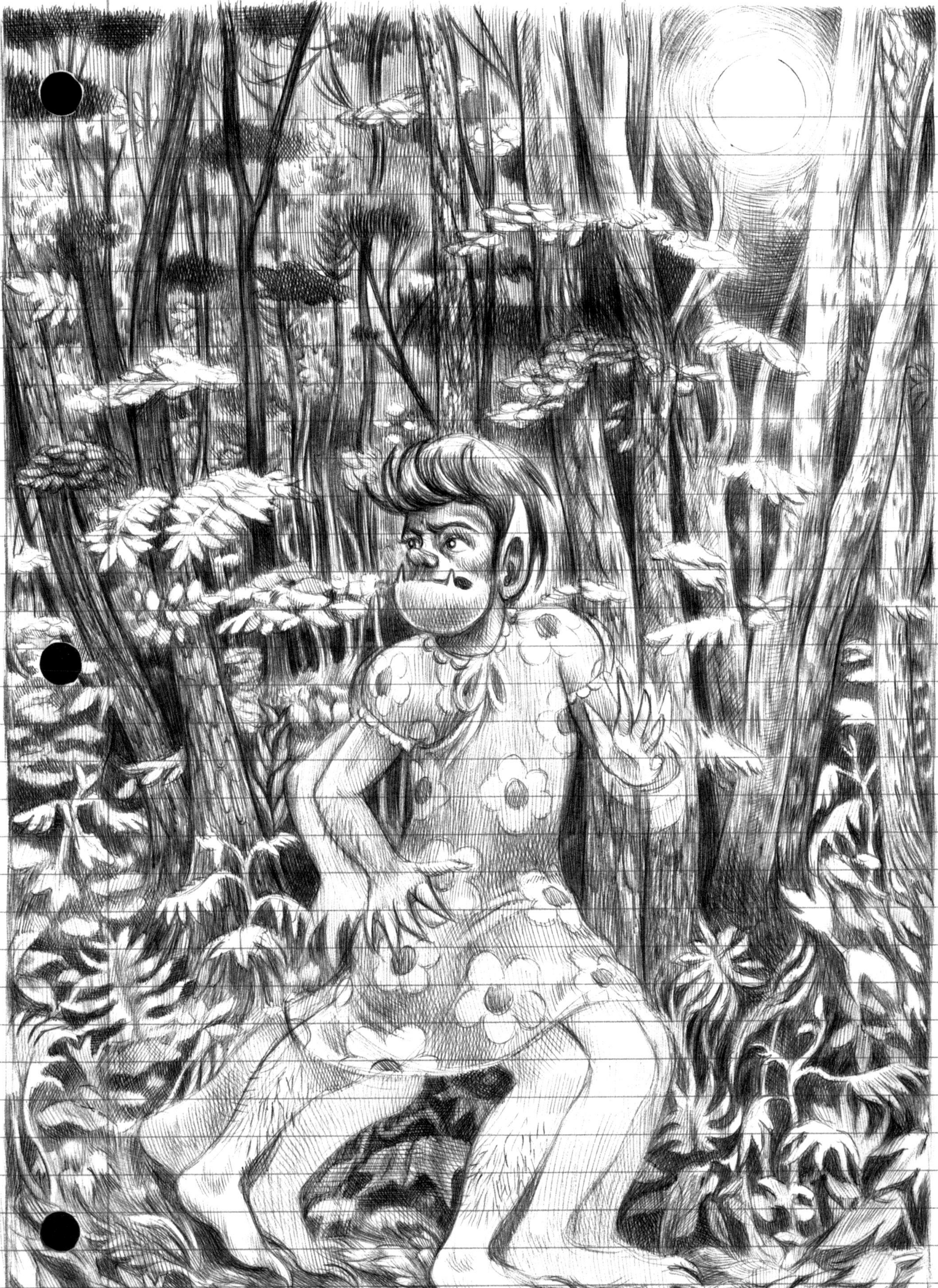

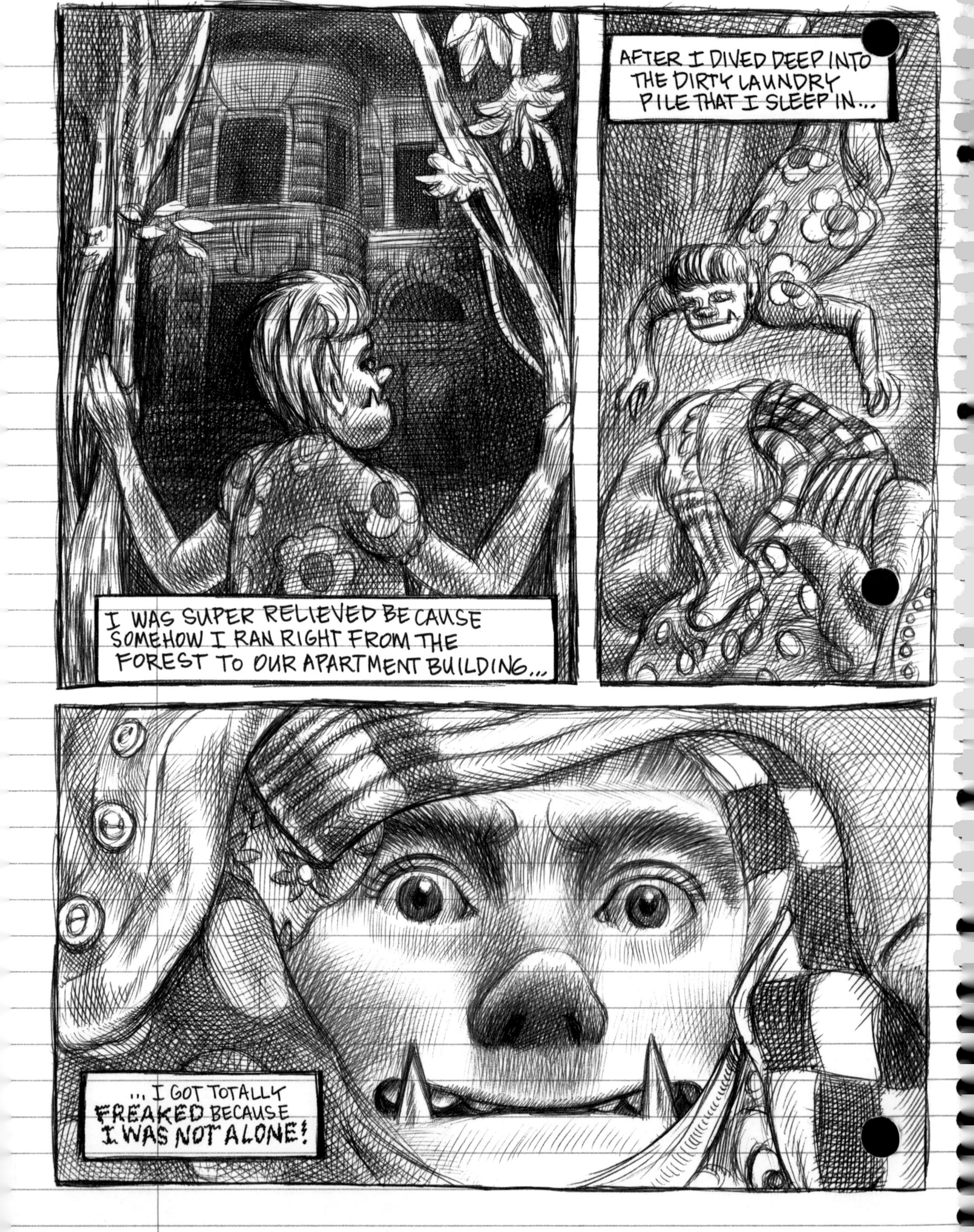
I WAS SUPER RELIEVED BECAUSE SOMEHOW I RAN RIGHT FROM THE FOREST TO OUR APARTMENT BUILDING...
AFTER I DIVED DEEP INTO THE DIRTY LAUNDRY PILE THAT I SLEEP IN...
... I GOT TOTALLY FREAKED BECAUSE I WAS NOT ALONE!

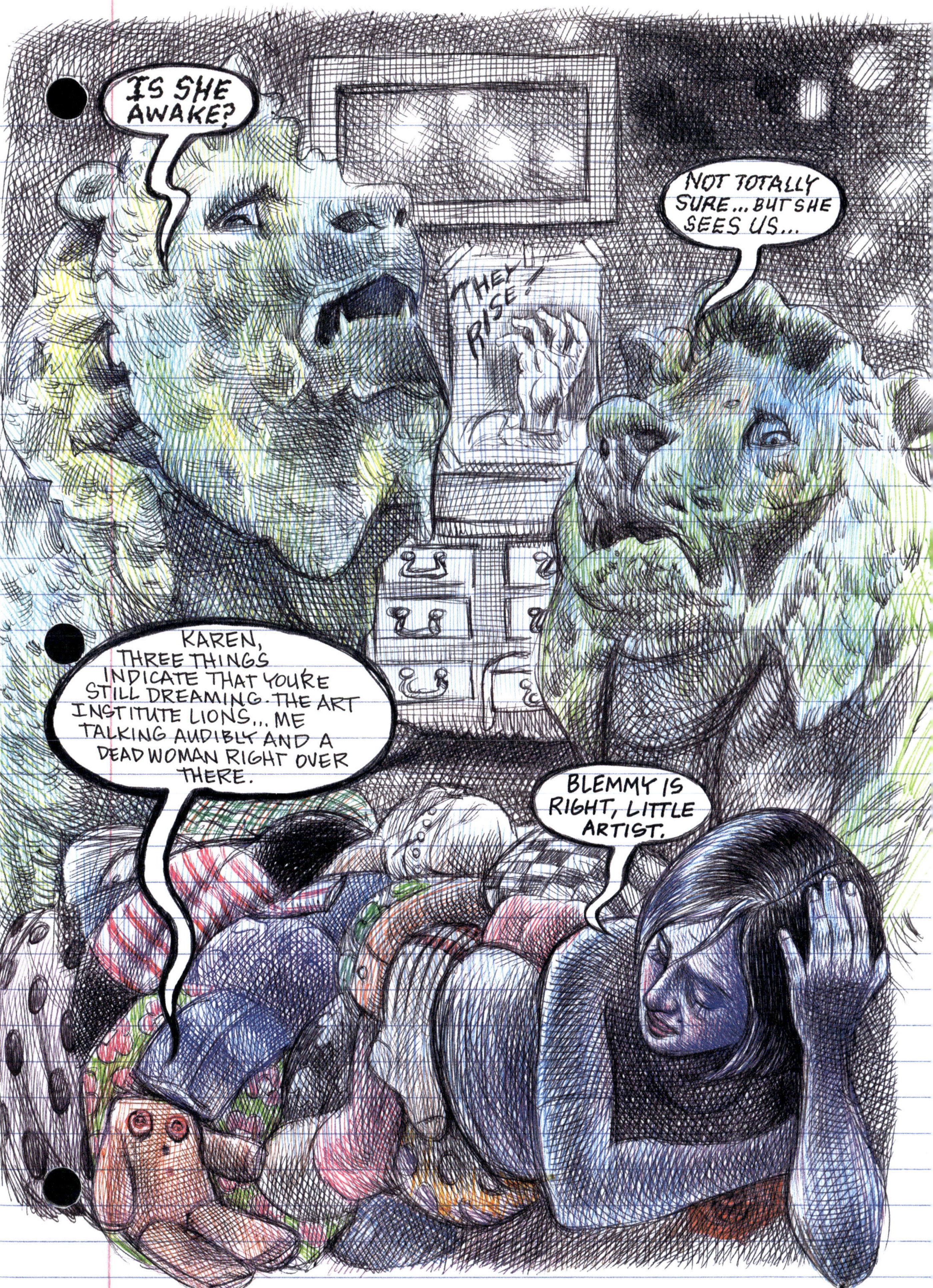
IS SHE AWAKE?
NOT TOTALLY SURE... BUT SHE SEES US...
THEY RISE!
KAREN, THREE THINGS INDICATE THAT YOU'RE STILL DREAMING. THE ART INSTITUTE LIONS... ME TALKING AUDIBLY AND A DEAD WOMAN RIGHT OVER THERE.
BLEMMY IS RIGHT, LITTLE ARTIST.

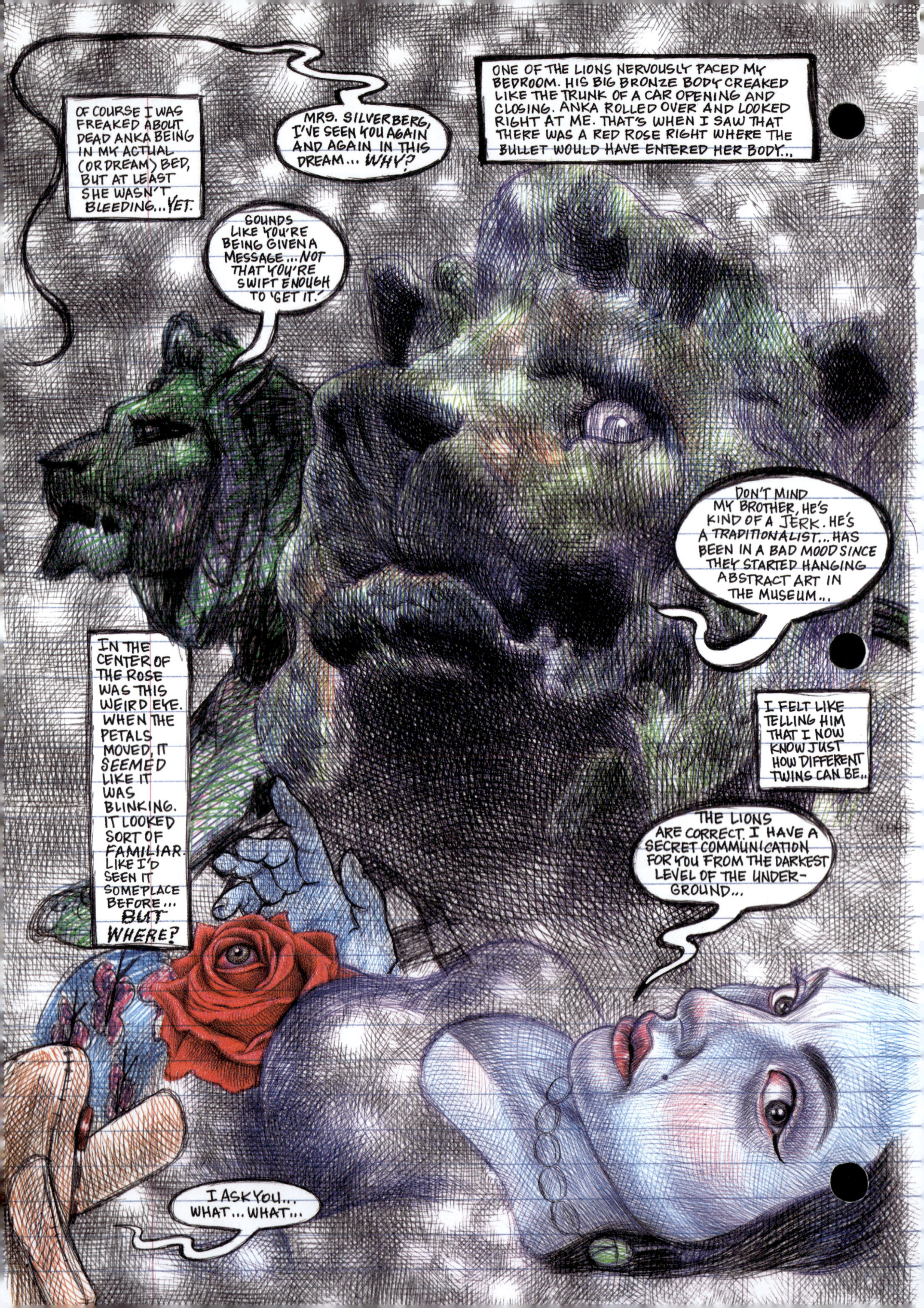
OF COURSE I WAS FREAKED ABOUT DEAD ANKA BEING IN MY ACTUAL (OR DREAM) BED, BUT AT LEAST SHE WASN'T BLEEDING... YET.
MRS. SILVERBERG, I'VE SEEN YOU AGAIN AND AGAIN IN THIS DREAM... WHY?
ONE OF THE LIONS NERVOUSLY PACED MY BEDROOM. HIS BIG BRONZE BODY CREAKED LIKE THE TRUNK OF A CAR OPENING AND CLOSING. ANKA ROLLED OVER AND LOOKED RIGHT AT ME. THAT'S WHEN I SAW THAT THERE WAS A RED ROSE RIGHT WHERE THE BULLET WOULD HAVE ENTERED HER BODY...
SOUNDS LIKE YOU'RE BEING GIVEN A MESSAGE... NOT THAT YOU'RE SWIFT ENOUGH TO 'GET IT.'
DON'T MIND MY BROTHER, HE'S KIND OF A JERK. HE'S A TRADITIONALIST... HAS BEEN IN A BAD MOOD SINCE THEY STARTED HANGING ABSTRACT ART IN THE MUSEUM...
IN THE CENTER OF THE ROSE WAS THIS WEIRD EYE. WHEN THE PETALS MOVED, IT SEEMED LIKE IT WAS BLINKING. IT LOOKED SORT OF FAMILIAR. LIKE I'D SEEN IT SOMEPLACE BEFORE... BUT WHERE?
I FELT LIKE TELLING HIM THAT I NOW KNOW JUST HOW DIFFERENT TWINS CAN BE...
THE LIONS ARE CORRECT. I HAVE A SECRET COMMUNICATION FOR YOU FROM THE DARKEST LEVEL OF THE UNDERGROUND...
I ASK YOU... WHAT... WHAT...

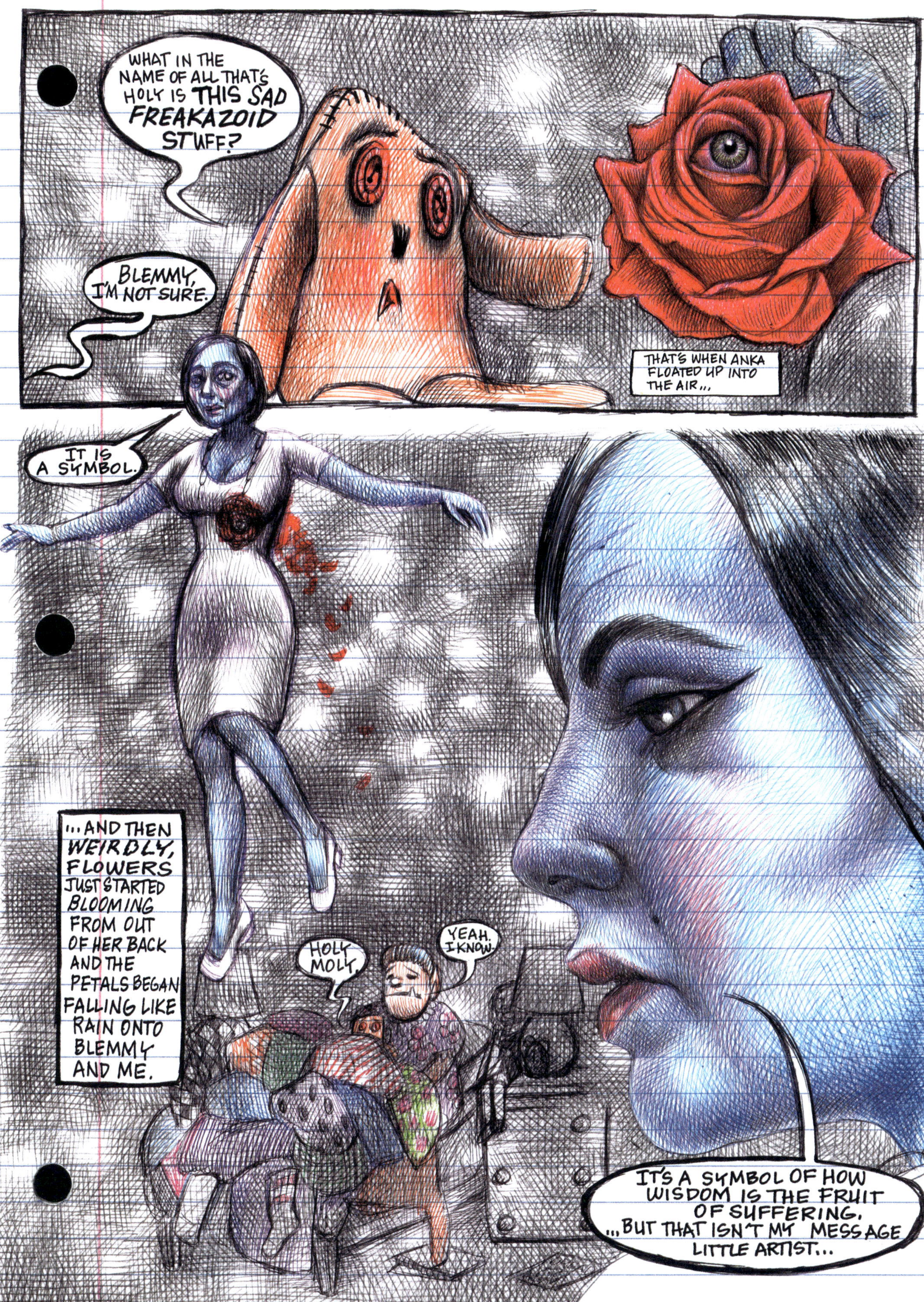
WHAT IN THE NAME OF ALL THAT'S HOLY IS THIS SAD FREAKAZOID STUFF?
BLEMMY, I'M NOT SURE.
THAT'S WHEN ANKA FLOATED UP INTO THE AIR...
IT IS A SYMBOL.
...AND THEN WEIRDLY, FLOWERS JUST STARTED BLOOMING FROM OUT OF HER BACK AND THE PETALS BEGAN FALLING LIKE RAIN ONTO BLEMMY AND ME.
HOLY MOLY.
YEAH. I KNOW.
IT'S A SYMBOL OF HOW WISDOM IS THE FRUIT OF SUFFERING. ...BUT THAT ISN'T MY MESSAGE LITTLE ARTIST...

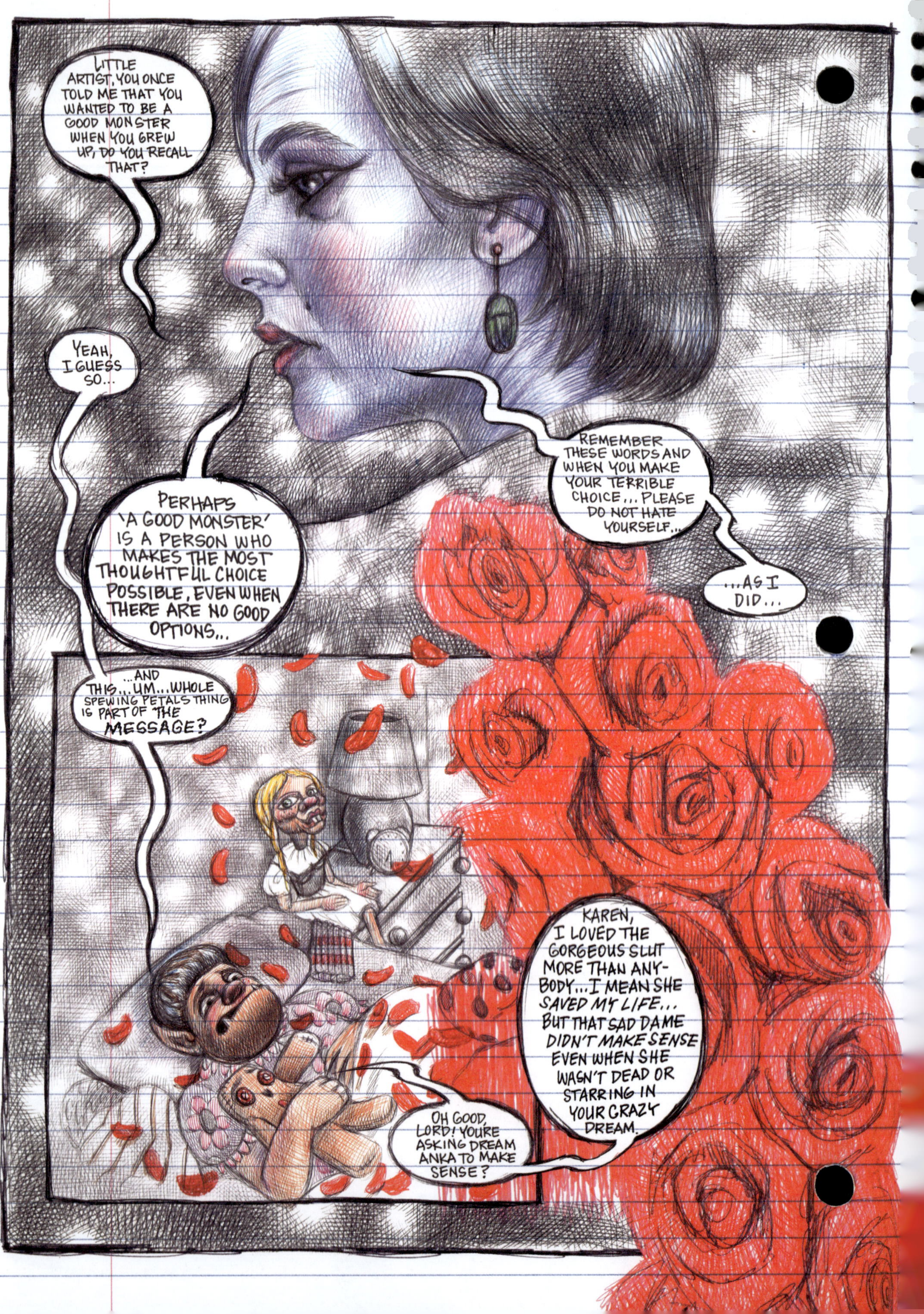
LITTLE ARTIST, YOU ONCE TOLD ME THAT YOU WANTED TO BE A GOOD MONSTER WHEN YOU GREW UP, DO YOU RECALL THAT?
YEAH, I GUESS SO...
PERHAPS 'A GOOD MONSTER' IS A PERSON WHO MAKES THE MOST THOUGHTFUL CHOICE POSSIBLE, EVEN WHEN THERE ARE NO GOOD OPTIONS...
REMEMBER THESE WORDS AND WHEN YOU MAKE YOUR TERRIBLE CHOICE... PLEASE DO NOT HATE YOURSELF...
...AS I DID...
...AND THIS...UM...WHOLE SPEWING PETALS THING IS PART OF THE MESSAGE?
KAREN, I LOVED THE GORGEOUS SLUT MORE THAN ANYBODY...I MEAN SHE SAVED MY LIFE... BUT THAT SAD DAME DIDN'T MAKE SENSE EVEN WHEN SHE WASN'T DEAD OR STARRING IN YOUR CRAZY DREAM.
OH GOOD, LORD! YOU'RE ASKING DREAM ANKA TO MAKE SENSE?

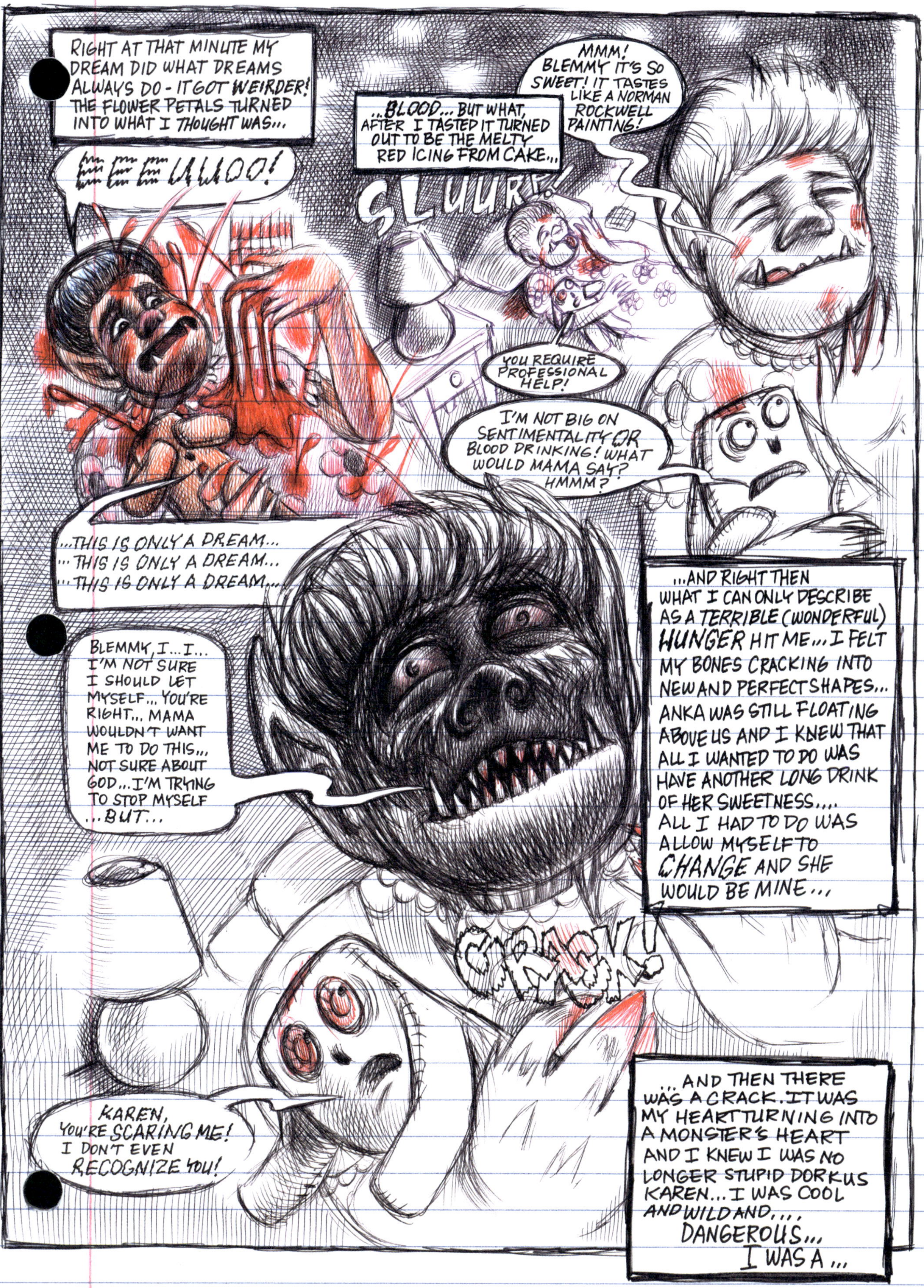
RIGHT AT THAT MINUTE MY DREAM DID WHAT DREAMS ALWAYS DO - IT GOT WEIRDER! THE FLOWER PETALS TURNED INTO WHAT I THOUGHT WAS...
EEEUUOO!
...BLOOD... BUT WHAT, AFTER I TASTED IT TURNED OUT TO BE THE MELTY RED ICING FROM CAKE...
MMM! BLEMMY IT'S SO SWEET! IT TASTES LIKE A NORMAN ROCKWELL PAINTING!
SLUURP!
YOU REQUIRE PROFESSIONAL HELP!
I'M NOT BIG ON SENTIMENTALITY OR BLOOD DRINKING! WHAT WOULD MAMA SAY? HMMM?
...THIS IS ONLY A DREAM... ...THIS IS ONLY A DREAM... ...THIS IS ONLY A DREAM...
BLEMMY, I...I... I'M NOT SURE I SHOULD LET MYSELF... YOU'RE RIGHT... MAMA WOULDN'T WANT ME TO DO THIS... NOT SURE ABOUT GOD... I'M TRYING TO STOP MYSELF ...BUT...
...AND RIGHT THEN WHAT I CAN ONLY DESCRIBE AS A TERRIBLE (WONDERFUL) HUNGER HIT ME... I FELT MY BONES CRACKING INTO NEW AND PERFECT SHAPES... ANKA WAS STILL FLOATING ABOVE US AND I KNEW THAT ALL I WANTED TO DO WAS HAVE ANOTHER LONG DRINK OF HER SWEETNESS.... ALL I HAD TO DO WAS ALLOW MYSELF TO CHANGE AND SHE WOULD BE MINE...
CRACK!
KAREN, YOU'RE SCARING ME! I DON'T EVEN RECOGNIZE YOU!
...AND THEN THERE WAS A CRACK. IT WAS MY HEART TURNING INTO A MONSTER'S HEART AND I KNEW I WAS NO LONGER STUPID DORKUS KAREN... I WAS COOL AND WILD AND.... DANGEROUS... I WAS A...

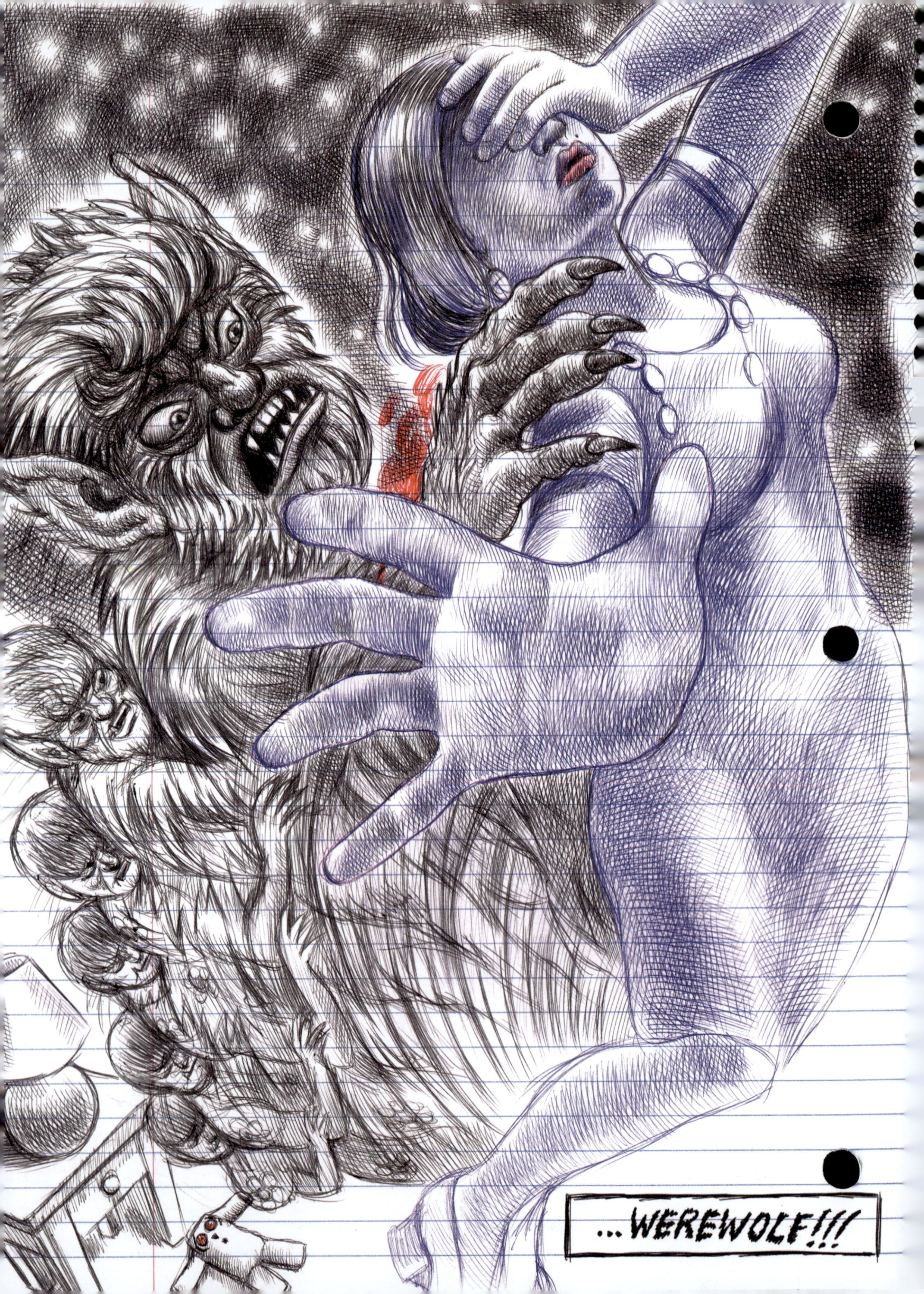
...WEREWOLF!!!

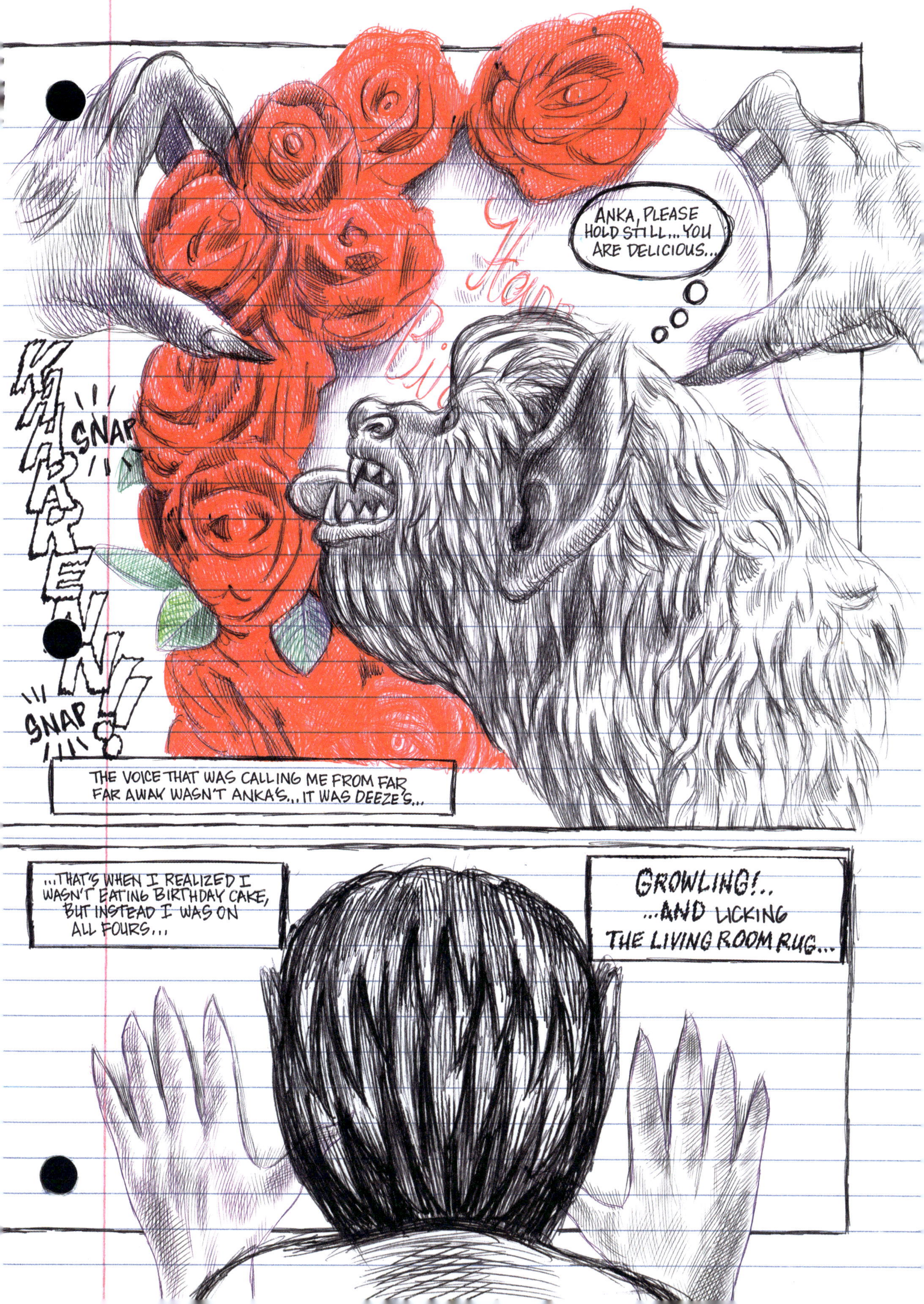
ANKA, PLEASE HOLD STILL... YOU ARE DELICIOUS...
KHAAKEVN!
SNAP
SNAP
THE VOICE THAT WAS CALLING ME FROM FAR FAR AWAK WASN'T ANKA'S... IT WAS DEEZE'S...
...THAT'S WHEN I REALIZED I WASN'T EATING BIRTHDAY CAKE, BUT INSTEAD I WAS ON ALL FOURS...
GROWLING!.. ...AND LICKING THE LIVING ROOM RUG...

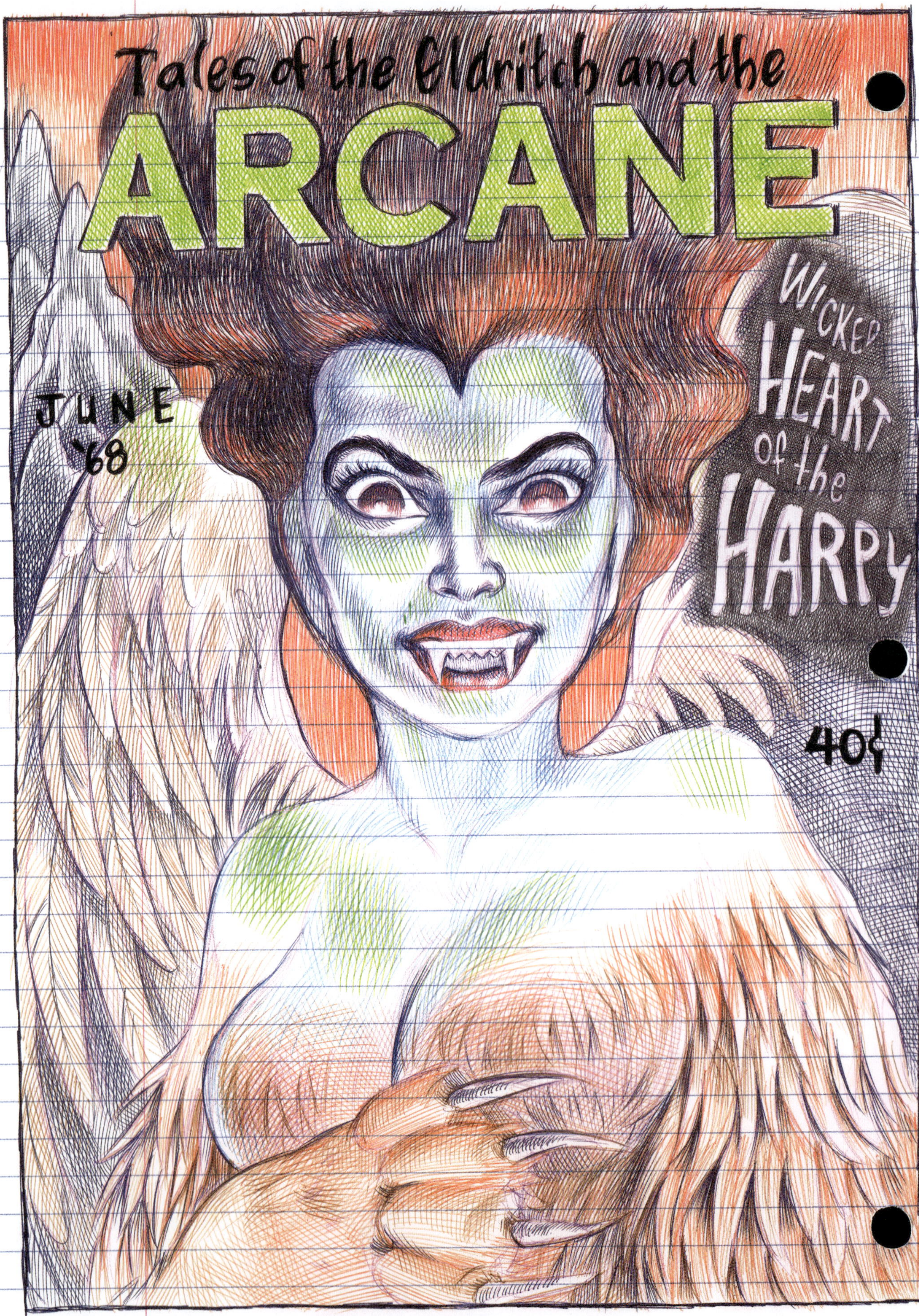
Tales of the Eldritch and the
ARCANE
JUNE
'68
WICKED
HEART
of the
HARPY
40¢

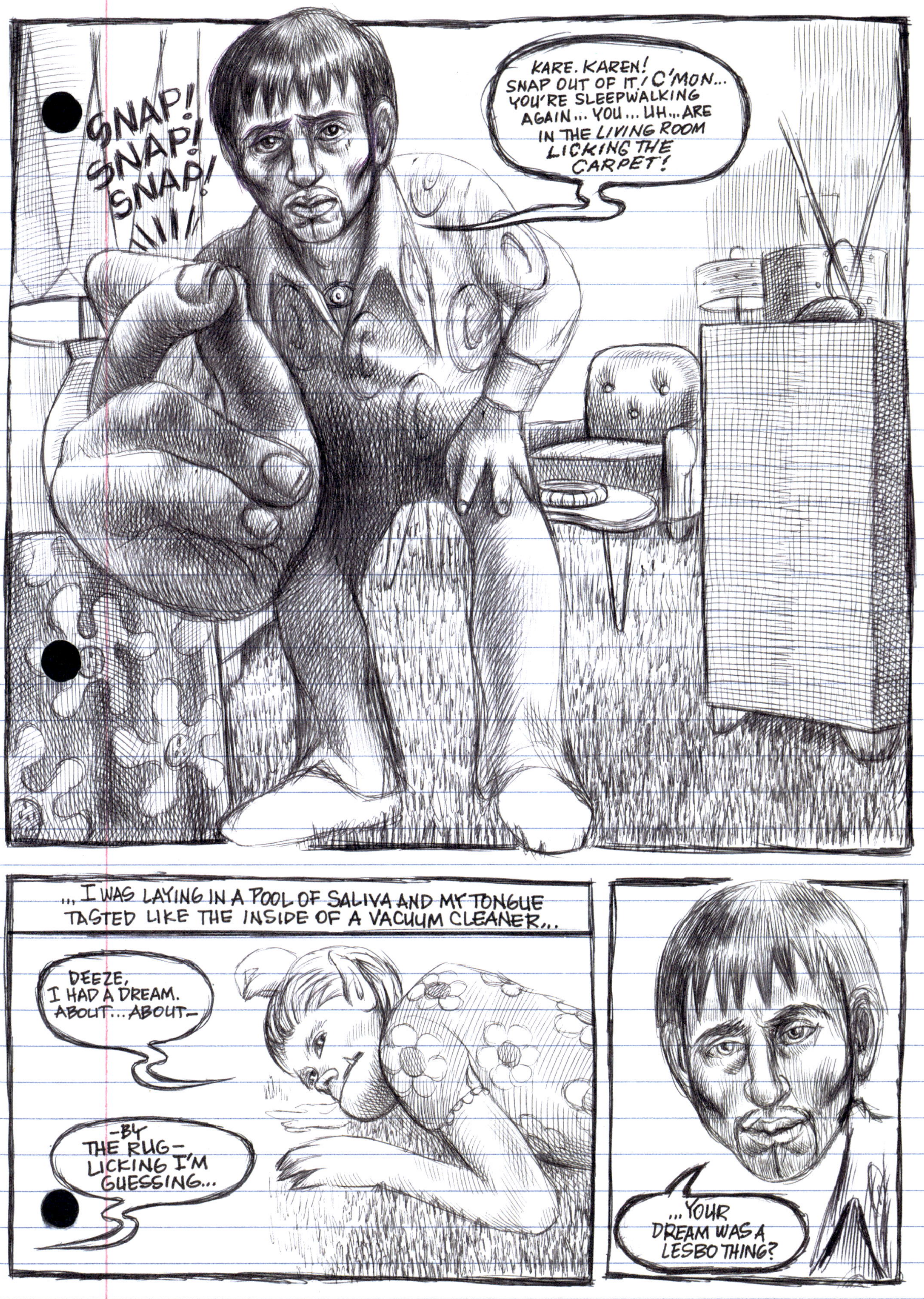
SNAP! SNAP! SNAP!
KARE. KAREN! SNAP OUT OF IT! C'MON... YOU'RE SLEEPWALKING AGAIN... YOU... UH... ARE IN THE LIVING ROOM LICKING THE CARPET!
...I WAS LAYING IN A POOL OF SALIVA AND MY TONGUE TASTED LIKE THE INSIDE OF A VACUUM CLEANER...
DEEZE, I HAD A DREAM. ABOUT... ABOUT—
—BY THE RUG-LICKING I'M GUESSING...
...YOUR DREAM WAS A LESBO THING?

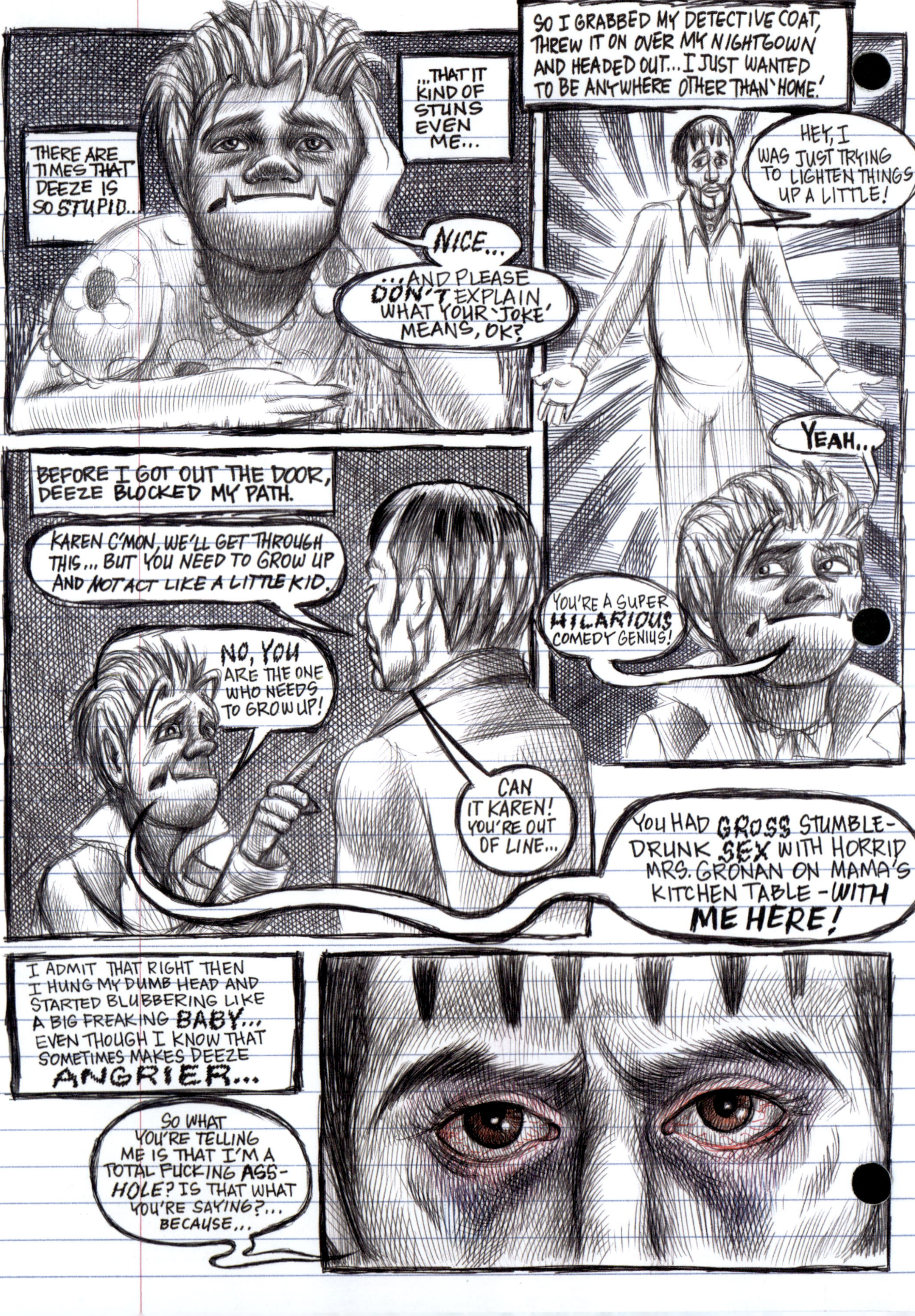
THERE ARE TIMES THAT DEEZE IS SO STUPID...
...THAT IT KIND OF STUNS EVEN ME...
NICE...
...AND PLEASE DON'T EXPLAIN WHAT YOUR 'JOKE' MEANS, OK?
SO I GRABBED MY DETECTIVE COAT, THREW IT ON OVER MY NIGHTGOWN AND HEADED OUT... I JUST WANTED TO BE ANYWHERE OTHER THAN 'HOME.'
HEY, I WAS JUST TRYING TO LIGHTEN THINGS UP A LITTLE!
YEAH...
YOU'RE A SUPER HILARIOUS COMEDY GENIUS!
BEFORE I GOT OUT THE DOOR, DEEZE BLOCKED MY PATH.
KAREN C'MON, WE'LL GET THROUGH THIS... BUT YOU NEED TO GROW UP AND NOT ACT LIKE A LITTLE KID.
NO, YOU ARE THE ONE WHO NEEDS TO GROW UP!
CAN IT KAREN! YOU'RE OUT OF LINE...
YOU HAD GROSS STUMBLE-DRUNK SEX WITH HORRID MRS. GRONAN ON MAMA'S KITCHEN TABLE - WITH ME HERE!
I ADMIT THAT RIGHT THEN I HUNG MY DUMB HEAD AND STARTED BLUBBERING LIKE A BIG FREAKING BABY... EVEN THOUGH I KNOW THAT SOMETIMES MAKES DEEZE ANGRIER...
SO WHAT YOU'RE TELLING ME IS THAT I'M A TOTAL FUCKING ASS-HOLE? IS THAT WHAT YOU'RE SAYING?... BECAUSE...

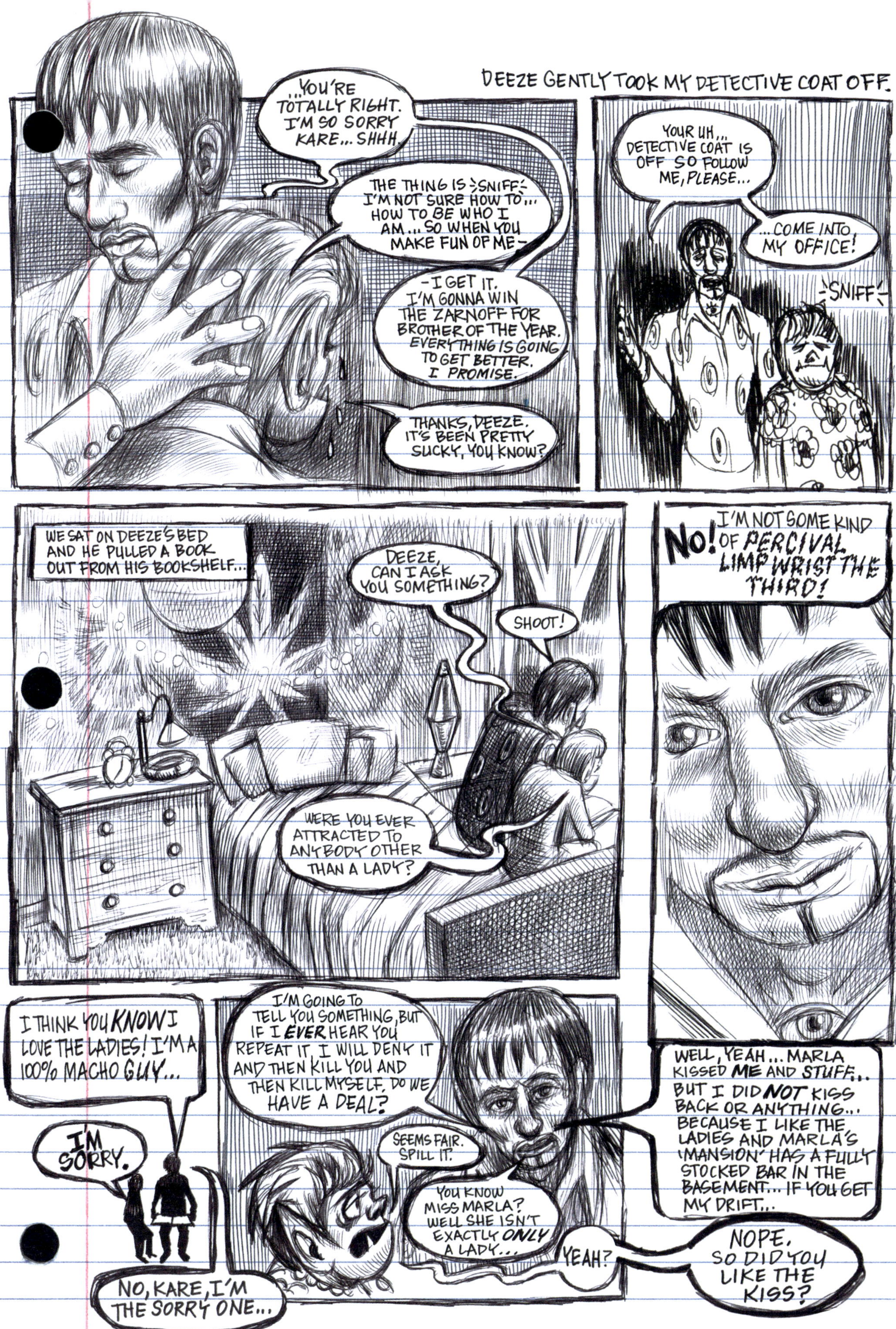

DEEZE GENTLY TOOK MY DETECTIVE COAT OFF.
...YOU'RE TOTALLY RIGHT. I'M SO SORRY KARE... SHHH.
THE THING IS -SNIFF- I'M NOT SURE HOW TO... HOW TO BE WHO I AM... SO WHEN YOU MAKE FUN OF ME-
-I GET IT. I'M GONNA WIN THE ZARNOFF FOR BROTHER OF THE YEAR. EVERYTHING IS GOING TO GET BETTER. I PROMISE.
THANKS, DEEZE. IT'S BEEN PRETTY SUCKY, YOU KNOW?
YOUR UH... DETECTIVE COAT IS OFF SO FOLLOW ME, PLEASE...
...COME INTO MY OFFICE!
-SNIFF-
WE SAT ON DEEZE'S BED AND HE PULLED A BOOK OUT FROM HIS BOOKSHELF...
DEEZE, CAN I ASK YOU SOMETHING?
SHOOT!
WERE YOU EVER ATTRACTED TO ANYBODY OTHER THAN A LADY?
NO! I'M NOT SOME KIND OF PERCIVAL LIMP WRIST THE THIRD!
I THINK YOU KNOW I LOVE THE LADIES! I'M A 100% MACHO GUY...
I'M SORRY.
NO, KARE, I'M THE SORRY ONE...
I'M GOING TO TELL YOU SOMETHING, BUT IF I EVER HEAR YOU REPEAT IT, I WILL DENY IT AND THEN KILL YOU AND THEN KILL MYSELF. DO WE HAVE A DEAL?
SEEMS FAIR. SPILL IT.
YOU KNOW MISS MARLA? WELL SHE ISN'T EXACTLY ONLY A LADY...
YEAH?
NOPE. SO DID YOU LIKE THE KISS?
WELL, YEAH... MARLA KISSED ME AND STUFF... BUT I DID NOT KISS BACK OR ANYTHING... BECAUSE I LIKE THE LADIES AND MARLA'S 'MANSION' HAS A FULLY STOCKED BAR IN THE BASEMENT... IF YOU GET MY DRIFT...

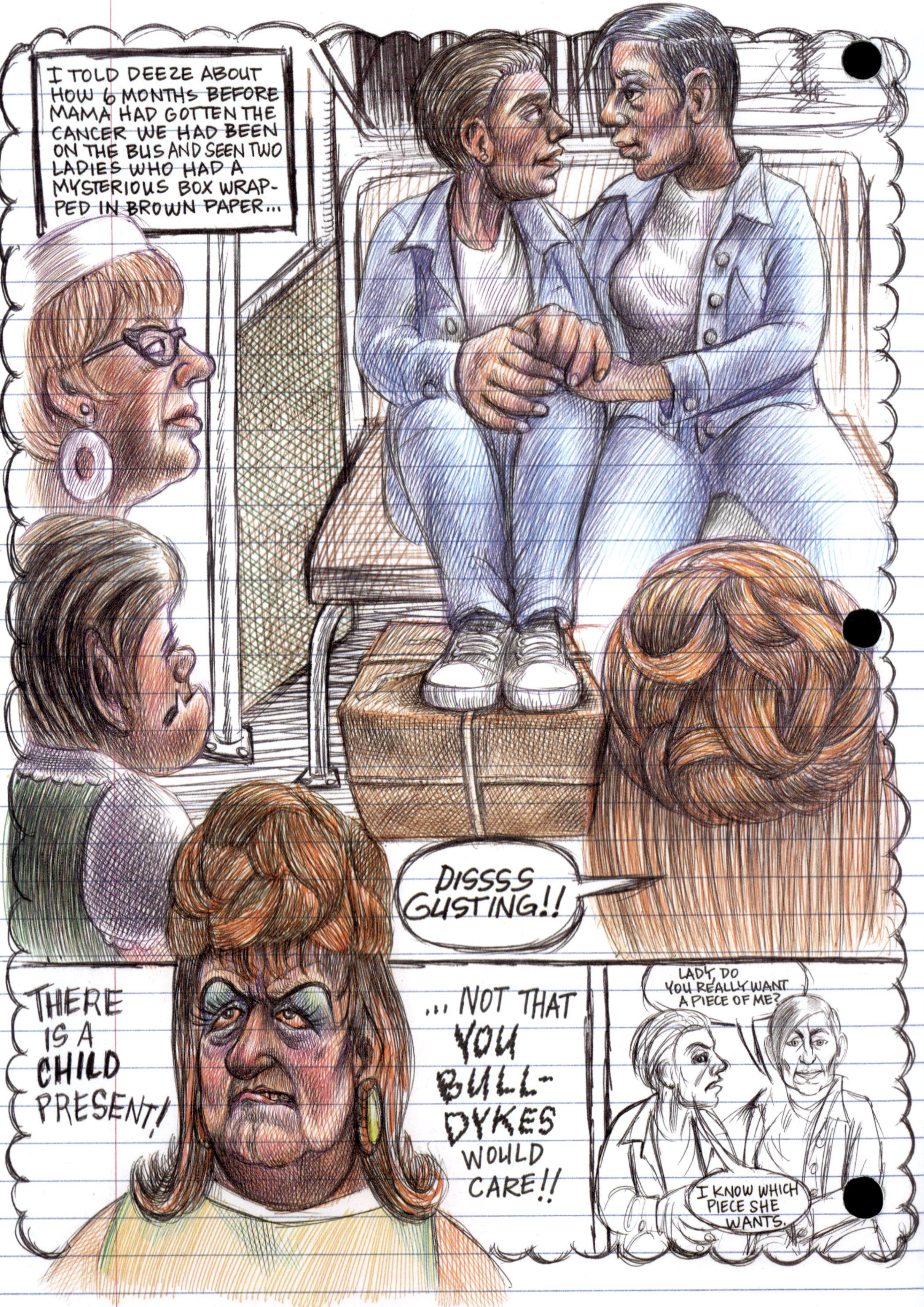
I TOLD DEEZE ABOUT HOW 6 MONTHS BEFORE MAMA HAD GOTTEN THE CANCER WE HAD BEEN ON THE BUS AND SEEN TWO LADIES WHO HAD A MYSTERIOUS BOX WRAPPED IN BROWN PAPER...
DISSSS GUSTING!!
THERE IS A CHILD PRESENT!
...NOT THAT YOU BULL-DYKES WOULD CARE!!
LADY, DO YOU REALLY WANT A PIECE OF ME?
I KNOW WHICH PIECE SHE WANTS.

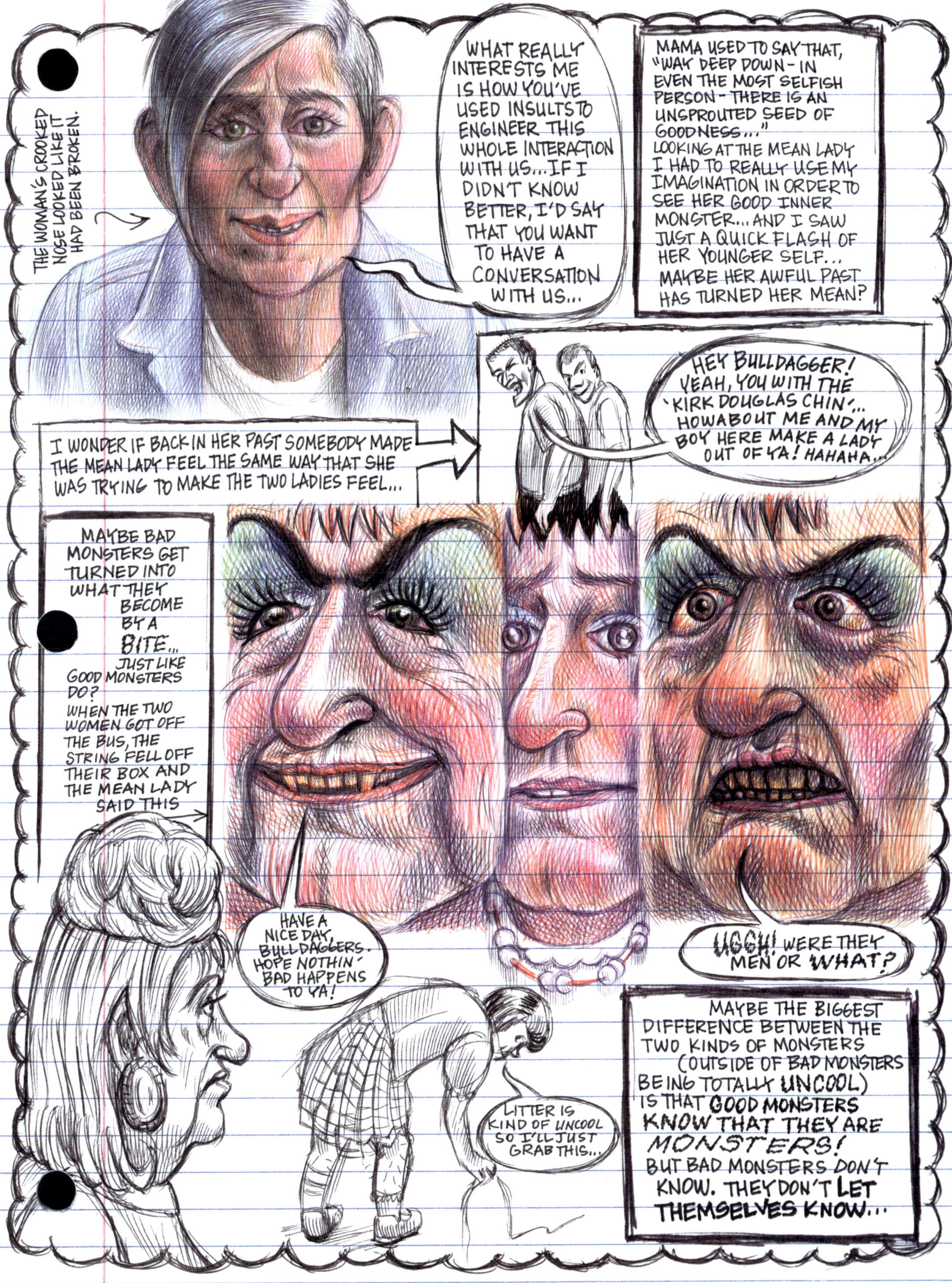

THE WOMAN'S CROOKED NOSE LOOKED LIKE IT HAD BEEN BROKEN.
WHAT REALLY INTERESTS ME IS HOW YOU'VE USED INSULTS TO ENGINEER THIS WHOLE INTERACTION WITH US... IF I DIDN'T KNOW BETTER, I'D SAY THAT YOU WANT TO HAVE A CONVERSATION WITH US...
MAMA USED TO SAY THAT, "WAY DEEP DOWN- IN EVEN THE MOST SELFISH PERSON- THERE IS AN UNSPROUTED SEED OF GOODNESS..." LOOKING AT THE MEAN LADY I HAD TO REALLY USE MY IMAGINATION IN ORDER TO SEE HER GOOD INNER MONSTER... AND I SAW JUST A QUICK FLASH OF HER YOUNGER SELF... MAYBE HER AWFUL PAST HAS TURNED HER MEAN?
I WONDER IF BACK IN HER PAST SOMEBODY MADE THE MEAN LADY FEEL THE SAME WAY THAT SHE WAS TRYING TO MAKE THE TWO LADIES FEEL...
HEY BULLDAGGER! YEAH, YOU WITH THE 'KIRK DOUGLAS CHIN'... HOWABOUT ME AND MY BOY HERE MAKE A LADY OUT OF YA! HAHAHA...
MAYBE BAD MONSTERS GET TURNED INTO WHAT THEY BECOME BY A BITE... JUST LIKE GOOD MONSTERS DO?
WHEN THE TWO WOMEN GOT OFF THE BUS, THE STRING FELL OFF THEIR BOX AND THE MEAN LADY SAID THIS
HAVE A NICE DAY, BULLDAGGERS. HOPE NOTHIN' BAD HAPPENS TO YA!
UGGH! WERE THEY MEN OR WHAT?
LITTER IS KIND OF UNCOOL SO I'LL JUST GRAB THIS...
MAYBE THE BIGGEST DIFFERENCE BETWEEN THE TWO KINDS OF MONSTERS (OUTSIDE OF BAD MONSTERS BEING TOTALLY UNCOOL) IS THAT GOOD MONSTERS KNOW THAT THEY ARE MONSTERS! BUT BAD MONSTERS DON'T KNOW. THEY DON'T LET THEMSELVES KNOW...

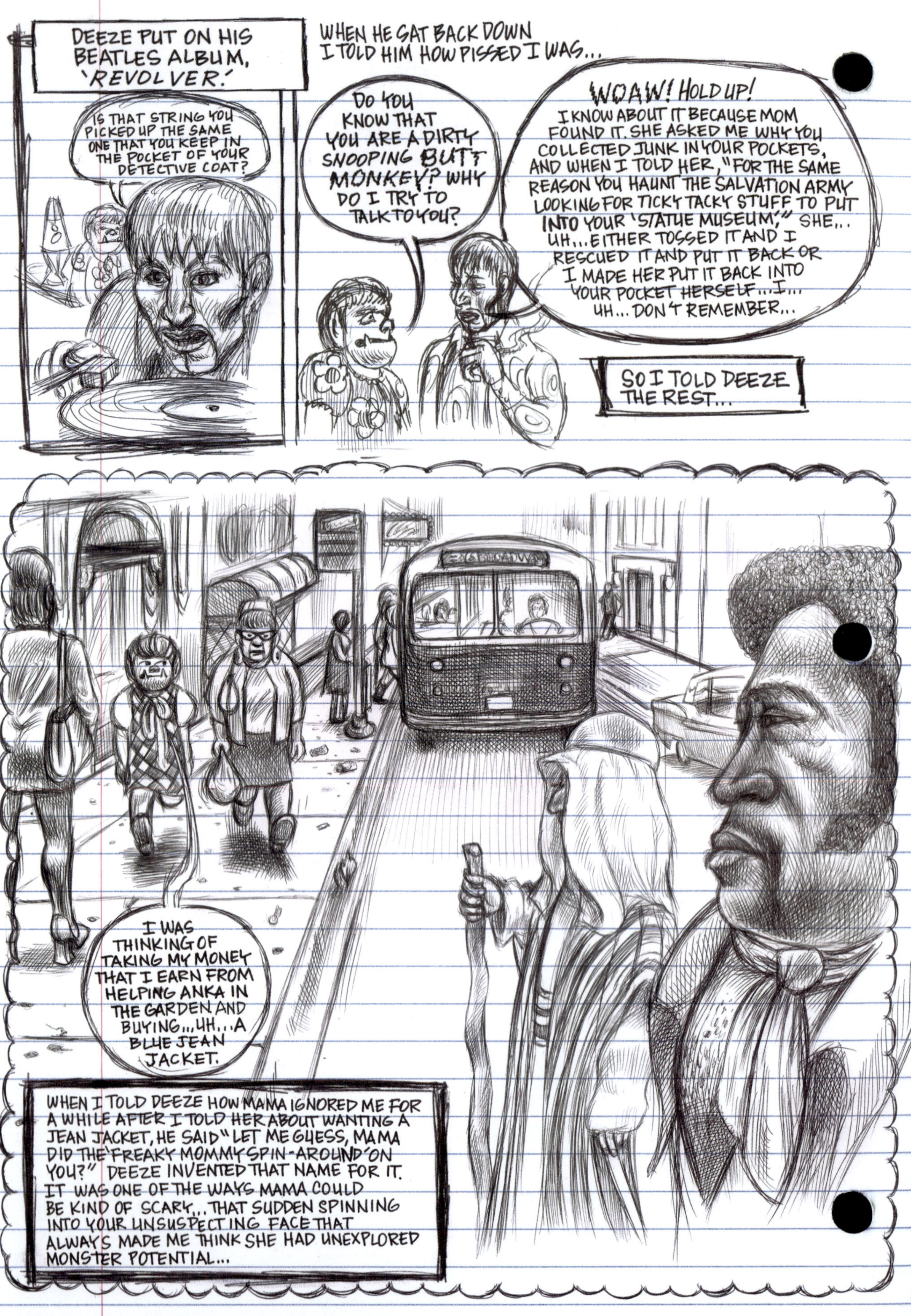
DEEZE PUT ON HIS BEATLES ALBUM, 'REVOLVER.'
IS THAT STRING YOU PICKED UP THE SAME ONE THAT YOU KEEP IN THE POCKET OF YOUR DETECTIVE COAT?
WHEN HE SAT BACK DOWN I TOLD HIM HOW PISSED I WAS...
DO YOU KNOW THAT YOU ARE A DIRTY SNOOPING BUTT MONKEY? WHY DO I TRY TO TALK TO YOU?
WOAW! HOLD UP! I KNOW ABOUT IT BECAUSE MOM FOUND IT. SHE ASKED ME WHY YOU COLLECTED JUNK IN YOUR POCKETS, AND WHEN I TOLD HER, "FOR THE SAME REASON YOU HAUNT THE SALVATION ARMY LOOKING FOR TICKY TACKY STUFF TO PUT INTO YOUR 'STATUE MUSEUM,'" SHE... UH... EITHER TOSSED IT AND I RESCUED IT AND PUT IT BACK OR I MADE HER PUT IT BACK INTO YOUR POCKET HERSELF... I... UH... DON'T REMEMBER...
SO I TOLD DEEZE THE REST...
I WAS THINKING OF TAKING MY MONEY THAT I EARN FROM HELPING ANKA IN THE GARDEN AND BUYING... UH... A BLUE JEAN JACKET.
WHEN I TOLD DEEZE HOW MAMA IGNORED ME FOR A WHILE AFTER I TOLD HER ABOUT WANTING A JEAN JACKET, HE SAID "LET ME GUESS, MAMA DID THE 'FREAKY MOMMY SPIN-AROUND' ON YOU?" DEEZE INVENTED THAT NAME FOR IT. IT WAS ONE OF THE WAYS MAMA COULD BE KIND OF SCARY... THAT SUDDEN SPINNING INTO YOUR UNSUSPECTING FACE THAT ALWAYS MADE ME THINK SHE HAD UNEXPLORED MONSTER POTENTIAL...

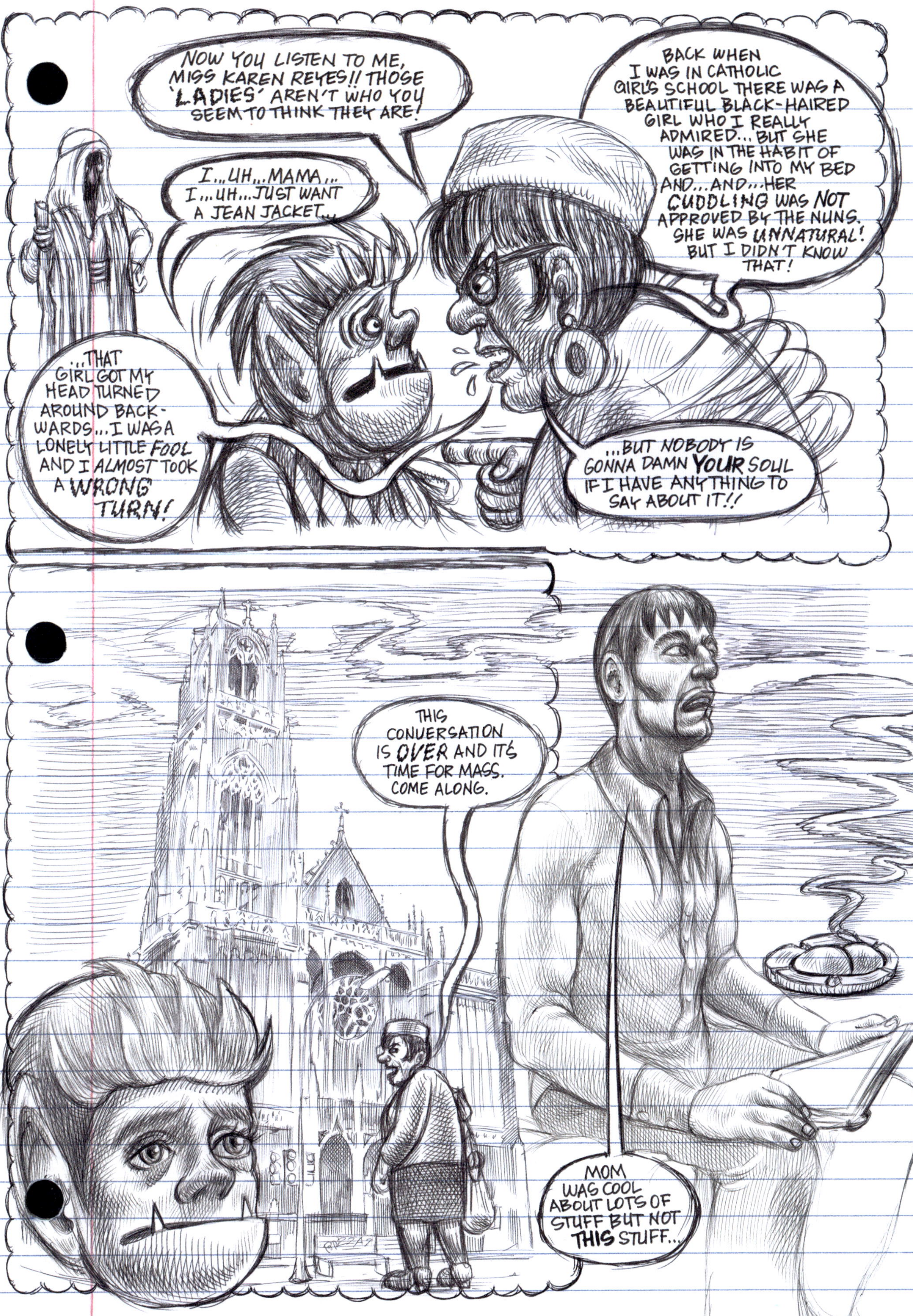
NOW YOU LISTEN TO ME, MISS KAREN REYES!! THOSE 'LADIES' AREN'T WHO YOU SEEM TO THINK THEY ARE!
I...UH...MAMA... I...UH...JUST WANT A JEAN JACKET...
BACK WHEN I WAS IN CATHOLIC GIRL'S SCHOOL THERE WAS A BEAUTIFUL BLACK-HAIRED GIRL WHO I REALLY ADMIRED... BUT SHE WAS IN THE HABIT OF GETTING INTO MY BED AND...AND...HER CUDDLING WAS NOT APPROVED BY THE NUNS. SHE WAS UNNATURAL! BUT I DIDN'T KNOW THAT!
...THAT GIRL GOT MY HEAD TURNED AROUND BACK-WARDS...I WAS A LONELY LITTLE FOOL AND I ALMOST TOOK A WRONG TURN!
...BUT NOBODY IS GONNA DAMN YOUR SOUL IF I HAVE ANYTHING TO SAY ABOUT IT!!
THIS CONVERSATION IS OVER AND IT'S TIME FOR MASS. COME ALONG.
MOM WAS COOL ABOUT LOTS OF STUFF BUT NOT THIS STUFF...

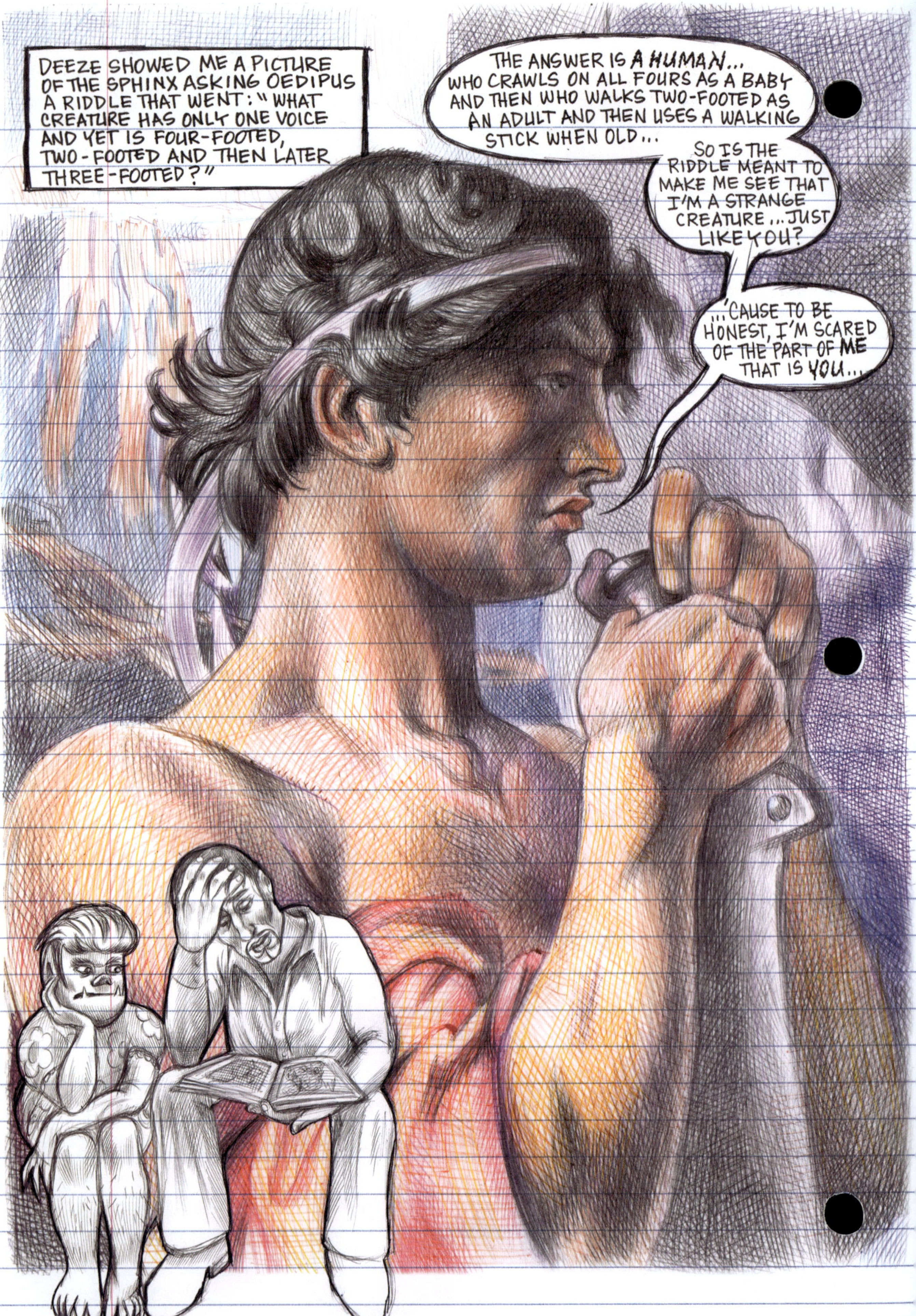
DEEZE SHOWED ME A PICTURE OF THE SPHINX ASKING OEDIPUS A RIDDLE THAT WENT: "WHAT CREATURE HAS ONLY ONE VOICE AND YET IS FOUR-FOOTED, TWO-FOOTED AND THEN LATER THREE-FOOTED?"
THE ANSWER IS A HUMAN... WHO CRAWLS ON ALL FOURS AS A BABY AND THEN WHO WALKS TWO-FOOTED AS AN ADULT AND THEN USES A WALKING STICK WHEN OLD...
SO IS THE RIDDLE MEANT TO MAKE ME SEE THAT I'M A STRANGE CREATURE... JUST LIKE YOU?
...'CAUSE TO BE HONEST, I'M SCARED OF THE PART OF ME THAT IS YOU...

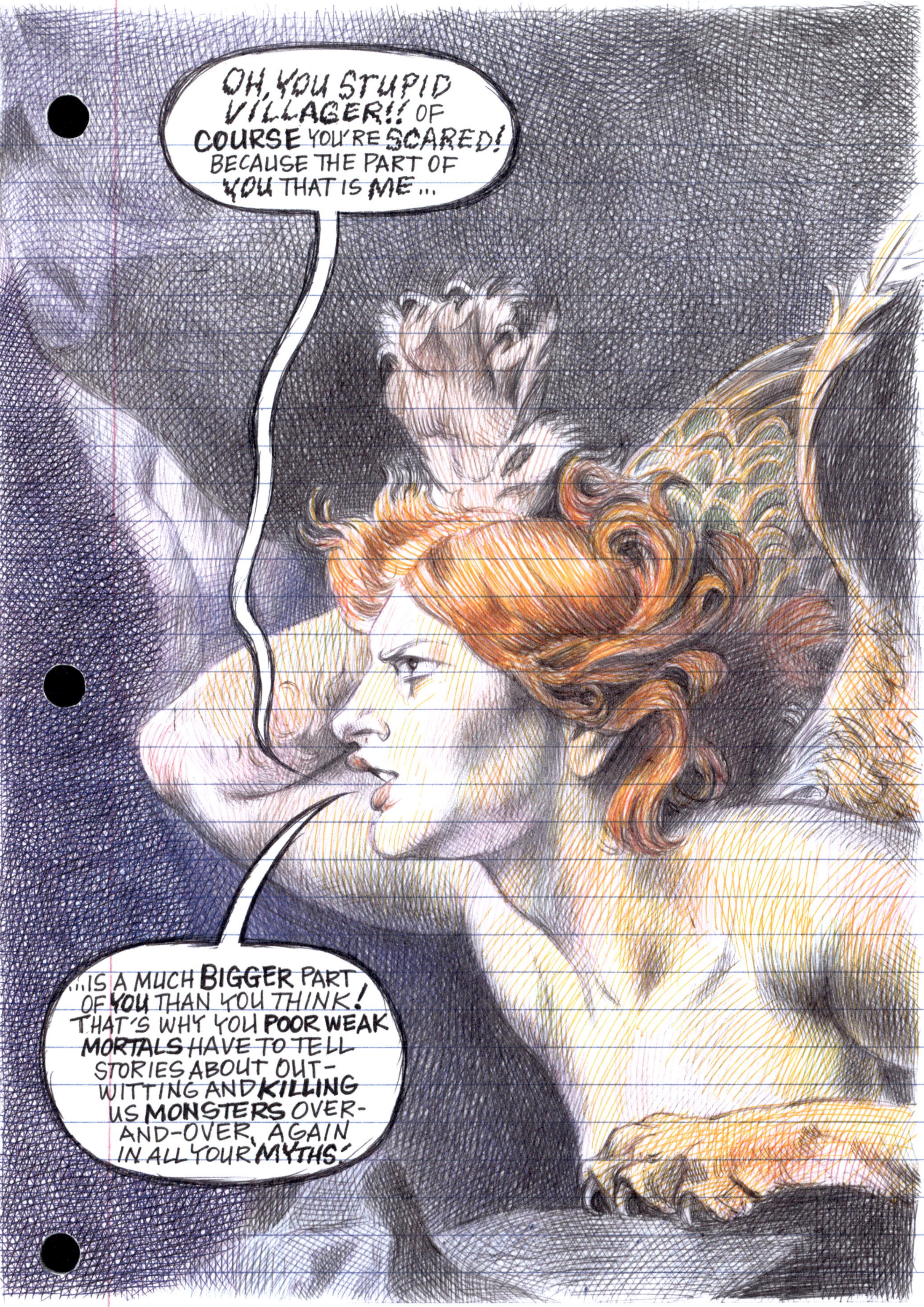
OH, YOU STUPID VILLAGER!! OF COURSE YOU'RE SCARED! BECAUSE THE PART OF YOU THAT IS ME...
...IS A MUCH BIGGER PART OF YOU THAN YOU THINK! THAT'S WHY YOU POOR WEAK MORTALS HAVE TO TELL STORIES ABOUT OUT-WITTING AND KILLING US MONSTERS OVER-AND-OVER, AGAIN IN ALL YOUR MYTHS!

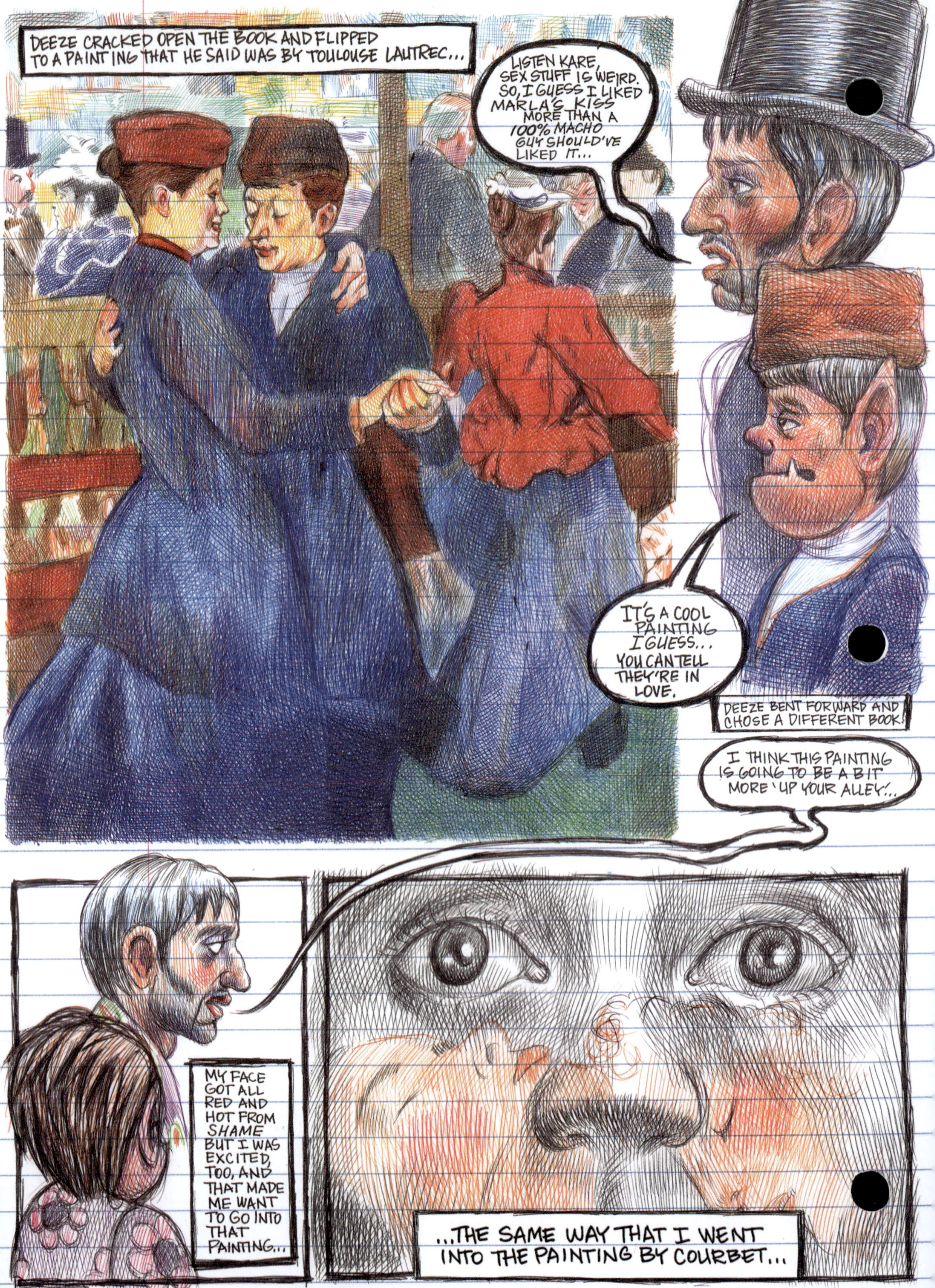

DEEZE CRACKED OPEN THE BOOK AND FLIPPED TO A PAINTING THAT HE SAID WAS BY TOULOUSE LAUTREC...
LISTEN KARE, SEX STUFF IS WEIRD. SO, I GUESS I LIKED MARLA'S KISS MORE THAN A 100% MACHO GUY SHOULD'VE LIKED IT...
IT'S A COOL PAINTING I GUESS... YOU CAN TELL THEY'RE IN LOVE.
DEEZE BENT FORWARD AND CHOSE A DIFFERENT BOOK!
I THINK THIS PAINTING IS GOING TO BE A BIT MORE 'UP YOUR ALLEY'...
MY FACE GOT ALL RED AND HOT FROM SHAME BUT I WAS EXCITED, TOO, AND THAT MADE ME WANT TO GO INTO THAT PAINTING...
...THE SAME WAY THAT I WENT INTO THE PAINTING BY COURBET...

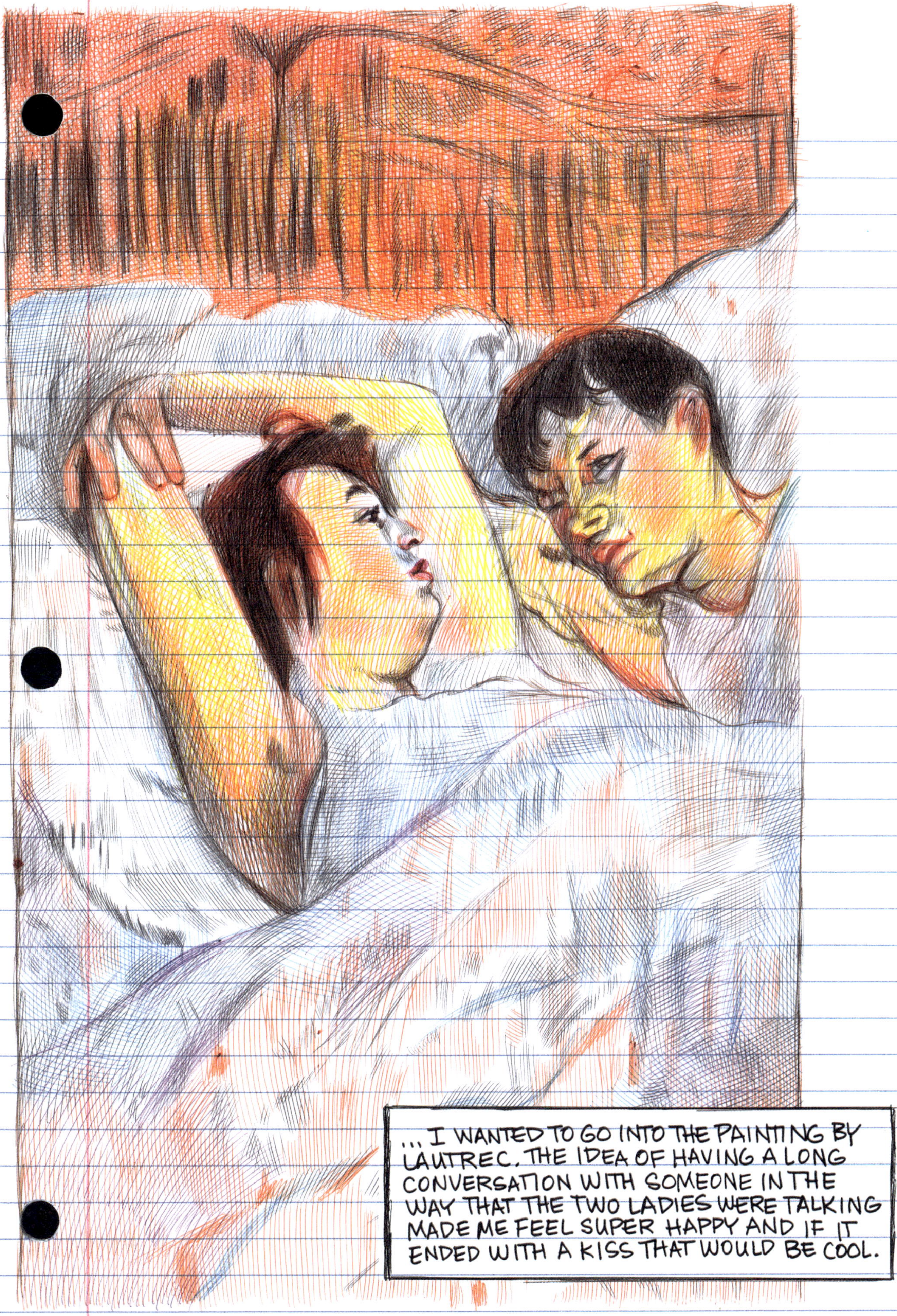
...I WANTED TO GO INTO THE PAINTING BY LAUTREC. THE IDEA OF HAVING A LONG CONVERSATION WITH SOMEONE IN THE WAY THAT THE TWO LADIES WERE TALKING MADE ME FEEL SUPER HAPPY AND IF IT ENDED WITH A KISS THAT WOULD BE COOL.

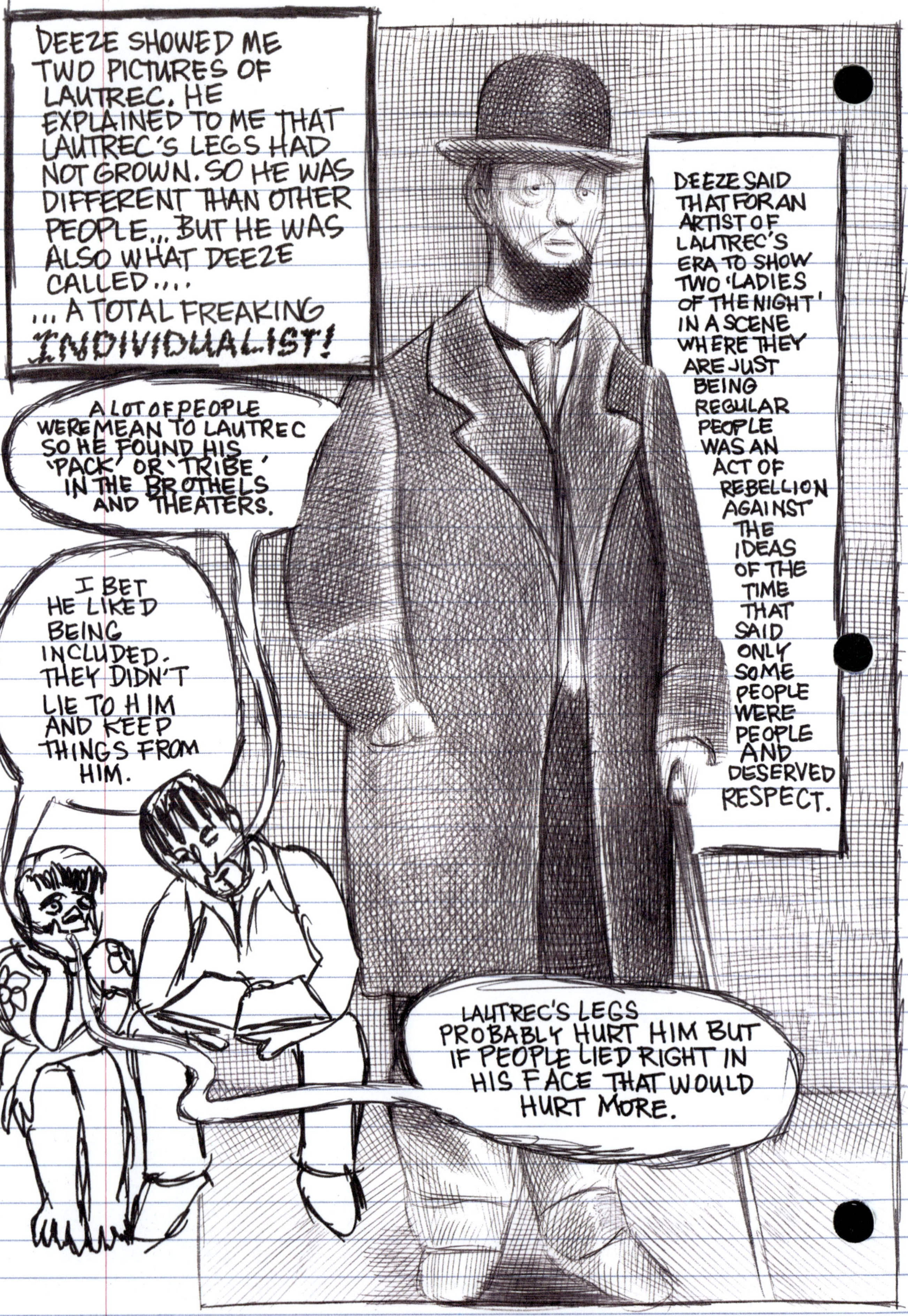
DEEZE SHOWED ME TWO PICTURES OF LAUTREC. HE EXPLAINED TO ME THAT LAUTREC'S LEGS HAD NOT GROWN. SO HE WAS DIFFERENT THAN OTHER PEOPLE... BUT HE WAS ALSO WHAT DEEZE CALLED.... ...A TOTAL FREAKING INDIVIDUALIST!
DEEZE SAID THAT FOR AN ARTIST OF LAUTREC'S ERA TO SHOW TWO 'LADIES OF THE NIGHT' IN A SCENE WHERE THEY ARE JUST BEING REGULAR PEOPLE WAS AN ACT OF REBELLION AGAINST THE IDEAS OF THE TIME THAT SAID ONLY SOME PEOPLE WERE PEOPLE AND DESERVED RESPECT.
A LOT OF PEOPLE WERE MEAN TO LAUTREC SO HE FOUND HIS 'PACK' OR 'TRIBE' IN THE BROTHELS AND THEATERS.
I BET HE LIKED BEING INCLUDED. THEY DIDN'T LIE TO HIM AND KEEP THINGS FROM HIM.
LAUTREC'S LEGS PROBABLY HURT HIM BUT IF PEOPLE LIED RIGHT IN HIS FACE THAT WOULD HURT MORE.

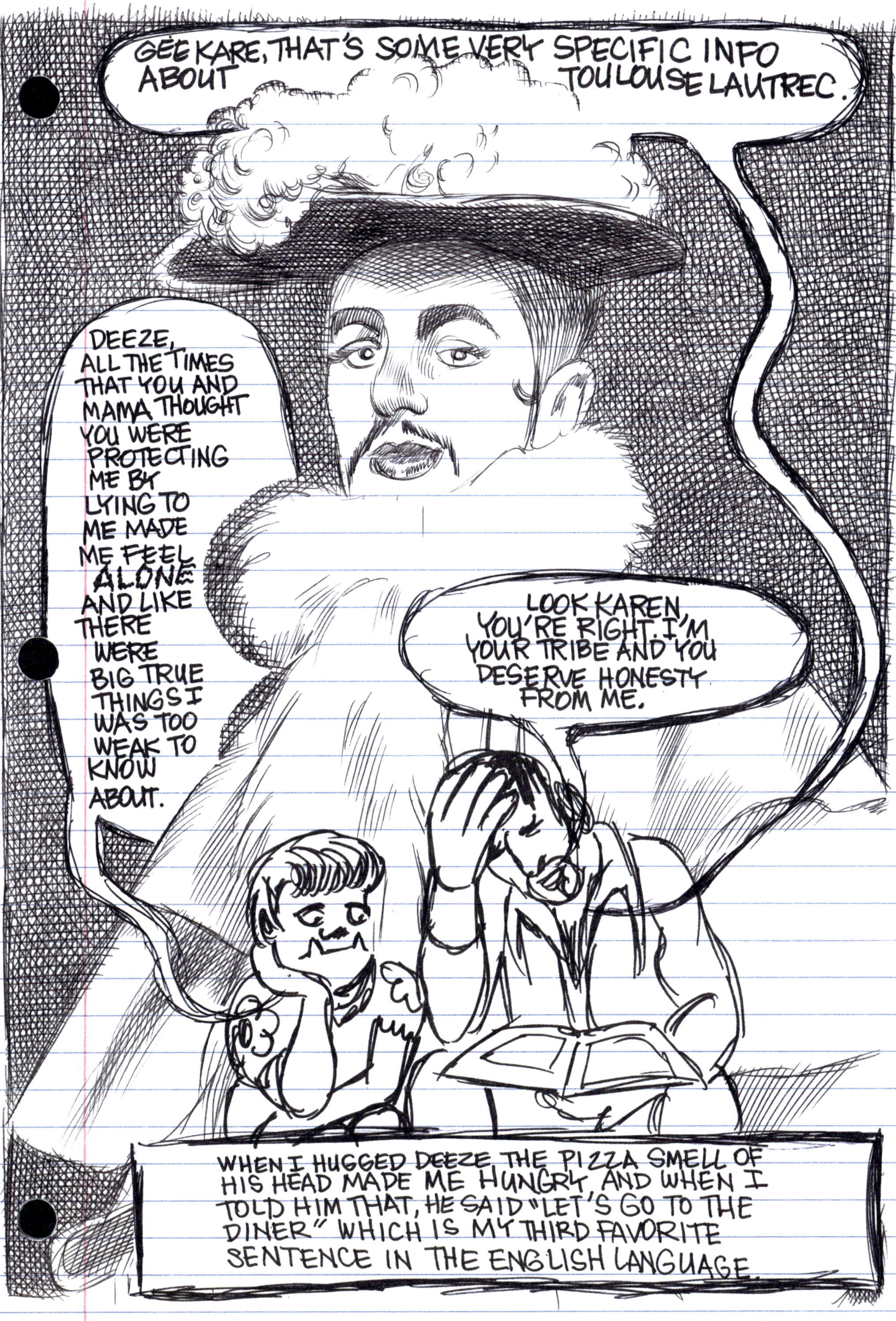
GEE KARE, THAT'S SOME VERY SPECIFIC INFO ABOUT TOULOUSE LAUTREC.
DEEZE, ALL THE TIMES THAT YOU AND MAMA THOUGHT YOU WERE PROTECTING ME BY LYING TO ME MADE ME FEEL ALONE AND LIKE THERE WERE BIG TRUE THINGS I WAS TOO WEAK TO KNOW ABOUT.
LOOK KAREN, YOU'RE RIGHT. I'M YOUR TRIBE AND YOU DESERVE HONESTY FROM ME.
WHEN I HUGGED DEEZE THE PIZZA SMELL OF HIS HEAD MADE ME HUNGRY, AND WHEN I TOLD HIM THAT, HE SAID "LET'S GO TO THE DINER" WHICH IS MY THIRD FAVORITE SENTENCE IN THE ENGLISH LANGUAGE.

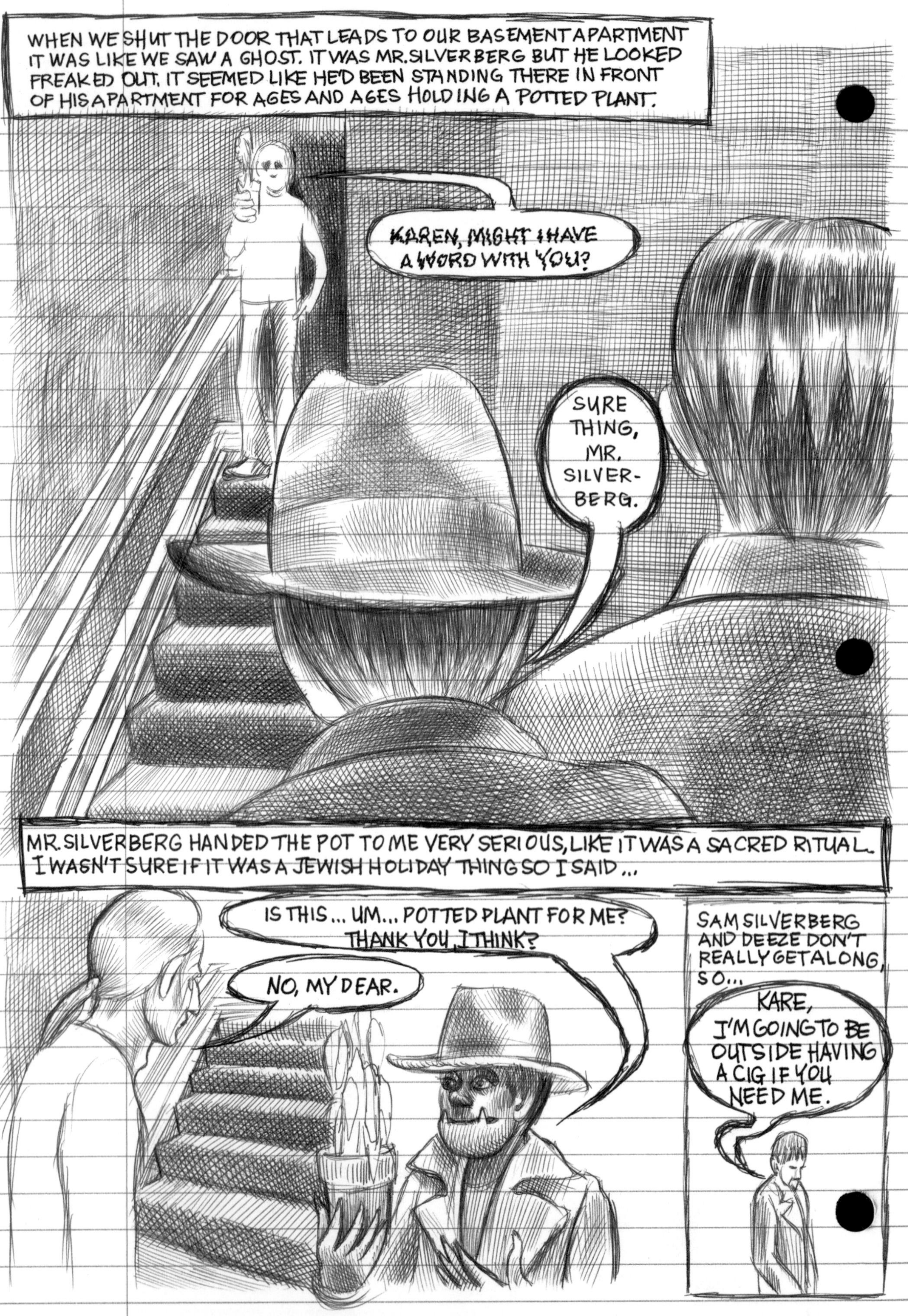
WHEN WE SHUT THE DOOR THAT LEADS TO OUR BASEMENT APARTMENT IT WAS LIKE WE SAW A GHOST. IT WAS MR. SILVERBERG BUT HE LOOKED FREAKED OUT. IT SEEMED LIKE HE'D BEEN STANDING THERE IN FRONT OF HIS APARTMENT FOR AGES AND AGES HOLDING A POTTED PLANT.
KAREN, MIGHT I HAVE A WORD WITH YOU?
SURE THING, MR. SILVERBERG.
MR. SILVERBERG HANDED THE POT TO ME VERY SERIOUS, LIKE IT WAS A SACRED RITUAL. I WASN'T SURE IF IT WAS A JEWISH HOLIDAY THING SO I SAID...
IS THIS... UM... POTTED PLANT FOR ME? THANK YOU, I THINK?
NO, MY DEAR.
SAM SILVERBERG AND DEEZE DON'T REALLY GET ALONG, SO...
KARE, I'M GOING TO BE OUTSIDE HAVING A CIG IF YOU NEED ME.

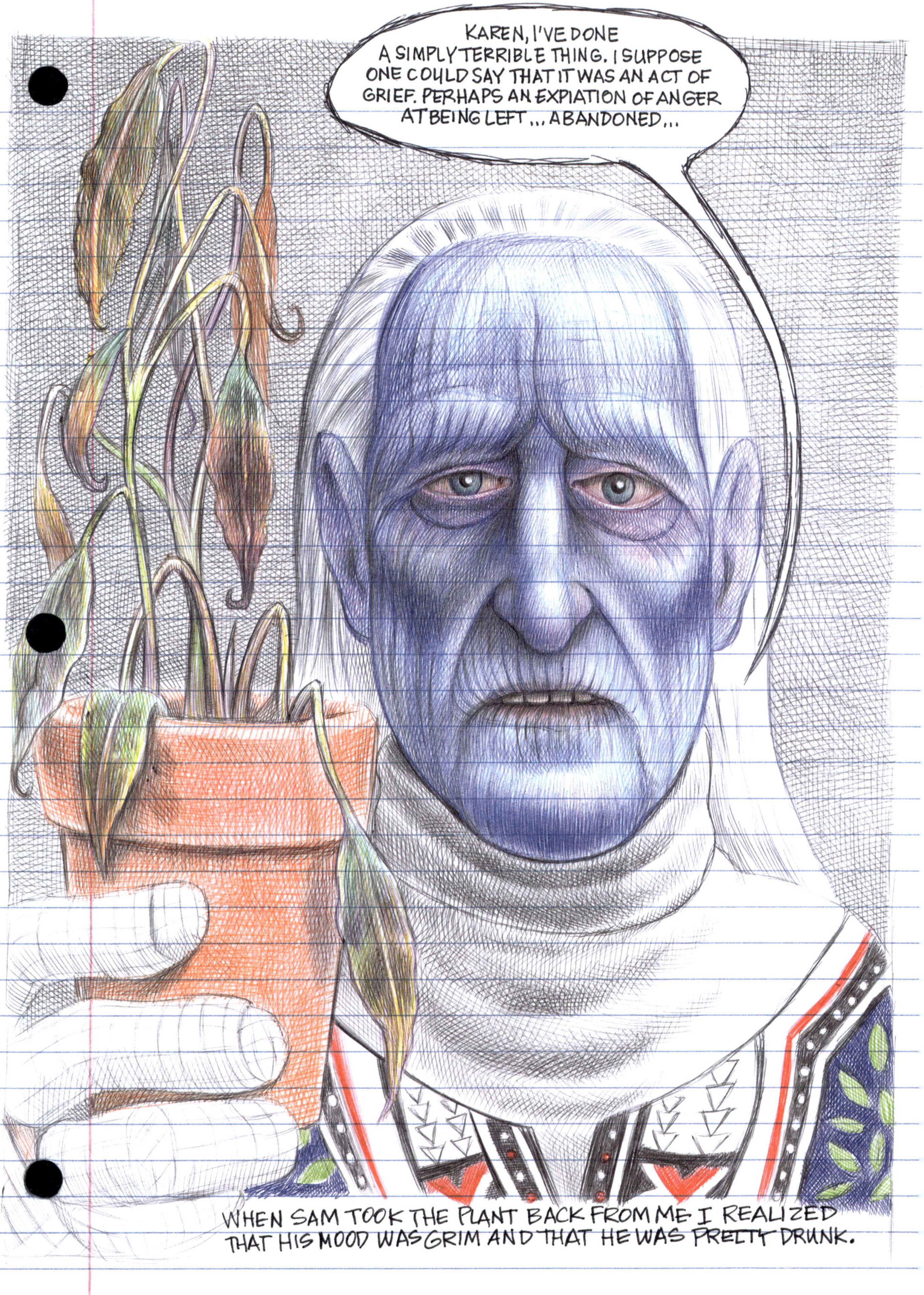
KAREN, I'VE DONE A SIMPLY TERRIBLE THING. I SUPPOSE ONE COULD SAY THAT IT WAS AN ACT OF GRIEF. PERHAPS AN EXPIATION OF ANGER AT BEING LEFT... ABANDONED...
WHEN SAM TOOK THE PLANT BACK FROM ME I REALIZED THAT HIS MOOD WAS GRIM AND THAT HE WAS PRETTY DRUNK.

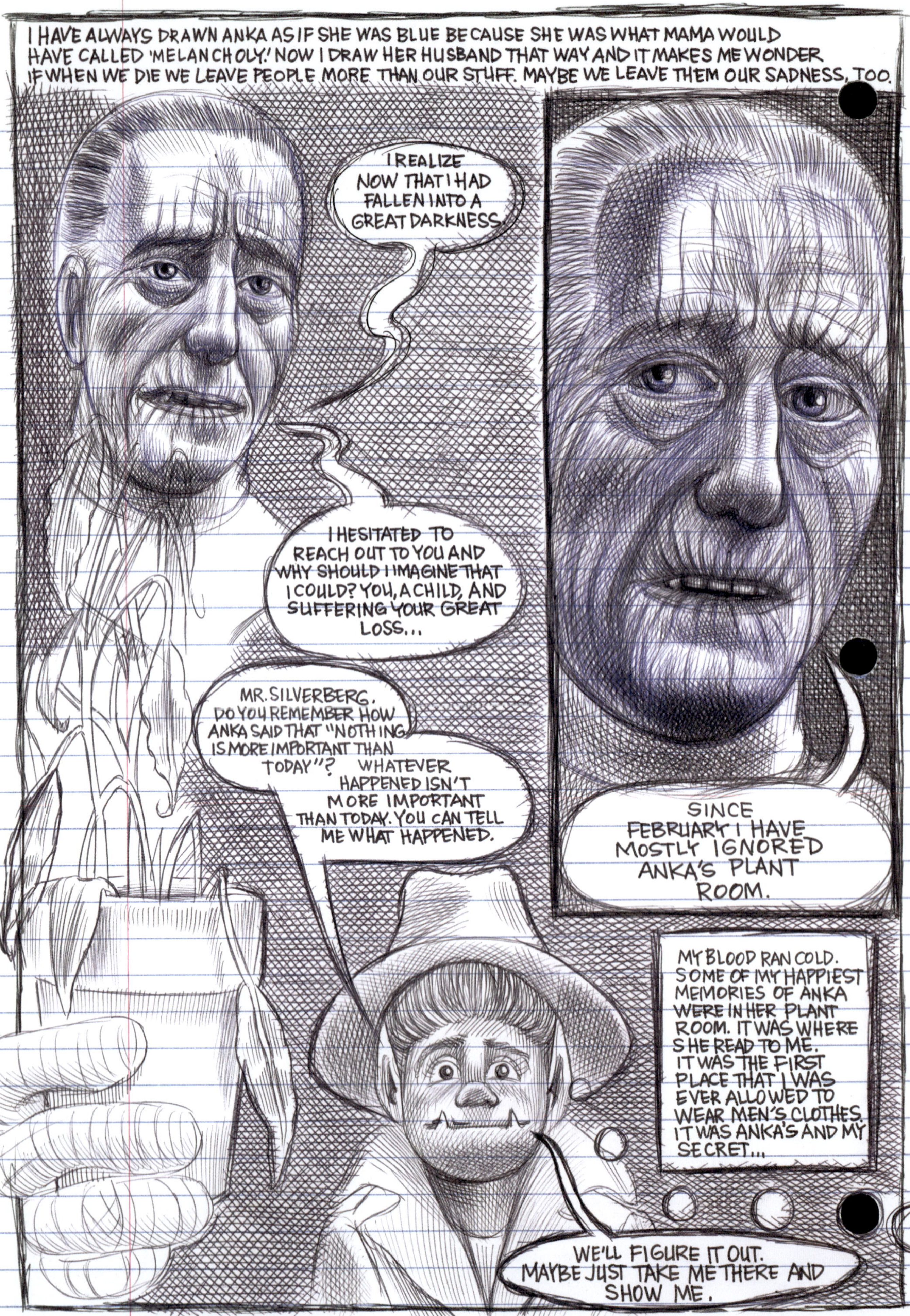
I HAVE ALWAYS DRAWN ANKA AS IF SHE WAS BLUE BECAUSE SHE WAS WHAT MAMA WOULD HAVE CALLED 'MELANCHOLY.' NOW I DRAW HER HUSBAND THAT WAY AND IT MAKES ME WONDER IF WHEN WE DIE WE LEAVE PEOPLE MORE THAN OUR STUFF. MAYBE WE LEAVE THEM OUR SADNESS, TOO.
I REALIZE NOW THAT I HAD FALLEN INTO A GREAT DARKNESS.
I HESITATED TO REACH OUT TO YOU AND WHY SHOULD I IMAGINE THAT I COULD? YOU, A CHILD, AND SUFFERING YOUR GREAT LOSS...
MR. SILVERBERG, DO YOU REMEMBER HOW ANKA SAID THAT "NOTHING IS MORE IMPORTANT THAN TODAY"? WHATEVER HAPPENED ISN'T MORE IMPORTANT THAN TODAY. YOU CAN TELL ME WHAT HAPPENED.
SINCE FEBRUARY I HAVE MOSTLY IGNORED ANKA'S PLANT ROOM.
MY BLOOD RAN COLD. SOME OF MY HAPPIEST MEMORIES OF ANKA WERE IN HER PLANT ROOM. IT WAS WHERE SHE READ TO ME. IT WAS THE FIRST PLACE THAT I WAS EVER ALLOWED TO WEAR MEN'S CLOTHES. IT WAS ANKA'S AND MY SECRET...
WE'LL FIGURE IT OUT. MAYBE JUST TAKE ME THERE AND SHOW ME.

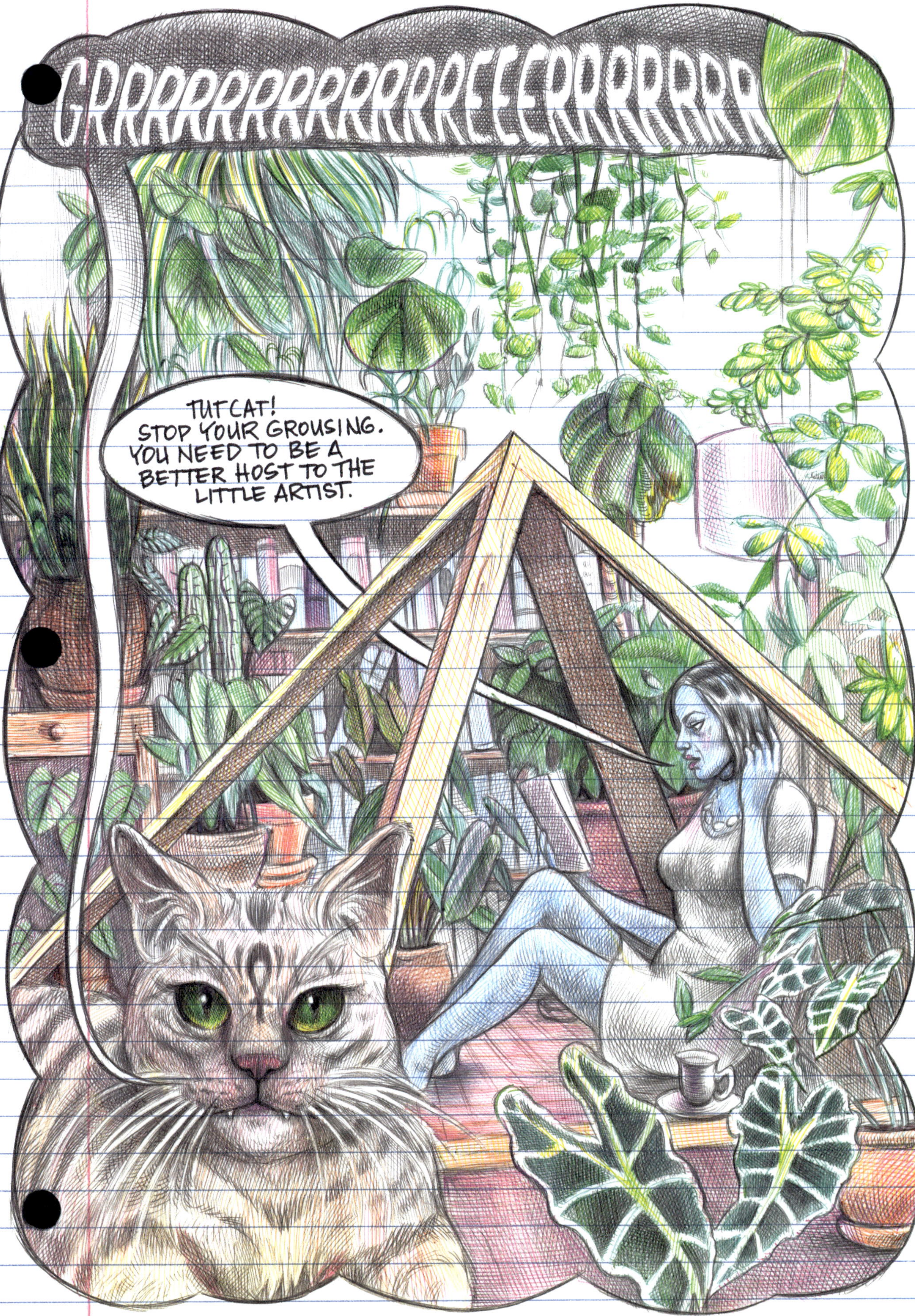
GRRRRRRRRRRRRRREEERRRRRRR
TUTCAT! STOP YOUR GROUSING. YOU NEED TO BE A BETTER HOST TO THE LITTLE ARTIST.

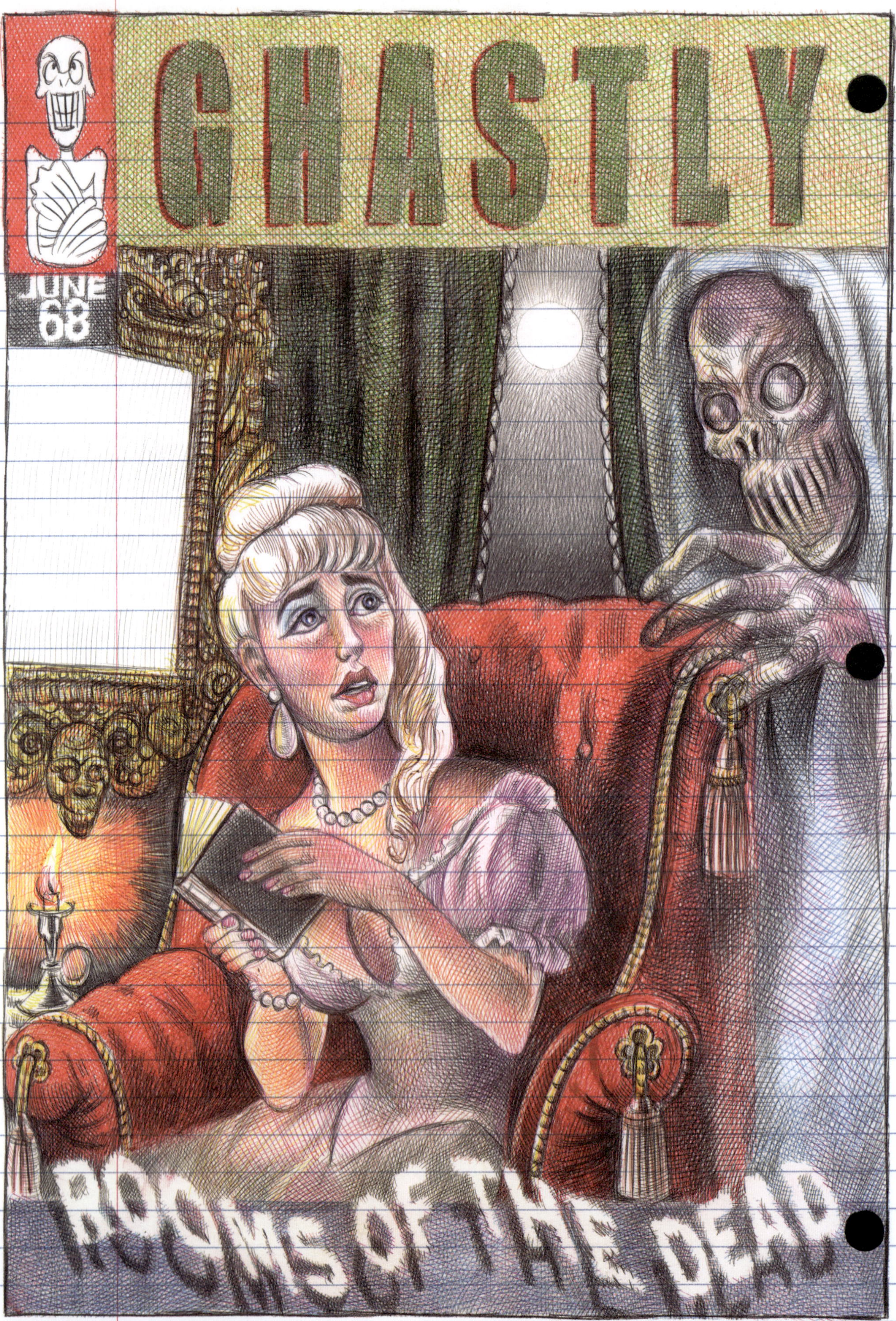
GHASTLY
JUNE
68
ROOMS OF THE DEAD

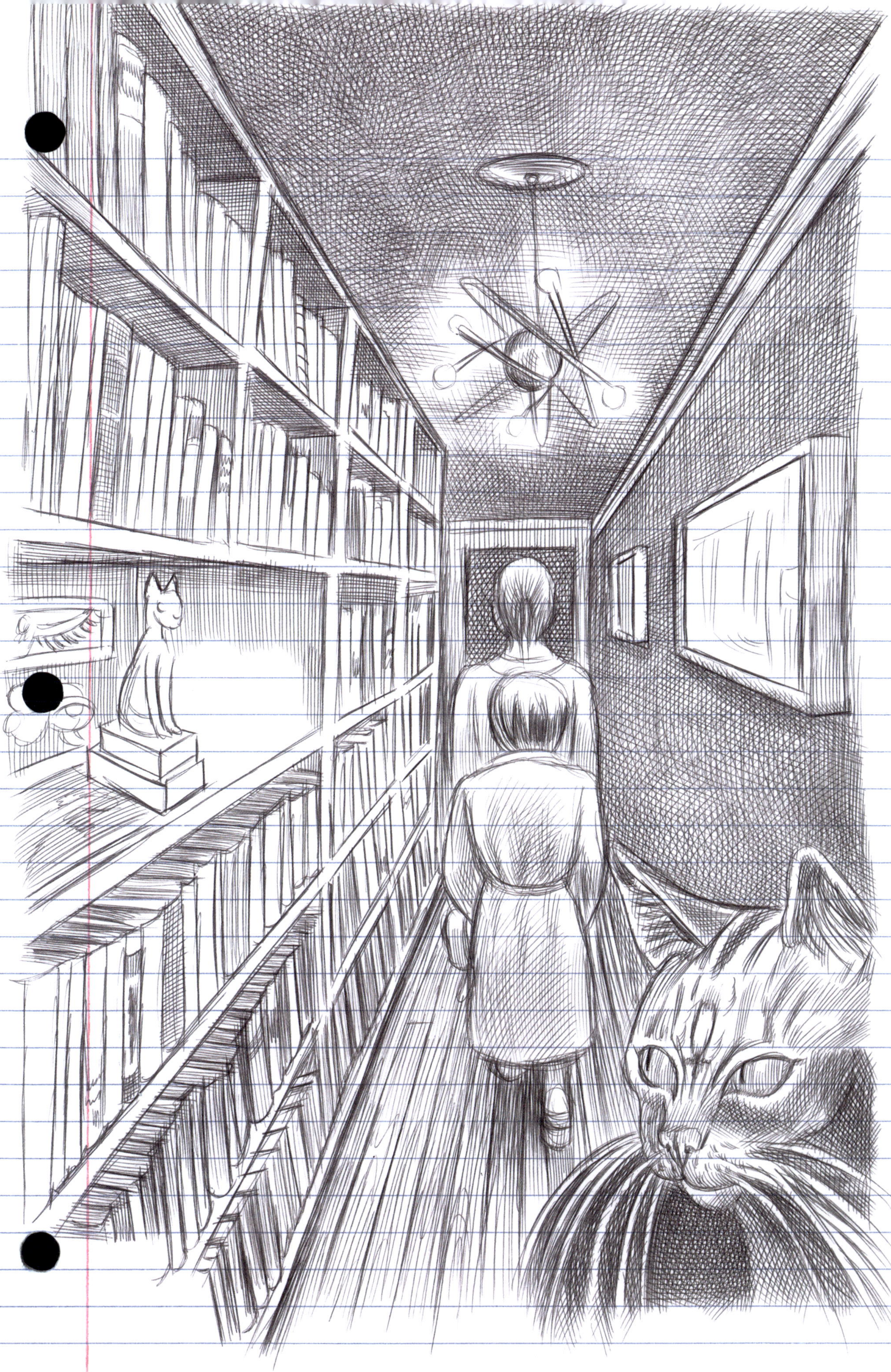

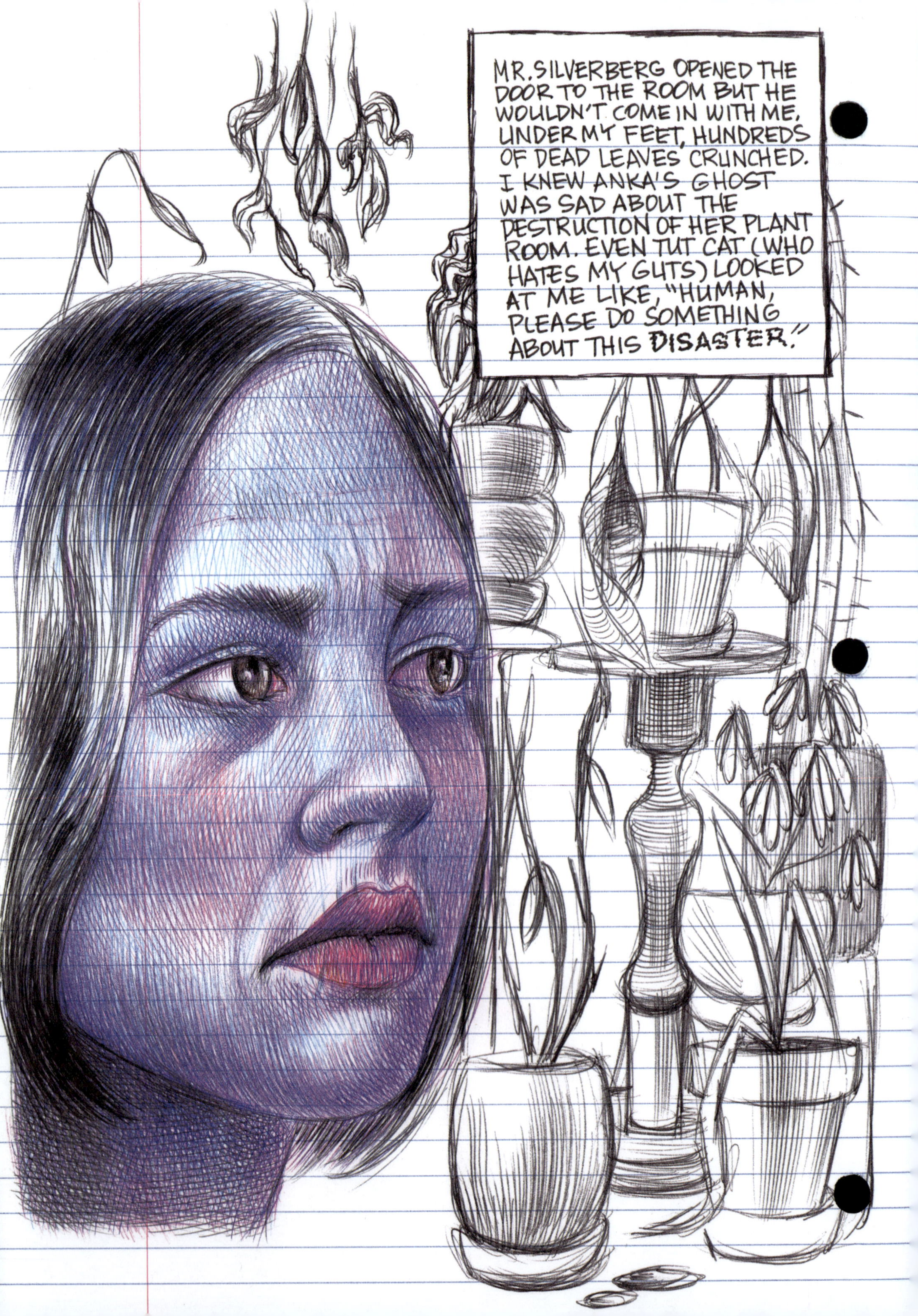
MR. SILVERBERG OPENED THE DOOR TO THE ROOM BUT HE WOULDN'T COME IN WITH ME. UNDER MY FEET, HUNDREDS OF DEAD LEAVES CRUNCHED. I KNEW ANKA'S GHOST WAS SAD ABOUT THE DESTRUCTION OF HER PLANT ROOM. EVEN TUT CAT (WHO HATES MY GUTS) LOOKED AT ME LIKE, "HUMAN, PLEASE DO SOMETHING ABOUT THIS DISASTER!"

> ANKA'S SECRET ROOM WITH ITS MAGICAL PYRAMID WAS NO LONGER GREEN. IT WAS A SICKLY YELLOW AND BROWN. ANKA HAD ALWAYS GIVEN ME DEAD LEAVES TO DRAW AND SHE'D TAUGHT ME...

> "...THAT THERE IS GREAT BEAUTY EVEN IN DEATH." SHE CALLED ME "LITTLE ARTIST" AND IT ALWAYS MADE ME FEEL VERY SPECIAL AND LIKE MY ART IS IMPORTANT. BUT STANDING IN HER RUINED INDOOR GARDEN I DID NOT FEEL THAT EVEN A GREAT ARTIST COULD FIND THE BEAUTY IN SO MUCH DEATH.

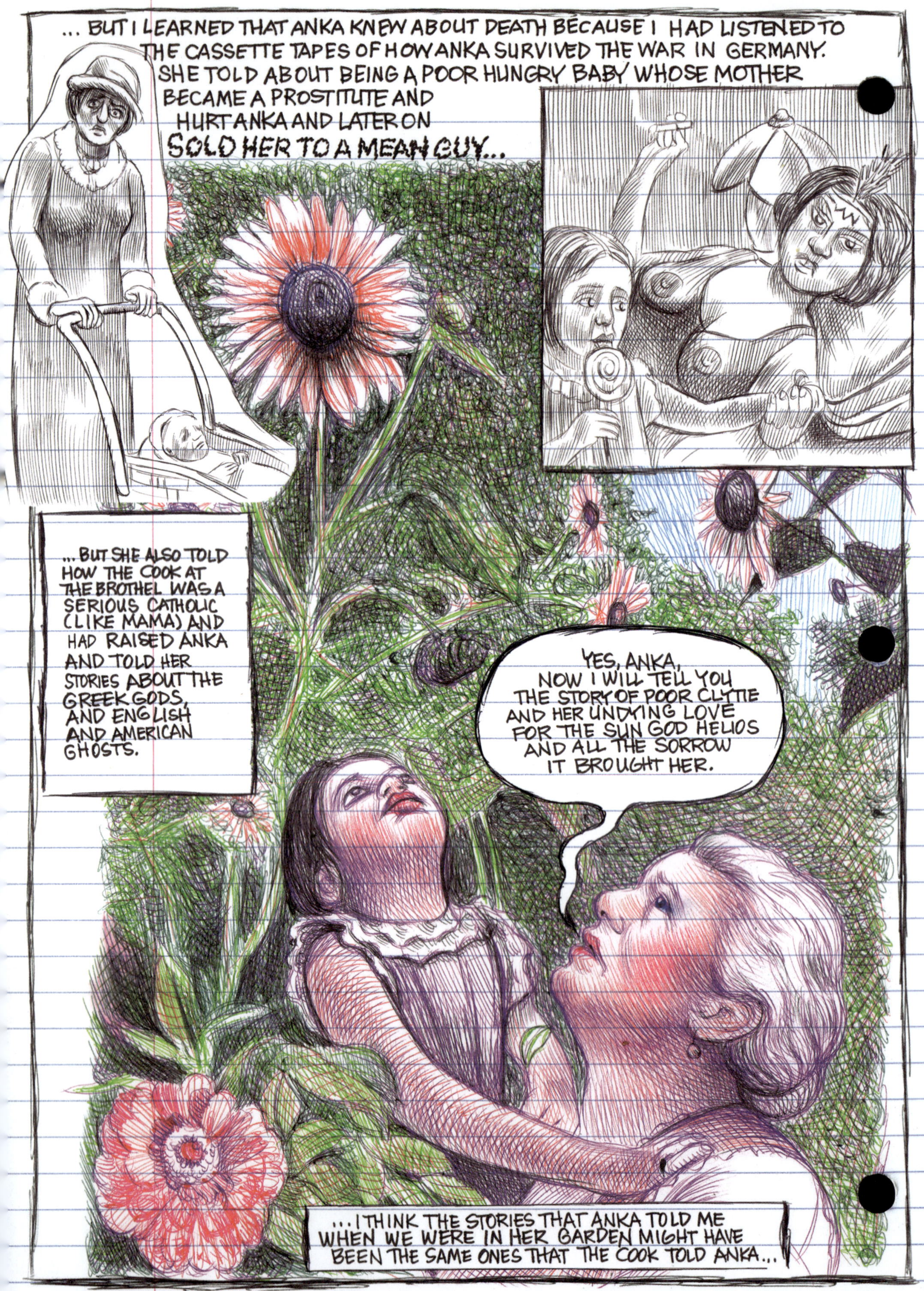

... BUT I LEARNED THAT ANKA KNEW ABOUT DEATH BECAUSE I HAD LISTENED TO THE CASSETTE TAPES OF HOW ANKA SURVIVED THE WAR IN GERMANY. SHE TOLD ABOUT BEING A POOR HUNGRY BABY WHOSE MOTHER BECAME A PROSTITUTE AND HURT ANKA AND LATER ON SOLD HER TO A MEAN GUY...
... BUT SHE ALSO TOLD HOW THE COOK AT THE BROTHEL WAS A SERIOUS CATHOLIC (LIKE MAMA) AND HAD RAISED ANKA AND TOLD HER STORIES ABOUT THE GREEK GODS, AND ENGLISH AND AMERICAN GHOSTS.
YES, ANKA, NOW I WILL TELL YOU THE STORY OF POOR CLYTIE AND HER UNDYING LOVE FOR THE SUN GOD HELIOS AND ALL THE SORROW IT BROUGHT HER.
... I THINK THE STORIES THAT ANKA TOLD ME WHEN WE WERE IN HER GARDEN MIGHT HAVE BEEN THE SAME ONES THAT THE COOK TOLD ANKA...

FROM THE CASSETTE TAPES THAT MR. SILVERBERG LET ME HEAR, I LEARNED ABOUT THIS TOTALLY CREEPY GUY NAMED MR. SCHUTZ WHO MESSED WITH ANKA BUT ALSO PROTECTED HER FROM AN EVEN WORSE PLACE CALLED A 'PHARMACY,' A BUSINESS WHERE THEY...

...ACTUALLY **SOLD** CHILDREN (WHICH IS SUPER SICK AND DISGUSTING). THE GUY NAMED SCHUTZ ALSO PROTECTED ANKA FROM DEVIL-WORSHIPPER GUYS (LIKE IN THE MOVIES 'THE WITCHES' OR 'HORROR HOTEL') -WHO WANTED TO DO HUMAN SACRIFICE ON ANKA!... ALL THAT ANKA WANTED TO DO WAS READ BOOKS AND PET HER CAT BUT BECAUSE SHE WAS PART JEWISH THE NAZIS BUTTED INTO HER LIFE, ARRESTED HER AND PUT HER ON A TRAIN. WHEN SHE GOT TO THE CONCENTRATION CAMP SHE CALLED SCHUTZ...

SCHUTZ WOULD HAVE JUST GOTTEN HER OUT OF THE CAMP BUT SHE TOLD HIM THAT IF HE WOULD GET OUT SOME OTHER GIRLS, TOO, ANKA WOULD START A PHARMACY WHERE THEY WOULD SELL THE CHILDREN. I DO NOT KNOW HOW I FEEL ABOUT THIS FACT. I DO NOT KNOW WHAT HAPPENED AFTER THAT. MR. SILVERBERG HAS BEEN WEIRD ABOUT LETTING ME HEAR MORE.

SO I HAVE BEEN WAITING TO HEAR ANKA ON THE TAPES TELL ABOUT WHAT SHE DID THOSE YEARS AGO. THIS IS THE REASON THAT WHAT MR. SILVERBERG DID NEXT WAS COMPLETELY UNCOOL...

"LITTLE ARTIST, HAVE I TOLD YOU THE SAD STORY OF POOR CLYTIE AND HER LOVE FOR THE SUN GOD HELIOS?"

"I'M GLAD TO HELP OUT, BUT I WAS WONDERING ABOUT LISTENING TO MORE OF MRS. SILVERBERG'S CASSETTE TAPES."

"AHHH, YES... WELL THE REMAINING TESTIMONY ON ANKA'S TAPES IS RATHER... ADULT IN NATURE..."

"MR. SILVERBERG, HOW CAN I HELP SOLVE THE MYSTERY OF HER DEATH IF I DON'T LISTEN?"

"YES, YES."

"PERHAPS IN A FEW YEARS WHEN YOU'RE A BIT OLDER... REALLY KAREN DEAR IT'S FOR THE BEST."

"OKAY MR. SILVERBERG I CAN RESPECT THAT... I JUST HOPE TUTCAT DOESN'T ATTACK ME WHEN I COME IN HERE..."

"...AND SEARCH THIS PLACE AND FIND THOSE TAPES AND LISTEN TO EVERY ONE!"

...BUT OF COURSE I ONLY THOUGHT THAT AND DIDN'T SAY IT OUT LOUD...

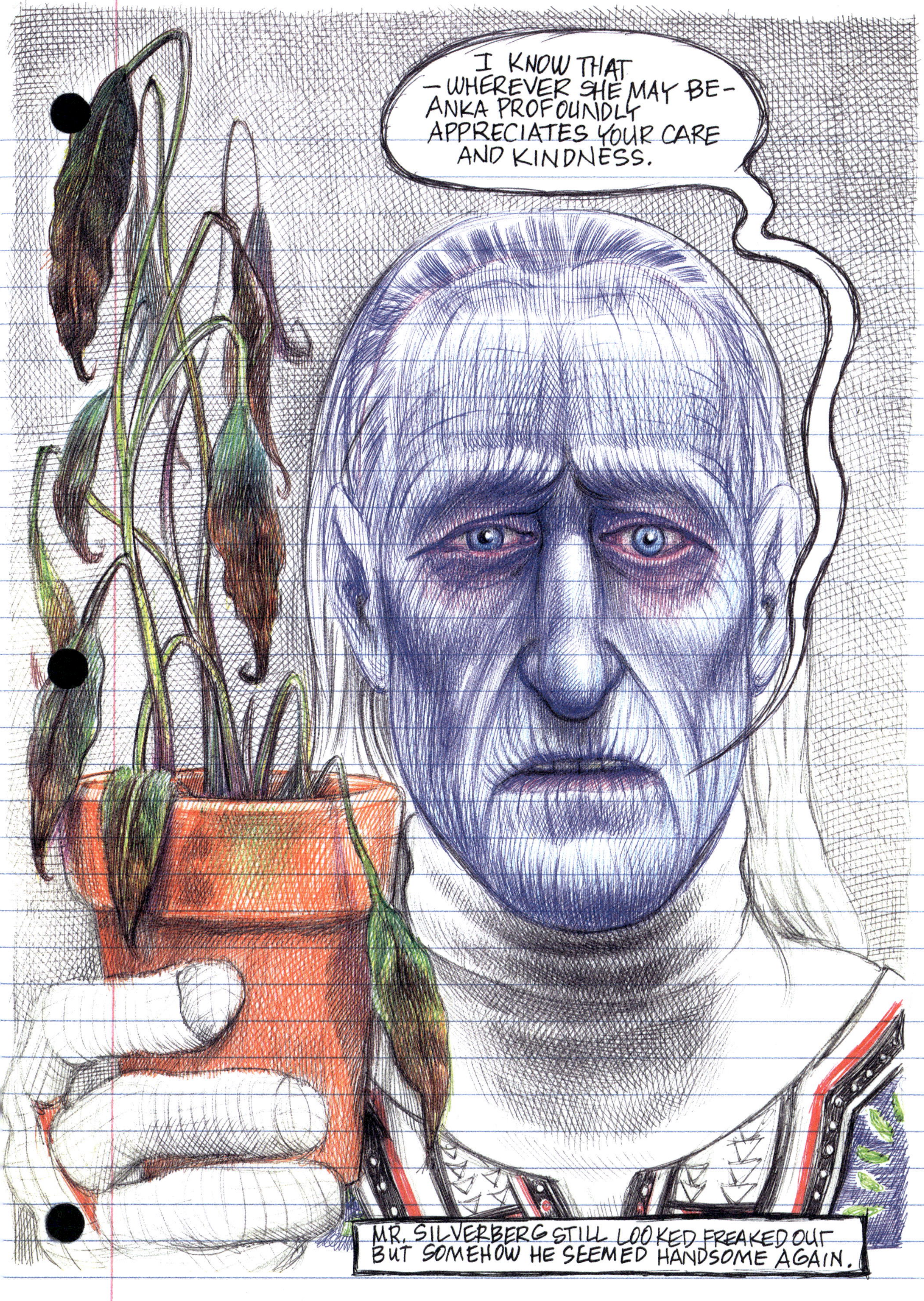
I KNOW THAT —WHEREVER SHE MAY BE— ANKA PROFOUNDLY APPRECIATES YOUR CARE AND KINDNESS.
MR. SILVERBERG STILL LOOKED FREAKED OUT BUT SOMEHOW HE SEEMED HANDSOME AGAIN.

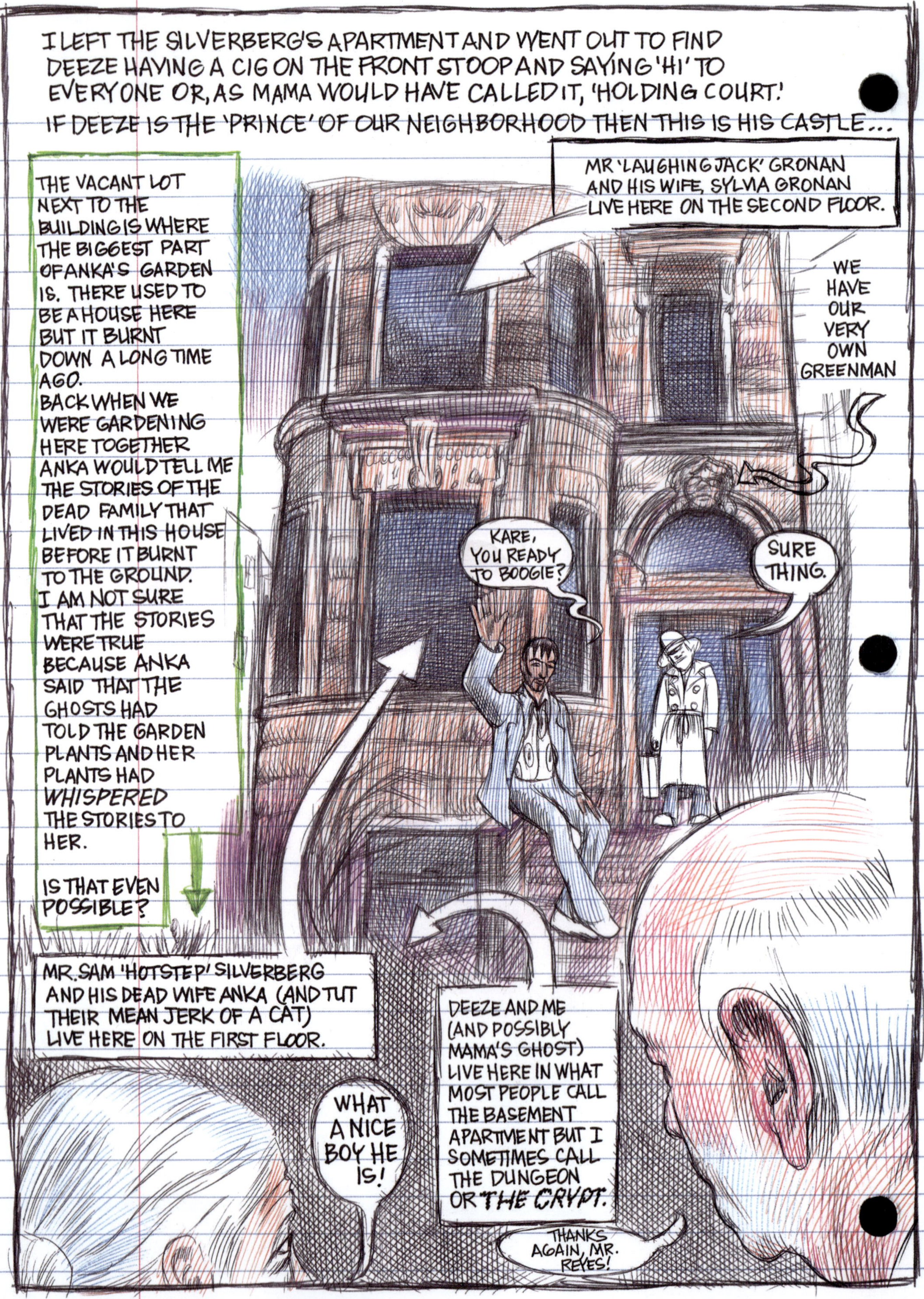

I LEFT THE SILVERBERG'S APARTMENT AND WENT OUT TO FIND DEEZE HAVING A CIG ON THE FRONT STOOP AND SAYING 'HI' TO EVERYONE OR, AS MAMA WOULD HAVE CALLED IT, 'HOLDING COURT.' IF DEEZE IS THE 'PRINCE' OF OUR NEIGHBORHOOD THEN THIS IS HIS CASTLE...
THE VACANT LOT NEXT TO THE BUILDING IS WHERE THE BIGGEST PART OF ANKA'S GARDEN IS. THERE USED TO BE A HOUSE HERE BUT IT BURNT DOWN A LONG TIME AGO. BACK WHEN WE WERE GARDENING HERE TOGETHER ANKA WOULD TELL ME THE STORIES OF THE DEAD FAMILY THAT LIVED IN THIS HOUSE BEFORE IT BURNT TO THE GROUND. I AM NOT SURE THAT THE STORIES WERE TRUE BECAUSE ANKA SAID THAT THE GHOSTS HAD TOLD THE GARDEN PLANTS AND HER PLANTS HAD *WHISPERED* THE STORIES TO HER.
IS THAT EVEN POSSIBLE?
MR 'LAUGHING JACK' GRONAN AND HIS WIFE, SYLVIA GRONAN LIVE HERE ON THE SECOND FLOOR.
WE HAVE OUR VERY OWN GREENMAN
KARE, YOU READY TO BOOGIE?
SURE THING.
MR. SAM 'HOTSTEP' SILVERBERG AND HIS DEAD WIFE ANKA (AND TUT THEIR MEAN JERK OF A CAT) LIVE HERE ON THE FIRST FLOOR.
DEEZE AND ME (AND POSSIBLY MAMA'S GHOST) LIVE HERE IN WHAT MOST PEOPLE CALL THE BASEMENT APARTMENT BUT I SOMETIMES CALL THE DUNGEON OR *THE CRYPT.*
WHAT A NICE BOY HE IS!
THANKS AGAIN, MR. REYES!

...SUDDENLY, STANDING RIGHT IN FRONT OF OUR BUILDING BUT REAL QUIET, THERE'S THIS BIG GUY AND HE JUST STARES AT DEEZE AND I'VE NEVER SEEN DEEZE CHANGE SO MUCH IN ONE SECOND. DEEZE IS INSTANTLY A COMPLETELY DIFFERENT PERSON. NO SMILES AND WAVES AND CHUCKLES (BY THE WAY I HATE THE WORD 'CHUCKLES,' BECAUSE REALLY ONLY CLOWNS CHUCKLE).

...WHEN DEEZE WENT TO TALK TO THE GUY HE WAS DEAD SERIOUS. DEEZE SENT ME ONE OF HIS E.S.P. MESSAGES **NOT** TO INTERRUPT THEM, SO INSTEAD I GOT DISTRACTED FOR A SECOND BY *THIS KIND OF DRUID IN A LONG ROBE* WHO I NEVER SAW BEFORE...

NOT PAYING ATTENTION WAS A GOOD MOVE BECAUSE I COULDN'T HEAR THEM ANYWAY.
...WHEN THE GUY WALKED AWAY, I COULD TELL THAT DEEZE DID NOT WANT ME TO ASK "WHO WAS THAT GUY?" SO I DIDN'T, BUT I WONDERED ABOUT IT ALL DAY. ALL I KNOW IS I HAVE A BAD FEELING ABOUT THE GUY.

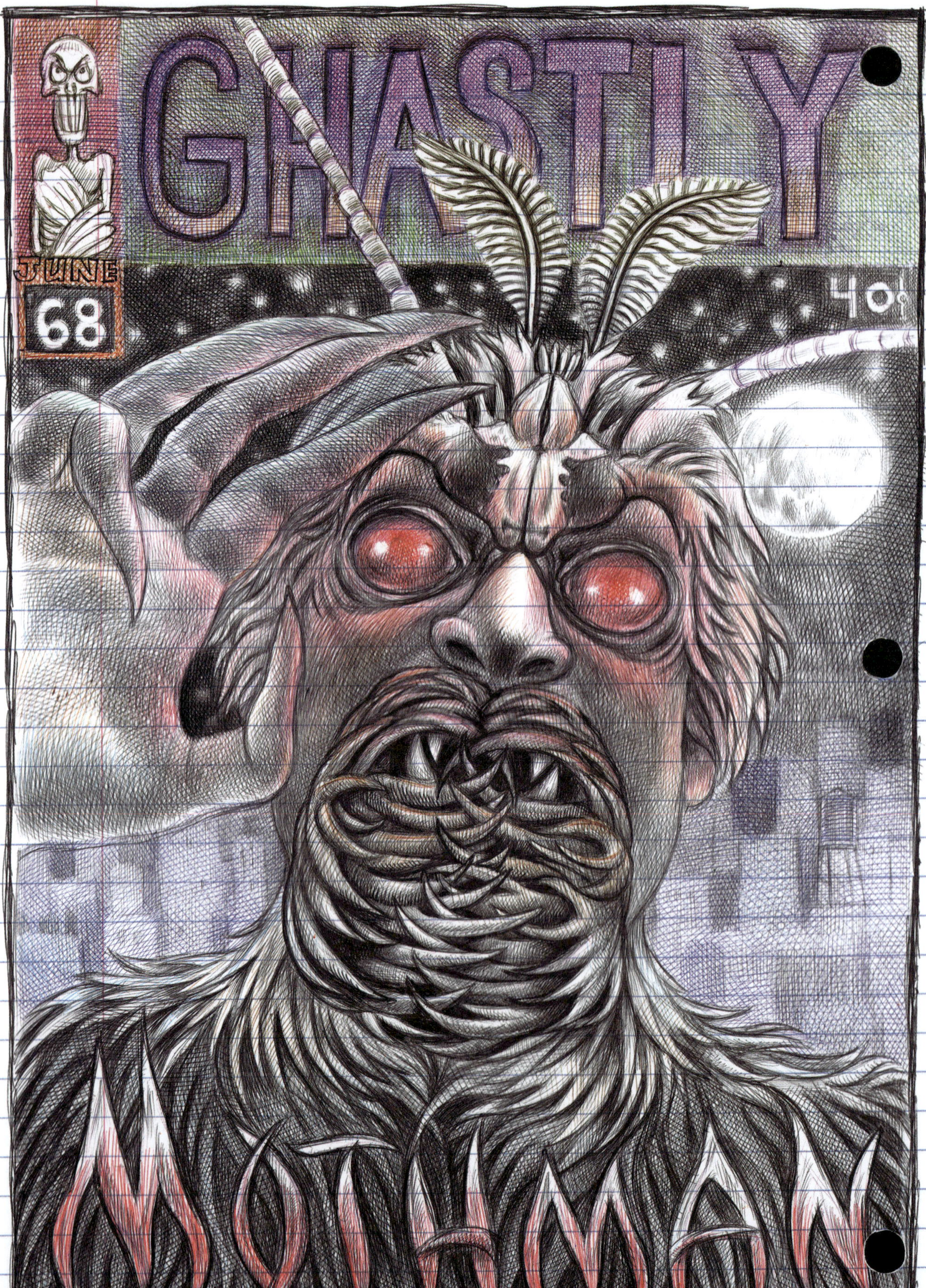
GHASTLY
JUNE
68
40¢
MOTHMAN

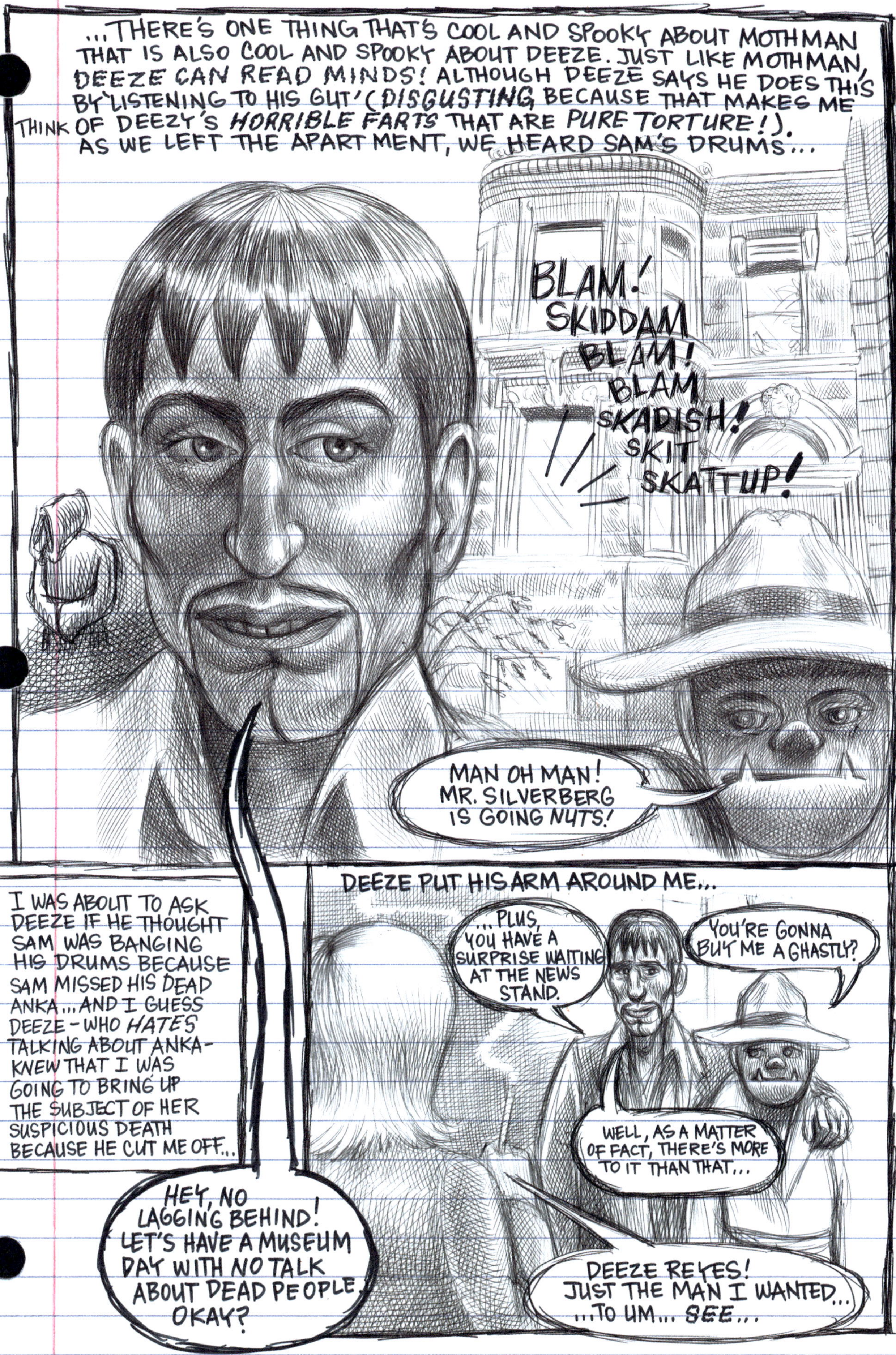
...THERE'S ONE THING THAT'S COOL AND SPOOKY ABOUT MOTHMAN THAT IS ALSO COOL AND SPOOKY ABOUT DEEZE. JUST LIKE MOTHMAN, DEEZE CAN READ MINDS! ALTHOUGH DEEZE SAYS HE DOES THIS BY 'LISTENING TO HIS GUT' (DISGUSTING, BECAUSE THAT MAKES ME THINK OF DEEZY'S HORRIBLE FARTS THAT ARE PURE TORTURE!). AS WE LEFT THE APARTMENT, WE HEARD SAM'S DRUMS...
BLAM! SKIDDAM BLAM! BLAM SKADISH! SKIT SKATTUP!
MAN OH MAN! MR. SILVERBERG IS GOING NUTS!
I WAS ABOUT TO ASK DEEZE IF HE THOUGHT SAM WAS BANGING HIS DRUMS BECAUSE SAM MISSED HIS DEAD ANKA... AND I GUESS DEEZE - WHO HATES TALKING ABOUT ANKA - KNEW THAT I WAS GOING TO BRING UP THE SUBJECT OF HER SUSPICIOUS DEATH BECAUSE HE CUT ME OFF...
HEY, NO LAGGING BEHIND! LET'S HAVE A MUSEUM DAY WITH NO TALK ABOUT DEAD PEOPLE. OKAY?
DEEZE PUT HIS ARM AROUND ME...
...PLUS, YOU HAVE A SURPRISE WAITING AT THE NEWS STAND.
YOU'RE GONNA BUY ME A GHASTLY?
WELL, AS A MATTER OF FACT, THERE'S MORE TO IT THAN THAT...
DEEZE REYES! JUST THE MAN I WANTED... ...TO UM... SEE...

WHILE DEEZE AND DORINE BLABBED ON AND ON, I SPACED OUT AND REMEMBERED WHAT MAMA HAD ONCE CALLED LADIES LIKE DORINE...

BLAH BLAH BLAH BLAH BLAH BLAH BLAH

BLAH BLAH BLAH BLAH BLAH BLAH BLAH BLAH BLAH

THEY'RE LADIES OF THE NIGHT AND YOU ARE FORBIDDEN FROM TALKING TO THEM EVER ABOUT ANYTHING!

WHEN MAMA DESCRIBED THEM LIKE THAT I GUESS I MIXED THEM UP WITH THE 'BRIDES OF DRACULA' AND WHEN SHE TOLD ME I COULD **NEVER** TALK TO THEM, TALKING TO THEM BECAME THE **ONLY** THING I WANTED TO DO...

HA HA HA HA! COULD A BRIDE OF DRACULA EVER FALL FOR A WEREWOLF? NOT SURE I EVER THOUGHT ABOUT THAT, KAREN...

AFTER I GOT CAUGHT SNEAKING OUT TO TALK TO THEM I GOT MY SECOND PRETEND WHIPPING FROM DEEZE... FOR A WHILE I WAS KIND OF POPULAR WITH THE LADIES AND I THINK DORINE EVEN LIKED ME BUT THEN I THINK DEEZE TOLD HER TO GIVE ME THE COLD SHOULDER AND I GUESS SHE WAS STILL DOING IT...

...BECAUSE DORINE DIDN'T SAY HELLO OR EVEN SEEM TO NOTICE ME.

WHEN THESE PEOPLE WALKED NEAR US, SHE GOT EVEN ANGRIER THAN SHE ALREADY WAS...

"WELL SPEAK OF THE DEVIL..."

"THEY ARE THE PROBLEM! I WANT IT TO BE NOTED THAT THEY'RE ON MY BLOCK! AND THEY'RE PRETEND RELIGIOUS NUTS..."

"OKAY, I'LL TELL THEM TO PEDDLE THEIR CLAPTRAP SOMEWHERE ELSE... FAR AWAY."

"IT AIN'T JUST THE PREACHING! CREEPY JOHN THE BAPTIST IS TURNING THEM GIRLS OUT! BUT I GUESS YOU ALREADY KNEW THAT."

"YEAH. HIYA KAREN, SORRY ABOUT YER MA."

"HEY! NOT THE TIME!"

WHEN DEEZE WALKED UP TO THE STREET PREACHER GUY, IT WAS LIKE HE SPOKE INTO MY MIND, JUST LIKE MOTHMAN DOES. "GET BEHIND ME, RIGHT THIS SECOND, KAREN" AND I DID.

MAMA AND DEEZE NEVER AGREED ABOUT RELIGION. MAMA THOUGHT DEEZE "BETTER GET HIMSELF SOME FIRE INSURANCE." (I THINK SHE MEANT SOMETHING ABOUT HELL.) AND DEEZE TEASED MAMA BY TELLING ME REAL LOUD THAT "ANNOYED BLONDE SURFER JESUS IS MAMA'S TEENY BOPPER FANTASY DATE."

EVEN THOUGH THE 'PREACHER GUY' **LOOKS** LIKE MAMA'S BLONDE SURFER JESUS, SOMETHING MORE THAN DEEZE'S E.S.P. MESSAGE TELLS ME THAT THE GUY ISN'T WHAT HE PRETENDS HE IS.
MAMA BELIEVED THAT EVEN THOUGH PEOPLE HIDE THINGS BEHIND THEIR FACES (SHE CALLED THEM 'THE MASK PEOPLE') IT'S POSSIBLE TO SEE WHAT'S INSIDE BY LOOKING INTO THEIR **EYES**.

WHEN I **FORCED** MYSELF TO LOOK INTO THE EYES OF 'THE PREACHER GUY' AND HIS GIRLFRIENDS, I GOT THE FEELING THAT I WAS A SPARROW TRYING TO STARE DOWN A PACK OF HUNGRY ALLEY CATS...

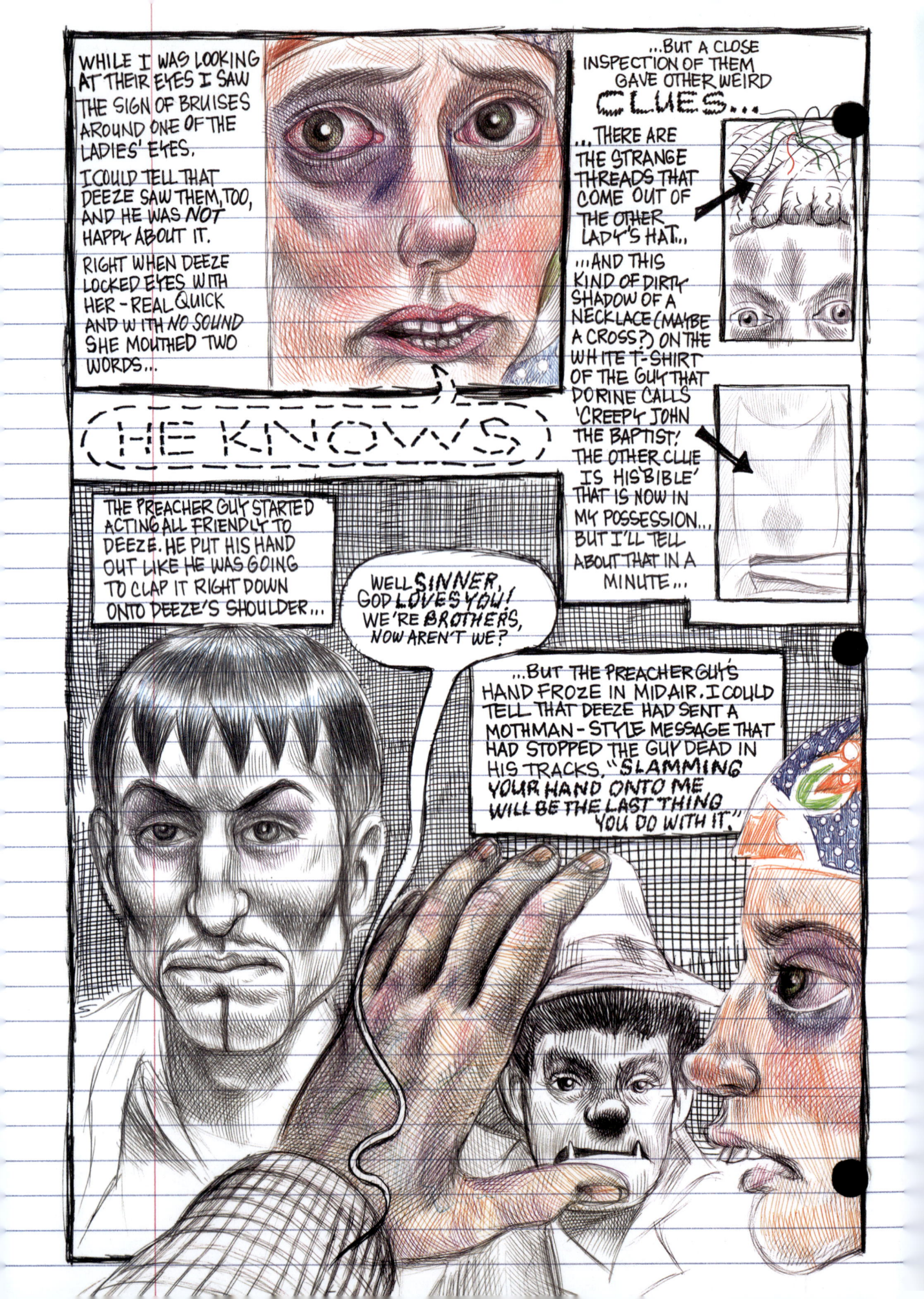

WHILE I WAS LOOKING AT THEIR EYES I SAW THE SIGN OF BRUISES AROUND ONE OF THE LADIES' EYES.

I COULD TELL THAT DEEZE SAW THEM, TOO, AND HE WAS *NOT* HAPPY ABOUT IT.

RIGHT WHEN DEEZE LOCKED EYES WITH HER — REAL QUICK AND WITH *NO SOUND* SHE MOUTHED TWO WORDS...

(HE KNOWS)

...BUT A CLOSE INSPECTION OF THEM GAVE OTHER WEIRD CLUES...

...THERE ARE THE STRANGE THREADS THAT COME OUT OF THE OTHER LADY'S HAT...

...AND THIS KIND OF DIRTY SHADOW OF A NECKLACE (MAYBE A CROSS?) ON THE WHITE T-SHIRT OF THE GUY THAT DORINE CALLS 'CREEPY JOHN THE BAPTIST'. THE OTHER CLUE IS HIS 'BIBLE' THAT IS NOW IN MY POSSESSION... BUT I'LL TELL ABOUT THAT IN A MINUTE...

THE PREACHER GUY STARTED ACTING ALL FRIENDLY TO DEEZE. HE PUT HIS HAND OUT LIKE HE WAS GOING TO CLAP IT RIGHT DOWN ONTO DEEZE'S SHOULDER...

WELL *SINNER*, GOD *LOVES YOU!* WE'RE *BROTHERS*, NOW AREN'T WE?

...BUT THE PREACHER GUY'S HAND FROZE IN MIDAIR. I COULD TELL THAT DEEZE HAD SENT A MOTHMAN-STYLE MESSAGE THAT HAD STOPPED THE GUY DEAD IN HIS TRACKS. "SLAMMING YOUR HAND ONTO ME WILL BE THE LAST THING YOU DO WITH IT."

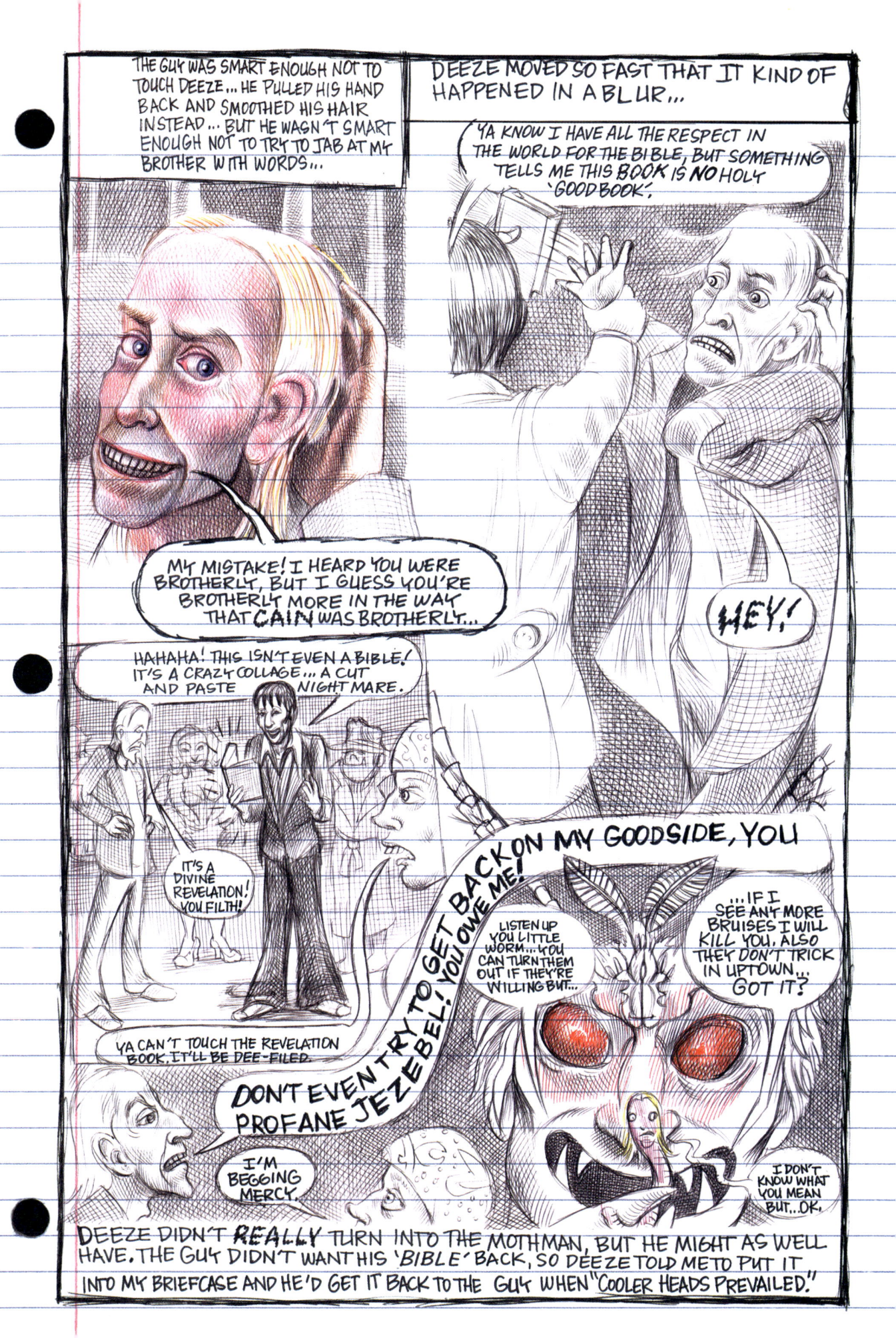

THE GUY WAS SMART ENOUGH NOT TO TOUCH DEEZE... HE PULLED HIS HAND BACK AND SMOOTHED HIS HAIR INSTEAD... BUT HE WASN'T SMART ENOUGH NOT TO TRY TO JAB AT MY BROTHER WITH WORDS...

DEEZE MOVED SO FAST THAT IT KIND OF HAPPENED IN A BLUR...

"YA KNOW I HAVE ALL THE RESPECT IN THE WORLD FOR THE BIBLE, BUT SOMETHING TELLS ME THIS BOOK IS NO HOLY 'GOOD BOOK'."

"MY MISTAKE! I HEARD YOU WERE BROTHERLY, BUT I GUESS YOU'RE BROTHERLY MORE IN THE WAY THAT CAIN WAS BROTHERLY..."

"HEY!"

"HAHAHA! THIS ISN'T EVEN A BIBLE! IT'S A CRAZY COLLAGE... A CUT AND PASTE NIGHTMARE."

"IT'S A DIVINE REVELATION! YOU FILTH!"

"DON'T EVEN TRY TO GET BACK ON MY GOODSIDE, YOU PROFANE JEZEBEL! YOU OWE ME!"

"LISTEN UP YOU LITTLE WORM... YOU CAN TURN THEM OUT IF THEY'RE WILLING BUT..."

"...IF I SEE ANY MORE BRUISES I WILL KILL YOU. ALSO THEY DON'T TRICK IN UPTOWN... GOT IT?"

"YA CAN'T TOUCH THE REVELATION BOOK, IT'LL BE DEE-FILED."

"I'M BEGGING MERCY."

"I DON'T KNOW WHAT YOU MEAN BUT...OK."

DEEZE DIDN'T REALLY TURN INTO THE MOTHMAN, BUT HE MIGHT AS WELL HAVE. THE GUY DIDN'T WANT HIS 'BIBLE' BACK, SO DEEZE TOLD ME TO PUT IT INTO MY BRIEFCASE AND HE'D GET IT BACK TO THE GUY WHEN "COOLER HEADS PREVAILED."

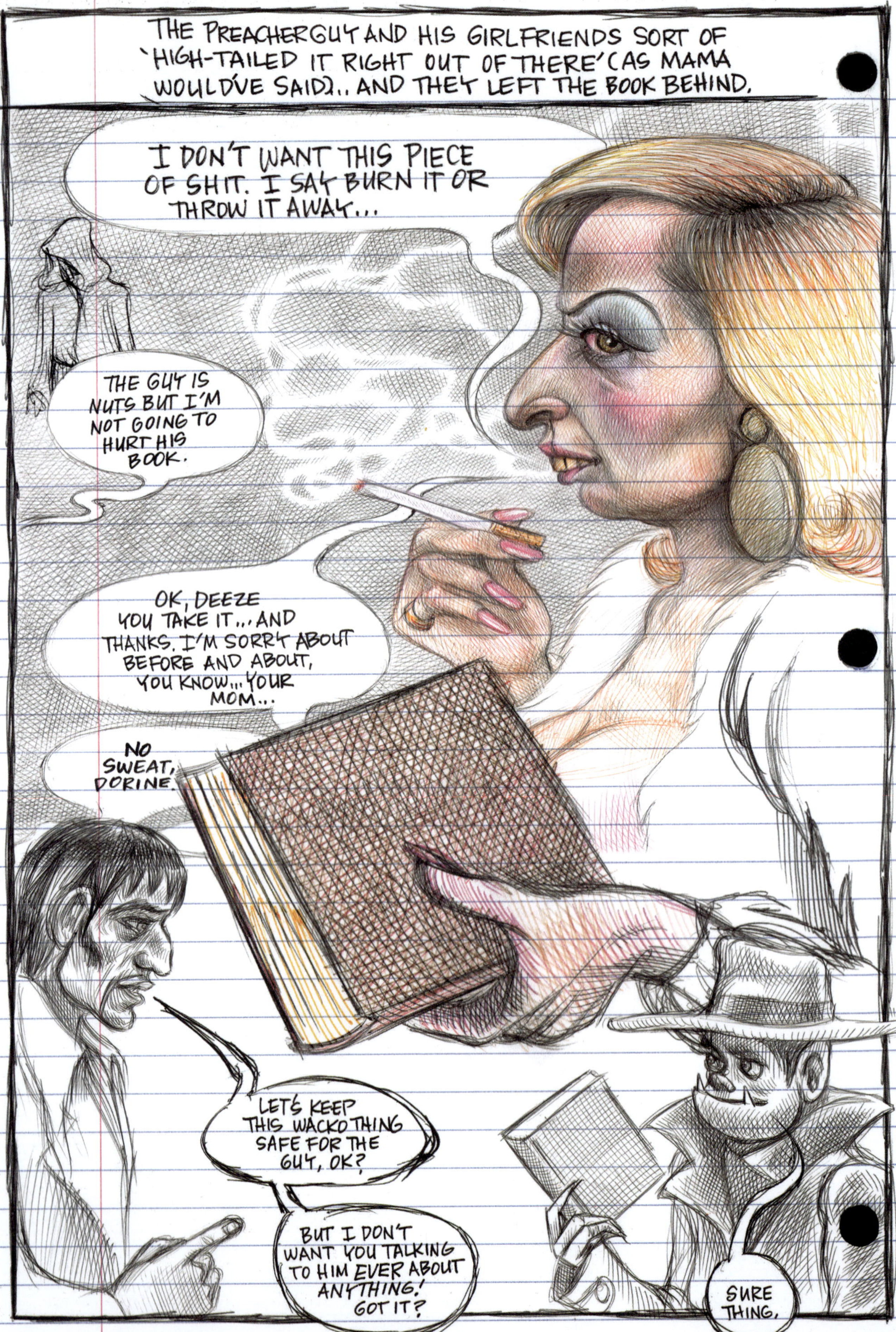
THE PREACHERGUY AND HIS GIRLFRIENDS SORT OF 'HIGH-TAILED IT RIGHT OUT OF THERE' (AS MAMA WOULD'VE SAID).. AND THEY LEFT THE BOOK BEHIND.
I DON'T WANT THIS PIECE OF SHIT. I SAY BURN IT OR THROW IT AWAY...
THE GUY IS NUTS BUT I'M NOT GOING TO HURT HIS BOOK.
OK, DEEZE YOU TAKE IT... AND THANKS. I'M SORRY ABOUT BEFORE AND ABOUT, YOU KNOW... YOUR MOM...
NO SWEAT, DORINE.
LET'S KEEP THIS WACKO THING SAFE FOR THE GUY, OK?
BUT I DON'T WANT YOU TALKING TO HIM EVER ABOUT ANYTHING! GOT IT?
SURE THING.

WHEN I PUT THE BOOK INTO MY BRIEFCASE THIS EXTREMELY CREEPY PAGE FELL OUT.

I KNOW THAT THE PREACHER GUY IS WEIRD AND MEAN BUT I HAVE TO ADMIT THAT I KIND OF LOVE THE PAGES IN HIS BOOK THAT HE TITLED "PICTURES OF SINNERS, DRAWN WITH PEN AND PENCIL." I HAVE SOME QUESTIONS ABOUT WHAT HIS BOOK MEANS.

WHEN WE GOT TO THE EL WE SAW OFFICER BRUMKIN YELLING AT DEEZE'S FRIEND 'THE BRAIN' AND TEARING UP THE POLITICAL PAMPHLETS THAT THE BRAIN HANDS OUT IN FRONT OF THE EL.

"COMMIE CRAP!"

"WELL KAREN, I'D THOUGHT WE COULD JUST SLIP OUT OF UPTOWN... BUT CLEARLY IT'S NOT GOING TO BE THAT SIMPLE..."

"LISTEN UP, *BOY!* KEEP AGITATING AND A STRAY BULLET'S GONNA GET FRIENDLY WITH YER BRAIN!"

"YOU TELL THAT GUY TO SHUT HIS TRAP!"

"GURDJIEFF SAID, 'BETTER TO DIE THAN LIVE IN SLEEP.'"

"I'D DO THAT BUT IT WOULD REALLY HURT HIS FEELINGS."

"I SAID, DO IT! AND TELL HIM HE'S A PIECE OF SHIT, TOO."

DEEZE AND OFFICER BRUMKIN WALKED DOWN THE BLOCK TO HAVE A PRIVATE CONVERSATION. EVERYONE IN UPTOWN KNOWS THAT DEEZE IS A FRIEND OF LAUGHING JACK GRONAN'S.

FOR A FEW MINUTES ME AND THE BRAIN STARED AT THE REMAINS OF HIS PAMPHLETS.

THE BRAIN HAS ALWAYS REMINDED ME OF AN ALIEN. →

"THE LITTER OF MY WRITING MAKES A RATHER PLEASING PATTERN WHEN COMBINED WITH THE GUM SPOTS."

"YOU'RE PRETTY CALM ABOUT THIS."

"I ASCRIBE TO THE BELIEF THAT THE PERSON WHO PUSHES YOUR BUTTONS IS YOUR OVERLORD."

"THAT'S DEEP."

"THE ONLY TRAGIC LOSS IS THE ORIGINAL PIECE OF ART THAT YOUR BROTHER DID FOR MY NOVEL."

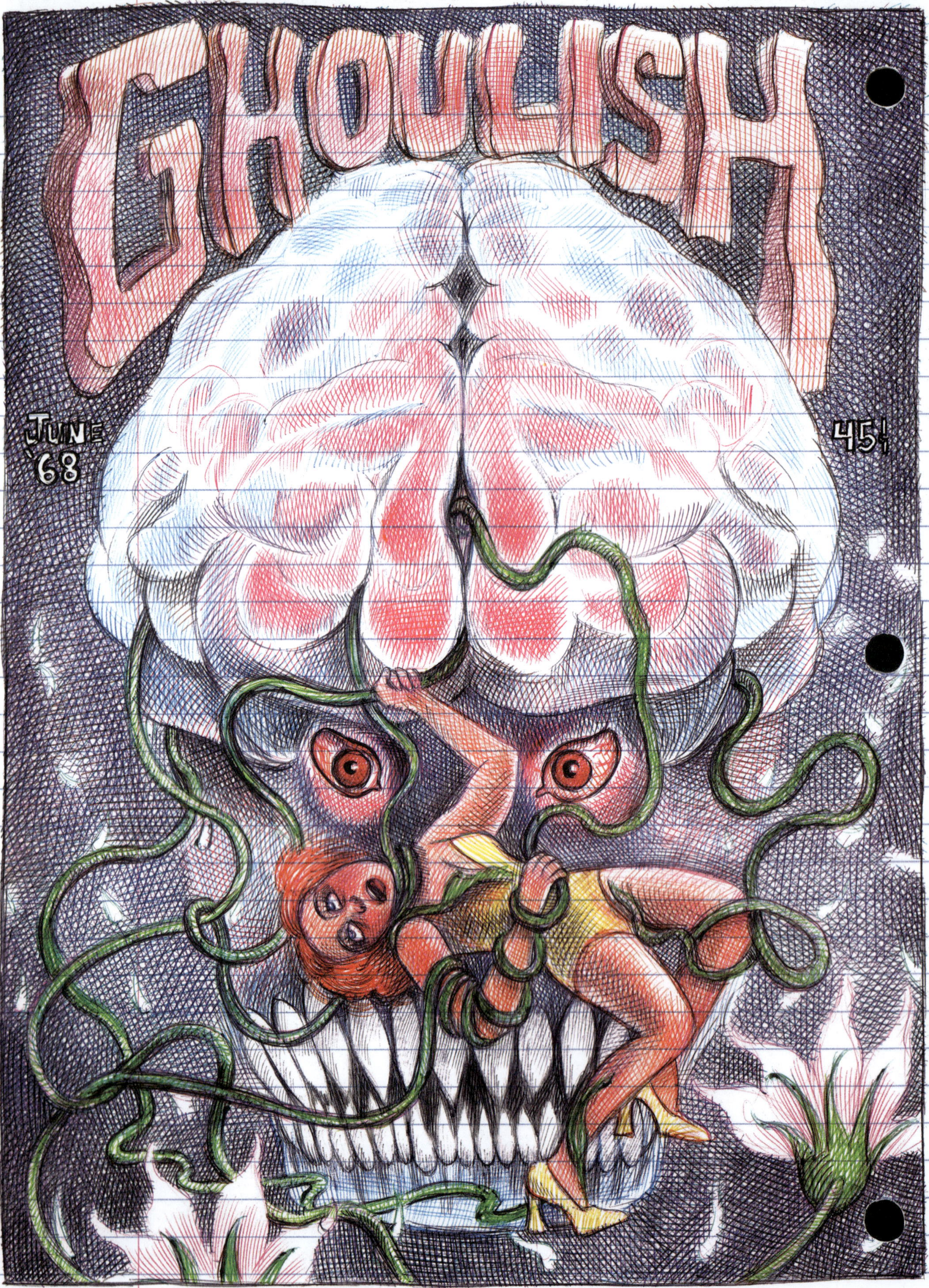
GHOULISH
JUNE '68
45¢

JEFFREY 'THE BRAIN' ALVAREZ IS A VERY WEIRD PERSON. HE HAS IDEAS AND OPINIONS THAT I NEVER HEARD BEFORE. FOR ONE THING HE DOES NOT EAT WHITE SUGAR, OR BREAD OR EVEN DRINK WATER FROM THE TAP. HE GOES TO CHINA TOWN TO BUY HIS TEA AND THE WATER HE USES FOR HIS TEA IS SPECIAL. THE BRAIN MADE A WATER FILTER WITH CHARCOAL IN IT THAT HE PUTS HIS TAP WATER INTO.
I REMEMBERED THE CONVERSATION WE HAD ABOUT IT...

"FLUORIDE ISN'T GOOD FOR THE HUMAN BRAIN."

"IT CAUSES A LOWER I.Q."

"EVERYBODY SAYS IT'S FOR OUR TEETH."

"NOPE. IT ISN'T GOOD FOR ANYONE'S TEETH, EITHER."

"THAT'S THE LIE THEY LIKE TO TELL."

"WHO IS THEY?"

"YOU HAVE TO ASK YOURSELF WHY ANYONE WOULD WANT TO POISON OUR WATER?"

"BUT WHO WOULD DO THAT?"

"THAT'S THE BIG QUESTION. IT'S THE QUESTION THAT WILL TAKE US RIGHT TO THE HARD TRUTH IF WE'RE BRAVE AND CURIOUS AND OPEN-MINDED."

A LOT OF THE TIME JEFFREY WEARS WILD COLORS LIKE THIS BUT TODAY HE WAS WEARING AN ARMY SURPLUS JACKET.

I'M NOT SURE IF JEFFERY IS RIGHT ABOUT ALL THAT STUFF, BUT HIS IDEAS ARE INTERESTING LIKE SCIENCE FICTION.

WE LOOKED REALLY HARD FOR THE PIECES OF THE ORIGINAL ART...

"WHAT IS YOUR NOVEL CALLED?"

"IT'S CALLED 'TRY ANNOYED ECSTASY'."

"NO, NOT RELIGIOUS. SPIRITUAL... YES... BUT IT'S SCIENCE FICTION..."

"LOOK, THAT IS A SCRAP OF THE COVER ART."

"'TRY ANNOYED ECSTASY'? A RELIGIOUS NOVEL? THAT ENCOURAGES... UM... ANNOYED ECSTASY?"

THEN I EXPLAINED HOW DEEZE THINKS THAT ALL OF MAMA'S SAINTS LOOK TOTALLY ANNOYED AND I WAS SURPRISED WHEN THE BRAIN LAUGHED.

"OH GAAWWD!! IT'S SOOO BORING HAVING A SWORD SPLITTING YOUR SKULL AND ALMOST CRAZY IMPOSSIBLE TO GET THROUGH A DOORWAY."

CARLO CRIVELLI 'SAINT PETER MARTYR' 1479

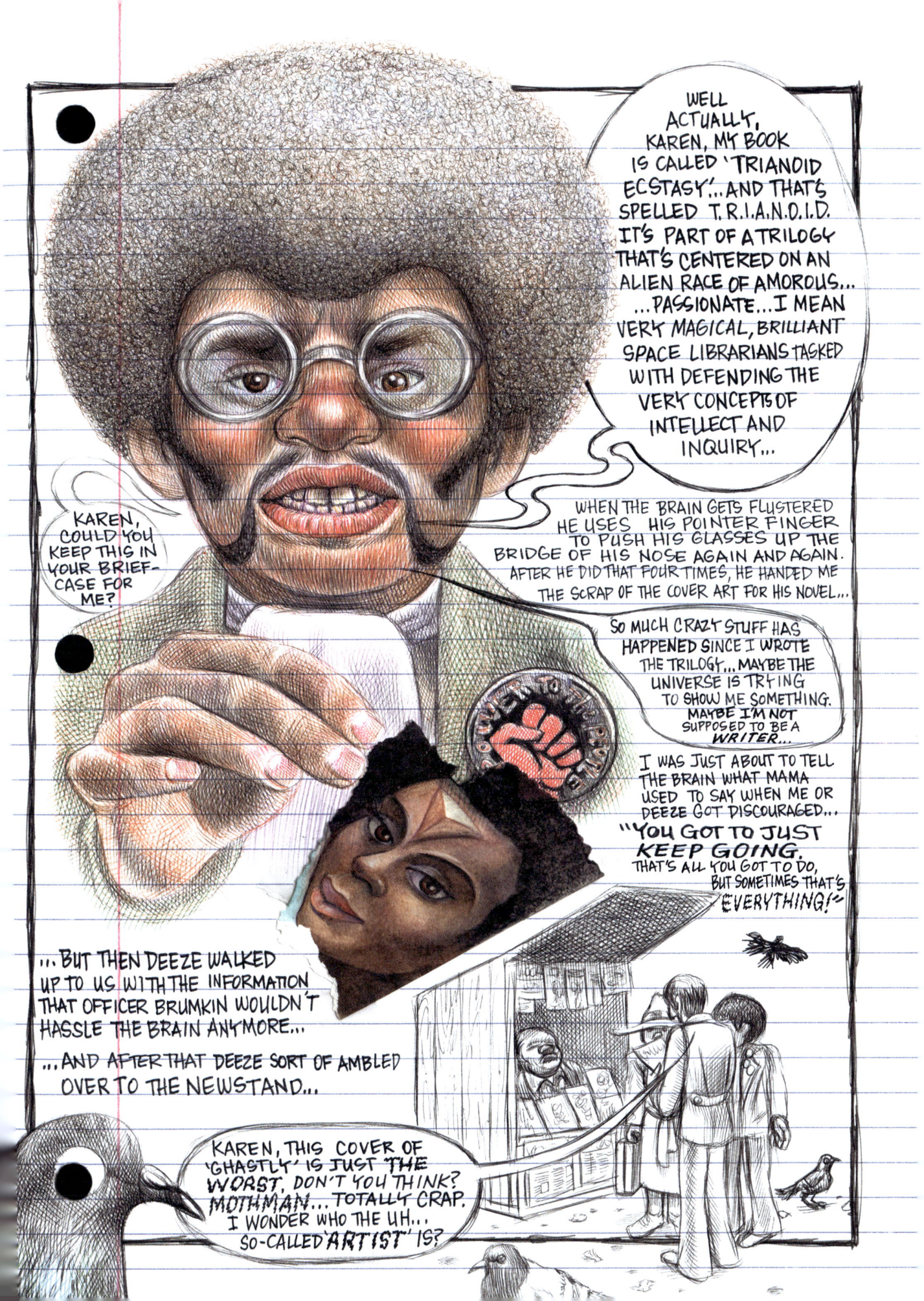

"WELL ACTUALLY, KAREN, MY BOOK IS CALLED 'TRIANOID ECSTASY'... AND THAT'S SPELLED T.R.I.A.N.O.I.D. IT'S PART OF A TRILOGY THAT'S CENTERED ON AN ALIEN RACE OF AMOROUS... ...PASSIONATE... I MEAN VERY MAGICAL, BRILLIANT SPACE LIBRARIANS TASKED WITH DEFENDING THE VERY CONCEPTS OF INTELLECT AND INQUIRY..."

"KAREN, COULD YOU KEEP THIS IN YOUR BRIEFCASE FOR ME?"

WHEN THE BRAIN GETS FLUSTERED HE USES HIS POINTER FINGER TO PUSH HIS GLASSES UP THE BRIDGE OF HIS NOSE AGAIN AND AGAIN. AFTER HE DID THAT FOUR TIMES, HE HANDED ME THE SCRAP OF THE COVER ART FOR HIS NOVEL...

"SO MUCH CRAZY STUFF HAS HAPPENED SINCE I WROTE THE TRILOGY... MAYBE THE UNIVERSE IS TRYING TO SHOW ME SOMETHING. MAYBE I'M NOT SUPPOSED TO BE A *WRITER*..."

I WAS JUST ABOUT TO TELL THE BRAIN WHAT MAMA USED TO SAY WHEN ME OR DEEZE GOT DISCOURAGED...

"YOU GOT TO JUST *KEEP GOING*. THAT'S ALL YOU GOT TO DO, BUT SOMETIMES THAT'S *EVERYTHING!*"

...BUT THEN DEEZE WALKED UP TO US WITH THE INFORMATION THAT OFFICER BRUMKIN WOULDN'T HASSLE THE BRAIN ANYMORE...

...AND AFTER THAT DEEZE SORT OF AMBLED OVER TO THE NEWSTAND...

"KAREN, THIS COVER OF 'GHASTLY' IS JUST *THE WORST*, DON'T YOU THINK? MOTHMAN... TOTALLY CRAP. I WONDER WHO THE UH... SO-CALLED '*ARTIST*' IS?"

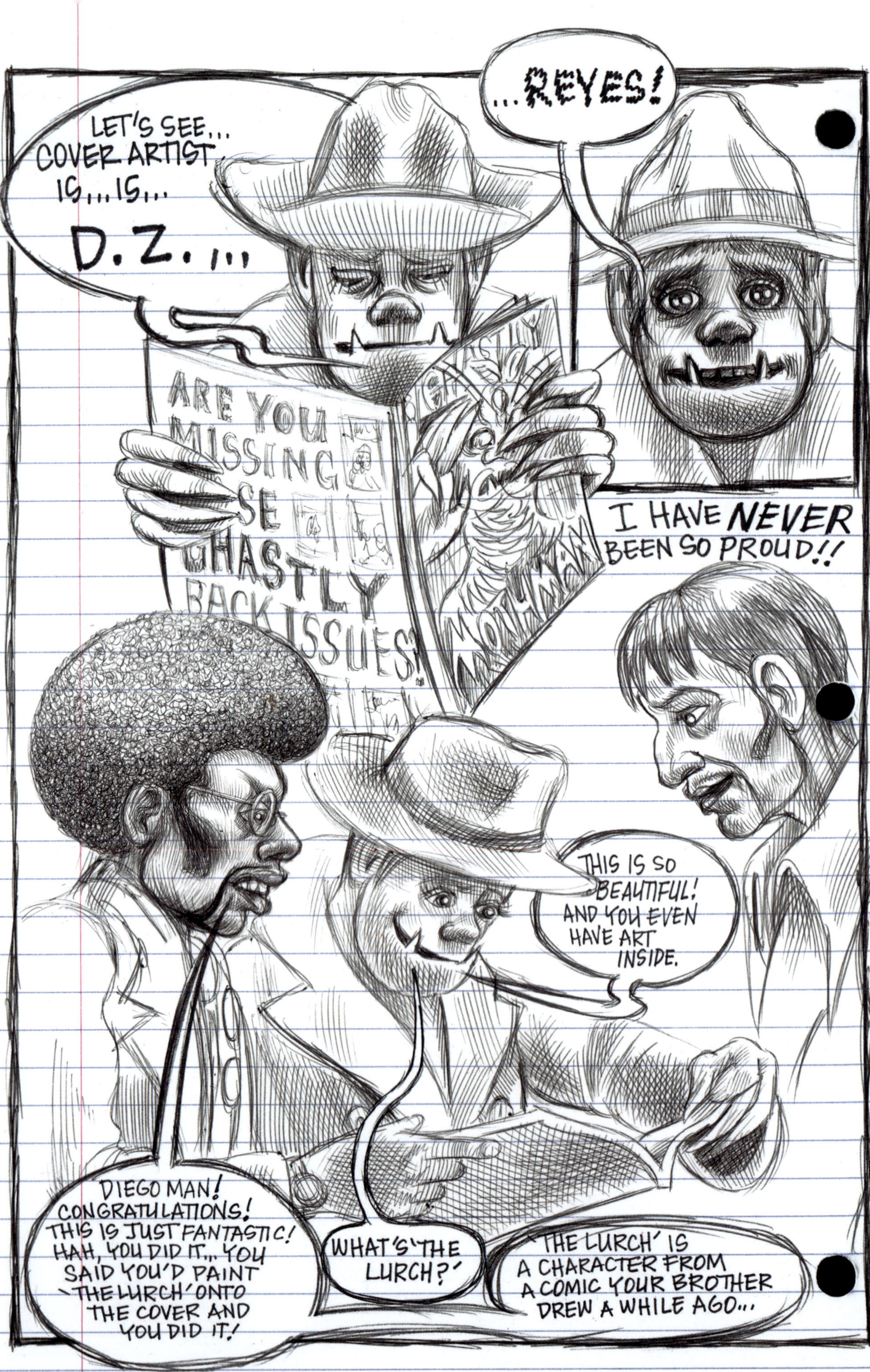
LET'S SEE... COVER ARTIST IS... IS... D.Z. ...
...REYES!
ARE YOU MISSING THESE GHASTLY BACK ISSUES!
GHASTLY
MOTHMAN
I HAVE NEVER BEEN SO PROUD!!
THIS IS SO BEAUTIFUL! AND YOU EVEN HAVE ART INSIDE.
DIEGO MAN! CONGRATULATIONS! THIS IS JUST FANTASTIC! HAH, YOU DID IT... YOU SAID YOU'D PAINT 'THE LURCH' ONTO THE COVER AND YOU DID IT!
WHAT'S 'THE LURCH?'
'THE LURCH' IS A CHARACTER FROM A COMIC YOUR BROTHER DREW A WHILE AGO...

WHEN DEEZE WENT OFF TO SHOW SOMEONE ELSE HIS GHASTLY, THE BRAIN DUG INTO HIS BAG AND PULLED THIS OUT AND HANDED IT TO ME...

LITTLE DICKEY WHITHERS IS LEFT IN THE LURCH

BY D. REYES

THE BRAIN SAID THAT IF I COMPARE 'LEFT IN THE LURCH' WITH THE MOTHMAN COVER OF GHASTLY MAGAZINE I WOULD SEE HOW MY BROTHER HID 'THE LURCH' IN PLAIN SIGHT... BUT THE BRAIN WOULDN'T TELL ME WHY DEEZE PLAYED THIS STRANGE TRICK ON THE WHOLE WORLD...

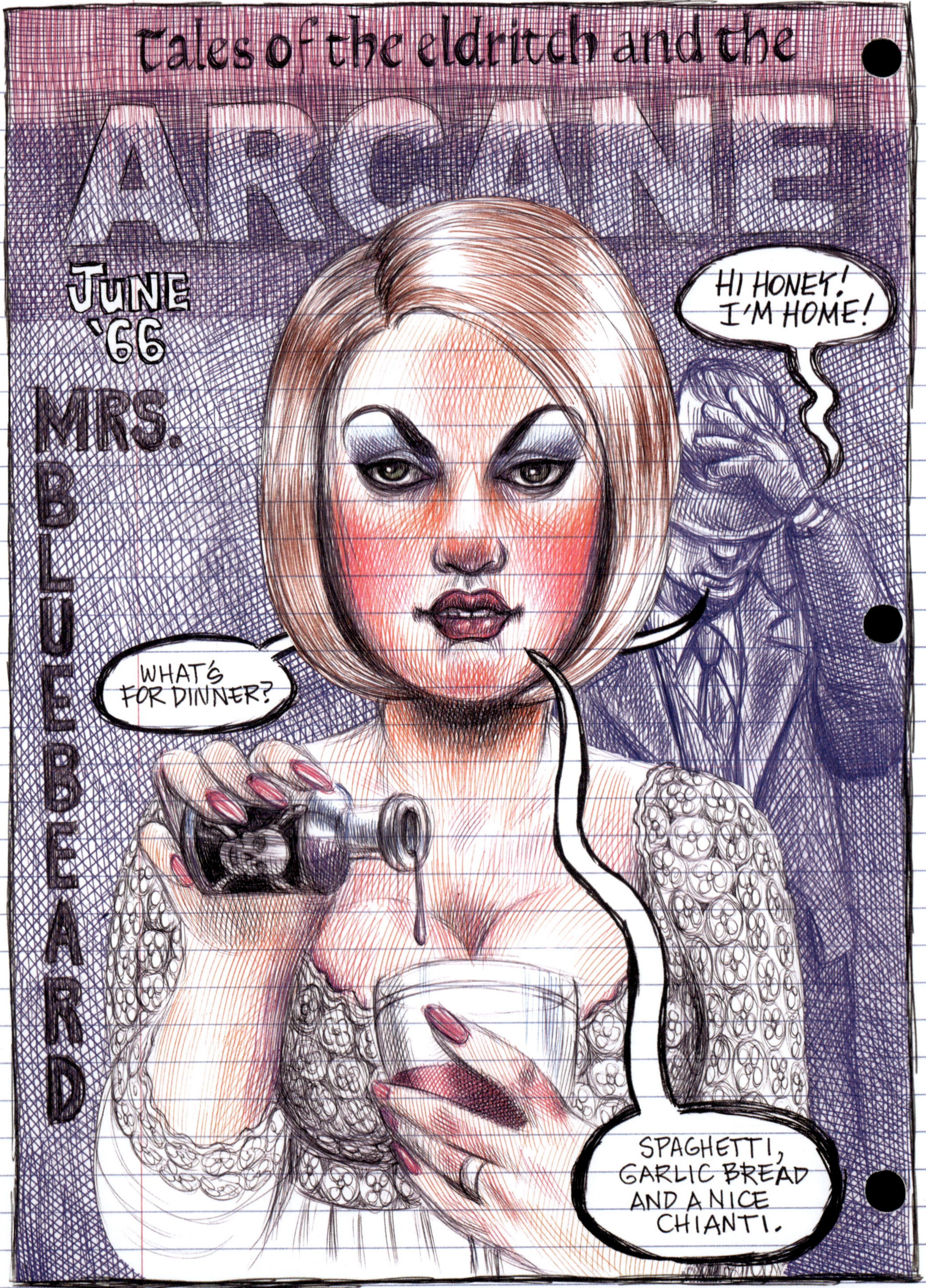
Tales of the eldritch and the
ARCANE
JUNE '66
MRS. BLUEBEARD
HI HONEY! I'M HOME!
WHAT'S FOR DINNER?
SPAGHETTI, GARLIC BREAD AND A NICE CHIANTI.

"HI KAREN REYES!"

AT THAT POINT I SAW A KID WHO I KNOW FROM THE NEIGHBORHOOD. HIS NAME IS DAN RICHWATER, BUT KIDS (MEAN ONES) CALL HIM "DANNY DITCHWATER." DAN ALWAYS SMILES LIKE CRAZY WHEN HE SEES ME AND HE ALWAYS WANTS TO PLAY WHAT HE CALLS "A MONSTER GAME." SOMETIMES I DO PLAY WITH HIM BECAUSE I FEEL SORRY FOR HIM BECAUSE OF HOW HARD HIS LIFE IS, SO I TRY NOT TO GET ANGRY WHEN HE OR HIS LITTLE BROTHER OR HIS SNAGGLE-TOOTH GRANNY SAY STUPID STUFF.

WHEN THE BLIND MUSICIAN WHO SITS IN FRONT OF THE EL STATION HEARD DAN'S VOICE HE STARTED SHAKING HIS HEAD CUZ HE KNEW WHAT WAS COMING...

"DAN-BOY YA AIN'T GONNA MESS WITH SPICS AND COLOREDS, ARE YA?"

"GRANNY, I'D LIKE TO TALK WITH KAREN REYES. PLEEASE?"

"IT AIN'T RIGHT..."

"...TO TRY TA POISON A CHILD'S INNOCENT MIND!"

"KIN I TALK TO HER?"

"IS SHE EVEN A *SHE*? IF YOUR PAP SEES YOU TALKING TO SPICS AND COLOREDS..."

"I KNOW. I'LL BE QUICK."

"THE HEART THAT WILL NOT BE DENIED CAN SURE ENOUGH EARN YOU A BEATING. ≷SIGH≶ GO AHEAD ON. I'LL WAIT."

"THANKS, GRAN."

"HI KAREN. I'M SORRY ABOUT THAT..."

"DANNY, I COULDN'T GET ANGRY ABOUT MUCH OF ANYTHING RIGHT NOW. MY BROTHER DID THE ART FOR THIS WHOLE MAGAZINE."

"LEMME SEE THAT?"

THEN DAN DID WHAT HE ALWAYS DOES.

I CALL IT HIS VERSION OF 'THE BIG HEIST.'

"THANKS FOR THE BRAND NEW MAGAZINE, KAREN REYES! SEE YA' AROUND, *SUCKER!*"

"NAW! I WAS JUS' FUNNIN' YOU, KAREN REYES."

DAN IS A TOTALLY GOOD-HEARTED KID BUT IT FEELS LIKE HE'S PRACTICING TO BE A REALLY ROTTEN ADULT.

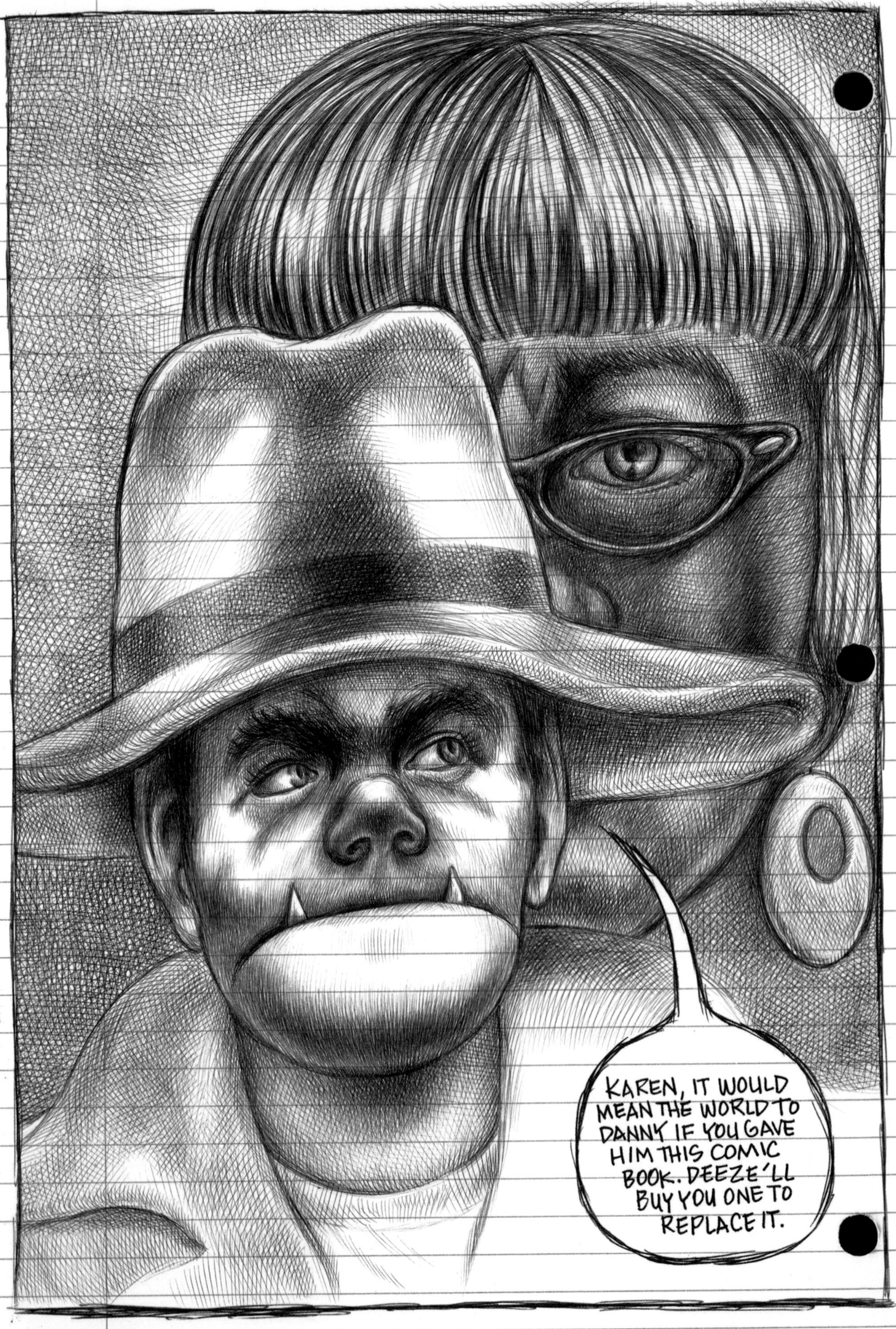
KAREN, IT WOULD MEAN THE WORLD TO DANNY IF YOU GAVE HIM THIS COMIC BOOK. DEEZE'LL BUY YOU ONE TO REPLACE IT.

"I'D LIKE TO GIVE THIS COPY TO YOU, DANNY."

"OH, I CAN'T, KAREN REYES... I WANT TO BUT IT'S YOUR SPECIAL BOOK YOUR BROTHER DONE MADE..."

"WELL, HOWABOUT I DROP IT BY YOUR HOUSE WHEN I'M DONE?"

THAT SETTLED IT. DANNY ACCEPTED HIS GIFT. I THOUGHT HE'D CRY. HE POINTED AT ONE GOOD DRAWING AFTER ANOTHER, BUT THEN HE SAID...

"LOOKIT THAT! YOUR BROTHER SURE IS A GOOD ARTIST! WHO WOULDA KNOWN A GANGSTER COULD DRAW?"

"HE IS A GREAT ARTIST, BUT HE ISN'T A GANGSTER, DANNY. HE'S JUST TOUGH, IS ALL."

"OKAY, KAREN REYES, IF'N YOU SAY SO."

I LET THE MATTER DROP BECAUSE I WAS SO HAPPY AND I WAS DISTRACTED BY HIS FINGERNAIL THAT WAS BITTEN DOWN TO THE BLOODY QUICK...

"KAREN REYES, I ALWAYS LIKE THE VILLAINS SO MUCH MORE THAN THE GOOD GUYS CUZ THE VILLAINS JUST DO SO MUCH MORE COOL STUFF AND THEY'VE ALWAYS GOT A GOOD REASON FOR ALL THE BAD STUFF THEY DO."

LATER ON, AFTER I READ THE ISSUE COVER-TO-COVER I REALIZED HOW MUCH DANNY WAS GOING TO LOVE THE VILLAIN OF "MOTHMAN." I WAS GLAD THAT I HAD LISTENED TO MAMA — EVEN IF DANNY WOULD HAVE TO READ HIS ISSUE OF GHASTLY IN SECRECY.

"WHY DID YA GIVE DANNY THAT THERE TRASH? AIN'T NOBODY EVER TOLD YA THAT THEM COMIC BOOKS ROT YER BRAIN? DAN, GIVE IT ON BACK TO THIS GIRL AND TELL HER YA DON'T WANT IT NO MORE."

"BUT GRAM, I DO WANT IT. IT'S JUST A STORY LIKE YOUR SOAP STORIES ON THE T.V. PLEASE GRAMMY, I WANT TA KEEP IT REAL BAD. I PROMISE TO KEEP IT HIDDEN. PLEEAASSE?"

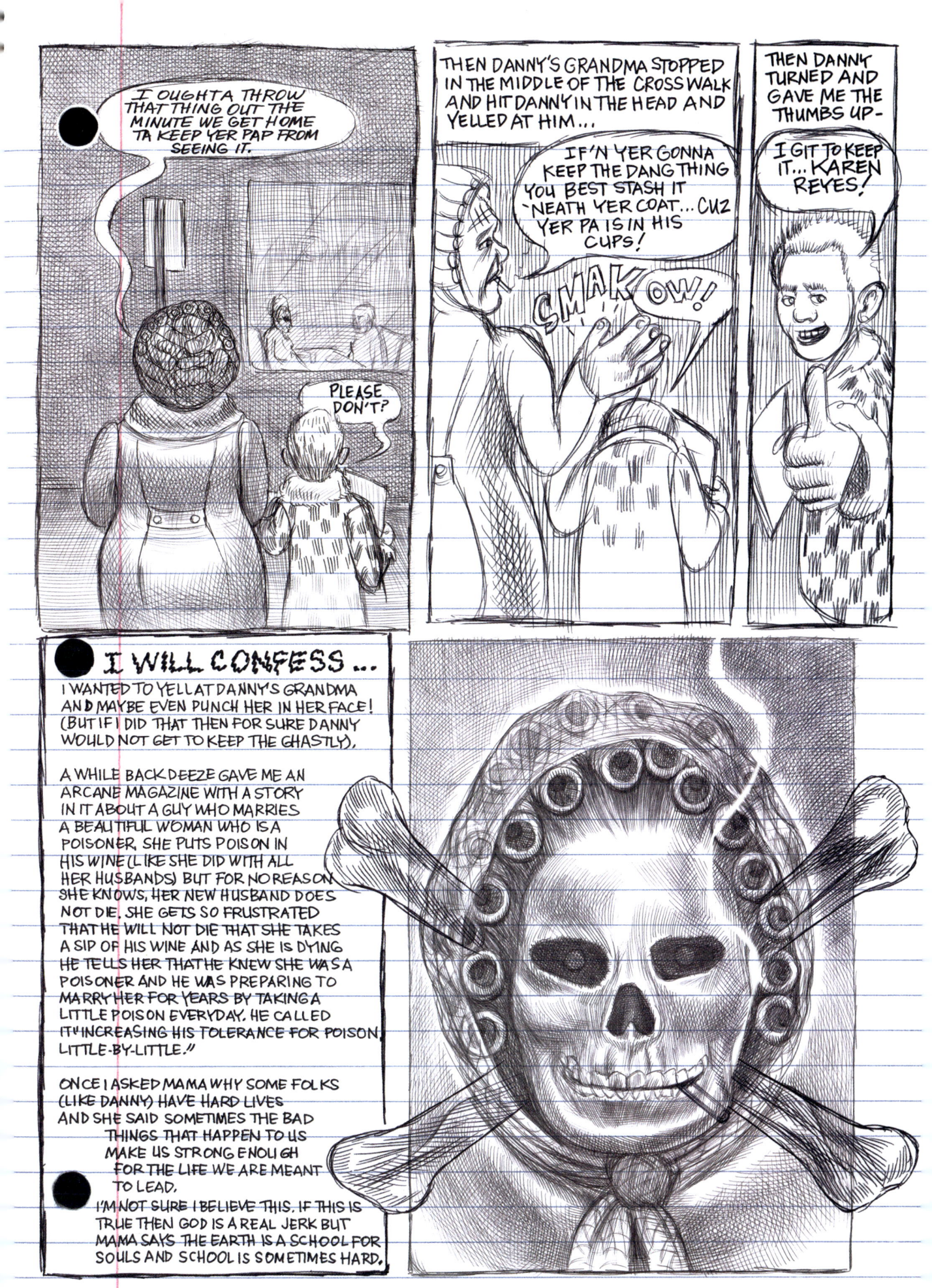

Panel 1:
"I OUGHTA THROW THAT THING OUT THE MINUTE WE GET HOME TA KEEP YER PAP FROM SEEING IT."

"PLEASE DON'T?"

Panel 2:
THEN DANNY'S GRANDMA STOPPED IN THE MIDDLE OF THE CROSSWALK AND HIT DANNY IN THE HEAD AND YELLED AT HIM...

"IF'N YER GONNA KEEP THE DANG THING YOU BEST STASH IT 'NEATH YER COAT... CUZ YER PA IS IN HIS CUPS!"

SMAK OW!

Panel 3:
THEN DANNY TURNED AND GAVE ME THE THUMBS UP—

"I GIT TO KEEP IT... KAREN REYES!"

Panel 4: I WILL CONFESS...

I WANTED TO YELL AT DANNY'S GRANDMA AND MAYBE EVEN PUNCH HER IN HER FACE! (BUT IF I DID THAT THEN FOR SURE DANNY WOULD NOT GET TO KEEP THE GHASTLY).

A WHILE BACK DEEZE GAVE ME AN ARCANE MAGAZINE WITH A STORY IN IT ABOUT A GUY WHO MARRIES A BEAUTIFUL WOMAN WHO IS A POISONER. SHE PUTS POISON IN HIS WINE (LIKE SHE DID WITH ALL HER HUSBANDS) BUT FOR NO REASON SHE KNOWS, HER NEW HUSBAND DOES NOT DIE. SHE GETS SO FRUSTRATED THAT HE WILL NOT DIE THAT SHE TAKES A SIP OF HIS WINE AND AS SHE IS DYING HE TELLS HER THAT HE KNEW SHE WAS A POISONER AND HE WAS PREPARING TO MARRY HER FOR YEARS BY TAKING A LITTLE POISON EVERYDAY. HE CALLED IT "INCREASING HIS TOLERANCE FOR POISON, LITTLE-BY-LITTLE."

ONCE I ASKED MAMA WHY SOME FOLKS (LIKE DANNY) HAVE HARD LIVES AND SHE SAID SOMETIMES THE BAD THINGS THAT HAPPEN TO US MAKE US STRONG ENOUGH FOR THE LIFE WE ARE MEANT TO LEAD.

I'M NOT SURE I BELIEVE THIS. IF THIS IS TRUE THEN GOD IS A REAL JERK BUT MAMA SAYS THE EARTH IS A SCHOOL FOR SOULS AND SCHOOL IS SOMETIMES HARD.

Tales of the eldritch and the ARCANE

JULY '68 — 40¢

HIDDEN SYMBOLS OF THE DARK LORDS

LEFT HAND OF THE DRUID

AS WE WALKED ALONG, I GOT THE FEELING OF WHAT IT WOULD BE LIKE TO HAVE A PACK.

...BUT A FEW STEPS ON, WHEN I TOLD THEM ABOUT THE DRUID POSSIBLY FOLLOWING ME AND TURNED BACK TO CHECK FOR HIM, DEEZE DISAPPOINTED ME BY NOT TAKING IT SERIOUSLY...

KAREN, *RELAX*. IT'S MORE THAN LIKELY JUST A HARMLESS HIPPIE.

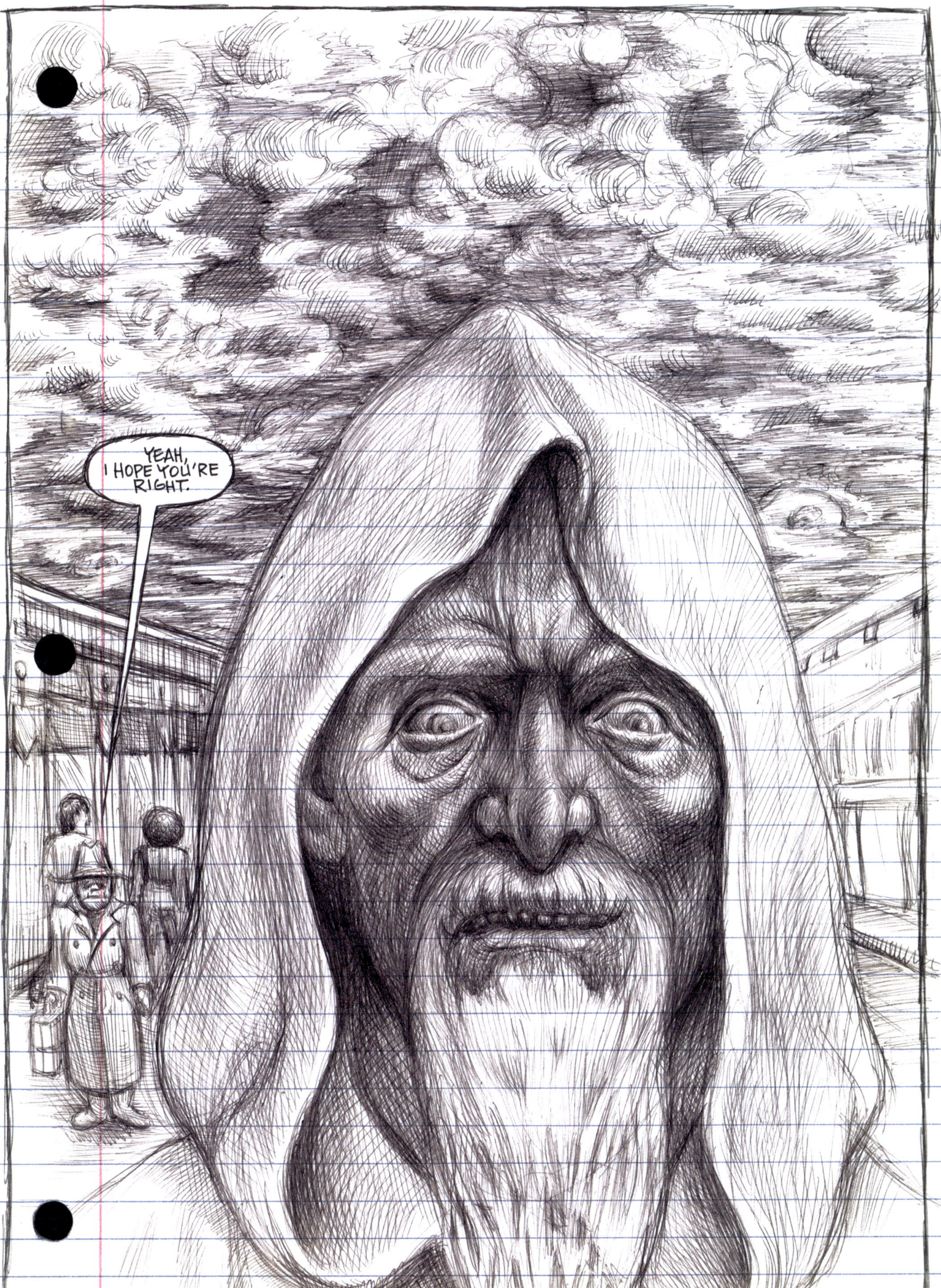
YEAH, I HOPE YOU'RE RIGHT.

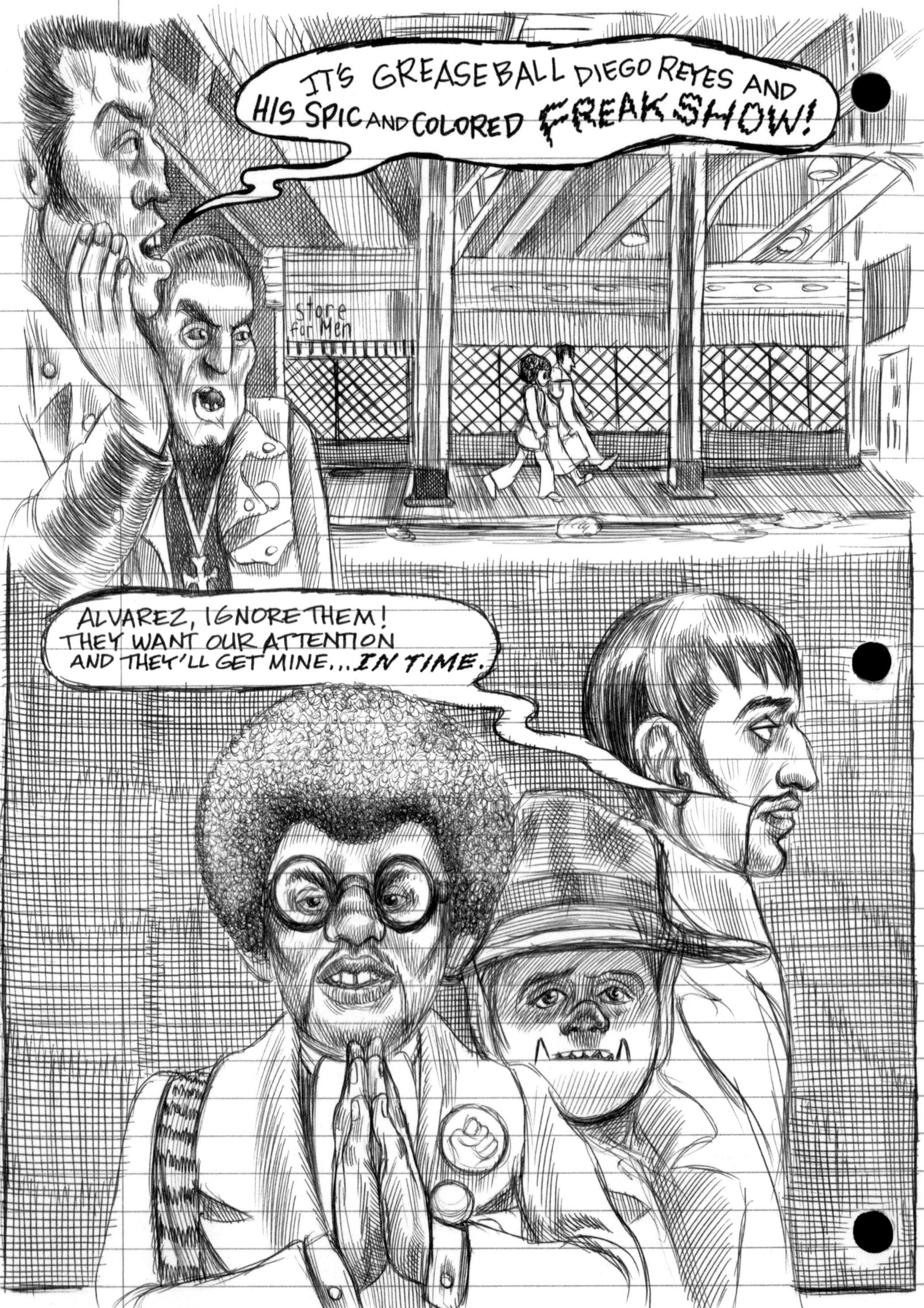

IT'S GREASEBALL DIEGO REYES AND HIS SPIC AND COLORED FREAK SHOW!
store for Men
ALVAREZ, IGNORE THEM! THEY WANT OUR ATTENTION AND THEY'LL GET MINE... IN TIME.

Panel 1:

Narration: I KNEW I SHOULD KEEP MY EYES OPEN JUST IN CASE THE DRUID WAS WATCHING ME FROM SOMEWHERE OUTSIDE.

Kare: WHAT'S THE DEAL WITH THE BRAIN DOING THE PRAYING HANDS THING AND THAT WEIRD BOW TO THOSE ICKY GUYS.

Deeze: OH HELL, KARE, I'VE NEVER TOTALLY FIGURED OUT ALVAREZ. MY HUNCH IS THAT HIS IDEA IS THAT HE'S BEING FORMED BY THE ABSURDITY... NO, THE WORD IS 'ADVERSITY.'

Panel 2:

Kare: FORMED BY ADVERSITY? SO THAT WAS HIM THANKING THOSE GUYS FOR CALLING HIM A BAD NAME?

Deeze: PRETTY MUCH, BUT THOSE 'INSANE POPE' WANNABEES WILL COME TO REGRET THAT BULLSHIT.

Narration: DEEZE LET ME ORDER COCA-COLA FOR BREAKFAST, WHICH MAMA WOULD NEVER HAVE DONE, SO EVEN THOUGH I WAS CURIOUS ABOUT WHAT DEEZE WAS GOING TO DO TO THOSE GUYS, I KEPT IT TO MYSELF...

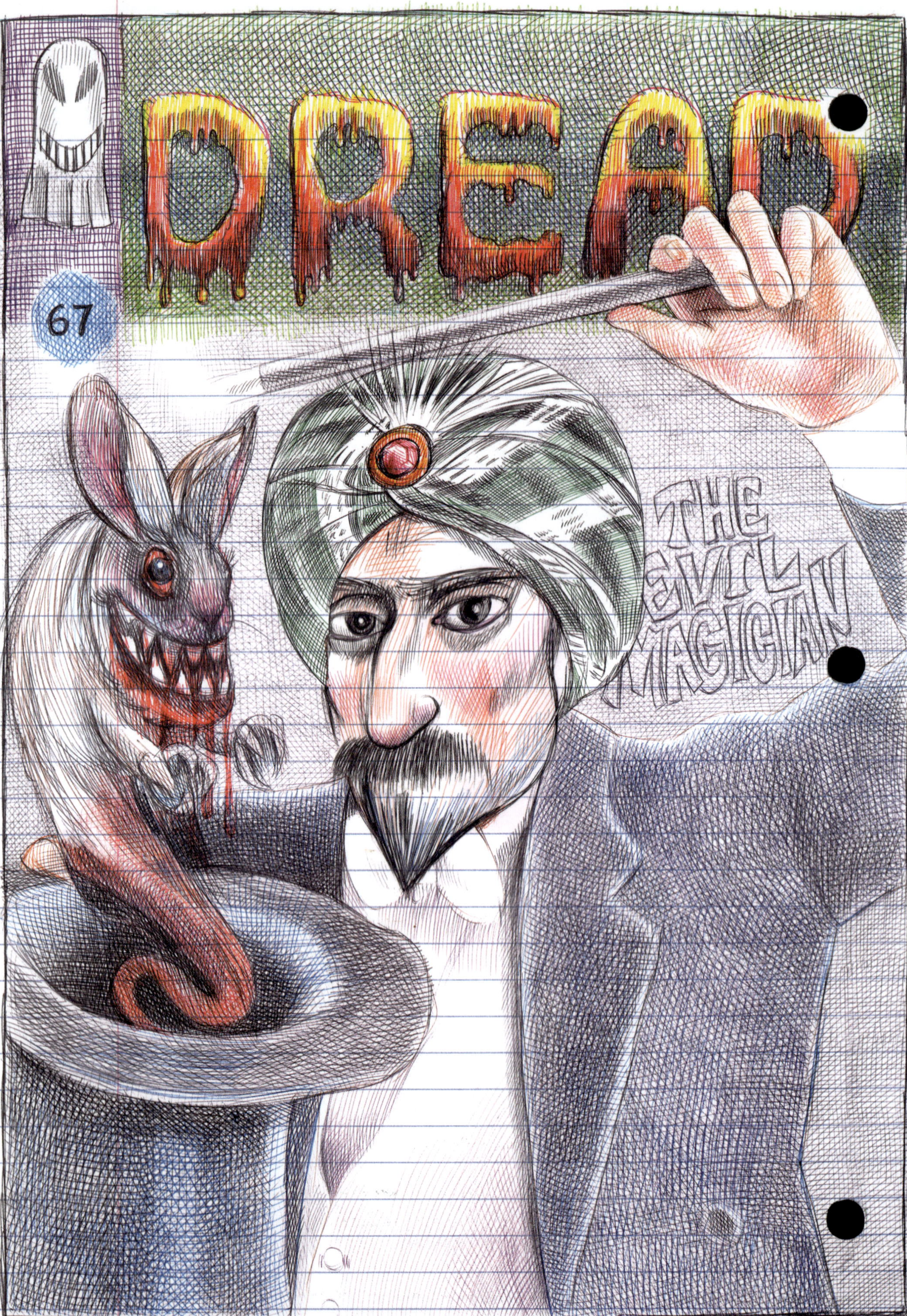
DREAD
67
THE EVIL MAGICIAN

DANTE THE MAGICIAN

DANTE IS THE CHEF AT THE DINER BUT THAT IS NOT HOW HE GOT HIS NICKNAME.

"HEY, DEEZE! AND KAREN! SO GOOD TO SEE YOU BOTH!"

"I'M GOING TO MAKE SOME SPECIAL STUFF FOR YOU TODAY."

"DEEZE, MAN, SO SORRY ABOUT GETTING TO THE FUNERAL LATE. YOU KNOW THE DAMN OWNER HERE HE WOULD NOT GIVE ME THE DAY OFF."

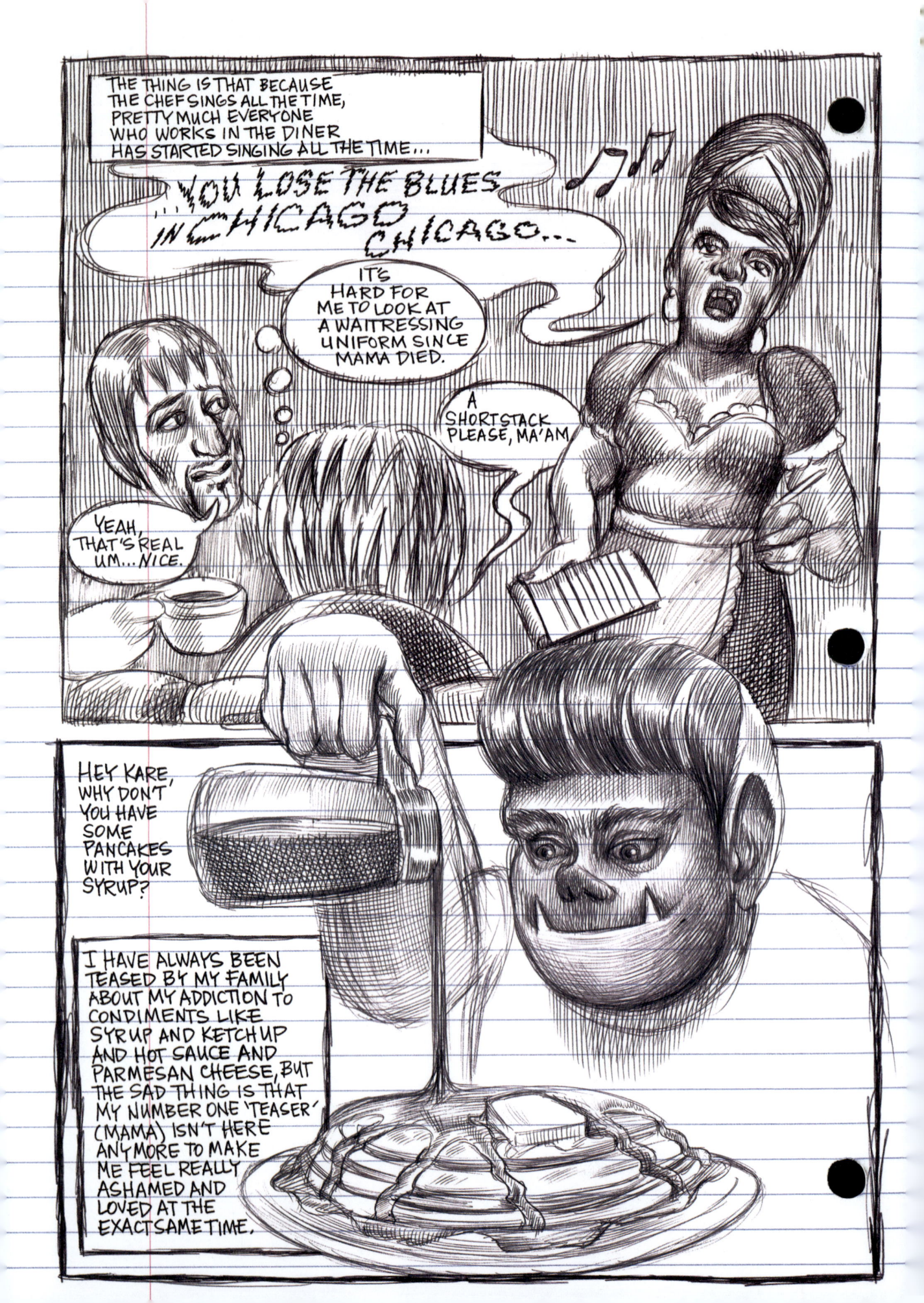

THE THING IS THAT BECAUSE THE CHEF SINGS ALL THE TIME, PRETTY MUCH EVERYONE WHO WORKS IN THE DINER HAS STARTED SINGING ALL THE TIME...

"YOU LOSE THE BLUES IN CHICAGO CHICAGO..."

IT'S HARD FOR ME TO LOOK AT A WAITRESSING UNIFORM SINCE MAMA DIED.

A SHORTSTACK PLEASE, MA'AM

YEAH, THAT'S REAL UM... NICE.

HEY KARE, WHY DON'T YOU HAVE SOME PANCAKES WITH YOUR SYRUP?

I HAVE ALWAYS BEEN TEASED BY MY FAMILY ABOUT MY ADDICTION TO CONDIMENTS LIKE SYRUP AND KETCHUP AND HOT SAUCE AND PARMESAN CHEESE, BUT THE SAD THING IS THAT MY NUMBER ONE 'TEASER' (MAMA) ISN'T HERE ANY MORE TO MAKE ME FEEL REALLY ASHAMED AND LOVED AT THE EXACT SAME TIME.

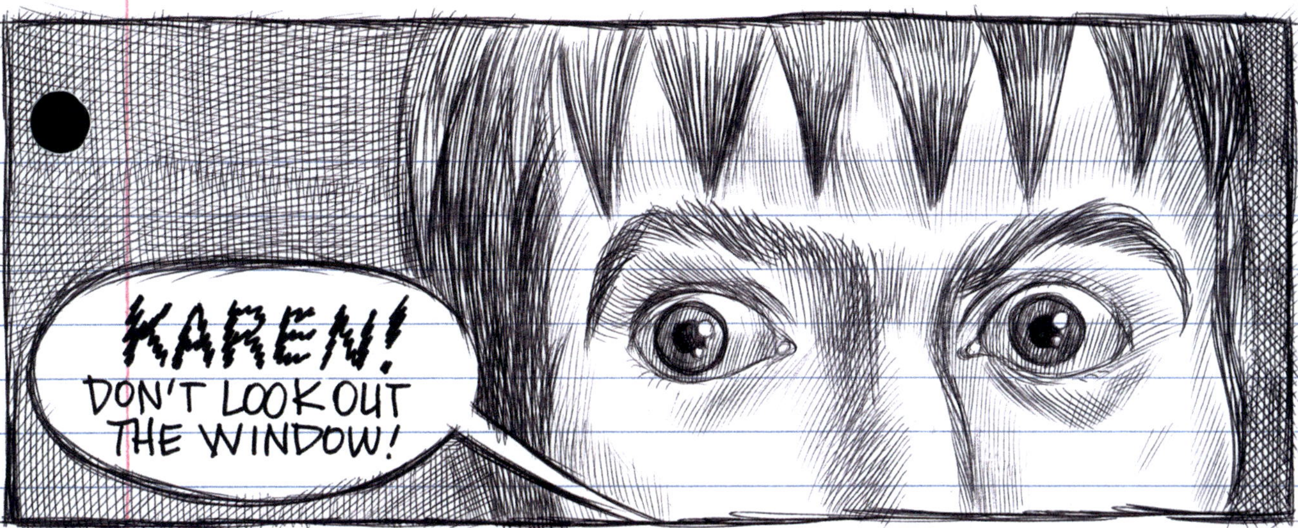
KAREN! DON'T LOOK OUT THE WINDOW!

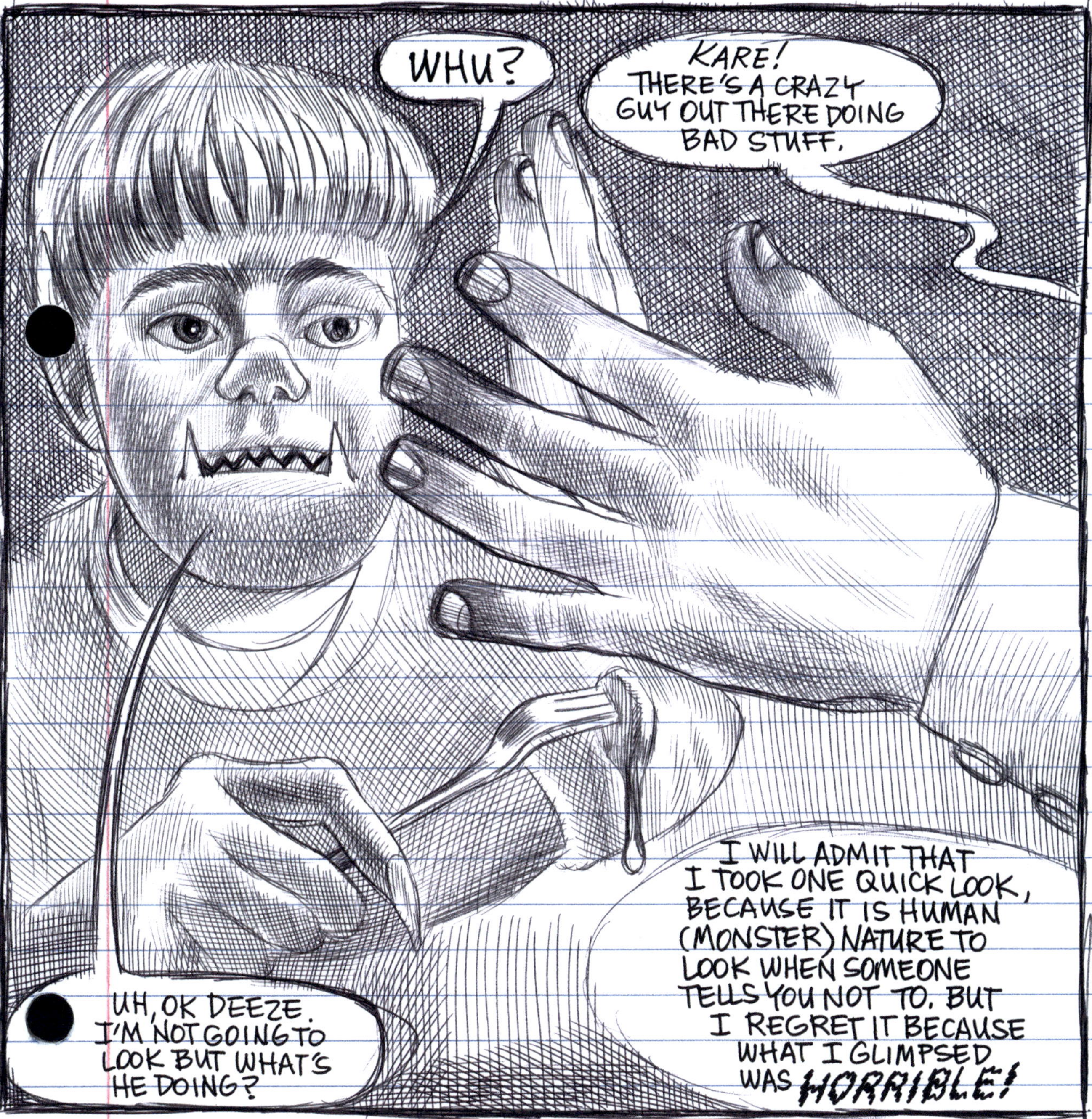
WHU?
KARE! THERE'S A CRAZY GUY OUT THERE DOING BAD STUFF.
UH, OK DEEZE. I'M NOT GOING TO LOOK BUT WHAT'S HE DOING?
I WILL ADMIT THAT I TOOK ONE QUICK LOOK, BECAUSE IT IS HUMAN (MONSTER) NATURE TO LOOK WHEN SOMEONE TELLS YOU NOT TO. BUT I REGRET IT BECAUSE WHAT I GLIMPSED WAS HORRIBLE!

AT FIRST I THOUGHT THE WEIRD DIRTY GUY WAS WASHING THE WINDOW BUT THEN I REALIZED HE WAS *PEEING* ON THE WINDOW!!

YAMBO FUMBO SO SKILLED MY TOY. SKILLED MY ONLY TOY!! FUCKING... BASHARDS...

THE GROSS PART WAS RIGHT HERE AND I DID NOT DRAW IT BECAUSE EW! THE WHOLE THING MADE DEEZE INTO HIS DRAGON SELF...

After Deeze went out of the restaurant, I wanted to follow, but Dante is one of Deeze's best friends and he didn't let me even get out of the booth. I could tell he was distracting me. Everyone in uptown always calls him 'Dante the Magician' because his singing has had the power to calm down the Latin Kings and the Insane Popes when they were just about to go to war.

"Karen, Karen I'm going to sing just for you. This is my song for you. Please listen only to me..."

AVE MARRRIA GRAT AI T PLENA MARIA GRATI A A PLEN A A A A MARIA GRATI A A A PLENA A A A

Mama used to say Dante's voice was like butter melting off a honey factory. Just hearing him sing made me feel calm and sad at the exact same time.

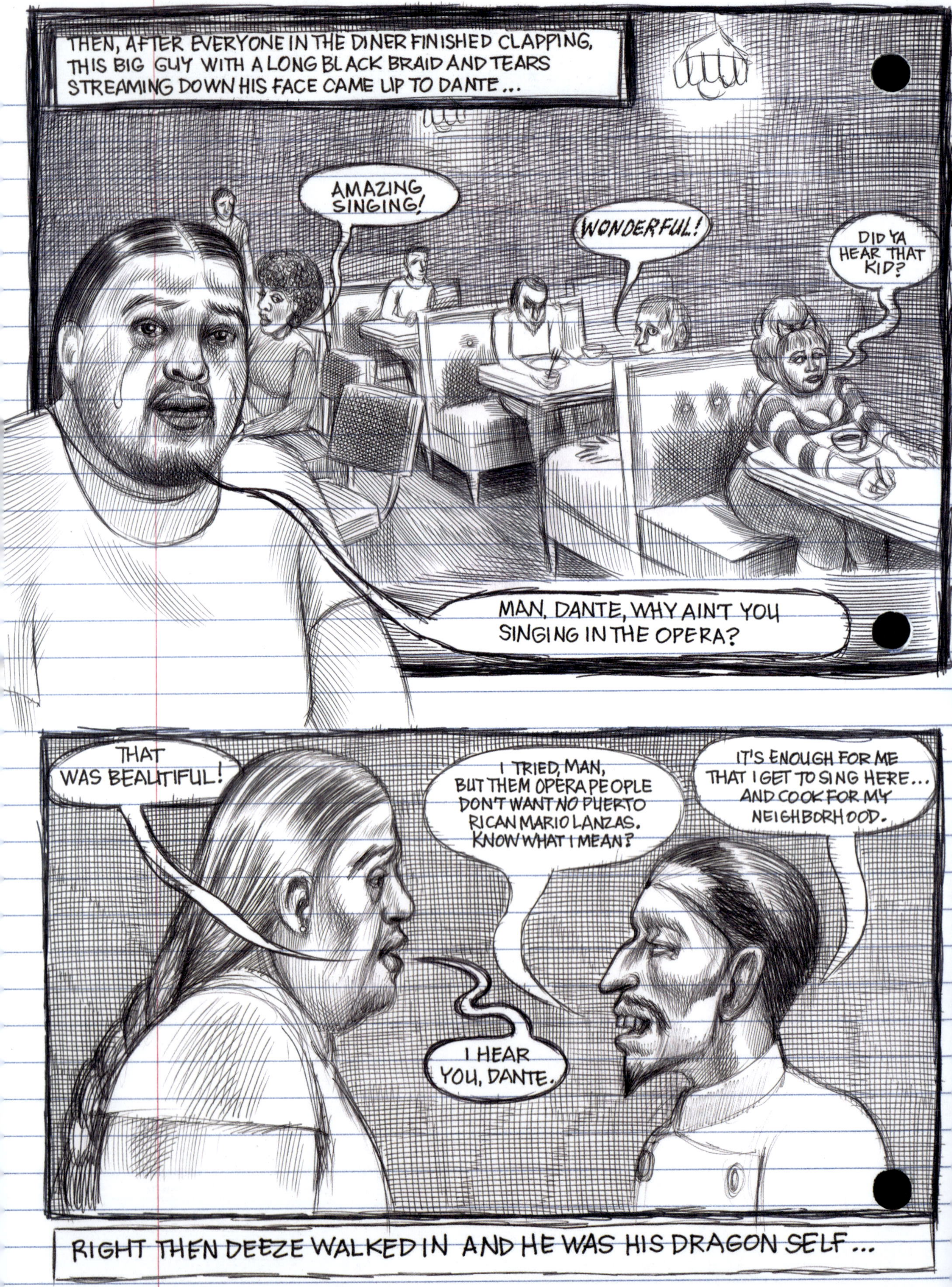
THEN, AFTER EVERYONE IN THE DINER FINISHED CLAPPING, THIS BIG GUY WITH A LONG BLACK BRAID AND TEARS STREAMING DOWN HIS FACE CAME UP TO DANTE...
AMAZING SINGING!
WONDERFUL!
DID YA HEAR THAT KID?
MAN, DANTE, WHY AIN'T YOU SINGING IN THE OPERA?
THAT WAS BEAUTIFUL!
I TRIED, MAN, BUT THEM OPERA PEOPLE DON'T WANT NO PUERTO RICAN MARIO LANZAS. KNOW WHAT I MEAN?
IT'S ENOUGH FOR ME THAT I GET TO SING HERE... AND COOK FOR MY NEIGHBORHOOD.
I HEAR YOU, DANTE.
RIGHT THEN DEEZE WALKED IN AND HE WAS HIS DRAGON SELF...

"THANKS, MAN."

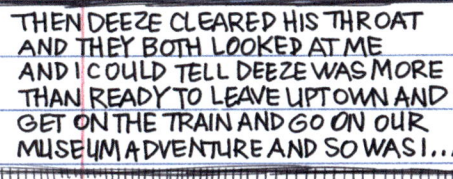

I THINK THAT DEEZE WAS THANKING DANTE FOR DISTRACTING ME FROM SEEING THE GUY'S GROSS PARTS AND MAYBE ALSO DISTRACTING ME FROM WATCHING DEEZE BEAT THE ICKY GUY UP...

"WHAT THE FUCKING FUCK WAS THAT BULLSHIT, MAN, I MEAN..."

"...AIN'T IT ENOUGH THAT YOU LOSE YOUR MOM? I'LL LAY YOU ODDS, MAN, THAT'S THE REASON THAT, UH—"

THEN DEEZE CLEARED HIS THROAT AND THEY BOTH LOOKED AT ME AND I COULD TELL DEEZE WAS MORE THAN READY TO LEAVE UPTOWN AND GET ON THE TRAIN AND GO ON OUR MUSEUM ADVENTURE AND SO WAS I...

WHEN DANTE LOOKED THROUGH THE WINDOW AND SAW HIS COUSIN 'THE BRAIN' WAITING FOR US OUTSIDE HE SAID...

"DEEZE, MAN, I DON'T KNOW WHY YOU WANT TO HANG OUT WITH THAT CREEP, ESPECIALLY WITH YOUR SISTER."

"CATCH YOU LATER, DANTE."

I KEPT TRYING TO DECIDE WHICH PAINTING I WAS GOING TO CLIMB INTO.

DANTE THE MAGICIAN IS A COOL GUY BUT WHY DOES HE HATE HIS OWN COUSIN SO MUCH?

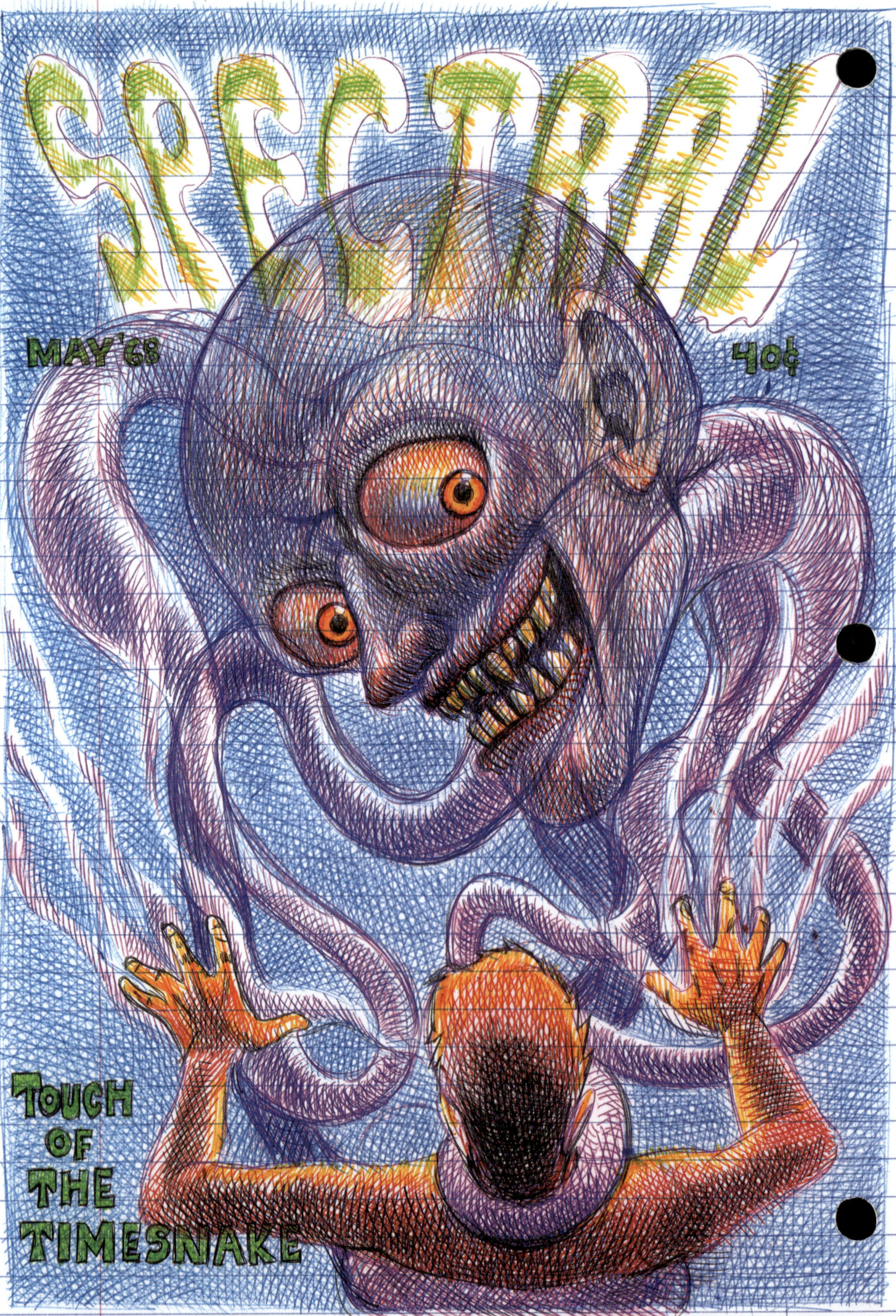
SPECTRAL
MAY '68
40¢
TOUCH OF THE TIMESNAKE

THE FACT IS THAT **PEOPLE ARE WEIRD** AND THE BRAIN IS WEIRDER THAN MOST. WHILE WE SAT IN THE RESTAURANT THE BRAIN HAD HANDED OUT HIS PAMPHETS BUT I GOT THE FEELING THAT HE WAS ACTUALLY *WATCHING ME AND DEEZE*. THEN HE WALKED US TO THE EL STATION *AND DIDN'T EVEN GET ON THE TRAIN.*

"I DON'T REALLY *GET* YOUR FRIEND THE BRAIN."

"LET'S FIND YOU A GOOD SEAT FOR STEALTH DRAWING."

WHEN WE SAT DOWN I SAW THE GRAFFITI.

I WILL CONFESS THAT BEFORE HE BECAME 'RESPONSIBLE,' DEEZE USED TO DO GRAFFITI WITH ME AS HIS ASSISTANT. SO I KNOW SOMETHING ABOUT THE SUBJECT. SOMETIMES PEOPLE MAKE BORING GRAFFITTI (WE DIDN'T) BUT OCCASIONALLY THEY TAKE IT REALLY SERIOUSLY AND TURN IN THEIR BEST EFFORT.

Karen: Wow, Deeze, that's impressive graffiti. It says, "Curtis, I gave your woman 3 orgasms."

Deeze: Karen, it didn't say that and do you have to read stuff like that for the whole train?

Karen: It did too say that and it was GIGANTIC! Didn't you read it, Deeze?

Deeze: I suppose I did read it but right now, Karen, I've got a lot of shit on my mind.

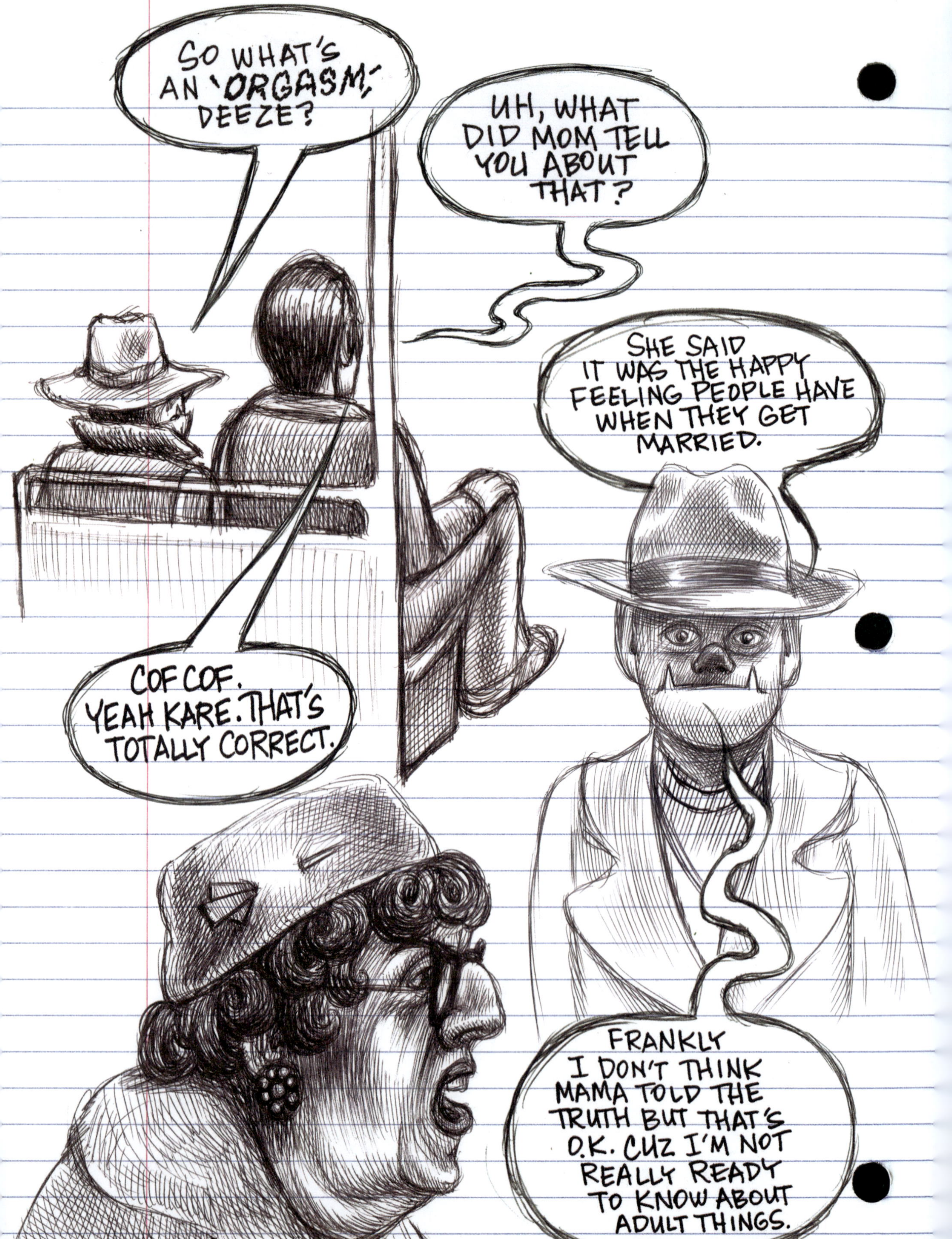
SO WHAT'S AN 'ORGASM,' DEEZE?
UH, WHAT DID MOM TELL YOU ABOUT THAT?
SHE SAID IT WAS THE HAPPY FEELING PEOPLE HAVE WHEN THEY GET MARRIED.
COF COF. YEAH KARE. THAT'S TOTALLY CORRECT.
FRANKLY I DON'T THINK MAMA TOLD THE TRUTH BUT THAT'S O.K. CUZ I'M NOT REALLY READY TO KNOW ABOUT ADULT THINGS.

"YOU KNOW YOU SHOULD START A NOTEBOOK THAT'S JUST FOR EL DRAWINGS."

"GOOD IDEA. UH OH."

"HEY KID, YOU DRAWING ME? DON'T WORRY, IT'S COOL."

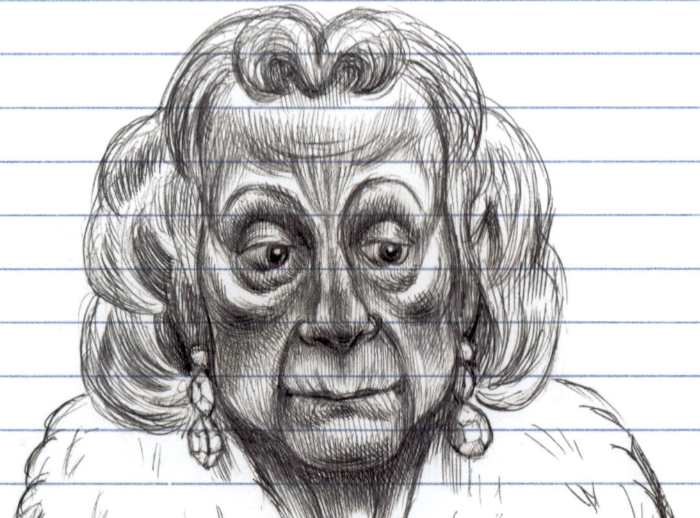

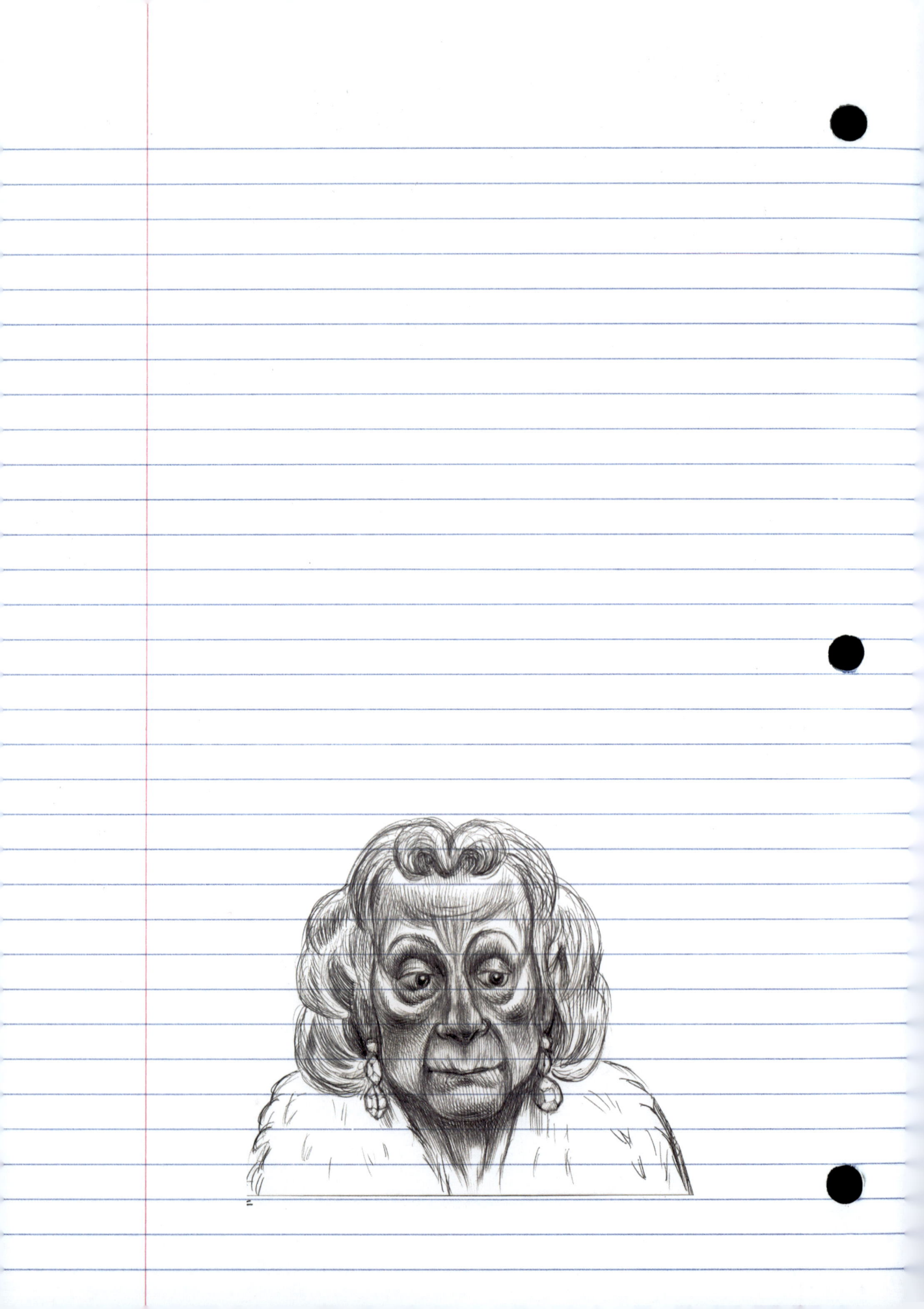

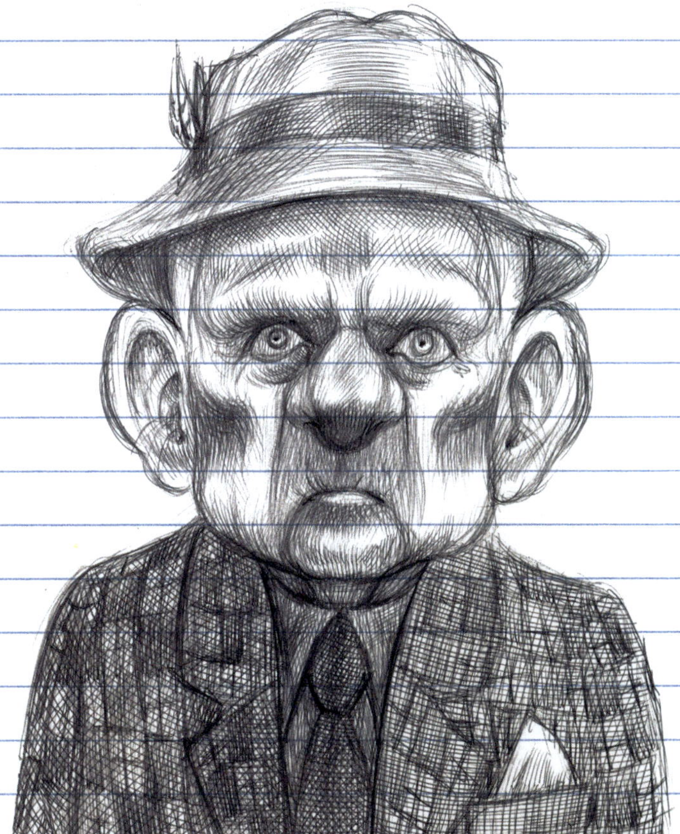

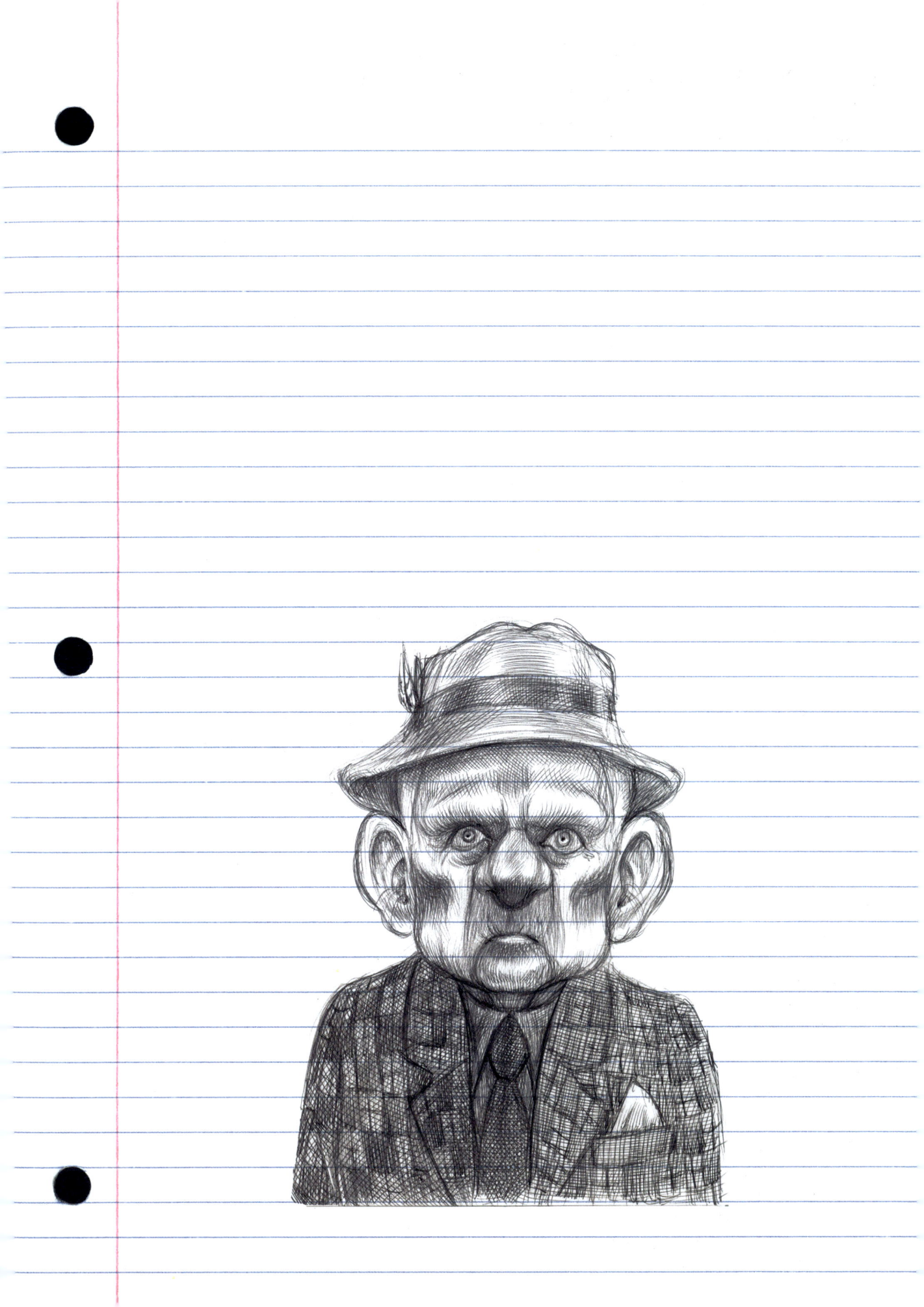

DRAWING IS THE WAY I UNDERSTAND THINGS. 'UNDERSTAND' IS A COOL WORD. IT ACTUALLY MEANS TO 'STAND UNDER' SOMETHING.

THE IDEA OF STANDING UNDER SOMETHING IN ORDER TO LEARN ABOUT IT MAKES ME THINK OF A STORY THAT ANKA TOLD ME. THE STORY WAS CALLED 'THE ENLIGHTENED FROG'. IT WAS ABOUT HOW BUDDHA WAS TAKING A WALK AND PAUSED OVER A LILY PAD ON WHICH A FROG WAS SITTING. AFTER BEING UNDER BUDDHA'S GREAT THOUGHTS THE FROG WAS FOREVER CHANGED.

I THINK DRAWING IS A WAY TO BE CHANGED LIKE THE FROG WAS CHANGED. RIGHT WHEN I THOUGHT I'D DRAWN EVERYONE ON THE TRAIN THIS REALLY BEAUTIFUL WOMAN *DANCED RIGHT INTO THE TRAIN CAR!*

"SHE'S A STUNNER!"

THE LADY LEAPT AND SPUN DOWN THE AISLE OF THE WHOLE CAR. (EVEN WHILE IT WAS MOVING) AND SHE WAS STILL AS GRACEFUL AS A SWAN.

SOMETIMES PEOPLE SAY MEAN THINGS ABOUT CHICAGO BUT MY CITY IS AN AMAZING PLACE WHERE A SUDDEN AND UNEXPECTED GIFT CAN BE GIVEN TO YOU WHEN YOU LEAST EXPECT IT.

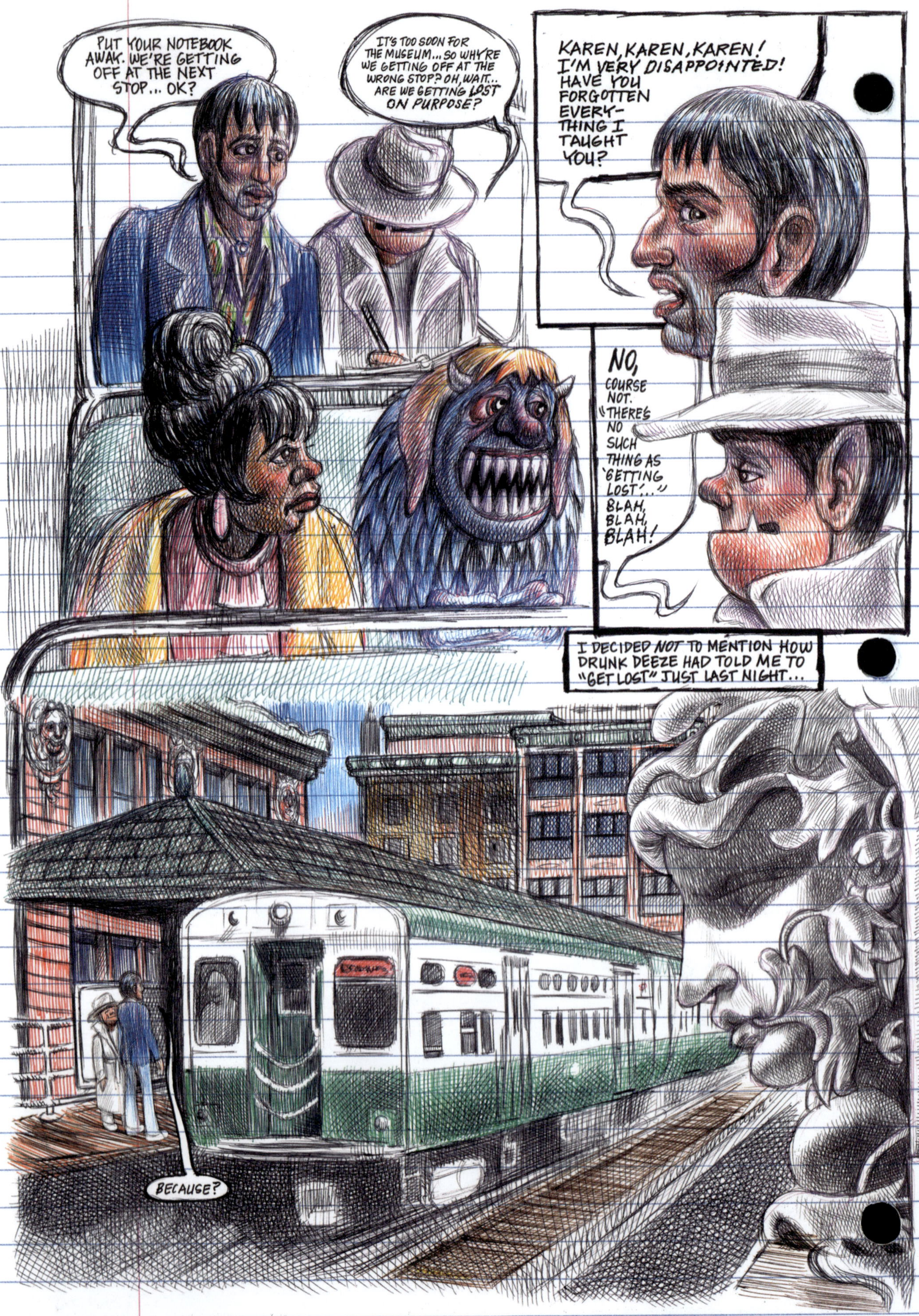

PUT YOUR NOTEBOOK AWAY. WE'RE GETTING OFF AT THE NEXT STOP... OK?
IT'S TOO SOON FOR THE MUSEUM... SO WHY'RE WE GETTING OFF AT THE WRONG STOP? OH, WAIT... ARE WE GETTING LOST ON PURPOSE?
KAREN, KAREN, KAREN! I'M VERY DISAPPOINTED! HAVE YOU FORGOTTEN EVERY-THING I TAUGHT YOU?
NO, COURSE NOT. "THERE'S NO SUCH THING AS 'GETTING LOST'..." BLAH, BLAH, BLAH!
I DECIDED NOT TO MENTION HOW DRUNK DEEZE HAD TOLD ME TO "GET LOST" JUST LAST NIGHT...
BECAUSE?

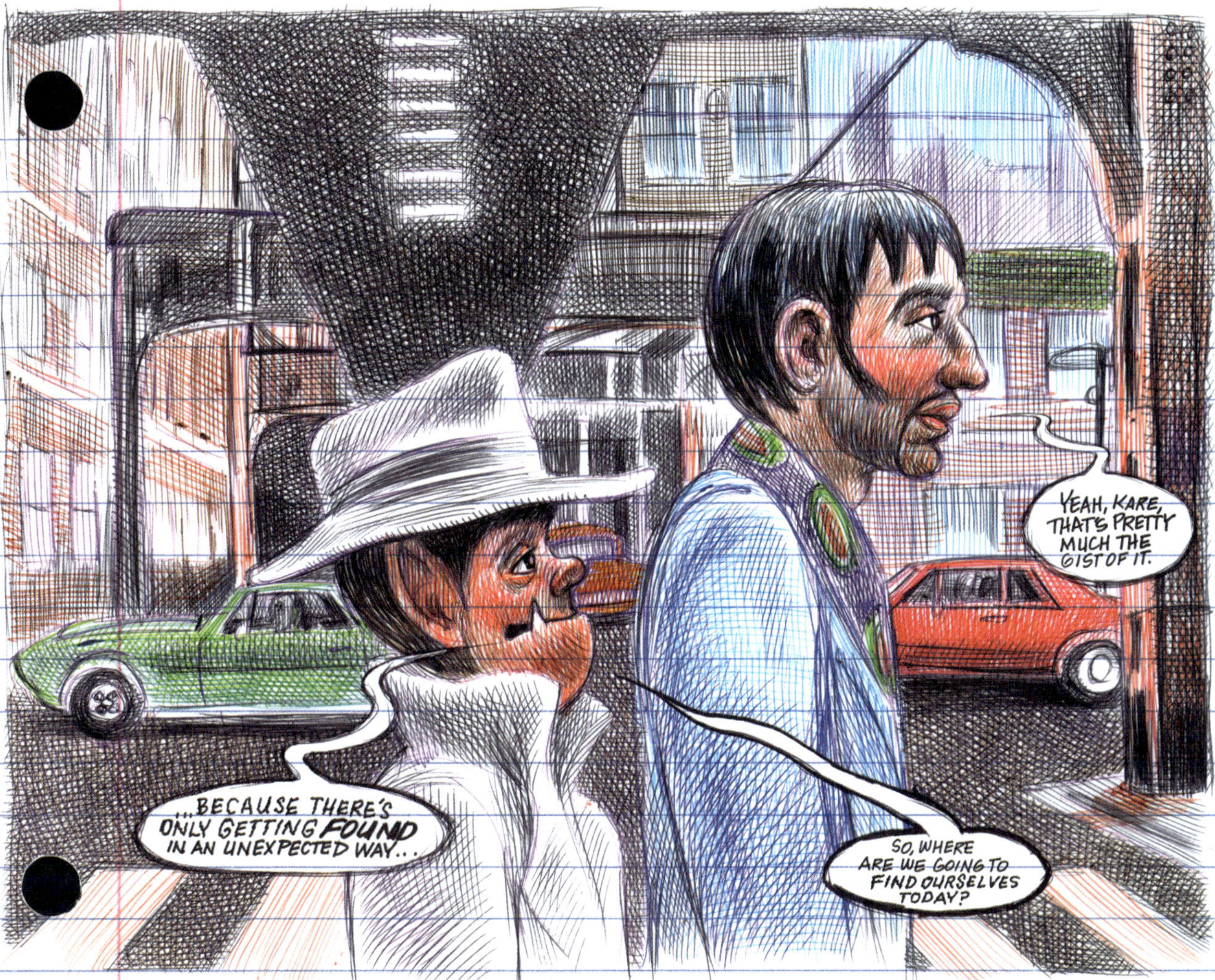
YEAH, KARE, THAT'S PRETTY MUCH THE GIST OF IT.
...BECAUSE THERE'S ONLY GETTING FOUND IN AN UNEXPECTED WAY...
SO, WHERE ARE WE GOING TO FIND OURSELVES TODAY?

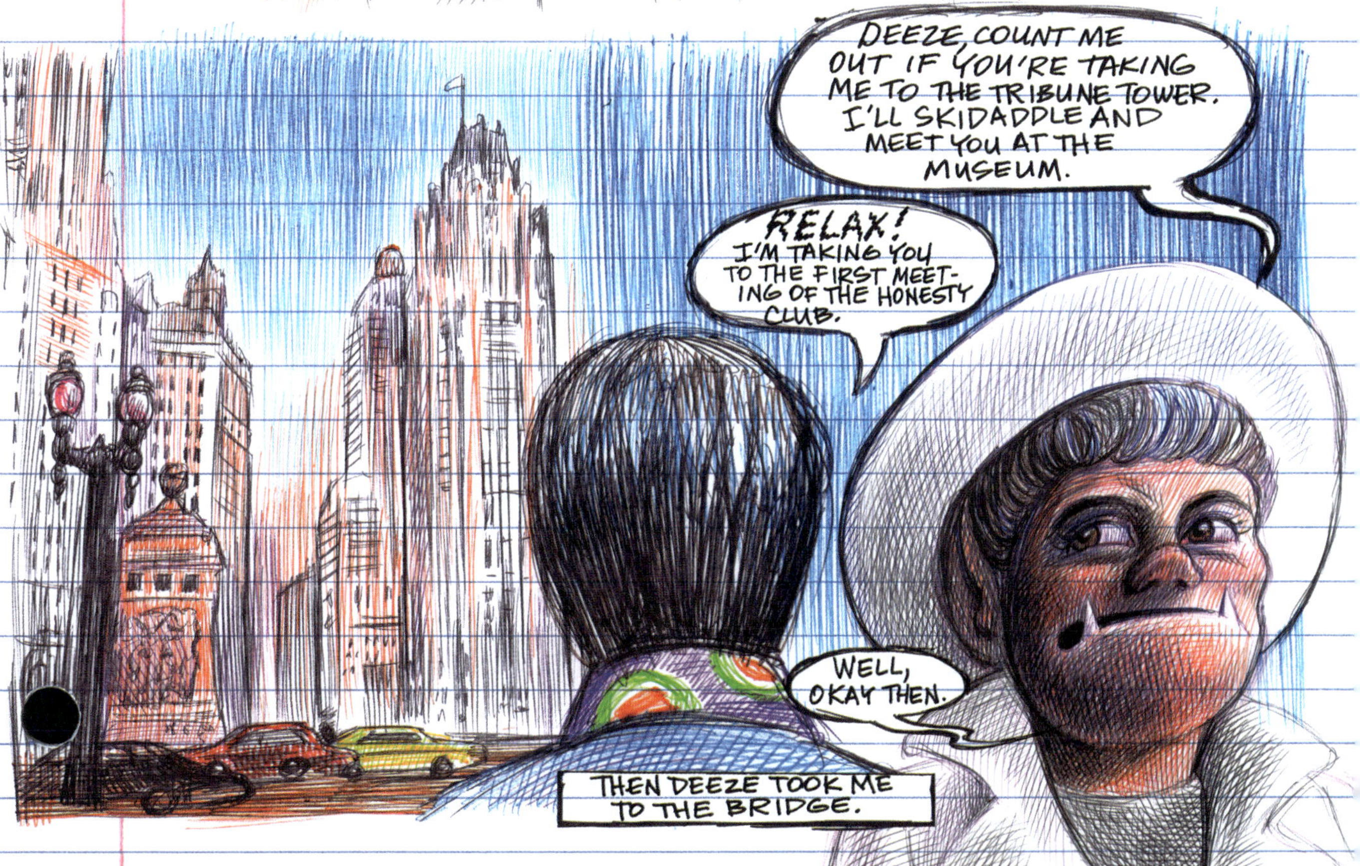
DEEZE, COUNT ME OUT IF YOU'RE TAKING ME TO THE TRIBUNE TOWER. I'LL SKIDADDLE AND MEET YOU AT THE MUSEUM.
RELAX! I'M TAKING YOU TO THE FIRST MEETING OF THE HONESTY CLUB.
WELL, OKAY THEN.
THEN DEEZE TOOK ME TO THE BRIDGE.

WHEN WE CAME TO THE FORT DEARBORN MASSACRE SCULPTURE, I TOLD DEEZE I WANTED TO DRAW IT. HE WAS O.K. WITH THAT AND SPENT THE FOLLOWING HALF HOUR 'PICKING UP CHICKS.'

"KIM? KIM, IS THAT... IS IT REALLY *YOU*?"

"NOPE. SORRY. NOT KIM."

"YOU SAW RIGHT THROUGH ME, DIDN'T YOU? AND I DELIVERED THE...UH... LINE BADLY, TOO..."

"YEAH. REALLY OBVIOUS AND WELL... PATHETIC."

AT THIS POINT DEEZE PUTS HIS HANDS ON HIS FACE AND 'LAUGH-CRIES.' HE SAYS, "OH GOD, I'M A *FOOL*, AN IDIOT... BUT YOU ARE SO LOVELY AND I JUST WANTED ...TO KNOW YOUR NAME..."
IF THE WOMAN IS STILL TALKING TO DEEZE SHE'LL START LAUGHING WITH HIM AND IN FIVE MINUTES HE'LL HAVE HER PHONE NUMBER...
AND IN ANOTHER FIVE MINUTES THEY'LL HAVE MADE PLANS TO GO ON A DATE.

I KNOW I SHOULD TELL THE WOMEN THAT THEY'D BE BETTER OFF JUMPING INTO THE RIVER RATHER THAN DATING MY BROTHER... BUT I DON'T. WE HAVE AN AGREEMENT. I DON'T WARN HIS LADIES OFF AND DEEZE DOESN'T TELL ME WHAT TO DRAW... *USUALLY*.

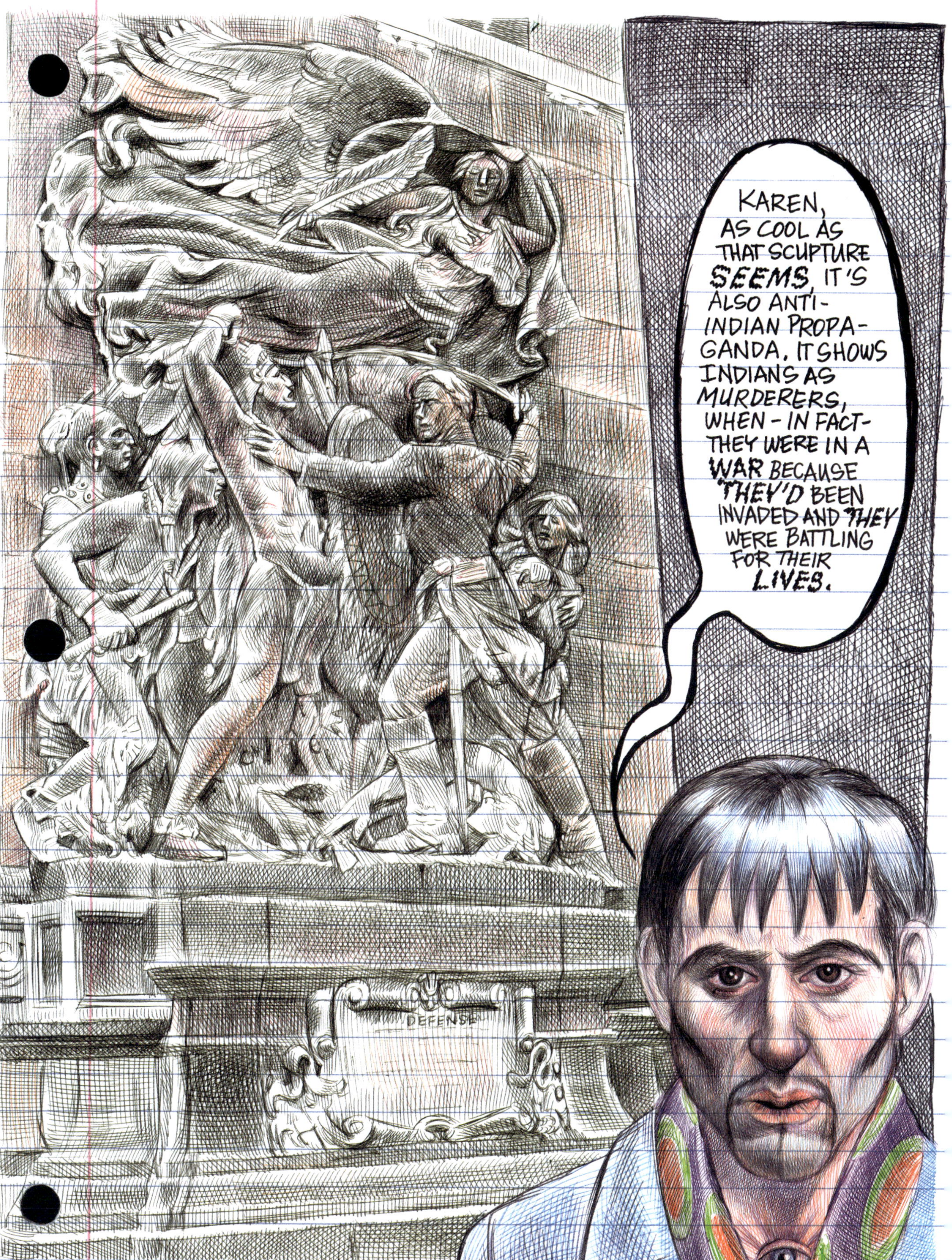
KAREN, AS COOL AS THAT SCUPTURE SEEMS, IT'S ALSO ANTI-INDIAN PROPA-GANDA. IT SHOWS INDIANS AS MURDERERS, WHEN - IN FACT- THEY WERE IN A WAR BECAUSE THEY'D BEEN INVADED AND THEY WERE BATTLING FOR THEIR LIVES.
DEFENSE

Tales of the Eldritch and the ARCANE

JUNE '68   45¢

JANUS – TRICKSTER GOD OF THE GATEWAY

"KAREN, YOU'VE HEARD THE SAYING, 'USE YOUR HEAD,' RIGHT? WELL, YOU'VE GOTTA UNDERSTAND, THE WHOLE FREAKING SYSTEM — THE CHURCHES, THE GOVERNMENT, THE T.V. AND DEFINITELY THE SCHOOLS — ARE TOTALLY DEDICATED TO TEACHING YOU...

...*NOT* TO USE YOUR HEAD. THEY WANT YOU TO BELIEVE *ONLY* WHAT YOU'RE TOLD BECAUSE THEY REALLY WANT TO CONTROL YOU. SO YOU NEED TO QUESTION EVERYTHING. ALWAYS ASK YOURSELF, HOW DO THESE FREAKS *BENEFIT* BY WHAT THEY WANT ME TO BELIEVE?"

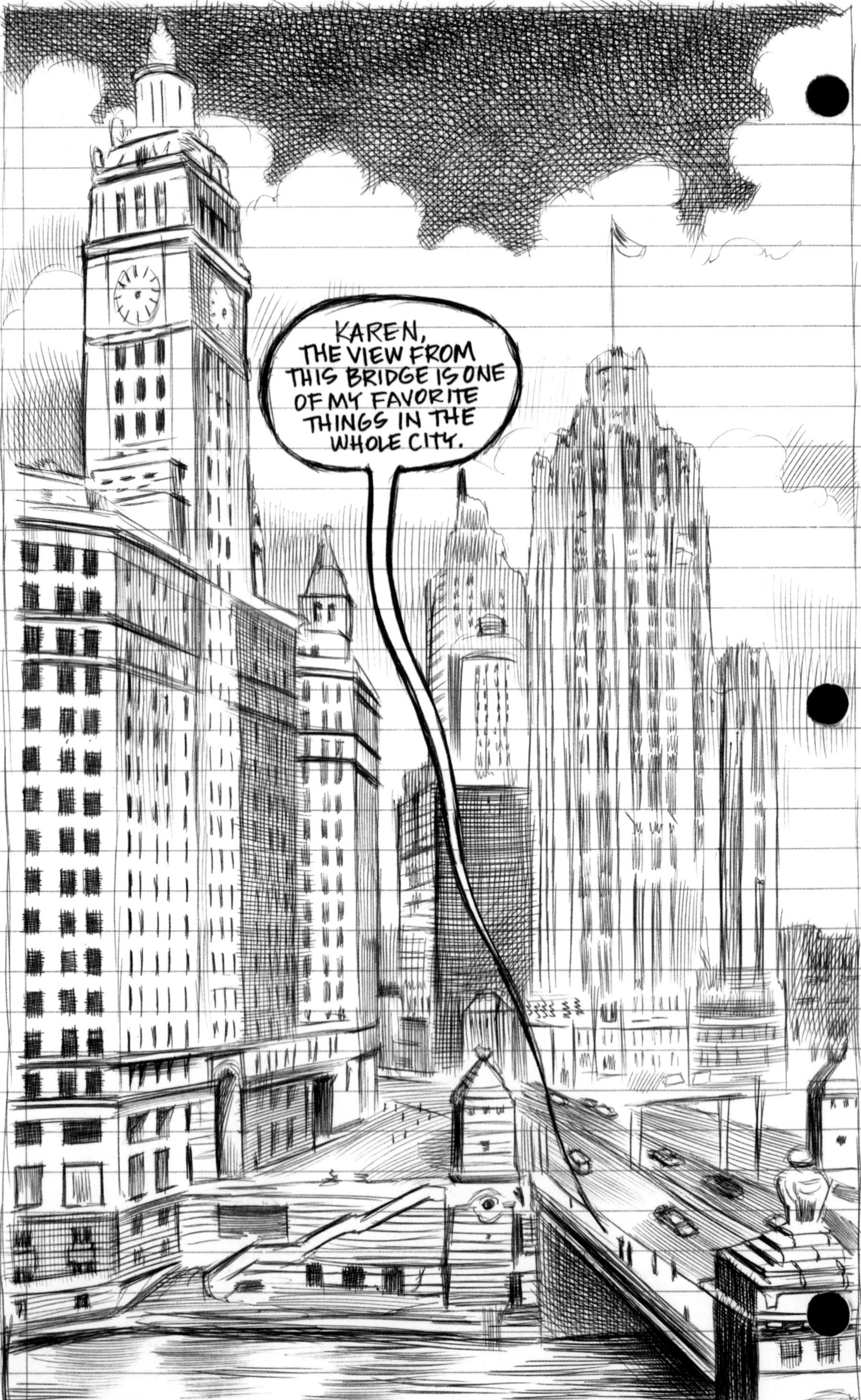
KAREN, THE VIEW FROM THIS BRIDGE IS ONE OF MY FAVORITE THINGS IN THE WHOLE CITY.

- IT'S KIND OF EXCITING BECAUSE WHEN YOU STAND ON THE BRIDGE YOUR LEGS VIBRATE FROM THE RUMBLE OF THE TRAFFIC AND IF YOU ARE WHAT DEEZE CALLS "A SUPER DARING MOTHER F@CKER," YOU CAN...

- ... PUT ONE FOOT ON EACH SIDE OF THE BRIDGE AND IF YOU LOOK DOWN PAST THE WIDE CRACK WHERE THE TWO PARTS OF THE BRIDGE JOIN, YOU CAN SEE THE RIVER FLOWING *FAR FAR* BELOW.

  I THINK IT WAS ON PURPOSE THAT DEEZE WALKED US TO THE BRIDGE IN ORDER TO TELL ME THE TRUTH ABOUT HOW HIS TWIN BROTHER NAMED 'VICTOR' HAD DIED.

GUIDE TO TELLING

HOLDS HEAD EXTRA EXTRA STILL

SKIN UNDER EYES CRINKLES A BIT AND EYES SQUINT SLIGHTLY.

HOLDS MOUTH LIKE HE HAS JUST TRIED (UNSUCCESSFULLY) TO SWALLOW A CHILDREN'S BUILDING BLOCK.

COF COF

YEAH KARE...

WHEN DEEZE IS LYING

... BUT THE EASIEST WAY TO TELL THAT HE IS LYING IS THAT RIGHT BEFORE DEEZE TELLS A LIE, HE KIND OF CLEARS HIS THROAT WITH THESE TWO LITTLE PHONY COUGHS AND THEN HE SAYS, "YEAH KARE..."

LIES DEEZE HAS TOLD ME THAT I HAVE FIGURED OUT ARE LIES...

COF COF
YEAH KARE, PEPPER IS ACTUALLY FLY SHIT

COF COF
YEAH KARE, OUR FATHER IS ACTUALLY THE INVISIBLE MAN

COF COF
YEAH KARE, WE'RE DESCENDED FROM MONTEZUMA, KING OF THE AZTECS

SO NOW, AFTER FOOLING ME FOR YEARS, DEEZE CLAIMS HE WILL TELL ME THE TRUTH ABOUT OUR BROTHER VICTOR THAT EVERYONE (INCLUDING MAMA) LIED ABOUT AND HID THE FACT OF HIS EXISTENCE FROM ME. SO THIS TIME I'M WATCHING DEEZE LIKE A HAWK FOR SIGNS THAT HE IS FIBBING. HE WON'T PULL THE WOOL OVER MY EYES **THIS TIME!**

"YOU KNOW KARE, JUST LIKE YOU CAN GET TWO COMPLETELY DIFFERENT VIEWS OF THE RIVER FROM THIS ONE BRIDGE, THE BRIDGE ITSELF OPENS INTO TWO PARTS. SO WHAT I'M SAYING IS THAT EVERY STORY HAS AT LEAST TWO DIFFERENT SIDES."

IN THE NIGHTMARE I HAD LAST NIGHT, VICTOR TOLD ME HIS SIDE OF THINGS. NOW DEEZE - WHO IS *THE OTHER SIDE OF THE BRIDGE* - WAS GOING TO TELL HIS TRUTH...

"DEEZE IS A *KILLER*."

"THERE'S MORE TO IT THAN THAT..."

That was when I got a clue that he would not be able to tell me anything if I was staring right at him, so I leaned on the railing and looked out at the river just like he was doing (and only when he was "deep in the telling of his story" as Mama would have said) did I sneak a few fast looks at him.

"When me and my twin Victor were kids our parents divided us. Victor was my father's favorite and - believe it or not - I was Mama's favorite. I don't think that Mama would have decided to play the favorites game but our father started it and I think Mama hated how much it hurt me, so she secretly called me 'her special guy' to make up for what my father was doing and I was a little fucking asshole - no surprise there, right? - so I may have told Victor that Mama loved me more than she loved him...

So my father was always giving Victor lots of extra stuff. My father would say that Victor was good and manly and I was a weakling - I was like a half inch shorter than Victor and not as muscular and maybe to be honest I was sort of gentle in comparison to Victor but our dad did not think that was a good thing. He always said, "If you're not the top dog then the top dog is shitting on your face." Nice, huh?
So I think he thought he was doing me a favor or something by toughening me up.

I mean Kare, with our father if you came home from school with a black eye and your knuckles weren't bleeding because you hadn't given as good or better than you got, well you could count on the belt from him right there and then. Sympathy was for weaklings.

So my father brought home an electric race car set ... very cool stuff like that and even though there were two race cars my father would say to Victor "Diego is a fuck up and he'll break your nice toy, so don't you dare let me catch you racing cars with Diego or I will whip your ass."

Our father knew that me and Victor LOVED all the western T.V. series - we just ate up 'The Cisco Kid,' 'Fury,' 'Bat Masterson,' 'The Rifleman' and 'Have Gun - Will Travel.' So one day our father brought home a really cool gunslinger outfit - but there was only one cowboy costume... and it was for VICTOR.

VICTOR →

"This ain't for YOU, Diego. Only Victor has been good enough to deserve this."

"Victor, since you have two guns, can I use one of them?"

Panel 1: NAW. DAD SAID IF I LENT YOU ONE, I'D LOSE THEM BOTH. YOU USE THE STICK, IT'S THE SAME THING. *POP POP POP POP POP POP*

Panel 2: EXCEPT A POPGUN AND A STICK AIN'T ONE BIT ALIKE AND VICTOR GOT A LOT OF JOY OUT OF SHOOTING ME OVER AND OVER AGAIN... *POP POP POP POP POP*

Panel 3: I GOT A PLAN SO WE'LL BE THE SAME.

Panel 4: BACK THEN WHEN YOU WERE A BABY, OUR FAMILY LIVED ON THE SECOND FLOOR — WHERE THE GRONANS LIVE NOW. I REMEMBER THAT I FIGURED OUT A WAY TO MAKE VICTOR AND ME EQUAL... I WENT UPSTAIRS AND GOT OUR DAD'S PISTOL.

Panel 5: KA-BLAM! UH-OH! I'LL KILL THAT LITTLE ASSHOLE DEAD!

I TOOK THE STORY THAT DEEZE TOLD ME AND I TURNED IT INTO A CARTOON. MAYBE BECAUSE CARTOONY PICTURES TELL SAD STORIES... BUT IN A WAY THAT DOESN'T HURT.

BUT DON'T IMAGINE THAT OUR FATHER SAW THAT HE WAS RESPONSIBLE FOR *ANY OF IT!*

WHEN I ASKED DEEZE WHAT HAPPENED AFTER HE SHOT OUR BROTHER VICTOR, THIS IS WHAT HE TOLD ME...

I RAN TO THE BASEMENT, TO THE SECRET UNDERGROUND TUNNEL. IN THOSE DAYS IT WASN'T LOCKED.

SO DEEZE, WHAT'S THAT TUNNEL *FOR*?

I'LL TELL YOU BUT YOU MUST PROMISE NOT TO GO DOWN THERE, O.K.?

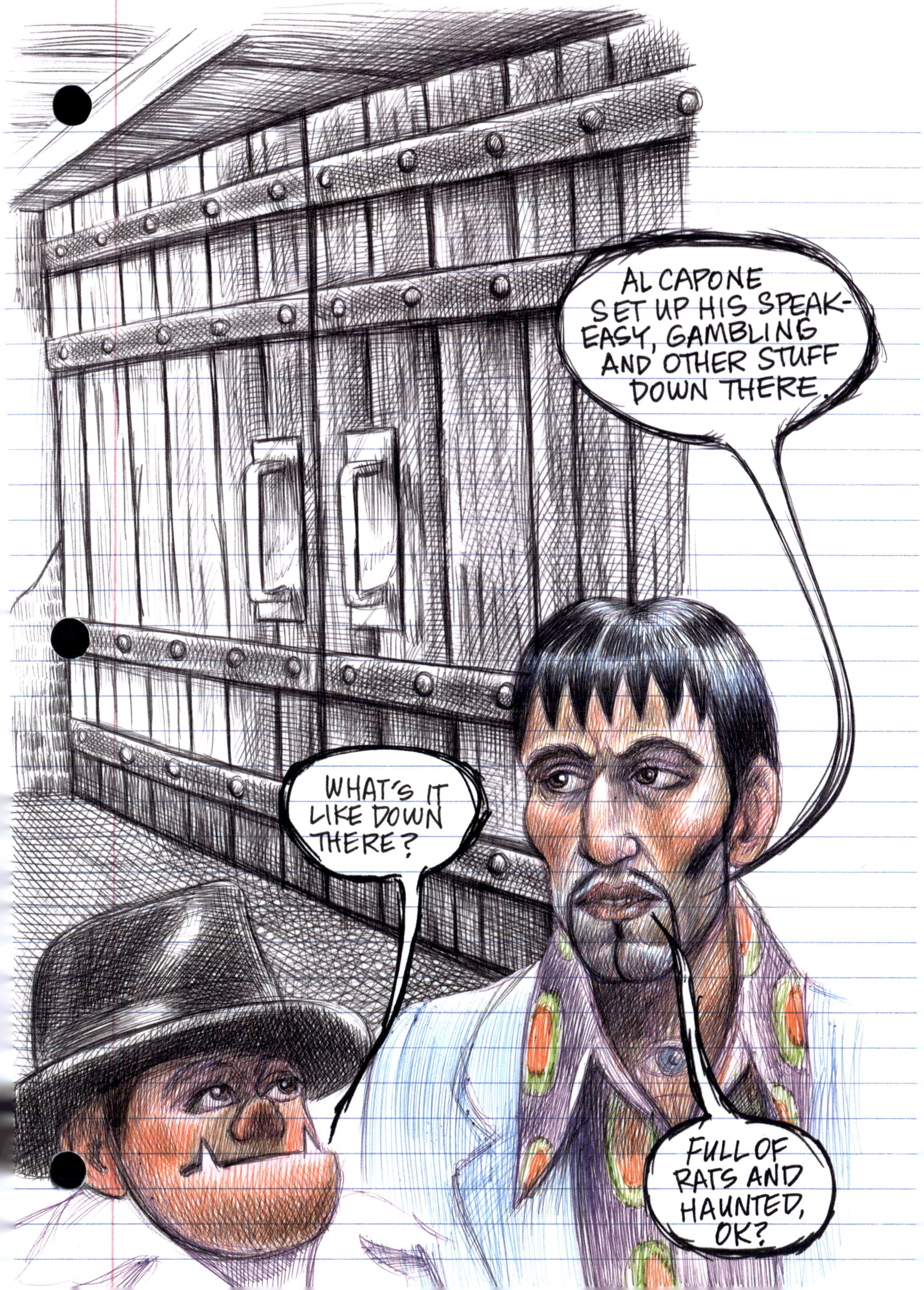
AL CAPONE SET UP HIS SPEAK-EASY, GAMBLING AND OTHER STUFF DOWN THERE.
WHAT'S IT LIKE DOWN THERE?
FULL OF RATS AND HAUNTED, OK?

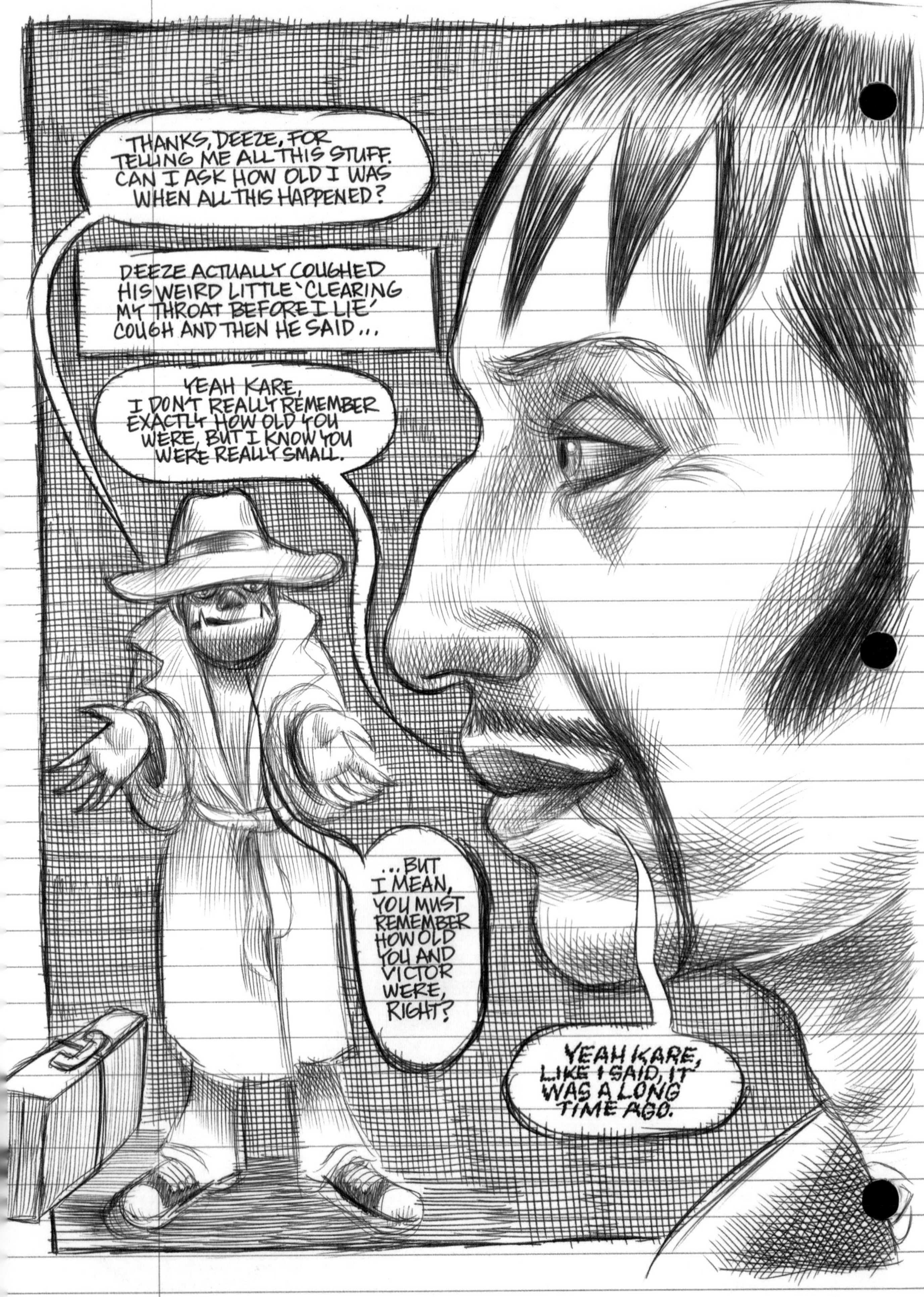
THANKS, DEEZE, FOR TELLING ME ALL THIS STUFF. CAN I ASK HOW OLD I WAS WHEN ALL THIS HAPPENED?
DEEZE ACTUALLY COUGHED HIS WEIRD LITTLE 'CLEARING MY THROAT BEFORE I LIE' COUGH AND THEN HE SAID...
YEAH KARE, I DON'T REALLY REMEMBER EXACTLY HOW OLD YOU WERE, BUT I KNOW YOU WERE REALLY SMALL.
...BUT I MEAN, YOU MUST REMEMBER HOW OLD YOU AND VICTOR WERE, RIGHT?
YEAH KARE, LIKE I SAID, IT WAS A LONG TIME AGO.

I WONDER IF THIS WAS WHY MAMA ALWAYS CRIED FOR NO GOOD REASON AT GUNSLINGER MOVIES...

BUT WE DON'T HAVE A GUN IN OUR HOUSE NOW, RIGHT?

YEAH KARE, THAT'S RIGHT. I'M NOT AGAINST GUNS. IT'S OUR RIGHT IN THE CONSTITUTION TO OWN A GUN BUT ONLY AN ASSHOLE WOULD LEAVE ONE OUT AROUND A KID.

I WONDER WHAT DEEZE IS LYING ABOUT.

A WHILE AGO (BEFORE MAMA GOT SICK) A MANAGER AT THE RESTAURANT WHERE MAMA WORKED BOTHERED HER. I KNOW THIS BECAUSE OF MY SPYING ABILITIES. I OVERHEARD MAMA BEGGING DEEZE "NOT TO GO OFF HALF-COCKED AND SHOOT THE GUY." I THINK THERE IS PROBABLY A GUN IN OUR APARTMENT...BUT WHERE WOULD DEEZE HIDE IT?

Tales of the Eldritch and the ARCANE

THE GREENMAN

As me and Deeze walked along Michigan Avenue I looked up and saw all the cool ornaments on the buildings. The ones we both like the most are the Greenmen. When we see them we always say to each other, 'Greenman,' and point it out, but today I was deep in thought about how my own family tricked me for years. So I didn't feel like pointing them out plus they looked like they were...

LAUGHING RIGHT AT ME!

"HAHAHA YOUR WHOLE FAMILY HAS LIED TO YOU FOR YEARS! AND YOU WERE TOO DUMB TO FIGURE IT OUT!!"

The other thing I thought about was all the greenmen that decorate the building that we live in. There is even a greenman on the secret door in our building's basement. I remembered the part of a dream where my dead neighbor Anka told me that I have to go down the stairs to that dark place to solve the mystery of her death. I'm scared to do it but maybe I WILL DO IT ANYWAY!

"IT'S A DRUID/HUMAN SACRIFICE THING. THE GUY TO ASK IS 'THE BRAIN!' HE KNOWS MORE ABOUT IT THAN I DO."

"WHAT'S THE DEAL WITH PUTTING THE GREENMEN ALL OVER THE PLACE, ANYWAY?"

"I READ A WHOLE ARCANE, SO I KNOW ABOUT WHAT THE GREENMAN IS. WHAT I'M ASKING IS, WHY PUT THEM ON BUILDINGS?"

Deeze didn't answer, so I guess he didn't know but that reminded me to see if the druid was following me...

"I WAS CHECKING TO SEE IF THE DRUID WAS STILL FOLLOWING ME WHEN I TOLD DEEZE—"

"ACTUALLY DEEZE, I KNOW ABOUT THE HUMAN SACRIFICE PART BECAUSE I READ A MAGAZINE ABOUT IT. MY QUESTION IS, WHY DO PEOPLE STILL PUT IT ON THEIR BUILDINGS?"

"WELL KARE, WHEN YOU WANT TO HIDE SOMETHING, THE BEST PLACE IS RIGHT OUT IN THE OPEN. IN PLAIN SIGHT WHERE PEOPLE WILL NEVER LOOK."

"WELL, YOU KNOW WHAT A CLOTHES HORSE YOUR BROTHER IS. EVEN AS A BABY HE HAD MORE SHOES THAN HE HAD NEED OF."

AS I RECALLED THERE HAD BEEN A BIG BLOTCH OF DRIED GLUE WHERE THE PLAQUE WITH DEEZE'S NAME WOULD HAVE BEEN... PROBABLY IT SAID 'DIEGO AND VICTOR REYES,' WITH THEIR BIRTHDAY ON IT. (DEEZE IS A *SCORPIO*... A FACT THAT HE SAYS IS ANOTHER REASON HE IS A 'SUPER-ROMEO').

THEN I REMEMBERED HOW WHEN MAMA WAS ALIVE I FOUND TWO PAIRS OF BRONZED BABY SHOES STUCK TO ONE WOODEN BOARD... I KNEW THAT THE EXTRA ONE WAS NOT MINE, BECAUSE I NEEDED SPECIAL SHOES WHEN I WAS A BABY...

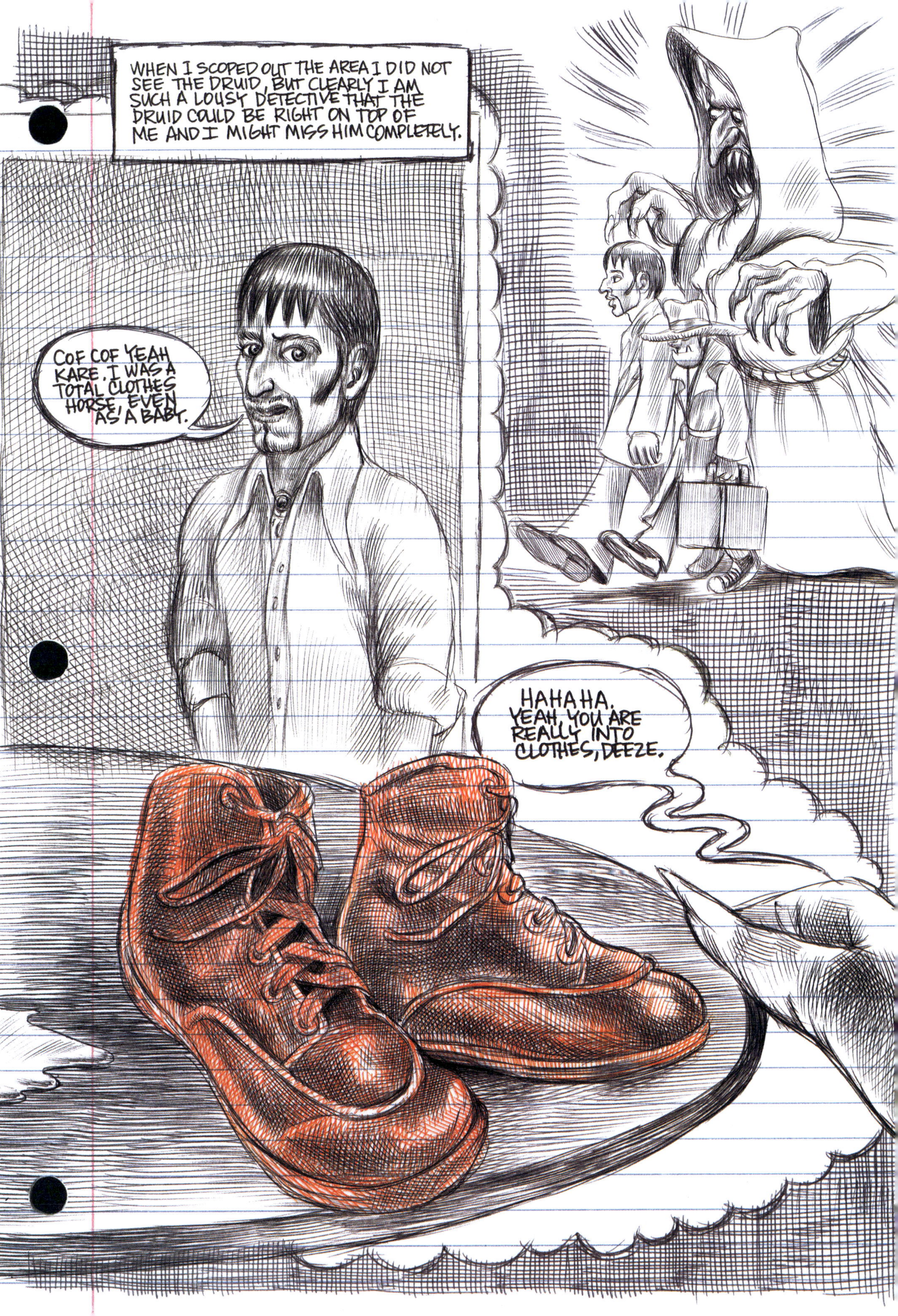
WHEN I SCOPED OUT THE AREA I DID NOT SEE THE DRUID, BUT CLEARLY I AM SUCH A LOUSY DETECTIVE THAT THE DRUID COULD BE RIGHT ON TOP OF ME AND I MIGHT MISS HIM COMPLETELY.
COF COF YEAH KARE. I WAS A TOTAL CLOTHES HORSE, EVEN AS A BABY.
HAHAHA. YEAH, YOU ARE REALLY INTO CLOTHES, DEEZE.

"KARE, SOME SHIT IS SO FREAKY THAT IT'S REALLY BETTER IF YOU DON'T LOOK INTO IT."

WHILE DEEZE SMOKED A CIG I LOOKED AROUND FOR THE DRUID. I DIDN'T SEE HIM BUT ALL OUR TALK ABOUT HUMAN SACRIFICE GOT ME FREAKED OUT.

IN THE ARCANE MAGAZINE ABOUT THE GREEN MEN THERE WAS THIS STORY ABOUT HOW IN OLDEN TIMES THEY USED TO SACRIFICE A PERSON AND BURY THEIR BODY IN THE FOUNDATION OF A NEW BUILDING. THEY THOUGHT IT GAVE THE BUILDING SPECIAL POWERS (IN THE ARTICLE IT GAVE THE BUILDING A SUPER PISSED OFF GHOST!) I WONDER IF THESE GREEN MEN ARE A WAY FOR THE SACRIFICERS TO SAY, "HEY FELLOW SECRET HUMAN SACRIFICE GUYS, WE DID IT HERE!"

THAT MAGAZINE GAVE ME NIGHTMARES.

SO WHEN I WAS LITTLE, DEEZE TOLD ME THAT THE ART INSTITUTE LIONS CAME TO MY BED WHEN I WAS ASLEEP IN ORDER TO WATCH OVER ME.

HE WAS TRYING TO MAKE ME UNDERSTAND THAT ART IS PROTECTION.

I THINK THAT ART AND STORIES ARE THE BEST INVENTIONS OF HUMAN BEINGS. THE GREATEST WAY TO BE A STRONG, EVIL-DEFEATING MONSTER IS TO MAKE ART AND TELL STORIES.

"SOMETIMES IT FEELS TO ME LIKE THE MUSEUM IS JUST SITTING HERE WAITING FOR YOU AND ME TO STOP BY AND LOVE IT."

"YOU NAILED IT!"

"I MISSED YOU TWO."

"I NEED ME SOME GAUGUIN!"

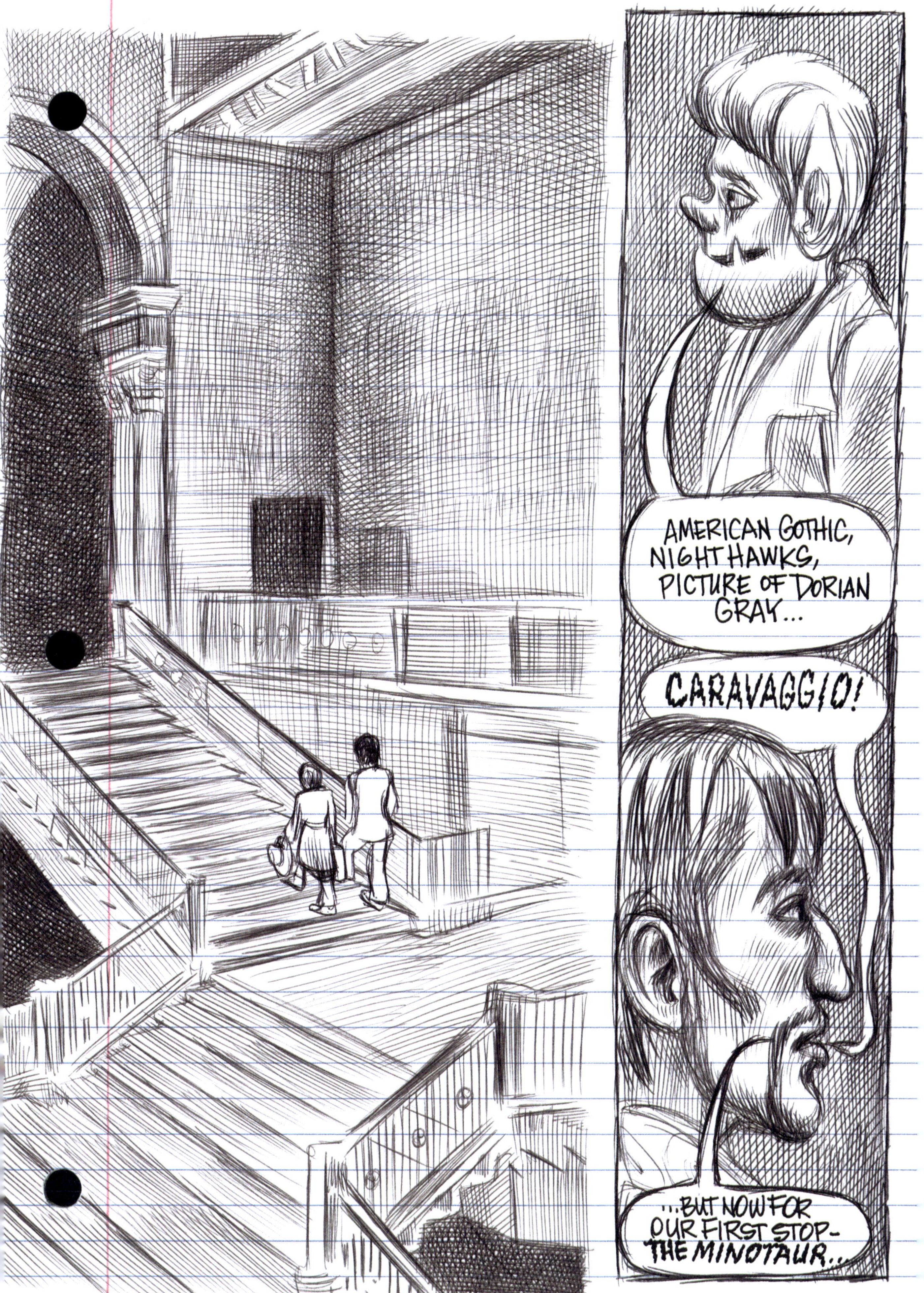
AMERICAN GOTHIC, NIGHTHAWKS, PICTURE OF DORIAN GRAY...
CARAVAGGIO!
...BUT NOW FOR OUR FIRST STOP- THE MINOTAUR...

EITHER YOU LET ME DO THIS OR YOU WILL GET ONLY ONE TABLE A NIGHT AND IT WILL BE THE ONE NEXT TO THE MEN'S ROOM.

YOU BETTER HOPE I DON'T TELL MY SON.

KARE, JUST LOOK AT THAT DRAWING HAND! ANY ARTIST COULD STAND AND DRINK THIS IN FOR THREE CONTINUOUS MINUTES AND I GUARANTEE THEIR ART WOULD BE RADICALLY IMPROVED!

SINCE THE ART INSTITUTE BOUGHT THIS NEW PICASSO ETCHING IN FEBRUARY, DEEZE HAS BEEN MAKING IT A STOP ON OUR FAVORITES TOUR. I DO NOT LIKE IT BECAUSE I DO NOT THINK IT'S 'SEXY.' (BUT I CAN TELL THAT DEEZE DOES.) THE LADY IS NOT LIKING WHAT THE MINOTAUR IS DOING, WHICH TO ME MAKES IT UNCOOL EXCEPT I THINK PICASSO (AND DEEZE) THINK IT IS *VERY GROOVY*. TODAY I COULD *NOT* KEEP QUIET ABOUT MY OPINION.

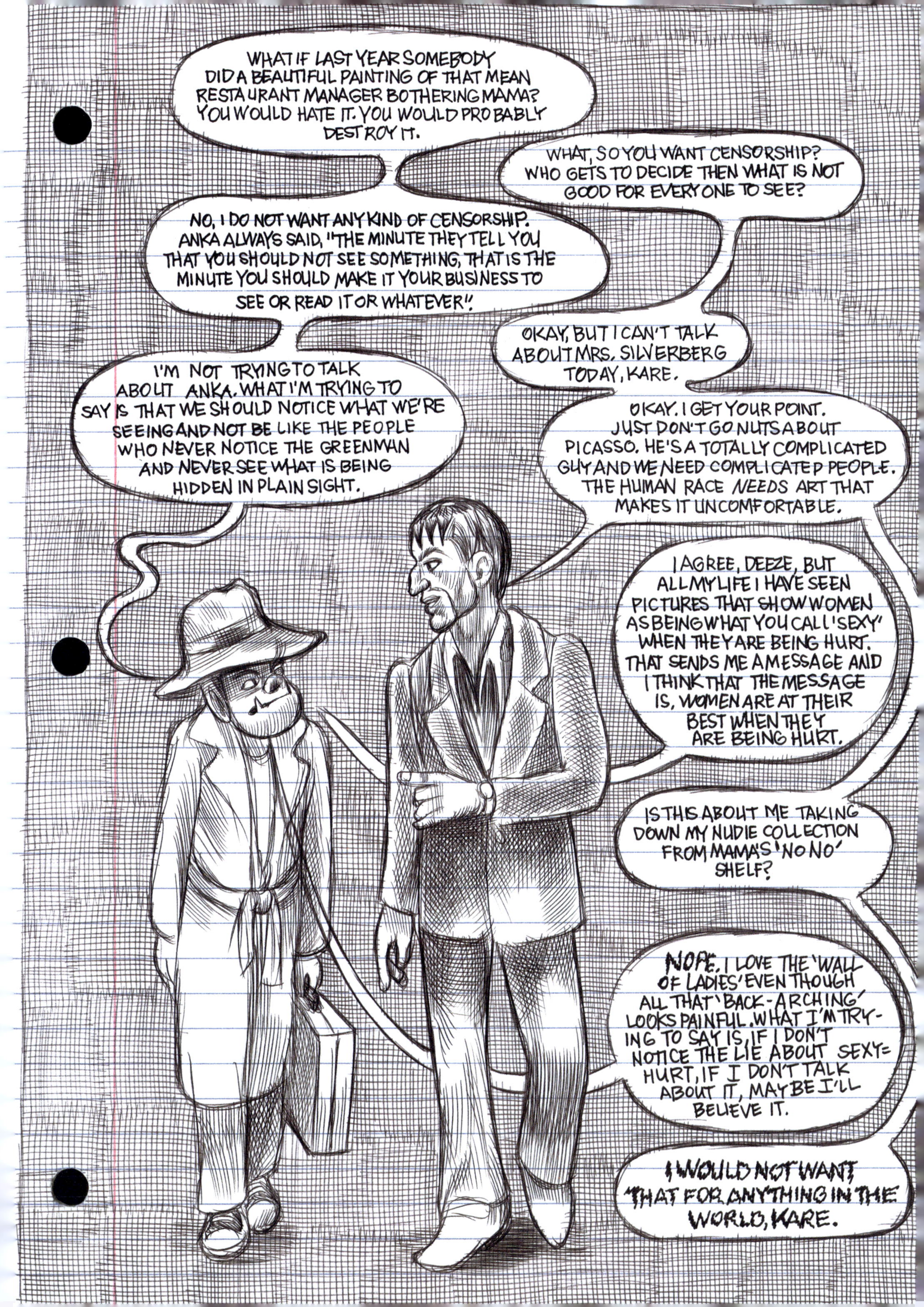
WHAT IF LAST YEAR SOMEBODY DID A BEAUTIFUL PAINTING OF THAT MEAN RESTAURANT MANAGER BOTHERING MAMA? YOU WOULD HATE IT. YOU WOULD PROBABLY DESTROY IT.
WHAT, SO YOU WANT CENSORSHIP? WHO GETS TO DECIDE THEN WHAT IS NOT GOOD FOR EVERYONE TO SEE?
NO, I DO NOT WANT ANY KIND OF CENSORSHIP. ANKA ALWAYS SAID, "THE MINUTE THEY TELL YOU THAT YOU SHOULD NOT SEE SOMETHING, THAT IS THE MINUTE YOU SHOULD MAKE IT YOUR BUSINESS TO SEE OR READ IT OR WHATEVER".
OKAY, BUT I CAN'T TALK ABOUT MRS. SILVERBERG TODAY, KARE.
I'M NOT TRYING TO TALK ABOUT ANKA. WHAT I'M TRYING TO SAY IS THAT WE SHOULD NOTICE WHAT WE'RE SEEING AND NOT BE LIKE THE PEOPLE WHO NEVER NOTICE THE GREENMAN AND NEVER SEE WHAT IS BEING HIDDEN IN PLAIN SIGHT.
OKAY. I GET YOUR POINT. JUST DON'T GO NUTS ABOUT PICASSO. HE'S A TOTALLY COMPLICATED GUY AND WE NEED COMPLICATED PEOPLE. THE HUMAN RACE *NEEDS* ART THAT MAKES IT UNCOMFORTABLE.
I AGREE, DEEZE, BUT ALL MY LIFE I HAVE SEEN PICTURES THAT SHOW WOMEN AS BEING WHAT YOU CALL 'SEXY' WHEN THEY ARE BEING HURT. THAT SENDS ME A MESSAGE AND I THINK THAT THE MESSAGE IS, WOMEN ARE AT THEIR BEST WHEN THEY ARE BEING HURT.
IS THIS ABOUT ME TAKING DOWN MY NUDIE COLLECTION FROM MAMA'S 'NO NO' SHELF?
NOPE. I LOVE THE 'WALL OF LADIES' EVEN THOUGH ALL THAT 'BACK-ARCHING' LOOKS PAINFUL. WHAT I'M TRYING TO SAY IS, IF I DON'T NOTICE THE LIE ABOUT SEXY=HURT, IF I DON'T TALK ABOUT IT, MAYBE I'LL BELIEVE IT.
I WOULD NOT WANT THAT FOR ANYTHING IN THE WORLD, KARE.

"THIS PARTICULAR VERSION OF JUDITH IS PRETTY MUCH THE CADILLAC COUPE DE VILLE OF ALL JUDITHS. NO SURPRISE IT'S IN CHICAGO.

SHE'D HANDLE LIKE A DREAM. HEAVY BODY CONSTRUCTION, V-8 ENGINE."

"I'M TRYING TO DECIDE IF YOU ARE DISGUSTING BECAUSE YOU'RE DISGUSTING OR BECAUSE SHE SCARES YOU."

"WELL, WE BOTH KNOW THAT I'M DISGUSTING BUT FACT IS SHE TERRIFIES ME.

SHE'D CALL ME 'BETSY,' WHIP MY ASS AND SEND ME HOME CRYING ON MONDAY...

...AND THE THING IS...

I'D BE BACK AGAIN FOR ANOTHER HELPING ON TUESDAY."

"THAT WAS GROSS, BUT IT'S AN IMPROVEMENT OVER LAST TIME WE WERE HERE AND HE SAID, 'SHE COULD KEEP MY BALLS IN HER KNAPSACK AND IT WOULD BE OK BY ME.'"

JAN SANDERS VAN HEMESSEN 'JUDITH', 1546

DEEZE IS WEIRD. HE SAYS THINGS THAT ARE NOT APPROPRIATE FOR HIM TO SAY AROUND ME, BUT IF I SAY A WORD LIKE '*FUCK*' THAT DEEZE THINKS A KID SHOULD NOT SAY, HE GETS *UPSET*. IT IS ESPECIALLY STRANGE BECAUSE EVERYTHING IS ABOUT S.E.X FOR DEEZE. ANKA ONCE TOLD ME THAT ALL THE *GREAT* WORKS OF ART HAVE BOTH SEX AND DEATH IN THEM. THIS JUDITH HAS BOTH BUT ALSO SHE IS *FEARLESS* WHICH NOT ALL JUDITHS I HAVE SEEN ARE...

WE WERE PRETTY MUCH ALONE IN THE MUSEUM, WHICH IS HOW WE LIKE IT.

KAREN, YOU DIDN'T GROOVE ON *THAT PARTICULAR* RENAISSANCE STORY-PAINTING? YA GOT DOZENS MORE TO CHOOSE FROM... PLUS...

...AN *EVEN HOTTER JUDITH!*

FELICE FICHERELLI, 'JUDITH WITH THE HEAD OF HOLOFERNES,' 1665

DEEZE THINKS THAT *THIS ONE* IS HOTTER?! TO ME SHE LOOKS LIKE A WORRIED KING CHARLES SPANIEL! *NOPE!* THIS JUDITH DOESN'T LOOK LIKE SHE COULD TELL OFF THE POSTMAN, EVEN IF HE LOST ALL HER MAIL, MUCH LESS ACTUALLY *USE* THAT SWORD OF HERS... BUT THEN I STARTED WONDERING WHAT JUDITH **HAD** DONE WITH HER SWORD...

"HEY, DEEZE... TELL ME WHO JUDITH WAS?"

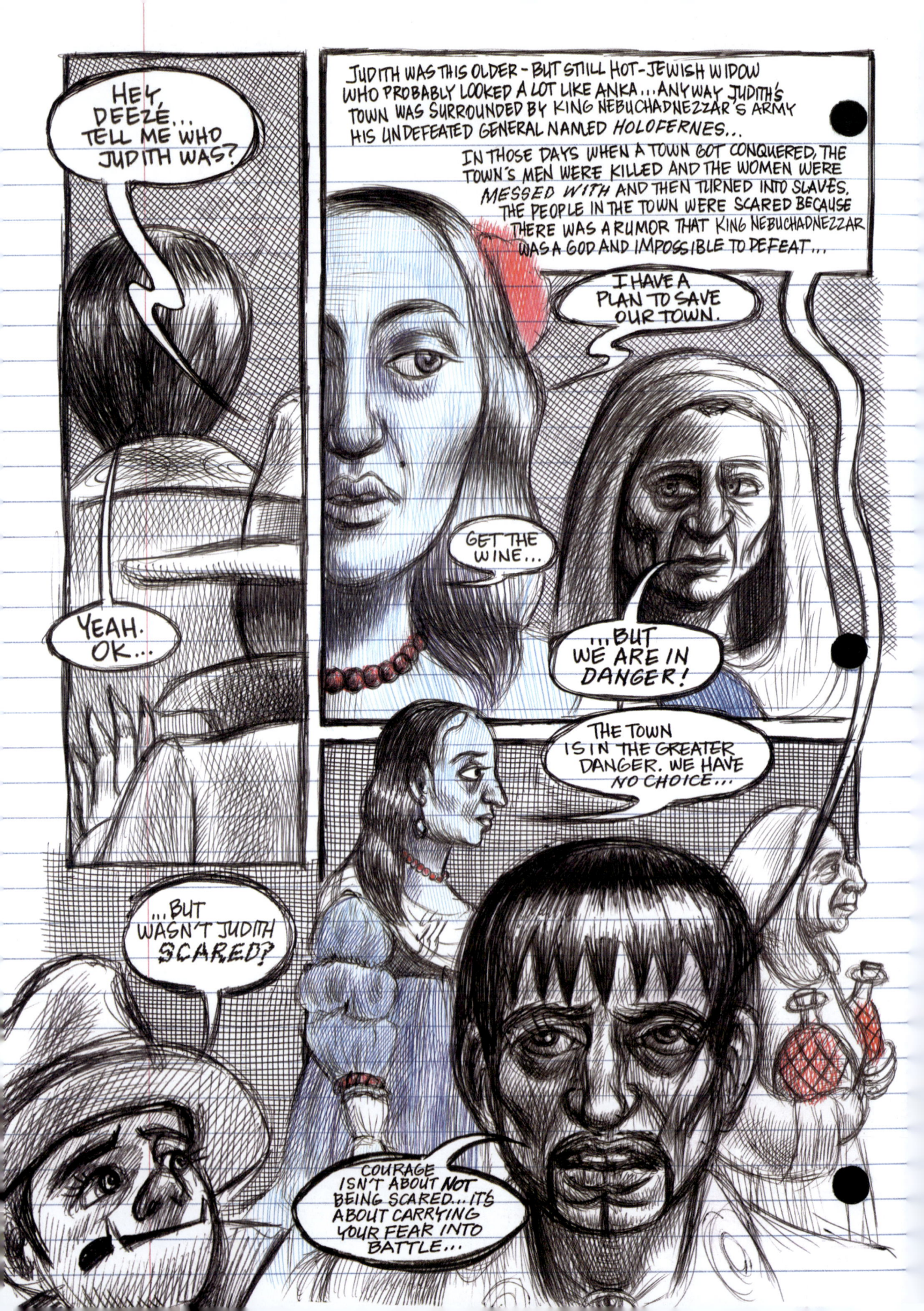

JUDITH WAS THIS OLDER - BUT STILL HOT- JEWISH WIDOW WHO PROBABLY LOOKED A LOT LIKE ANKA... ANYWAY JUDITH'S TOWN WAS SURROUNDED BY KING NEBUCHADNEZZAR'S ARMY HIS UNDEFEATED GENERAL NAMED *HOLOFERNES*...

IN THOSE DAYS WHEN A TOWN GOT CONQUERED, THE TOWN'S MEN WERE KILLED AND THE WOMEN WERE *MESSED WITH* AND THEN TURNED INTO SLAVES. THE PEOPLE IN THE TOWN WERE SCARED BECAUSE THERE WAS A RUMOR THAT KING NEBUCHADNEZZAR WAS A GOD AND IMPOSSIBLE TO DEFEAT...

"I HAVE A PLAN TO SAVE OUR TOWN."

"GET THE WINE..."

"YEAH. OK..."

"...BUT WE ARE IN DANGER!"

"THE TOWN IS IN THE GREATER DANGER. WE HAVE NO CHOICE..."

"...BUT WASN'T JUDITH *SCARED*?"

"COURAGE ISN'T ABOUT *NOT* BEING SCARED...IT'S ABOUT CARRYING YOUR FEAR INTO BATTLE..."

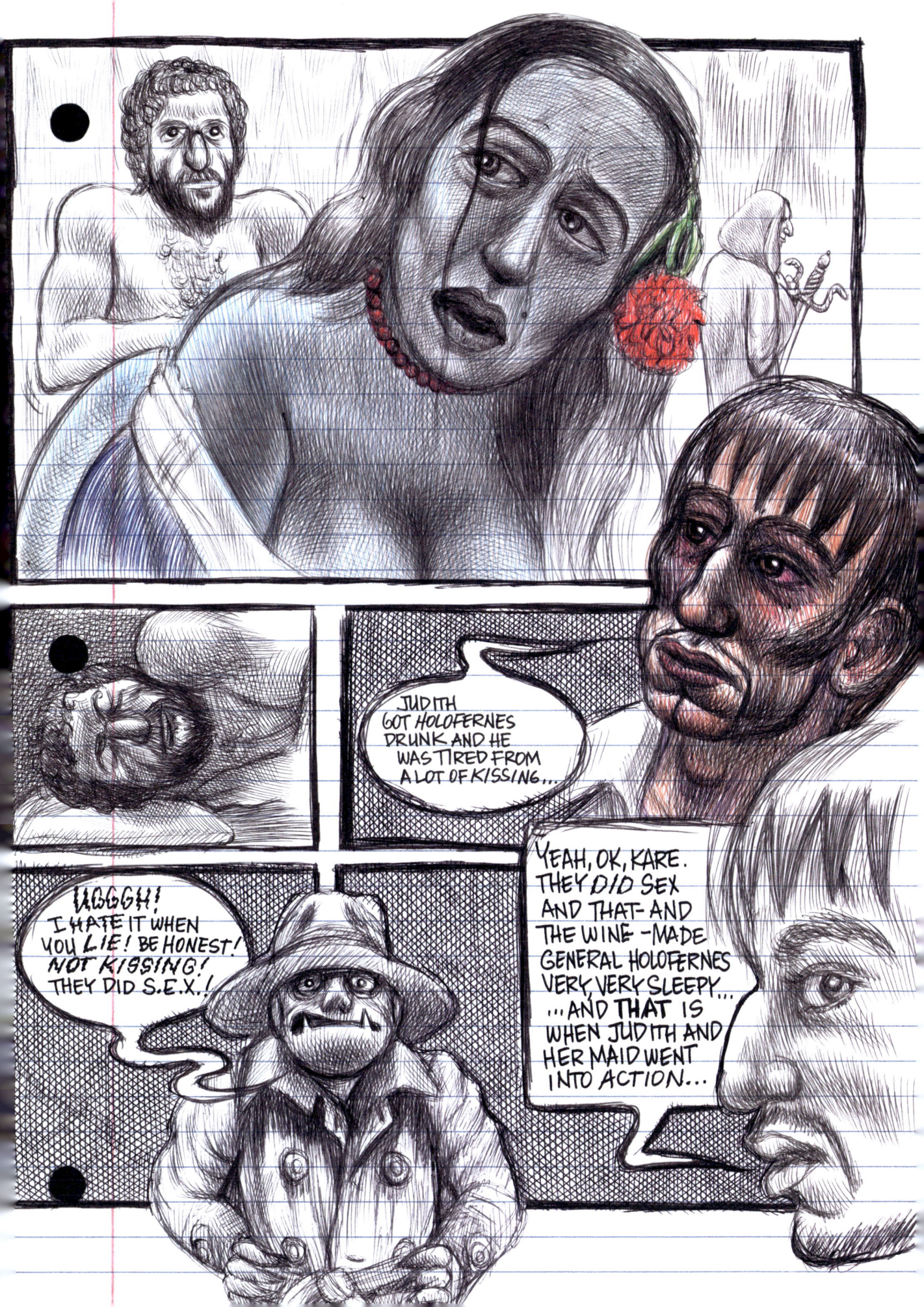

JUDITH GOT HOLOFERNES DRUNK AND HE WAS TIRED FROM A LOT OF KISSING...

UGGGH! I HATE IT WHEN YOU LIE! BE HONEST! NOT KISSING! THEY DID S.E.X.!

YEAH, OK, KARE. THEY DID SEX AND THAT— AND THE WINE —MADE GENERAL HOLOFERNES VERY, VERY SLEEPY... ...AND THAT IS WHEN JUDITH AND HER MAID WENT INTO ACTION...

ALTHOUGH I CAN'T IMAGINE GOING INTO THE PAINTING TO **BE** JUDITH, (MOSTLY BECAUSE OF ALL THE ICKY CLOTHES AND THE GROSS SEX STUFF) I **CAN** IMAGINE BEING JUDITH'S LOYAL SERVANT.

WAIT A MINUTE, SO 'GOING INTO ACTION' MEANS **CUTTING HOLOFERNES'** HEAD COMPLETELY **OFF**? I JUST GOTTA WRAP MY MIND AROUND IT ALL.

DOING SOMETHING LIKE THIS IS REALLY **SERIOUS**. WHEN YOU CUT SOMEBODY'S HEAD OFF THERE ARE NO 'TAKE-SEE BACK-SEES' ON SOMETHING LIKE THAT.

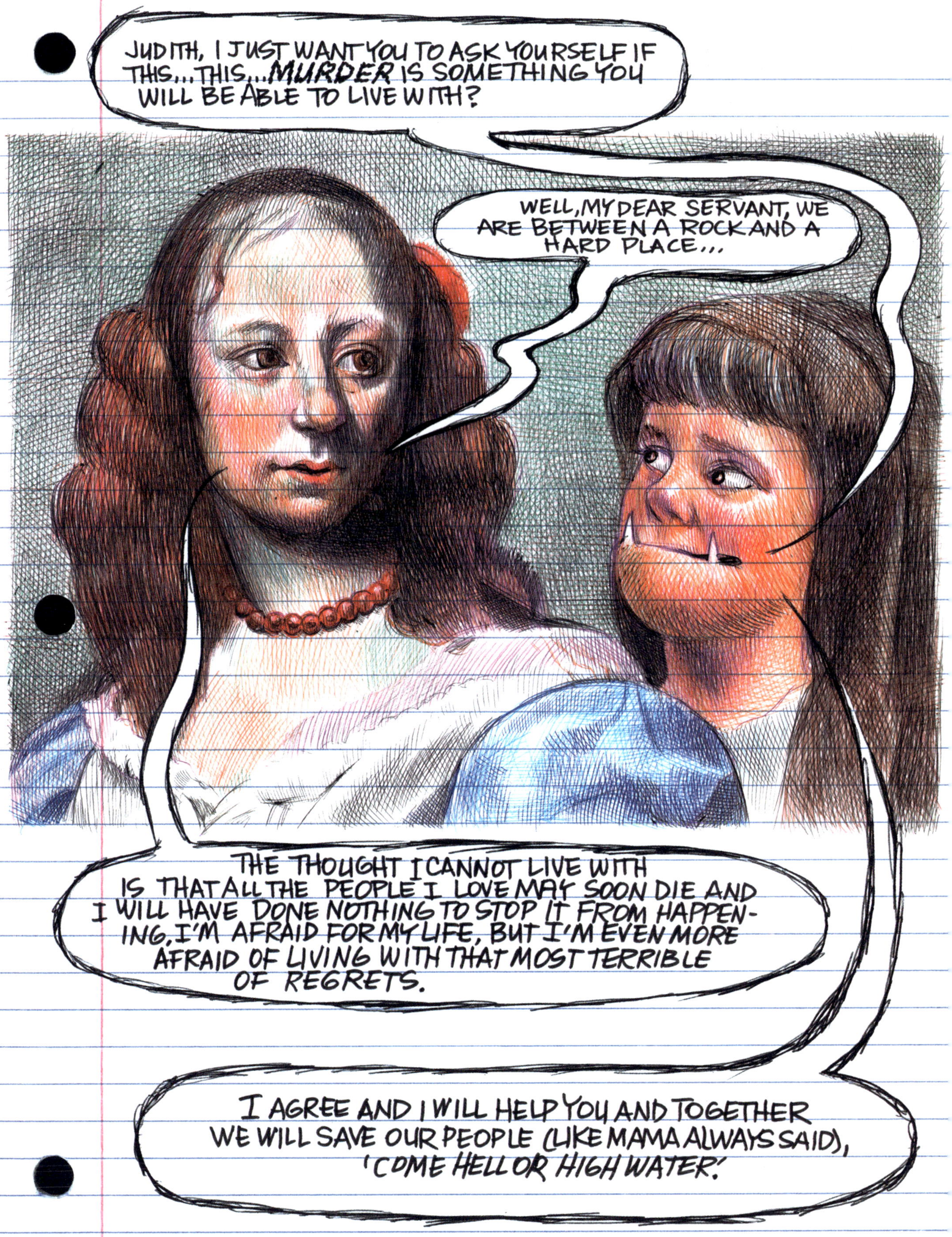
JUDITH, I JUST WANT YOU TO ASK YOURSELF IF THIS... THIS... *MURDER* IS SOMETHING YOU WILL BE ABLE TO LIVE WITH?
WELL, MY DEAR SERVANT, WE ARE BETWEEN A ROCK AND A HARD PLACE...
THE THOUGHT I CANNOT LIVE WITH IS THAT ALL THE PEOPLE I LOVE MAY SOON DIE AND I WILL HAVE DONE NOTHING TO STOP IT FROM HAPPENING. I'M AFRAID FOR MY LIFE, BUT I'M EVEN MORE AFRAID OF LIVING WITH THAT MOST TERRIBLE OF REGRETS.
I AGREE AND I WILL HELP YOU AND TOGETHER WE WILL SAVE OUR PEOPLE (LIKE MAMA ALWAYS SAID), 'COME HELL OR HIGH WATER.'

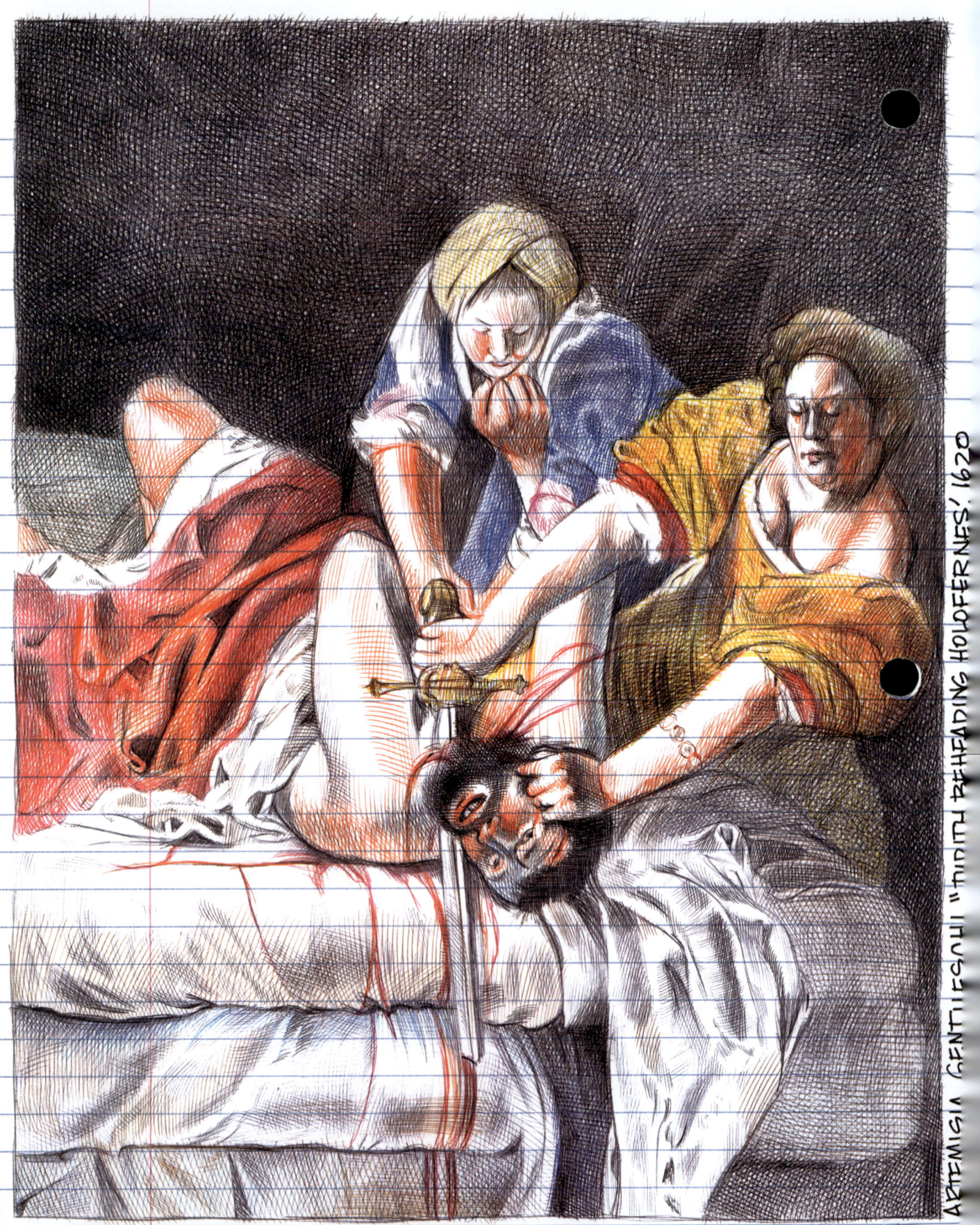

ARTEMISIA GENTILESCHI "JUDITH BEHEADING HOLOFERNES", 1620

EVEN THOUGH THIS PAINTING BY THE GREAT ARTEMESIA GENTILESCHI ISN'T IN THE ART INSTITUTE OF CHICAGO, I DREW IT FROM ONE OF DEEZE'S ART BOOKS. IT IS SO GOOD THAT IT COULD BE THE COVER OF A VERY CREEPY ISSUE OF GHASTLY.

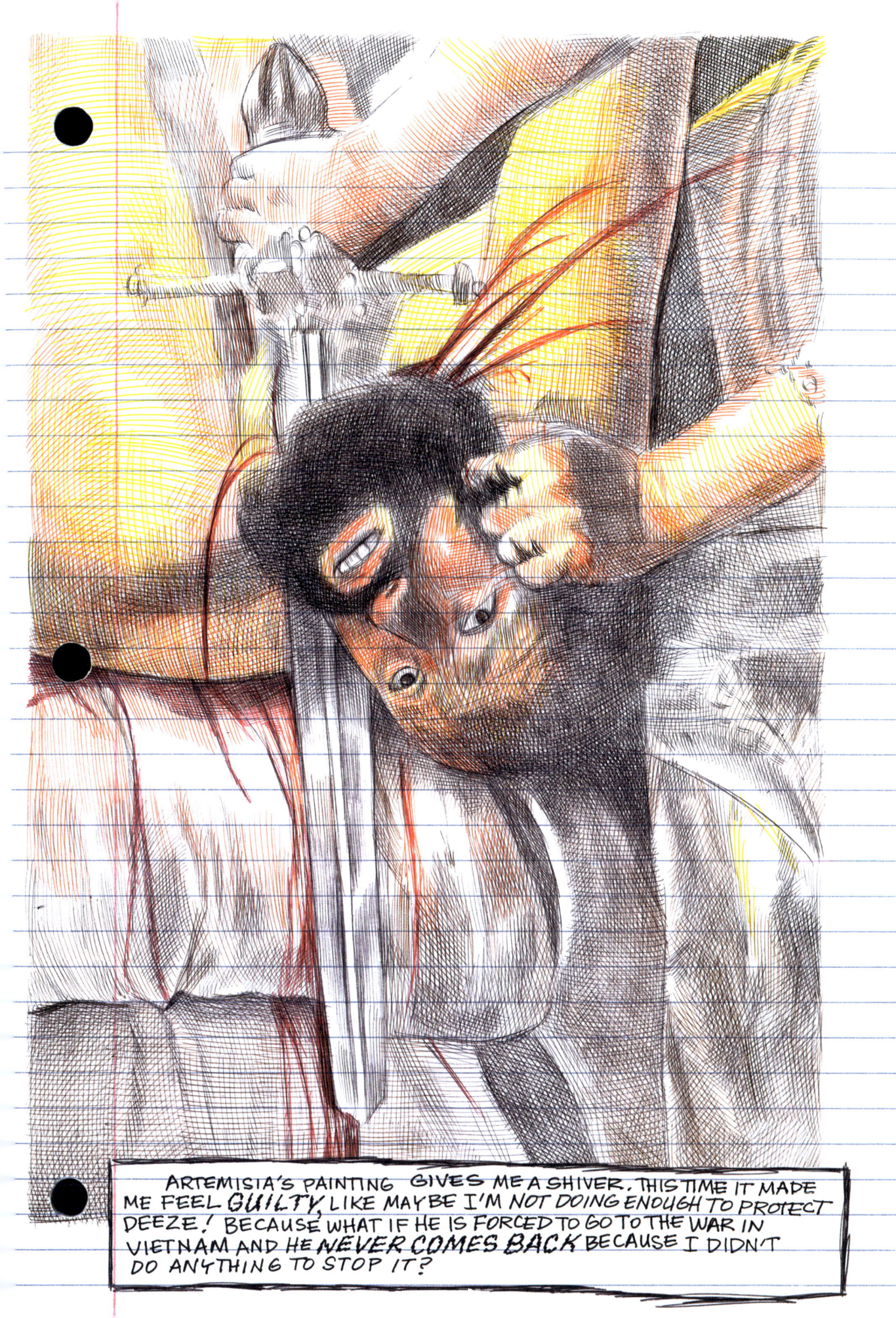

ARTEMISIA'S PAINTING GIVES ME A SHIVER. THIS TIME IT MADE ME FEEL *GUILTY*, LIKE MAYBE I'M *NOT DOING ENOUGH* TO PROTECT DEEZE! BECAUSE WHAT IF HE IS FORCED TO GO TO THE WAR IN VIETNAM AND HE *NEVER COMES BACK* BECAUSE I DIDN'T DO ANYTHING TO STOP IT?

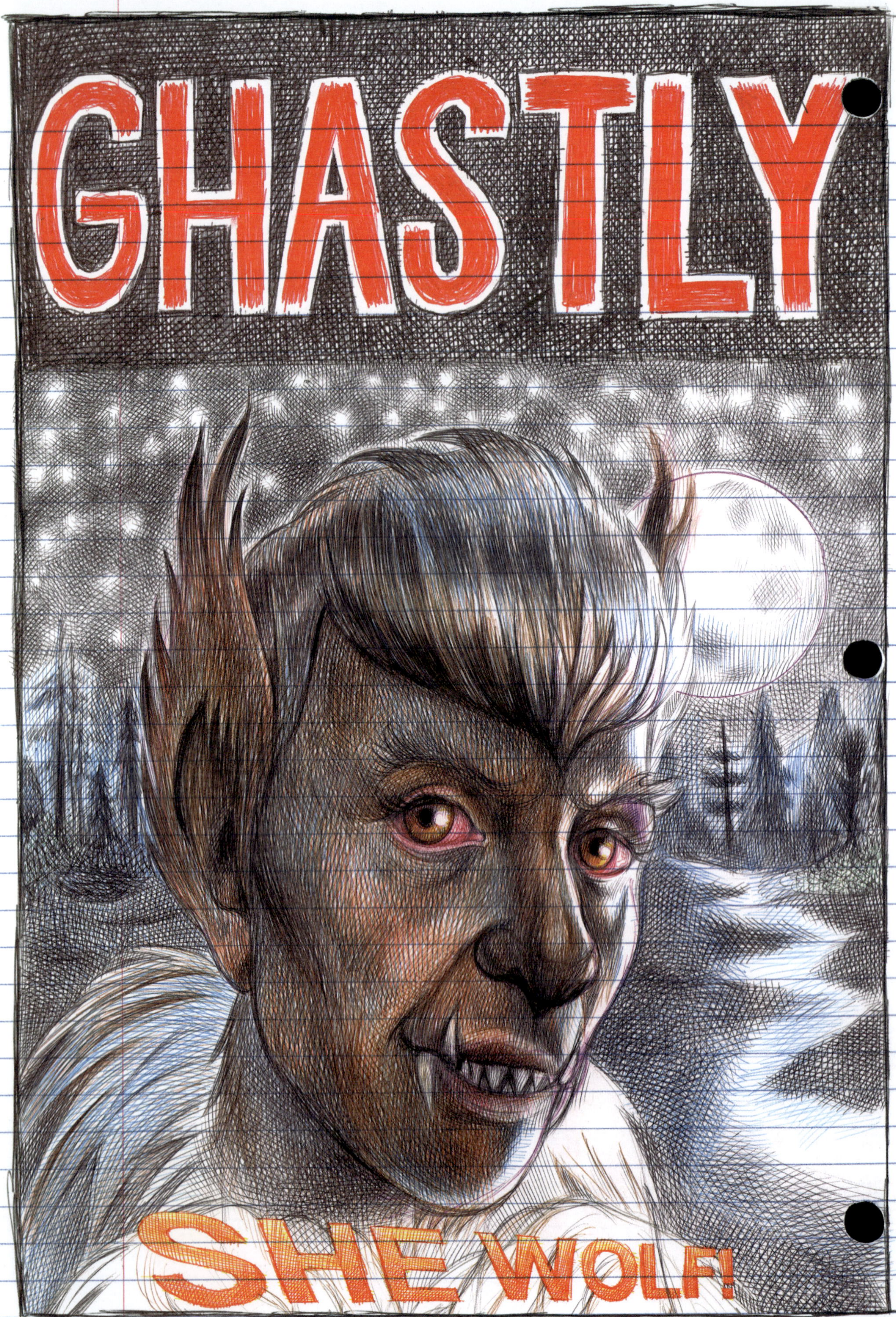
GHASTLY
SHE WOLF!

MAMA DIDN'T USUALLY BREAK ANY RULES BUT SHE HATED PAY TOILETS. MAMA WAS A WAITRESS AND SOMETIMES AT THE END OF THE MONTH A DIME WAS ALL THAT KEPT US FROM GOING HUNGRY. SHE WOULD ALWAYS TELL ME TO GO UNDER THE DOOR, USE THE FACILITIES AND THEN LET HER IN. "THE RICH MAKE US PAY THEM FOR EVERYTHING BUT THEY AIN'T MAKING US PAY TO PEE," MAMA ALWAYS SAID. SO IN MAMA'S HONOR...

ALL OF A SUDDEN I GOT A REAL *SHOCK*. THE DRUID WAS IN THE LADIES ROOM AND WENT RIGHT PAST THE DOOR OF THE STALL I WAS IN! I CALLED OUT...

"STOP DRUID!"

JUST AS I RACED OUT OF THE STALL I HEARD ALL THESE COINS CLANKING AND RIGHT THAT SECOND I THOUGHT MAYBE A DRUID IS LIKE A LEPRECHAUN AND CAN KIND OF MAKE COINS APPEAR...

...SO I WAS FULLY EXPECTING TO SEE THIS TYPE OF THING BUT WHAT I SAW INSTEAD WAS...

...A KID WHO WAS USING A KEY THAT WAS STRUNG ON A REALLY LONG SHOELACE. THE KEY WAS OPENING A PAY TOILET LOCKBOX AND THE COINS INSIDE IT WERE SPILLING INTO A CANVAS BAG SHE WAS HOLDING.

SHE DIDN'T EVEN LOOK AT ME, BUT SHE SAID...

"HEY, WANNA BE MY LOOKOUT?"

"BUT IS WHAT YOU'RE DOING ILLEGAL?"

"COMPLETELY AND TOTALLY. IT'S CALLED 'STEALING' BY SOME."

OF ALL THE UNCOOL MOMENTS OF MY UNCOOL LIFE, SAYING THOSE WORDS MADE ME THE SQUAREST PERSON ALIVE.

Tales of the eldritch and the ARCANE

IT'S WEIRD BUT I THINK THAT THE MOST IMPORTANT THING OF MY WHOLE ENTIRE LIFETIME HAPPENED TODAY IN THE MUSEUM BATHROOM   BECAUSE TODAY I MET...

SHELLEY

WHILE I WAS THE KID'S LOOKOUT (AT THAT POINT I DIDN'T KNOW HER NAME) ONLY ONE LADY CAME IN TO THE BATHROOM AND I DISTRACTED HER SO THAT SHE DIDN'T SEE THE LOCKBOXES WERE BEING ROBBED — BUT MAYBE I WILL TELL MORE ABOUT THAT LATER ON.

AFTER THE KID GOT HER STEALING DONE, SHE GOT A WILD EXPRESSION ON HER FACE AND SHE SAID...

"MAYBE I KIND OF HAVE E.S.P. AND I KNOW THAT YOU HAVE A RECORD OF WAGNER'S MUSIC IN YOUR RECORD COLLECTION."

"HOW WOULD YOU KNOW THAT? A FEW YEARS AGO — EVEN THOUGH SHE WAS A TOTAL STRANGER — A NICE OLD LADY BOUGHT ME THAT RECORD."

"IT WASN'T REALLY MY E.S.P. I KNOW ABOUT IT BECAUSE THE LADY WHO BOUGHT YOU THAT RECORD IS MY GRANDMOTHER."

MIND BLOWN

"WOW, BUT HOW DID YOU KNOW IT WAS ME THAT SHE BOUGHT IT FOR?"

"I SAW YOU FROM OUR WINDOW WHEN YOU WALKED MY GRANDMOTHER HOME AND SHE TOLD ME THAT YOU WERE THE KID WHO SHE BOUGHT A RECORD FOR."

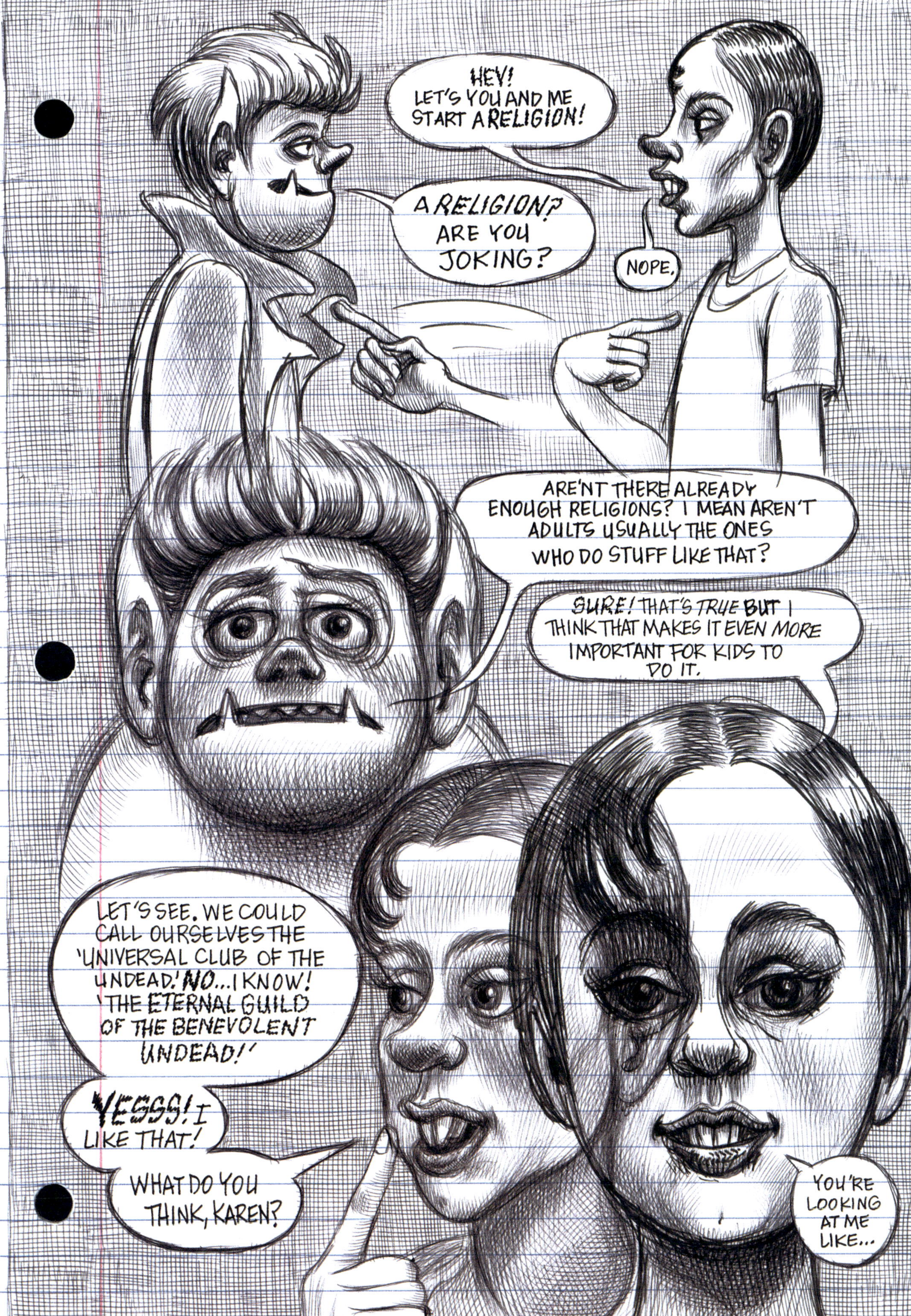
HEY! LET'S YOU AND ME START A RELIGION!
A RELIGION? ARE YOU JOKING?
NOPE.
AREN'T THERE ALREADY ENOUGH RELIGIONS? I MEAN AREN'T ADULTS USUALLY THE ONES WHO DO STUFF LIKE THAT?
SURE! THAT'S TRUE BUT I THINK THAT MAKES IT EVEN MORE IMPORTANT FOR KIDS TO DO IT.
LET'S SEE. WE COULD CALL OURSELVES THE 'UNIVERSAL CLUB OF THE UNDEAD.' NO... I KNOW! 'THE ETERNAL GUILD OF THE BENEVOLENT UNDEAD!'
YESSS! I LIKE THAT!
WHAT DO YOU THINK, KAREN?
YOU'RE LOOKING AT ME LIKE...

YOU DIDN'T REALIZE THAT I'M A 'MONSTER KID' JUST LIKE YOU, DID YOU?

NO, WHEN YOU SAID THE UNDEAD THING I WAS KIND OF SURPRISED. SO YOU'RE A MONSTER KID? WHICH MONSTER IS *YOUR* MONSTER?

SHE JUST LOOKED AT ME IN A STRANGE WAY AND PUT ON HER HEAVY BACKPACK AND TURNED TO GO. I PANICKED WHILE TRYING TO THINK OF SOMETHING TO SAY.

EGOTBU!

EGOT...?

OHHH YEAH. ETERNAL GUILD OF THE BENEVOLENT UNDEAD. EGOTBU!

I IMITATED PULLING A STAKE OUT OF MY HEART AND I HELD IT UP AND MADE A LONG LOW VICTORY HOWL.

LIKE ME, SHE PULLED THE INVISIBLE STAKE OUT OF HER HEART AND HOWLED (LOUDER THAN I'D EXPECTED) AND SHE SAID...

"I TOTALLY LOVE THAT IDEA!"

"I THINK WE SHOULD HAVE AN INSIGNIA, A SYMBOL. I PROPOSE MEDUSA WITH HER HEAD RE-ATTACHED IN HONOR OF SOMEONE SPECIAL WHO I'LL TELL YOU ABOUT IF I... ...IF I... SEE YOU AGAIN..."

...AND THEN SUDDENLY THE KID WAS JUST ON ME, *ACTUALLY HUGGING ME!*

"EGOTBU!"

"YOU'LL SEE ME AGAIN, KAREN REYES!"

...AND SHE WHISPERED INTO MY EAR.

"THE NEXT TIME I SEE YOU, I'LL HAVE A PRESENT FOR YOU."

...AND THEN SHE WAS GONE. I WANTED TO RUN AFTER HER BUT THAT WOULD'VE BEEN *MAGNA UNCOOL.*

DEEZE HAS THIS THEORY THAT THE ARTIST'S GHOST CAN BE REACHED WHEN YOU'RE STANDING RIGHT IN FRONT OF THEIR PAINTING. SINCE MR. HOPPER DIED LAST YEAR, EVERY TIME WE VISIT HIS PAINTING CALLED 'NIGHTHAWKS' DEEZE HAS BEEN TALKING TO EDWARD HOPPER— **RIGHT OUT LOUD!**

DAMMIT! EDWARD HOPPER— YOU B-YOO-TI-FULL FUCKING BASTARD!

"HIYA KAREN! LOOKIT THIS BIG OL' PILE OF CAN-PAKES I GOT ME!"

"WELL SON, I CAN'T SAY I'VE BEEN REFERRED TO IN THAT WAY BEFORE, BUT THANKS ANYWHO!"

DEEZE TALKED TO ME SO MUCH ABOUT ALL OF THE PAINTING'S 'VISUAL MAGIC' (AS DEEZE CALLS IT) THAT A CROWD KIND OF FORMED TO HEAR WHAT HE SAID. WHILE HE TALKED I LOOKED AT THE PAINTING AND I SAW THAT THERE WAS MORE MAGIC TO THE PAINTING AND EVEN MORE **GHOSTS** THAN MR. HOPPER.

THE CROWD SITUATION MEANT THAT I DIDN'T HAVE THE PRIVACY I NEEDED TO CLIMB INTO THE PAINTING. IT LOOKED TO ME LIKE ALL THE PEOPLE IN THE PAINTING WERE PEOPLE I KNOW... BUT ALSO PEOPLE WHO ARE **DEAD**...

...EXCEPT FOR MY FRIEND SANDY WHO WAS PROBABLY IN THE RESTAURANT BECAUSE SHE'S ALWAYS HUNGRY. (SHE ALWAYS CALLS 'PANCAKES' 'CANPAKES' BUT I'M NOT SURE WHY).

> THE GUY SERVING THE COFFEE LOOKED LIKE VICTOR SO DON'T GET ME STARTED ON HIM! IS **HE** THE GOOD ONE (LIKE HE SAYS) OR IS DEEZE THE GOOD ONE?

THROUGH MY MIND'S EYE I COULD SEE THAT MAMA AND ANKA WERE SITTING AT THE COUNTER. UNLIKE SANDY THEY SEEMED TO BE IGNORING ME AND THIS MADE ME WONDER IF BEING DEAD IS A KIND OF SNOOTY HIGHFALUTIN CLUB. SO DESPITE CREATING THE 'ETERNAL GUILD OF THE BENEVOLENT UNDEAD' WITH SHELLEY, I FELT A FLASH OF **RAGE** AT STUPID MONSTERS WHO **TOTALLY** LET ME DOWN BY NOT BITING MAMA AND I FELT ANGER AT *GHOSTS* WHO NOW LIVE ON THE OTHER SIDE AS HAPPY AS INVISIBLE CLAMS WHILE THE ONES THEY LEFT BEHIND SUFFER!

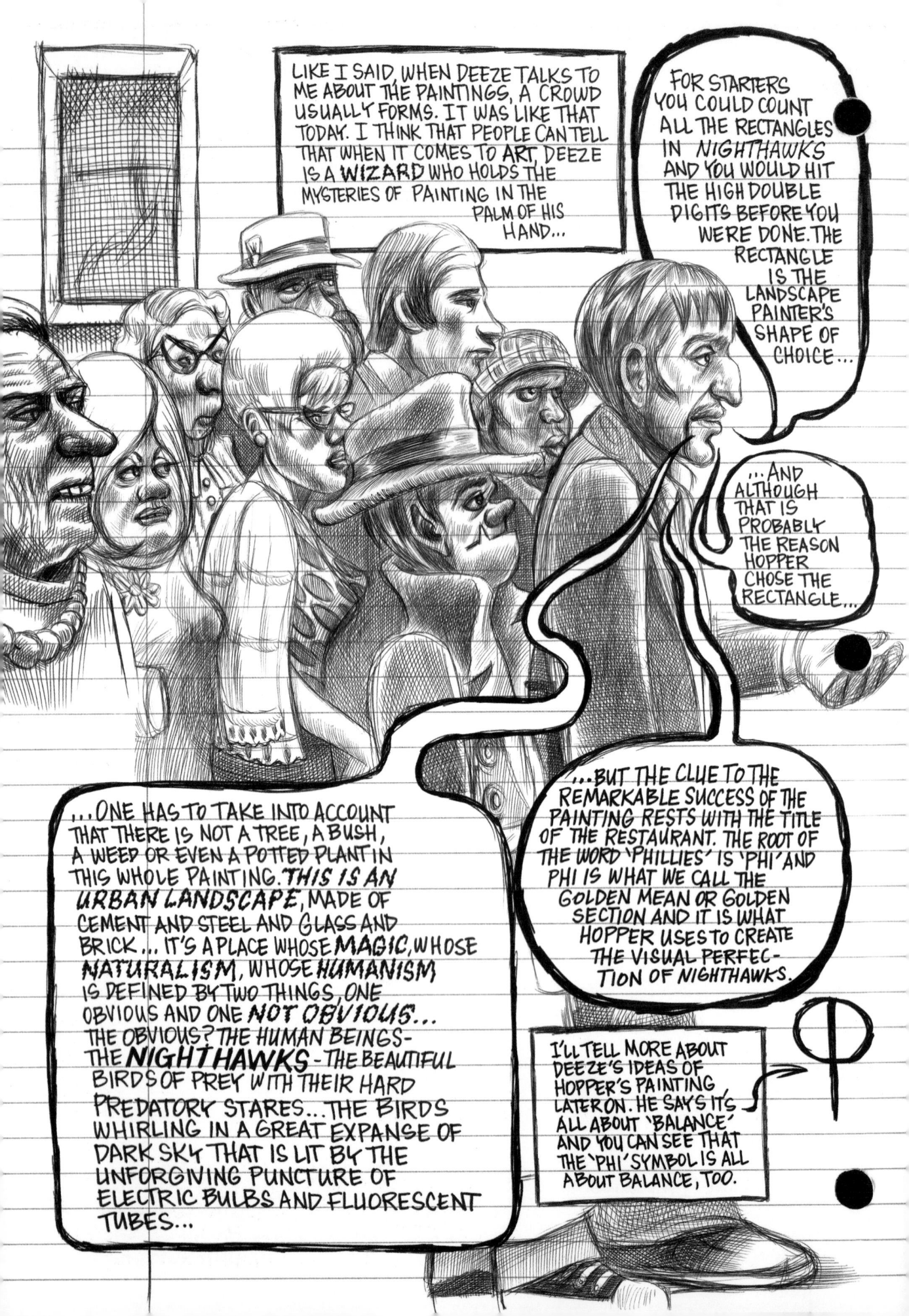

LIKE I SAID, WHEN DEEZE TALKS TO ME ABOUT THE PAINTINGS, A CROWD USUALLY FORMS. IT WAS LIKE THAT TODAY. I THINK THAT PEOPLE CAN TELL THAT WHEN IT COMES TO ART, DEEZE IS A **WIZARD** WHO HOLDS THE MYSTERIES OF PAINTING IN THE PALM OF HIS HAND...

FOR STARTERS YOU COULD COUNT ALL THE RECTANGLES IN *NIGHTHAWKS* AND YOU WOULD HIT THE HIGH DOUBLE DIGITS BEFORE YOU WERE DONE. THE RECTANGLE IS THE LANDSCAPE PAINTER'S SHAPE OF CHOICE...

...AND ALTHOUGH THAT IS PROBABLY THE REASON HOPPER CHOSE THE RECTANGLE...

...BUT THE CLUE TO THE REMARKABLE SUCCESS OF THE PAINTING RESTS WITH THE TITLE OF THE RESTAURANT. THE ROOT OF THE WORD 'PHILLIES' IS 'PHI' AND PHI IS WHAT WE CALL THE GOLDEN MEAN OR GOLDEN SECTION AND IT IS WHAT HOPPER USES TO CREATE THE VISUAL PERFECTION OF NIGHTHAWKS.

...ONE HAS TO TAKE INTO ACCOUNT THAT THERE IS NOT A TREE, A BUSH, A WEED OR EVEN A POTTED PLANT IN THIS WHOLE PAINTING. *THIS IS AN URBAN LANDSCAPE*, MADE OF CEMENT AND STEEL AND GLASS AND BRICK... IT'S A PLACE WHOSE **MAGIC**, WHOSE **NATURALISM**, WHOSE **HUMANISM** IS DEFINED BY TWO THINGS, ONE OBVIOUS AND ONE *NOT OBVIOUS*... THE OBVIOUS? THE HUMAN BEINGS- THE **NIGHTHAWKS** - THE BEAUTIFUL BIRDS OF PREY WITH THEIR HARD PREDATORY STARES... THE BIRDS WHIRLING IN A GREAT EXPANSE OF DARK SKY THAT IS LIT BY THE UNFORGIVING PUNCTURE OF ELECTRIC BULBS AND FLUORESCENT TUBES...

I'LL TELL MORE ABOUT DEEZE'S IDEAS OF HOPPER'S PAINTING LATER ON. HE SAYS IT'S ALL ABOUT 'BALANCE' AND YOU CAN SEE THAT THE 'PHI' SYMBOL IS ALL ABOUT BALANCE, TOO.

BEFORE WE LEFT DOWNTOWN DEEZE AND ME STOPPED AT THE ORIENTAL THEATER BUILDING. DEEZE SAID THAT THIS WAS WHERE HIS PUBLISHER'S OFFICE IS LOCATED. WE DROPPED OFF THE PACKAGE HE HAD ME CARRY FOR HIM (WHICH IT TURNS OUT WAS SOME VERY BEAUTIFUL ART THAT DEEZE MADE FOR AN UPCOMING ISSUE!) DEEZE SAID WE WOULD COME BACK AND SEE 'ROSEMARY'S BABY' SOON.
I TOLD DEEZE HOW ONCE I CAME DOWN HERE WITH ANKA AND ME AND HER SAW A GHOST IN THIS VERY BUILDING, BUT I WILL TELL ABOUT THAT LATER ON.

WHEN WE GOT HOME DEEZE PUT ON MAMA'S APRON AND HE MADE US SALAMI SANDWICHES WITH MUSTARD AND TANG TO DRINK AND WHILE HE DID THE DISHES, I LOOKED IN THE T.V. GUIDE TO SEE WHAT THE DOUBLE FEATURE WOULD BE ON THE LATE NIGHT CREEPSHOW.

"GOOD NEWS, DEEZE! TONIGHT THEY'RE PLAYING 'BRIDE OF FRANKENSTEIN' AND 'A PICTURE OF DORIAN GRAY'. I'LL POP THE POPCORN AND— GUESS WHAT— WE'VE GOT *REAL* BUTTER!"

"KARE, I'VE GOT A BIT OF BAD NEWS. I'M GOING TO HAVE TO BE OUT LATE AT A DELIVERY JOB I'M DOING FOR MR. GRONAN. SO I'LL HAVE TO MISS CREATURE FEATURES..., OK? BUT NEXT WEEK— *FOR SURE*— WE'LL WATCH IT TOGETHER...I ABSOLUTELY *PROMISE*, OK?"

"BUT YOU PROMISED! YOU TOTALLY SAID!"

"KAREN, NOW I'M UNSAYING! GET OVER IT RIGHT NOW AND ONE MORE FREAKING THING..."

"IT WAS FUNNY AND **CUTE** HOW YOU'D WANDER **OUT** OF THIS APARTMENT WHEN YOU WERE A LITTLE KID AND I'D RUN OUT AND FIND YOU TALKING TO 'THE LADIES,' AS YOU CALLED THEM. BUT YOU'RE NOT A FREAKING LITTLE KID ANYMORE. SO IF YOU GO OUT OF THIS BUILDING WHILE I'M GONE, IT WILL NOT BE FUNNY BECAUSE I WILL HURT YOU! AND **THAT** KAREN IS A STRAIGHT UP **PROMISE** FROM ME TO YOU. YOU GET IT? HAVE I MADE MYSELF UNDERSTOOD?"

"YEAH, DEEZE. I GET IT."

"BUT WHEN WILL YOU GET BACK? I GET SORT OF WORRIED WHEN I'M ALONE A LOT."

"HEY DEEZE, MAYBE YOU WOULD WANNA..."

"KARE, IT'S NOT ALWAYS GOING TO BE LIKE THIS."

SLAM!

"MAYBE YOU WOULD WANNA TAKE OFF MAMA'S APRON BEFORE YOU GO ON THE STREET."

FOR A FEW MINUTES AFTER DEEZE STOMPED OUT OF THE APARTMENT I WAS INCREDIBLY BUMMED OUT BUT THEN I REMEMBERED HOW I HAD MR. SILVERBERG'S KEY AND HOW HE LEFT A NOTE ON OUR DOOR SAYING HE'D BE GONE FOR THE WEEKEND TO ONE OF HIS JAZZ GIGS. I COULD KEEP MY PROMISE TO DEEZE ABOUT NOT LEAVING THE BUILDING BUT STILL GET OUT OF OUR APARTMENT, AND MAYBE, JUST MAYBE, I WOULD FIND ANKA'S CASSETTE TAPES...

THERE IS SOMETHING EXCITING ABOUT TURNING THE KEY TO GO INTO A NEIGHBOR'S APARTMENT. THE SMELLS ARE ALL DIFFERENT. AT THE SILVERBERG'S PLACE EVERYTHING KIND OF STINKS. WHEN ANKA WAS ALIVE I COULD SMELL HER PERFUME, BUT NOW IT IS MOSTLY GONE, EXCEPT FOR IN HER BEDROOM. (WHICH IS WHERE THEY FOUND HER BODY.

ANKA'S CAT NAMED 'TUT' WAS RIGHT ON MY HEELS.
I THINK TUT IS REALLY LONELY SO THIS TIME HIS ATTITUDE HAD A LITTLE LESS OF "I WANT TO MURDER YOU" IN IT.

USUALLY
TUT HUNTS ME LIKE A RAT WHO SNEAKED ONTO HIS TURF.

TODAY
WAS MORE LIKE I WAS A PATHETIC TOOTHLESS DOG WHO REQUIRED CAREFUL WATCHING BECAUSE I MIGHT LIFT MY LEG ON THE FURNITURE.

WHILE I PUT ON GARDENING CLOTHES I THOUGHT ABOUT HOW THINGS BETWEEN ME AND TUT HAVE IMPROVED...

I ALSO THOUGHT ABOUT HOW TUT STARES AT ANKA'S BED AND HOW YOU CAN STILL SEE THE BLOOD STAIN ON THE CARPET AND ALSO HOW COLD THE BEDROOM IS.

I KNEW MY MISSION WAS TO *SOMEHOW* SAVE WHAT I COULD OF THE PLANT ROOM.

ANKA WAS SENSITIVE TO LIVING THINGS IN A WAY I HAD NEVER SEEN BEFORE.

ANKA SAID, "THE ENERGY OF A PLACE IS *UNIQUE* TO THE PEOPLE WHO LIVE THERE."

SHE SAID THINGS LIKE THAT WHEN WE SNUCK INTO PEOPLE'S BACKYARDS TO STEAL THEIR DYING PLANTS (THAT ANKA WOULD USE HER *SUPER GREEN THUMB* TO BRING BACK TO LIFE).

EVER SINCE THE FIRST TIME I HEARD ANKA TELL HER STORY ON THE CASSETTE TAPES I KNEW I WOULD *HAVE TO HEAR EVERY WORD*. SO TODAY I SEARCHED THROUGH MY DEAD NEIGHBOR'S BELONGINGS SO I COULD LEARN THE TRUTH ABOUT HER LIFE (AND MAYBE HER DEATH). *THE ONLY PROBLEM WAS...*

"WHERE WOULD MR. SILVERBERG HAVE STASHED THOSE CASSETTE TAPES?"

WHILE I WAS STANDING AT THE SILVERBERG'S FRONT WINDOW AND ABSENTMINDEDLY THINKING ABOUT WHERE THE TAPE MIGHT BE HIDDEN...

EXCEPT FOR TUT, I AM TOTALLY ALONE IN THIS BUILDING!!

I WATCHED THE ACTUAL DRUID WALK RIGHT UP MY BUILDING'S FRONT STEPS!

I ADMIT THAT RIGHT THAT MINUTE I WAS SCARED OUT OF MY WITS! I FELT LIKE I AGED 50 YEARS! WOULD THE DRUID USE HIS DRUID POWERS TO BE IN THE APARTMENT (AND SACRIFICING ME AND POSSIBLY EVEN TUT) **IN ONLY SECONDS?** THEN THE OUTER DOOR SLAMMED AND THE DRUID WAS **LEAVING**.

THINKING THAT MAYBE THE DRUID LEFT A BOMB IN THE FOYER, I RAN INTO THE FOYER AND LOOKED AND I DID FIND SOMETHING THERE AND THAT'S WHEN I FIGURED OUT WHAT WAS GOING ON, I TOOK OFF RUNNING AFTER THAT DRUID LIKE THERE WAS NO TOMORROW (AS MAMA WOULD HAVE SAID).

"STOP DRUID!"

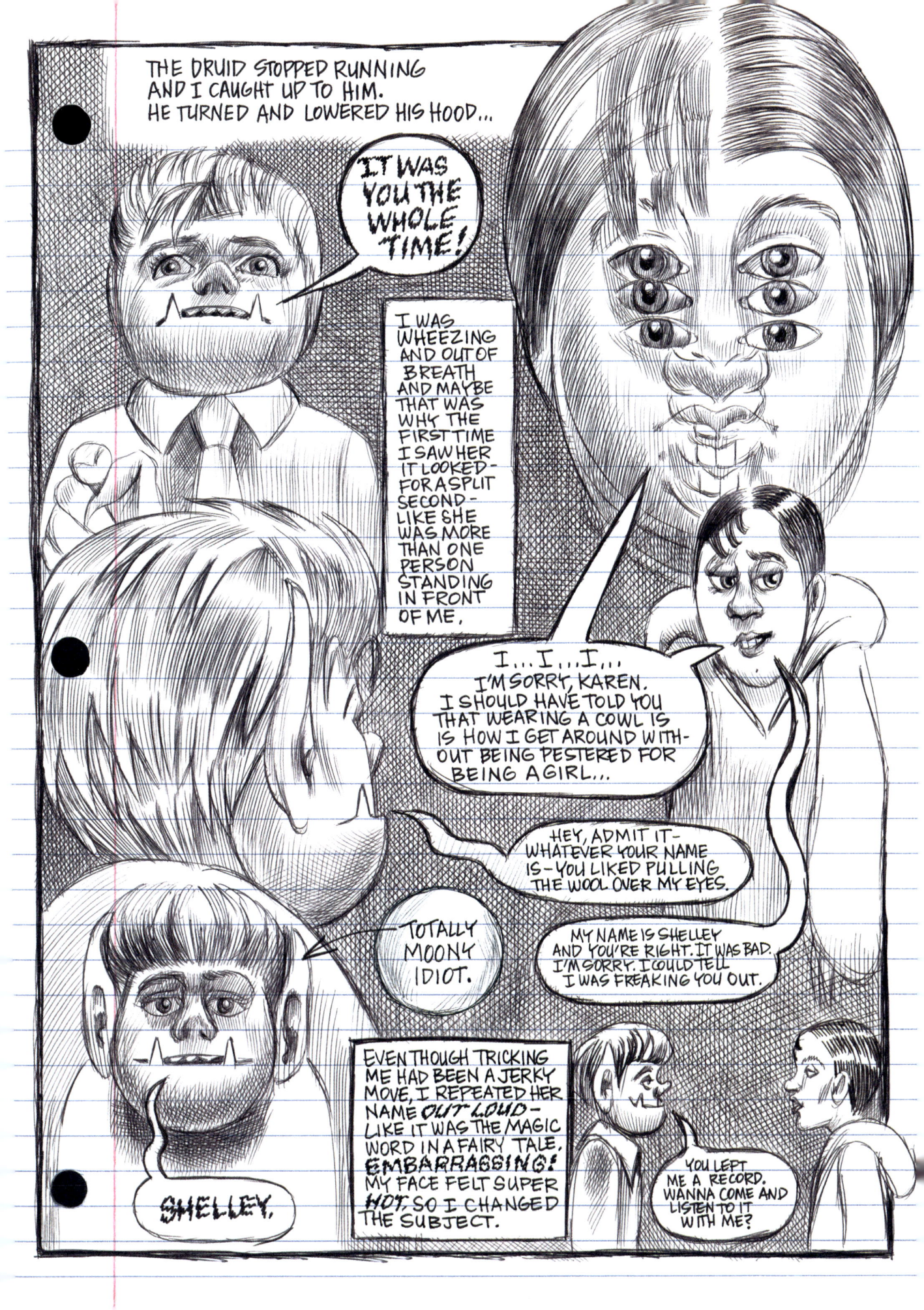

THE DRUID STOPPED RUNNING AND I CAUGHT UP TO HIM. HE TURNED AND LOWERED HIS HOOD...

"IT WAS YOU THE WHOLE TIME!"

I WAS WHEEZING AND OUT OF BREATH AND MAYBE THAT WAS WHY THE FIRST TIME I SAW HER IT LOOKED — FOR A SPLIT SECOND — LIKE SHE WAS MORE THAN ONE PERSON STANDING IN FRONT OF ME.

"I... I... I... I'M SORRY, KAREN. I SHOULD HAVE TOLD YOU THAT WEARING A COWL IS HOW I GET AROUND WITHOUT BEING PESTERED FOR BEING A GIRL..."

"HEY, ADMIT IT — WHATEVER YOUR NAME IS — YOU LIKED PULLING THE WOOL OVER MY EYES."

"TOTALLY MOONY IDIOT."

"MY NAME IS SHELLEY AND YOU'RE RIGHT. IT WAS BAD. I'M SORRY. I COULD TELL I WAS FREAKING YOU OUT."

EVEN THOUGH TRICKING ME HAD BEEN A JERKY MOVE, I REPEATED HER NAME *OUT LOUD* — LIKE IT WAS THE MAGIC WORD IN A FAIRY TALE. *EMBARRASSING!* MY FACE FELT SUPER *HOT*, SO I CHANGED THE SUBJECT.

"SHELLEY."

"YOU LEFT ME A RECORD. WANNA COME AND LISTEN TO IT WITH ME?"

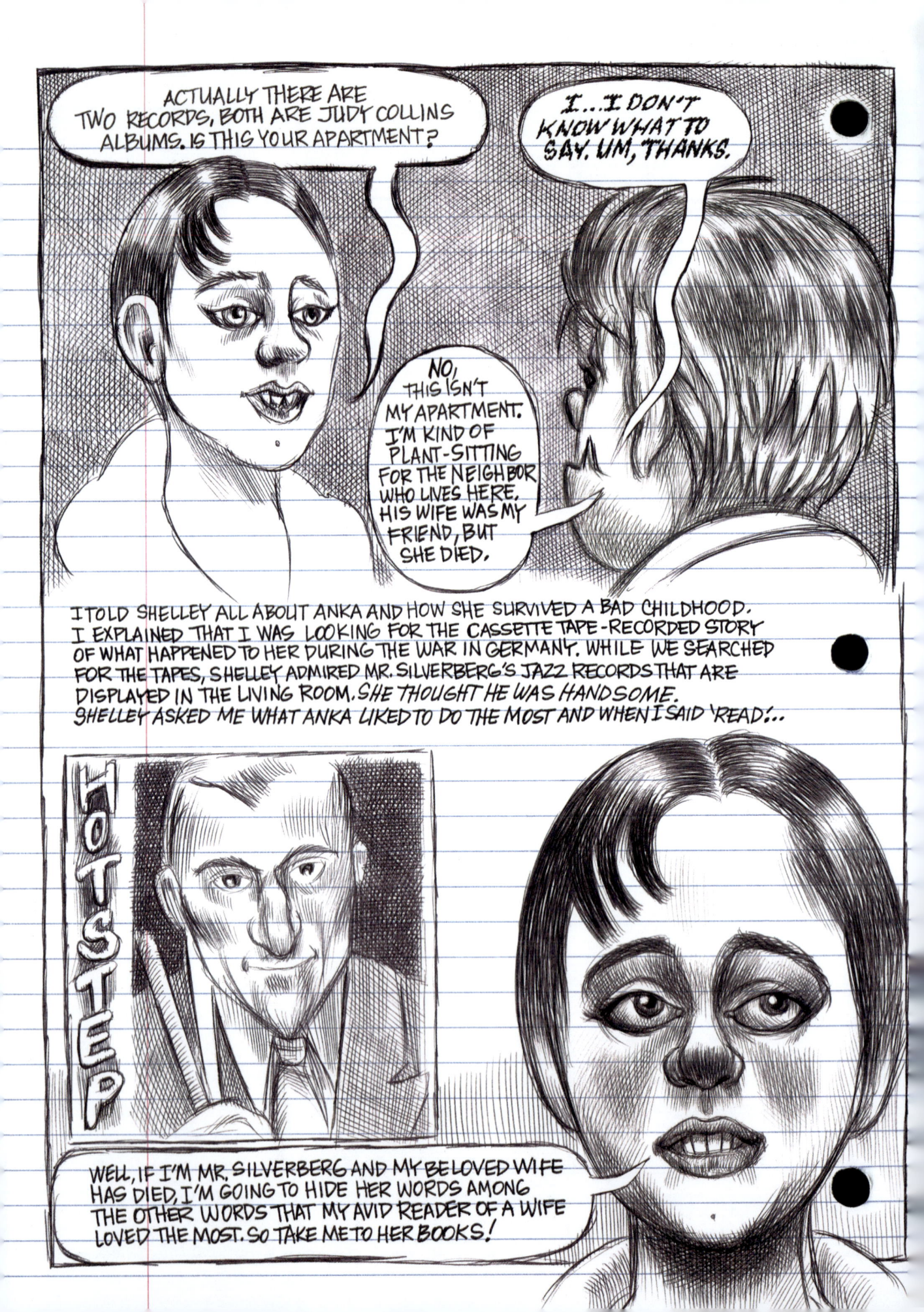

"ACTUALLY THERE ARE TWO RECORDS, BOTH ARE JUDY COLLINS ALBUMS. IS THIS YOUR APARTMENT?"

"I...I DON'T KNOW WHAT TO SAY. UM, THANKS."

"NO, THIS ISN'T MY APARTMENT. I'M KIND OF PLANT-SITTING FOR THE NEIGHBOR WHO LIVES HERE. HIS WIFE WAS MY FRIEND, BUT SHE DIED."

I TOLD SHELLEY ALL ABOUT ANKA AND HOW SHE SURVIVED A BAD CHILDHOOD. I EXPLAINED THAT I WAS LOOKING FOR THE CASSETTE TAPE-RECORDED STORY OF WHAT HAPPENED TO HER DURING THE WAR IN GERMANY. WHILE WE SEARCHED FOR THE TAPES, SHELLEY ADMIRED MR. SILVERBERG'S JAZZ RECORDS THAT ARE DISPLAYED IN THE LIVING ROOM. SHE THOUGHT HE WAS HANDSOME. SHELLEY ASKED ME WHAT ANKA LIKED TO DO THE MOST AND WHEN I SAID 'READ'...

"WELL, IF I'M MR. SILVERBERG AND MY BELOVED WIFE HAS DIED, I'M GOING TO HIDE HER WORDS AMONG THE OTHER WORDS THAT MY AVID READER OF A WIFE LOVED THE MOST. SO TAKE ME TO HER BOOKS!"

WHEN WE PULLED BACK THE BOOKS BY GOETHE WE FOUND THE CASSETTE TAPES.

"SHELLEY, WHAT I DIDN'T TELL YOU IS THAT I BELIEVE ANKA WAS MURDERED AND I THINK..."

"...THESE TAPES MIGHT CONTAIN A CLUE AS TO WHO HER KILLER IS. THEY ARE KIND OF UPSETTING SO IF THEY START TO MAKE YOU FEEL WEIRD, I CAN TURN THEM OFF. NO PROBLEM."

CLICK

I TURNED ON THE TAPE PLAYER.

"I WAS TAKEN TO A COMPLEX OF BUILDINGS..."

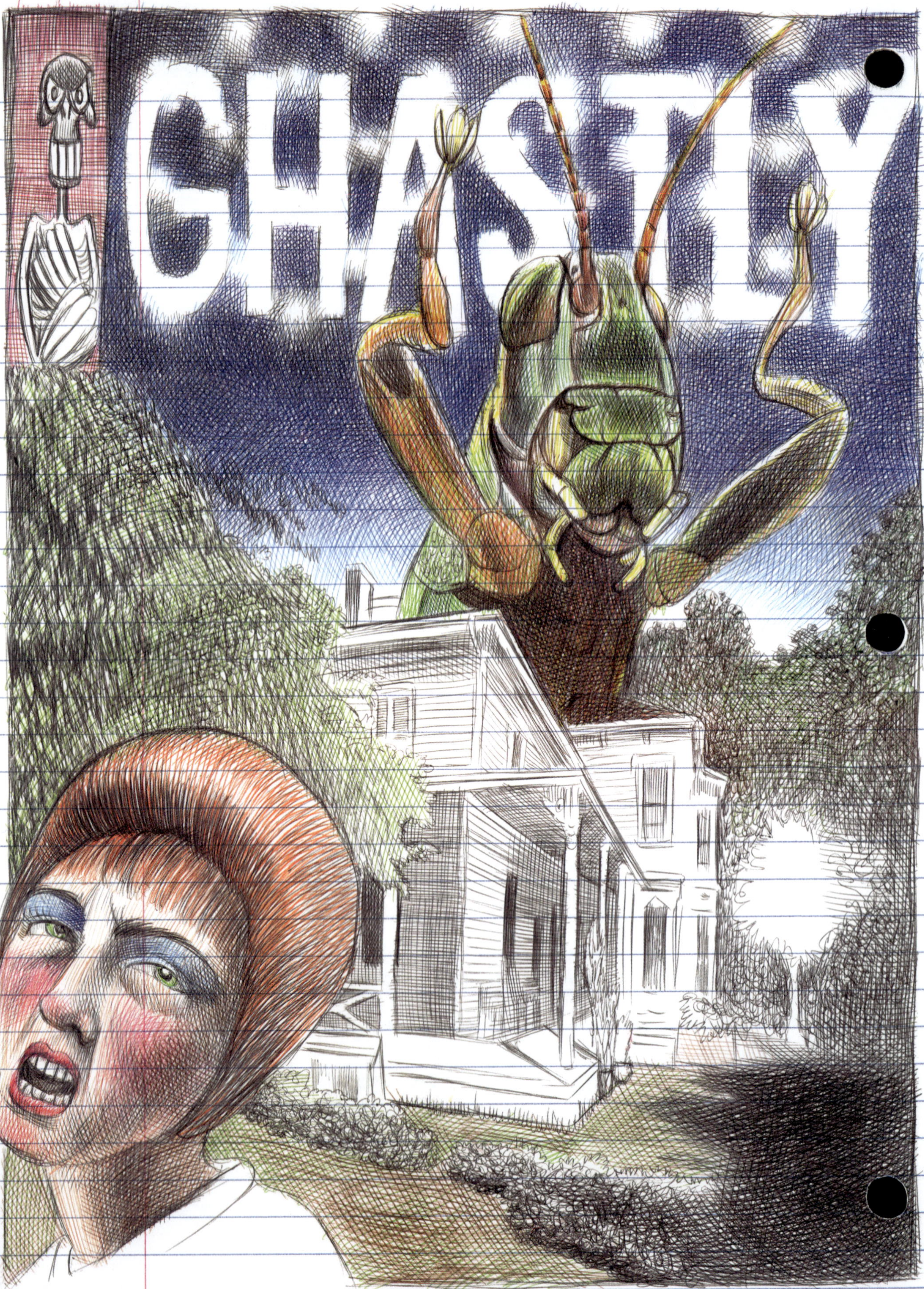
GHASTLY

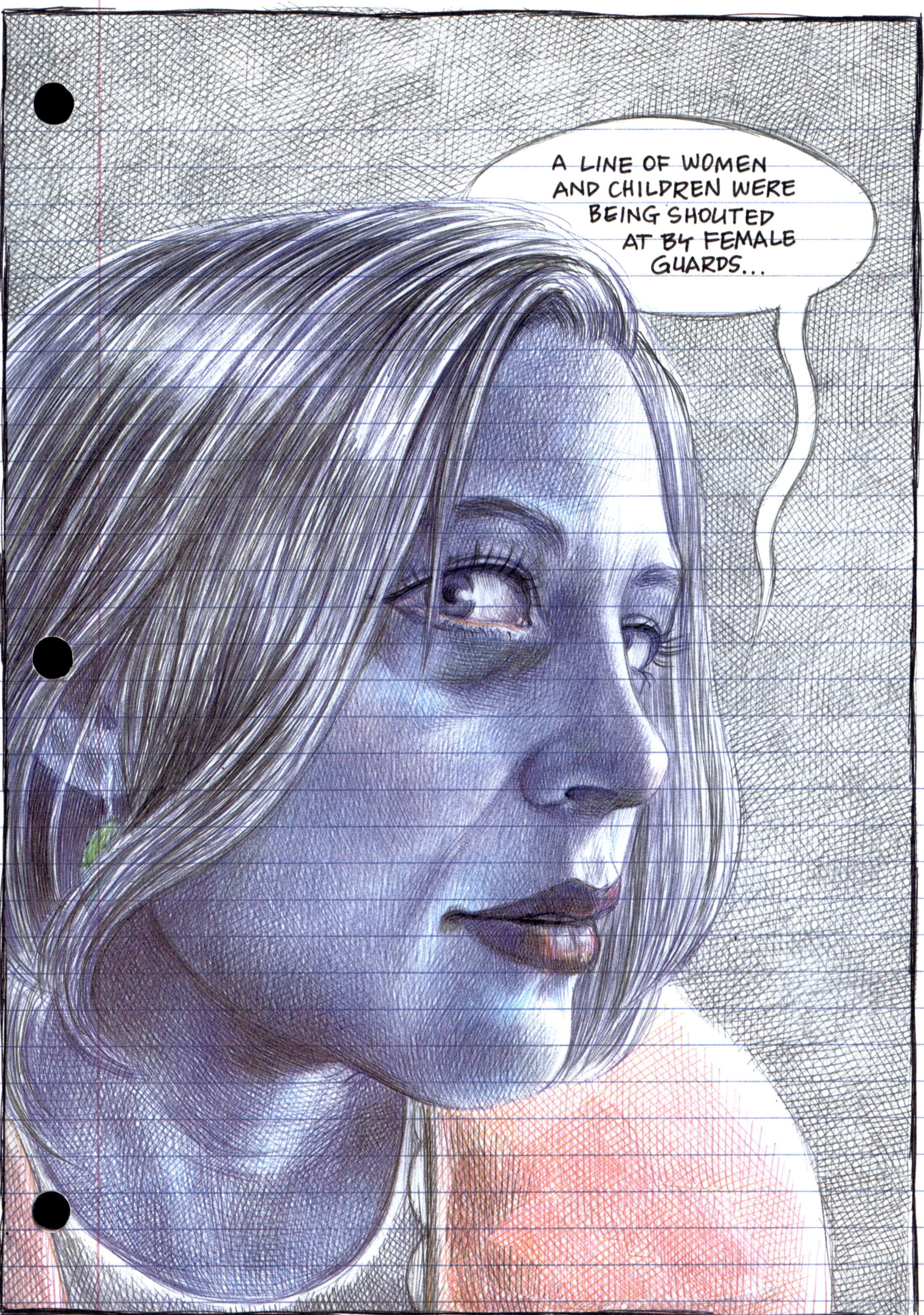
A LINE OF WOMEN AND CHILDREN WERE BEING SHOUTED AT BY FEMALE GUARDS...

One of the guards who escorted me was handsome, the other one was tall with large bright pink ears.

We passed women and children standing in a long long line.

"Quiet!"

"You don't have the proper authorization to be here!"

"Move! Our orders come from the top!"

The signs posted in the halls had a confidential tone.

HAVE PATIENCE! SOON YOU WILL BE A USEFUL PART OF GERMANY'S FUTURE.

One of the signs was smeared with blood..

WE ALL WANT A FUTURE OF CLEANLINESS, DON'T WE?

I recognized the mother and daughter beside the bloody sign. I'd seen them last near the 'Market Street.' Clearly the mother had been clubbed for some infraction. One of her daughters must've been ordered to use their coats to clean up the blood.

WE ALL WANT A FUTURE OF CLEANLINESS, DON'T WE?

IF YOUR DAUGHTERS COME WITH ME IT MIGHT BE SAFER FOR THEM...

TAKE THEM!

PLEASE FIND MY SISTER!

I PICKED TWO GIRLS. ONE WHO WOULD WORK WELL AS GYPSY BLACK. AND THE OTHER WHO WAS BRUNETTE...

I KEPT THE THREE GIRLS CLOSE TO ME WHILE WE LOOKED FOR THE SISTER. WE HEARD A DULL STEADY HUMMING THAT GREW LOUDER AND LOUDER. IT WAS AS IF WE WERE WALKING TOWARDS A NEST OF...

GIANT WASPS

ZUZZZZ

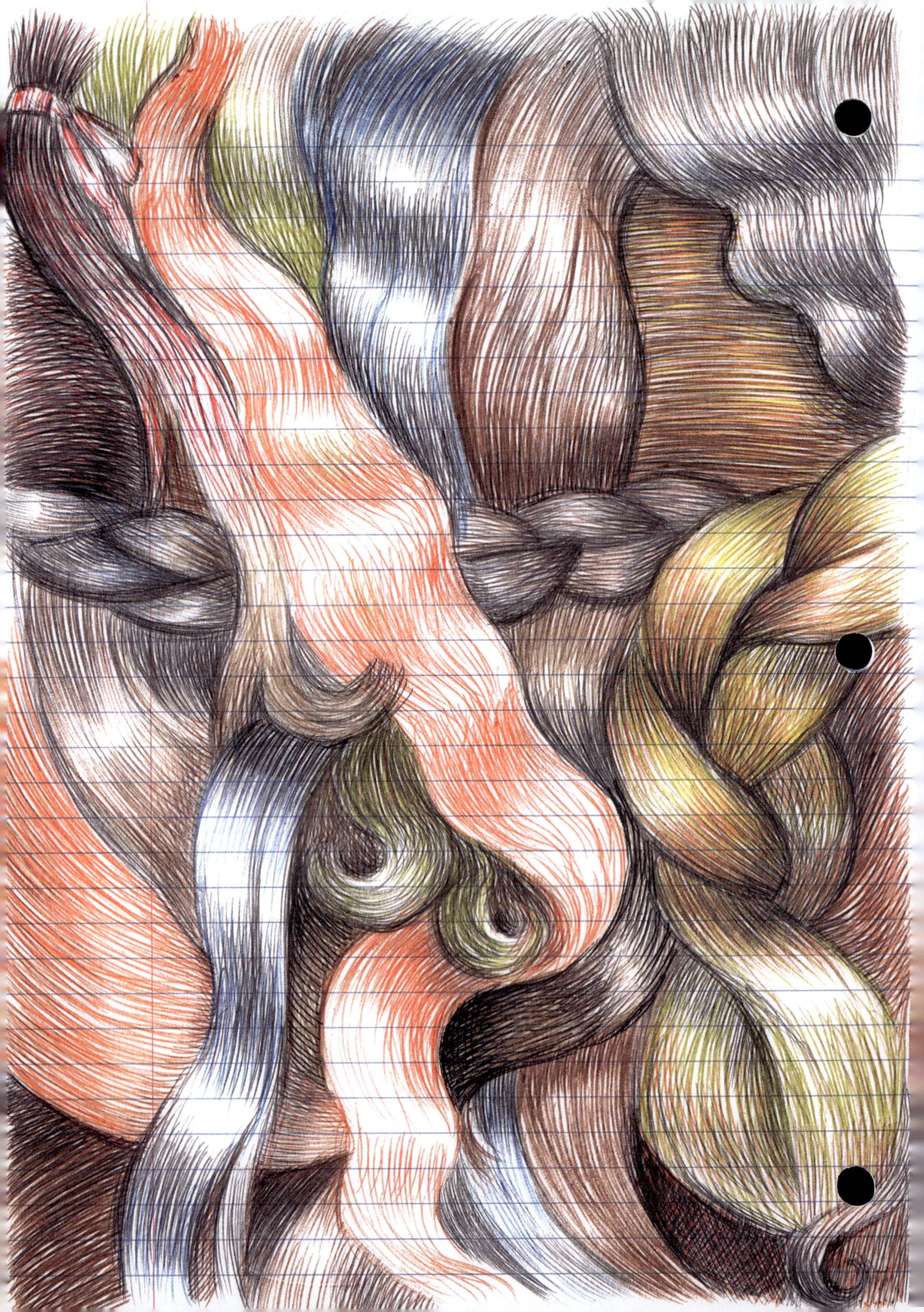

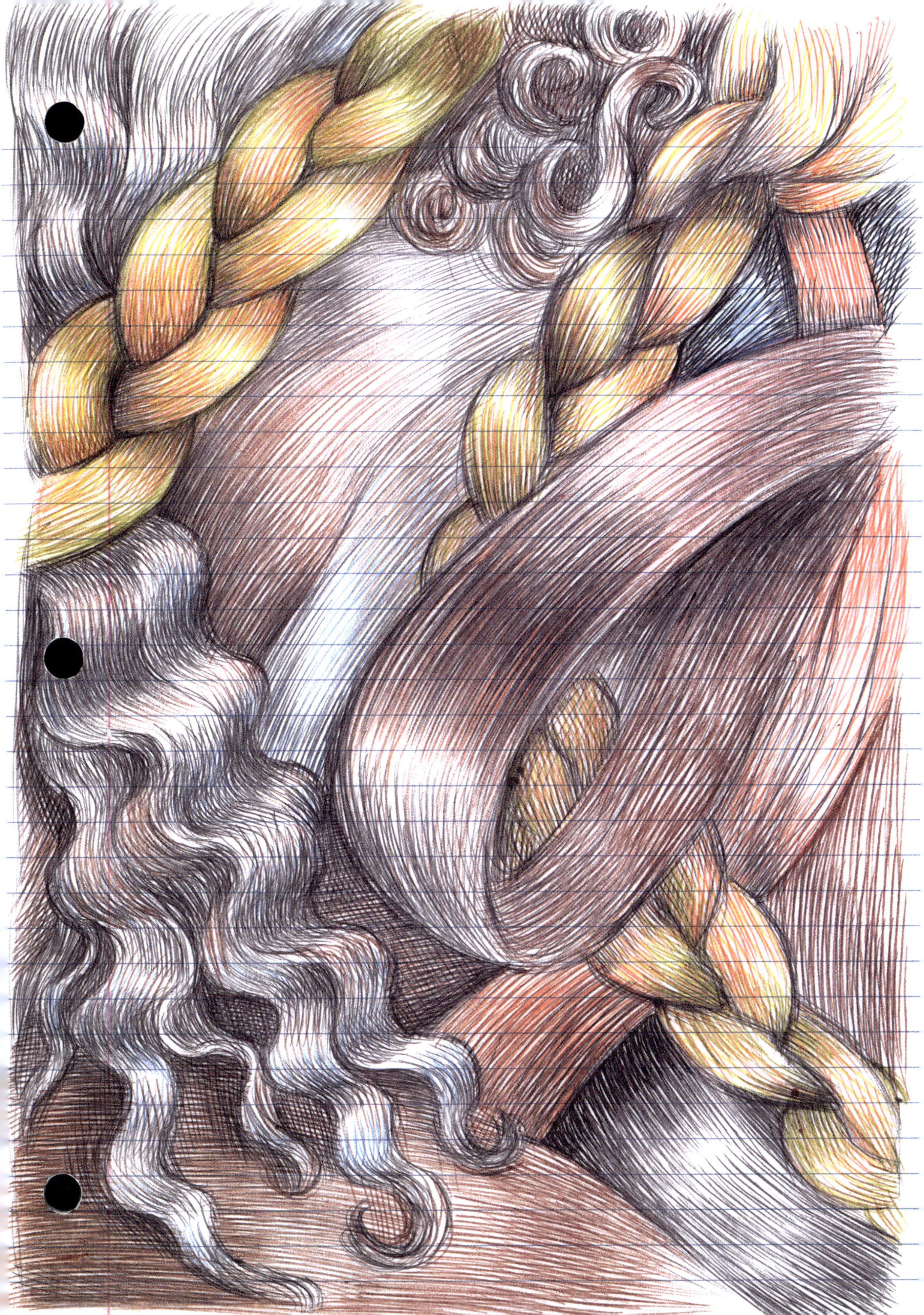

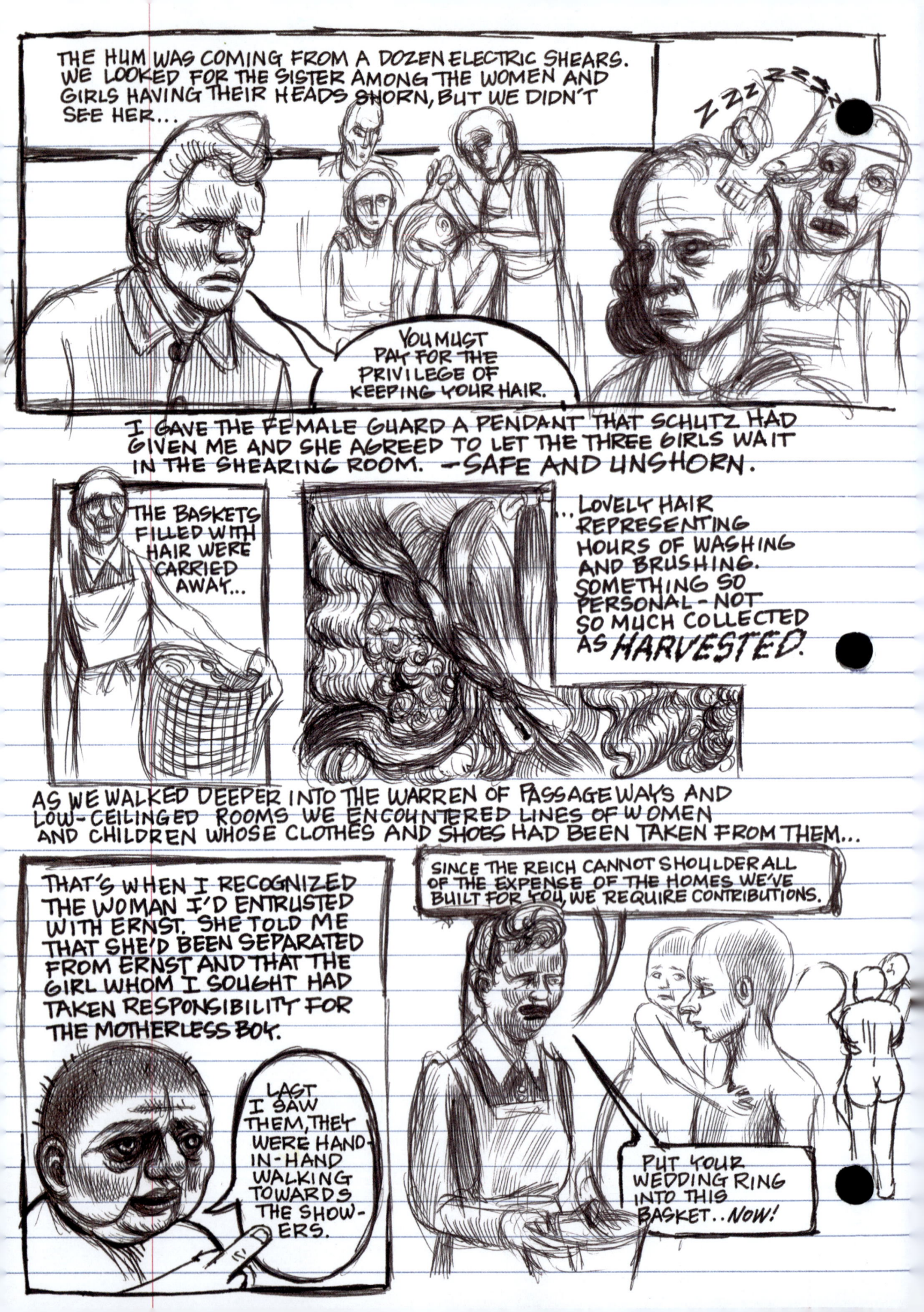

THE HUM WAS COMING FROM A DOZEN ELECTRIC SHEARS. WE LOOKED FOR THE SISTER AMONG THE WOMEN AND GIRLS HAVING THEIR HEADS SHORN, BUT WE DIDN'T SEE HER...

"YOU MUST PAY FOR THE PRIVILEGE OF KEEPING YOUR HAIR."

I GAVE THE FEMALE GUARD A PENDANT THAT SCHUTZ HAD GIVEN ME AND SHE AGREED TO LET THE THREE GIRLS WAIT IN THE SHEARING ROOM. —SAFE AND UNSHORN.

THE BASKETS FILLED WITH HAIR WERE CARRIED AWAY...

...LOVELY HAIR REPRESENTING HOURS OF WASHING AND BRUSHING. SOMETHING SO PERSONAL — NOT SO MUCH COLLECTED AS *HARVESTED*.

AS WE WALKED DEEPER INTO THE WARREN OF PASSAGEWAYS AND LOW-CEILINGED ROOMS WE ENCOUNTERED LINES OF WOMEN AND CHILDREN WHOSE CLOTHES AND SHOES HAD BEEN TAKEN FROM THEM...

THAT'S WHEN I RECOGNIZED THE WOMAN I'D ENTRUSTED WITH ERNST. SHE TOLD ME THAT SHE'D BEEN SEPARATED FROM ERNST AND THAT THE GIRL WHOM I SOUGHT HAD TAKEN RESPONSIBILITY FOR THE MOTHERLESS BOY.

"LAST I SAW THEM, THEY WERE HAND-IN-HAND WALKING TOWARDS THE SHOWERS."

"SINCE THE REICH CANNOT SHOULDER ALL OF THE EXPENSE OF THE HOMES WE'VE BUILT FOR YOU, WE REQUIRE CONTRIBUTIONS."

"PUT YOUR WEDDING RING INTO THIS BASKET.. *NOW!*"

Panel 1: "JEWESS..."

I remember how the handsome one's wide-spaced teeth began to look to me...

Panel 2: "I DON'T KNOW WHAT BIG OFFICIAL IS CAUGHT IN YOUR *PUBIC HAIR*... ...LIKE TOMBSTONES."

Panel 3: "...BUT THIS PLACE IS A KIND OF *MACHINE* AND GOOD CONNECTIONS WON'T NECESSARILY KEEP YOU FROM BEING CAUGHT IN IT."

"THAT'S WHY WE MUST HELP HER."

Panel 4: We came to the end of a long passage where behind a door labeled "DISINFECTION," hundreds of naked women and children stood with panic written on their faces.

"NO ENTRANCE! THEY MUST STAY! THE LIST CANNOT BE AMENDED!"

But Pink Ears simply pushed past the guards and we were in the "shower" room that stank of excrement and *FEAR*.

THE GUARDS CALLED OUT THE NAME 'CLARA' BUT WHEN NO ANSWER CAME....

WELL, I THINK WE HAVE OUR ANSWER AND CAN LEAVE NOW.

CLARA!

THAT'S ENOUGH OF THAT.

PLEASE COME FORWARD. WE WANT TO REUNITE YOU WITH YOUR SISTER. NO ONE WILL...

...HARM YOU, I... SWEAR!

THIS IS A TERRIBLE ABUSE OF THE RULES!

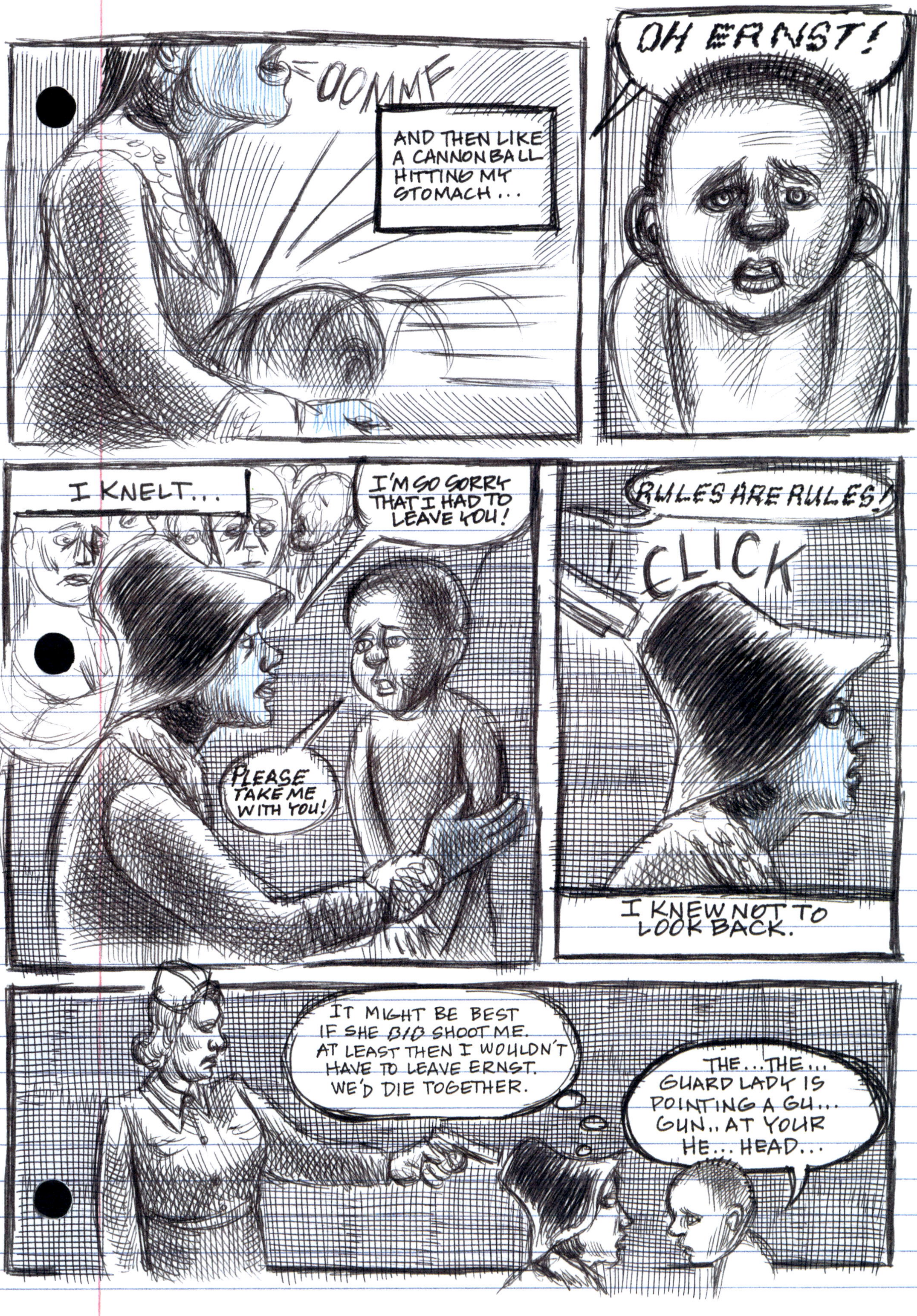
OOMMF
AND THEN LIKE A CANNON BALL HITTING MY STOMACH...
OH ERNST!
I KNELT...
I'M SO SORRY THAT I HAD TO LEAVE YOU!
PLEASE TAKE ME WITH YOU!
RULES ARE RULES!
CLICK
I KNEW NOT TO LOOK BACK.
IT MIGHT BE BEST IF SHE DID SHOOT ME. AT LEAST THEN I WOULDN'T HAVE TO LEAVE ERNST. WE'D DIE TOGETHER.
THE...THE... GUARD LADY IS POINTING A GU... GUN.. AT YOUR HE... HEAD...

Panel 1:
"THE MAN WHO WANTS *SIX* GIRLS WILL NOT CARE IF YOU KILL ME..."

IT WAS NEVER ENOUGH FOR THE NAZIS TO SIMPLY ROB AND KILL. THEY *NEEDED* TO INSPIRE *FEAR*.

Panel 2:
"...I'M ONLY HIS SERVANT, BUT HE *WILL* WANT TO KNOW WHY HE NEITHER HAS MY SERVICE NOR THE EXACT TYPE OF GIRLS FOR WHOM HE ASKED AND YOU SHOULD KNOW THAT THIS MAN TO WHOM I ANSWER IS POWERFUL, CRUEL AND VERY, VERY *UNFORGIVING*."

Panel 3:
"SHE IS TELLING THE TRUTH!"

Panel 4:
"MY GUN POINTING AT HER HEAD WILL GET HER JOB DONE QUICKER..."

Panel 5:
"ERNST, I'M SO SORRY I HAD TO LEAVE!"

"DID YOU FIND MY MOTHER?"

Panel 6:
I RECALLED A PREGNANT WOMAN BEING CARRIED FROM THE TRAIN. IT HADN'T BEEN CLEAR TO ME IF THE WOMAN HAD BEEN ALIVE. I SUSPECTED THAT THE WOMAN AND THE MAN WHO CARRIED HER HAD BEEN ERNST'S PARENTS.

AFTERWARDS WE HEARD TWO GUNSHOTS.

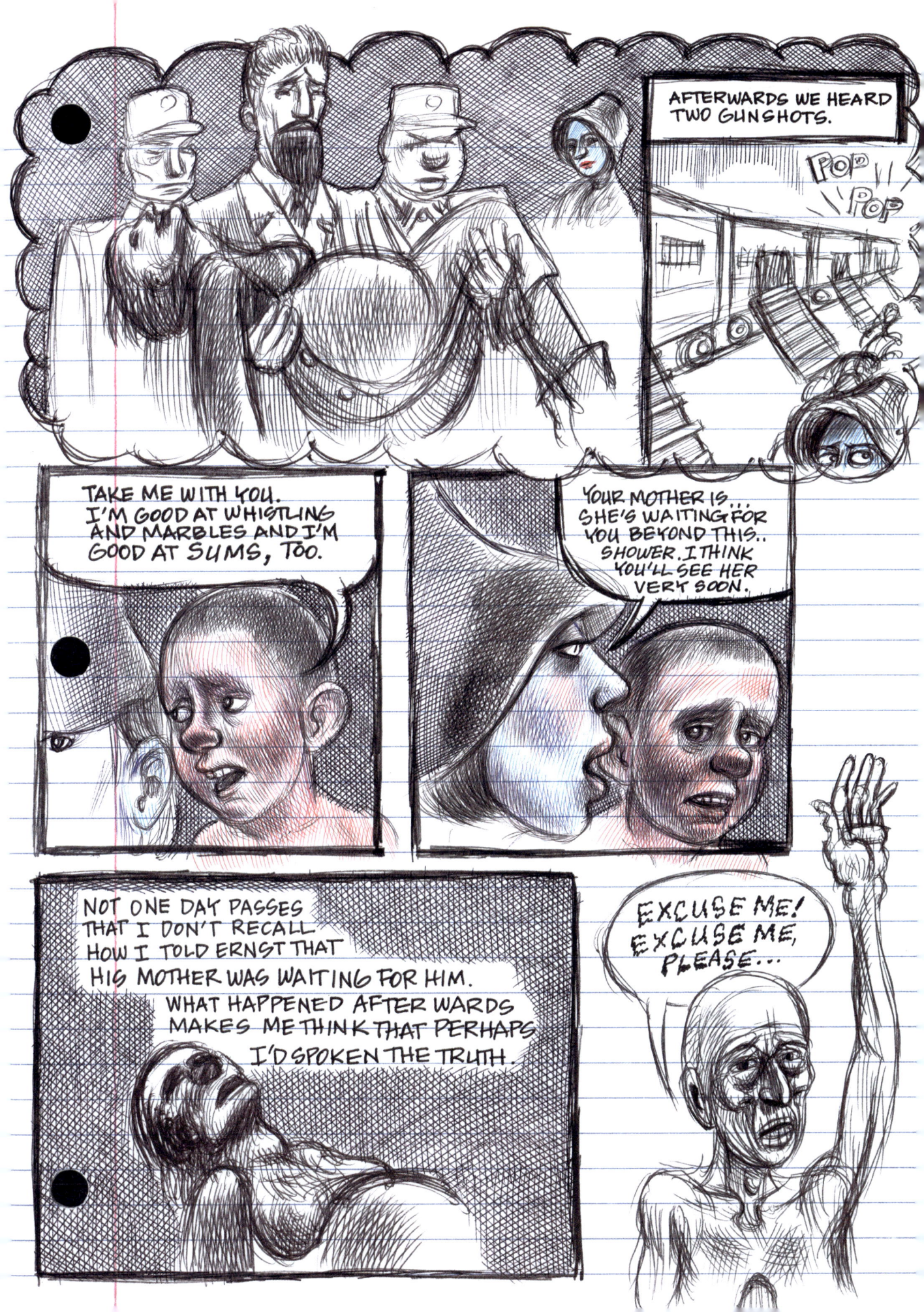

POP POP

"TAKE ME WITH YOU. I'M GOOD AT WHISTLING AND MARBLES AND I'M GOOD AT SUMS, TOO."

"YOUR MOTHER IS... SHE'S WAITING FOR YOU BEYOND THIS... SHOWER. I THINK YOU'LL SEE HER VERY SOON."

NOT ONE DAY PASSES THAT I DON'T RECALL HOW I TOLD ERNST THAT HIS MOTHER WAS WAITING FOR HIM. WHAT HAPPENED AFTERWARDS MAKES ME THINK THAT PERHAPS I'D SPOKEN THE TRUTH.

"EXCUSE ME! EXCUSE ME, PLEASE..."

> DURING CHICAGO SUMMERS THERE'S A SUFFOCATING CLOSENESS, LIKE A STRONG PERSON IS PRESSING A HEAVY PILLOW ACROSS YOUR FACE... TIMES LIKE THAT... REMIND ME... OF IT.

WHEN THE CROWD OF WOMEN REALIZED WE WERE CHOOSING YOUNG GIRLS TO BE TAKEN OUT OF THAT PLACE, THEY BEGAN CRYING OUT.
"MY GIRL IS FIFTEEN AND GOOD AT SEWING,"
"MINE IS THIRTEEN AND A GOOD DANCER,"
"MY NIECE IS ELEVEN AND HAS A GOOD VOICE,"...
"PLAYS THE PIANO,"..."WRITES POETRY,"...

I'LL NEVER STOP HEARING THEIR VOICES. LOUD, DESPERATE, STRAINED... AND I WANTED ALL THE GIRLS, EVERY CHILD, ALL THE MOTHERS, ALL THE GRANDMOTHERS. I WANTED EVERYONE. I STILL WANT THEM. I'M... I'M STILL *THERE*... BECAUSE THERE ARE PLACES THAT YOU ESCAPE, BUT THAT YOU NEVER *LEAVE*.

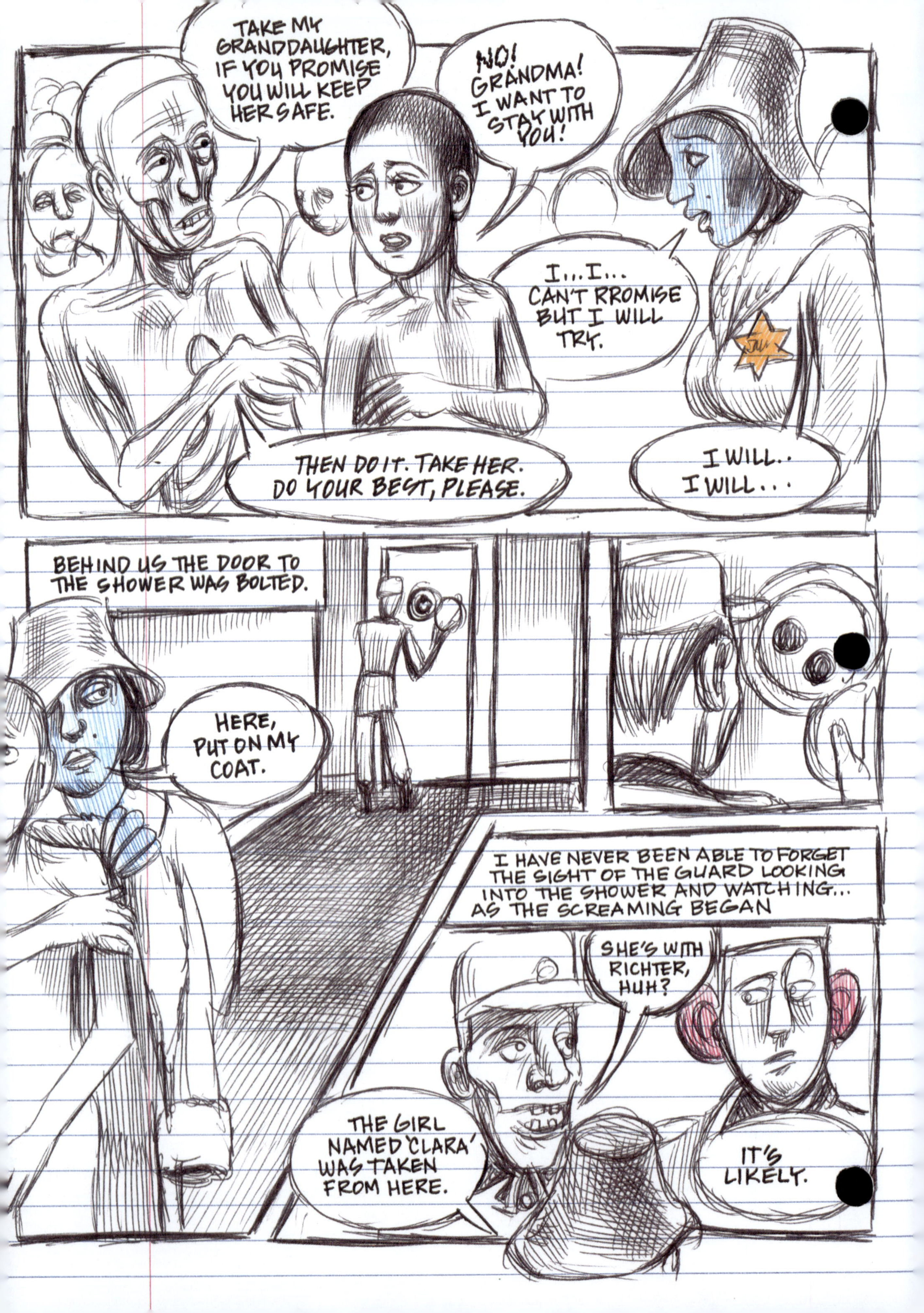
TAKE MY GRANDDAUGHTER, IF YOU PROMISE YOU WILL KEEP HER SAFE.
NO! GRANDMA! I WANT TO STAY WITH YOU!
I... I... CAN'T RROMISE BUT I WILL TRY.
THEN DO IT. TAKE HER. DO YOUR BEST, PLEASE.
I WILL.. I WILL...
BEHIND US THE DOOR TO THE SHOWER WAS BOLTED.
HERE, PUT ON MY COAT.
I HAVE NEVER BEEN ABLE TO FORGET THE SIGHT OF THE GUARD LOOKING INTO THE SHOWER AND WATCHING... AS THE SCREAMING BEGAN
SHE'S WITH RICHTER, HUH?
THE GIRL NAMED 'CLARA' WAS TAKEN FROM HERE.
IT'S LIKELY.

WE BROUGHT THE FOUR GIRLS THAT I'D ALREADY CHOSEN TO THE SHEARING ROOM. FOR THE PROMISE OF A REWARD, THE GUARDS OF THAT ROOM AGREED TO KEEP THEM UNTIL OUR RETURN...

"YOU MUST STAY HERE AND *NOT* FOLLOW!"

"PLEASE FIND HER."

MY HUSBAND HATES IT WHEN I TALK ABOUT WHAT I SAW THERE. I DON'T BLAME HIM...

WHILE THE PRISONERS SEARCHED THE DEAD FOR GOLD TEETH AND HIDDEN VALUABLES, FLECKS OF PALE ASH DRIFTED DOWN FROM ABOVE LIKE AIMLESS GREY BUTTERFLIES.

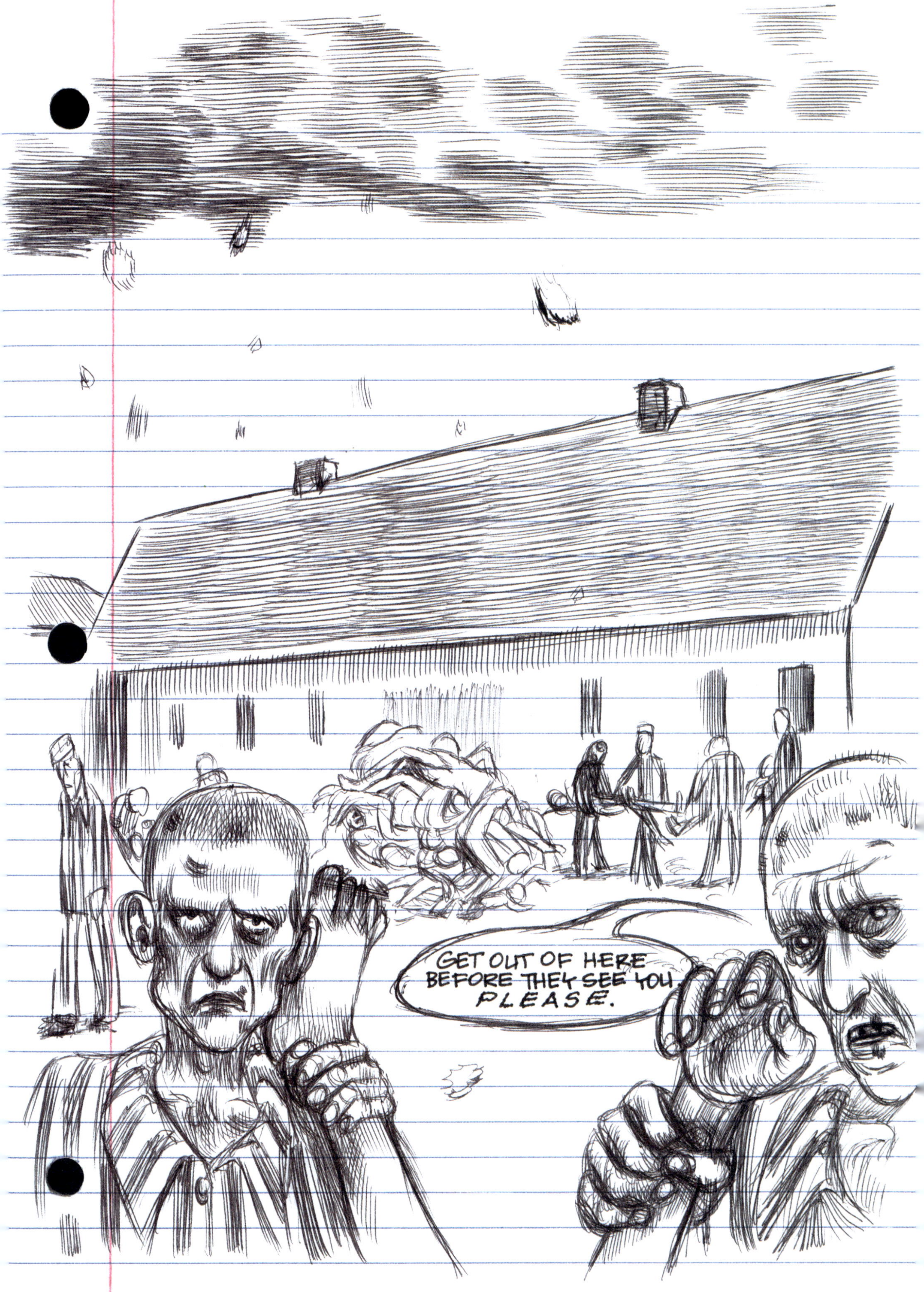
GET OUT OF HERE BEFORE THEY SEE YOU PLEASE.

"KAREN."

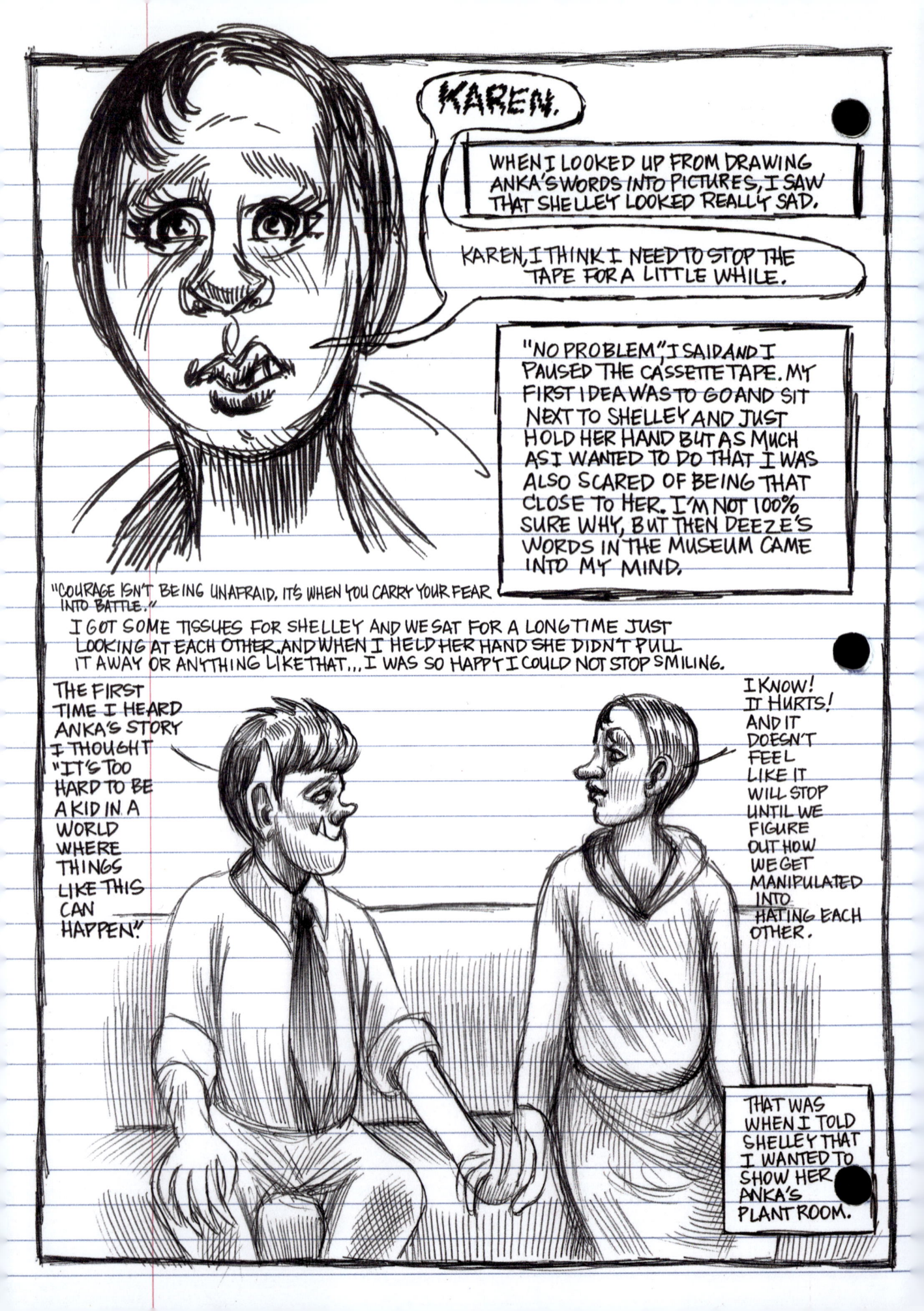

When I looked up from drawing Anka's words into pictures, I saw that Shelley looked really sad.

Karen, I think I need to stop the tape for a little while.

"No problem", I said and I paused the cassette tape. My first idea was to go and sit next to Shelley and just hold her hand but as much as I wanted to do that I was also scared of being that close to her. I'm not 100% sure why, but then Deeze's words in the museum came into my mind.

"Courage isn't being unafraid, it's when you carry your fear into battle.."

I got some tissues for Shelley and we sat for a long time just looking at each other. And when I held her hand she didn't pull it away or anything like that... I was so happy I could not stop smiling.

The first time I heard Anka's story I thought "It's too hard to be a kid in a world where things like this can happen."

I know! It hurts! And it doesn't feel like it will stop until we figure out how we get manipulated into hating each other.

That was when I told Shelley that I wanted to show her Anka's plant room.

EVEN THOUGH ANKA'S PLANT ROOM IS MOSTLY DEAD SHELLEY SAID SHE COULD SEE HOW LUSH IT ONCE WAS. I SHOWED SHELLEY ANKA'S RECORD COLLECTION AND ANKA'S RECORD PLAYER, THEN I TOLD HER THE STORY OF JUDITH AND HOLOFERNES...

> I THINK WOMEN JUST HAVE TO STEP UP AGAINST THE WAR IN VIETNAM. IF WE GAVE THE WAR-MONGERS WHAT JUDITH GAVE HOLOFERNES, IT WOULD BE A FAR BETTER WORLD... WELL MAYBE NOT *VIOLENCE*... BUT I DON'T KNOW.

...SHELLEY PLAYED A FEW OF HER FAVORITE SONGS FROM THE RECORDS SHE GAVE ME. ONE OF THE SONGS WAS CALLED 'LA COLUMBE'. IT WAS ABOUT PEOPLE BEING SENT TO WAR. I GUESS SHELLEY COULD TELL THAT SOMETHING WAS BOTHERING ME. I TOLD HER ABOUT HOW MY 'INVISIBLE MAN' OF A FATHER IS TRYING TO FORCE DEEZE INTO GOING TO VIETNAM. I TOLD HER HOW I'M TRYING TO MAKE A PLAN FOR SAVING DEEZE. THE QUESTION THAT HUNG IN THE ROOM UNANSWERED WAS IF I WOULD USE VIOLENCE TO PROTECT DEEZE. I WAS GLAD SHE DIDN'T ASK ME BECAUSE RIGHT NOW **I DON'T HAVE AN ANSWER.** (ALSO THIS HAPPENED)

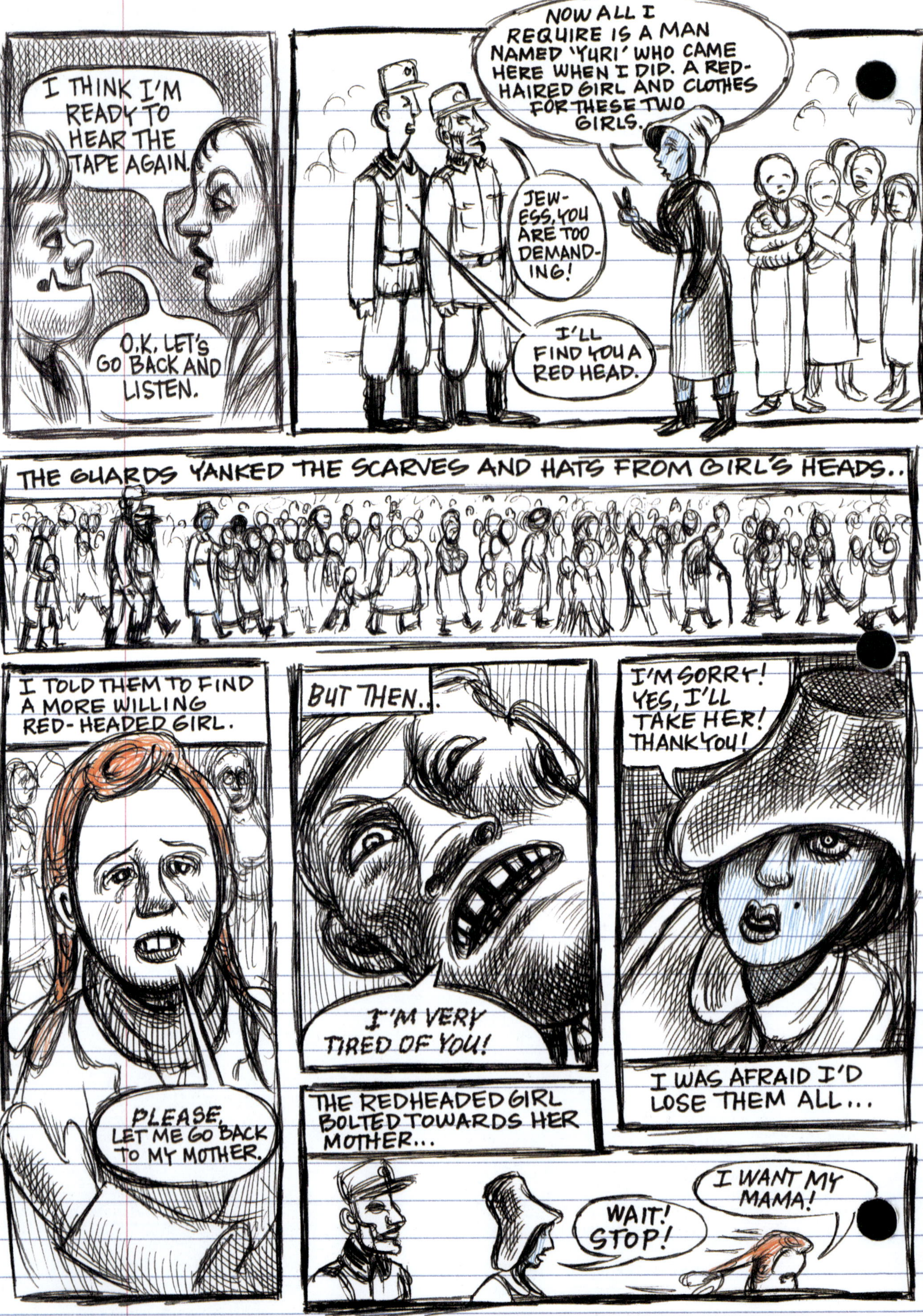
I THINK I'M READY TO HEAR THE TAPE AGAIN.
O.K, LET'S GO BACK AND LISTEN.
NOW ALL I REQUIRE IS A MAN NAMED 'YURI' WHO CAME HERE WHEN I DID. A RED-HAIRED GIRL AND CLOTHES FOR THESE TWO GIRLS.
JEW-ESS, YOU ARE TOO DEMAND-ING!
I'LL FIND YOU A RED HEAD.
THE GUARDS YANKED THE SCARVES AND HATS FROM GIRL'S HEADS..
I TOLD THEM TO FIND A MORE WILLING RED-HEADED GIRL.
PLEASE, LET ME GO BACK TO MY MOTHER.
BUT THEN..
I'M VERY TIRED OF YOU!
I'M SORRY! YES, I'LL TAKE HER! THANK YOU!
I WAS AFRAID I'D LOSE THEM ALL...
THE REDHEADED GIRL BOLTED TOWARDS HER MOTHER...
WAIT! STOP!
I WANT MY MAMA!

THE GUARD WITH THE GRAVESTONE TEETH POINTED HIS GUN AT THE GIRL. I KNOCKED HIS ARM WITH MY SHOULDER...

NO!

BANG!

FWMP!

...I HAVE NOT HEARD OUT OF MY RIGHT EAR SINCE THEN, BUT A FEW OTHER BYSTANDERS PAID A GREATER PRICE.

THE GIRLS IN MY CARE WERE CRYING AND TREMBLING.

SHE NEEDS A DOCTOR!

DO YOU WISH TO ACCOMPANY THE OLD WOMAN TO HER DESTINATION? I WILL ARRANGE IT FOR YOU.

YES, YES I'LL GO WITH HER...

VERY WELL, THEN..

...THIS GUN IS MY MEDICAL DEGREE.

THE GUN COUGHED TWICE AND THE WOMEN SUDDENLY LOOKED LIKE TWO PILES OF BLOODY LAUNDRY HEAPED ON THE GROUND.

PLEASE CONSIDER RELEASING YOUR DAUGHTER TO MY CARE. I CAN'T PROMISE MUCH BUT..I'LL TRY TO...

...KEEP HER SAFE.

YES, THIS PLACE IS NO LABOR CAMP. TAKE HER!

I..I.. HATE YOU SO VERY MUCH!

Tales of the Eldritch and the ARCANE

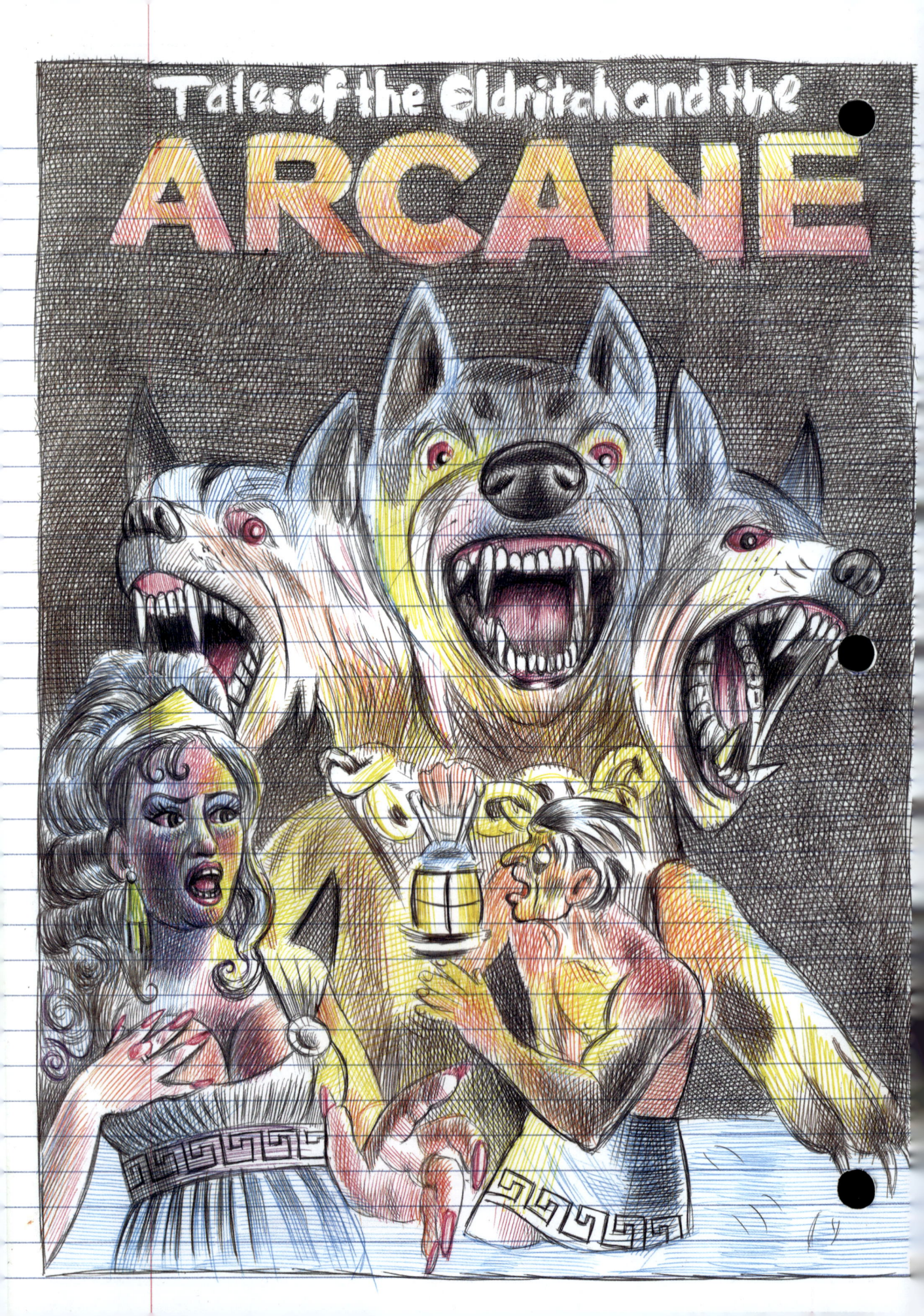

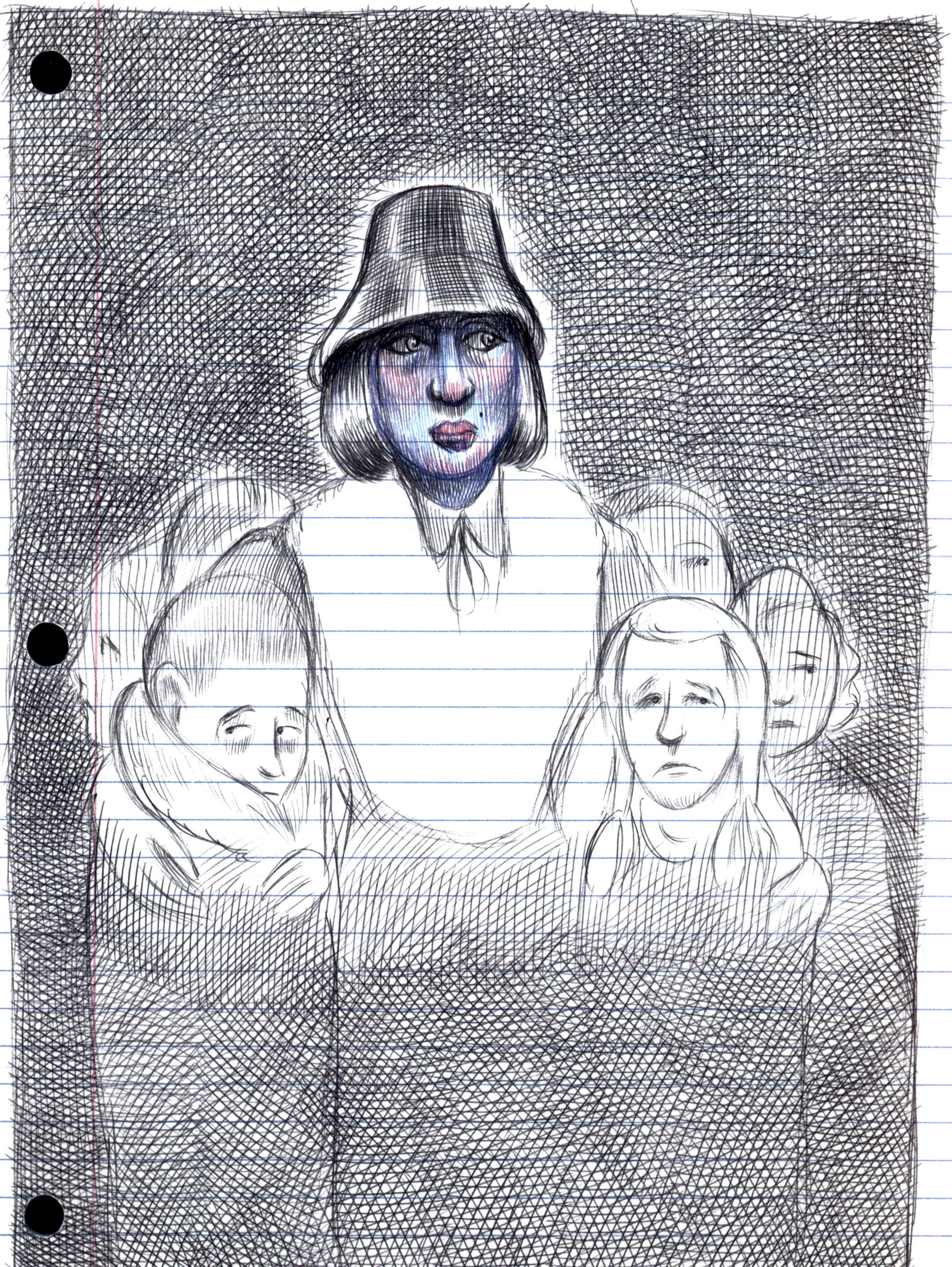

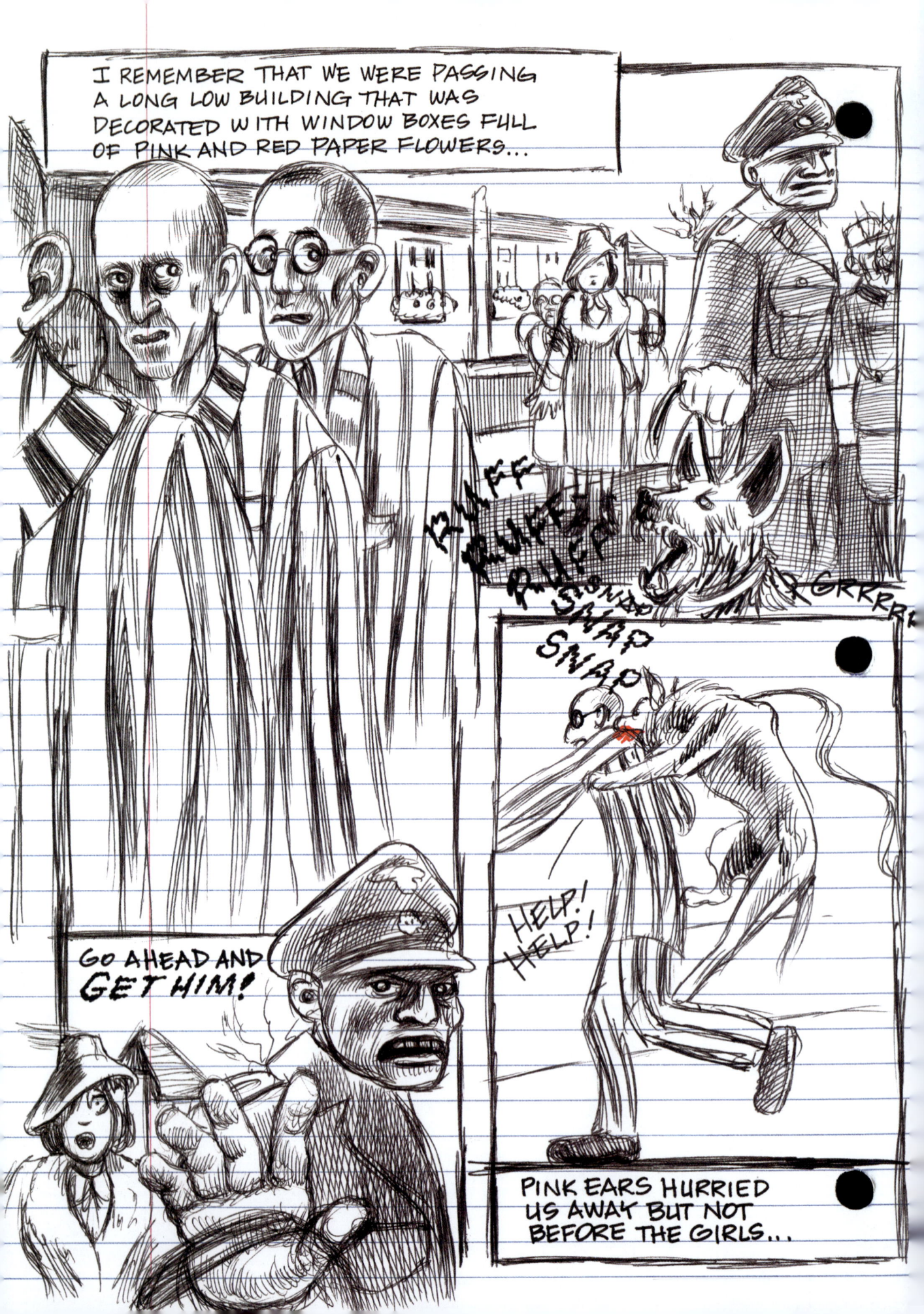

I REMEMBER THAT WE WERE PASSING A LONG LOW BUILDING THAT WAS DECORATED WITH WINDOW BOXES FULL OF PINK AND RED PAPER FLOWERS...

RUFF RUFF RUFF SNARL SNAP SNAP GRRRR

HELP! HELP!

GO AHEAD AND *GET HIM!*

PINK EARS HURRIED US AWAY BUT NOT BEFORE THE GIRLS...

...HAD HEARD THE TANGLE OF SCREAMS AND GROWLS AND RIPPING CLOTH AND SNAPPING BONES AND THE CRUEL LAUGHTER OF THE GUARDS...

WHEN WE GOT TO THE TRAIN PLATFORM...

HUH?

TO THIS DAY THE SIGHT OF PAPER FLOWERS MAKES ME NAUSEOUS.

YURI STOOD BEHIND ME. IN MY HEART I CALLED HIM THE SNOW MAN!

LOOK IT'S HERR LAUREL HARDY!

CLOWNY BASTARD!

I INTRODUCED YURI AND GABBY.

HOW DID YOU END UP WITH *THOSE* CLOTHES?

THEY TOOK OUR CLOTHES AND GAVE US PRISON UNIFORMS. WHEN THEY LEARNED THAT I WAS BEING RELEASED THE GUARDS ALLOWED ME TO CHOOSE A SUIT FROM THE PILE.

...AND YOU *CHOSE THAT?*

SURE! IT'S MUCH HARDER TO TAKE GOOD AIM WHEN YOU'RE *LAUGHING.*

AFTER WE WERE LOADED ONTO THE TRAIN, ONE OF THE GUARDS TOSSED YURI A LOAF OF BREAD AND A BOTTLE OF SCHNAPPS. THEN 'PINK EARS' APPEARED...

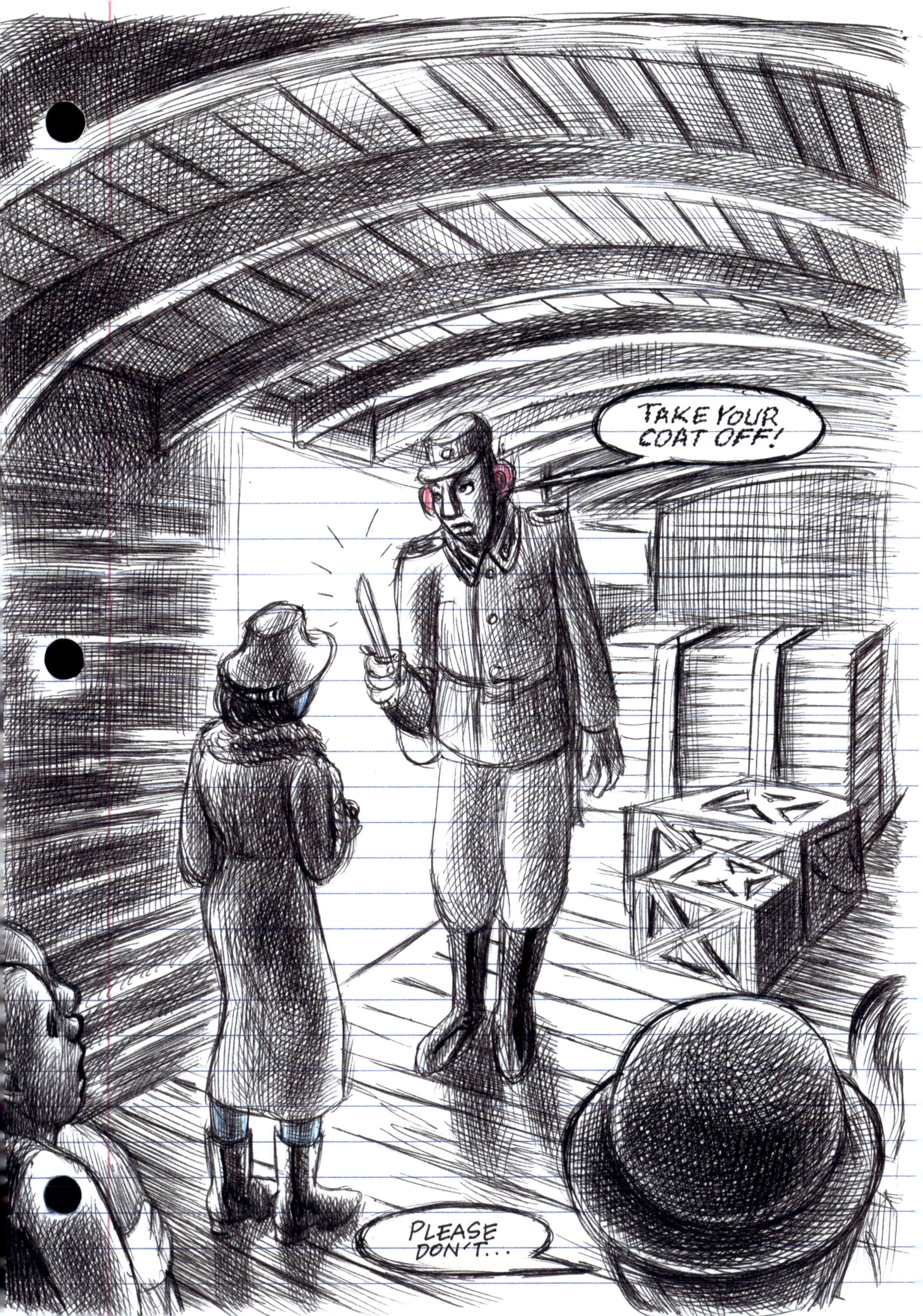
TAKE YOUR COAT OFF!
PLEASE DON'T...

..OFFICER, PLEASE LET HER ALONE.

SHUT UP! TAKE OFF THE COAT!

PLEASE ALLOW THE GIRLS TO TURN AWAY...

GIVE IT TO ME.

'PINK EARS' TOSSED ME THE STAR, BUT HE HELD ONTO MY COAT.

MAKE SURE YOU PIN IT TO YOUR BLOUSE..

BEFORE THE TRAIN ARRIVES IN BERLIN.

'PINK EARS' HELD MY COAT TO HIS NOSE.

FLOWERS

SSSNIIIFF

AFTER 'PINK EARS' LEFT THE TRAIN - WITH MY COAT - I TOOK ACCOUNT OF THE SIX GIRLS I'D CHOSEN TO BRING WITH ME OUT OF THE CAMP. I REALIZED THAT I DIDN'T EVEN KNOW ALL OF THEIR NAMES.

JUST MOMENTS EARLIER THE GIRLS HAD WITNESSED AN INNOCENT MAN SET UPON BY ATTACK DOGS. THEY ALL SEEMED SHAKEN BY THE HORRORS THEY'D SEEN IN THE CAMP. I LOOKED DOWN AT THE STAR IN MY HAND. IT REMINDED ME OF...

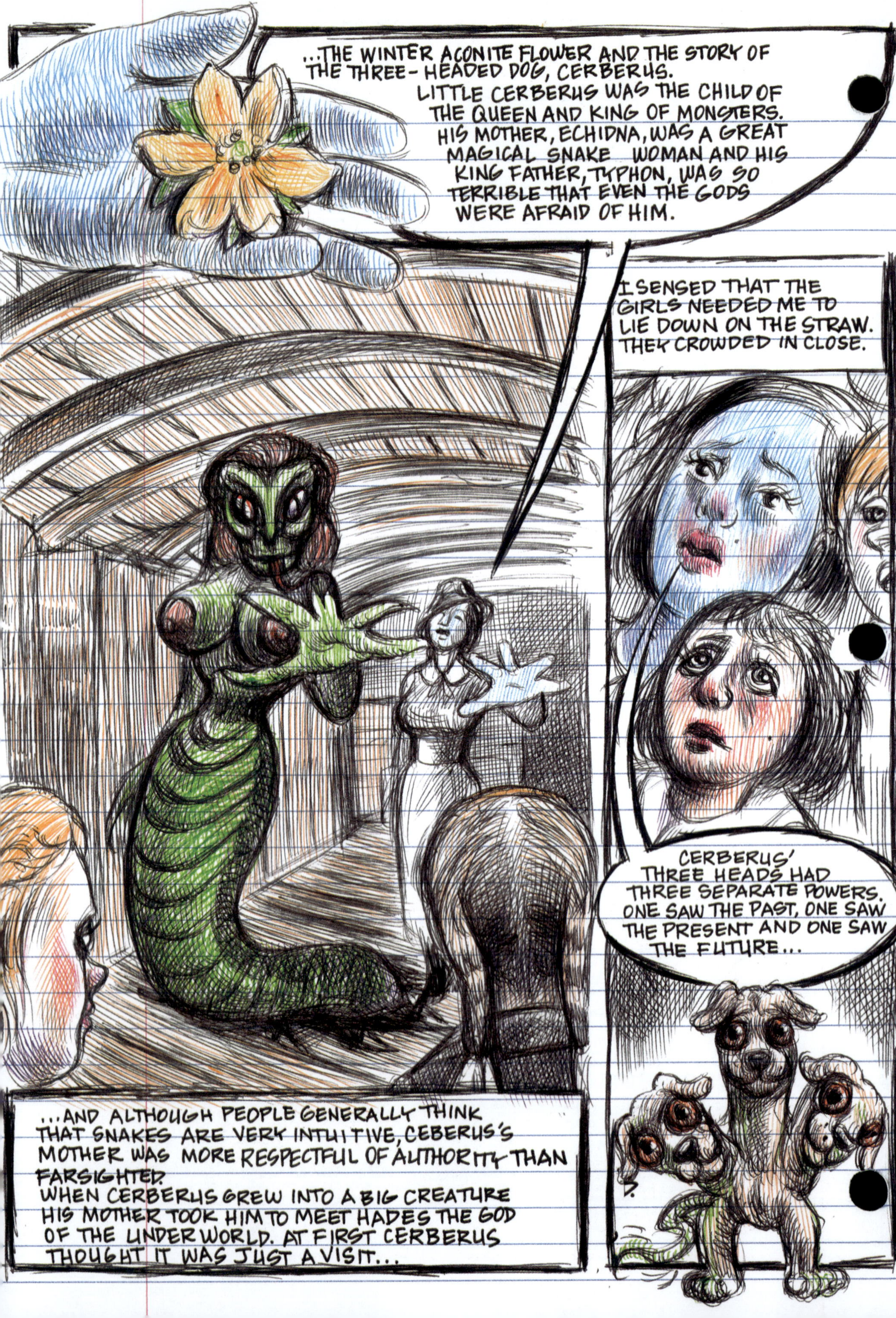
...THE WINTER ACONITE FLOWER AND THE STORY OF THE THREE-HEADED DOG, CERBERUS.
LITTLE CERBERUS WAS THE CHILD OF THE QUEEN AND KING OF MONSTERS. HIS MOTHER, ECHIDNA, WAS A GREAT MAGICAL SNAKE WOMAN AND HIS KING FATHER, TYPHON, WAS SO TERRIBLE THAT EVEN THE GODS WERE AFRAID OF HIM.
I SENSED THAT THE GIRLS NEEDED ME TO LIE DOWN ON THE STRAW. THEY CROWDED IN CLOSE.
CERBERUS' THREE HEADS HAD THREE SEPARATE POWERS. ONE SAW THE PAST, ONE SAW THE PRESENT AND ONE SAW THE FUTURE...
...AND ALTHOUGH PEOPLE GENERALLY THINK THAT SNAKES ARE VERY INTUITIVE, CEBERUS'S MOTHER WAS MORE RESPECTFUL OF AUTHORITY THAN FARSIGHTED.
WHEN CERBERUS GREW INTO A BIG CREATURE HIS MOTHER TOOK HIM TO MEET HADES THE GOD OF THE UNDERWORLD. AT FIRST CERBERUS THOUGHT IT WAS JUST A VISIT...

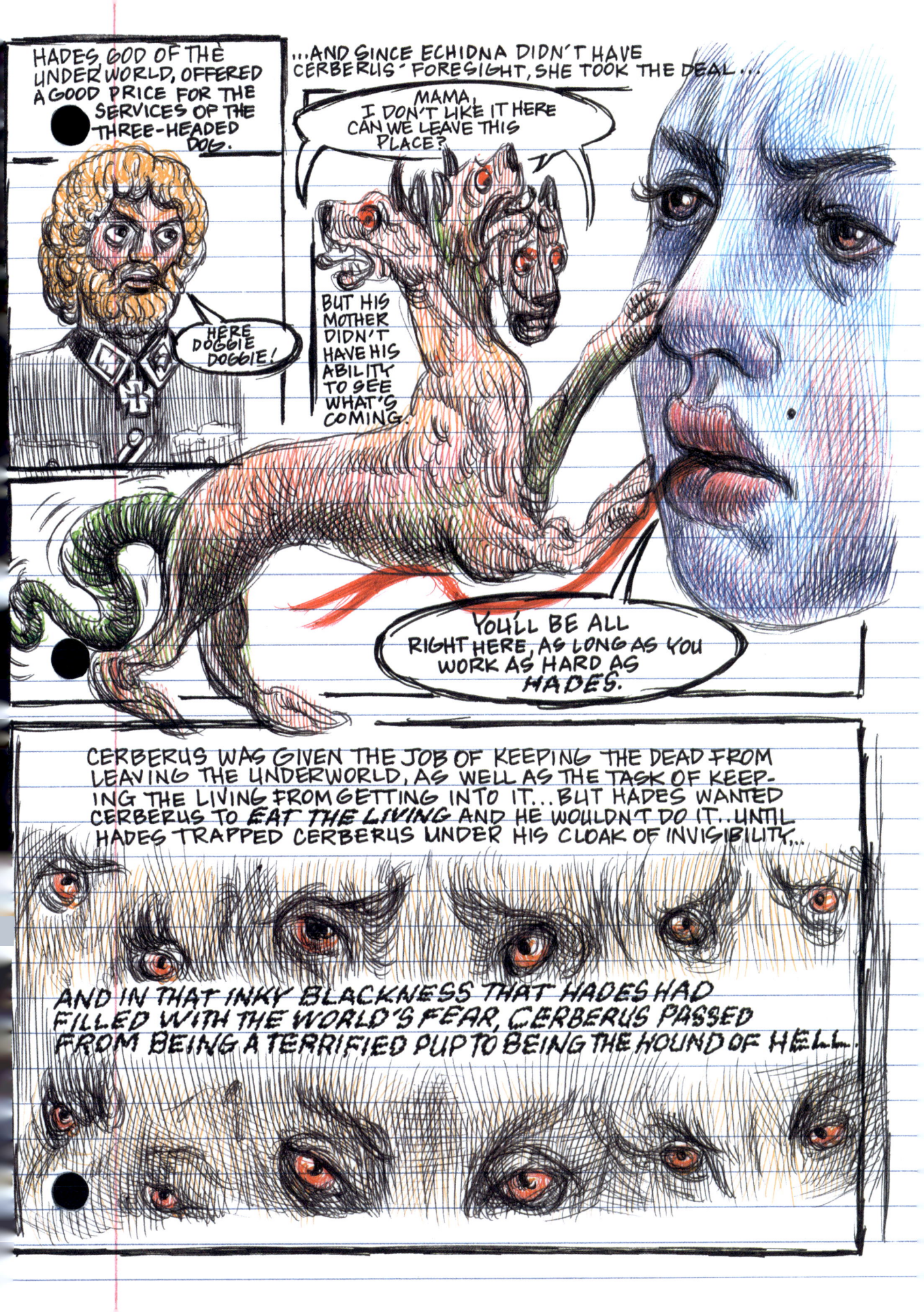

HADES, GOD OF THE UNDERWORLD, OFFERED A GOOD PRICE FOR THE SERVICES OF THE THREE-HEADED DOG.

"HERE DOGGIE DOGGIE!"

...AND SINCE ECHIDNA DIDN'T HAVE CERBERUS' FORESIGHT, SHE TOOK THE DEAL...

"MAMA, I DON'T LIKE IT HERE, CAN WE LEAVE THIS PLACE?"

BUT HIS MOTHER DIDN'T HAVE HIS ABILITY TO SEE WHAT'S COMING.

"YOU'LL BE ALL RIGHT HERE, AS LONG AS YOU WORK AS HARD AS *HADES.*"

CERBERUS WAS GIVEN THE JOB OF KEEPING THE DEAD FROM LEAVING THE UNDERWORLD, AS WELL AS THE TASK OF KEEPING THE LIVING FROM GETTING INTO IT... BUT HADES WANTED CERBERUS TO *EAT THE LIVING* AND HE WOULDN'T DO IT... UNTIL HADES TRAPPED CERBERUS UNDER HIS CLOAK OF INVISIBILITY...

AND IN THAT INKY BLACKNESS THAT HADES HAD FILLED WITH THE WORLD'S FEAR, CERBERUS PASSED FROM BEING A TERRIFIED PUP TO BEING THE HOUND OF HELL.

But Cerberus did not like being the...

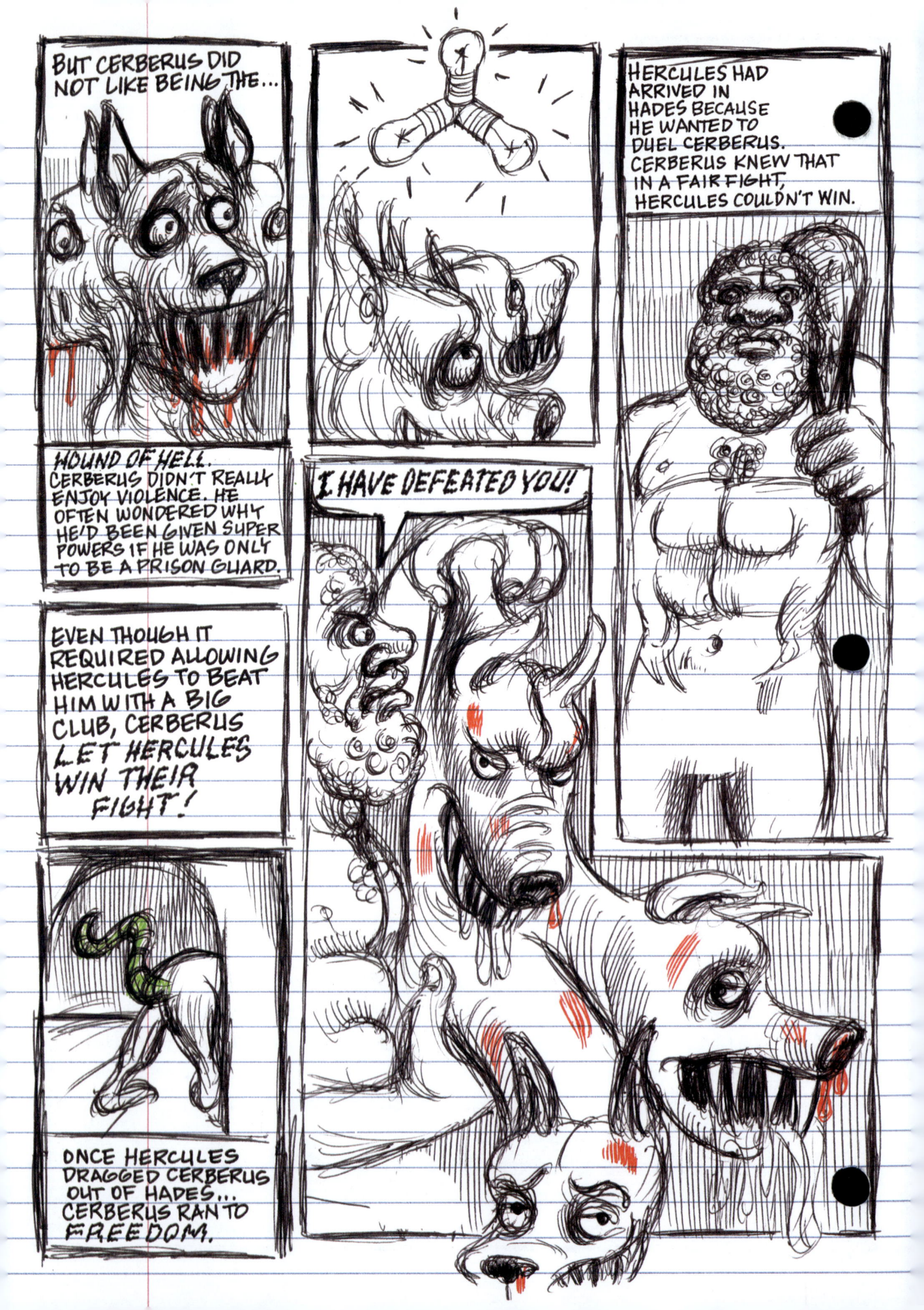

Hound of Hell. Cerberus didn't really enjoy violence. He often wondered why he'd been given super powers if he was only to be a prison guard.

Even though it required allowing Hercules to beat him with a big club, Cerberus *let Hercules win their fight!*

Once Hercules dragged Cerberus out of Hades... Cerberus ran to FREEDOM.

I HAVE DEFEATED YOU!

Hercules had arrived in Hades because he wanted to duel Cerberus. Cerberus knew that in a fair fight, Hercules couldn't win.

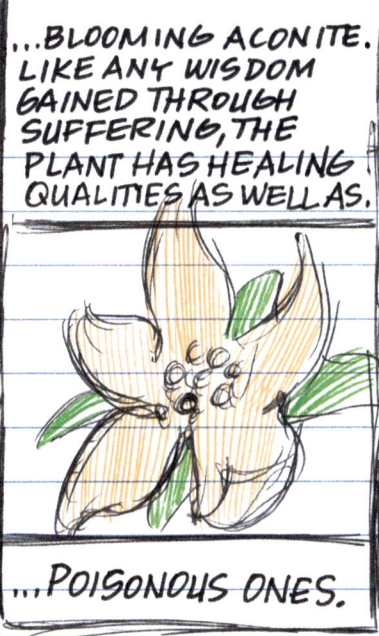

WELL, IN TRUTH, HE LIMPED TO FREEDOM. BECAUSE	CERBERUS WAS INJURED. ...AND WHEN HIS BLOOD HIT THE GROUND, IT BECAME THE...	...BLOOMING ACONITE. LIKE ANY WISDOM GAINED THROUGH SUFFERING, THE PLANT HAS HEALING QUALITIES AS WELL AS... ...POISONOUS ONES.
FROM LOOKING INTO THE PAST, CERBERUS GAINED COMPASSION. FROM LOOKING INTO THE PRESENT HE GOT JOY AND FROM LOOKING INTO THE FUTURE HE ACQUIRED IMAGINATION...	...ALL OF THESE GAVE CERBERUS WISDOM.	DID IT TAKE LONG FOR HIM TO GET WELL? I DON'T KNOW...

...BUT THE REASON I TOLD YOU THIS STORY IS TWOFOLD. FOR ONE THING I DON'T WANT YOU TO BE FRIGHTENED OF DOGS, BUT THE BIGGEST REASON IS THAT I WANT YOU TO THINK ABOUT HOW IT'D FEEL TO PRETEND TO BE DEFEATED...

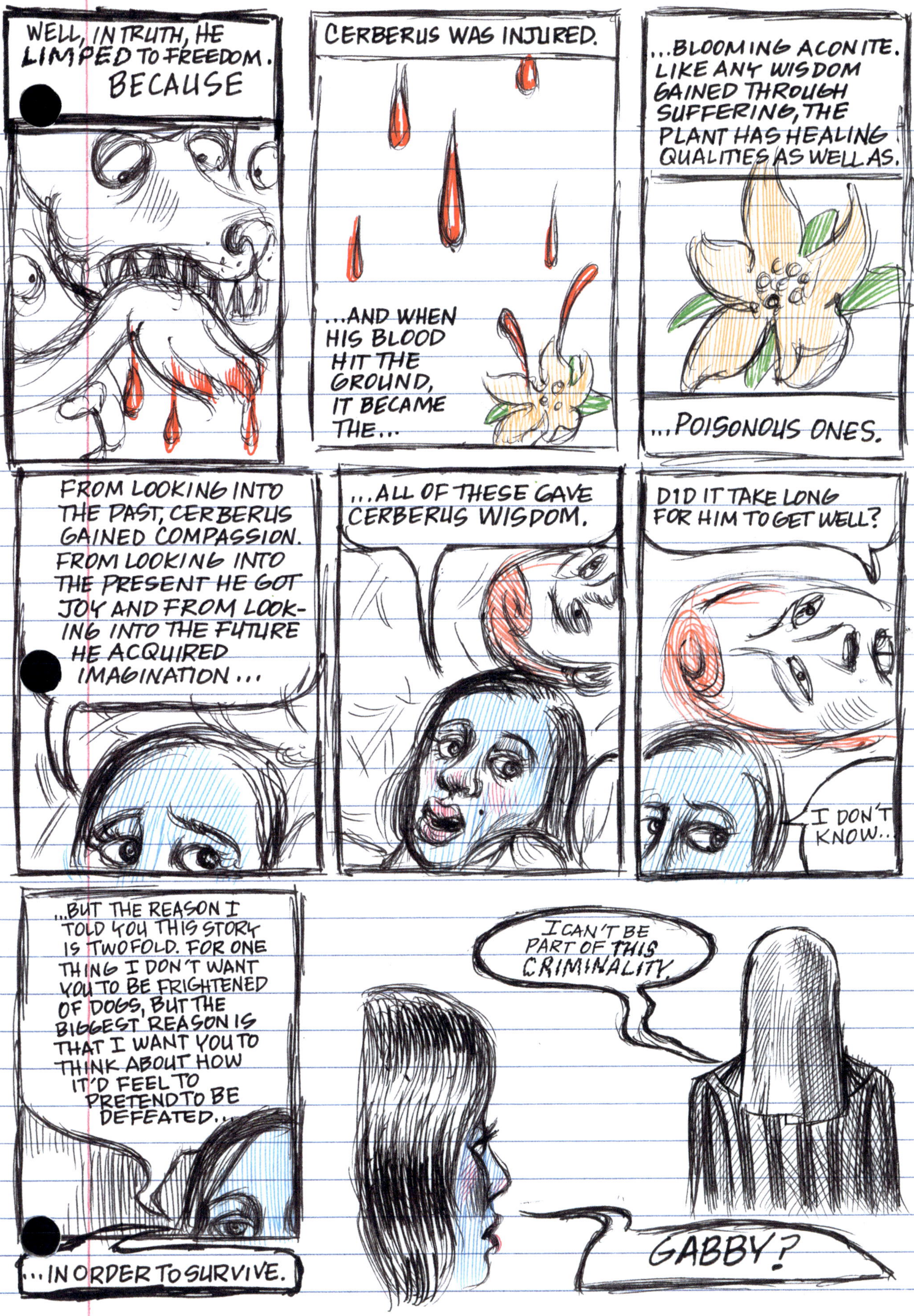

...IN ORDER TO SURVIVE.

"I CAN'T BE PART OF THIS CRIMINALITY."

GABBY?

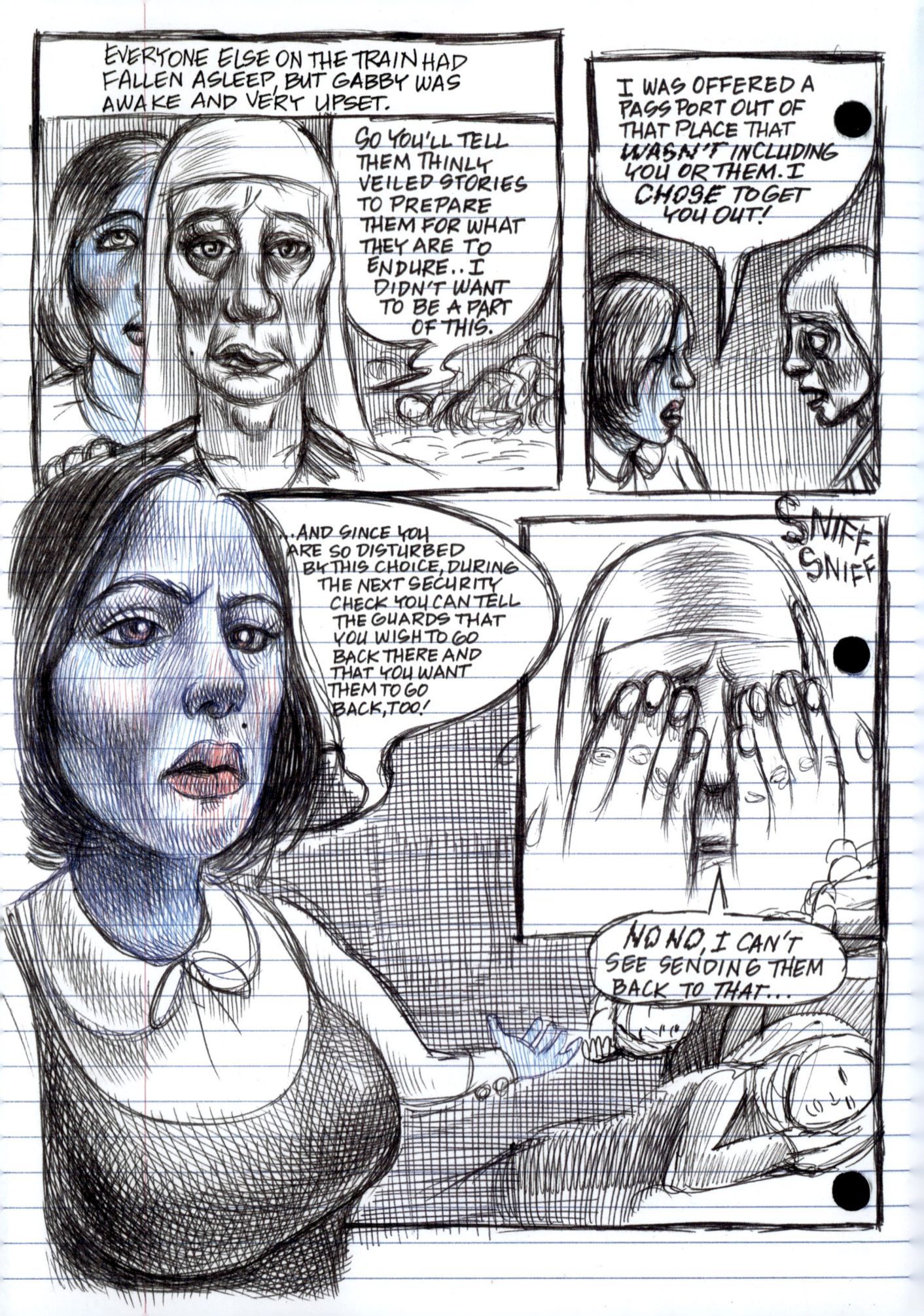

EVERYONE ELSE ON THE TRAIN HAD FALLEN ASLEEP, BUT GABBY WAS AWAKE AND VERY UPSET.

"SO YOU'LL TELL THEM THINLY VEILED STORIES TO PREPARE THEM FOR WHAT THEY ARE TO ENDURE.. I DIDN'T WANT TO BE A PART OF THIS."

"I WAS OFFERED A PASSPORT OUT OF THAT PLACE THAT WASN'T INCLUDING YOU OR THEM. I CHOSE TO GET YOU OUT!"

"..AND SINCE YOU ARE SO DISTURBED BY THIS CHOICE, DURING THE NEXT SECURITY CHECK YOU CAN TELL THE GUARDS THAT YOU WISH TO GO BACK THERE AND THAT YOU WANT THEM TO GO BACK, TOO!"

SNIFF SNIFF

"NO NO, I CAN'T SEE SENDING THEM BACK TO THAT..."

WE STOOD AND WATCHED THE GIRLS SLEEP. I REMEMBER EXPLAINING MY PLAN TO RAISE MONEY AND BUY EACH OF THEM A NEW IDENTITY.

I TOLD HIM WE'D GET THEM ALL SAFELY INTO THE HANDS OF THE UNDERGROUND RESISTANCE AND THAT THEY'D BE TAKEN IN BY FAMILIES WHO WERE BEYOND THE REACH OF THE NAZIS. I WAS ONLY A FEW YEARS OLDER THAN THE GIRLS I THOUGHT I COULD SAVE.

EVERYONE SLEPT. I WAS DROWSING OR PERHAPS I WAS DREAMING... I DON'T KNOW...

ERNST?

I WATCHED AS HIS SMALL HAND SLID SOMETHING INTO A GAP IN THE FLOORBOARDS...

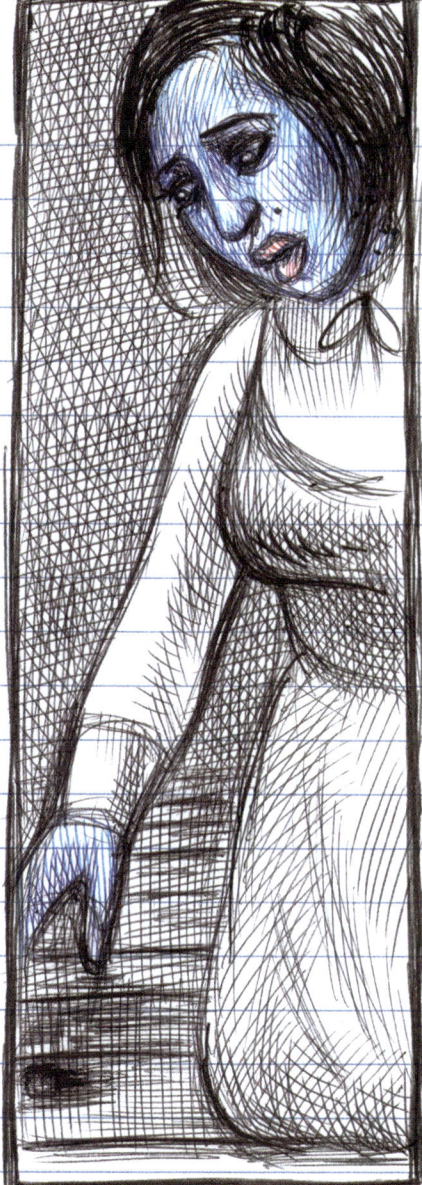

"WHEN THE WASPS SWARM CLOSE, HIDE IN THE SUNFLOWERS."

AFTER ERNST WHISPERED THIS TO ME HE TURNED TOWARDS THE CORNER OF THE CATTLE CAR AND HE SMILED AT A BRIGHT WOMAN-SHAPED LIGHT. I THINK IT MIGHT HAVE BEEN HIS MOTHER... BECAUSE HE WALKED INTO THAT LIGHT AND WAS GONE. I FOUND MYSELF KNEELING WHERE ERNST....

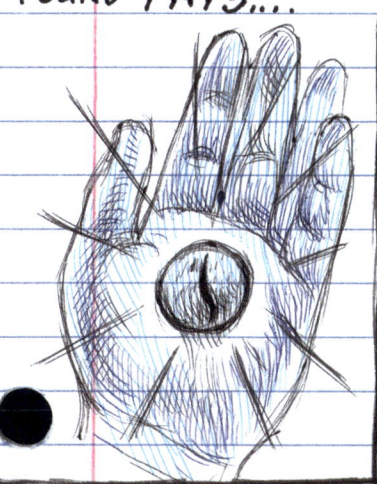

...HAD STOOD AND I FOUND THIS....

WHEN WE ARRIVED IN BERLIN A NAZI OFFICIAL APPEARED IN OUR PATH AND SAID THERE'D BEEN A REPORT THAT A JEW WAS WEARING FUR. IT WAS PROBABLY A PLOY TO ARREST US AND THEN WRING MORE MONEY FROM SCHUTZ BUT PINKEARS MUST'VE KNOWN AND HE'D SAVED US FROM DETENTION.

"THERE'S NO FUR HERE? THERE MUST BE FUR... CHECK AGAIN..."

I LOVED THE HEAVY HITLER LOOK-ALIKE'S DEEP DISAPPOINTMENT...

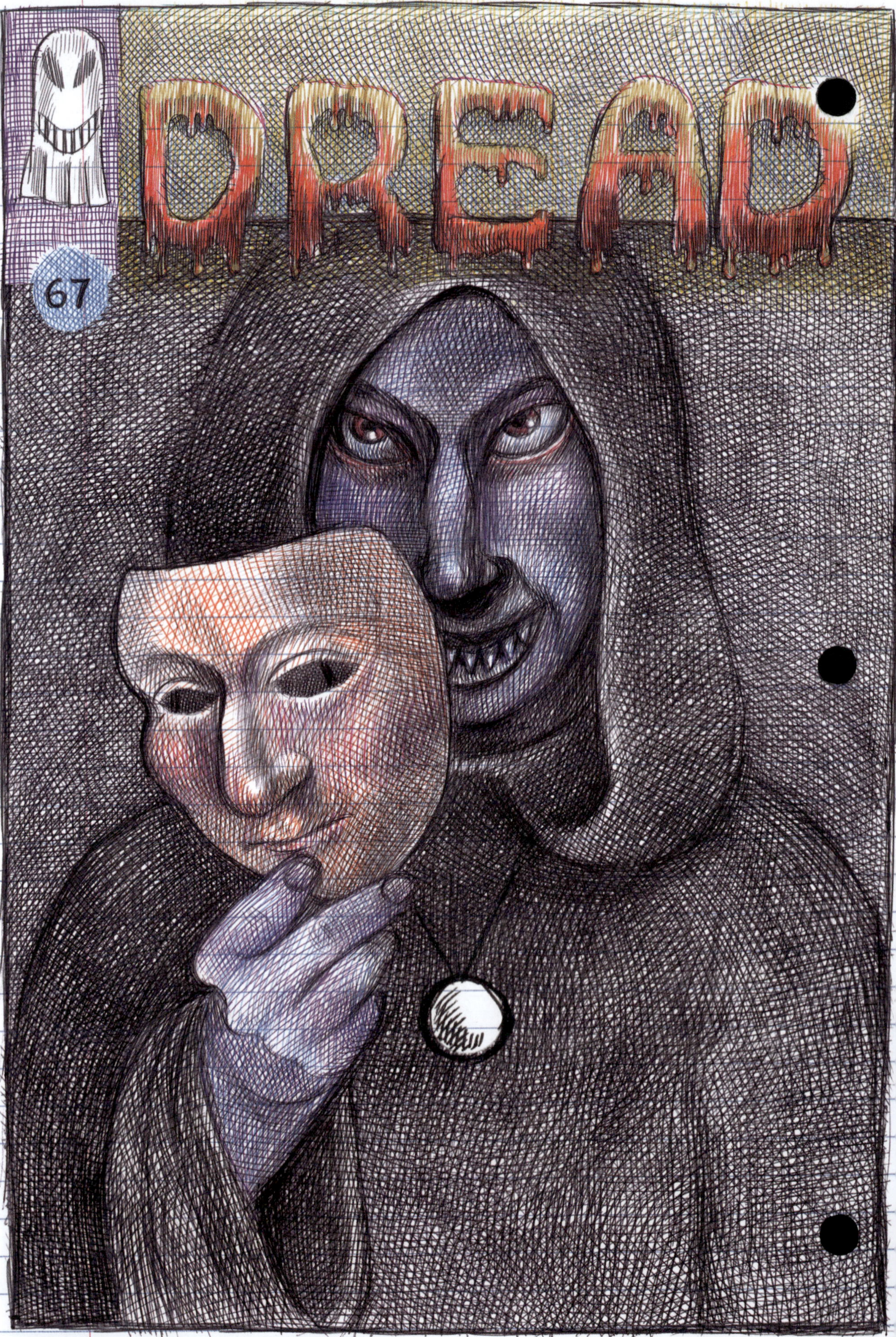
DREAD
67

THE PERSON WHO WAS INTERVIEWING ANKA ASKED HER A QUESTION...

DO YOU THINK THAT THE MAN YOU DESCRIBED AS 'PINK EARS' TOOK THE FUR-COLLARED COAT BECAUSE HE WAS TRYING TO SAVE YOU?

IT'S BEEN MY EXPERIENCE THAT PEOPLE WILL SURPRISE YOU. AS OFTEN AS PEOPLE DO TERRIBLE THINGS, THEY ALSO DO SMALL ACTS OF KINDNESS. I BELIEVE THAT SPIRITS OF EVIL AND GOOD WHISPER TO US ALL THE TIME.

SO YOU THINK HE LISTENED TO AN ANGEL?

PERHAPS. IT'S THE ONLY WAY I CAN EXPLAIN IT.

KNOCK KNOCK KNOCK

BAANNNG! BANG! BANG!

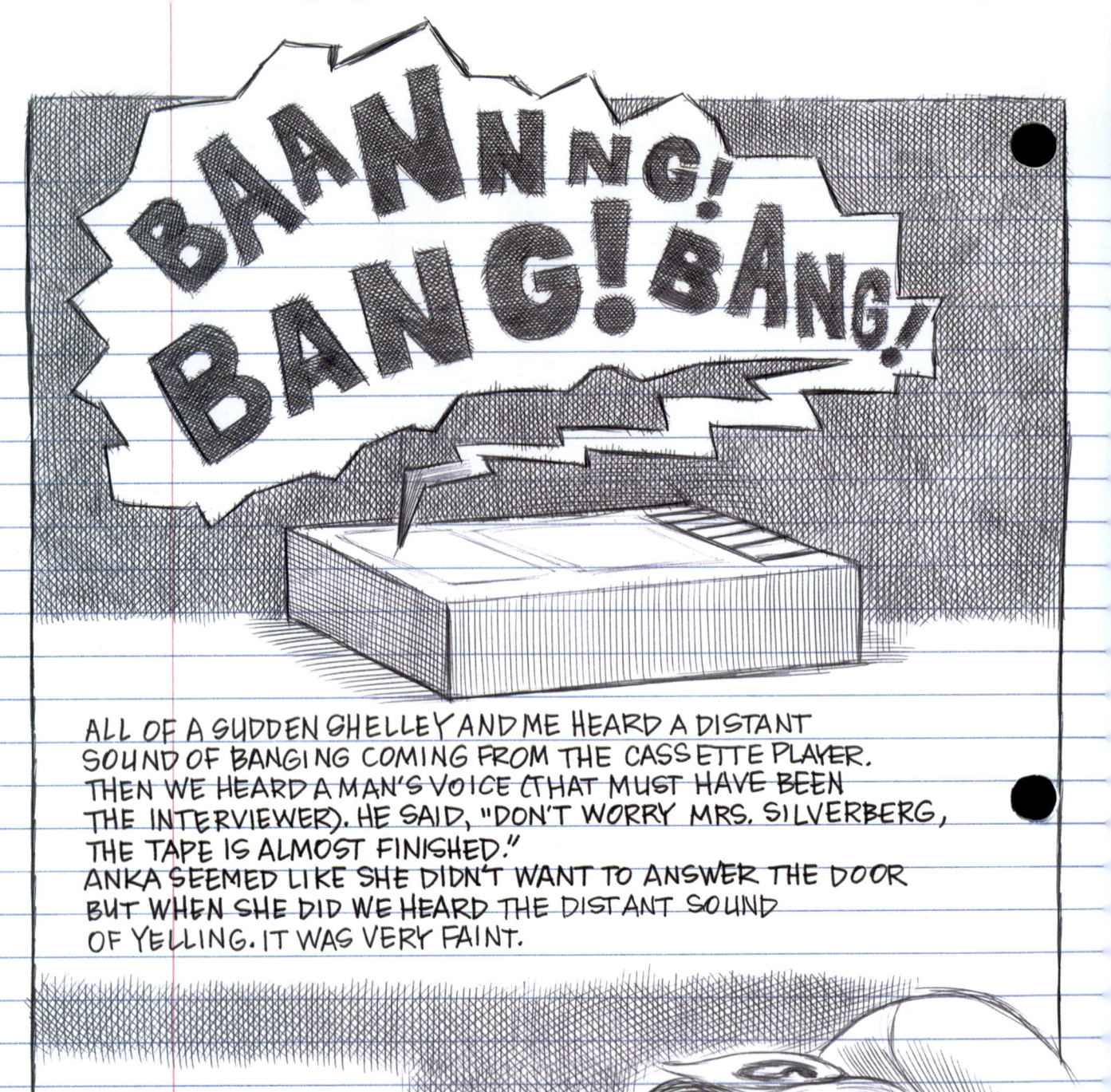

All of a sudden Shelley and me heard a distant sound of banging coming from the cassette player. Then we heard a man's voice (that must have been the interviewer). He said, "Don't worry Mrs. Silverberg, the tape is almost finished."
Anka seemed like she didn't want to answer the door but when she did we heard the distant sound of yelling. It was very faint.

When I turned the sound up I heard Anka and a person whose voice I recognized. The person on the tape was **THREATENING** Anka!!!

WHO WAS ON THE TAPE?

UM. IT WAS A NEIGHBOR WHO WAS UPSET BECAUSE ANKA'S CAT WAS KILLING THE BIRDS IN HIS YARD.

I HATED TO LIE TO SHELLEY, BUT I REALLY HAD TO DO IT. SHELLEY *CLEARLY DIDN'T BUY IT!* IT WORRIED ME THAT SHE HAD FIGURED OUT WHOSE VOICE SHE HEARD BEFORE I TURNED IT DOWN.

NO! YOU CAN'T DO THIS NOW... I'M DOING AN INTERVIEW AND THAT'S ALL!

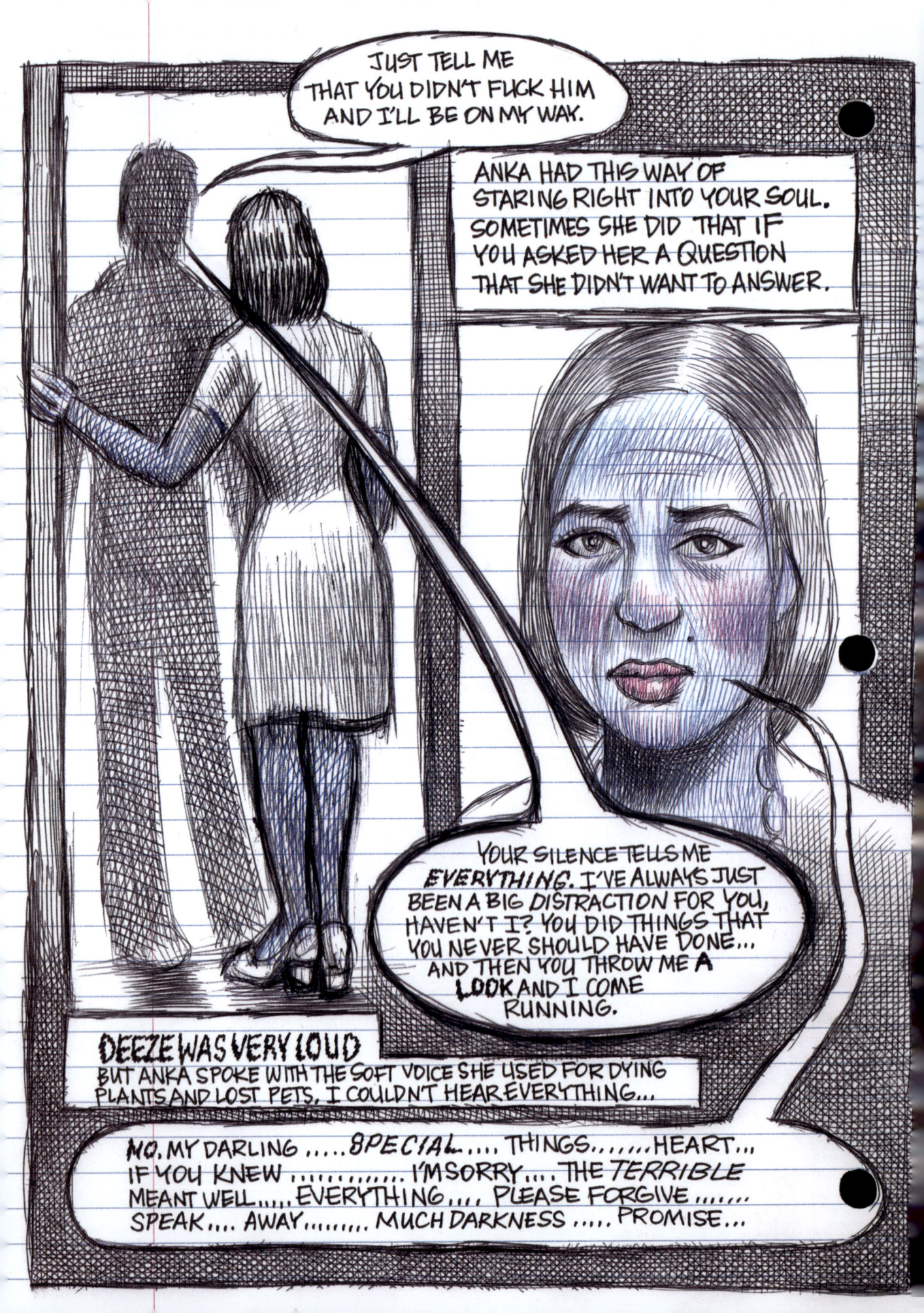

"JUST TELL ME THAT YOU DIDN'T FUCK HIM AND I'LL BE ON MY WAY."

ANKA HAD THIS WAY OF STARING RIGHT INTO YOUR SOUL. SOMETIMES SHE DID THAT IF YOU ASKED HER A QUESTION THAT SHE DIDN'T WANT TO ANSWER.

"YOUR SILENCE TELLS ME *EVERYTHING*. I'VE ALWAYS JUST BEEN A BIG *DISTRACTION* FOR YOU, HAVEN'T I? YOU DID THINGS THAT YOU NEVER SHOULD HAVE DONE... AND THEN YOU THROW ME A *LOOK* AND I COME RUNNING."

DEEZE WAS VERY LOUD
BUT ANKA SPOKE WITH THE SOFT VOICE SHE USED FOR DYING PLANTS AND LOST PETS, I COULDN'T HEAR EVERYTHING...

*NO, MY DARLING ..... SPECIAL..... THINGS......... HEART...
IF YOU KNEW .... I'M SORRY.... THE TERRIBLE
MEANT WELL..... EVERYTHING.... PLEASE FORGIVE.......
SPEAK.... AWAY......... MUCH DARKNESS..... PROMISE...*

BUT NOT MUCH WORKS TO CALM HIM DOWN ONCE DEEZE IS IN A RAGE. IT WASN'T ONLY FURY. WHEN DEEZE YELLED BACK AT ANKA HE SOUNDED LIKE HE WAS TRYING NOT TO CRY. HIS VOICE CRACKED LIKE A WOUNDED TEENAGER'S.

I SHOULD PUT A GODDAM BULLET IN YOUR...IN YOUR HEART!

AFTER I HEARD THE DOOR SHUT I ALSO HEARD ANKA SAYING THAT SHE NEEDED A BREAK. IT SEEMED LIKE A GOOD TIME FOR US TO TAKE A BREAK, TOO.

"IT'S COOL ABOUT TAKING A BREAK FROM THE TAPE. INSTEAD WE COULD WATCH CREATURE FEATURES. THEY'RE PLAYING, 'THE PICTURE OF DORIAN GRAY.'"

"OK. I'VE READ THE BOOK BUT I'VE NEVER SEEN THE MOVIE. THE AUTHOR—OSCAR WILDE—WENT TO JAIL..."

"...JUST FOR BEING HOMOSEXUAL. 'SODOMY' IS STILL A CRIME IN MOST OF THE U.S.A."

"IT REALLY FREAKS ME OUT THAT PEOPLE LIKE YOU AND ME CAN GO TO JAIL JUST FOR BEING WHO WE ARE. THAT'S THE FAULT OF RELIGION."

"NOT EVERY RELIGIOUS PERSON THINKS THAT WAY. MAMA WASN'T COOL ABOUT ME BEING DIFFERENT BUT SHE WOULDN'T HAVE LET THEM TAKE ME TO JAIL..."

...AT LEAST I HOPE THAT MAMA WOULDN'T HAVE LET ANYONE TAKE ME TO JAIL. THE THING THAT I COULDN'T STOP THINKING ABOUT WAS WHAT SHELLEY HAD SAID...

The PICTURE of DORIAN GRAY

"SHE USED THE WORDS, 'PEOPLE LIKE YOU AND ME!' I ALMOST CAN'T KEEP MYSELF FROM SMILING LIKE AN IDIOT. ALSO IT'S HANDY TO KNOW THAT ME LOVING SHELLEY IS CALLED 'SODOMY.'"

"THAT'S A RUBAI OF OMAR KHAYYAM.

I sent my soul through the invisible,
Some letter of that after-life to spell.
And by and by my soul returned to me
And answered "I myself am Heaven and Hell."

"WHAT IS A RUBAI AND WHO IS OMAR KHAYYAM?"

IN PERSIAN POETRY A RUBAI IS A QUATRAIN. A QUATRAIN IS A POEM OF FOUR LINES. OMAR KHAYYAM WAS AN ASTRONOMER AND A POET.

THE MOVIE WAS ABOUT THIS RICH AND HANDSOME GUY WHO KEPT DOING ROTTEN THINGS. ALL THE TOTALLY TERRIBLE THINGS HE DID NEVER CHANGED HIS FACE *BUT DID* CHANGE THIS PORTRAIT OF HIM. HIS BAD ACTIONS TURNED THE PICTURE SUPER HORRID. SHELLEY NOTICED HOW THE MOVIE WAS LIKE A MUSEUM FULL OF MASTERPIECES. EACH OF THE SCENES WAS FRAMED AND LAID OUT LIKE THE COMPOSITION OF A FAMOUS PAINTING.
WHEN IT WAS OVER I WANTED TO BE SMART ABOUT SOMETHING, LIKE SHELLEY IS SMART, SO I TOLD HER...

"YOU PROBABLY KNOW THIS BUT THE PAINTING FROM THE FILM IS RIGHT OVER AT THE ART MUSEUM. WE COULD GO THERE AND LOOK AT IT ANYTIME YOU WANT TO."

"ARE YOU KIDDING? *I DID NOT KNOW THAT!* SURE. I'D LOVE TO SEE IT WITH YOU!"

AFTER THE MOVIE SHELLEY SUDDENLY BROUGHT UP THE SUBJECT OF ANKA'S STORY...

I'M OF TWO MINDS. ON ONE HAND I WANT TO KNOW WHAT HAPPENED AND ON THE OTHER, I'M JUST NOT SURE I WANT TO KNOW ABOUT IT IF SHE DID NOT SAVE THOSE KIDS.

SHE SAID, "THE GIRLS *I THOUGHT I COULD SAVE.*"

YOU CAN COME BACK AND LISTEN WHENEVER YOU WANT TO. I WON'T LISTEN TO ANY MORE OF IT UNTIL YOU DECIDE.

OKAY, THANKS KAREN.

I SHOULD PROBABLY GO. MY DAD WORKS NIGHTS AND IF I CALL HIM BEFORE HIS SHIFT ENDS HE'LL PICK ME UP ON HIS WAY BACK FROM HIS JOB.

I MEAN YOU CAN ALSO COME BACK TO LISTEN TO THE JUDY COLLINS RECORDS... OR FOR ANY REASON.

OKAY.

I'M *SO SOPHISTICATED* THAT 'OKAY' WOULD HAVE BEEN THE LAST WORDS I SAID TO HER YESTERDAY, BUT LUCKILY AFTER SHE CALLED HER DAD AND AFTER HIS CAR PULLED UP IN FRONT AND RIGHT AS SHE WAS LEAVING, I REMEMBERED TO SAY...

"EGOTBU!"

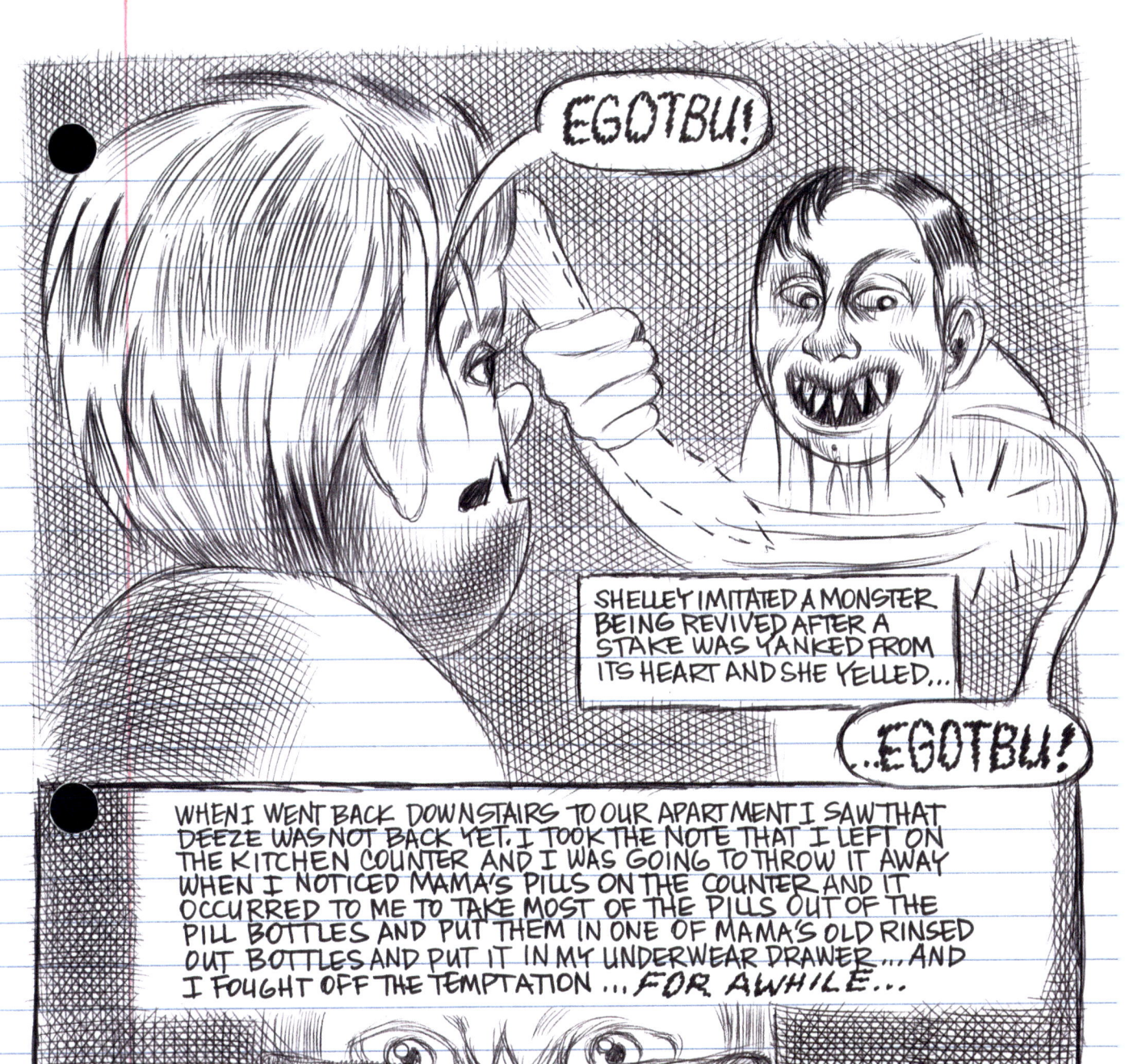

SHELLEY IMITATED A MONSTER BEING REVIVED AFTER A STAKE WAS YANKED FROM ITS HEART AND SHE YELLED...

"..EGOTBU!"

WHEN I WENT BACK DOWNSTAIRS TO OUR APARTMENT I SAW THAT DEEZE WAS NOT BACK YET. I TOOK THE NOTE THAT I LEFT ON THE KITCHEN COUNTER AND I WAS GOING TO THROW IT AWAY WHEN I NOTICED MAMA'S PILLS ON THE COUNTER AND IT OCCURRED TO ME TO TAKE MOST OF THE PILLS OUT OF THE PILL BOTTLES AND PUT THEM IN ONE OF MAMA'S OLD RINSED OUT BOTTLES AND PUT IT IN MY UNDERWEAR DRAWER... AND I FOUGHT OFF THE TEMPTATION ...*FOR AWHILE*...

...BECAUSE I STARTED WONDERING WHAT MAMA WOULD SAY ABOUT HOW DEEZE (AND ME) ARE LIVING OUR LIVES AND IT WAS ALMOST MORNING AND DEEZE WAS STILL NOT BACK AND I GOT UP AND DID WHAT I DESCRIBED ABOVE WITH THE PILLS. I ALSO TOOK ONLY A HALF OF ONE...
BUT THAT WAS ENOUGH TO GIVE ME CRAZY DREAMS...

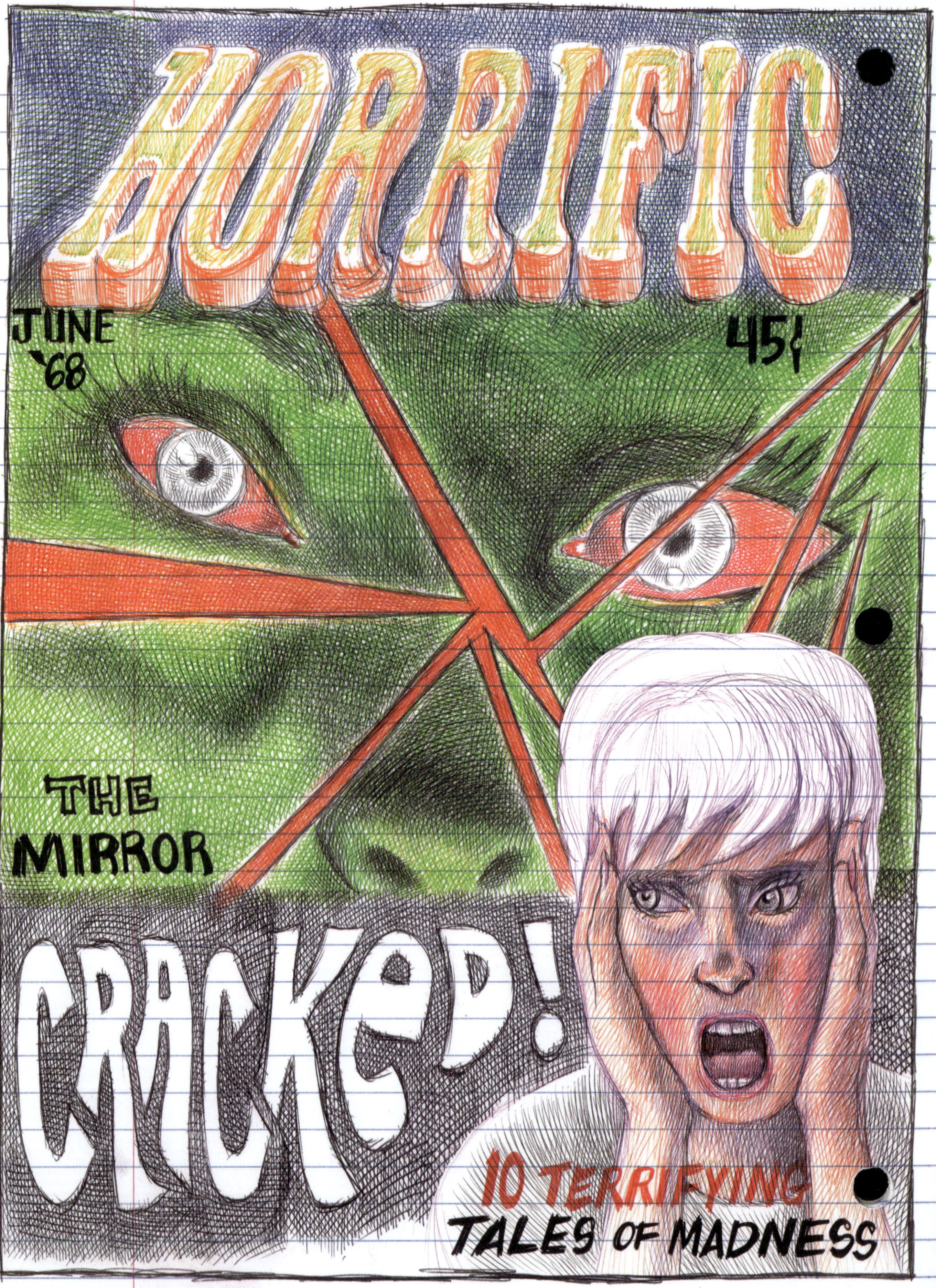
HORRIFIC
JUNE '68
45¢
THE MIRROR
CRACKED!
10 TERRIFYING
TALES OF MADNESS

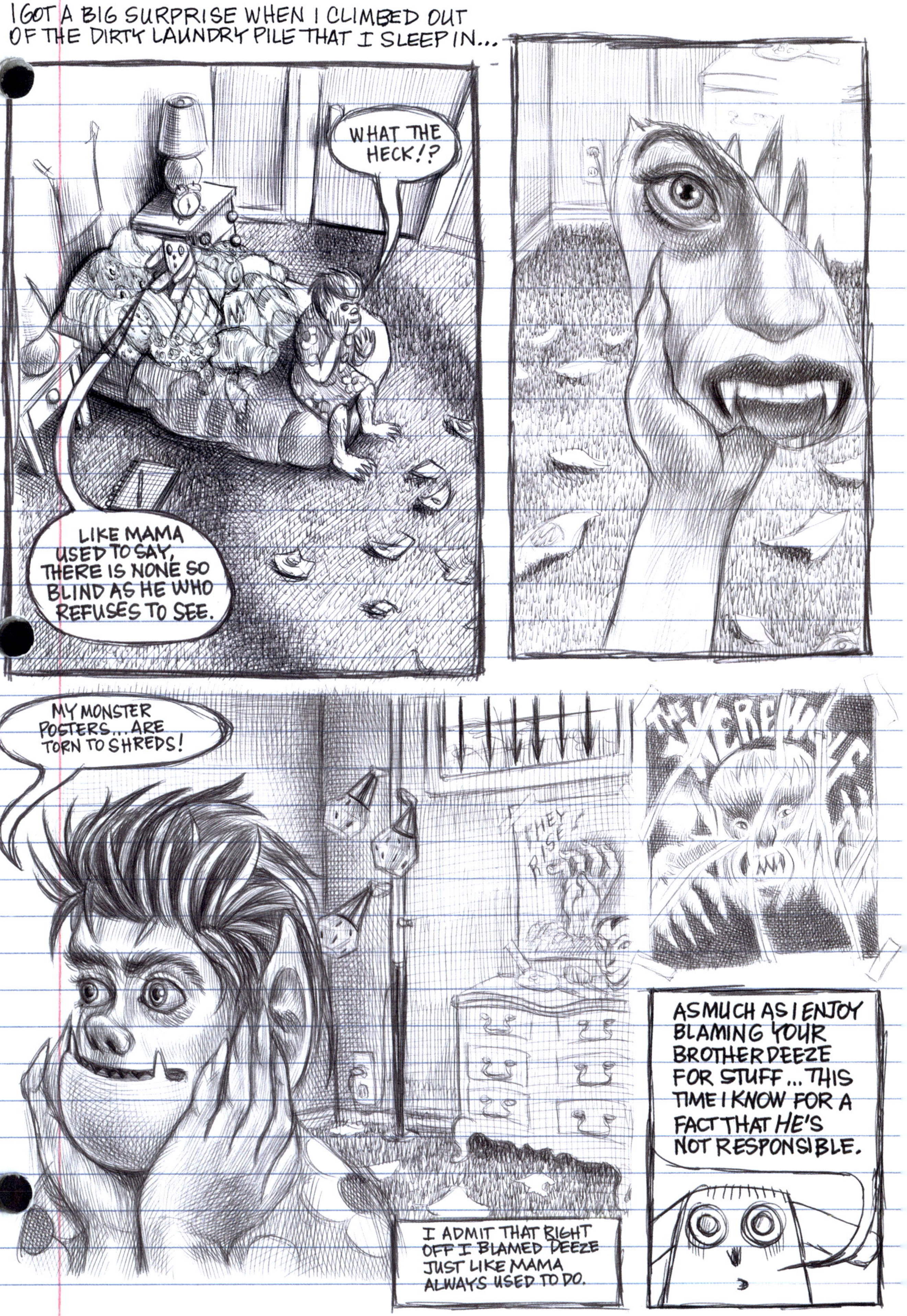
I GOT A BIG SURPRISE WHEN I CLIMBED OUT OF THE DIRTY LAUNDRY PILE THAT I SLEEP IN...
WHAT THE HECK!?
LIKE MAMA USED TO SAY, THERE IS NONE SO BLIND AS HE WHO REFUSES TO SEE.
MY MONSTER POSTERS... ARE TORN TO SHREDS!
I ADMIT THAT RIGHT OFF I BLAMED DEEZE JUST LIKE MAMA ALWAYS USED TO DO.
AS MUCH AS I ENJOY BLAMING YOUR BROTHER DEEZE FOR STUFF... THIS TIME I KNOW FOR A FACT THAT HE'S NOT RESPONSIBLE.

AND THEN I REMEMBERED. IT WAS THE SECOND TIME I HAD THE DREAM WHERE I WAS **SO ANGRY** AT MONSTERS FOR *NOT* BITING MAMA SO SHE COULD BE **UNDEAD** AND *NOT DIE*...

THE WHOLE TIME I WAS DOING THE HORRIBLE MURDERS I HEARD JUDITH'S VOICE WHISPERING TO ME THAT TO KILL THESE MONSTERS WOULDN'T SAVE DEEZE...

"YOU NEED TO BE MORE THAN INVISIBLE...

...YOU NEED TO ACTUALLY DISAPPEAR FROM THE PLANET OF EARTH!

O STOP!

BLAM!

...IT WAS THE ONLY WAY TO SAVE YOUR BROTHER FROM THE WAR...

BUT WHEN I KILLED THE INVISIBLE MAN I GOT REALLY REALLY **SAD** AND JUDITH'S WORDS DIDN'T STOP MY TEARS.

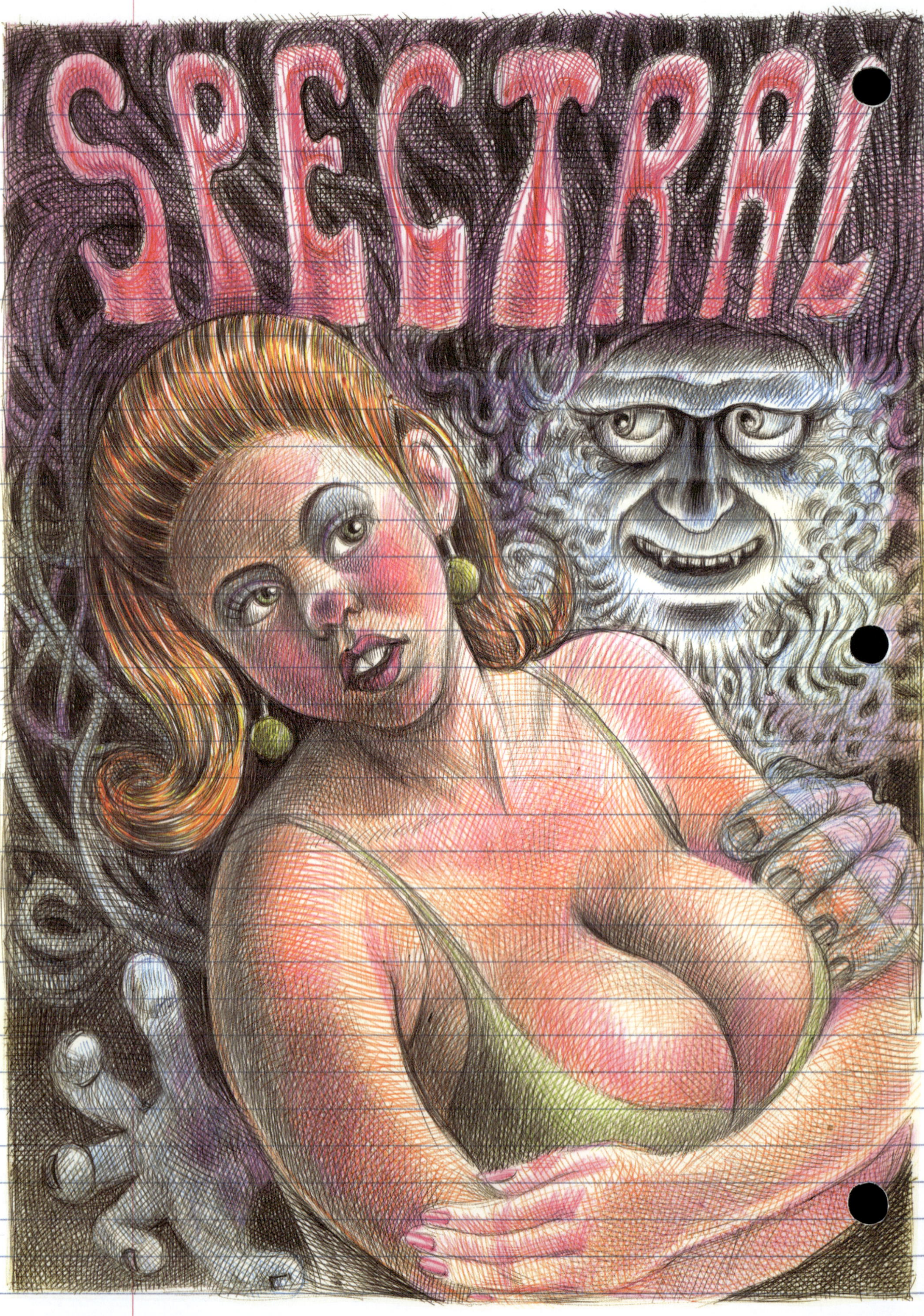
SPECTRAL

> IF I HAD BEEN IN YOUR NIGHTMARE I WOULD'VE ZAPPED THOSE MONSTERS WITH MY FISTS AND KICKED THEM WITH MY MEGA STRONG FEET!!

I'M PROBABLY THE ONLY PERSON WHO CAN TELL WHEN BLEMMY IS ANGRY.

AFTER BLEMMY GOES TOTALLY *NUTS* HE ALWAYS GET COMPLETELY WORN OUT.

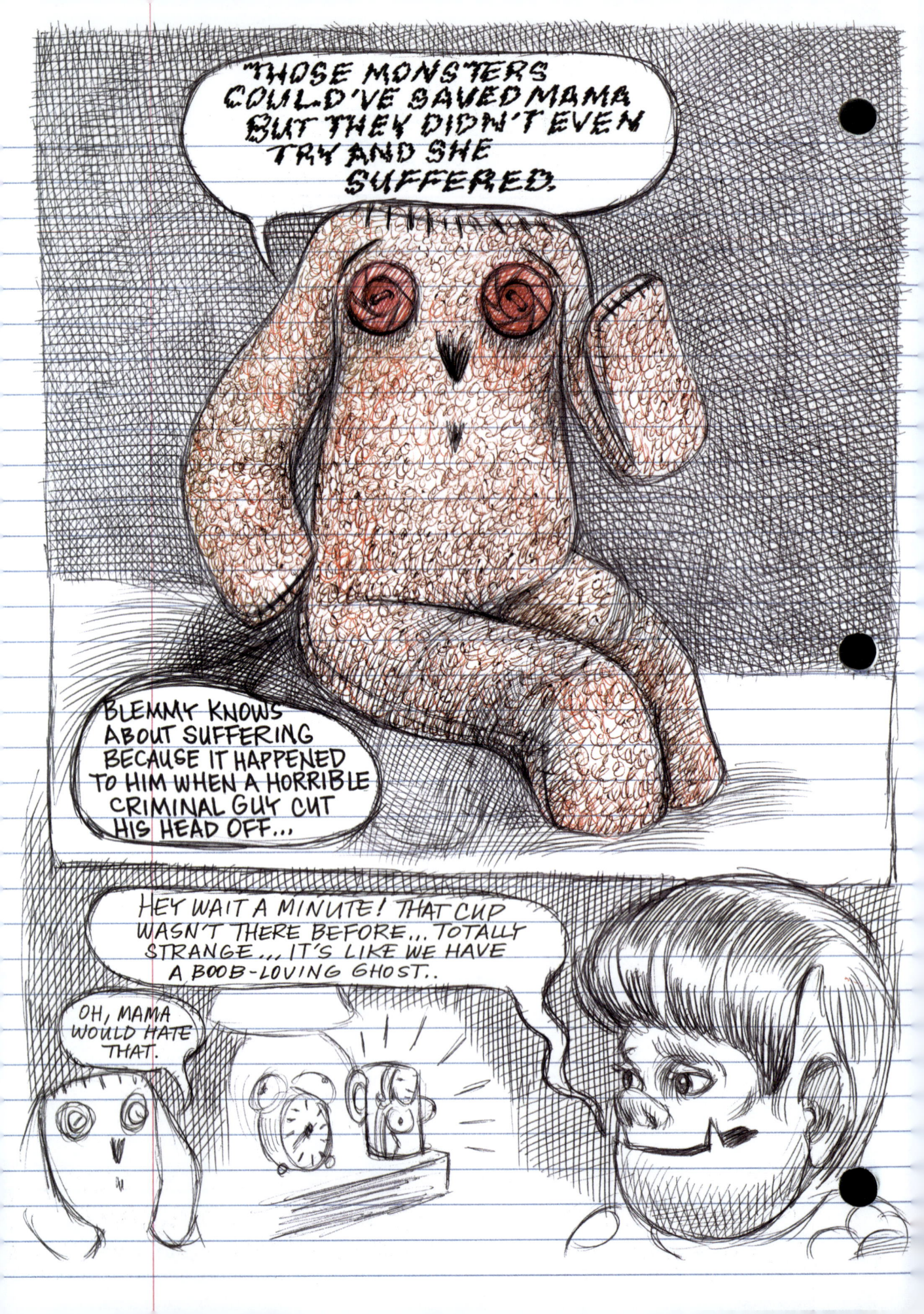

"THOSE MONSTERS COULD'VE SAVED MAMA BUT THEY DIDN'T EVEN TRY AND SHE SUFFERED.

BLEMMY KNOWS ABOUT SUFFERING BECAUSE IT HAPPENED TO HIM WHEN A HORRIBLE CRIMINAL GUY CUT HIS HEAD OFF...

HEY WAIT A MINUTE! THAT CUP WASN'T THERE BEFORE... TOTALLY STRANGE... IT'S LIKE WE HAVE A BOOB-LOVING GHOST..

OH, MAMA WOULD HATE THAT.

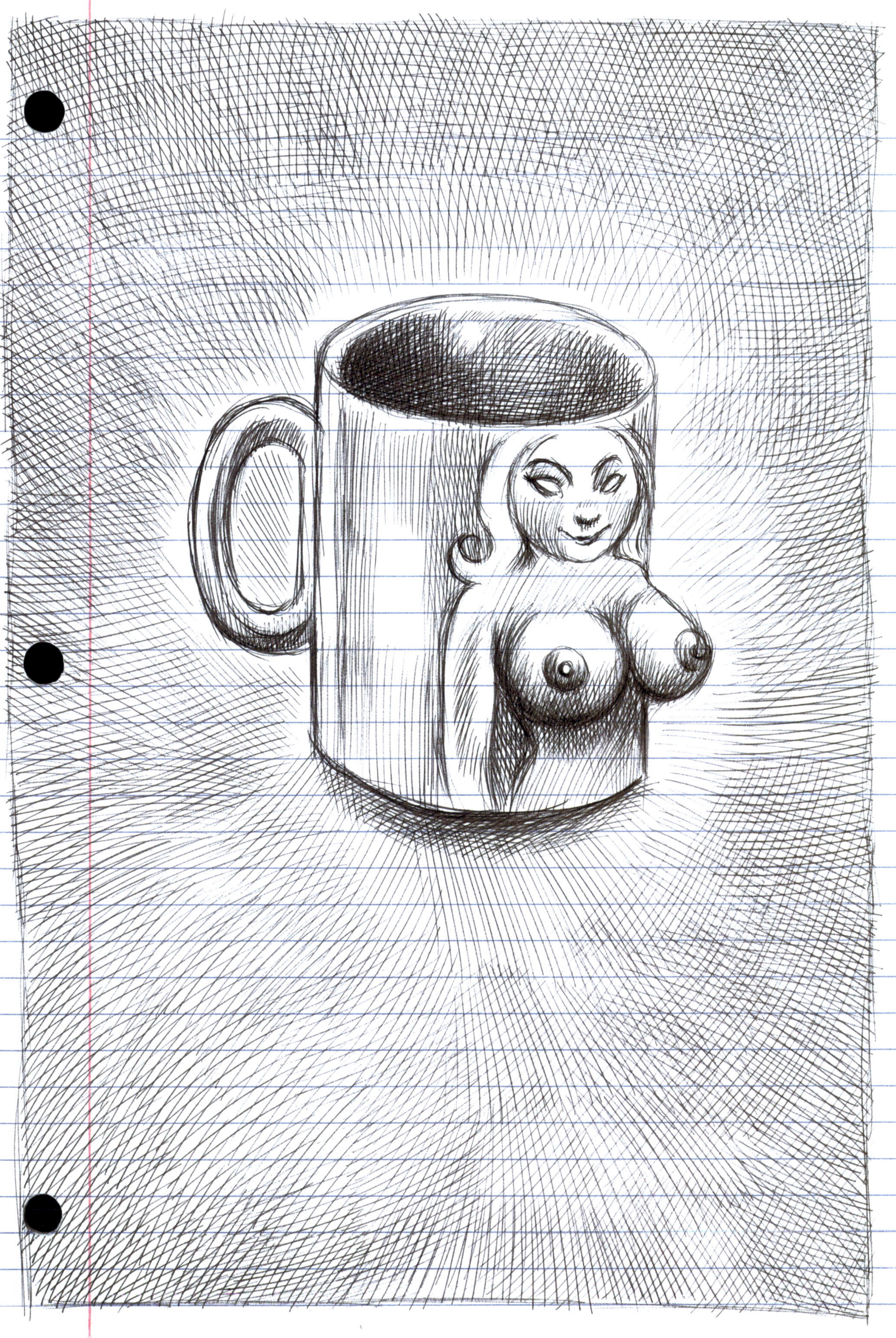

THE DAY AFTER MAMA PASSED AWAY, DEEZE TOOK ALL OF THE 'NAUGHTY THINGS' THAT MAMA HAD BANNED OUT OF HIDING. I FEEL TWO COMPLETELY DIFFERENT WAYS ABOUT WHAT DEEZE DID - IT FEELS TOO SOON AND I ALSO LIKE THE 'NAUGHTY THINGS' FOR REASONS THAT MAMA WOULD HATE... EVEN SO, I KNOW FOR SURE THAT I DIDN'T BRING THE CUP IN HERE.

BOOBS! COMPLETELY INAPPROPRIATE!!!

I LIKE THEM.

WELL, OF COURSE YOU LIKE THEM. YOU'RE A TOTAL QUEER.

KAREN!

TWO CIGARETTE BUTTS?

I HAVE SOMETHING IMPORTANT TO SAY! YOU NEED TO FACE WHAT YOU DID LAST NIGHT!

I'M PUTTING YOU TO BED NOW.

OH GAWD NWOOO!

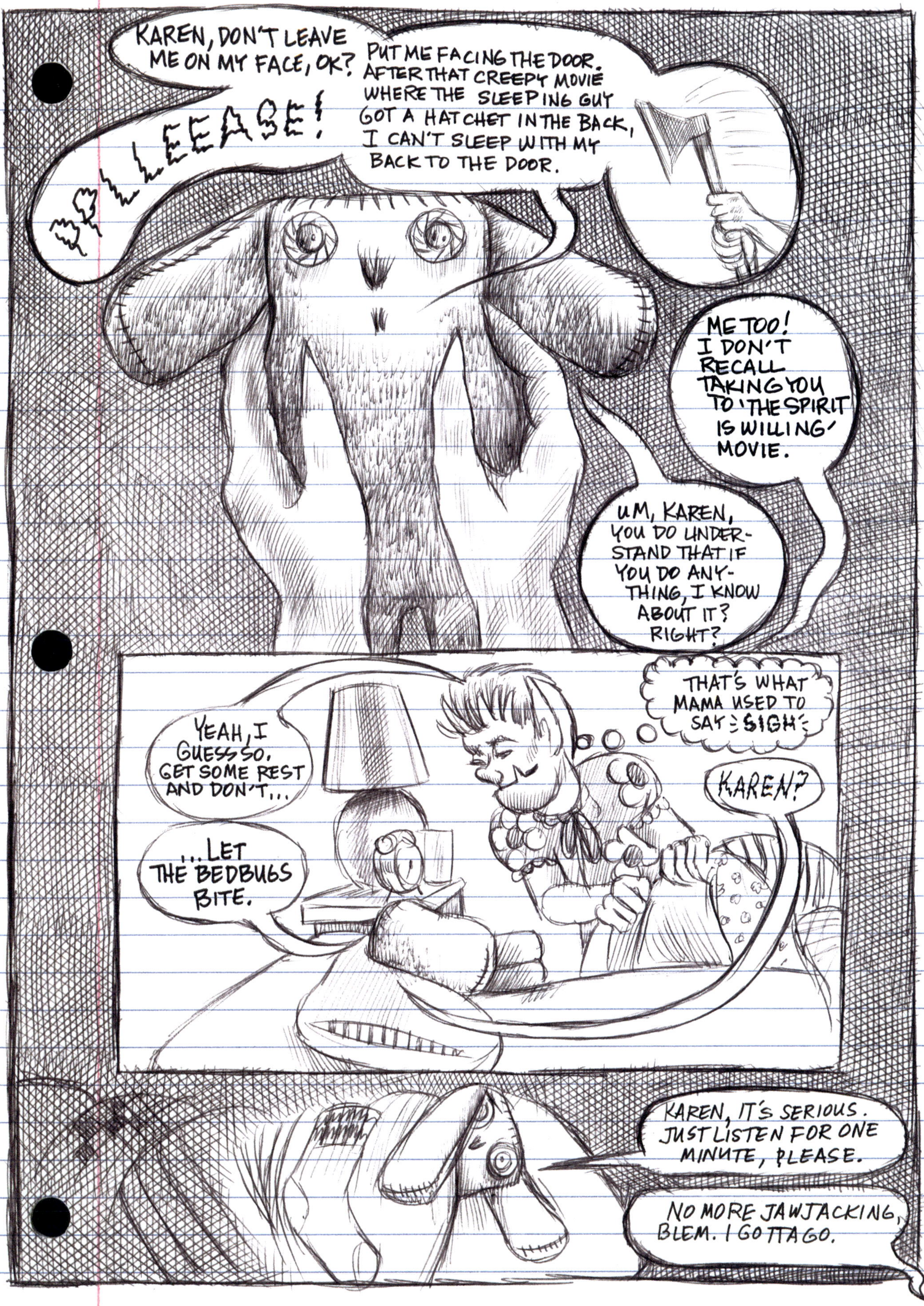
KAREN, DON'T LEAVE ME ON MY FACE, OK?
PLLEEASE!
PUT ME FACING THE DOOR. AFTER THAT CREEPY MOVIE WHERE THE SLEEPING GUY GOT A HATCHET IN THE BACK, I CAN'T SLEEP WITH MY BACK TO THE DOOR.
ME TOO! I DON'T RECALL TAKING YOU TO 'THE SPIRIT IS WILLING' MOVIE.
UM, KAREN, YOU DO UNDER-STAND THAT IF YOU DO ANY-THING, I KNOW ABOUT IT? RIGHT?
YEAH, I GUESS SO. GET SOME REST AND DON'T...
...LET THE BEDBUGS BITE.
THAT'S WHAT MAMA USED TO SAY. SIGH
KAREN?
KAREN, IT'S SERIOUS. JUST LISTEN FOR ONE MINUTE, PLEASE.
NO MORE JAWJACKING, BLEM. I GOTTA GO.

THE WHOLE SITUATION WITH THE GOVERNMENT TRYING TO SEND DEEZE TO THE WAR IN VIETNAM SCARES ME. IT MAKES ME FEEL LIKE I'M STANDING ON THE EDGE OF THE WORLD AND COULD FALL OFF ANY SECOND...

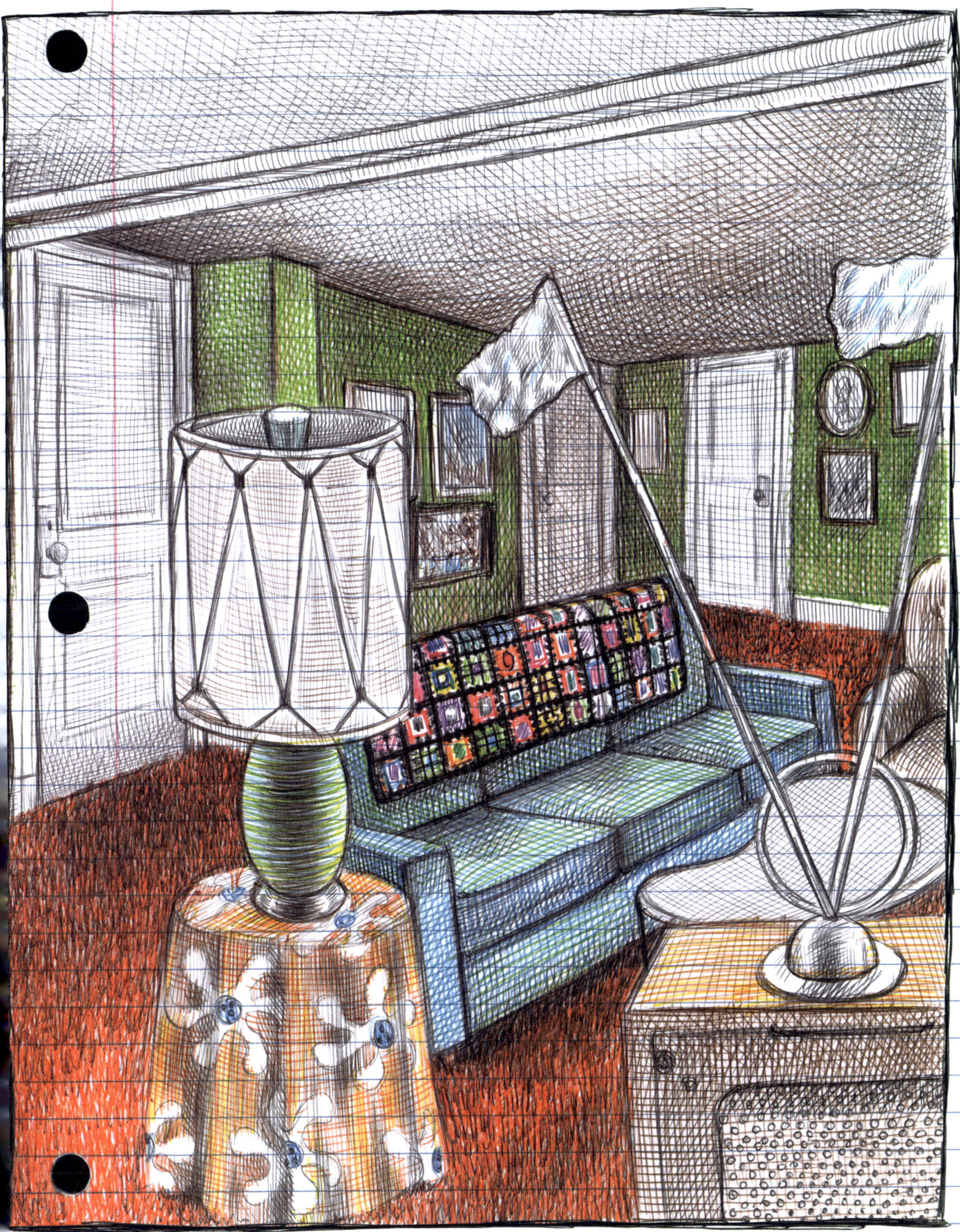

BEFORE GOING INTO DEEZE'S ROOM (WHICH WAS KIND OF OFF LIMITS WHEN MAMA WAS ALIVE) I WENT AND GOT MY DRAWING STUFF. MY IDEA WAS...

...TO DRAW DEEZE IN HIS NATURAL HABITAT AND MAYBE DO SOME SNOOPING, TOO. LOTS OF PEOPLE SAY THAT DEEZE IS HANDSOME. I THINK THAT IS TRUE BUT I AM THE ONE WHO KNOWS THE REAL SIDE OF DEEZE — THE NASTY PARTS SIDE OF HIM.

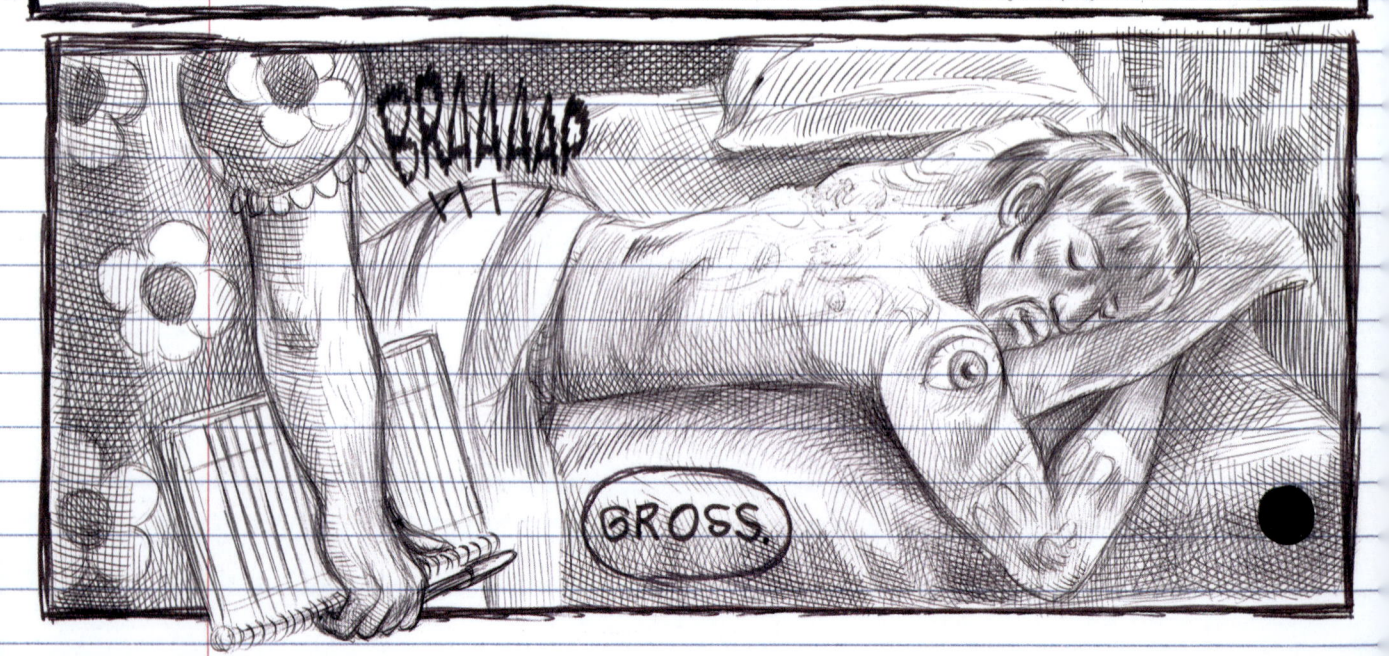

BRAAAAP

GROSS.

"SO I DID DRAW DEEZE BUT I ALSO LOOKED AT 'THE WALL OF LADIES,' AS MAMA CALLED IT, THAT ALWAYS HAD TO BE HIDDEN FROM MY "TENDER EYES."

LIKE I SAID, RIGHT AFTER MAMA DIED, DEEZE UNCOVERED ALL OF HIS NUDITY STUFF. DEEZE KNOWS THAT I LIKE GIRLS AND I USUALLY HAVE TO...

...BE A CLOSED BOOK AROUND MOST PEOPLE, BUT NOT AROUND DEEZE. HE GETS WHO I AM AND WHAT I FEEL ABOUT THINGS...

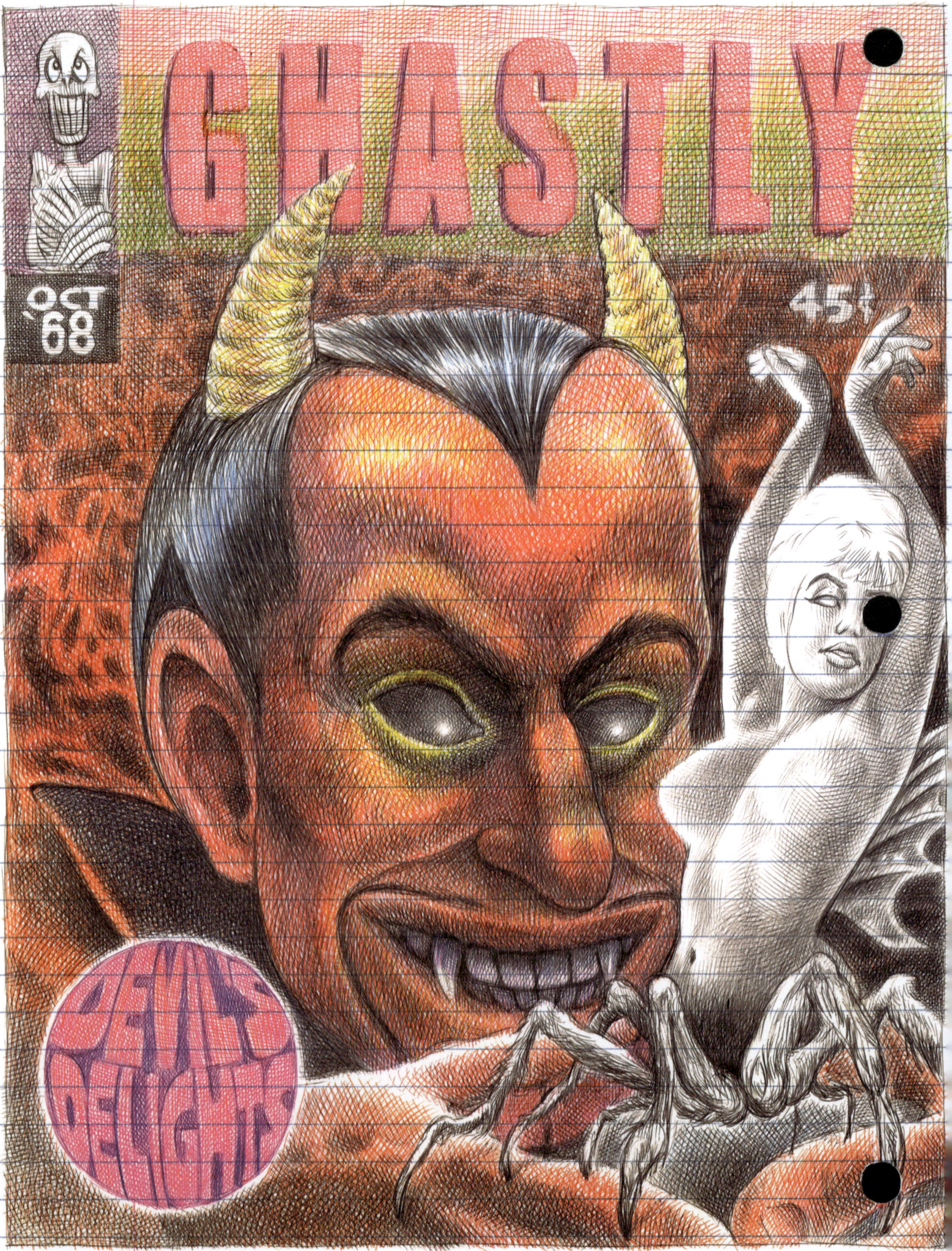
GHASTLY
OCT '68
45¢
DEVIL'S DELIGHTS

I LIKE TO LOOK AT THE 'WALL OF LADIES.' MAYBE I DON'T THINK THE SAME THINGS THAT DEEZE DOES WHEN HE SEES THEM. I ALWAYS IMAGINE THEM APPRECIATING THE FACT THAT I WANT TO GET TO KNOW THEM AND NOT JUST ADMIRE THEIR SKILLS AT TWIRLING THEIR BOOB TASSELS...

... BUT THERE IS ONE PICTURE THAT I LOVE MORE THAN ALL THE OTHERS. IT IS A PRINT OF A PAINTING AND BECAUSE THE LADIES LOVE EACH OTHER SO MUCH IT GIVES ME MORE HOPE THAN EVEN THE PIECE OF TWINE I KEEP IN MY DETECTIVE COAT (HOPEFULLY I WILL TELL ABOUT THAT LATER)...

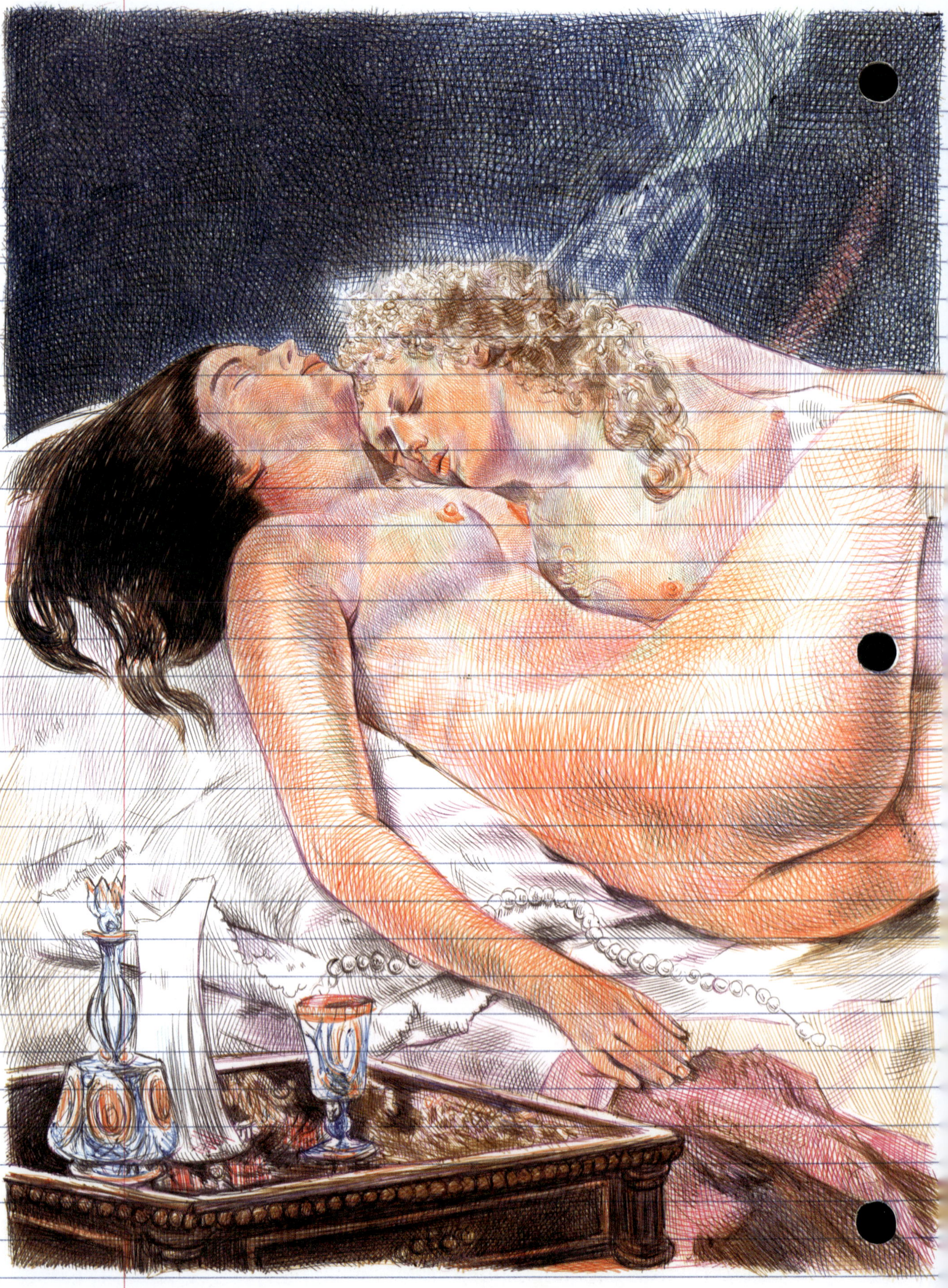

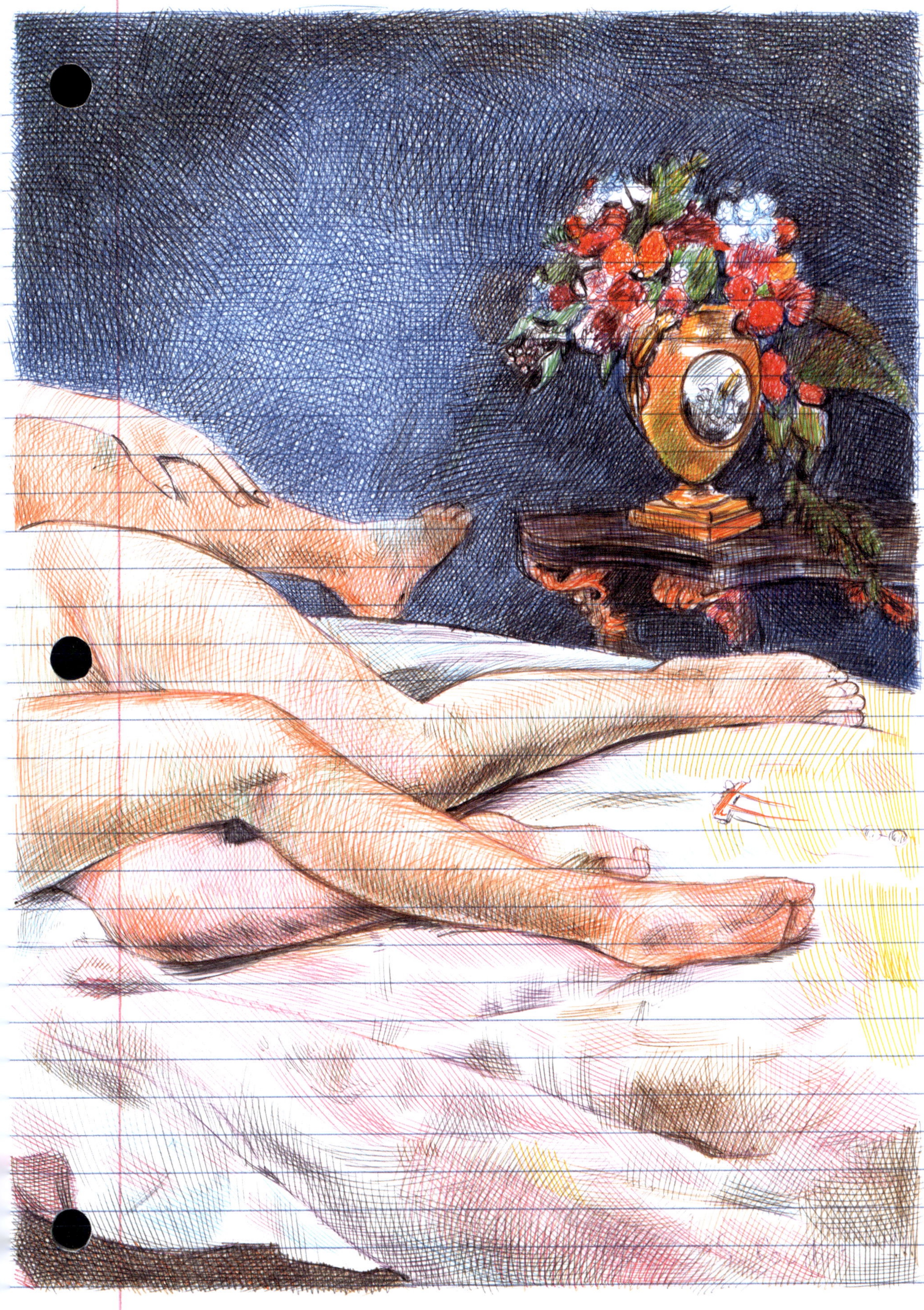

I LIKE THE PICTURE BUT NOT IN A 'PLAYBOY' KIND OF WAY. I LIKE IT BECAUSE THE LOVE THAT THE LADIES HAVE FOR ONE ANOTHER IS THE KIND THAT ENDS UP IN HOLY MATRIMONY — A SUBJECT THAT MAMA DIDN'T LIKE...

ONCE WHEN I WAS REALLY LITTLE I TOLD MAMA THAT I WANTED TO MARRY A GIRL. MAMA GOT PRETTY UPSET. SHE TOLD ME THAT TWO LADIES COULD NOT GET MARRIED AND WHEN I ASKED HER IF SHE WOULD COME TO MY WEDDING WHEN I DO MARRY A GIRL, SHE SAID SHE WOULD BE TOO ASHAMED OF ME. THEN I REMEMBERED THE *JEAN JACKET FIGHT*...

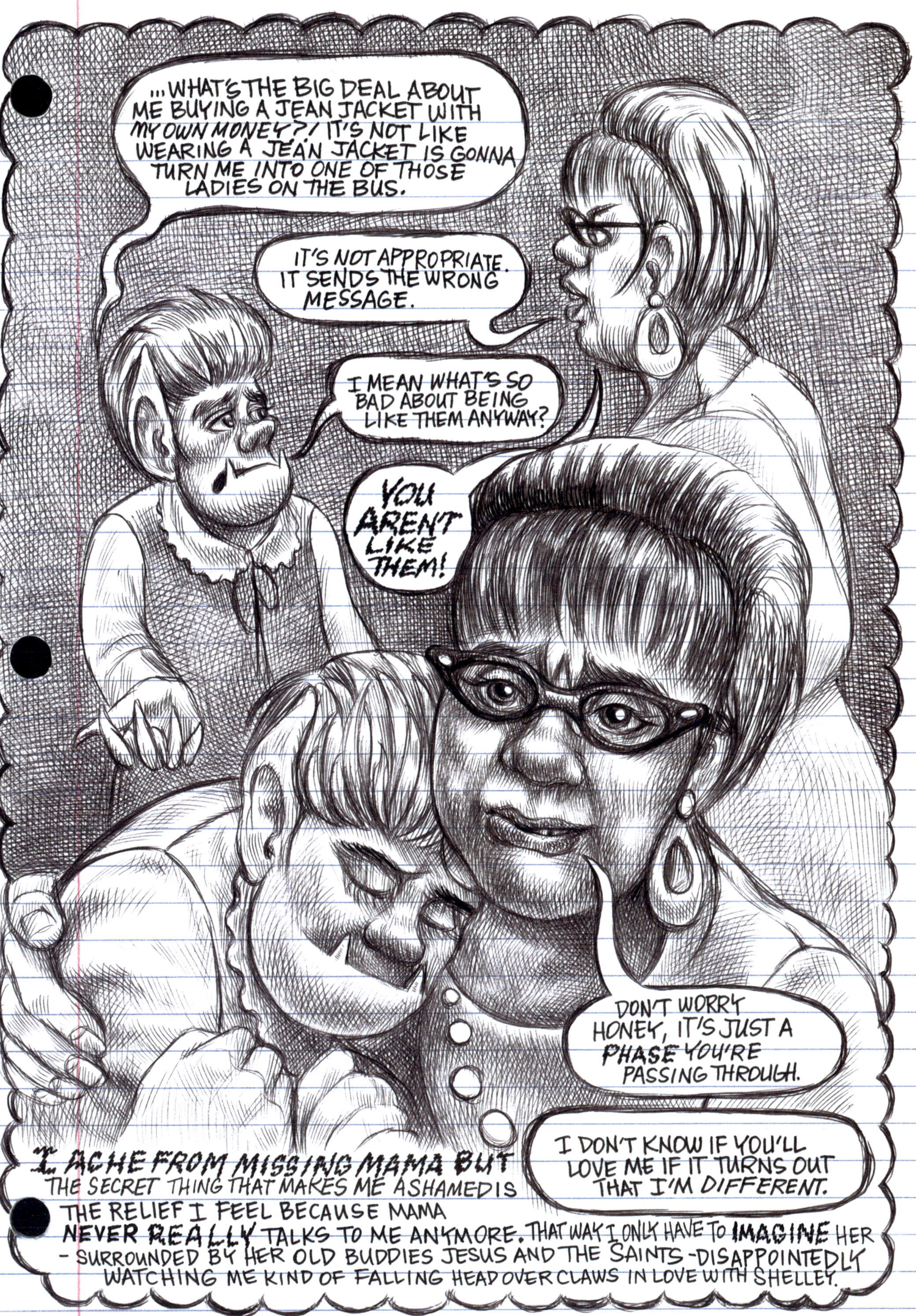
...WHAT'S THE BIG DEAL ABOUT ME BUYING A JEAN JACKET WITH MY OWN MONEY?! IT'S NOT LIKE WEARING A JEAN JACKET IS GONNA TURN ME INTO ONE OF THOSE LADIES ON THE BUS.
IT'S NOT APPROPRIATE. IT SENDS THE WRONG MESSAGE.
I MEAN WHAT'S SO BAD ABOUT BEING LIKE THEM ANYWAY?
YOU AREN'T LIKE THEM!
DON'T WORRY HONEY, IT'S JUST A PHASE YOU'RE PASSING THROUGH.
I DON'T KNOW IF YOU'LL LOVE ME IF IT TURNS OUT THAT I'M DIFFERENT.
I ACHE FROM MISSING MAMA BUT THE SECRET THING THAT MAKES ME ASHAMED IS THE RELIEF I FEEL BECAUSE MAMA NEVER REALLY TALKS TO ME ANYMORE. THAT WAY I ONLY HAVE TO IMAGINE HER - SURROUNDED BY HER OLD BUDDIES JESUS AND THE SAINTS - DISAPPOINTEDLY WATCHING ME KIND OF FALLING HEAD OVER CLAWS IN LOVE WITH SHELLEY.

SWAMP THING

"THE PENNY TREATMENT" IS WHERE I TAKE DEEZE'S PENNY JAR AND PITCH THE PENNIES ONTO HIS BACK AND BUTT (AND SOMETIMES HIS HEAD).

BAY-BEE...

...AND WHILE I DO THIS I LIKE TO SING...

IT'S A GOOD TECHNIQUE BECAUSE IF DEEZE WAKES UP PISSED OFF THEN I AM FAR ENOUGH AWAY FROM HIM TO RUN BEFORE HE CAN GET TO ME. I CAN LOCK MYSELF IN THE BATHROOM AND MAKE HIM PROMISE TO TAKE NO REVENGE IN EXCHANGE FOR BEING ABLE TO PEE...

PLINK

PLINK

"KARE, STOP 'THE PENNY TREATMENT' RIGHT NOW AND I PROBABLY WON'T KILL YOU!"

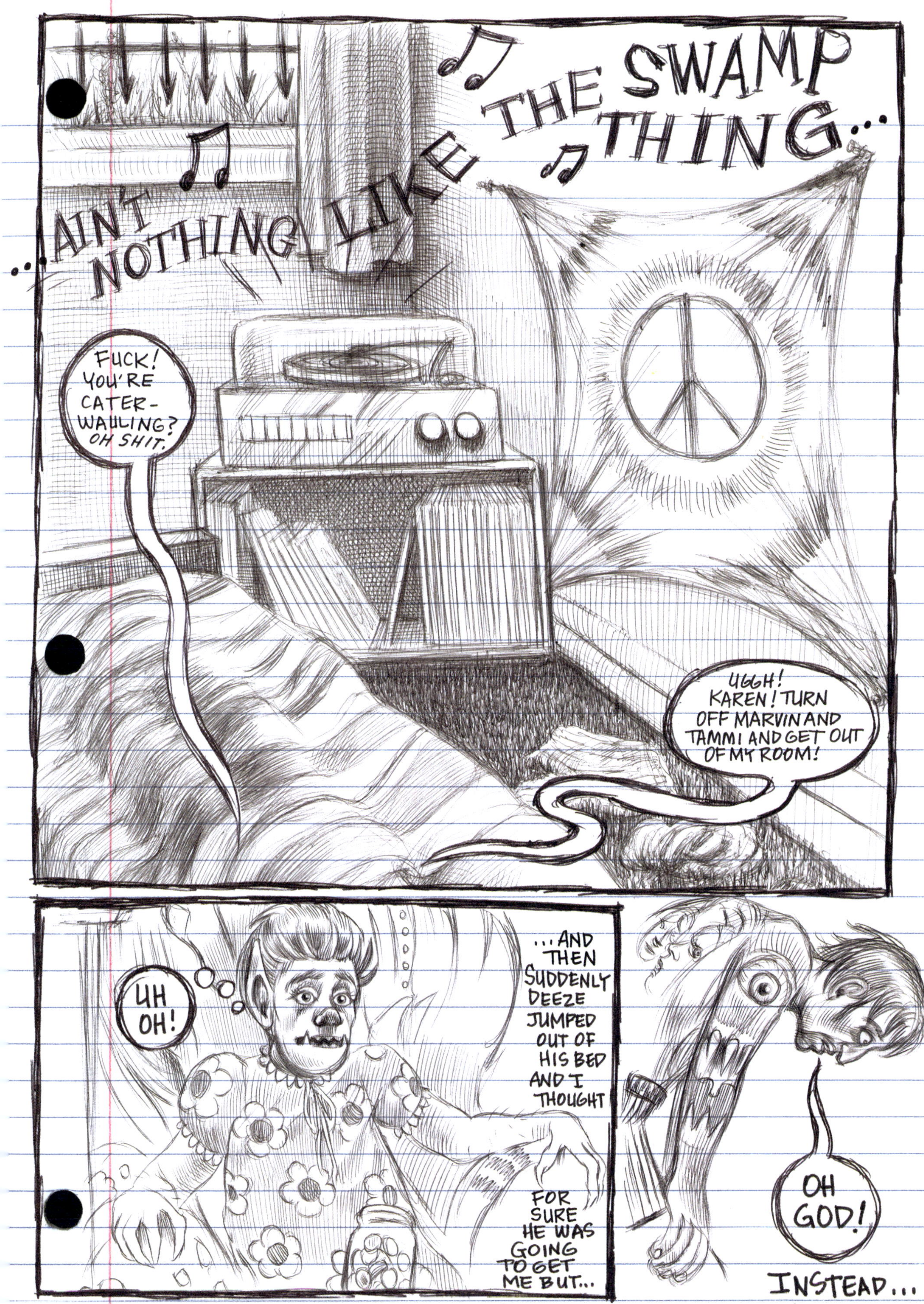

...AIN'T NOTHING LIKE THE SWAMP THING...
FUCK! YOU'RE CATER-WAULING? OH SHIT.
UGGH! KAREN! TURN OFF MARVIN AND TAMMI AND GET OUT OF MY ROOM!
UH OH!
...AND THEN SUDDENLY DEEZE JUMPED OUT OF HIS BED AND I THOUGHT
FOR SURE HE WAS GOING TO GET ME BUT...
OH GOD!
INSTEAD...

Panel 1:
COF COF HURG HURG

"Deeze, can I come in? I'm sorry you're sick..."

"Kare, wait. I'll be out in a bit."

Panel 2: But the door wasn't locked, so...

"It's so great that you barged right in here..."

HURGG

"...what could possibly be as cool as watching me drive the porcelain school bus?"

Panel 3:

"Kare, c'mon. JUST LET ME FUCKING PUKE IN PEACE, OK?"

"I just wanted to check on you. Do you think you're sick?"

"You mean, am I sick like Mom was sick? This is just a hangover. YOU KNOW I GOT PLOWED YESTERDAY...what's the deal with you?"

"It's just that I'm sort of freaked because someone tore up all my monster posters and then taped up the Wolfman poster."

Panel 4:

"...You don't remember last night? Do you?"

"YOU EVEN TORE UP THE WOLFMAN POSTER I GOT YOU."

"I don't... I don't remember that...hey I have to pee so I'll wait my turn in the living room."

"It's official. I've gone totally and completely coo coo."

"Don't worry about that Kare. You were probably sleep walking. Go out and wait and... ...UNLIKE YOU I'LL EVEN GIVE YOU YOUR 'PIRACY.'"

AFTER DEEZE WAS DONE PUKING HE LET ME PEE AND HE WAS GOOD ON HIS WORD BECAUSE HE GAVE ME MY 'PIRACY.' (THE REASON MAMA AND DEEZE ALWAYS SAY 'PIRACY' INSTEAD OF 'PRIVACY' IS BECAUSE THAT WAS SOMETHING I SAID WHEN I WAS A STUPID LITTLE KID AND WANTED TO BE LEFT ALONE. I'M SURE I THOUGHT THAT THE WORD ACTUALLY WAS 'PIRACY.' MAMA AND DEEZE COULDN'T STOP SAYING STUFF LIKE... AND THEN THEY'D LAUGH LIKE HYENAS. I STARTED LOVING IT, TOO. IT MADE ME THINK OF US AS A PIRATE FAMILY AND THE APARTMENT AS OUR PIRATE SHIP, SAILING THE HIGH SEAS AND LOOKING FOR TREASURE.)

"ARGH MATEY."
"AND SHIVER ME TIMBERS."

AFTER I WAS DONE PEEING DEEZE CAME BACK AND GOT IN THE TUB AND PULLED SHUT THE SHOWER CURTAIN AND THEN HE TOSSED OUT HIS ICKY UNDERWEAR....

"IT TOTALLY SMELLS LIKE VOMIT IN HERE."

"WOW KARE, THAT'S A *REAL* PUZZLER."

"HEY KARE, COULD YOU DO ME A FAVOR?"

"THERE WAS SOMEONE IN MY DREAM WHO LOOKED JUST LIKE YOU..."

"CAN YOU LOAD ME A TOOTHBRUSH AND BLIND PASS IT TO ME?"

"YEAH KARE, A TOTAL HUNK HUH?"

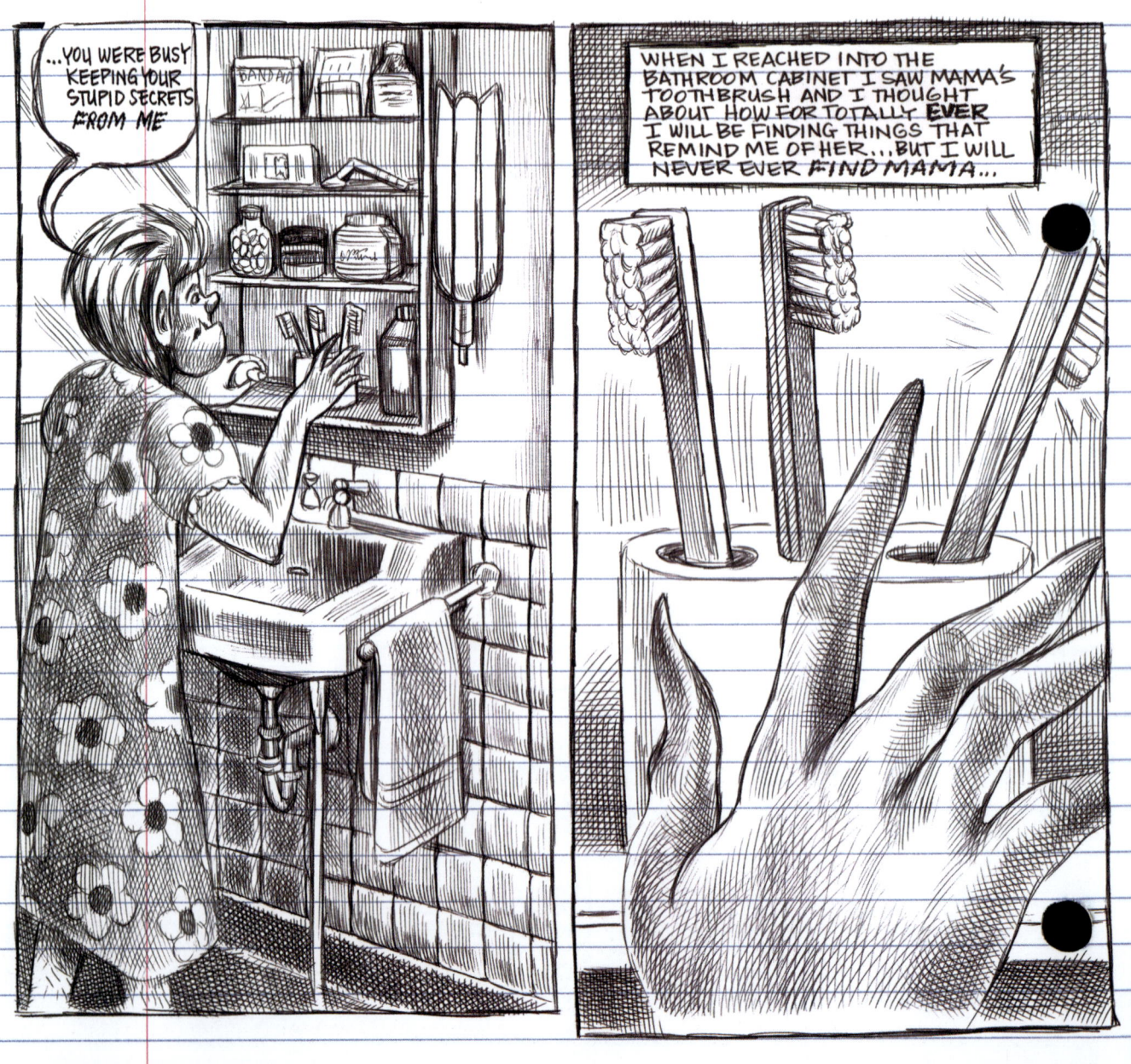

"DEEZE EVERYTHING HAS TO CHANGE. I MEAN EITHER YOU AND MAMA WERE HAVING YOUR *WAR* WITH EACH OTHER OR...

...YOU WERE BUSY KEEPING YOUR STUPID SECRETS FROM ME"

WHEN I REACHED INTO THE BATHROOM CABINET I SAW MAMA'S TOOTHBRUSH AND I THOUGHT ABOUT HOW FOR TOTALLY *EVER* I WILL BE FINDING THINGS THAT REMIND ME OF HER... BUT I WILL NEVER EVER *FIND MAMA*...

"DEEZE, I THINK SCHOOL IS A BAD IDEA."

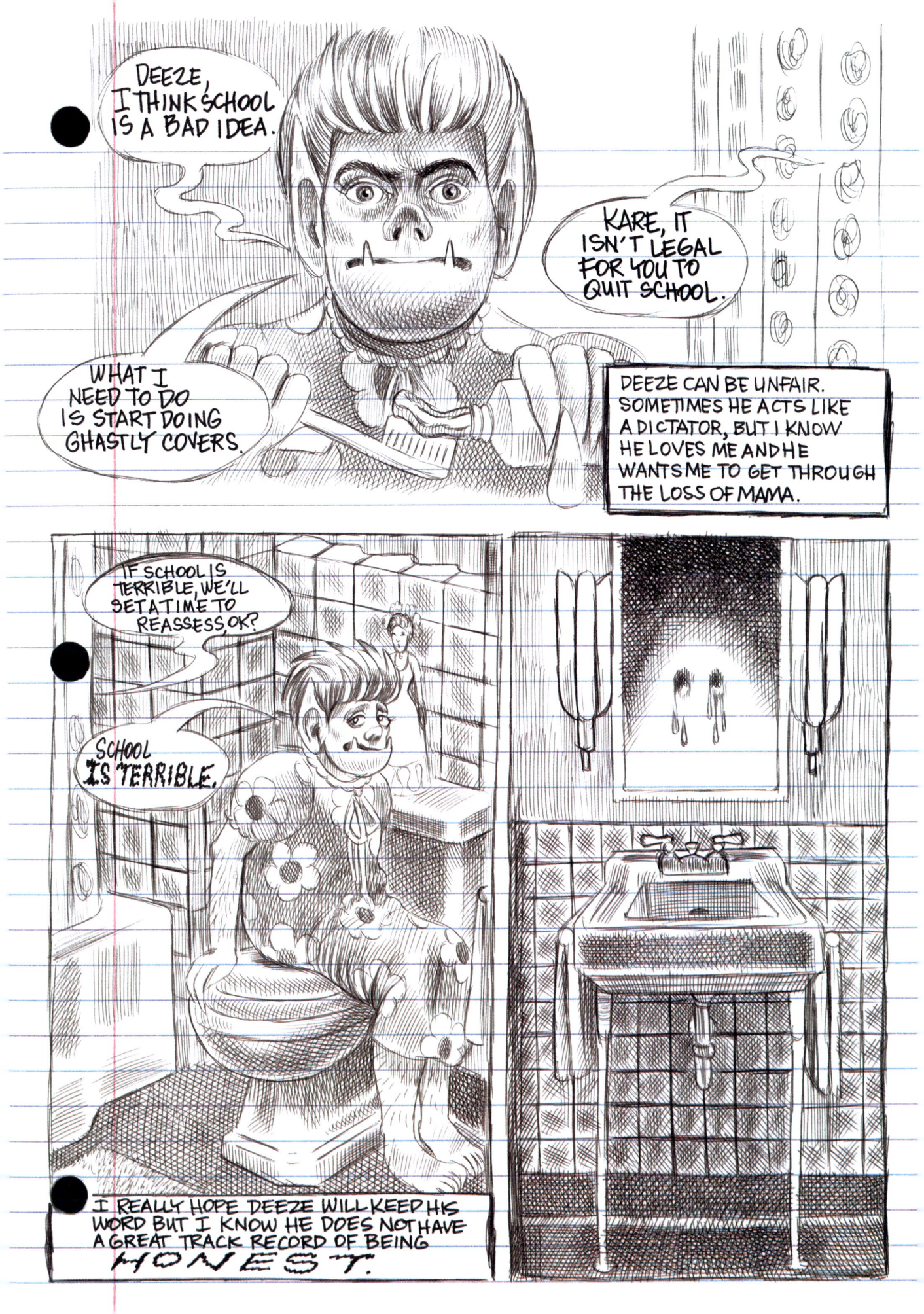

"KARE, IT ISN'T LEGAL FOR YOU TO QUIT SCHOOL."

"WHAT I NEED TO DO IS START DOING GHASTLY COVERS."

DEEZE CAN BE UNFAIR. SOMETIMES HE ACTS LIKE A DICTATOR, BUT I KNOW HE LOVES ME AND HE WANTS ME TO GET THROUGH THE LOSS OF MAMA.

"IF SCHOOL IS TERRIBLE, WE'LL SET A TIME TO REASSESS, OK?"

"SCHOOL IS TERRIBLE."

I REALLY HOPE DEEZE WILL KEEP HIS WORD BUT I KNOW HE DOES NOT HAVE A GREAT TRACK RECORD OF BEING *HONEST.*

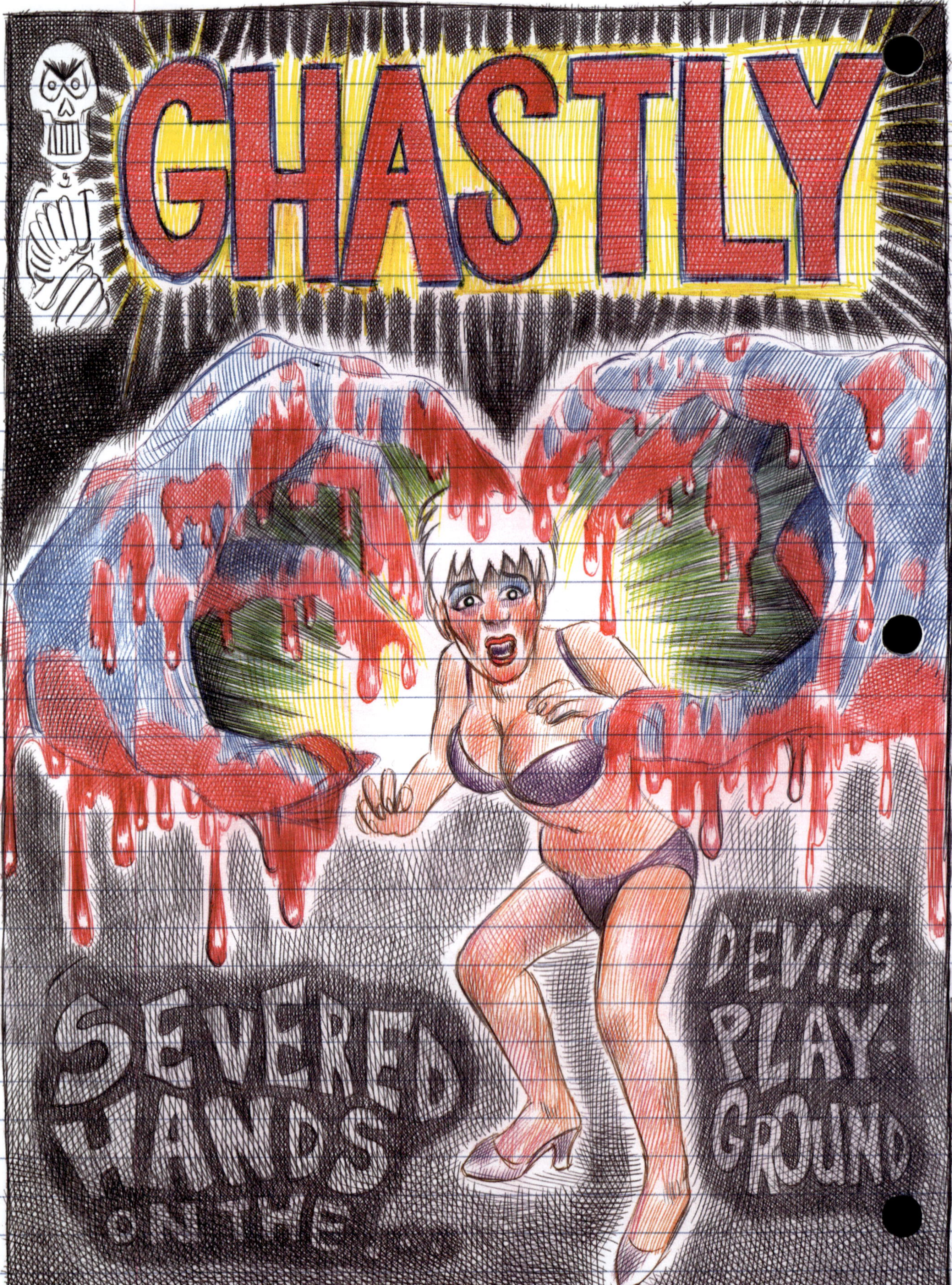
GHASTLY
SEVERED HANDS ON THE
DEVIL'S PLAYGROUND

SO TODAY WAS THE FIRST TIME SINCE MAMA DIED THAT DEEZE MADE ME GO TO *HELL*...

I GOT YOU A NEW NOTEBOOK.

THANKS!

DEEZE, YOU CAN CONTINUE THE HONESTY POLICY BY TELLING ME WHY THERE ARE TWO CIGARETTE BUTTS IN A BOOB CUP IN MY BEDROOM.

DEEZE GOT ME THE WRONG KIND. INSTEAD OF WIDE-RULED HE GOT ME COLLEGE-RULED. DEEZE SAID MAMA DYING MEANS I GRADUATED INTO COLLEGE-RULED...

MIJA MIJA MIJA

COME HERE, KAREN. LAST NIGHT YOU WENT TOTALLY *LOCA*. YOU WERE HOWLING LIKE A BANSHEE. YOU TORE UP YOUR MONSTER POSTERS... I THINK YOU BLAMED THE MONSTERS FOR NOT SAVING MA...

I GOT YOU TO CALM DOWN THE WAY I USED TO WHEN YOU WERE A LITTLE KID AND HAD NIGHT TERRORS. I PUT YOU IN MY ARMS AND I STROKED YOUR HAIR. THE CIGS WERE BECAUSE I STAYED TO MAKE SURE YOU WERE OKAY.

THAT WAS WHAT I DID IN MY DREAM. I KILLED ALL THE MONSTERS I LOVE.

YA KNOW, KARE, YOU'RE GOING TO HAVE TO FIND A WAY TO FORGIVE THE MONSTERS FOR NOT BITING MAMA...

...MAYBE WE NEED TO WATCH CREATURE FEATURES TOGETHER TONIGHT. LET'S LOOK IN THE TV GUIDE AND SEE WHAT'S PLAYING, OK?

WHILE I WAS GONE FROM SCHOOL I DECIDED THAT IF DEEZE MADE ME GO BACK I WOULD START CARRYING A BIG STICK ON THE WAY TO AND FROM SCHOOL.

REYES, DO YA THINK THAT STICK IS GONNA *PROTECT YA?*

WELL, WHY DON'T YOU COME HERE AND *FIND OUT?*

THE ONLY PERSON I WAS LOOKING FORWARD TO SEEING WHEN I GOT TO SCHOOL WAS FRANKLIN.

KAREN, I REALLY MISSED YOU SO MUCH! *PLEASE* COME TO MY HOUSE AFTER SCHOOL? I JUST MADE THE MOST *AMAZING* OUTFIT AND I WANT *YOU* TO BE THE FIRST PERSON I MODEL IT FOR.

THESE TWO SAY THINGS ABOUT WHO THE DEVIL IS AND WHAT IS WRONG AND RIGHT, THAT KIND OF DRIVE ME CRAZY. SOMETIMES I THINK ABOUT CREATING COMIC BOOKS WITH THESE TWO AS 'SUPER HEROES' BATTLING THE DEVIL AND WHEN I DECIDE I NO LONGER WANT TO BE AT THIS SCHOOL, THAT IS EXACTLY WHAT I'LL DO.

BEFORE I LEFT FROM SCHOOL TO BE AT HOME WITH MAMA UNTIL SHE DIED, THIS WAS THE ART TEACHER FOR MY SCHOOL.
IF YOU WANTED TO DRAW A SINGLE BOAT ON A CALM SEA,
THAT WAS OKEY DOKEY.
IF YOU WANTED TO PAINT A PICTURE OF A FLOWER ON A CROSS... GROOVY.
IF YOU WANTED TO DRAW A SINGLE TREE GROWING IN A PASTURE OR A CAT LICKING IT'S PAW...
YOU WERE GOLDEN.
YOU DRAW A **MONSTER?**
DO THAT AND YOU ARE GOING TO FATHER McGUNKLIN'S OFFICE AND YOUR MOM AND BROTHER WILL BE CALLED.

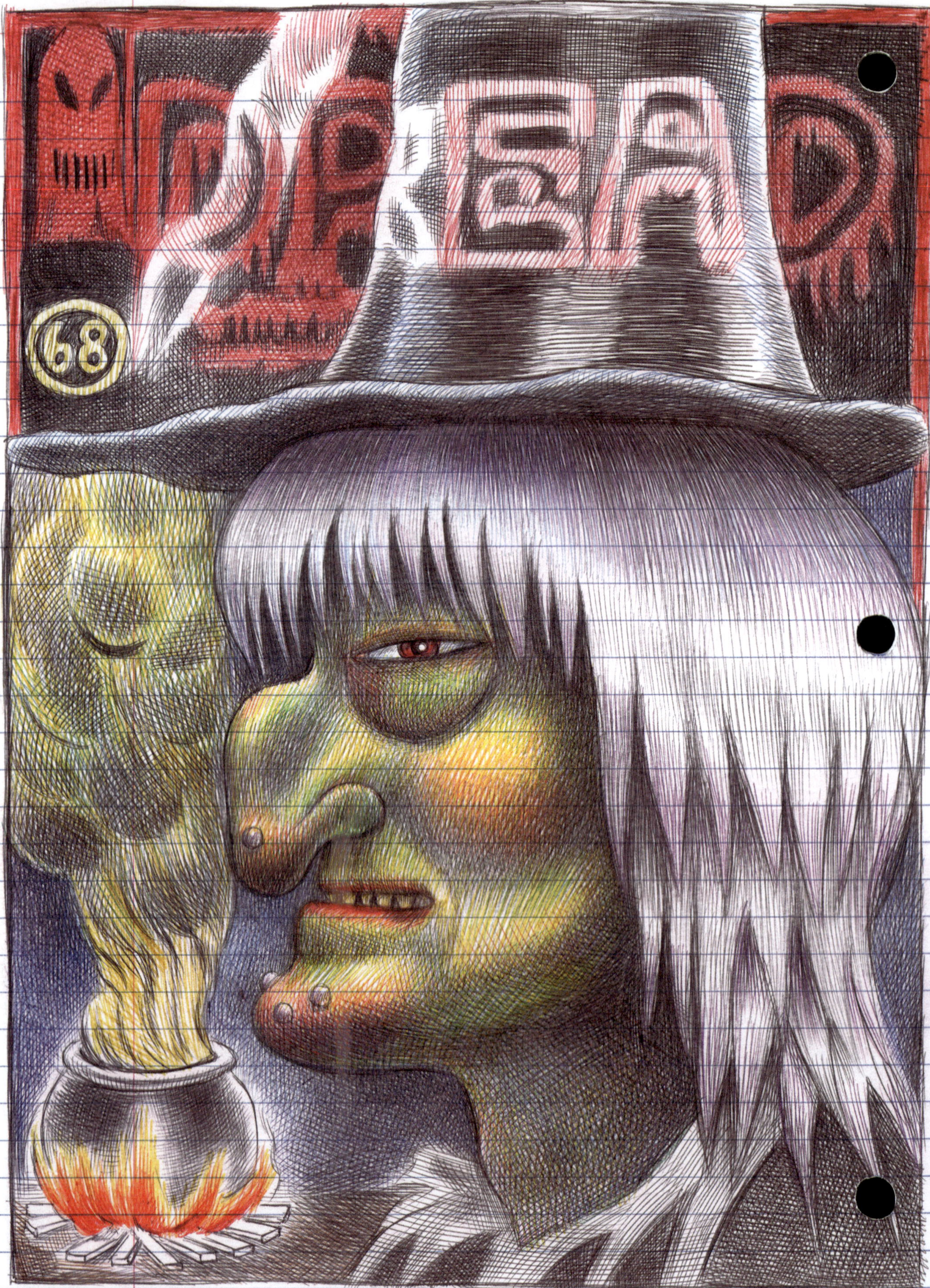
DREAD
68

THERE ARE REALLY CRAPPY THINGS ABOUT BEING BACK IN SCHOOL, BUT THERE IS ONE GOOD THING. THE NUNS HAVE HIRED A LAY TEACHER TO TEACH ART AND SHE LIKES MY DRAWINGS... AND SHE LIKES THEM A LOT.

"YOU'VE DRAWN THEM SO WELL THAT I ALMOST FEEL LIKE I KNOW THESE LADIES."

HER NAME IS MRS. WIDJIEWSKI BUT THAT'S DIFFICULT TO SAY, SO EVERYONE CALLS HER...

MRS. WITCH...

SHE PLAYS CHOPIN FOR US WHILE WE WORK ON OUR ART PROJECTS. SHE IS VERY PROUD OF BEING POLISH...

CHOPIN IS POLISH LIKE MRS. WITCH.

"KAREN, WOULD YOU MIND IF I BORROWED YOUR DRAWING FOR A FEW WEEKS?"

"SURE."

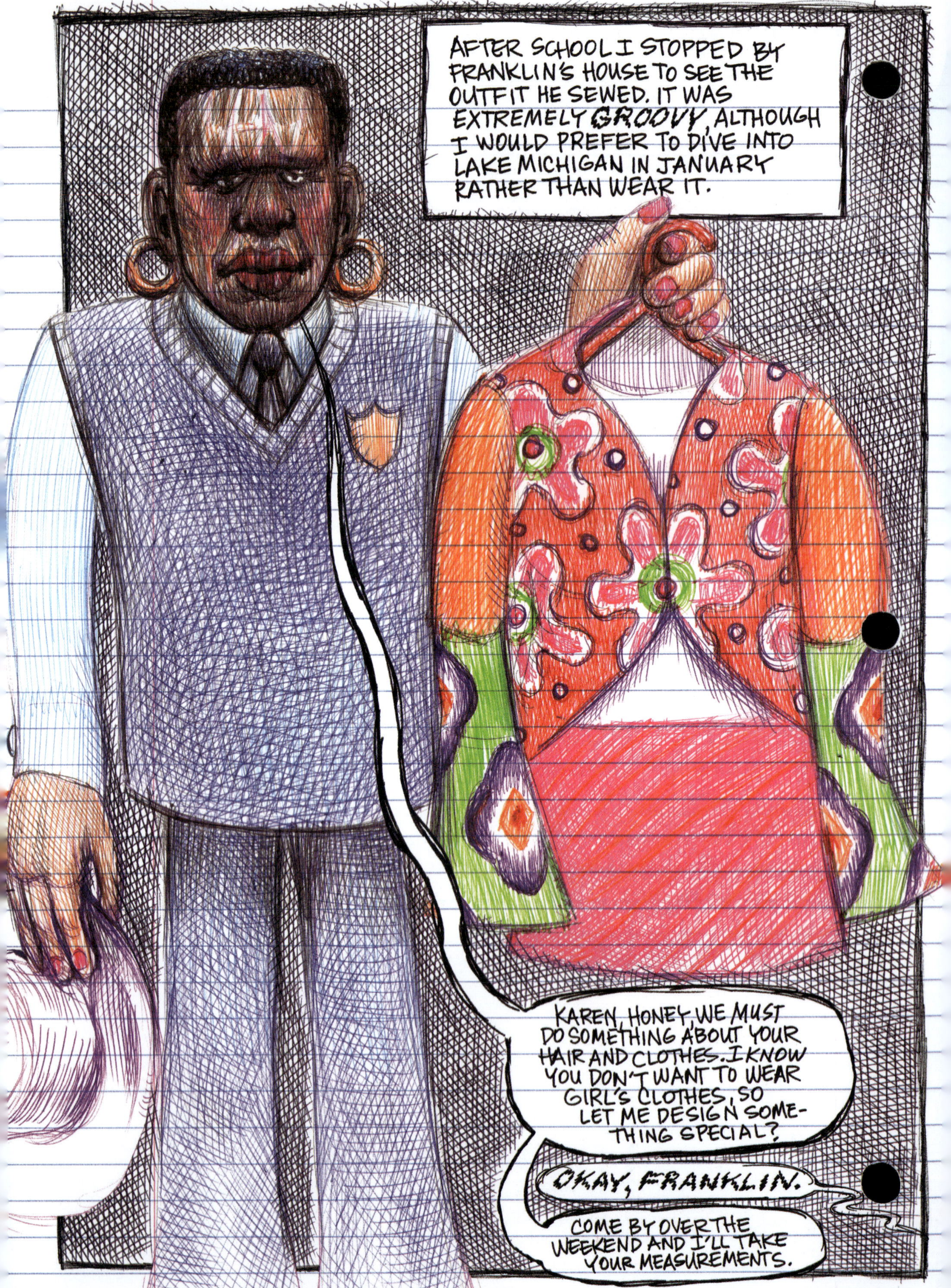
AFTER SCHOOL I STOPPED BY FRANKLIN'S HOUSE TO SEE THE OUTFIT HE SEWED. IT WAS EXTREMELY GROOVY, ALTHOUGH I WOULD PREFER TO DIVE INTO LAKE MICHIGAN IN JANUARY RATHER THAN WEAR IT.
KAREN, HONEY, WE MUST DO SOMETHING ABOUT YOUR HAIR AND CLOTHES. I KNOW YOU DON'T WANT TO WEAR GIRL'S CLOTHES, SO LET ME DESIGN SOMETHING SPECIAL?
OKAY, FRANKLIN.
COME BY OVER THE WEEKEND AND I'LL TAKE YOUR MEASUREMENTS.

WHEN I GOT TO MY APARTMENT THERE WAS A NOTE FROM SHELLEY TAPED TO OUR MAILBOX. IT SAID THAT THERE IS AN ANTI-WAR FESTIVAL THIS SATURDAY IN GRANT PARK AND THAT MAYBE COULD WE GO TO IT TOGETHER? I DO NOT HAVE WORDS FOR HOW HAPPY I AM... I ONLY HAVE THIS DRAWING, WHICH SAYS IT ALL.

SOMEHOW I GOT THROUGH THE WEEK AND ALL OF IT'S STUPIDNESS AND I MADE IT DOWNTOWN TO MEET SHELLEY IN FRONT OF THE ART INSTITUTE. UNLIKE SHELLEY I DO NOT HAVE TOILET MONEY SO I COULDN'T GET HER AS NICE A GIFT AS SHE BOUGHT ME. I COULD ONLY AFFORD THESE FORTUNE TELLING FISH FROM CHINATOWN.

FORTUNE FISH

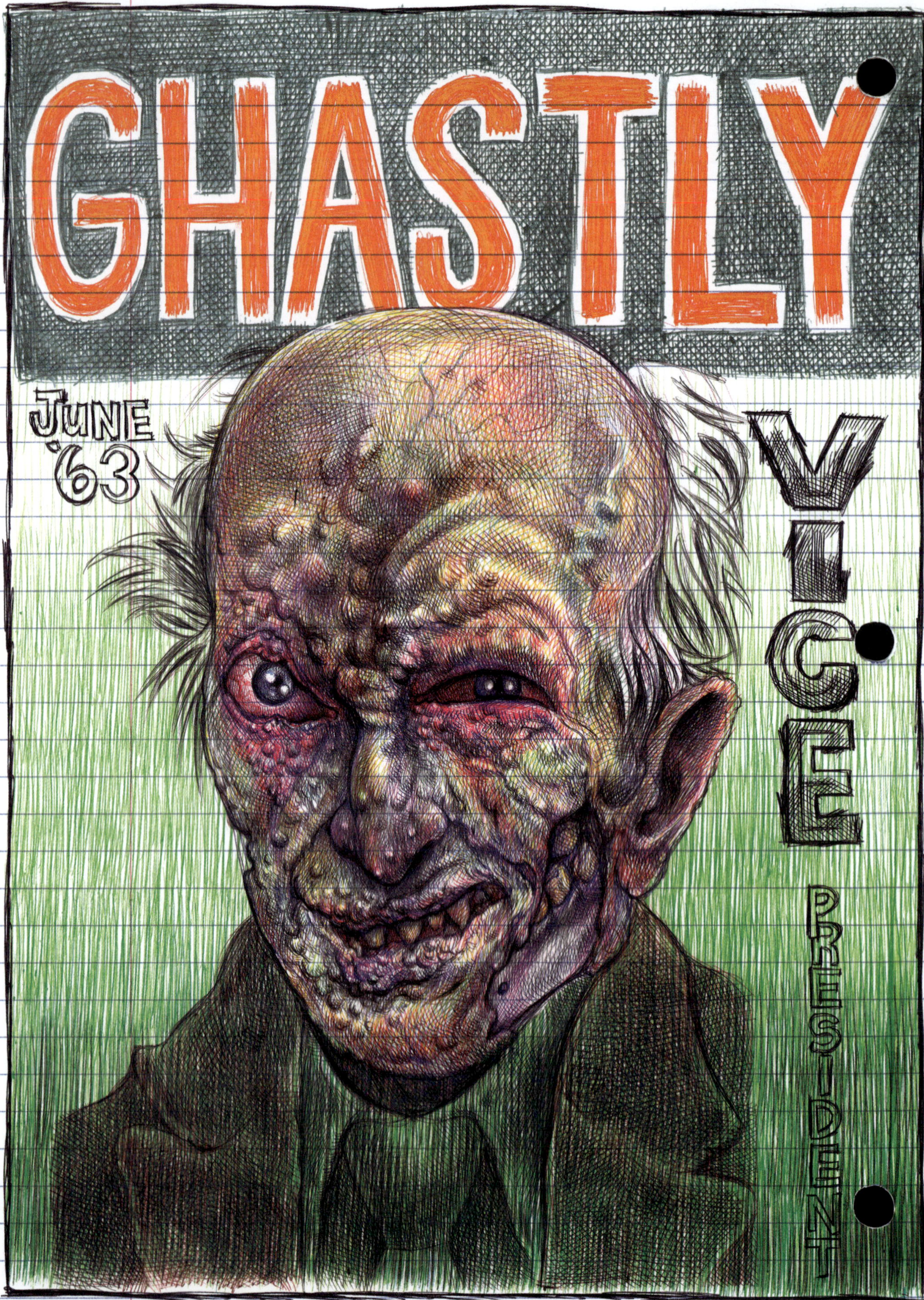

GHASTLY
JUNE '63
VICE
PRESIDENT

"KAREN, I THOUGHT YOU WEREN'T GOING TO SHOW. IT SEEMED LIKE YOU HAD... STOOD ME UP."

I EXPLAINED TO SHELLEY THAT THERE WERE SO MANY PEOPLE COMING TO THE PROTEST IN GRANT PARK THAT THE SUBWAY TRAINS WERE ALL DELAYED BUT I COULD SEE THAT SHELLEY WAS STILL UPSET BY ME BEING LATE TO MEET HER.

"YOU SHOULD KNOW THAT I'M NOT GREAT AT WAITING."

WHEN SHELLEY SAID THIS I EXPLAINED TO HER THAT IN THE FUTURE THERE MIGHT BE CIRCUMSTANCES BEYOND MY CONTROL. I GUESS THIS WAS OUR FIRST FIGHT AND I WILL TELL ABOUT IT LATER ON...

"THIS IS THE ACTUAL PAINTING THAT WAS IN THE MOVIE. I KNOW ONE INTERESTING SECRET ABOUT THIS PAINTING..."

TELL ME YOUR SECRET!

...BACK WHEN I WAS A LITTLE KID AND MY BROTHER DEEZE WOULD BRING ME HERE... A FEW TIMES I SAW... IVAN ALBRIGHT...

...THE ARTIST WHO PAINTED THIS PAINTING *ACTUALLY PAINTING ON THIS ARTWORK WHILE IT HUNG ON THE WALL!* THE MUSEUM WOULD LET HIM COME IN HERE EVERY ONCE IN A WHILE TO ADD THINGS TO IT!

KAREN, DO YOU THINK THAT MR. ALBRIGHT WAS PUTTING HIS CRIMES INTO THE PAINTING?

NAW. HE SEEMED LIKE A GREAT GUY... HE WAS PROBABLY JUST A PERFECTION-LOVER TYPE.

KAREN, DO YOU MEAN A PERFECTIONIST? KEEP IN MIND THAT ALL PEOPLE ARE FLAWED,... EVEN ARTISTS.

I KNOW. CARAVAGGIO WAS A KILLER... AND HE WASN'T THE ONLY ONE EITHER.

WOW! I DIDN'T KNOW THAT.

AFTER I TOOK SHELLEY TO SEE THE CARAVAGGIO WE WENT DOWN TO THE PAY TOILETS AND HELPED OURSELVES TO ALL THE CHANGE IN THE LOCKBOXES. WHILE I WAS HER LOOKOUT I WONDERED IF BY STEALING I WAS MESSING UP A PORTRAIT OF ME THAT EXISTS SOMEWHERE. SHELLEY SURPRISED ME WHEN SHE PUT THE NECKLACE THAT HAS THE LOCKBOX KEY ON IT *AROUND MY NECK!*

IT'S YOURS NOW, KAREN.

WOW, THANKS!

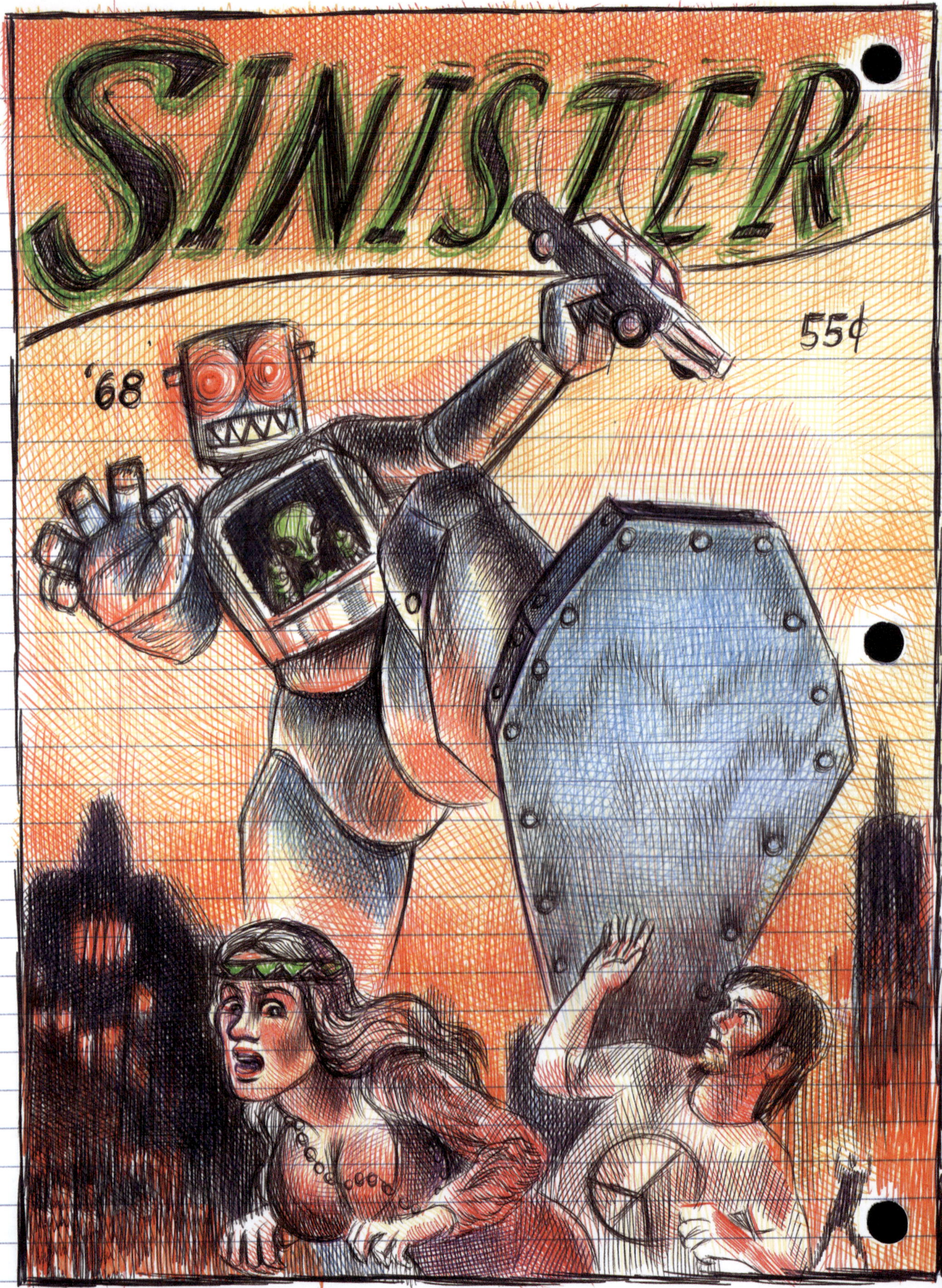
SINISTER
'68
55¢

WHEN ME AND SHELLEY LEFT THE MUSEUM WE RAN INTO 'THE BRAIN' WHO WAS HANDING OUT HIS PAMPHLETS ON THE CORNER. WHILE I WAS INTRODUCING SHELLEY TO HIM, THIS LADY OFFERED ME AND SHELLEY A COPY OF MAO'S LITTLE RED BOOK.
SHELLEY TOOK A COPY BUT I COULD TELL THAT THE BRAIN DIDN'T WANT ME TO TAKE ONE AND THAT CONFUSED ME.

"IF YOU WANT A BETTER WORLD, CHAIRMAN MAO WANTS TO GIVE YOU A GIFT."

"BUT I THOUGHT YOU **WERE** A **COMMUNIST**."

"WHAT GAVE YOU THAT IDEA?"

"I GUESS IT WAS WHAT OFFICER PUMPKIN SAID."

"YEAH, BUT I MEAN *EXCUSE ME* BUT WHAT'S THE PROBLEM WITH COMMUNISM?"

"I CAN'T SUPPORT ANY IDEOLOGY THAT'S PREDICATED ON **COLLECTIVISM** OVER PERSONAL INDIVIDUAL AUTONOMY AND FREEDOM..."

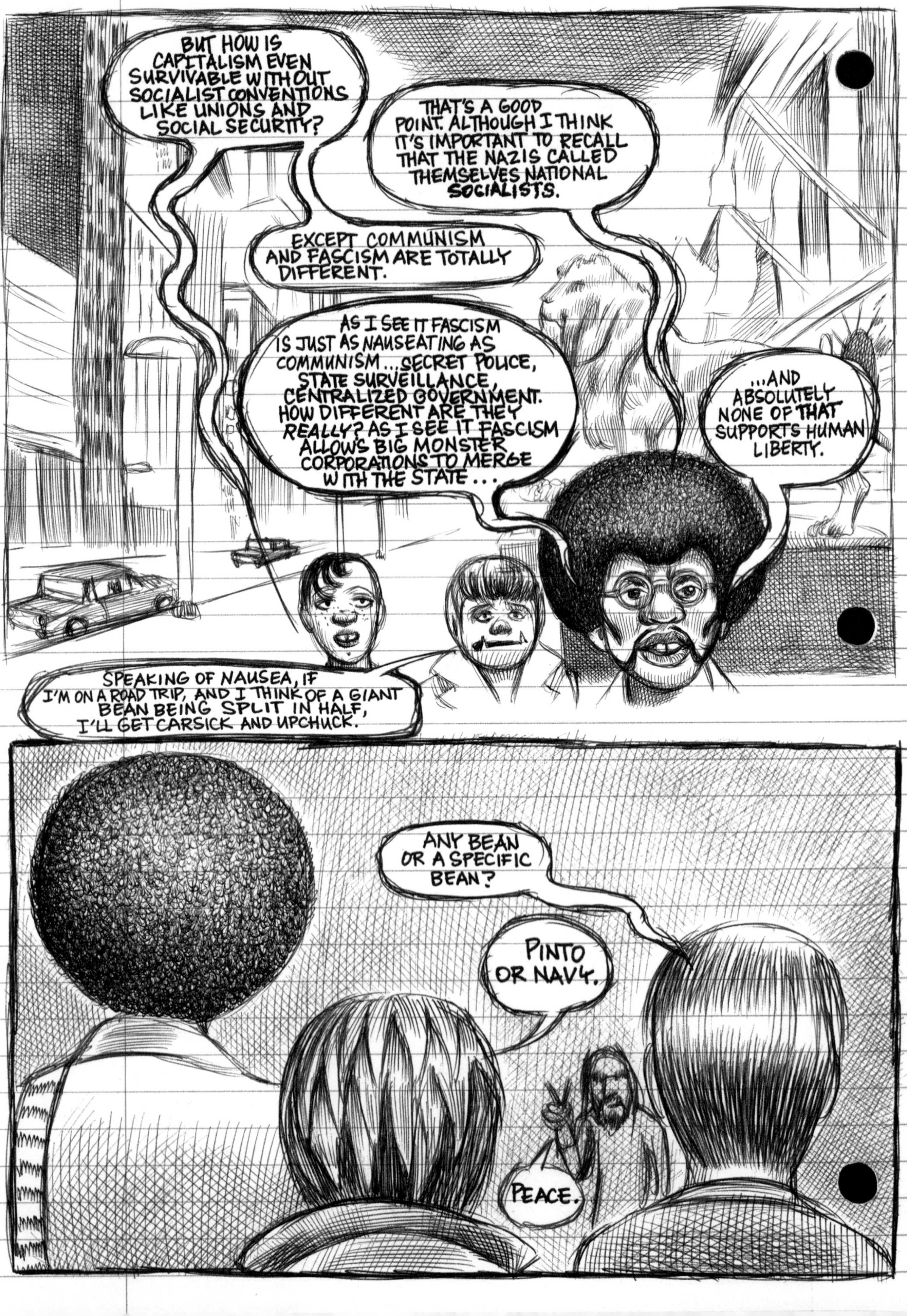
BUT HOW IS CAPITALISM EVEN SURVIVABLE WITHOUT SOCIALIST CONVENTIONS LIKE UNIONS AND SOCIAL SECURITY?
THAT'S A GOOD POINT. ALTHOUGH I THINK IT'S IMPORTANT TO RECALL THAT THE NAZIS CALLED THEMSELVES NATIONAL SOCIALISTS.
EXCEPT COMMUNISM AND FASCISM ARE TOTALLY DIFFERENT.
AS I SEE IT FASCISM IS JUST AS NAUSEATING AS COMMUNISM... SECRET POLICE, STATE SURVEILLANCE, CENTRALIZED GOVERNMENT. HOW DIFFERENT ARE THEY REALLY? AS I SEE IT FASCISM ALLOWS BIG MONSTER CORPORATIONS TO MERGE WITH THE STATE...
...AND ABSOLUTELY NONE OF THAT SUPPORTS HUMAN LIBERTY.
SPEAKING OF NAUSEA, IF I'M ON A ROAD TRIP, AND I THINK OF A GIANT BEAN BEING SPLIT IN HALF, I'LL GET CARSICK AND UPCHUCK.
ANY BEAN OR A SPECIFIC BEAN?
PINTO OR NAVY.
PEACE.

"YOU WILL KNOW THAT THE U.S. IS UNDER ATTACK WHEN THE FORCES AT THE TOP ENGAGE IN THE CENSORSHIP OF AMERICAN'S FREE SPEECH. *NO GOVERNMENT EVER CENSORS LIES.* THEY DO ATTEMPT TO CENSOR THE TRUTH, THOUGH."

"PEACE."

"PEACE."

"IF CENSORSHIP IS WRONG, WHY DID YOU CENSOR KAREN FROM HAVING MAO'S BOOK?"

JEFFREY SIGHED AND SAID THAT COMMUNISM WAS JUST A TOOL THAT 'THE ELITES' WOULD USE TO TRICK US INTO GIVING UP OUR FREEDOM AND BECOMING...

...SLAVES!

GRANT PARK WAS FULL OF HIPPIES. IT KIND OF REMINDED ME OF A GEORGIA O'KEEFE PAINTING.

DUMP THE HUMP

SEND THE TROOPS HOME

WHEN WE GOT TO GRANT PARK THE BRAIN SAW SOME FRIENDS. WHEN ANYBODY SHOT HIM A PEACE SIGN, I NOTICED THAT HE ONLY RAISED HIS POINTER FINGER AND SAID...

"INDIVID- UALISM."

...BUT THE HIPPIE SCENE DIDN'T SEEM LIKE 'INDIVIDUALISM' TO ME. IT *LOOKS* JUST LIKE ANOTHER SCENE THAT WOULDN'T WANT *ME* ANYWAY. **ALTHOUGH** I WILL GIVE THE HIPPIES CREDIT, THEY ARE REALLY SUPER GOOD AT **DECORATING A JEAN JACKET.**

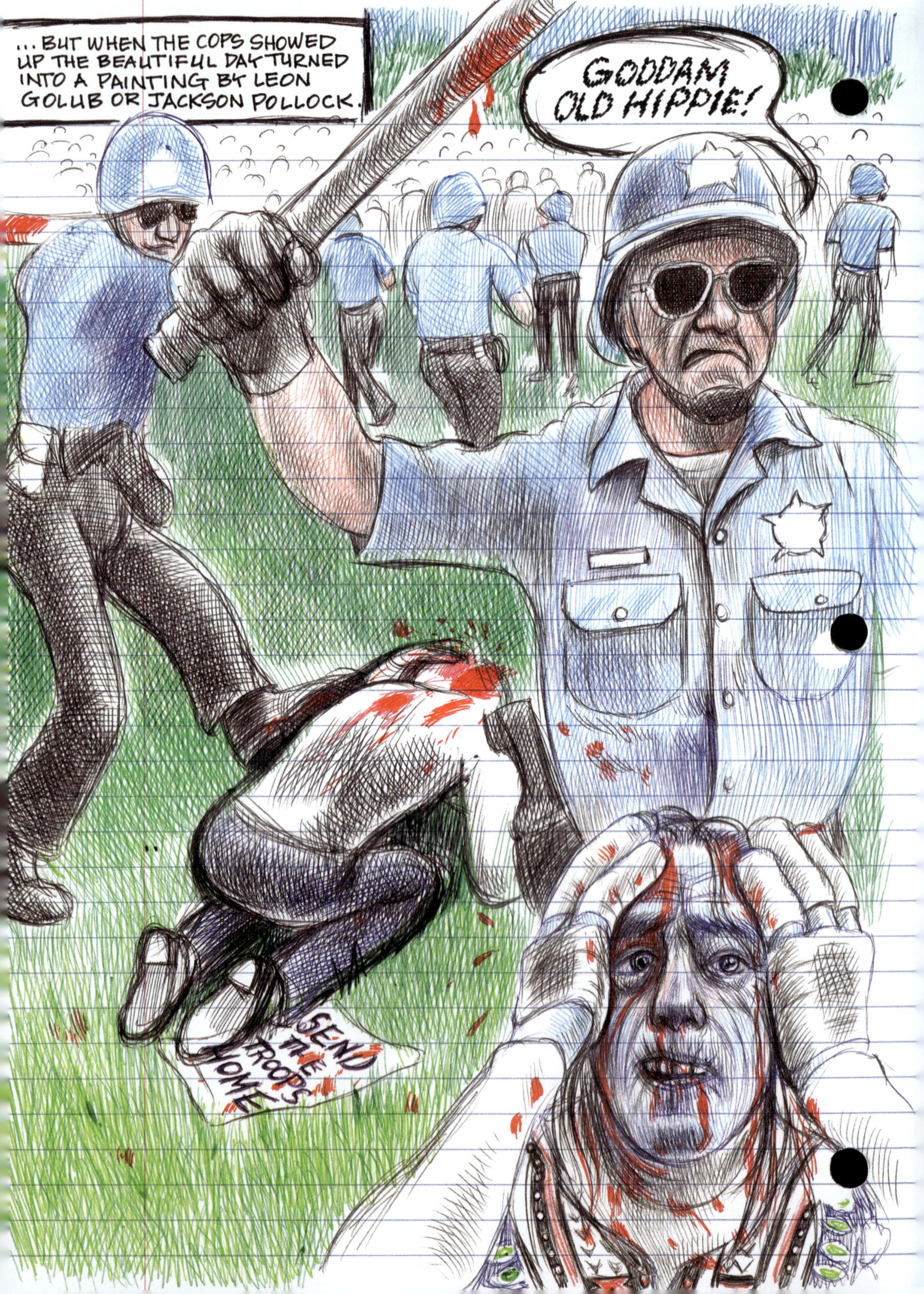

...BUT WHEN THE COPS SHOWED UP THE BEAUTIFUL DAY TURNED INTO A PAINTING BY LEON GOLUB OR JACKSON POLLOCK.
GODDAM OLD HIPPIE!
SEND THE TROOPS HOME

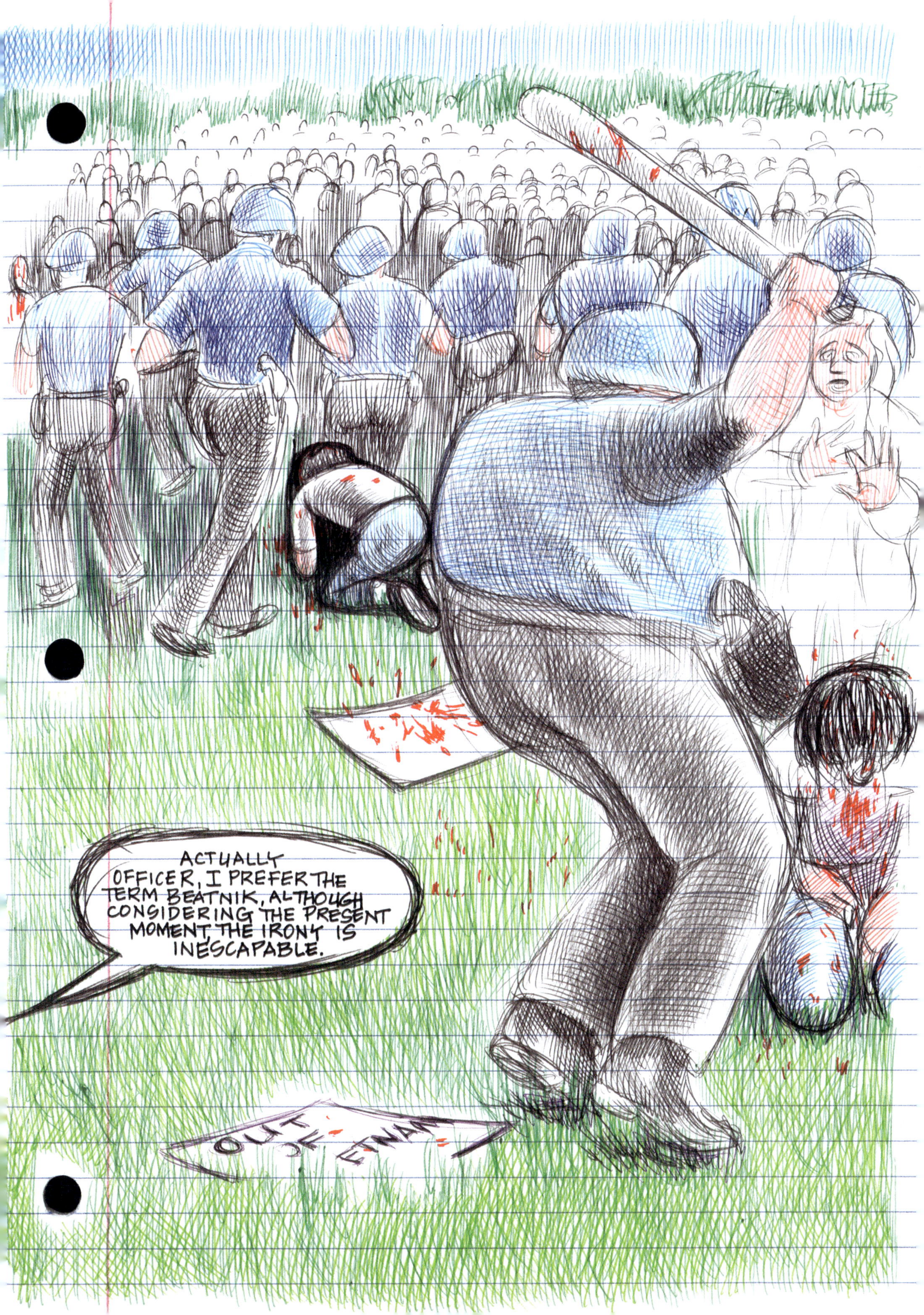
ACTUALLY OFFICER, I PREFER THE TERM BEATNIK, ALTHOUGH CONSIDERING THE PRESENT MOMENT, THE IRONY IS INESCAPABLE.
OUT OF ETNAM

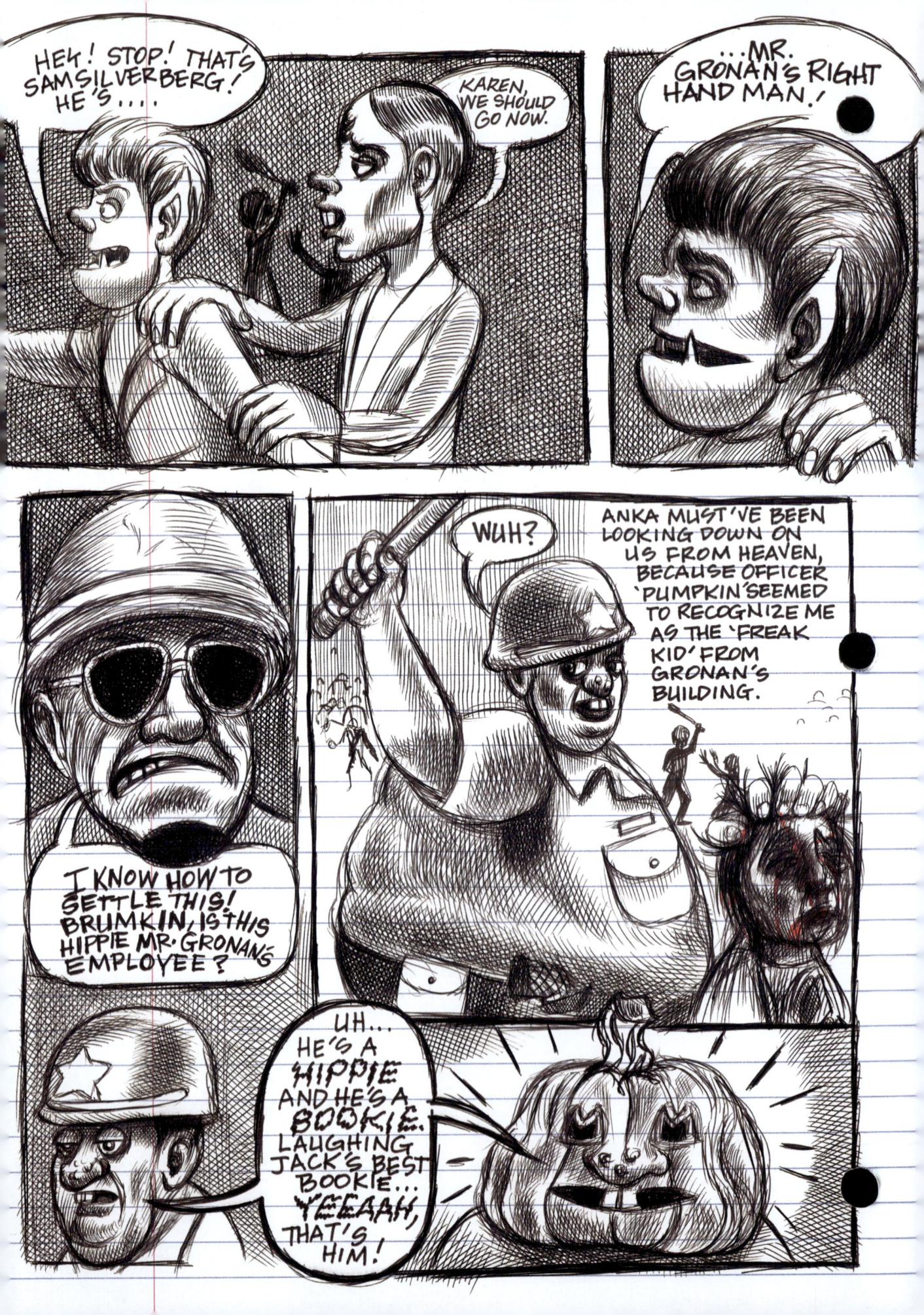

Panel 1: HEY! STOP! THAT'S SAM SILVERBERG! HE'S.... / KAREN, WE SHOULD GO NOW.

Panel 2: ...MR. GRONAN'S RIGHT HAND MAN.!

Panel 3: I KNOW HOW TO SETTLE THIS! BRUMKIN, IS THIS HIPPIE MR. GRONAN'S EMPLOYEE?

Panel 4: WUH? / ANKA MUST'VE BEEN LOOKING DOWN ON US FROM HEAVEN, BECAUSE OFFICER 'PUMPKIN' SEEMED TO RECOGNIZE ME AS THE 'FREAK KID' FROM GRONAN'S BUILDING.

Panel 5: UH... HE'S A *HIPPIE* AND HE'S A *BOOKIE*. LAUGHING JACK'S BEST BOOKIE... YEEAAH, THAT'S HIM!

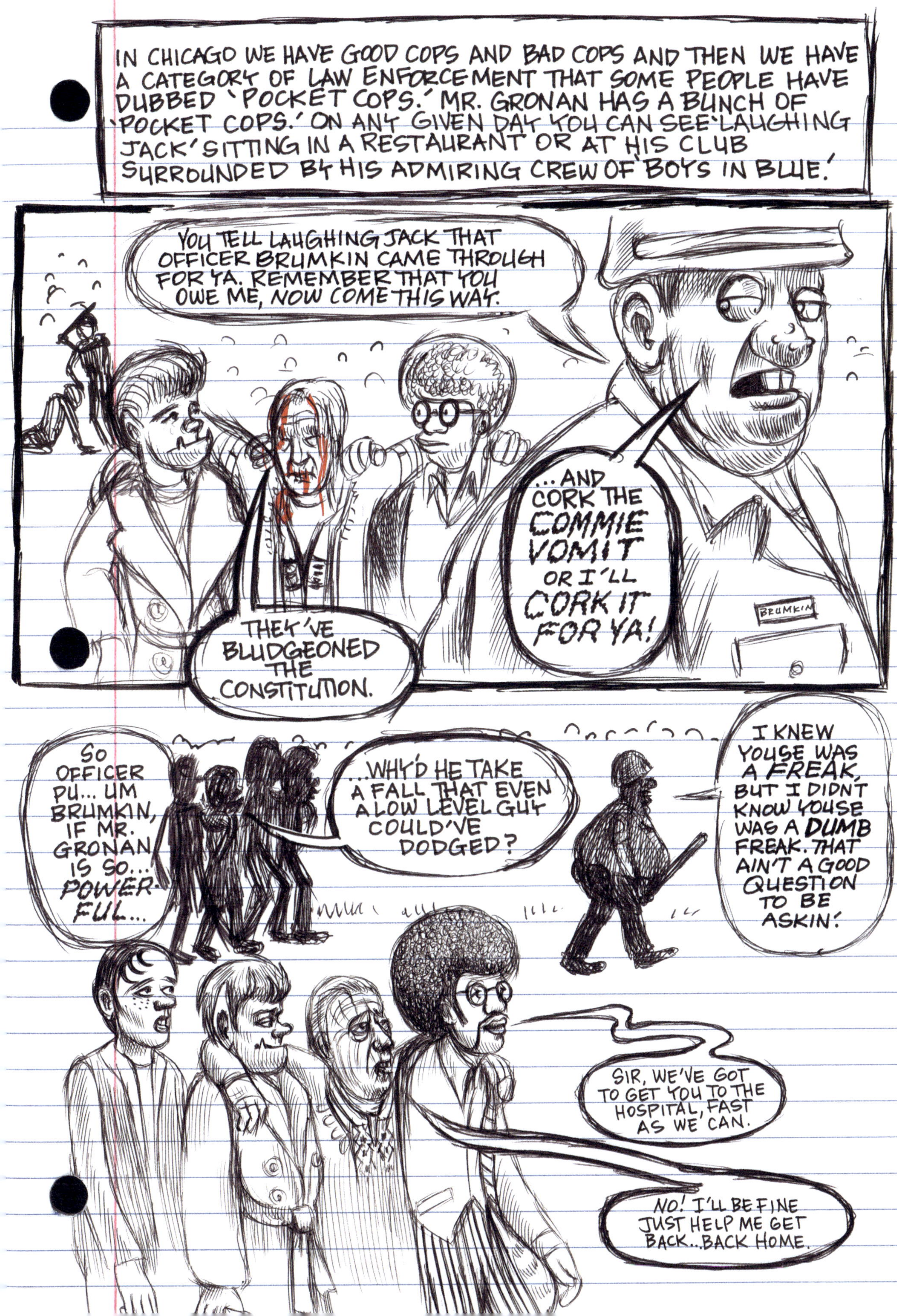
IN CHICAGO WE HAVE GOOD COPS AND BAD COPS AND THEN WE HAVE A CATEGORY OF LAW ENFORCEMENT THAT SOME PEOPLE HAVE DUBBED 'POCKET COPS.' MR. GRONAN HAS A BUNCH OF 'POCKET COPS.' ON ANY GIVEN DAY YOU CAN SEE 'LAUGHING JACK' SITTING IN A RESTAURANT OR AT HIS CLUB SURROUNDED BY HIS ADMIRING CREW OF 'BOYS IN BLUE.'
YOU TELL LAUGHING JACK THAT OFFICER BRUMKIN CAME THROUGH FOR YA. REMEMBER THAT YOU OWE ME, NOW COME THIS WAY.
...AND CORK THE COMMIE VOMIT OR I'LL CORK IT FOR YA!
BRUMKIN
THEY'VE BLUDGEONED THE CONSTITUTION.
SO OFFICER PU... UM BRUMKIN, IF MR. GRONAN IS SO... POWERFUL...
...WHY'D HE TAKE A FALL THAT EVEN A LOW LEVEL GUY COULD'VE DODGED?
I KNEW YOUSE WAS A FREAK, BUT I DIDN'T KNOW YOUSE WAS A DUMB FREAK. THAT AIN'T A GOOD QUESTION TO BE ASKIN'.
SIR, WE'VE GOT TO GET YOU TO THE HOSPITAL, FAST AS WE CAN.
NO! I'LL BE FINE JUST HELP ME GET BACK...BACK HOME.

AFTER THE BRAIN AND SHELLEY HELPED ME GET MR. SILVERBERG HOME, THE BRAIN **SORT OF DISAPPEARED** AND I WALKED SHELLEY HOME. I WAS STUMBLING AROUND BECAUSE I SENSED THAT SHELLEY DIDN'T WANT TO INVITE ME IN TO HER APARTMENT AND THEN I REMEMBERED THE **FORTUNE TELLING FISH**. I TOLD HER I HAD A SMALL PRESENT FOR HER BUT IT WOULD BLOW AWAY IF I DIDN'T GIVE IT TO HER **IN HER APARTMENT**.

THIS WAS FRANKLY THE KIND OF MOVE THAT DRACULA (AND DEEZE) WOULD HAVE BEEN PROUD OF BUT I DESPERATELY WANTED TO SEE WHERE SHELLEY LIVED! HER APARTMENT WAS KIND OF REGULAR AND JUST AS BORING AS OURS BUT HER BEDROOM WAS AS COOL (AND COOLER) THAN I THOUGHT IT WOULD BE.

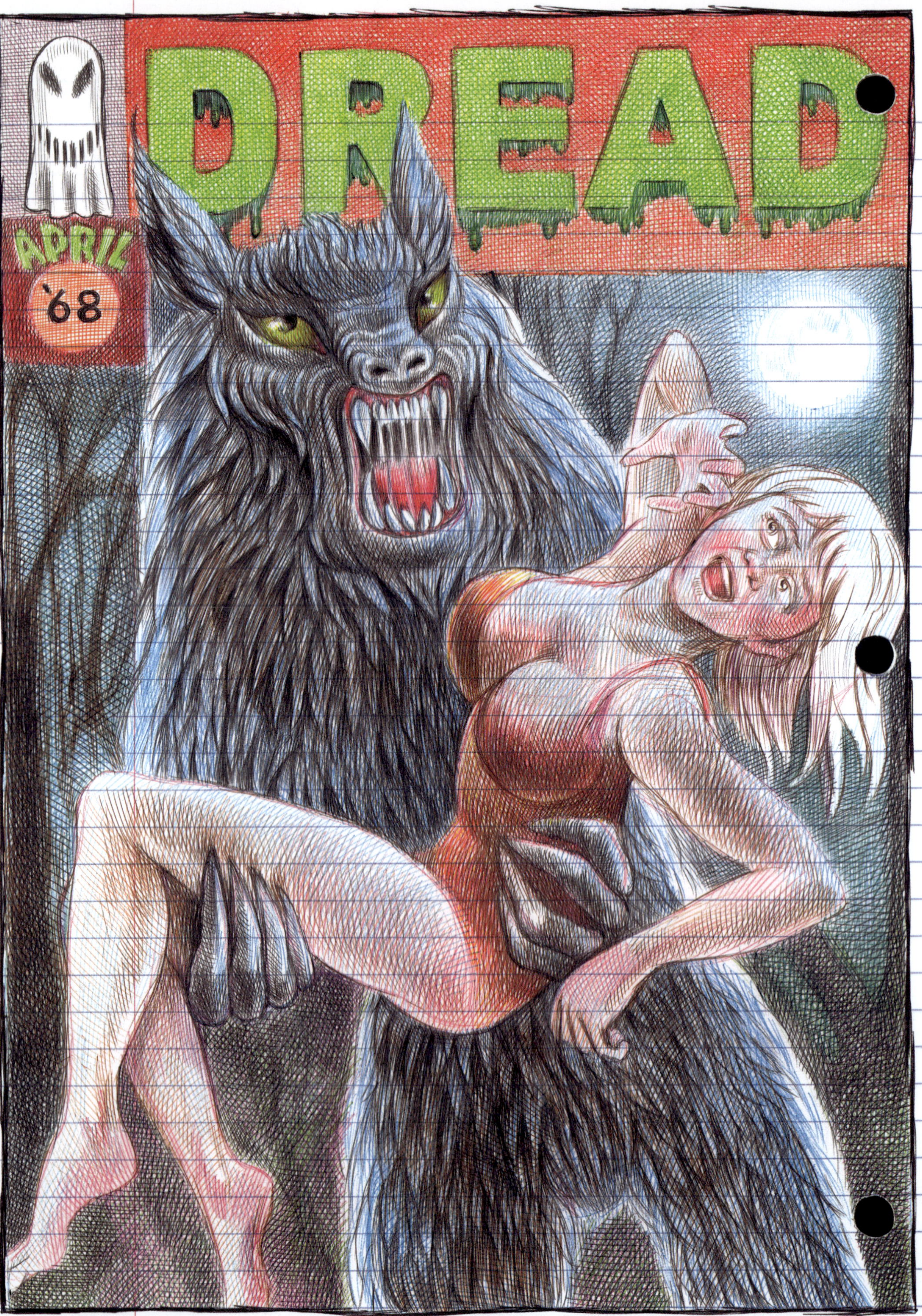
DREAD
APRIL
'68

ONE OF THE COOLEST THINGS IN SHELLEY'S ROOM WAS DRAWINGS OF LEAVES TAPED TO THE WALL. SHELLEY EXPLAINED HOW SHE FINDS THE LEAVES ON THE STREET AND MAKES A DRAWING OF EACH LEAF WHICH INSPIRES A POEM. SHELLEY TAPES THE TITLES OF HER POEMS NEXT TO THE DRAWINGS. SHELLEY LET ME READ A FEW OF HER POEMS. I WILL TELL MORE ABOUT THEM LATER.

"YOUR POETRY IS SUPER GOOD BUT I HAVE TO BE HONEST. I DON'T TOTALLY UNDERSTAND IT."

"WELL, IT'S SUPPOSED TO ELICIT AN EMOTIONAL RESPONSE FROM THE READER."

"IT DEFINITELY DID THAT."

AFTER I READ HER POETRY SHELLEY ASKED TO SEE MY NOTEBOOK.

Panel 1:

"OK, BUT YOU'RE THE FIRST ONE WHO'LL SEE IT."

"I'M HONORED."

"JUST SO YOU KNOW I DRAW MYSELF THE WAY I ACTUALLY *AM* AND NOT THE WAY OTHER PEOPLE SEE ME."

SHELLEY MOVED CLOSE TO ME WHICH MADE ME HAPPY BUT ALSO MADE ME BLUSH.

Panel 2:

"WHO IS THIS LADY WITH THE SWORD?"

"THAT'S A PAINTING OF JUDITH."

"JUDITH? I DON'T KNOW HER STORY."

"JUDITH WAS A PERSON FROM BIBLE TIMES WHOSE CITY WAS THREATENED BY THIS TOUGH GENERAL AND HIS BIG ARMY. GENERAL HOLOFERNES HAD THIS REPUTATION OF BEING UNDEFEATABLE..."

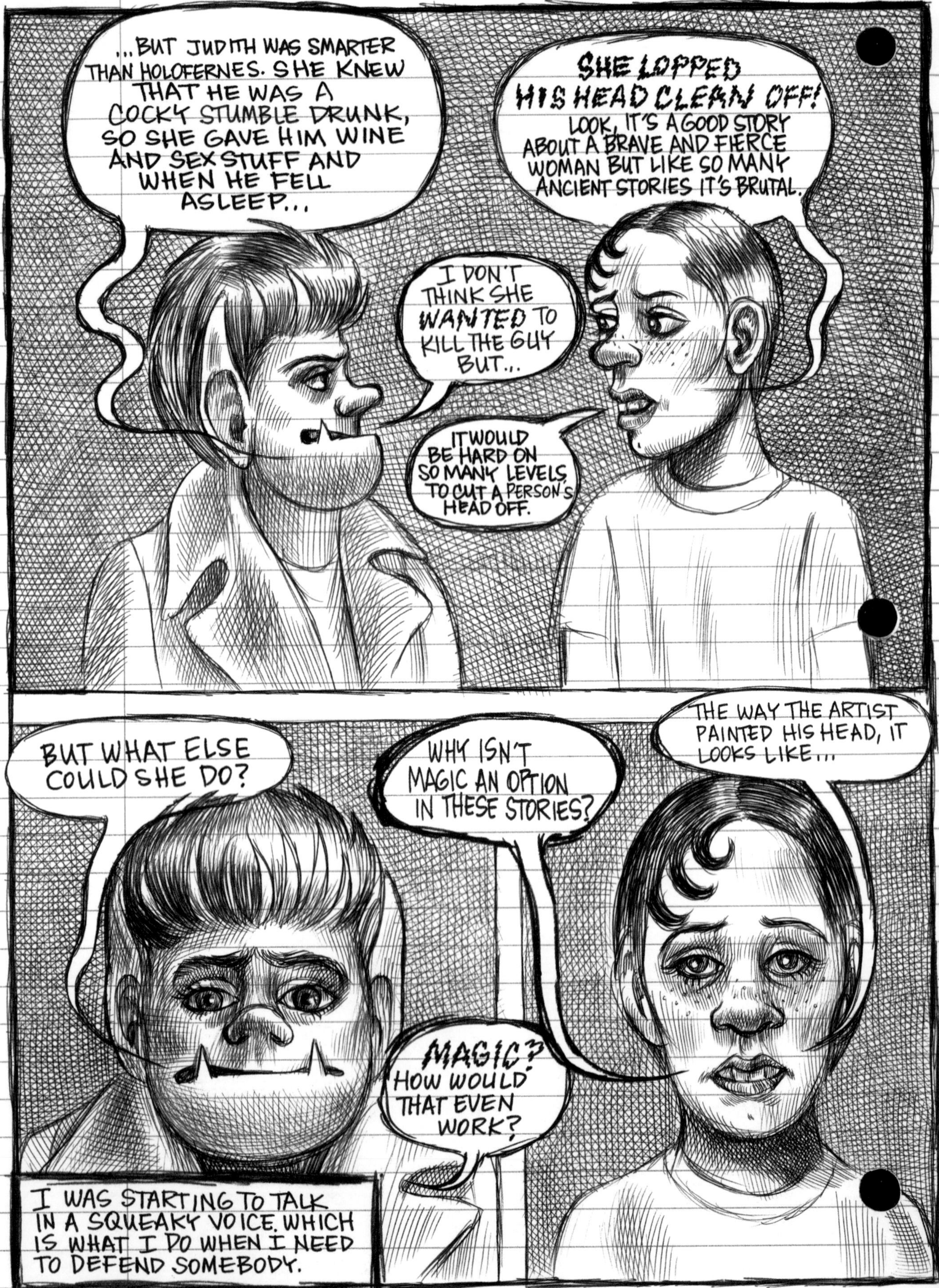
...BUT JUDITH WAS SMARTER THAN HOLOFERNES. SHE KNEW THAT HE WAS A COCKY STUMBLE DRUNK, SO SHE GAVE HIM WINE AND SEX STUFF AND WHEN HE FELL ASLEEP...
SHE LOPPED HIS HEAD CLEAN OFF!
LOOK, IT'S A GOOD STORY ABOUT A BRAVE AND FIERCE WOMAN BUT LIKE SO MANY ANCIENT STORIES IT'S BRUTAL.
I DON'T THINK SHE WANTED TO KILL THE GUY BUT...
IT WOULD BE HARD ON SO MANY LEVELS TO CUT A PERSON'S HEAD OFF.
BUT WHAT ELSE COULD SHE DO?
WHY ISN'T MAGIC AN OPTION IN THESE STORIES?
THE WAY THE ARTIST PAINTED HIS HEAD, IT LOOKS LIKE...
MAGIC? HOW WOULD THAT EVEN WORK?
I WAS STARTING TO TALK IN A SQUEAKY VOICE, WHICH IS WHAT I DO WHEN I NEED TO DEFEND SOMEBODY.

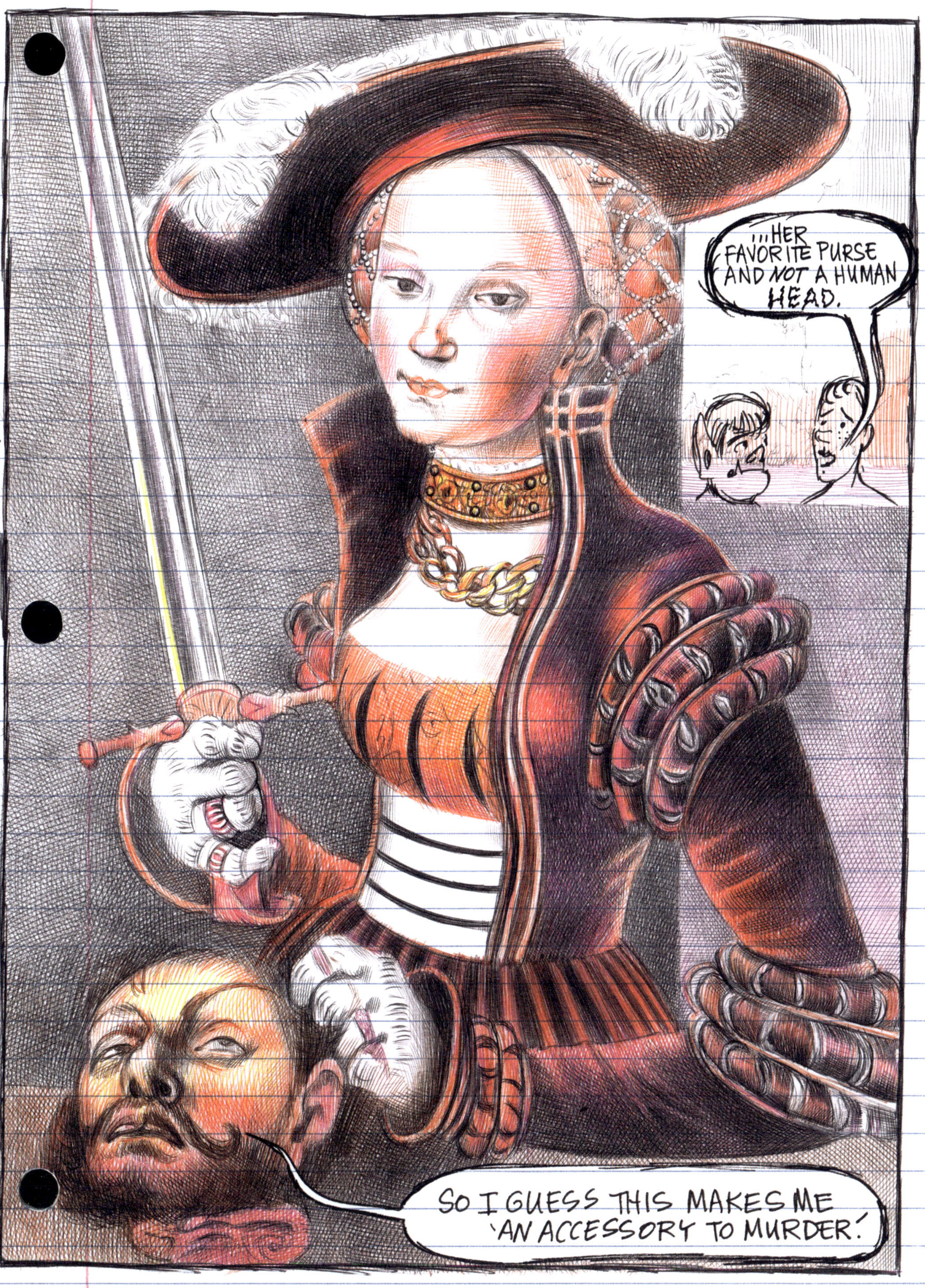

LUCAS CRANACH THE ELDER, JUDITH WITH THE HEAD OF HOLOFERNES 1530

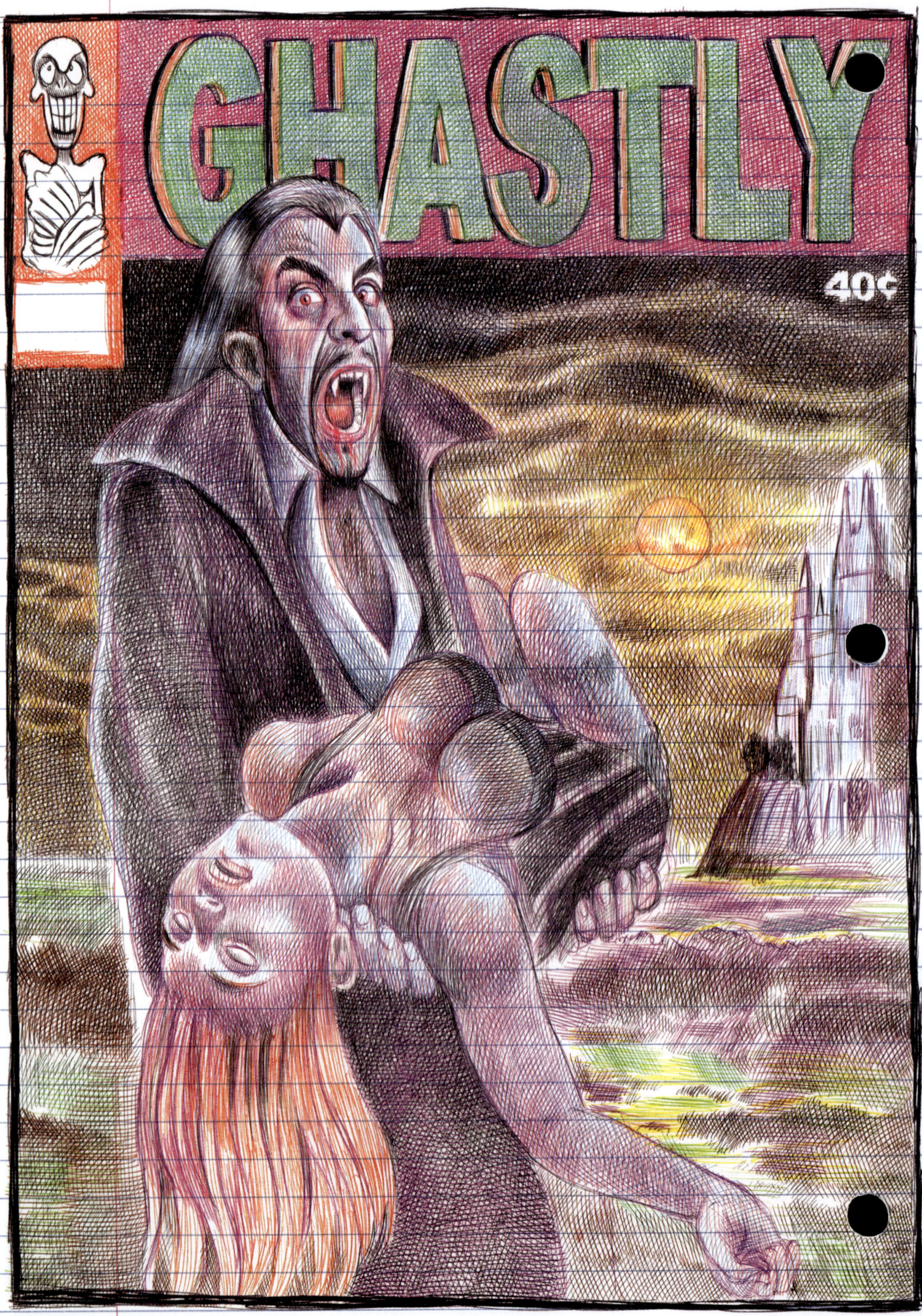
GHASTLY
40¢

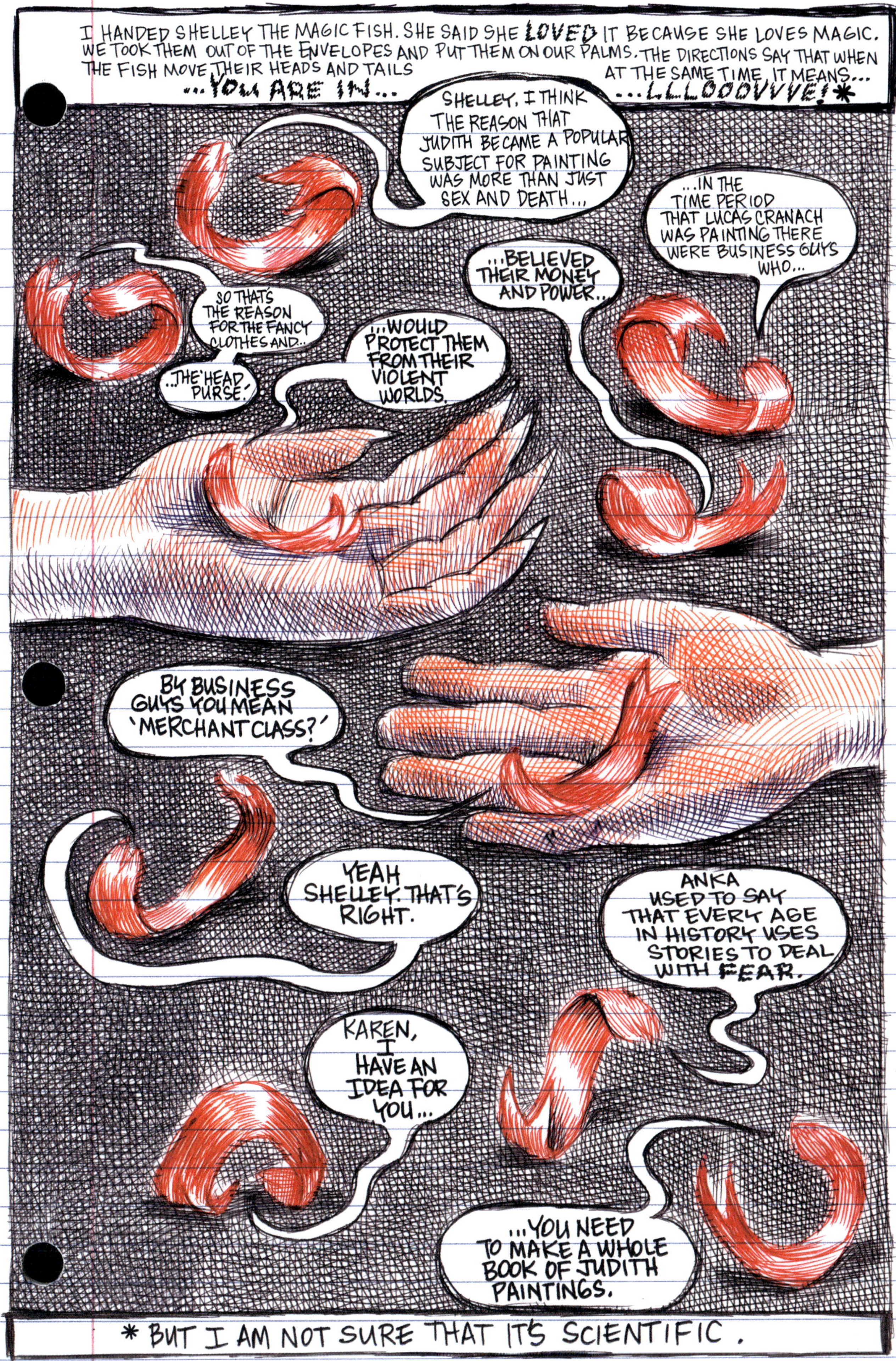
I HANDED SHELLEY THE MAGIC FISH. SHE SAID SHE LOVED IT BECAUSE SHE LOVES MAGIC. WE TOOK THEM OUT OF THE ENVELOPES AND PUT THEM ON OUR PALMS. THE DIRECTIONS SAY THAT WHEN THE FISH MOVE THEIR HEADS AND TAILS AT THE SAME TIME, IT MEANS... ...YOU ARE IN... ...LLLOOOVVVE!*
SHELLEY, I THINK THE REASON THAT JUDITH BECAME A POPULAR SUBJECT FOR PAINTING WAS MORE THAN JUST SEX AND DEATH...,
...IN THE TIME PERIOD THAT LUCAS CRANACH WAS PAINTING THERE WERE BUSINESS GUYS WHO...
...BELIEVED THEIR MONEY AND POWER...
...WOULD PROTECT THEM FROM THEIR VIOLENT WORLDS.
SO THAT'S THE REASON FOR THE FANCY CLOTHES AND...
...THE 'HEAD PURSE.'
BY BUSINESS GUYS YOU MEAN 'MERCHANT CLASS?'
YEAH SHELLEY. THAT'S RIGHT.
ANKA USED TO SAY THAT EVERY AGE IN HISTORY USES STORIES TO DEAL WITH FEAR.
KAREN, I HAVE AN IDEA FOR YOU...
...YOU NEED TO MAKE A WHOLE BOOK OF JUDITH PAINTINGS.
* BUT I AM NOT SURE THAT IT'S SCIENTIFIC.

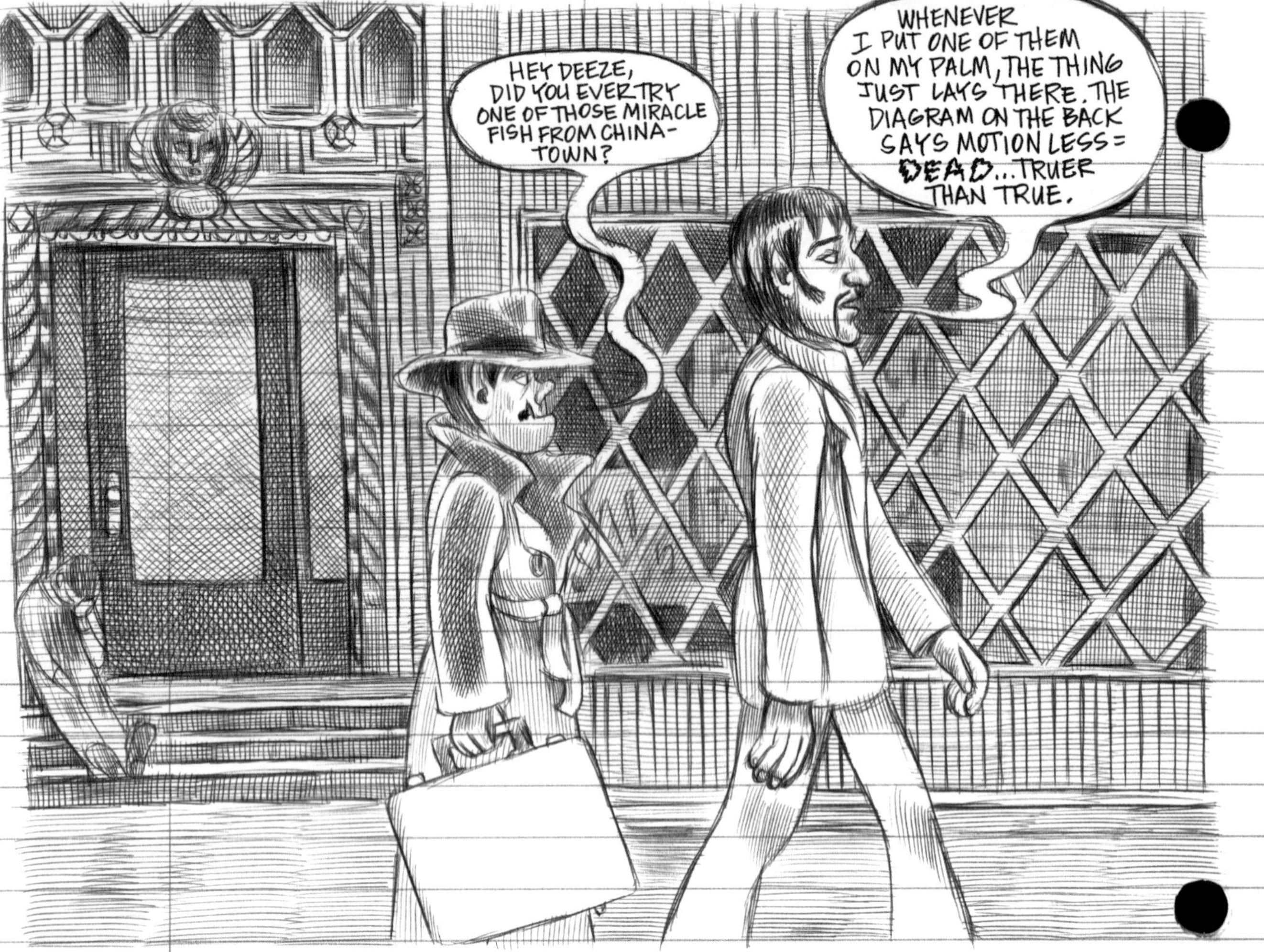
HEY DEEZE, DID YOU EVER TRY ONE OF THOSE MIRACLE FISH FROM CHINA-TOWN?
WHENEVER I PUT ONE OF THEM ON MY PALM, THE THING JUST LAYS THERE. THE DIAGRAM ON THE BACK SAYS MOTION LESS = DEAD... TRUER THAN TRUE.

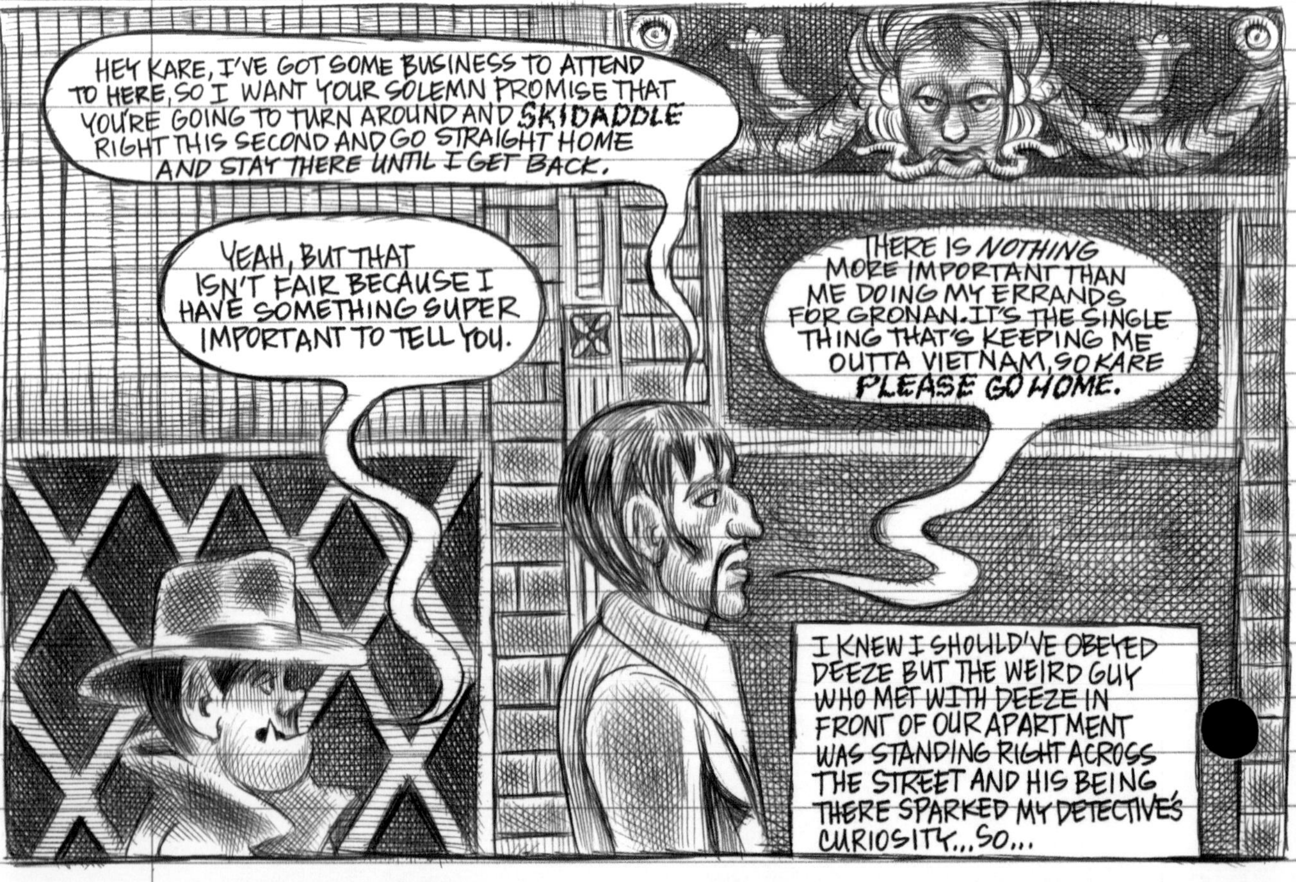
HEY KARE, I'VE GOT SOME BUSINESS TO ATTEND TO HERE, SO I WANT YOUR SOLEMN PROMISE THAT YOU'RE GOING TO TURN AROUND AND SKIDADDLE RIGHT THIS SECOND AND GO STRAIGHT HOME AND STAY THERE UNTIL I GET BACK.
YEAH, BUT THAT ISN'T FAIR BECAUSE I HAVE SOMETHING SUPER IMPORTANT TO TELL YOU.
THERE IS NOTHING MORE IMPORTANT THAN ME DOING MY ERRANDS FOR GRONAN. IT'S THE SINGLE THING THAT'S KEEPING ME OUTTA VIETNAM, SO KARE PLEASE GO HOME.
I KNEW I SHOULD'VE OBEYED DEEZE BUT THE WEIRD GUY WHO MET WITH DEEZE IN FRONT OF OUR APARTMENT WAS STANDING RIGHT ACROSS THE STREET AND HIS BEING THERE SPARKED MY DETECTIVE'S CURIOSITY... SO...

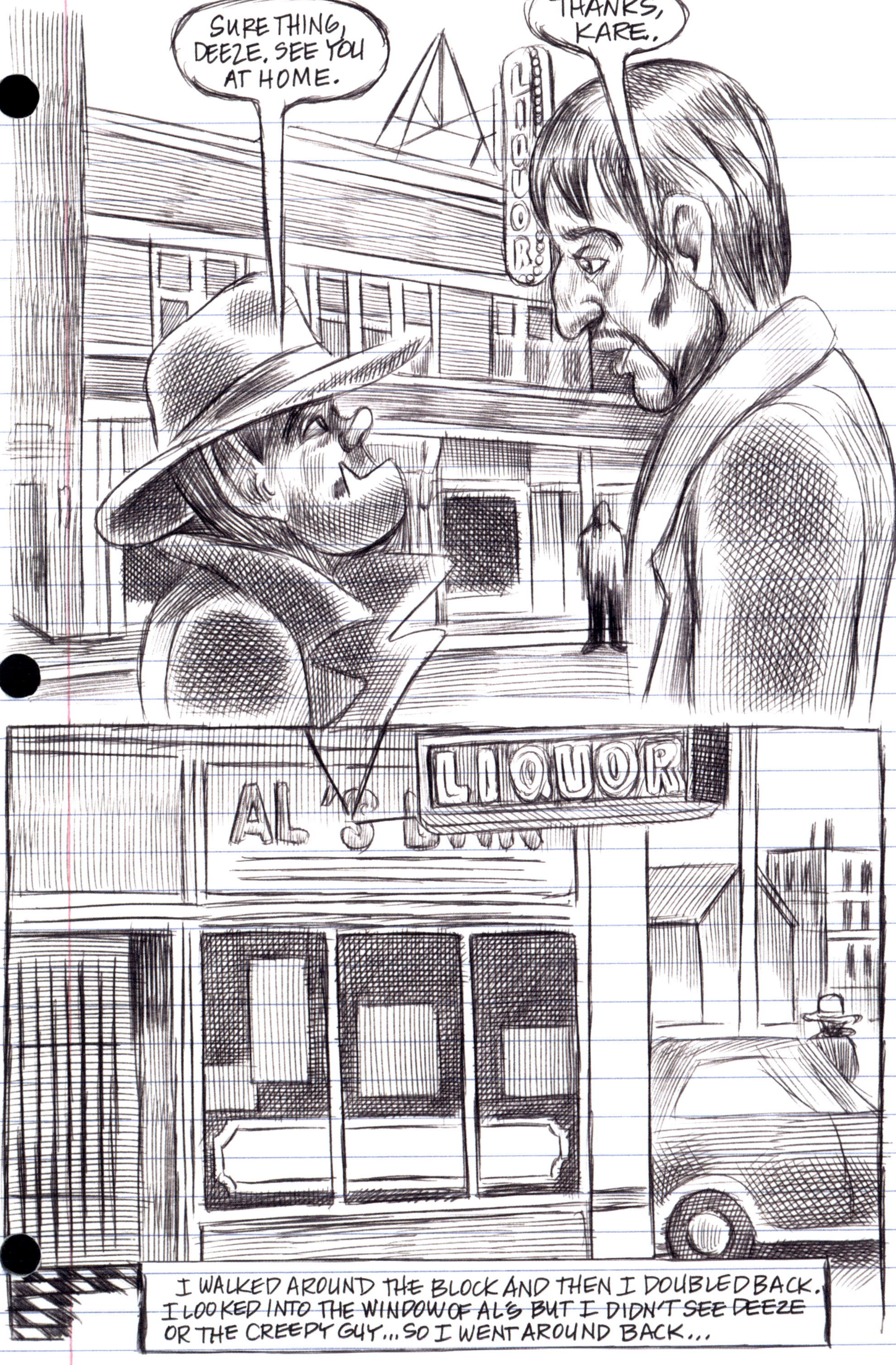
SURE THING, DEEZE. SEE YOU AT HOME.
THANKS, KARE.
LIQUOR
LIQUOR
AL'S
I WALKED AROUND THE BLOCK AND THEN I DOUBLED BACK. I LOOKED INTO THE WINDOW OF AL'S BUT I DIDN'T SEE DEEZE OR THE CREEPY GUY... SO I WENT AROUND BACK...

Panel 1 (narration): I FOLLOWED DEEZE'S VOICE. WHEN I GOT HALF WAY ACROSS THE PARKING LOT I SAW DEEZE AND I REAL QUICK DUCKED DOWN BESIDE A PARKED CAR. I LOOKED THROUGH THE CAR WINDOWS...

Deeze: DIEGO, SON, I THOUGHT YOU WAS AN *ARTIST!*

Diego: AL, I AM AN ARTIST. I'M A SHAKE-DOWN ARTIST AND I'M...

Diego (cont.): ...HERE TO PAINT YOU A PICTURE OF WHAT'S GOING TO HAPPEN TO YOU BECAUSE YOU HAVEN'T PAID LAUGHING JACK WHAT YOU OWE HIM... LET ME SEE... FOR THIS PICTURE...

Diego: ...I'M GOING TO NEED A LOT OF CARMINE RED, CADMIUM RED AND MAYBE EVEN SOME ALIZARIN CRIMSON.

Panel 2:

Al: NO, NO, NO! I'LL PAY! I JUST NEED ONE MORE WEEK IS ALL...

Diego: THIS IS THE SONG YOU SANG LAST WEEK.

Al: ...BUT IT'S TRUE. I'LL HAVE THE MONEY. IN ONE WEEK... REALLY!

Diego: DO YOU HAVE ANY FUCKING IDEA HOW MUCH I HATE WHAT I HAVE TO DO NOW?

Al: NO, PLEASE! I KNEW YOUR DAD AND I KNEW YOU SINCE YOU WAS A KID.

THE SOUND OF DEEZE HITTING AL WAS HORRIBLE. WHEN HE DID IT AL SAID SOMETHING THAT SOUNDED LIKE 'CLARK' AND FOR A MINUTE I THOUGHT HE WAS CALLING CLARK KENT. THEN THE GUY WHO HAD BEEN WAITING FOR DEEZE AT THE FRONT OF THE LIQUOR STORE HANDED DEEZE *A GUN!* THE WAY THEY DID IT - NO WORDS AND VERY SMOOTH - GAVE ME THE FEELING THEY'D DONE THIS LOTS OF TIMES BEFORE.

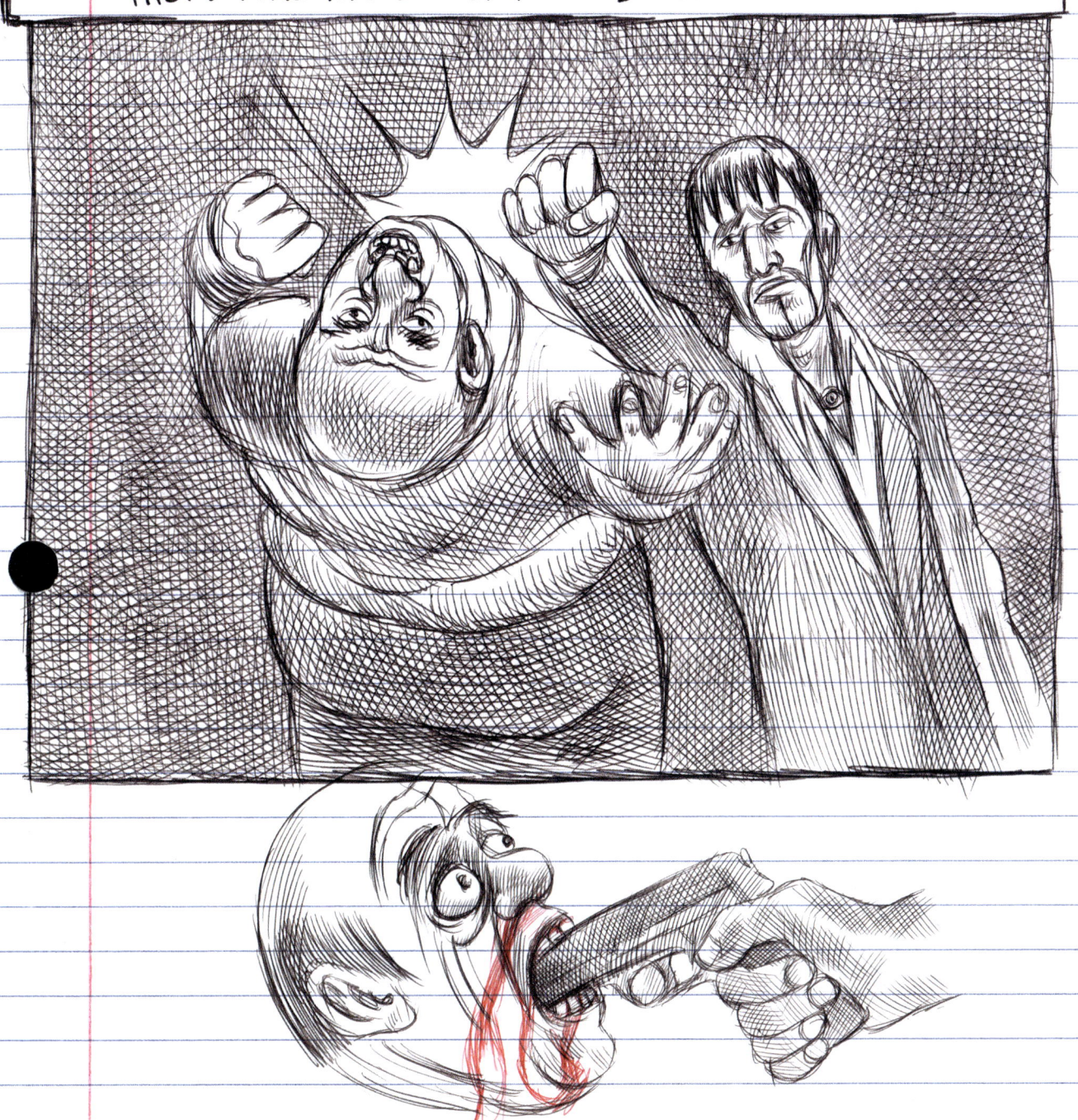

NOW YOU LISTEN TO ME, AL! YOU WILL SELL YOUR WIFE'S JEWELRY. YOU WILL SELL YOUR CAR, HELL, YOU WILL ROB A GAS STATION AS LONG AS IT ISN'T ONE OF GRONAN'S, YOU WILL DO WHATEVER IT TAKES TO GET THE CASH, BECAUSE IN FIVE DAYS I HAVE TO *KILL YOU, AL.* I DON'T WANT TO, BUT I WILL DO IT IF YOU STILL OWE GRONAN!
GOT THAT?

WHEN DEEZE AND THE GUY STARTED WALKING TO THE PARKING LOT I REALLY QUICK SCUTTLED AROUND THE CAR TO A SPOT WHERE DEEZE COULDN'T SEE ME. AS HE PASSED I GOT A LOOK AT DEEZE, HIS FACE WAS LIKE A STONE. FOR A MINUTE IT SEEMED LIKE HE WAS NOT REALLY MY BROTHER, LIKE MAYBE THERE WAS A DEMON IN HIM WHO WAS USING MY BROTHER TO MAKE MORE SUFFERING IN THE WORLD.

OH GOD, OH GOD, OHHH GOD!

I GUESS I WAS CRYING, TOO, BUT I KNEW BETTER THAN TO GO AND HELP AL. IF HE RECOGNIZED ME, HE MIGHT TELL DEEZE OR EVEN THE POLICE. I KNEW I WOULD LIE IF THE POLICE ASKED ME WHAT I SAW.

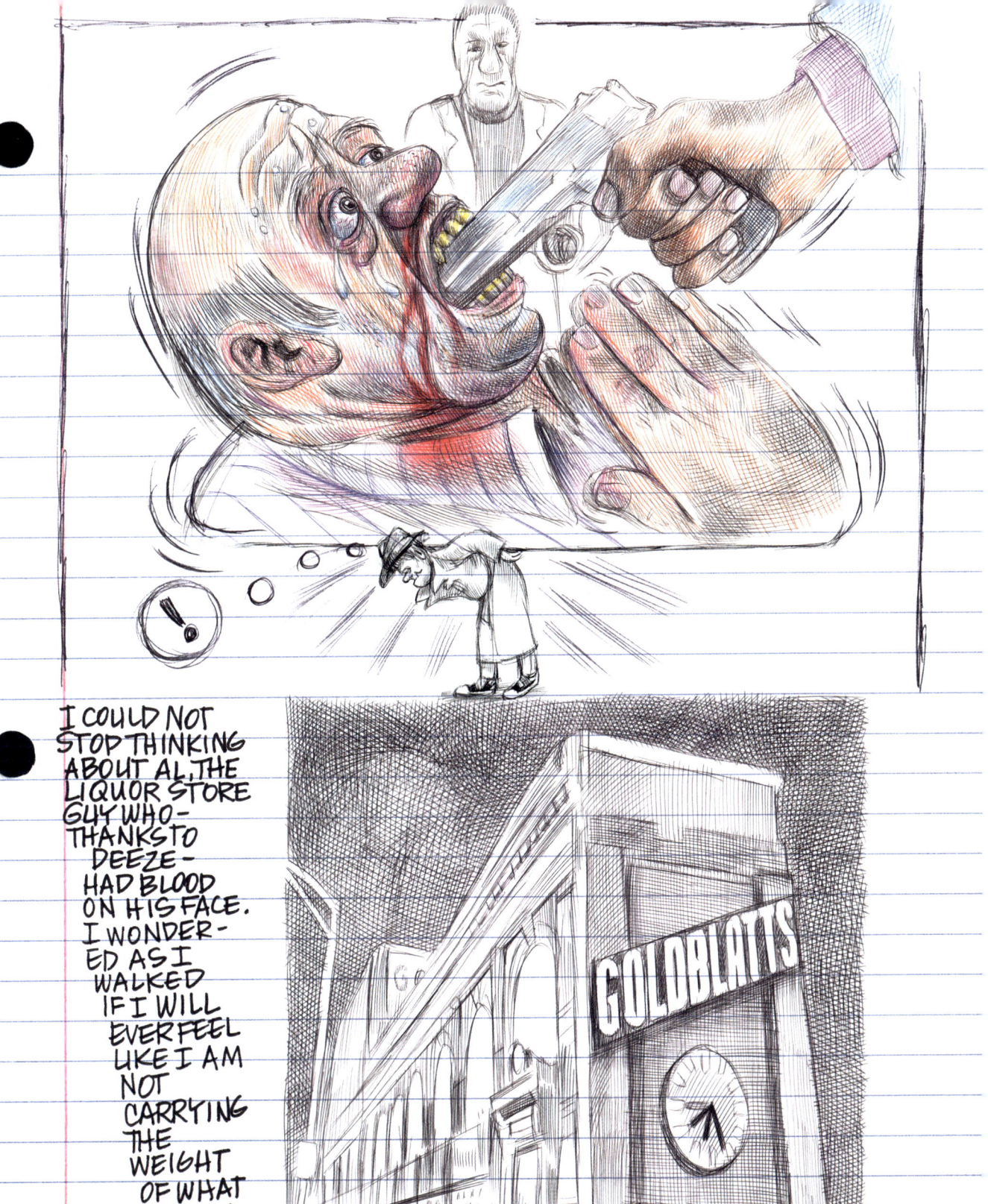

I COULD NOT STOP THINKING ABOUT AL, THE LIQUOR STORE GUY WHO - THANKS TO DEEZE - HAD BLOOD ON HIS FACE. I WONDERED AS I WALKED IF I WILL EVER FEEL LIKE I AM NOT CARRYING THE WEIGHT OF WHAT I SAW.

I FELT SO ALONE AND I NEEDED TO TALK TO SOMEBODY. THERE WAS ONLY ONE PERSON WHO I KNEW WOULD NEVER TELL THE COPS ABOUT DEEZE.

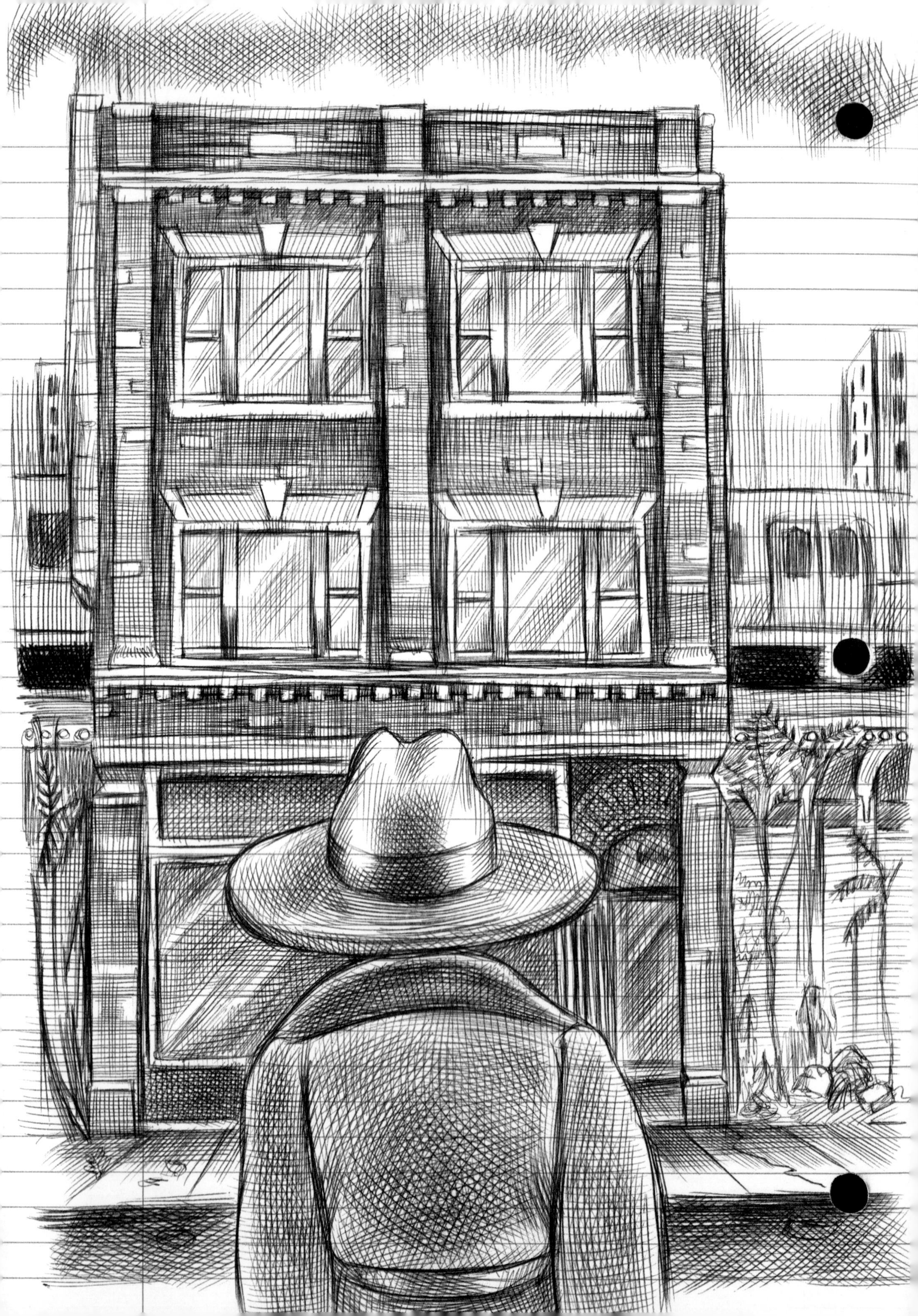

I BUZZED THE BRAIN'S BUZZER BUT WHEN HE ANSWERED THE DOOR HE HESITATED ABOUT LETTING ME COME IN. I GUESS HE COULD SEE HOW UPSET I WAS. PLUS IT WAS UNUSUAL FOR ME TO SHOW UP ON HIS DOORSTEP (I NEVER DID IT BEFORE NOW). ALSO WRITERS **HATE** INTERRUPTIONS.

THE BRAIN'S APARTMENT IS JUST THE WAY YOU'D THINK A WRITER'S HOME WOULD BE. HE HAS TONS OF PICTURES, MAPS AND FAMOUS QUOTES TACKED TO HIS WALLS.

THE BRAIN SAID THAT RAYGUN KNOWS WHEN PEOPLE NEED HIM AND ALSO I PROBABLY SMELL LIKE MY MOM WHO RAYGUN TOTALLY LOVED.

THE BRAIN TOLD ME THAT RAYGUN WAS MY MOM'S 'PSYCHOPOMP.' HE SAID A PSYCHOPOMP HELPS PEOPLE WHO ARE DYING. MAYBE RAYGUN LIKES ME NOW BECAUSE HE SENSES THAT SOMEHOW I AM **DYING**.

JEFFREY 'THE BRAIN' ALVAREZ ISN'T AN ALIEN - IN ANY WAY - BUT HE **LOVES** TO TALK ABOUT ALIENS AND SCIENCE FICTION STUFF AND SINCE WE'RE FRIENDS (KIND OF) I GUESS I LIKE TO TALK ABOUT OTHER SPECIES, TOO...

GHASTLY

45¢

THE LONE SPACE TRAVELER

MUTANT MENACE

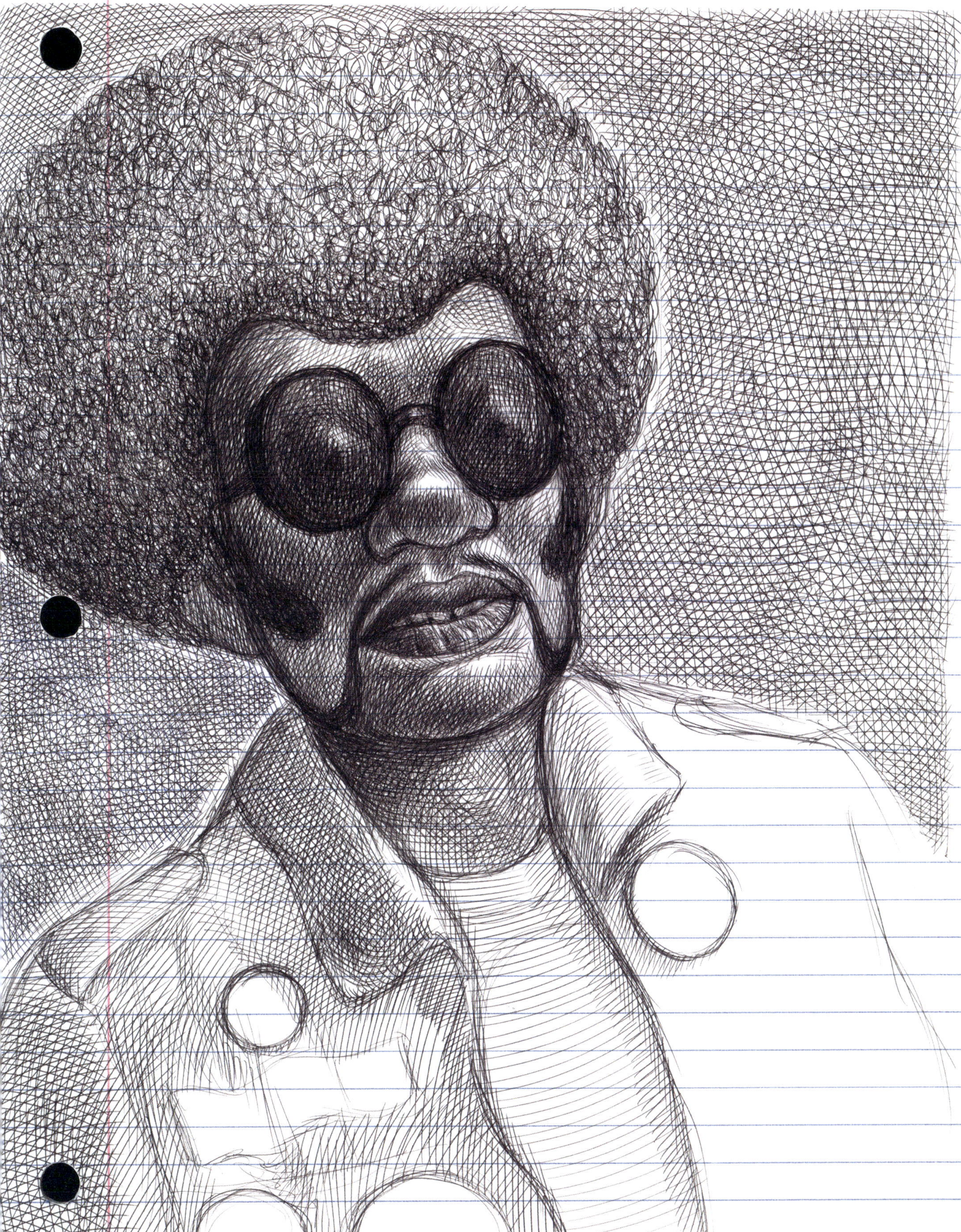

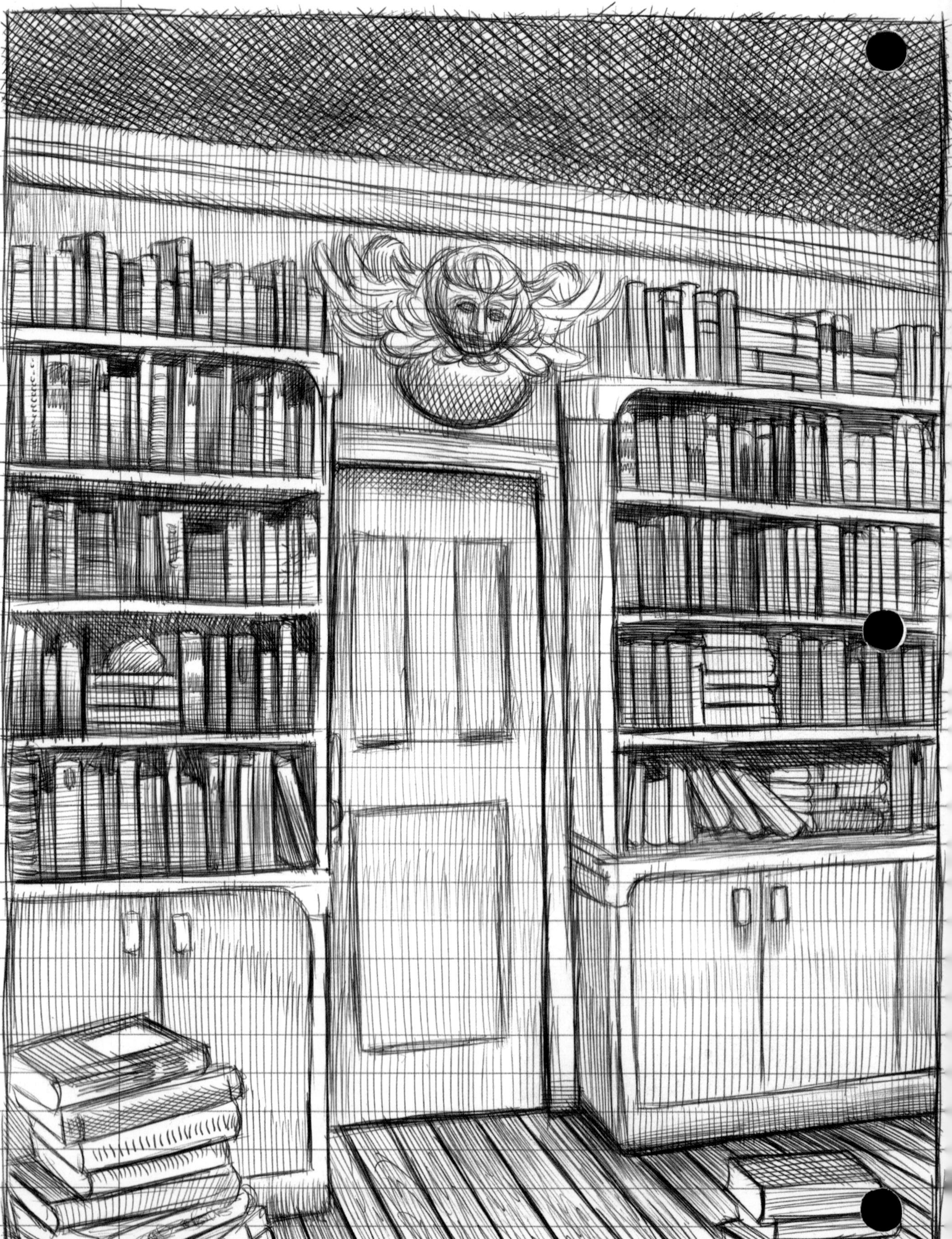

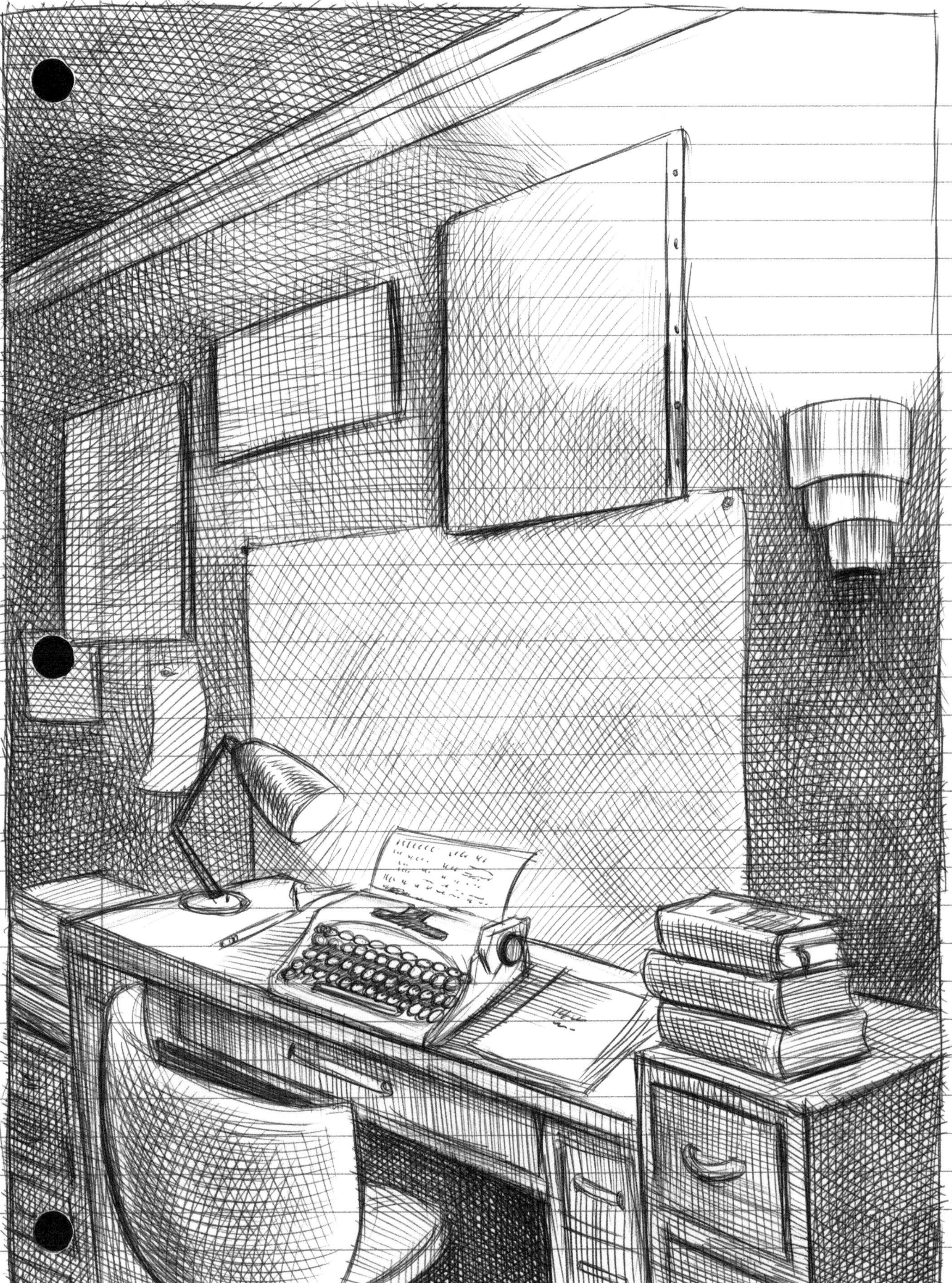

I TOLD THE BRAIN ALL ABOUT WHAT I'D SEEN DEEZE DO AND HE LISTENED TO EVERYTHING WITHOUT COMMENTING. HE PETTED RAYGUN AND WE WAITED FOR THE TRAIN TO PASS.

CLIC CLAAACK CLAAACK CLAAACK CLIC

KAREN, THIS IS WHAT I CAN TELL YOU. YOUR BROTHER IS IN A TOUGH SPOT. HE'S FIGHTING BEING SHIPPED OFF TO NAM. HE'S ENOUGH OF A **LUNKHEAD** THAT IF SOMEBODY COULD TAKE CARE OF YOU, HE MIGHT ACTUALLY GO TO VIETNAM. BUT, AS WE BOTH KNOW, THERE'S NOBODY HE COULD LEAVE YOU WITH.

THEN ANOTHER TRAIN WENT PAST...

CLICCLAAACK   CLICCLAAACK   CLICCLAAACK

I KNOW ABOUT MY FATHER, WHO HATES DEEZE SO MUCH THAT HE'S TRYING TO FORCE DEEZE TO GO TO THE WAR. I ALSO KNOW THAT MRS. GRONAN IS MAKING DEEZE DO OTHER STUFF WHICH IS DANGEROUS BECAUSE MR. GRONAN IS A GANGSTER.

WELL, THAT'S ABOUT THE WHOLE ENCHILADA.

OKAY, BUT WHAT DO I DO ABOUT IT?

THE BRAIN TOLD ME THAT THE BEST I COULD HOPE FOR IS TO LOVE DEEZE BY KEEPING HIS SECRETS AND NOT PUTTING TOO MUCH PRESSURE ON HIM. THE BRAIN SAID THAT WHEN SOMEBODY IS IN A DARK PLACE THE BEST THING YOU CAN DO FOR THEM IS TO ALWAYS TRY TO REMEMBER THEIR BETTER, MOST BEAUTIFUL AND KINDEST SELVES.

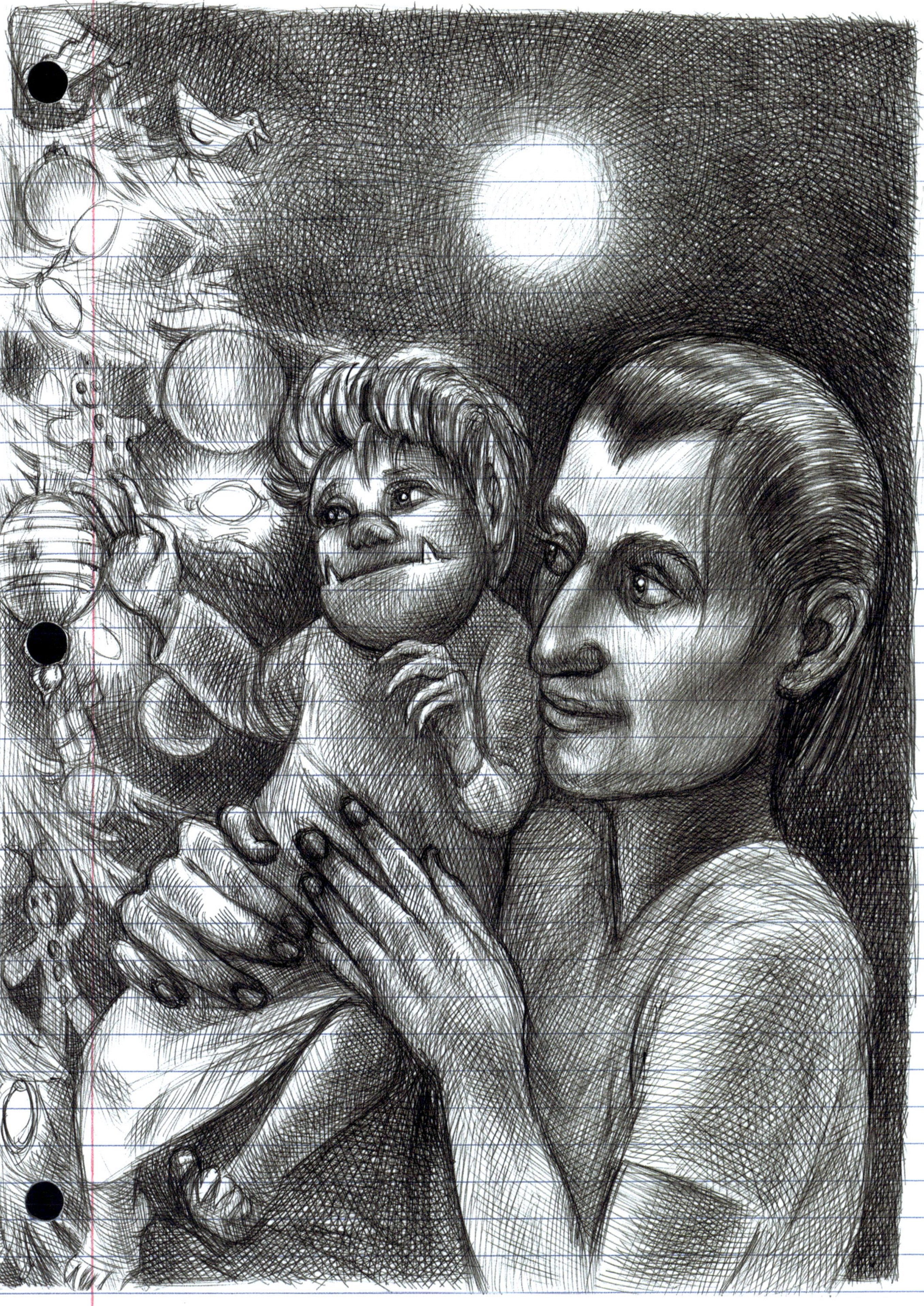

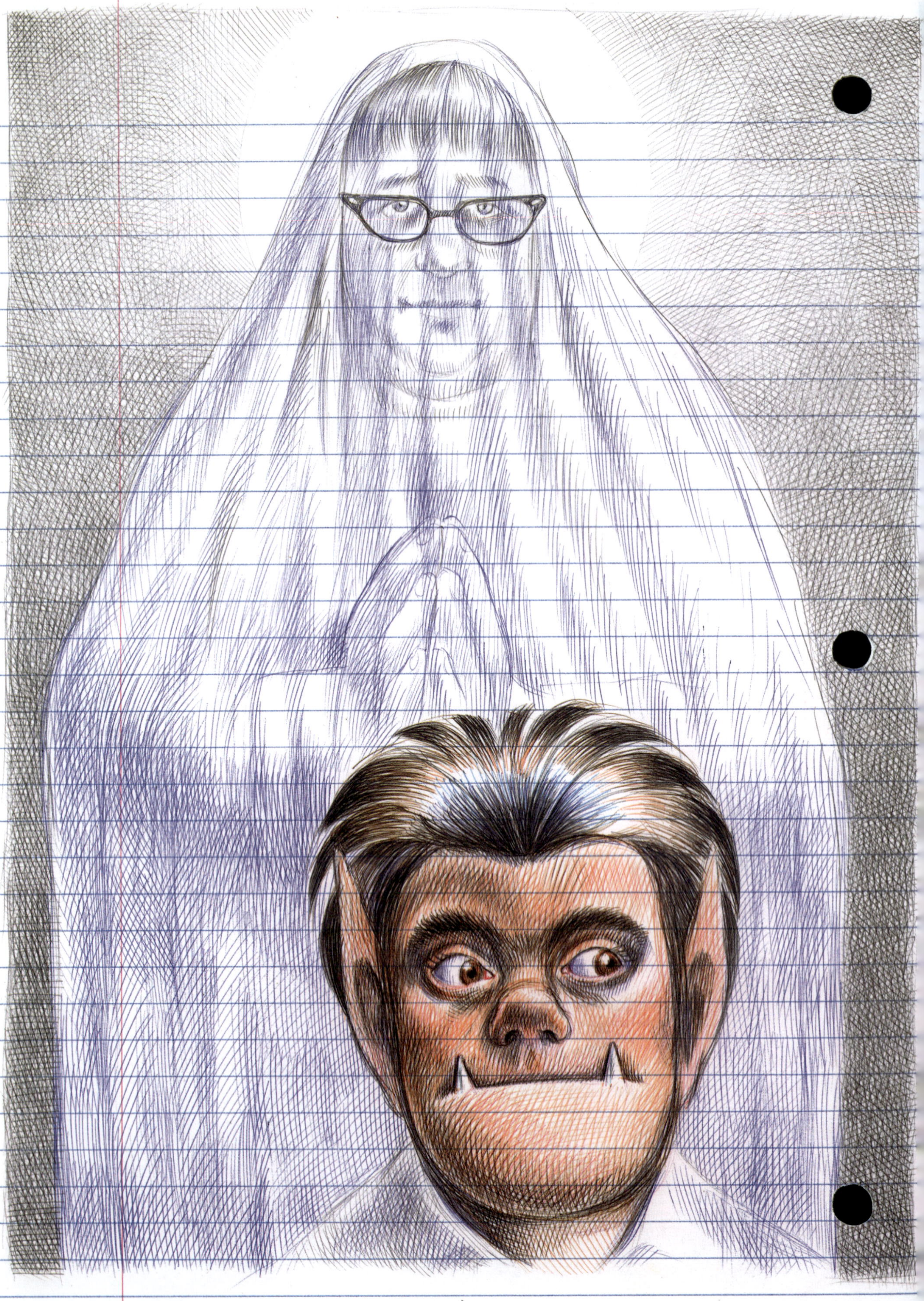

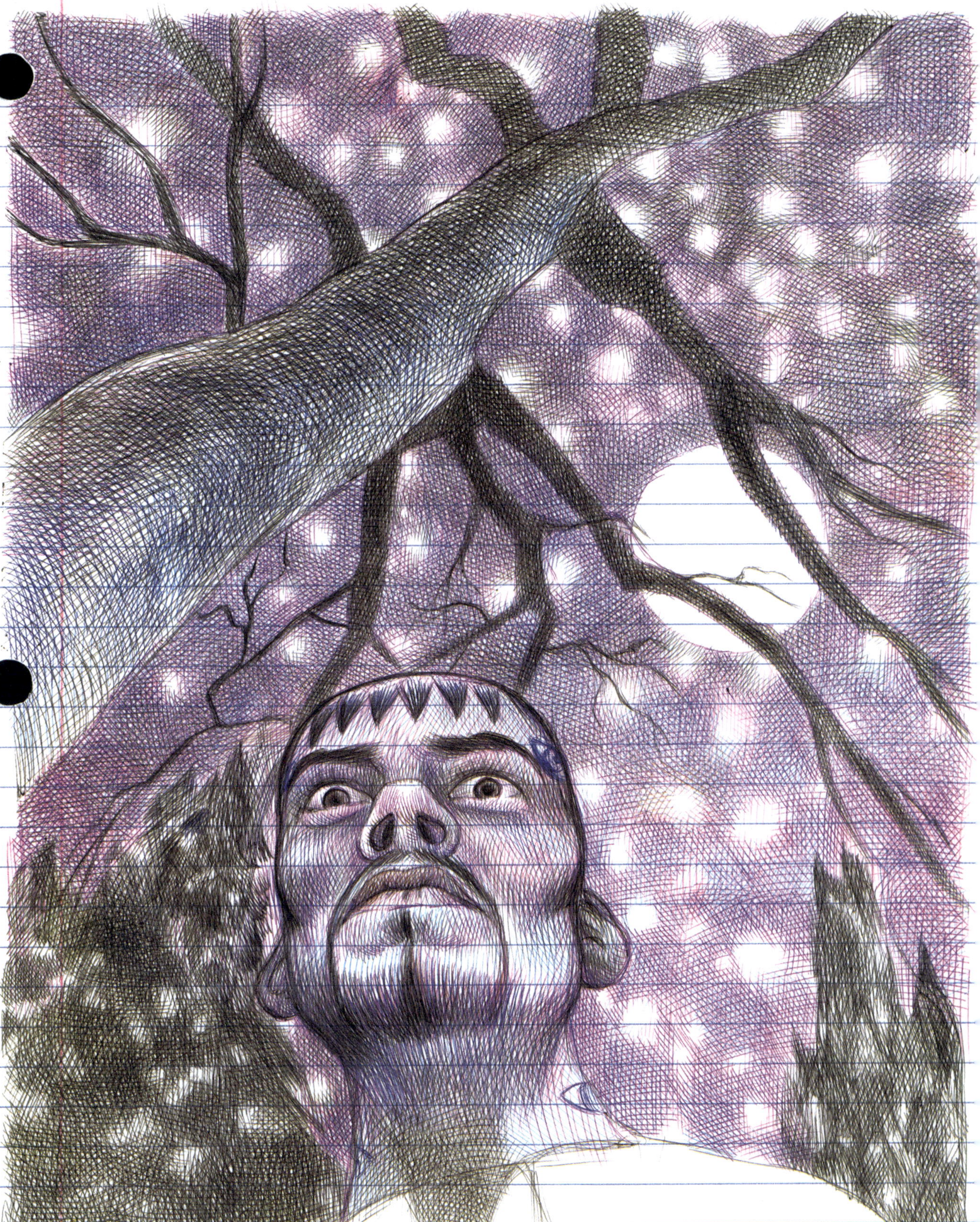

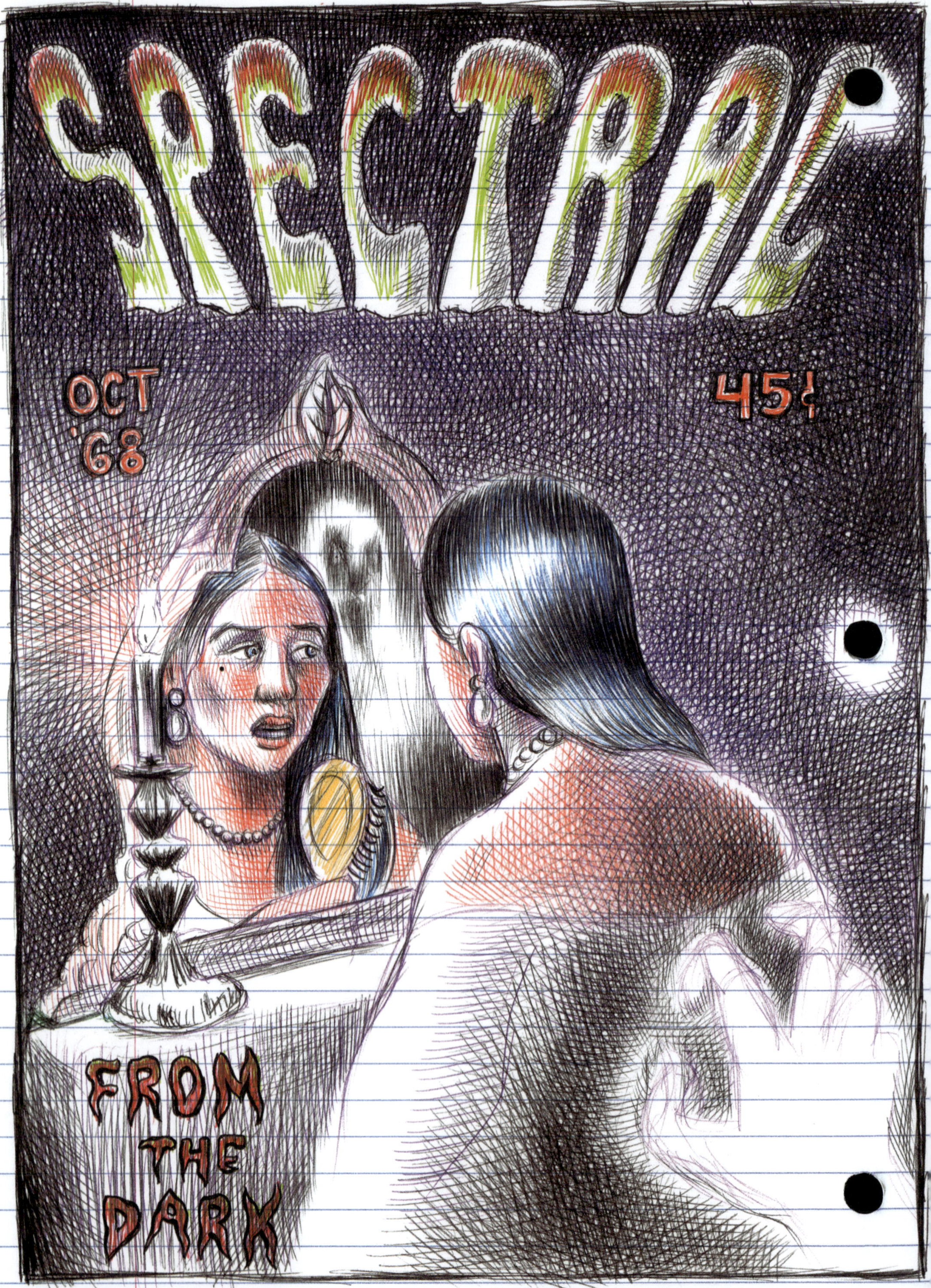
SPECTRAL
OCT '68
45¢
FROM THE DARK

"THE BRAIN SAID HE WOULD WALK ME HOME AND WHILE HE PUT HIS RABBIT INTO A CAGE I THOUGHT ABOUT HOW EVERYONE IN MY FAMILY (EXCEPT ME AND DEEZE) IS NOW INVISIBLE AND ALSO HAVE KIND OF BAD OPINIONS OF DEEZE. THAT MADE ME THINK OF MY FRIEND SANDY...

DEEZE CALLS OUR DAD 'THE INVISIBLE MAN.'

...WHO I HAVEN'T SEEN FOR A WHILE. AND I DECIDED TO ASK THE BRAIN FOR HIS HELP.

HEY, UM DO YOU THINK YOU COULD WALK ME TO MY FRIEND SANDY'S PLACE? I'M SORT OF WORRIED ABOUT HER..

NO PROBLEM, KAREN.

I COULDN'T UNDERSTAND WHY I HAD TO WALK *BEHIND* 'THE BRAIN' BUT THEN I THOUGHT ABOUT IT AND REALIZED THAT THE BRAIN CAN'T WALK NEXT TO ME AND HE CAN'T *LOOK* LIKE HE'S FOLLOWING ME, BECAUSE THIS IS THE WORLD WE LIVE IN... *UGGGHH!*

Panel 2: I WENT INTO ABE'S AND BOUGHT CANDY.

ABE'S LIQUORS

Panel 4: ...AND AS ALWAYS NOBODY WAS HOME AT SANDY'S APARTMENT

KNOCK KNOCK KNOCK

Panel 6: SANDY CALLED 'CANDY BARS' 'KINDY BARS.' AFTER LISTENING WITH MY EAR TO THE DOOR (AND HEARING NOTHING) I LEFT THE CANDY NEXT TO THE DOOR AND WE LEFT.

Panel 7:
— PARDON ME, MA'AM BUT...
— WHAT'S THE STORY ON THE FAMILY THAT LIVES OVER THE STORE?
— MOVED.

Panel 1: SO SANDY MOVED, WELL THAT MAKES SENSE BUT I WISH SHE'D SAID—

Panel 2: (silent, close-up of eyes)

Panel 3: SANDY!? YOU SAID... WAIT WE CAN'T BE TALKIN ABOUT THE SAME KID...

Panel 4: A KID THAT MY MOM WOULD'VE DESCRIBED AS NO BIGGER THAN A MINUTE... BLONDE.
DEAR GOD!

Panel 5: THAT'S HER... ABE! I'M TAKIN A CIG. BREAK.

Panel 6: YOU WANT ONE KID? I GOT A FULL PACK.
NAW.

Panel 7: ABE'S
WELL AS YOU RECALL, SANDY WAS ALWAYS HUNGRY WE MET WHEN...

Panel 8: ...I CAUGHT HER STEALIN'...
STOP THIEF!
I DIDN'T DO IT!

Panel 9: YOU CALLIN' THE COPS?
WHEN SHE LIFTED HER SHIRT SHE WAS BONES IS ALL SHE WAS...

Panel 10: DID YOU CALL THE POLICE ON HER PARENTS?
SUDDENLY THE LADY GROWLED HER WORDS.

Panel 11: NO, THOSE TWO WEREN'T PARENTS. AND AS FOR CALLING THE POLICE... WHAT? SO SANDY GOES INTO THE FOSTER HOMES?

"...OR SHOULD I SAY FOSTER *HELL*... A GOOD PLACE TO DESTROY A KID, SOMEONE THERE TO BEAT EM, FIDDLE WITH EM, I KNOW CUZ I WAS IN THOSE 'HOMES.' SOME ARE OK, BUT A LOT AIN'T... NO I WAS FEEDING SANDY AND I WAS JUST ABOUT TO BRING HER HOME..."

"...WHEN I GOT INTO A BAD CAR ACCIDENT. MY HEAD WAS HURT..."

"...GOT A SCAR UP HERE... WOKE UP LIKE I'D BEEN ASLEEP..."

WHILE SHE TALKED SHE CASUALLY SHOWED ME WHAT LOOKED LIKE CIGARETT BURNS ON THE BACKS OF HER UPPER ARMS....

"...FOR AN HOUR... BUT THE NURSE SAYS, 'NO HONEY, YOU BEEN OUT OF IT FOR WEEKS... I RACE BACK HERE RUN UP..."

"...THOSE STAIRS... AND I FOUND HER THERE CURLED UP IN A CLOSET =SNIFF= POOR LITTLE GIRL.

OH GOD NO!

"I FEEL SO TERRIBLE... IF I'D HAVE REALIZED HOW BAD IT WAS FOR HER..."

"OH HONEY THAT'S THE WEIRD THING... ALL OF THIS HAPPENED YEARS AGO... SO YOU SEE..."

MUST'VE BEEN PRETTY RECENT—THAT MOVE—MY FRIEND SANDY WAS LIVING UP THERE TWO WEEKS AGO.

THERE IS NO WAY IT'S THE SAME KID... I HAFTA GO BACK TO WORK.

WITHOUT ANOTHER WORD, THE LADY WENT BACK INTO THE LIQUOR STORE AND ME AND THE BRAIN STARTED WALKING TOWARDS MY HOME.

KAREN, I'M SORRY THAT WE DIDN'T SOLVE THE MYSTERY SURROUNDING YOUR FRIEND.

THAT'S OK. THANKS ANYWAY. I JUST KIND OF FEEL STUPID. I KNOW IT'S IMPOSSIBLE THAT SANDY IS A GHOST.

THERE ARE MORE THINGS IN HEAVEN AND EARTH, HORATIO, THAN ARE DREAMT OF IN YOUR PHILOSOPHY.

THERE WAS A WEIRD SILENCE AFTER THE BRAIN SAID THAT BECAUSE MY NAME ISN'T HORATIO AND ALSO I WAS THINKING ABOUT HOW 'HORATIO' WOULD BE A GOOD NAME FOR A CARTOON HIPPO.

AS I'M SURE YOU KNOW THAT'S A LINE FROM THE FIRST ACT OF THE PLAY 'HAMLET'. I THINK YOU TAKE MY MEANING THAT MUCH MORE IS POSSIBLE THAN MOST PEOPLE WANT TO ALLOW THEMSELVES TO BELIEVE...

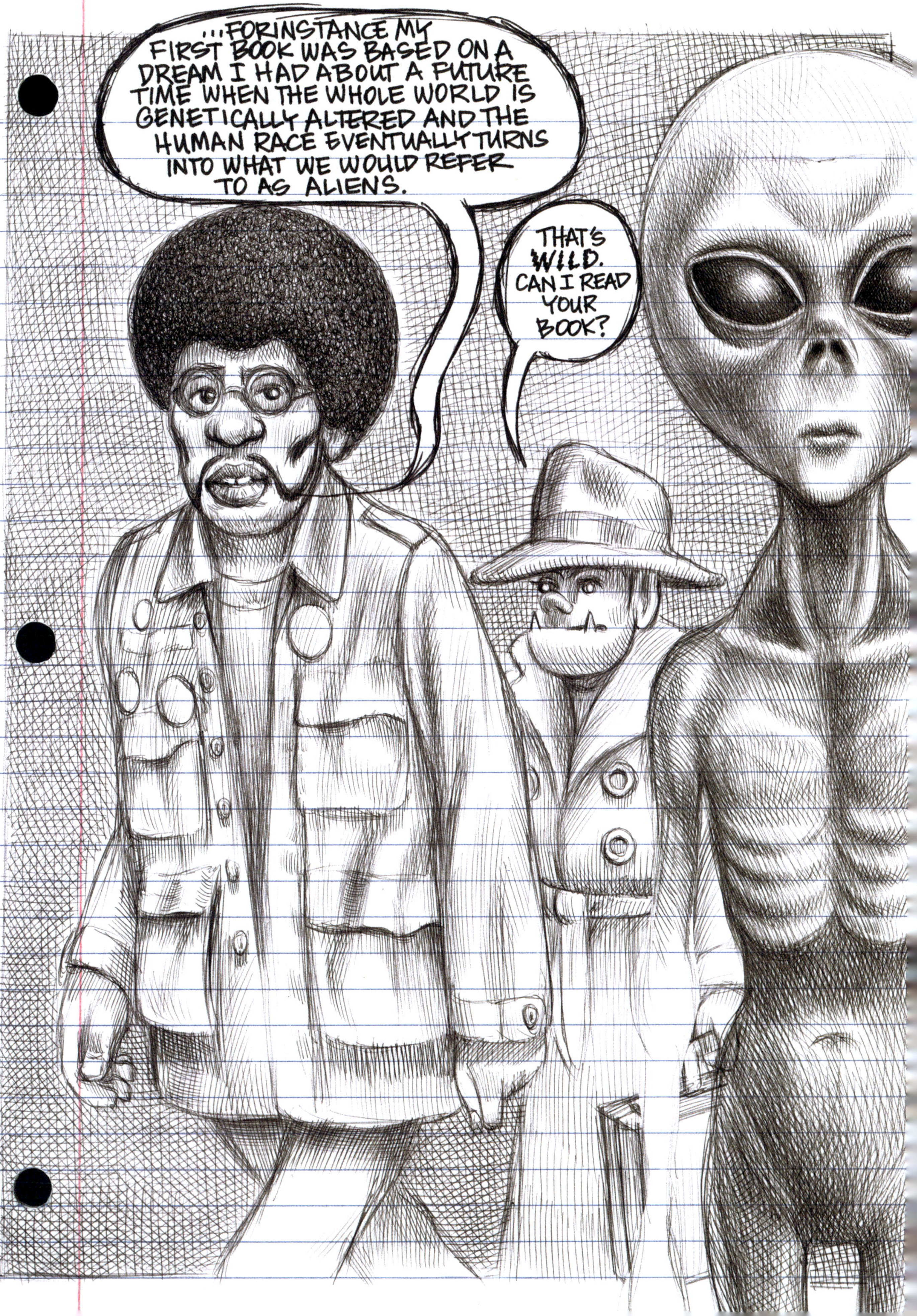
...FOR INSTANCE MY FIRST BOOK WAS BASED ON A DREAM I HAD ABOUT A FUTURE TIME WHEN THE WHOLE WORLD IS GENETICALLY ALTERED AND THE HUMAN RACE EVENTUALLY TURNS INTO WHAT WE WOULD REFER TO AS ALIENS.
THAT'S WILD. CAN I READ YOUR BOOK?

WHEN ME AND THE BRAIN WERE WALKING PAST THE CHURCH THAT DEEZE ALWAYS CALLS THE "CHRIST DIED CHURCH," I THOUGHT ABOUT HOW MAMA WOULD GET UPSET THAT DEEZE DIDN'T READ THE 'FOR OUR SINS' PART.

IT IS SPOOKY, KAREN. IF YOU LOOK AT THE PLANS BEING MADE FOR THE HUMANS OF THE WORLD, IT'S ALWAYS ABOUT CONTROL. THEY DON'T WANT US TO HAVE ANY FREEDOM. THEY WANT TO CONTROL EVERY ASPECT OF OUR LIVES.

BUT BRAIN, I MEAN JEFFREY, WHO IS THIS *THEY* THAT YOU ARE ALWAYS TALKING ABOUT?

THEY ARE *MURDEROUS* 'YOU-JEN-UH-SISSTS' WHO HATE HUMANITY.

I'M SORRY BUT THAT DOESN'T REALLY ANSWER MY QUESTION. CAN YOU GIVE ME A NAME OF ONE OF THESE PEOPLE WHO YOU SAY IS TRYING TO MESS UP OUR LIVES?

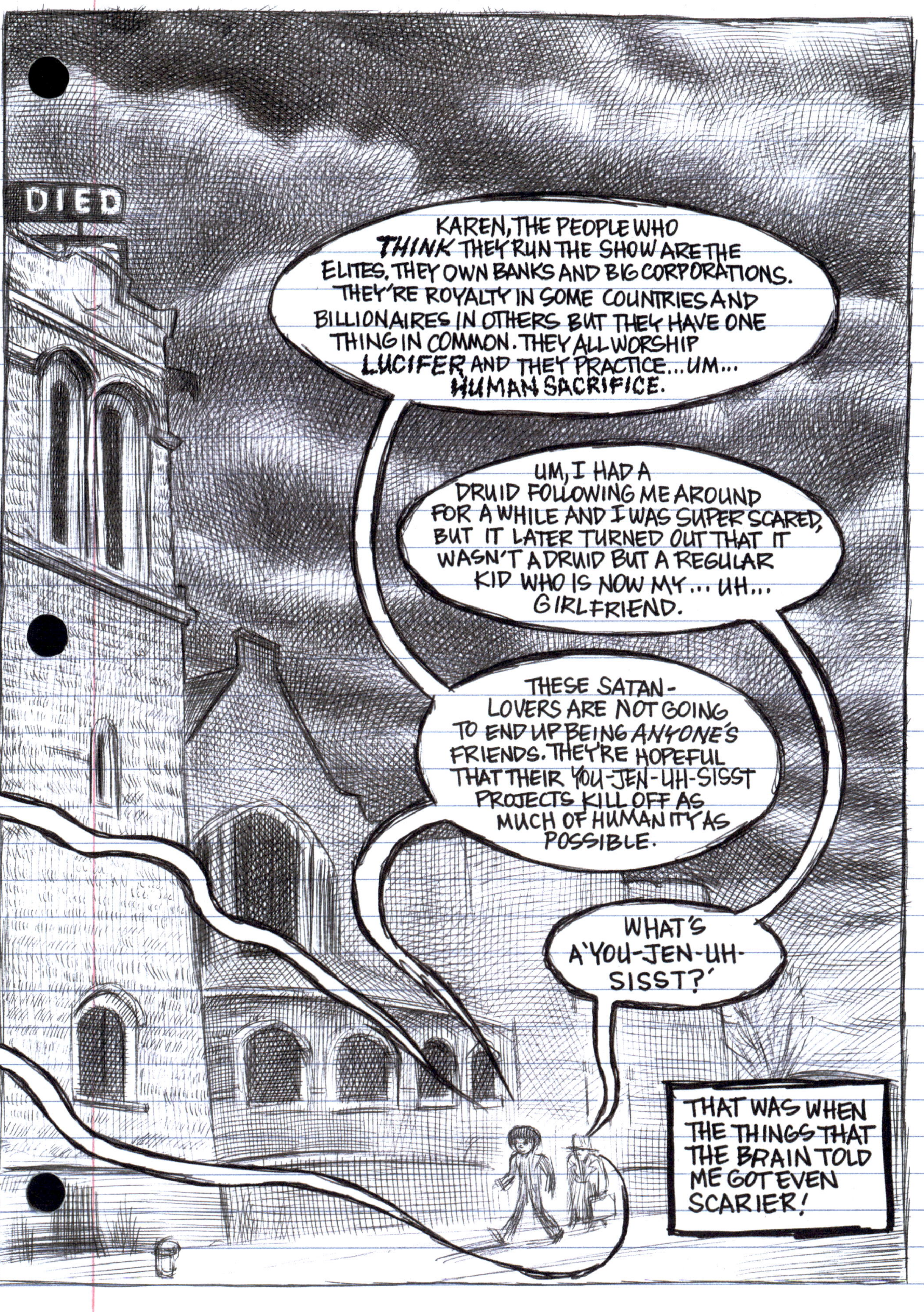
DIED
KAREN, THE PEOPLE WHO *THINK* THEY RUN THE SHOW ARE THE ELITES. THEY OWN BANKS AND BIG CORPORATIONS. THEY'RE ROYALTY IN SOME COUNTRIES AND BILLIONAIRES IN OTHERS BUT THEY HAVE ONE THING IN COMMON. THEY ALL WORSHIP **LUCIFER** AND THEY PRACTICE... UM... **HUMAN SACRIFICE.**
UM, I HAD A DRUID FOLLOWING ME AROUND FOR A WHILE AND I WAS SUPER SCARED, BUT IT LATER TURNED OUT THAT IT WASN'T A DRUID BUT A REGULAR KID WHO IS NOW MY... UH... GIRLFRIEND.
THESE SATAN-LOVERS ARE NOT GOING TO END UP BEING *ANYONE'S* FRIENDS. THEY'RE HOPEFUL THAT THEIR YOU-JEN-UH-SISST PROJECTS KILL OFF AS MUCH OF HUMANITY AS POSSIBLE.
WHAT'S A 'YOU-JEN-UH-SISST?'
THAT WAS WHEN THE THINGS THAT THE BRAIN TOLD ME GOT EVEN SCARIER!

WHEN JEFFREY SPELLED THE WORD 'EUGENICIST' FOR ME I REMEMBERED HOW DEEZE LIKES TO TEASE JEFFREY BY CALLING HIM 'DORIS THESAURUS.'

"'EUGENICS' MEANS 'GOOD CREATION' IN GREEK. THIS BELIEF PUTS FORWARD THE IDEA THAT *SOME* PEOPLE ARE MORE WORTHY OF LIFE THAN *OTHERS*."

"NEXT TIME YOU'RE AT THE LIBRARY LOOK UP 'MALTHUS' AND 'SIR FRANCIS GALTON.' THEIR *DUMB* IDEAS ARE STILL POPULAR IN ACADEMIC CIRCLES..."

"...BECAUSE THE AGENDA IS TO TEACH US THAT WE'RE WEAK STUPID EVIL AND WORTHLESS ALTHOUGH *NOTHING* COULD BE A BIGGER *LIE*."

"I KNOW A LITTLE BIT ABOUT THAT FROM SOME TAPES OF ANKA SILVERBERG'S WARTIME EXPERIENCES. THE NAZIS STARTED KILLING DISABLED PEOPLE."

"AT THE NUREMBERG TRIALS IT CAME OUT THAT HITLER GOT HIS IDEAS FROM *AMERICAN EUGENICISTS*."

"IF THE NAZIS EVER COME BACK THEY'LL TRY TO KILL ME BECAUSE MY SPINE IS CROOKED."

"THEY ARE ALWAYS TRYING TO RESURRECT SLAVERY AND THE INDIAN GENOCIDE, BECAUSE THOSE WERE THE 'GOOD OLD DAYS' TO THE SERIAL KILLER ELITES."

"KAREN, *PLEASE*, DON'T EVER SAY WORDS THAT INVOKE *BAD THINGS*! SPOKEN WORDS ARE *SPELLS*. I WOULDN'T... YOUR BROTHER WOULDN'T ALLOW ANYONE TO HURT YOU LIKE THAT."

I GUESS WHAT I SAID HAD UPSET THE BRAIN BECAUSE HE DID THE THING WHERE HE TOUCHES HIS POINTER FINGER TO THE BRIDGE OF HIS EYEGLASSES THREE TIMES.

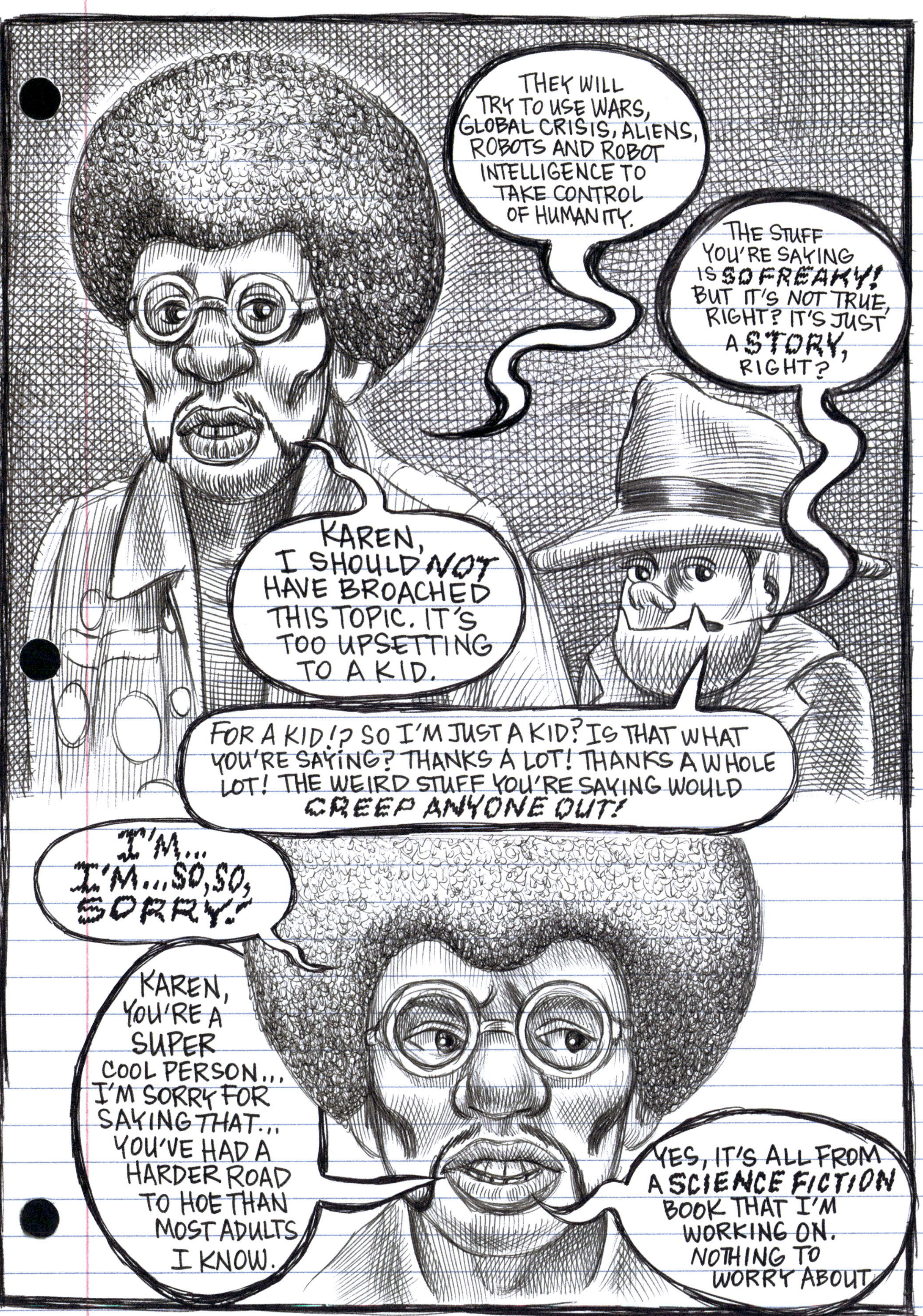
THEY WILL TRY TO USE WARS, GLOBAL CRISIS, ALIENS, ROBOTS AND ROBOT INTELLIGENCE TO TAKE CONTROL OF HUMANITY.
THE STUFF YOU'RE SAYING IS SO FREAKY! BUT IT'S NOT TRUE, RIGHT? IT'S JUST A STORY, RIGHT?
KAREN, I SHOULD NOT HAVE BROACHED THIS TOPIC. IT'S TOO UPSETTING TO A KID.
FOR A KID!? SO I'M JUST A KID? IS THAT WHAT YOU'RE SAYING? THANKS A LOT! THANKS A WHOLE LOT! THE WEIRD STUFF YOU'RE SAYING WOULD CREEP ANYONE OUT!
I'M... I'M...SO, SO, SORRY!
KAREN, YOU'RE A SUPER COOL PERSON... I'M SORRY FOR SAYING THAT... YOU'VE HAD A HARDER ROAD TO HOE THAN MOST ADULTS I KNOW.
YES, IT'S ALL FROM A SCIENCE FICTION BOOK THAT I'M WORKING ON. NOTHING TO WORRY ABOUT.

I COULD TELL THAT JEFFREY 'THE BRAIN' ALVAREZ WAS NOT THRILLED ABOUT GOING INSIDE OUR BUILDING, WHICH IS WEIRD BECAUSE HE'S VISITED US A BUNCH OF TIMES.

KAREN, I, UH, JUST CAN'T — IN GOOD CONSCIENCE — LEAVE YOU TO WALK IN THERE TOTALLY ALONE.

TECHNICALLY, I WOULDN'T BE ALONE. ALTHOUGH MRS. GRONAN IS AT HER JOB AT THE MOUNT VESUVIUS CLUB AND ALTHOUGH SILVERBERG IS AT A GIG IN PEORIA...

...AND ALTHOUGH THE GHOSTS ARE THERE, TOO, THERE IS ANOTHER LIVING BEING IN THE BUILDING... TUT THE CAT *WHO HATES MY GUTS!*

WELL, RAYGUN USED TO... NOT EXACTLY GROOVE ON YOU, BUT NOW HE SEEMS TO *LOVE* YOU, SO MAYBE TUT WILL COME AROUND.

THE BRAIN SHOT ME A LOOK WITH A QUESTION MARK INSIDE IT AND I THINK HE WAS WONDERING WHY ANIMALS DON'T LIKE ME. THE FACT IS THAT REGULAR CREATURES *DO NOT USUALLY LIKE SUPERNATURAL CREATURES* SUCH AS WEREWOLVES. I SUPPOSE THAT THEY CAN SENSE OUR DIFFERENTNESS TO THEM.

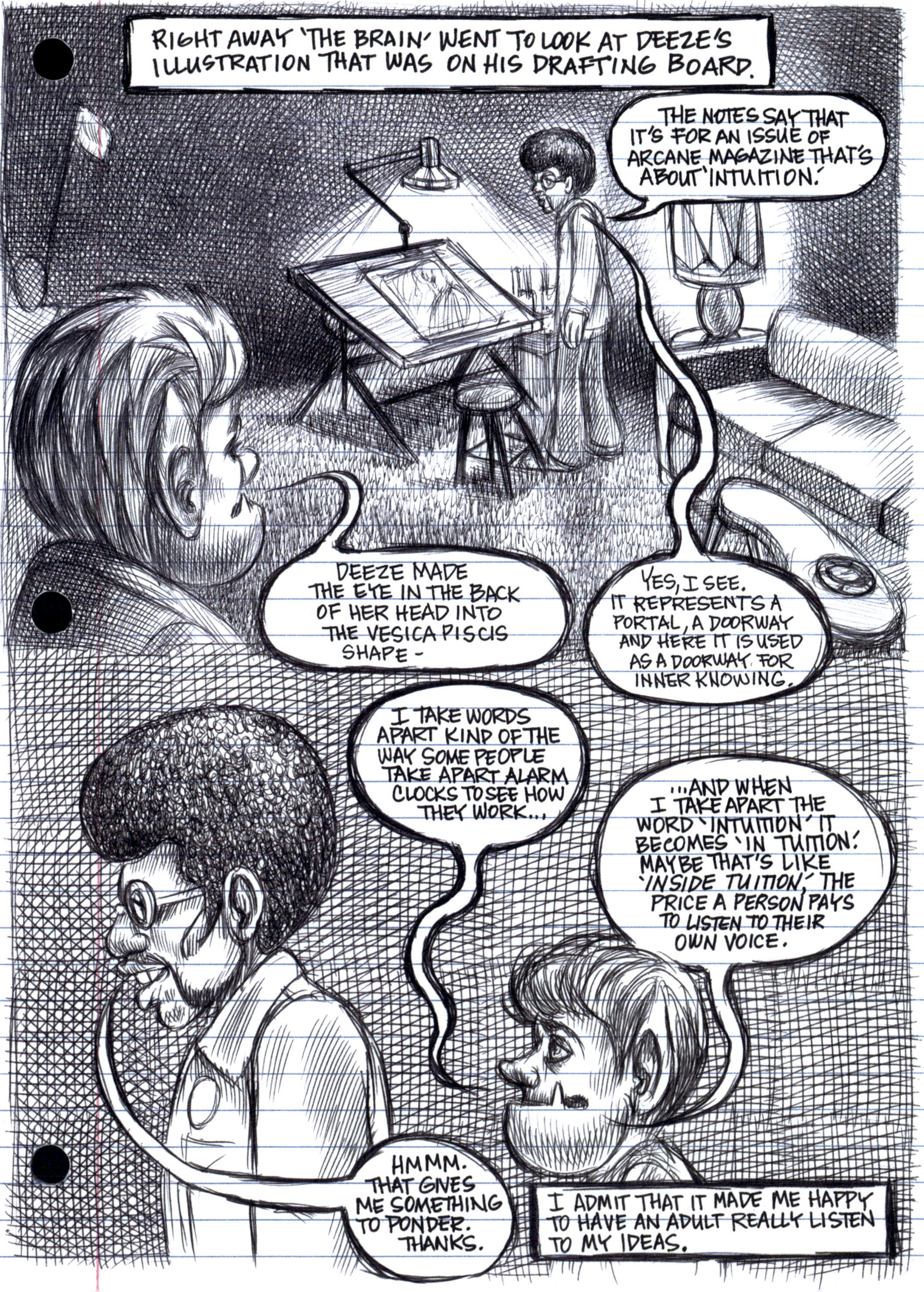
RIGHT AWAY 'THE BRAIN' WENT TO LOOK AT DEEZE'S ILLUSTRATION THAT WAS ON HIS DRAFTING BOARD.
THE NOTES SAY THAT IT'S FOR AN ISSUE OF ARCANE MAGAZINE THAT'S ABOUT 'INTUITION.'
DEEZE MADE THE EYE IN THE BACK OF HER HEAD INTO THE VESICA PISCIS SHAPE -
YES, I SEE. IT REPRESENTS A PORTAL, A DOORWAY AND HERE IT IS USED AS A DOORWAY FOR INNER KNOWING.
I TAKE WORDS APART KIND OF THE WAY SOME PEOPLE TAKE APART ALARM CLOCKS TO SEE HOW THEY WORK...
...AND WHEN I TAKE APART THE WORD 'INTUITION' IT BECOMES 'IN TUITION.' MAYBE THAT'S LIKE 'INSIDE TUITION,' THE PRICE A PERSON PAYS TO LISTEN TO THEIR OWN VOICE.
HMMM. THAT GIVES ME SOMETHING TO PONDER. THANKS.
I ADMIT THAT IT MADE ME HAPPY TO HAVE AN ADULT REALLY LISTEN TO MY IDEAS.

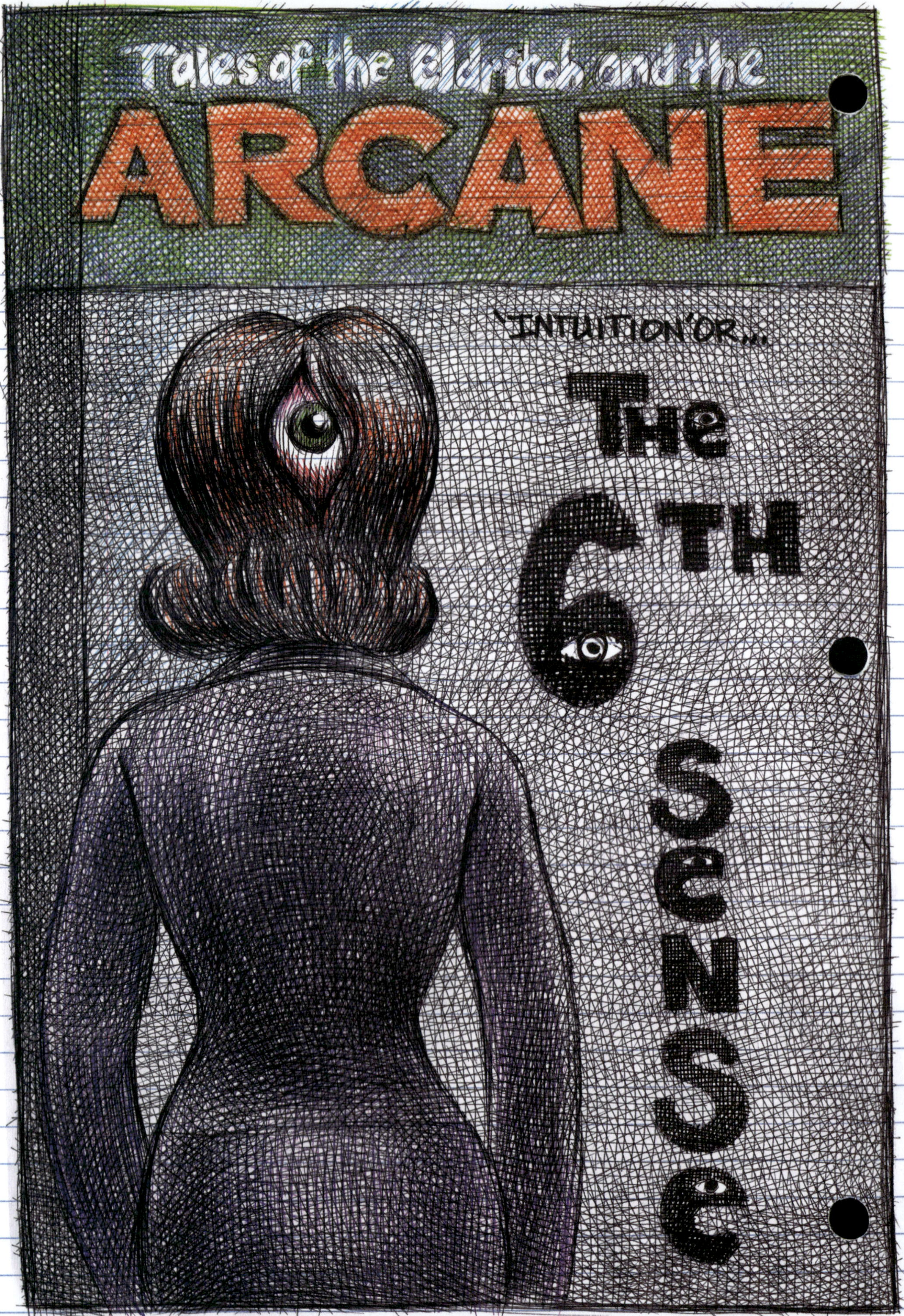
Tales of the Eldritch and the
ARCANE
'INTUITION' OR...
THE 6TH SENSE

"YOUR THOUGHTS ON INTUITION REMIND ME OF A PASSAGE OF THE CHRISTIAN BIBLE. 'BEHOLD, I SEND YOU OUT AS SHEEP IN THE MIDST OF WOLVES. THEREFORE BE WISE AS SERPENTS AND GENTLE AS DOVES.'"

"NO OFFENSE TO JESUS BUT—I WOULD RATHER BE A WEREWOLF THAN A SHEEP."

"TO MY MIND JESUS' WORDS ARE MEANT TO HIGHLIGHT TWO WAYS OF KNOWING. THE SERPENT REPRESENTS THE LOWER WAY OR THE 'GUT INSTINCT' AND THE DOVE IS AN ENCOURAGEMENT TO LOOK AT THINGS AS THOUGH FROM ABOVE."

AFTER WE TALKED FOR A WHILE THE BRAIN SAID HE WAS GOING TO WATCH THE LATE MOVIE. HE SAID I COULD STAY UP IF I WANTED TO AND I DID AND WHEN THE CAR DEALER COMMERCIALS PLAYED, WE TURNED DOWN THE SOUND AND CONTINUED OUR CONVERSATION. I'LL TELL ABOUT THAT LATER. WHEN I WENT TO BED THE BRAIN STAYED AROUND AND WATCHED MORE T.V.

"HEY, BRAIN! WHAT ARE YOU DOING HERE? NOT THAT I'M NOT GLAD TO SEE YOU... BY THE WAY, THANKS FOR WHAT YOU DID AT THE DINER."

DEEZE LOOKED IN ON ME. I LAID VERY STILL SO HE CLOSED THE DOOR BUT NOT ALL THE WAY. BLEMMY SAID THAT HE HAD THIS WEIRD FEELING THAT I SHOULDN'T SNOOP...

...BUT I DIDN'T LISTEN TO BLEMMY...

HEY DIEGO, WHAT IF I COULD FIND YOU MORE ILLUSTRATION WORK? UNTIL THEN KAREN COULD STAY WITH MY COUSIN DANTE AND HIS WIFE...

MAN, I'D LIKE NOTHING BETTER BUT— AS YOU KNOW— I'M A MORON WHO CAN'T *EVEN READ.* I'D NEED LOTS OF HELP...

YOU KNOW, JUST WHEN YOU HAVE *OUTSIDE WORK.*

YOU KNOW THAT I THINK YOU'RE A GENIUS AND I'LL *ALWAYS* HELP WITH THAT.

...AND AS FOR ME PUTTING KAREN IN SOME OTHER SITUATION, RIGHT NOW SHE'S SAFER HERE THAN ANYWHERE. GRONAN IS WEIRD BUT HE CONSIDERS HER FAMILY.

ALVAREZ, YOU ARE EASILY THE SMARTEST GUY I'VE EVER KNOWN BUT CLEARLY YOU JUST DON'T GET THE WAY THINGS WORK, SO LET ME BREAK IT DOWN FOR YOU...

I BECAME JACK GRONAN'S PROPERTY THE DAY I SHOT MY BROTHER IN HIS EVIL FREAKING HEAD. INSTEAD OF DOING IT HIMSELF, MY FATHER -THE POCKET COP- TOOK OUT A HIT ON ME BUUUT JACK GRONAN FROZE THE HIT COLD AS LAKE MICHIGAN IN WINTER - ALTHOUGH HE CAN UNFREEZE IT WITH THE SNAP OF HIS FINGERS.

LOOK MAN, THERE **HAS** TO BE A WAY THROUGH THIS. YOU WEREN'T AN ADULT SO THEY CAN'T CHARGE YOU FOR IT. YOU DEAL WITH YOUR FATHER IN WHATEVER WAY YOU HAVE TO AND YOU TAKE KAREN AND YOU LEAVE, GET NEW IDENTITIES—

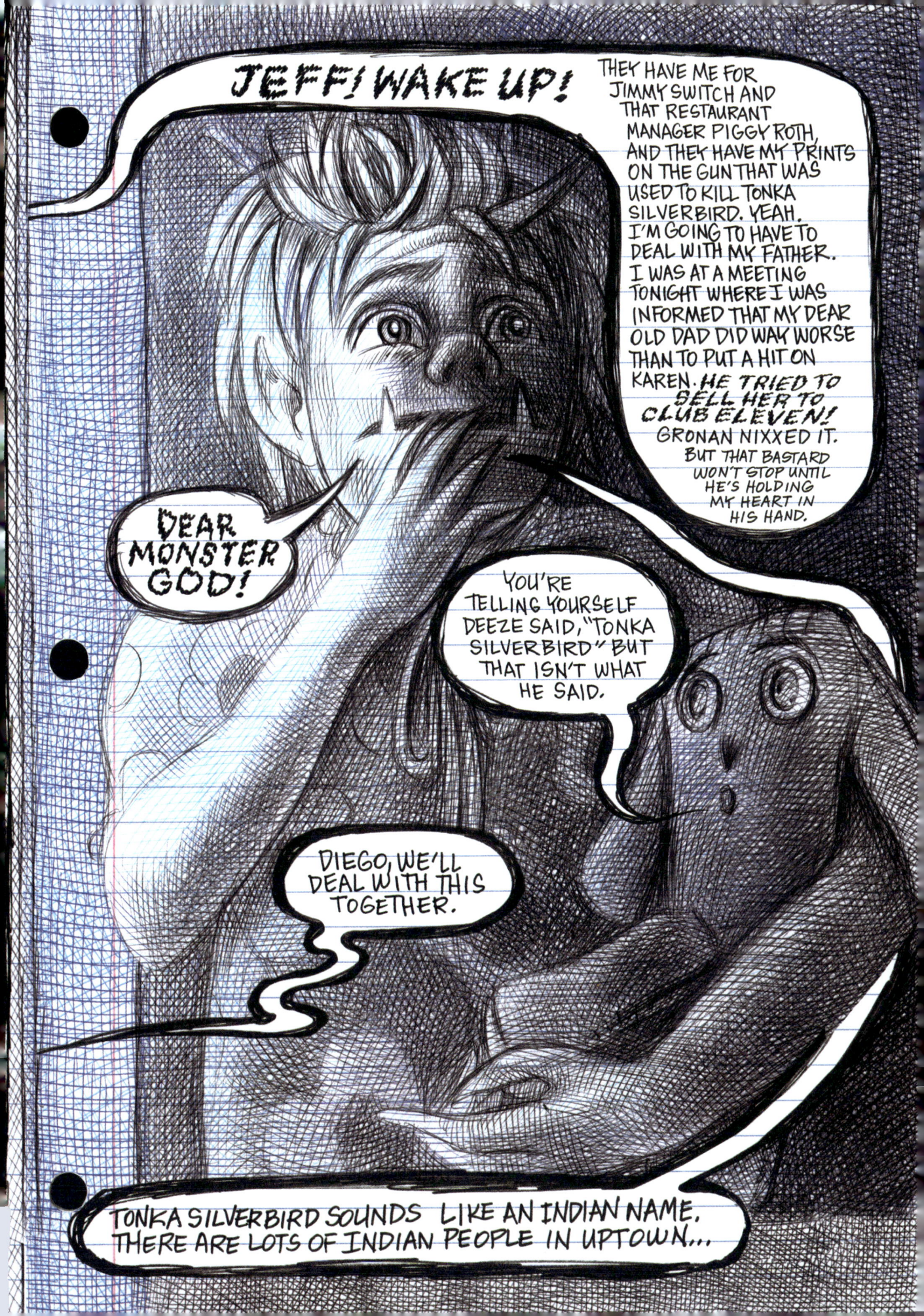

JEFF! WAKE UP! THEY HAVE ME FOR JIMMY SWITCH AND THAT RESTAURANT MANAGER PIGGY ROTH, AND THEY HAVE MY PRINTS ON THE GUN THAT WAS USED TO KILL TONKA SILVERBIRD. YEAH. I'M GOING TO HAVE TO DEAL WITH MY FATHER. I WAS AT A MEETING TONIGHT WHERE I WAS INFORMED THAT MY DEAR OLD DAD DID WAY WORSE THAN TO PUT A HIT ON KAREN. *HE TRIED TO SELL HER TO CLUB ELEVEN!* GRONAN NIXXED IT. BUT THAT BASTARD WON'T STOP UNTIL HE'S HOLDING MY HEART IN HIS HAND.

DEAR MONSTER GOD!

YOU'RE TELLING YOURSELF DEEZE SAID, "TONKA SILVERBIRD" BUT THAT ISN'T WHAT HE SAID.

DIEGO, WE'LL DEAL WITH THIS TOGETHER.

TONKA SILVERBIRD SOUNDS LIKE AN INDIAN NAME. THERE ARE LOTS OF INDIAN PEOPLE IN UPTOWN...

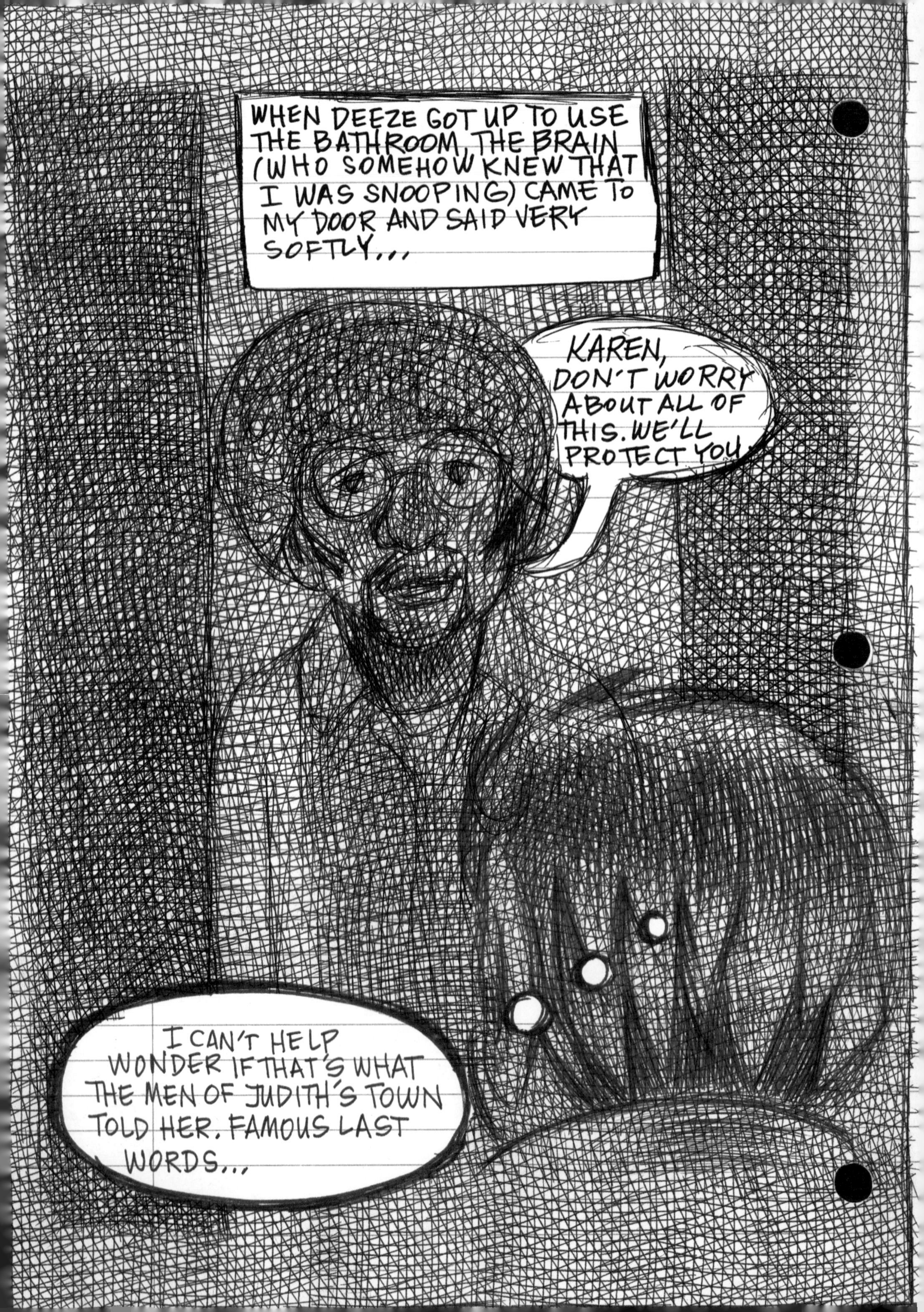
WHEN DEEZE GOT UP TO USE THE BATHROOM, THE BRAIN (WHO SOMEHOW KNEW THAT I WAS SNOOPING) CAME TO MY DOOR AND SAID VERY SOFTLY...
KAREN, DON'T WORRY ABOUT ALL OF THIS. WE'LL PROTECT YOU.
I CAN'T HELP WONDER IF THAT'S WHAT THE MEN OF JUDITH'S TOWN TOLD HER. FAMOUS LAST WORDS...

"DEEZY CAN'T *READ*?"

"THAT *WOULD* EXPLAIN WHY YOUR #1 DUTY AS 'CO-PILOT' OF DEEZE'S CAR IS BEING THE STREET SIGN READER."

"ALL MY FAMILY DOES IS HIDE STUFF FROM ME."

'SLEEP OF REASON PRODUCES MONSTERS' FRANCISCO JOSE DE GOYA Y LUCIENTES

...I COULDN'T SLEEP RIGHT AWAY, SO I COPIED A GOYA INTO MY NOTEBOOK. GOYA'S LIFE WASN'T AN EASY ONE. THINKING ABOUT THAT MAKES ME WANT TO TRY AND HANG ON, EVEN WHEN THINGS ARE SCARY.

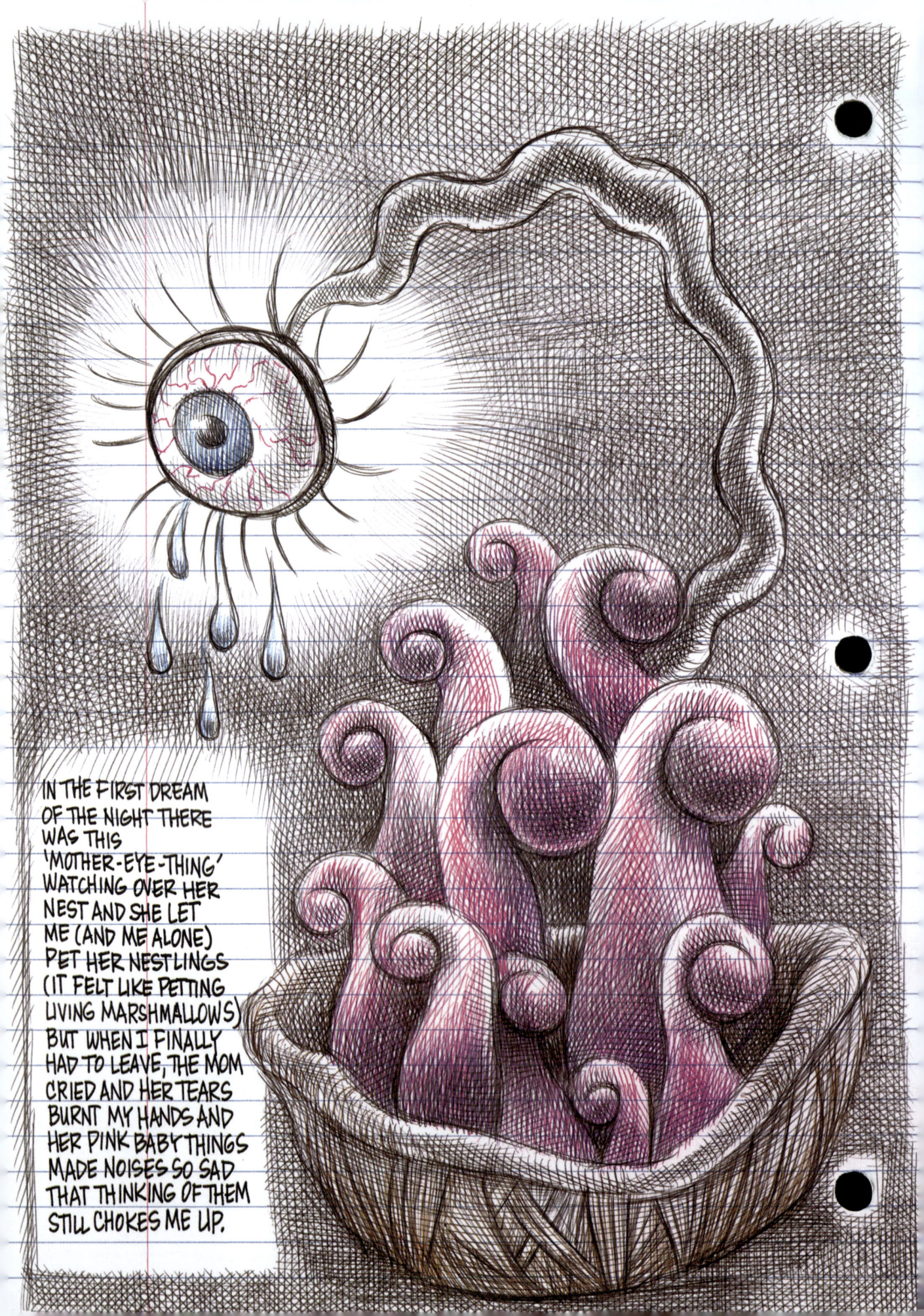

IN THE FIRST DREAM OF THE NIGHT THERE WAS THIS 'MOTHER-EYE-THING' WATCHING OVER HER NEST AND SHE LET ME (AND ME ALONE) PET HER NESTLINGS (IT FELT LIKE PETTING LIVING MARSHMALLOWS) BUT WHEN I FINALLY HAD TO LEAVE, THE MOM CRIED AND HER TEARS BURNT MY HANDS AND HER PINK BABY THINGS MADE NOISES SO SAD THAT THINKING OF THEM STILL CHOKES ME UP.

...IN THE SECOND DREAM, SHELLEY AND ME HAD OUR FIRST KISS AND IT WAS **WONDERFUL**, BUT THEN...

I TOLD YOU, THEM UNNATURAL GIRLS COULD TURN YOUR HEAD AROUND BACKWARDS... AND *NOW* JUST LOOK AT YERSELF.

WHEN I WENT TO LOOK INTO A MIRROR I SAW THAT I HAD CHANGED...

WUH? WAIT A SEC. WHAT'S HAPPENING...

...TO MY *HEAD?*

...BUT MAMA I'M ONE OF THOSE TYPE OF GIRLS!

"HEY KARE, WANNA GRAB SOME EGGS OUT OF THE FRIDGE?"

"WHO IS TONKA SILVERBIRD? WHAT IS 'CLUB ELEVEN?'"

WHEN I SAID THAT I COULD TELL THAT DEEZE WAS FREAKING OUT... I KNEW HE'D TRY TO TURN IT ALL AROUND ON ME.

"SO WHAT I'M GETTING FROM THIS IS THAT YOU HAVE NO PROBLEM AT ALL SPYING ON PRIVATE CONVERSATIONS!"

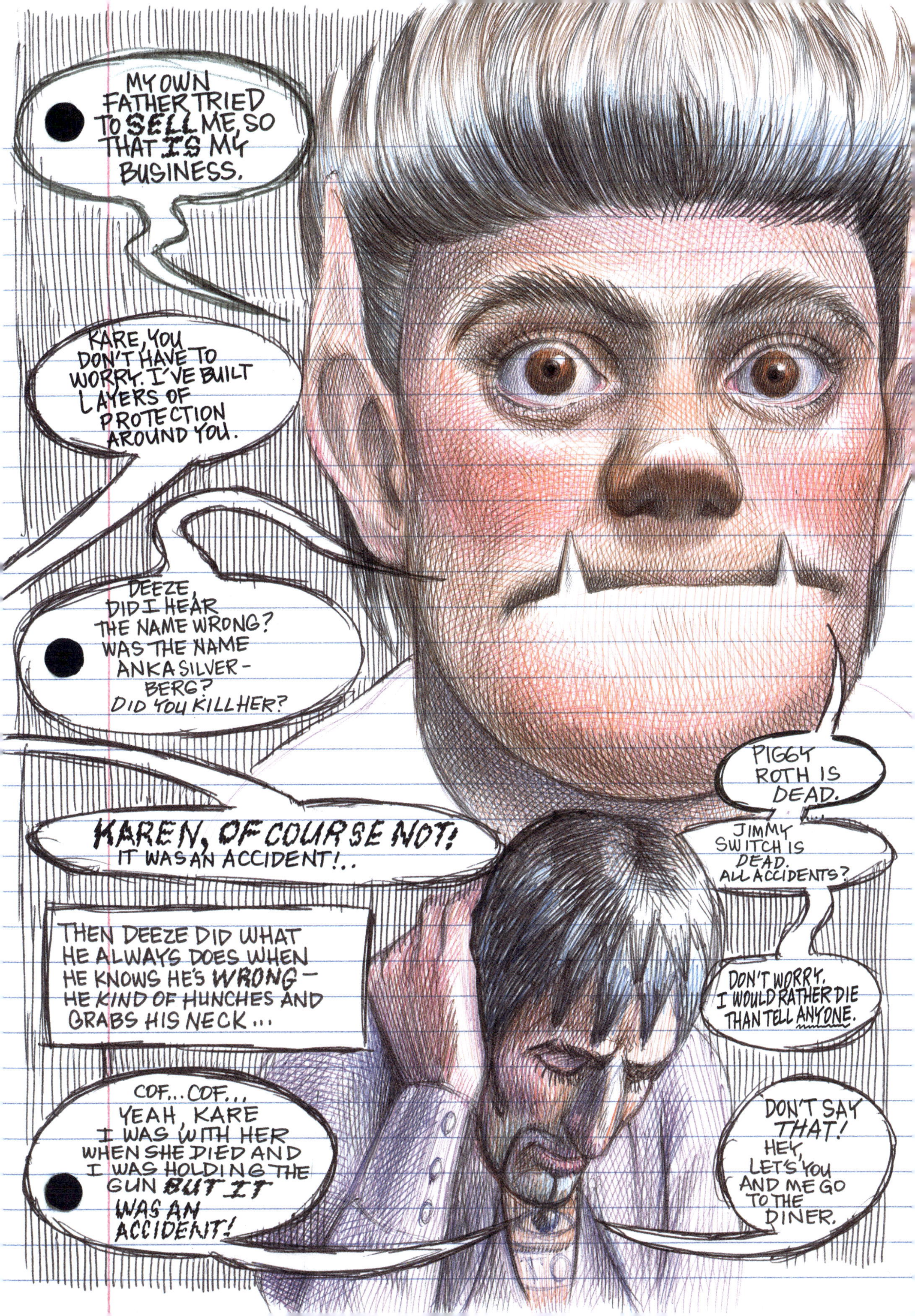
MY OWN FATHER TRIED TO SELL ME, SO THAT IS MY BUSINESS.
KARE, YOU DON'T HAVE TO WORRY. I'VE BUILT LAYERS OF PROTECTION AROUND YOU.
DEEZE, DID I HEAR THE NAME WRONG? WAS THE NAME ANKA SILVER-BERG? DID YOU KILL HER?
KAREN, OF COURSE NOT! IT WAS AN ACCIDENT!..
PIGGY ROTH IS DEAD.
JIMMY SWITCH IS DEAD. ALL ACCIDENTS?
THEN DEEZE DID WHAT HE ALWAYS DOES WHEN HE KNOWS HE'S WRONG— HE KIND OF HUNCHES AND GRABS HIS NECK...
DON'T WORRY. I WOULD RATHER DIE THAN TELL ANYONE.
COF...COF... YEAH, KARE I WAS WITH HER WHEN SHE DIED AND I WAS HOLDING THE GUN BUT IT WAS AN ACCIDENT!
DON'T SAY THAT! HEY, LET'S YOU AND ME GO TO THE DINER.

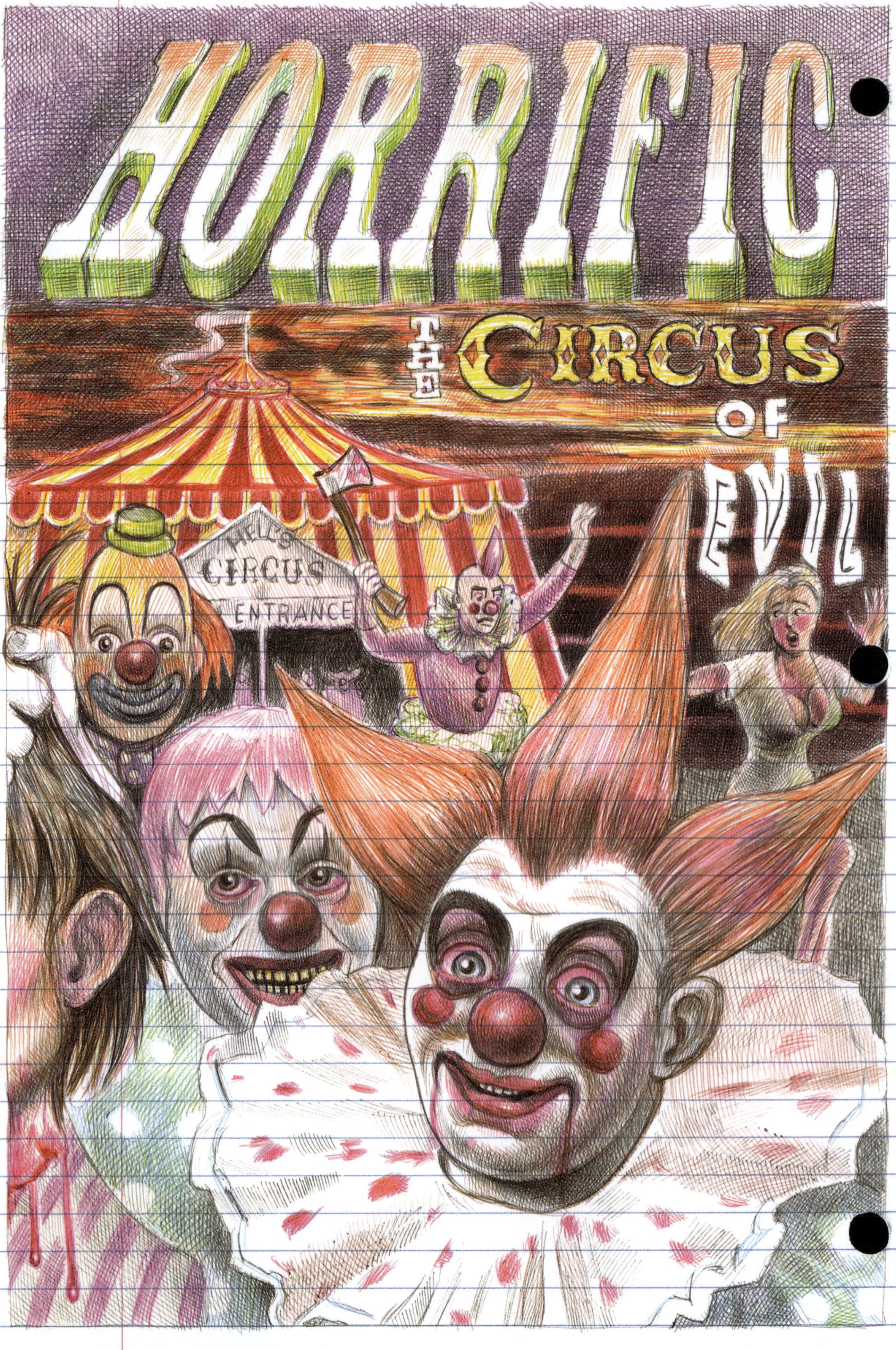
HORRIFIC
THE CIRCUS OF EVIL
HELL'S
CIRCUS
ENTRANCE

FROM NOW ON I WILL BE SUSPICIOUS WHEN DEEZE SAYS, "HEY, LET'S GO TO THE DINER!"

KARE, I'VE BEEN LEAVING YOU ON YOUR OWN FAR TOO MUCH. IT'S GOTTA STOP.

YEAH DEEZE, IT MAKES ME LONELY AND I MISS YOU, SO THANKS.

IT WOULD BE BEST IF YOU HAD AN ADULT AROUND.

I'VE GIVEN THIS SOME DEEP THOUGHT.

YEAH, SO I'M NOT SURE I'D DESCRIBE YOU AS AN ADULT. NO OFFENSE...

NO OFFENSE TAKEN, BUT I WAS THINKING MORE OF MRS. GRONAN...

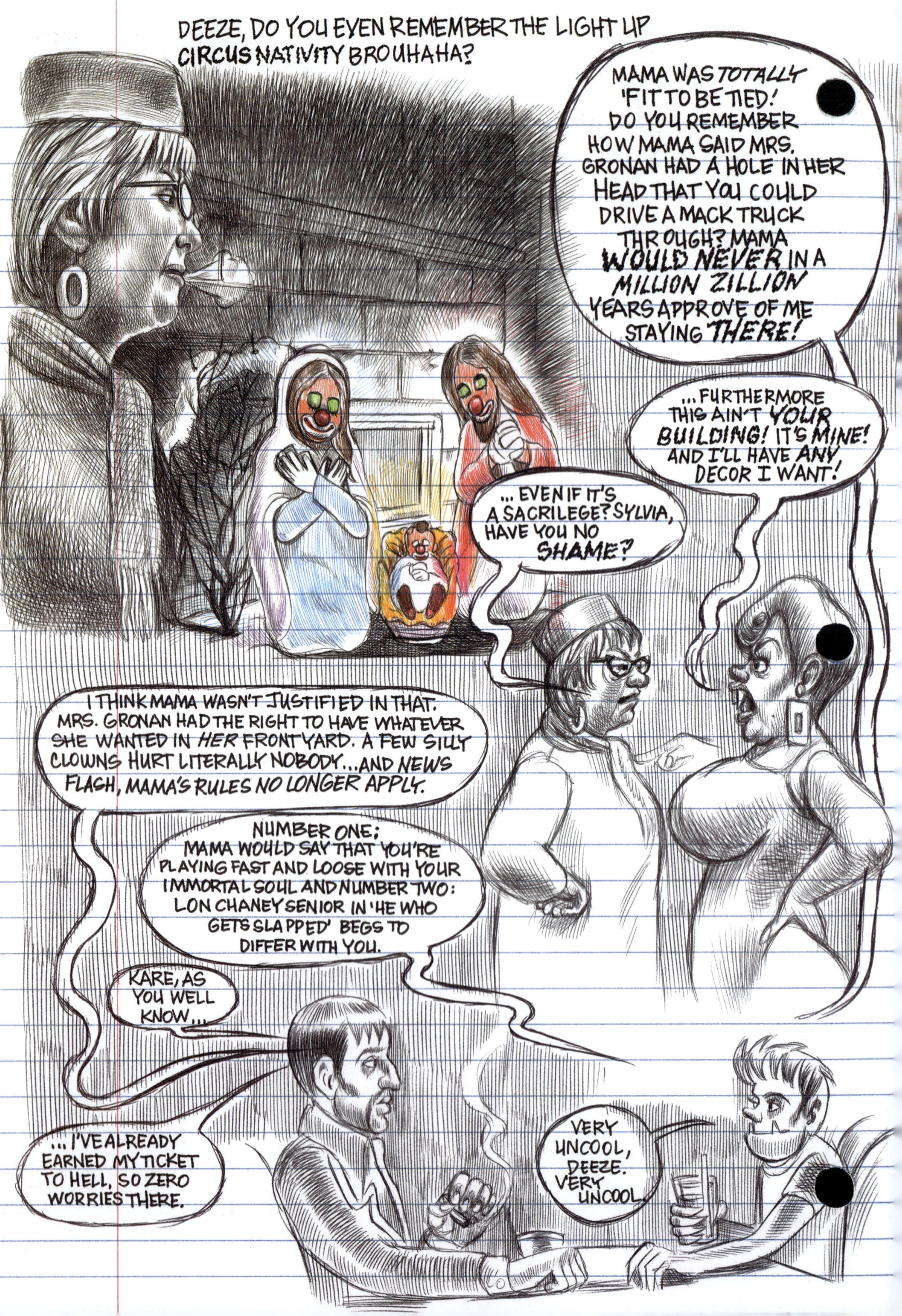
DEEZE, DO YOU EVEN REMEMBER THE LIGHT UP CIRCUS NATIVITY BROUHAHA?
MAMA WAS TOTALLY 'FIT TO BE TIED.' DO YOU REMEMBER HOW MAMA SAID MRS. GRONAN HAD A HOLE IN HER HEAD THAT YOU COULD DRIVE A MACK TRUCK THROUGH? MAMA WOULD NEVER IN A MILLION ZILLION YEARS APPROVE OF ME STAYING THERE!
... FURTHERMORE THIS AIN'T YOUR BUILDING! IT'S MINE! AND I'LL HAVE ANY DECOR I WANT!
... EVEN IF IT'S A SACRILEGE? SYLVIA, HAVE YOU NO SHAME?
I THINK MAMA WASN'T JUSTIFIED IN THAT. MRS. GRONAN HAD THE RIGHT TO HAVE WHATEVER SHE WANTED IN HER FRONT YARD. A FEW SILLY CLOWNS HURT LITERALLY NOBODY... AND NEWS FLASH, MAMA'S RULES NO LONGER APPLY.
NUMBER ONE; MAMA WOULD SAY THAT YOU'RE PLAYING FAST AND LOOSE WITH YOUR IMMORTAL SOUL AND NUMBER TWO: LON CHANEY SENIOR IN 'HE WHO GETS SLAPPED' BEGS TO DIFFER WITH YOU.
KARE, AS YOU WELL KNOW...
... I'VE ALREADY EARNED MY TICKET TO HELL, SO ZERO WORRIES THERE.
VERY UNCOOL, DEEZE. VERY UNCOOL.

DEEZE MADE ME PACK MY STUFF FOR MY WONDERFUL VISIT TO 'CIRCUS HELL' (WHICH IS WHAT I CALL THE GRONAN'S APARTMENT).

HEY, DEEZE, I HAVE A JOKE FOR YOU.

OK, KARE, SHOOT.

WHAT HAPPENS WHEN YOU COMBINE PRESIDENT RICHARD NIXON AND A POTATO.

NO IDEA.

YOU GET A *TRICKY DICK-TATER.* GET IT?

HILARIOUS, KARE. WAS THE JOKE MEANT AS A MESSAGE FOR ME?

NO, DEEZE. WHY **EVER** WOULD YOU THINK *THAT*?

WHEN I PUT BLEMMY IN THE BAG TO GO UPSTAIRS HE WENT *NUTS!*

KAREN, YOU COULD HAVE STOPPED THIS. WHY DIDN'T YOU?!

BLEMMY, THERE WAS NOTHING I COULD DO. IT WAS A DONE DEAL.

GHASTLY

JULY 68

50¢

GALLERY OF BLOOD

MURDER MAZE

KEY TO HELL'S TOMB

INTO THE FUNHOUSE MIRROR

THE THIRTEEN LORDS OF THE LEAGUE OF DEATH

SECRETS OF THE HOUSE ON THE HILL

THE BLACK VELVET SMILE

THE WORLD ACCORDING TO MRS. GRONAN

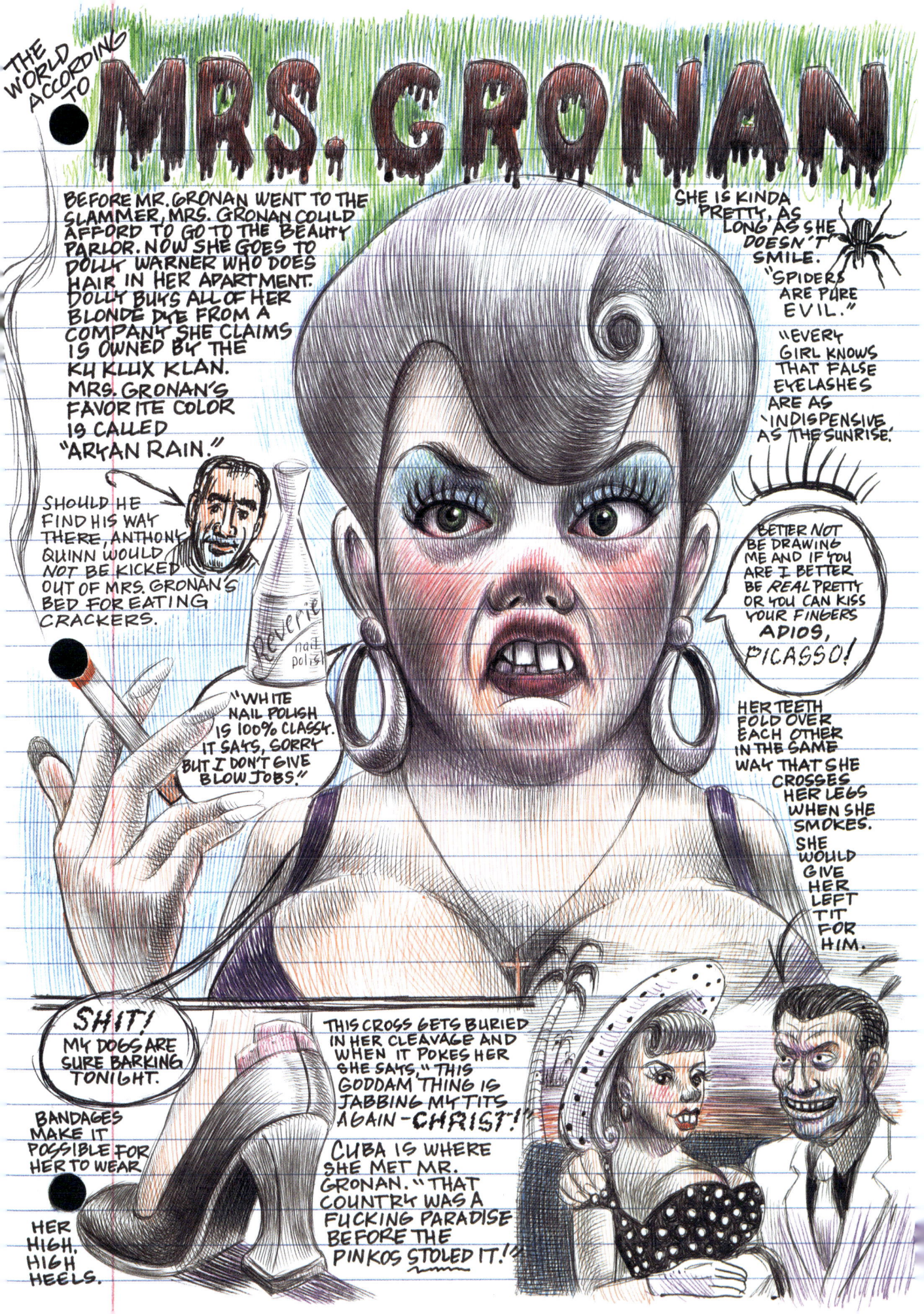

BEFORE MR. GRONAN WENT TO THE SLAMMER, MRS. GRONAN COULD AFFORD TO GO TO THE BEAUTY PARLOR. NOW SHE GOES TO DOLLY WARNER WHO DOES HAIR IN HER APARTMENT. DOLLY BUYS ALL OF HER BLONDE DYE FROM A COMPANY SHE CLAIMS IS OWNED BY THE KU KLUX KLAN. MRS. GRONAN'S FAVORITE COLOR IS CALLED "ARYAN RAIN."

SHE IS KINDA PRETTY, AS LONG AS SHE DOESN'T SMILE.

"SPIDERS ARE PURE EVIL."

"EVERY GIRL KNOWS THAT FALSE EYELASHES ARE AS INDISPENSIBLE AS THE SUNRISE."

SHOULD HE FIND HIS WAY THERE, ANTHONY QUINN WOULD NOT BE KICKED OUT OF MRS. GRONAN'S BED FOR EATING CRACKERS.

"BETTER NOT BE DRAWING ME AND IF YOU ARE I BETTER BE *REAL* PRETTY OR YOU CAN KISS YOUR FINGERS ADIOS, PICASSO!"

"WHITE NAIL POLISH IS 100% CLASSY. IT SAYS, SORRY BUT I DON'T GIVE BLOW JOBS."

HER TEETH FOLD OVER EACH OTHER IN THE SAME WAY THAT SHE CROSSES HER LEGS WHEN SHE SMOKES. SHE WOULD GIVE HER LEFT TIT FOR HIM.

"SHIT! MY DOGS ARE SURE BARKING TONIGHT."

BANDAGES MAKE IT POSSIBLE FOR HER TO WEAR HER HIGH, HIGH HEELS.

THIS CROSS GETS BURIED IN HER CLEAVAGE AND WHEN IT POKES HER SHE SAYS, "THIS GODDAM THING IS JABBING MY TITS AGAIN — CHRIST!"

CUBA IS WHERE SHE MET MR. GRONAN. "THAT COUNTRY WAS A FUCKING PARADISE BEFORE THE PINKOS STOLED IT!"

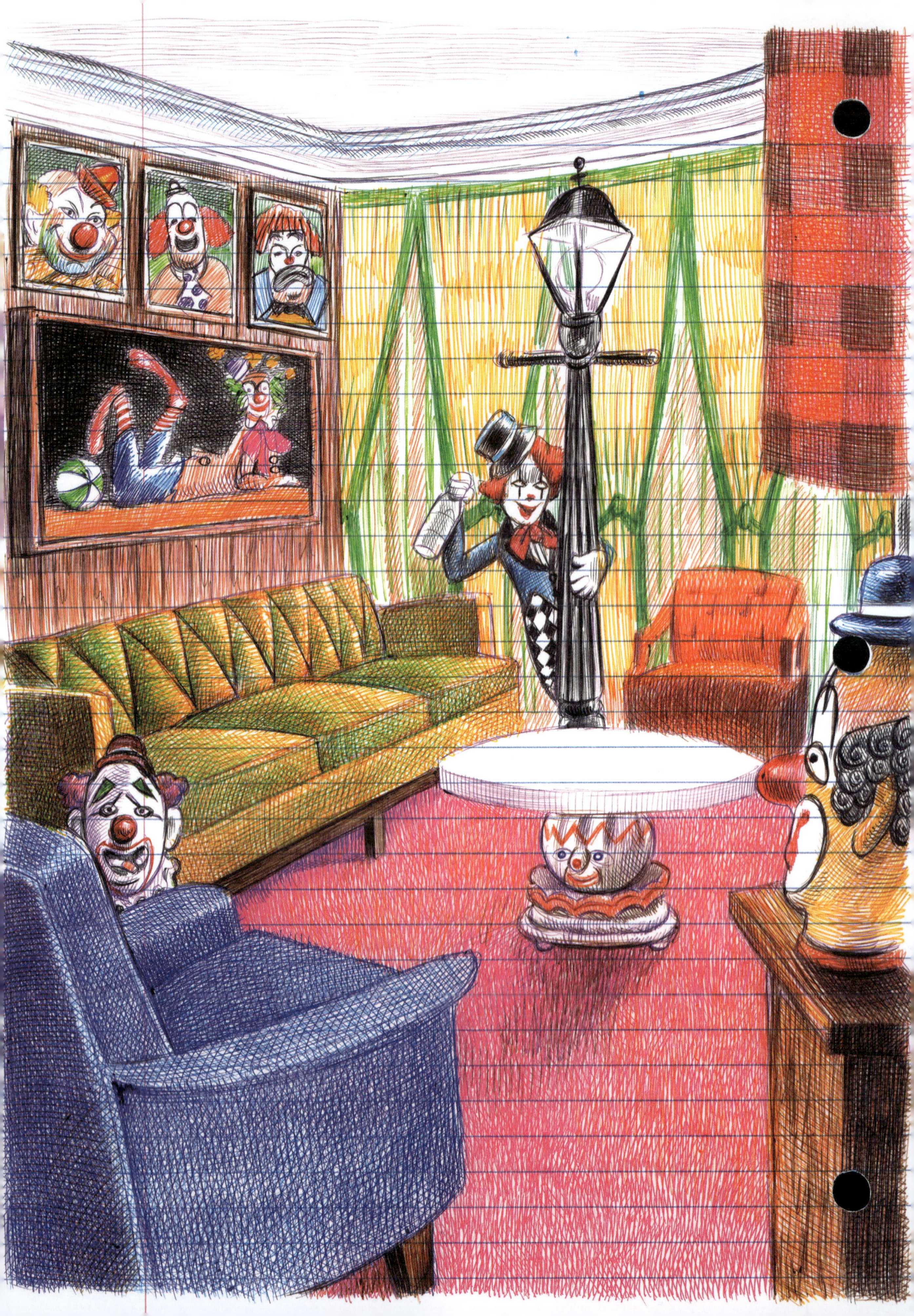

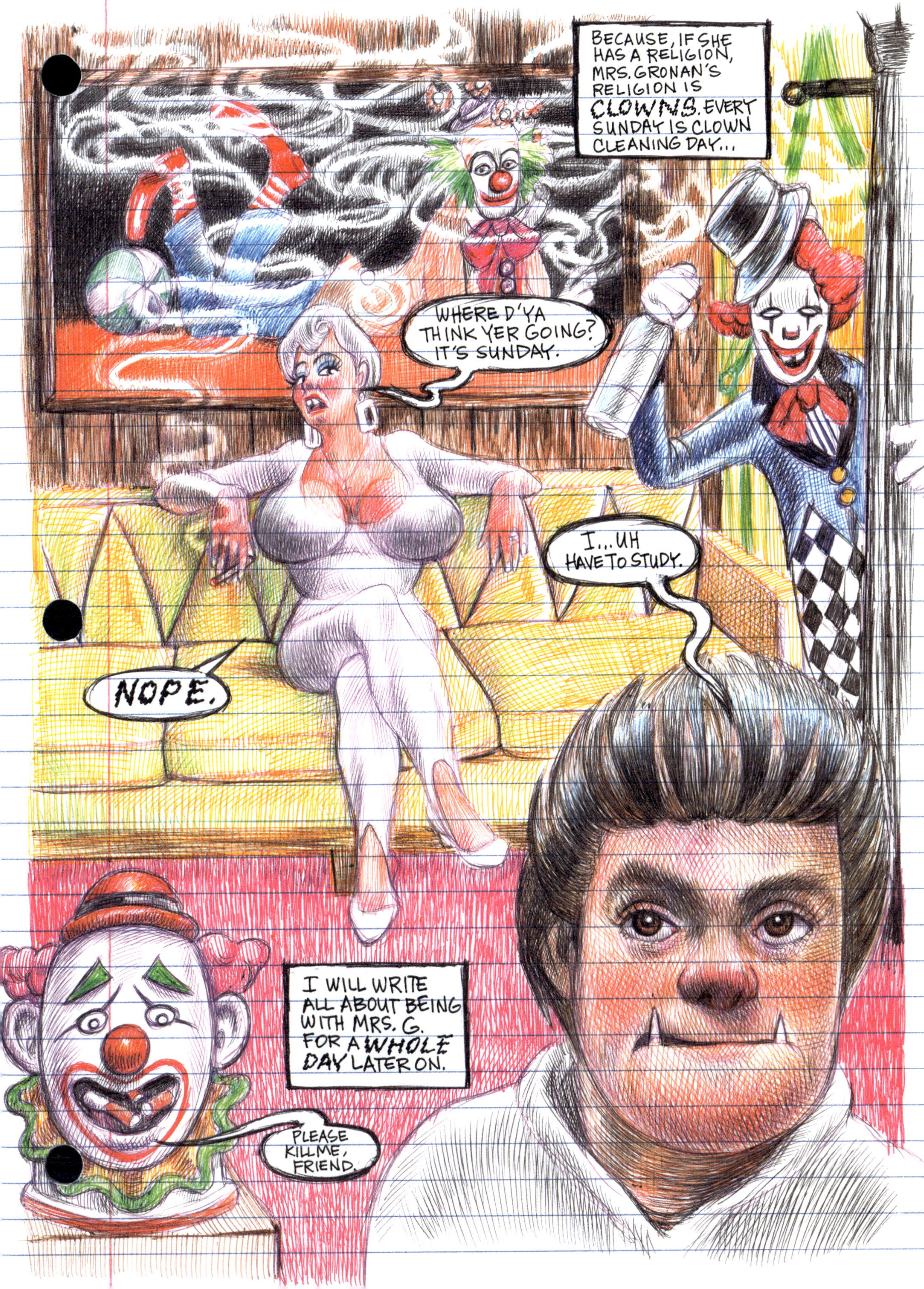
BECAUSE, IF SHE HAS A RELIGION, MRS. GRONAN'S RELIGION IS CLOWNS. EVERY SUNDAY IS CLOWN CLEANING DAY...
WHERE D'YA THINK YER GOING? IT'S SUNDAY.
I...UH HAVE TO STUDY.
NOPE.
I WILL WRITE ALL ABOUT BEING WITH MRS. G. FOR A WHOLE DAY LATER ON.
PLEASE KILL ME, FRIEND.

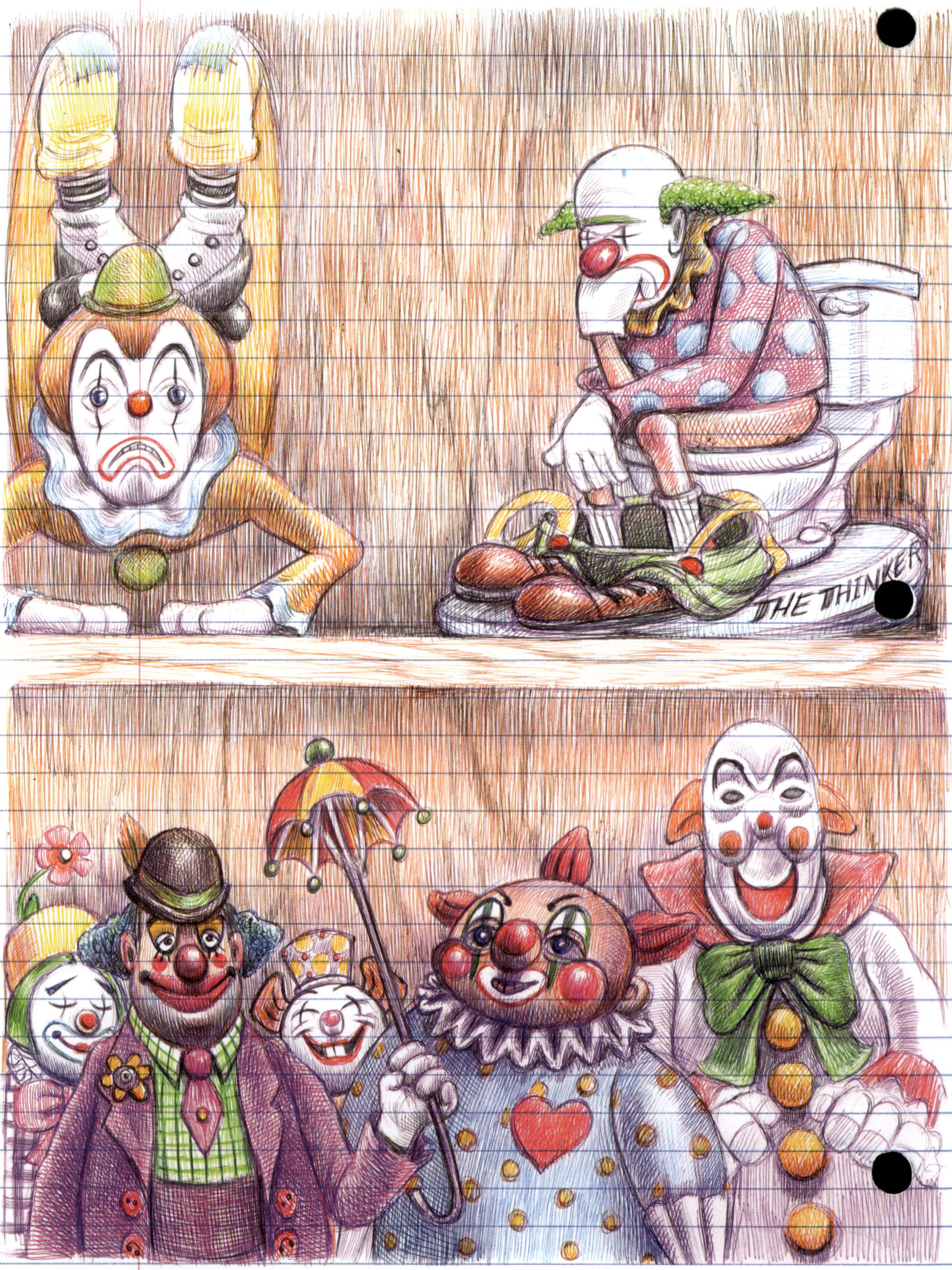
THE THINKER

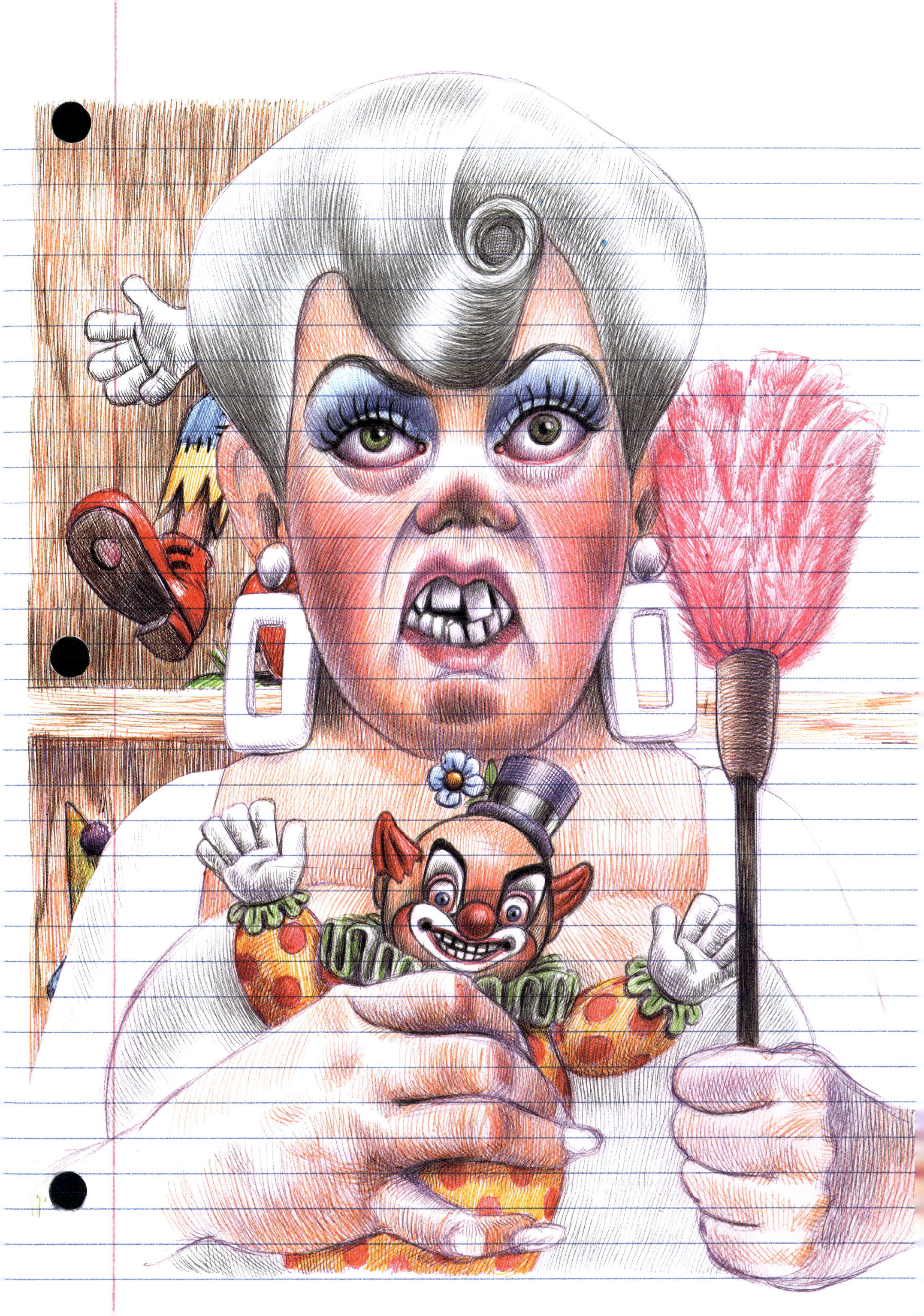

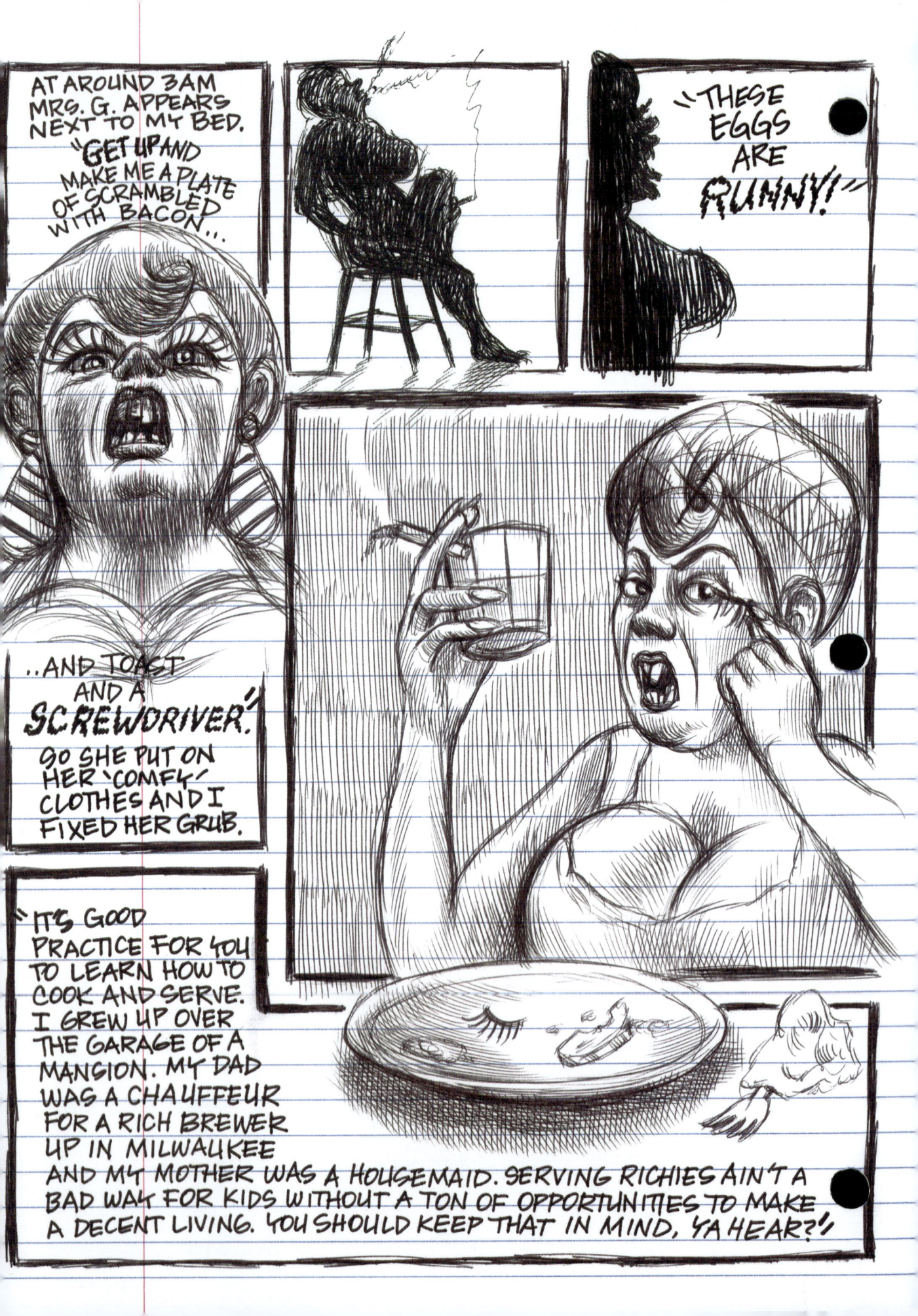

AT AROUND 3AM MRS. G. APPEARS NEXT TO MY BED. "GET UP AND MAKE ME A PLATE OF SCRAMBLED WITH BACON...

"THESE EGGS ARE RUNNY!"

..AND TOAST AND A SCREWDRIVER." SO SHE PUT ON HER 'COMFY' CLOTHES AND I FIXED HER GRUB.

"IT'S GOOD PRACTICE FOR YOU TO LEARN HOW TO COOK AND SERVE. I GREW UP OVER THE GARAGE OF A MANSION. MY DAD WAS A CHAUFFEUR FOR A RICH BREWER UP IN MILWAUKEE AND MY MOTHER WAS A HOUSEMAID. SERVING RICHIES AIN'T A BAD WAY FOR KIDS WITHOUT A TON OF OPPORTUNITIES TO MAKE A DECENT LIVING. YOU SHOULD KEEP THAT IN MIND, YA HEAR?!"

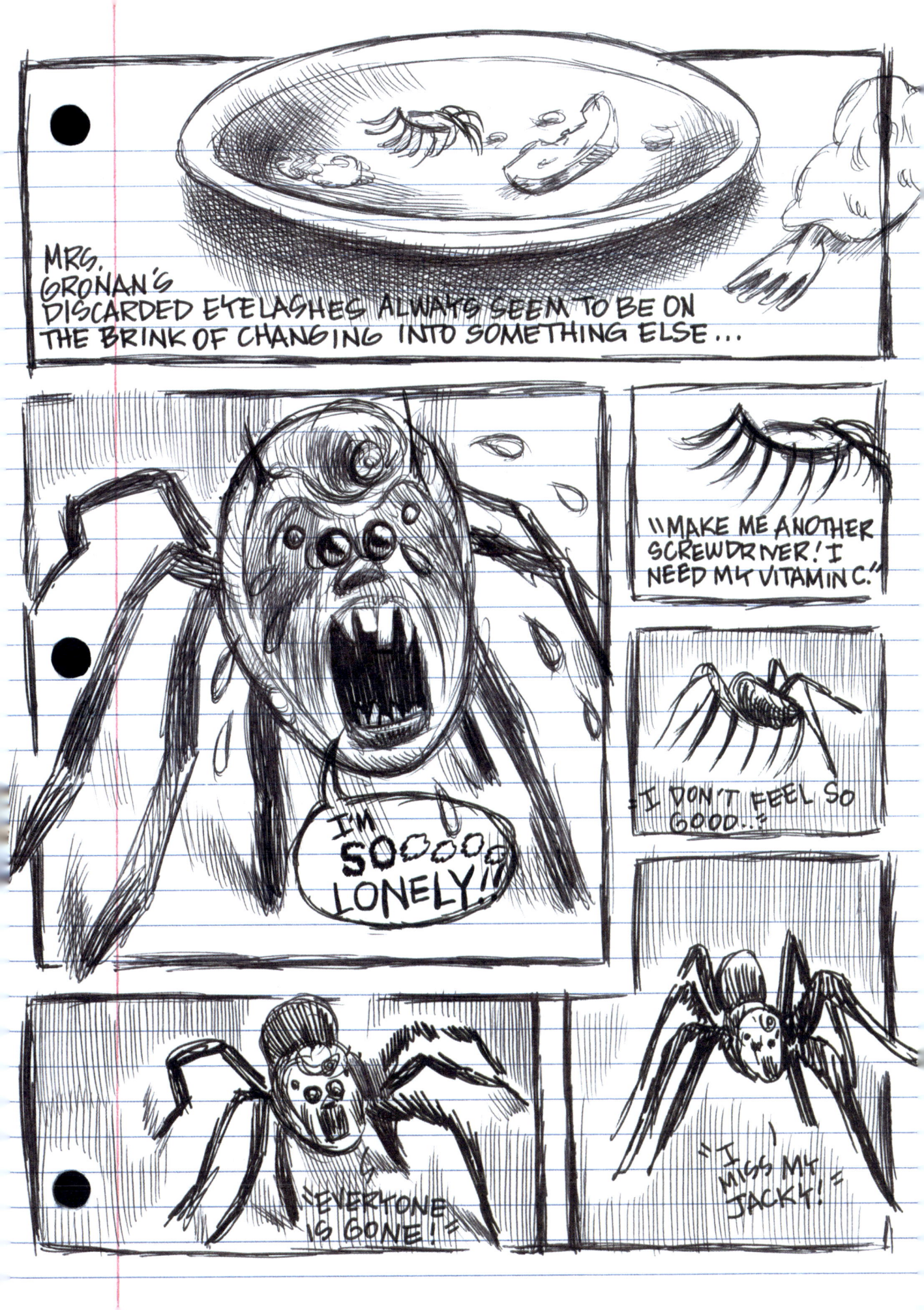

MRS. GRONAN'S DISCARDED EYELASHES ALWAYS SEEM TO BE ON THE BRINK OF CHANGING INTO SOMETHING ELSE...

"I'M SOOOOO LONELY!"

"MAKE ME ANOTHER SCREWDRIVER! I NEED MY VITAMIN C."

"I DON'T FEEL SO GOOD."

"EVERYONE IS GONE!"

"I MISS MY JACK!"

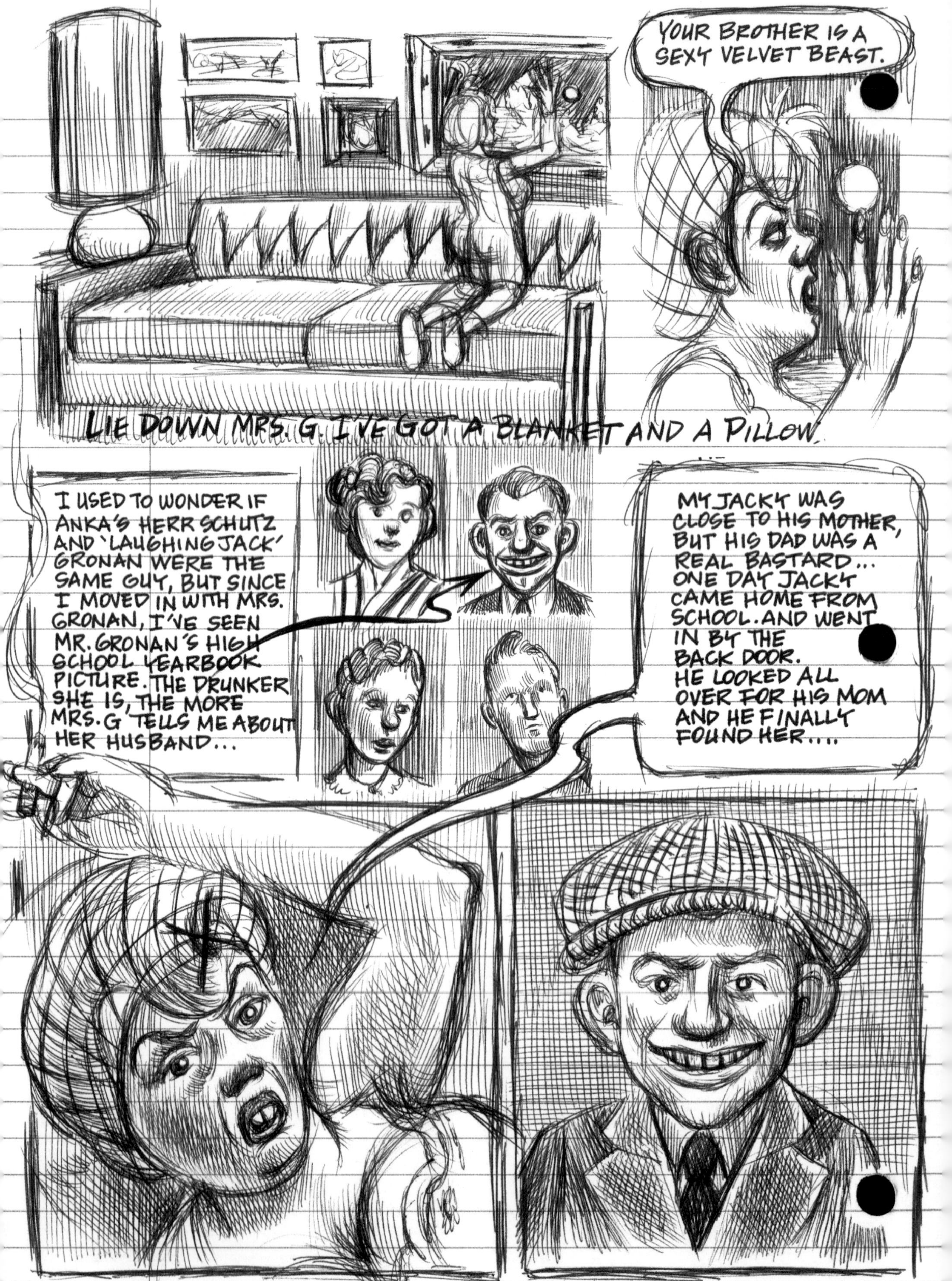
YOUR BROTHER IS A SEXY VELVET BEAST.
LIE DOWN MRS. G. I'VE GOT A BLANKET AND A PILLOW.
I USED TO WONDER IF ANKA'S HERR SCHUTZ AND 'LAUGHING JACK' GRONAN WERE THE SAME GUY, BUT SINCE I MOVED IN WITH MRS. GRONAN, I'VE SEEN MR. GRONAN'S HIGH SCHOOL YEARBOOK PICTURE. THE DRUNKER SHE IS, THE MORE MRS. G TELLS ME ABOUT HER HUSBAND...
MY JACKY WAS CLOSE TO HIS MOTHER, BUT HIS DAD WAS A REAL BASTARD... ONE DAY JACKY CAME HOME FROM SCHOOL. AND WENT IN BY THE BACK DOOR. HE LOOKED ALL OVER FOR HIS MOM AND HE FINALLY FOUND HER....

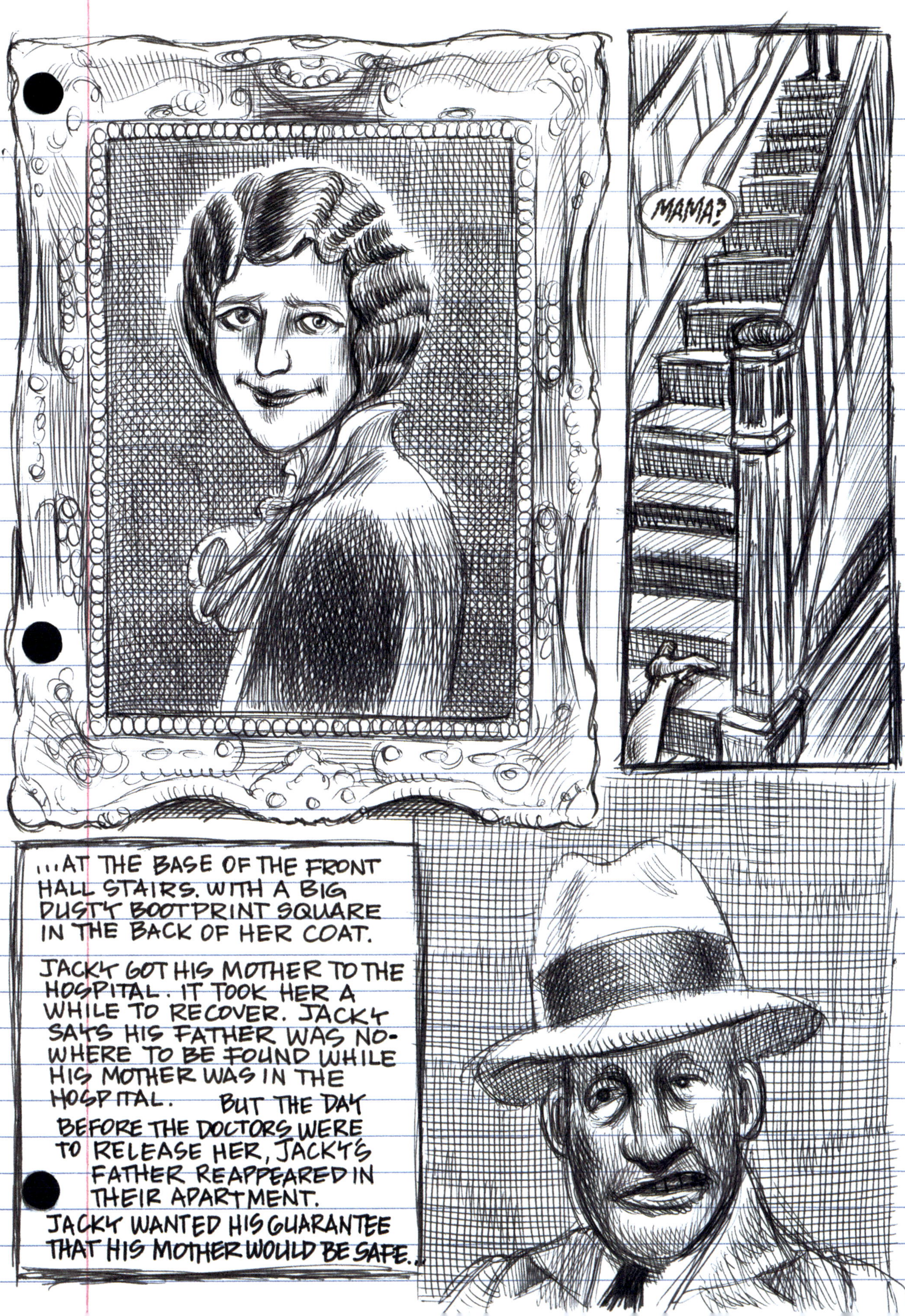
MAMA?
...AT THE BASE OF THE FRONT HALL STAIRS. WITH A BIG DUSTY BOOTPRINT SQUARE IN THE BACK OF HER COAT.
JACKY GOT HIS MOTHER TO THE HOSPITAL. IT TOOK HER A WHILE TO RECOVER. JACKY SAYS HIS FATHER WAS NOWHERE TO BE FOUND WHILE HIS MOTHER WAS IN THE HOSPITAL. BUT THE DAY BEFORE THE DOCTORS WERE TO RELEASE HER, JACKY'S FATHER REAPPEARED IN THEIR APARTMENT.
JACKY WANTED HIS GUARANTEE THAT HIS MOTHER WOULD BE SAFE...

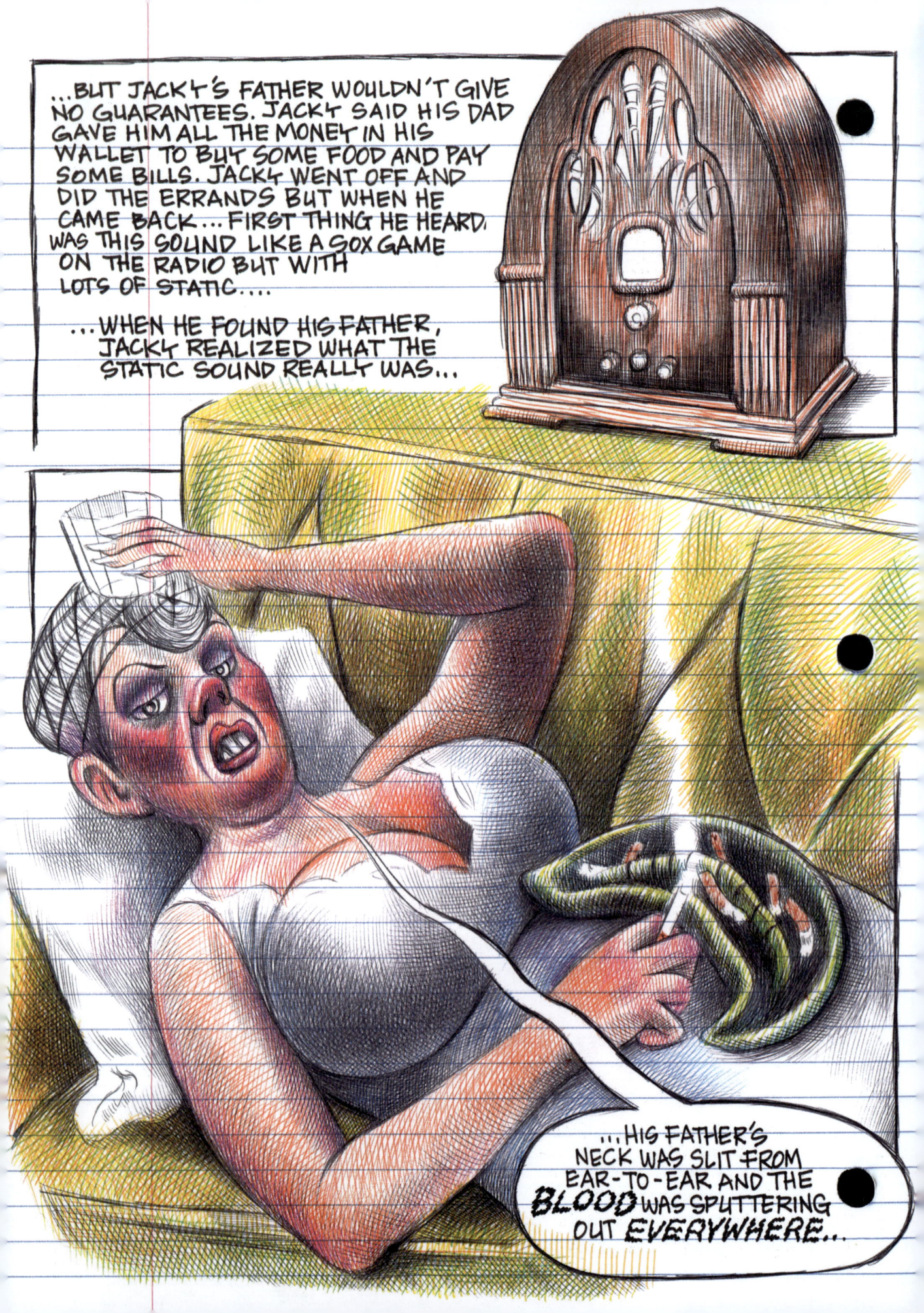

...BUT JACKY'S FATHER WOULDN'T GIVE NO GUARANTEES. JACKY SAID HIS DAD GAVE HIM ALL THE MONEY IN HIS WALLET TO BUY SOME FOOD AND PAY SOME BILLS. JACKY WENT OFF AND DID THE ERRANDS BUT WHEN HE CAME BACK... FIRST THING HE HEARD WAS THIS SOUND LIKE A SOX GAME ON THE RADIO BUT WITH LOTS OF STATIC....

...WHEN HE FOUND HIS FATHER, JACKY REALIZED WHAT THE STATIC SOUND REALLY WAS...

...HIS FATHER'S NECK WAS SLIT FROM EAR-TO-EAR AND THE **BLOOD** WAS SPUTTERING OUT *EVERYWHERE*...

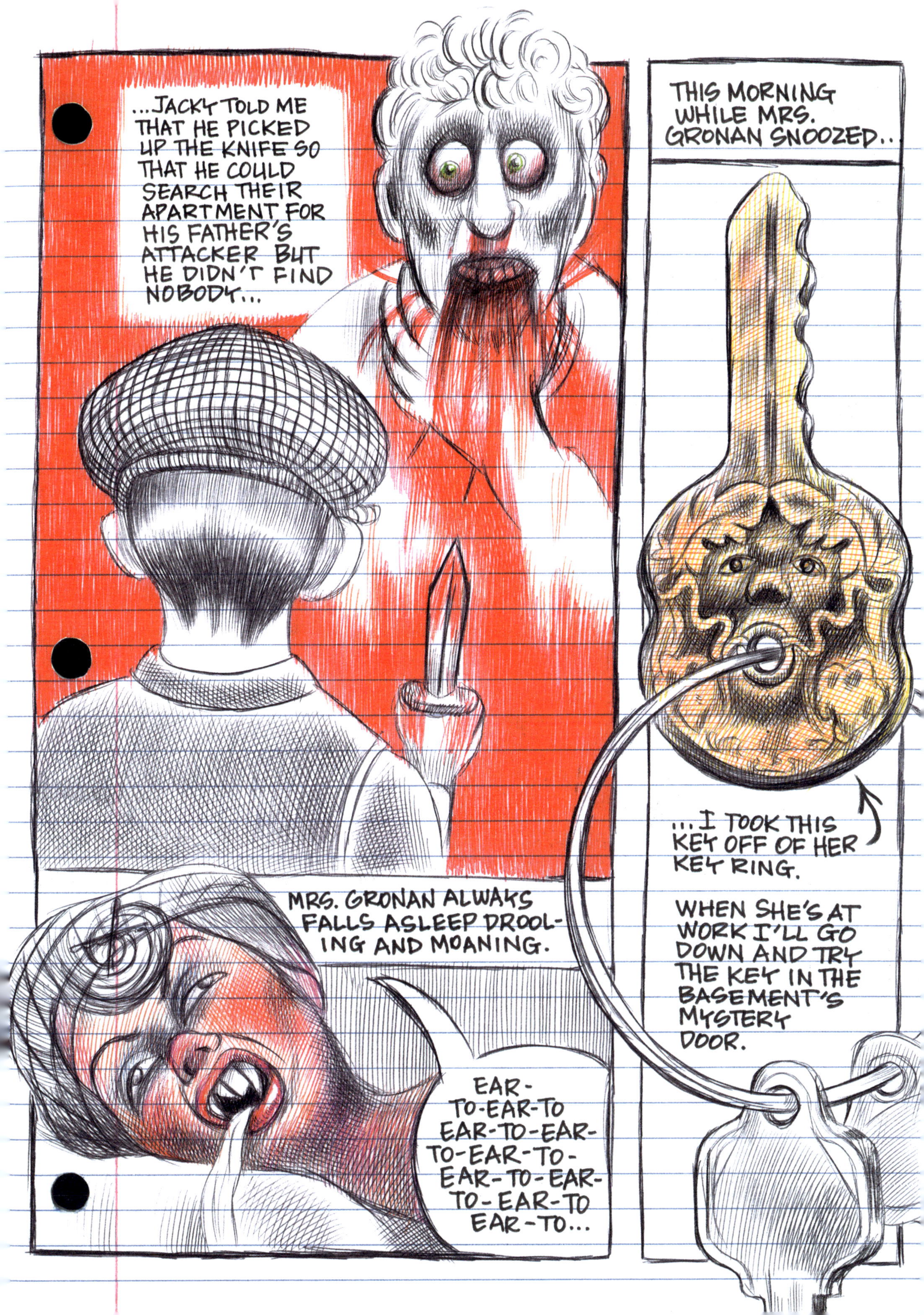
...JACKY TOLD ME THAT HE PICKED UP THE KNIFE SO THAT HE COULD SEARCH THEIR APARTMENT FOR HIS FATHER'S ATTACKER BUT HE DIDN'T FIND NOBODY...
MRS. GRONAN ALWAYS FALLS ASLEEP DROOL-ING AND MOANING.
EAR-TO-EAR-TO EAR-TO-EAR-TO-EAR-TO-EAR-TO-EAR-TO-EAR-TO EAR-TO...
THIS MORNING WHILE MRS. GRONAN SNOOZED...
...I TOOK THIS KEY OFF OF HER KEY RING.
WHEN SHE'S AT WORK I'LL GO DOWN AND TRY THE KEY IN THE BASEMENT'S MYSTERY DOOR.

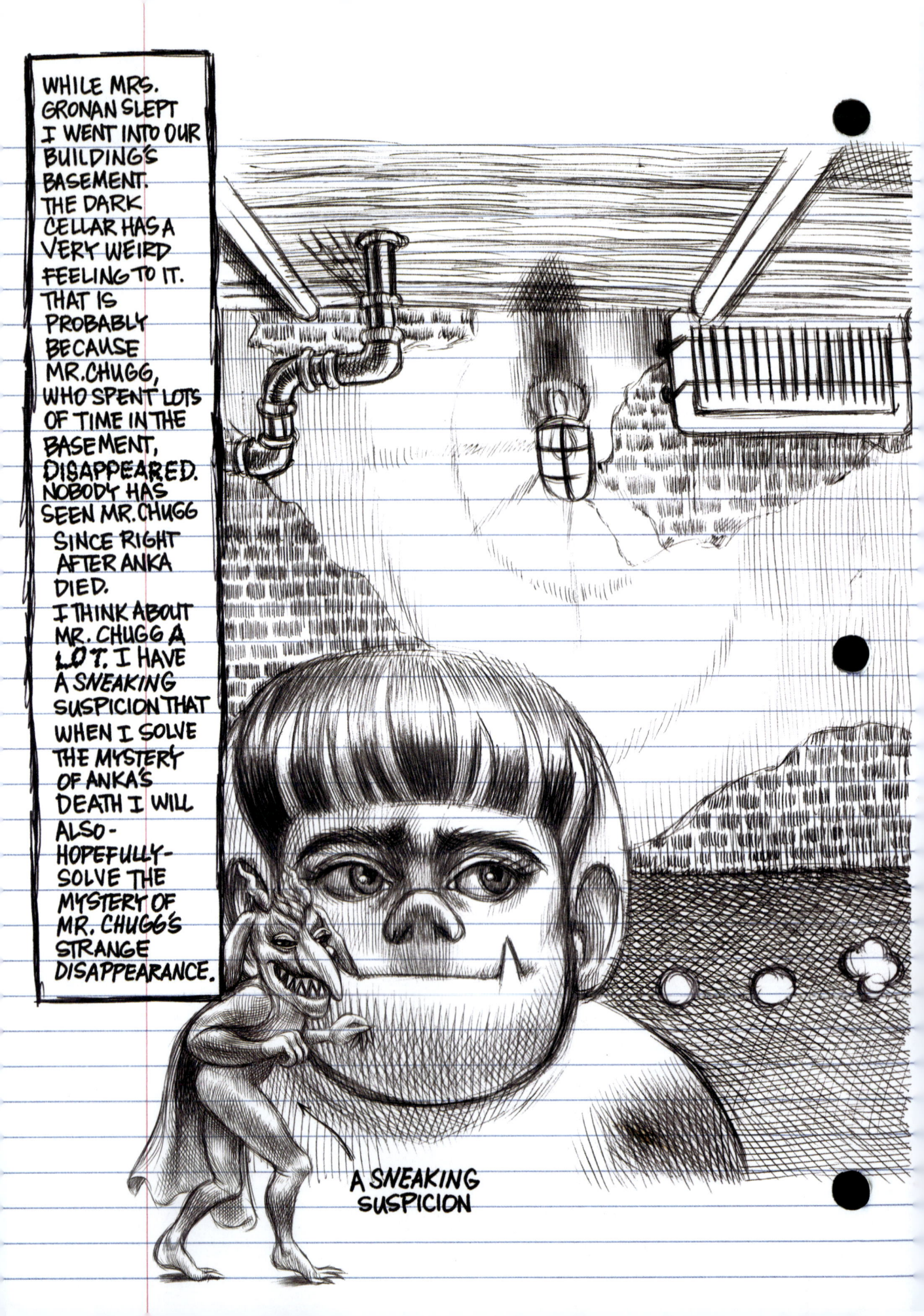

WHILE MRS. GRONAN SLEPT I WENT INTO OUR BUILDING'S BASEMENT. THE DARK CELLAR HAS A VERY WEIRD FEELING TO IT. THAT IS PROBABLY BECAUSE MR. CHUGG, WHO SPENT LOTS OF TIME IN THE BASEMENT, DISAPPEARED. NOBODY HAS SEEN MR. CHUGG SINCE RIGHT AFTER ANKA DIED. I THINK ABOUT MR. CHUGG A *LOT*. I HAVE A SNEAKING SUSPICION THAT WHEN I SOLVE THE MYSTERY OF ANKA'S DEATH I WILL ALSO - HOPEFULLY - SOLVE THE MYSTERY OF MR. CHUGG'S STRANGE DISAPPEARANCE.

A SNEAKING SUSPICION

CHUGG'S GLASS EYE

MR. CHUGG AND HIS DUMMY C.J.

THE BORING LOOKING KEY OPENED THE PADLOCK!

THE HEAVY WOODEN DOORS SWUNG OPEN
REVEALING ANOTHER - EVEN COOLER - DOOR.
IT'S WHAT I CALL 'THE GRAPE MONSTER
DOOR' EVEN THOUGH I'VE LEARNED IT IS
CALLED A **GREEN MAN**.
IT'S MADE OF BRASS OR BRONZE
AND IT'S BEAUTIFUL BUT ALSO **EXTREMELY
CREEPY** ESPECIALLY WHEN
YOU ARE THE ONLY ONE IN THE BASEMENT.
THERE IS ANOTHER GREEN PERSON DECORATION
ABOVE THE FRONT DOOR OF OUR BUILDING.
SINCE ME AND DEEZE NOW HAVE THE 'HONESTY
CLUB' I WILL ASK HIM WHY SOMEBODY PUT
THESE THINGS ON THE BUILDING WE LIVE IN...

THE GREEN MAN DOOR SQUEALED LIKE IT ALWAYS DOES WHEN IT'S OPENED. I SHIVERED FROM A GUST OF CHILLED MUSTY AIR THAT ROLLED UP THE STAIRS **RIGHT AT ME!!**

THAT WAS WHEN *TWO ODD THINGS* HAPPENED AT ONE TIME. I HEARD FAINT MUSIC COMING FROM THE DARKNESS BELOW. THE MUSIC SOUNDED LIKE THE BILLIE HOLIDAY RECORDS THAT MR. SILVERBERG HAS PLAYED FOR ME IN THE PAST.

"MR. CHUGG?"

THE SECOND STRANGE THING WAS THAT I HEARD THE SOUND OF KNOCKING COME FROM INSIDE OF THE FRONT DOOR OF MR. CHUGG'S EMPTY APARTMENT THAT IS ON THE OTHER SIDE OF THE BASEMENT. WHEN I WENT TO SEE WHO HAD MADE THE SOUND I FOUND THAT THE DOOR WAS UNLOCKED. AND EVEN THOUGH THERE WAS NOBODY *I COULD SEE* I AM NOW WONDERING IF WHAT I HEARD WAS MR. CHUGG'S **GHOST.**

HORRIFIC

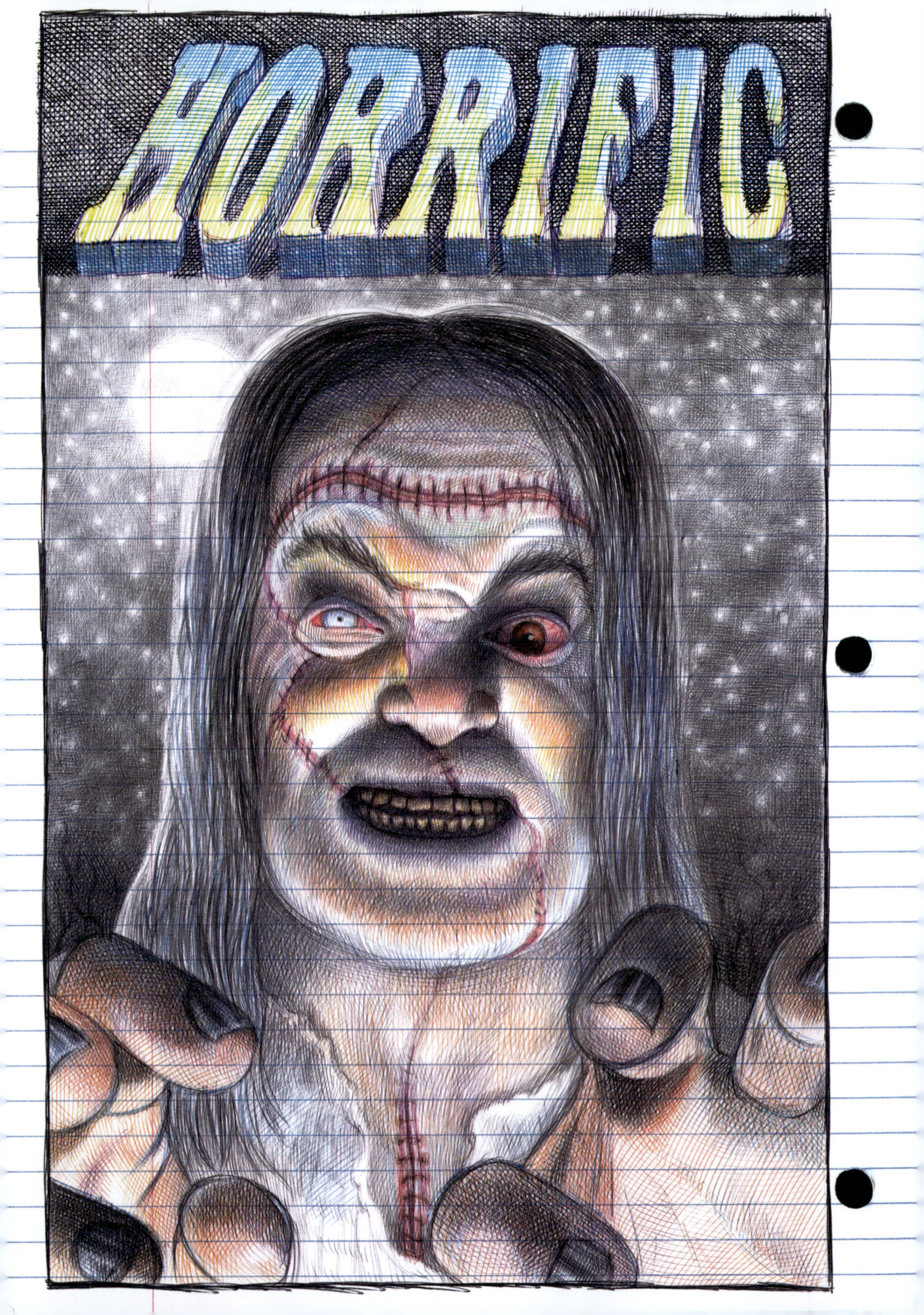

FRANKLIN'S APARTMENT IS BEAUTIFUL. HIS MOM HAS DECORATED IT WITH WONDERFUL COLORS. THE FOOD I ATE WAS FROM JAMAICA AND THE FLAVORS WERE STRANGE BUT GOOD.

I'M GOING TO BE PERFORMING AT THE CLUB DOWNSTAIRS AND I'D LIKE TO INVITE YOU.

CAN I BRING A FRIEND?

SURE. IT'S KIND OF FANCY SO I'D LIKE TO DESIGN AN OUTFIT FOR YOU, IF YOU'D LIKE.

FRANKLIN TOLD ME THAT HIS MOM OWNS THE CLUB DOWNSTAIRS. HE SAID THAT IT IS CALLED 'CLUB ALEXZANDRA' AND THAT HIS MOM MADE IT A GLAMOROUS PLACE WHERE PEOPLE CAN BE THEIR TRUEST SELVES. THAT WAS WHEN I TOLD HIM ABOUT...

"I KIND OF THINK I MIGHT HAVE A...UM...A KIND OF ACTUAL GIRLFRIEND...SO GOING TO YOUR MOM'S CLUB WILL BE OUR FIRST DATE."

"OH MY GOD!! THAT'S GREAT! WHAT'S SHE LIKE? HOW COME YOU SEEM A BIT UNHAPPY ABOUT IT?"

"HER NAME IS SHELLEY, SHE'S REAL SMART AND FUNNY AND TALENTED AND... ...AND VERY BEAUTIFUL."

"YEAH, YOU'RE RIGHT. MAMA WOULD BE REALLY DISAPPOINTED IN ME, IF SHE WAS HERE."

"...BUT THERE'S MORE TO IT THAN THAT, RIGHT? BECAUSE OF COURSE YOU KNOW THAT *YOU* HAVE TO LEAD *YOUR* LIFE AND *NOT* YOUR MOM'S LIFE...SO WHAT'S THE *OTHER* PROBLEM?"

"FRANKLIN, I'M NOT GOOD ENOUGH FOR SHELLEY. SHE'S SO *COOL* AND EVERY TIME I'M WITH HER I WONDER WHEN SHE'LL JUST LOOK AT ME AND SAY, 'I JUST REALIZED HOW UNCOOL AND *GROSS* YOU ARE, KAREN, AND NOW I HAVE TO RUN SCREAMING INTO THE NIGHT TO GET AWAY FROM YOU.'"

OH HONEY! YOU'RE GOING TO NEED A MAGICAL SUIT.

KAREN, I'D LIKE YOU TO DO SOMETHING FOR ME. COULD YOU CALL ME BY A DIFFERENT NAME? COULD YOU CALL ME 'FRAN-SWAAZ?'

FRAN-SWAAZ? BUT WHAT'S SO BAD ABOUT THE NAME 'FRANKLIN?'

PLEEASE! 'FRANKLIN' IS SUCH A CLUNKY NAME. WHEN A HEAVY BRICK FALLS ON YOUR FOOT IT SHOULD BE CALLED, 'A FRANKLIN.'

...BUT FRAN-SWAAZ COULD BE THE SOUND THAT A SILK SCARF MAKES WHEN IT GLIDES OFF THE NAKED SHOULDER OF A BEAUTIFUL WOMAN.

FRANK... UM I MEAN FRAN-SWAAZ, IT MIGHT TAKE ME A WHILE TO GET USED TO IT.

LET ME SHOW YOU THE SPECIAL WAY IT'S SPELLED.

THEN FRAN-SWAAZ WROTE ON THE PAPER OF A DRESS PATTERN 'HER NAME IS FRANÇOISE.'

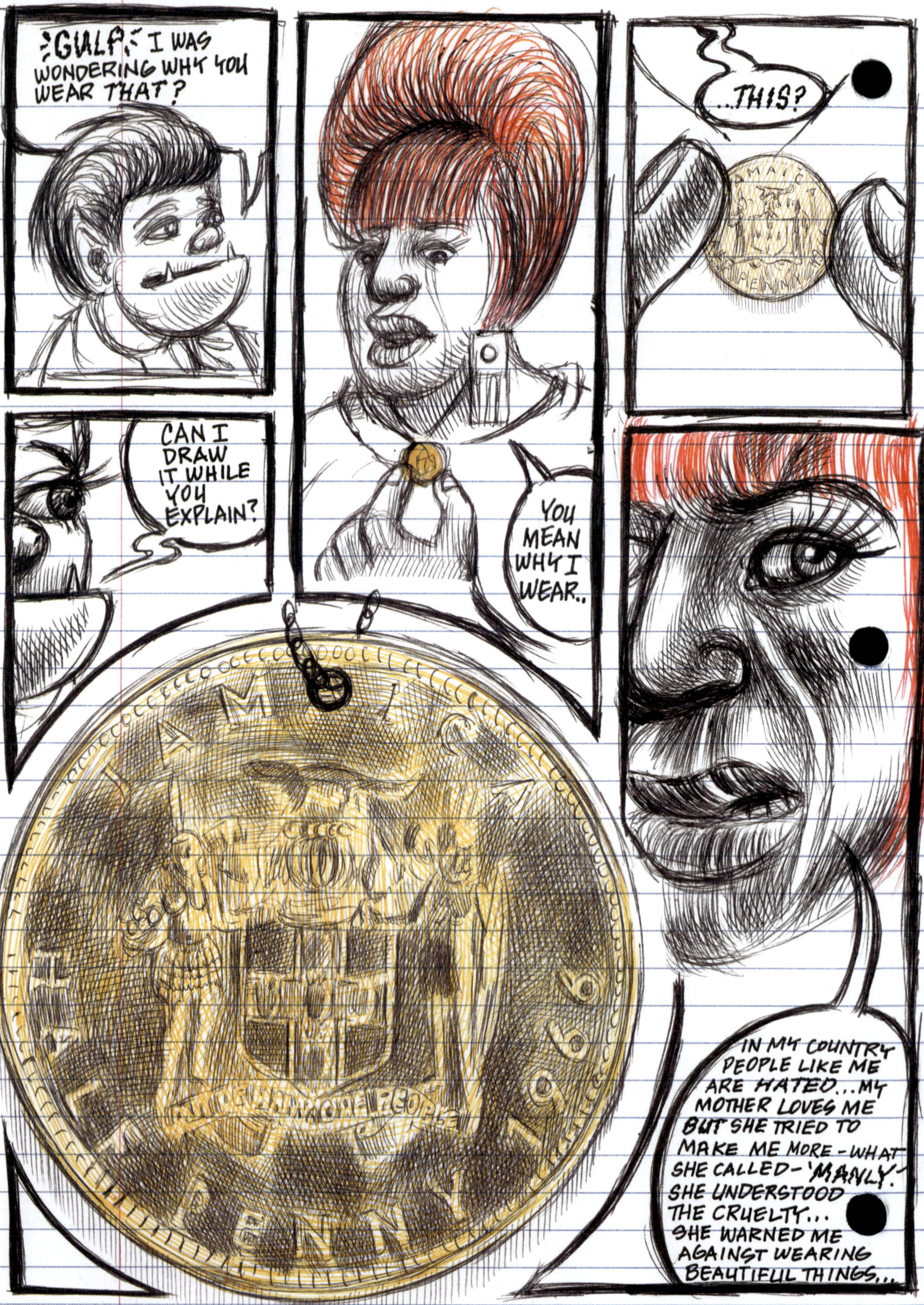
GULP I WAS WONDERING WHY YOU WEAR THAT?
YOU MEAN WHY I WEAR..
...THIS?
CAN I DRAW IT WHILE YOU EXPLAIN?
IN MY COUNTRY PEOPLE LIKE ME ARE HATED... MY MOTHER LOVES ME BUT SHE TRIED TO MAKE ME MORE - WHAT SHE CALLED - 'MANLY.' SHE UNDERSTOOD THE CRUELTY... SHE WARNED ME AGAINST WEARING BEAUTIFUL THINGS...

AFTER THE NEIGHBORHOOD MEN WERE FINISHED WITH ME, THEY DUMPED ME IN A FIELD. I TOLD THE CLOUDS TO TELL MY MOTHER WHERE I WAS...

...BUT I DIDN'T LISTEN.

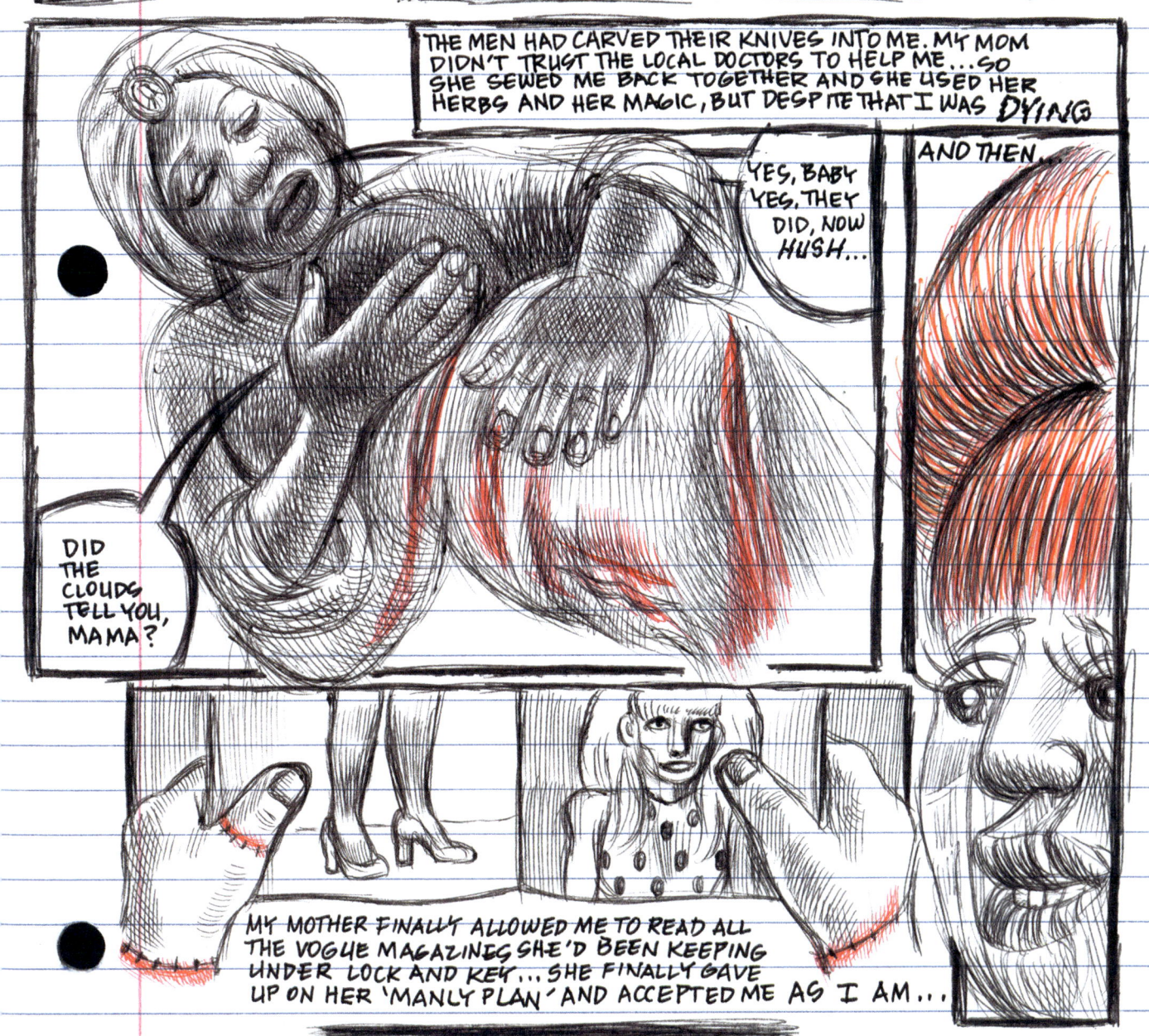

THE MEN HAD CARVED THEIR KNIVES INTO ME. MY MOM DIDN'T TRUST THE LOCAL DOCTORS TO HELP ME... SO SHE SEWED ME BACK TOGETHER AND SHE USED HER HERBS AND HER MAGIC, BUT DESPITE THAT I WAS *DYING*

YES, BABY YES, THEY DID, NOW *HUSH*...

AND THEN...

DID THE CLOUDS TELL YOU, MAMA?

MY MOTHER FINALLY ALLOWED ME TO READ ALL THE VOGUE MAGAZINES SHE'D BEEN KEEPING UNDER LOCK AND KEY... SHE FINALLY GAVE UP ON HER 'MANLY PLAN' AND ACCEPTED ME AS I AM...

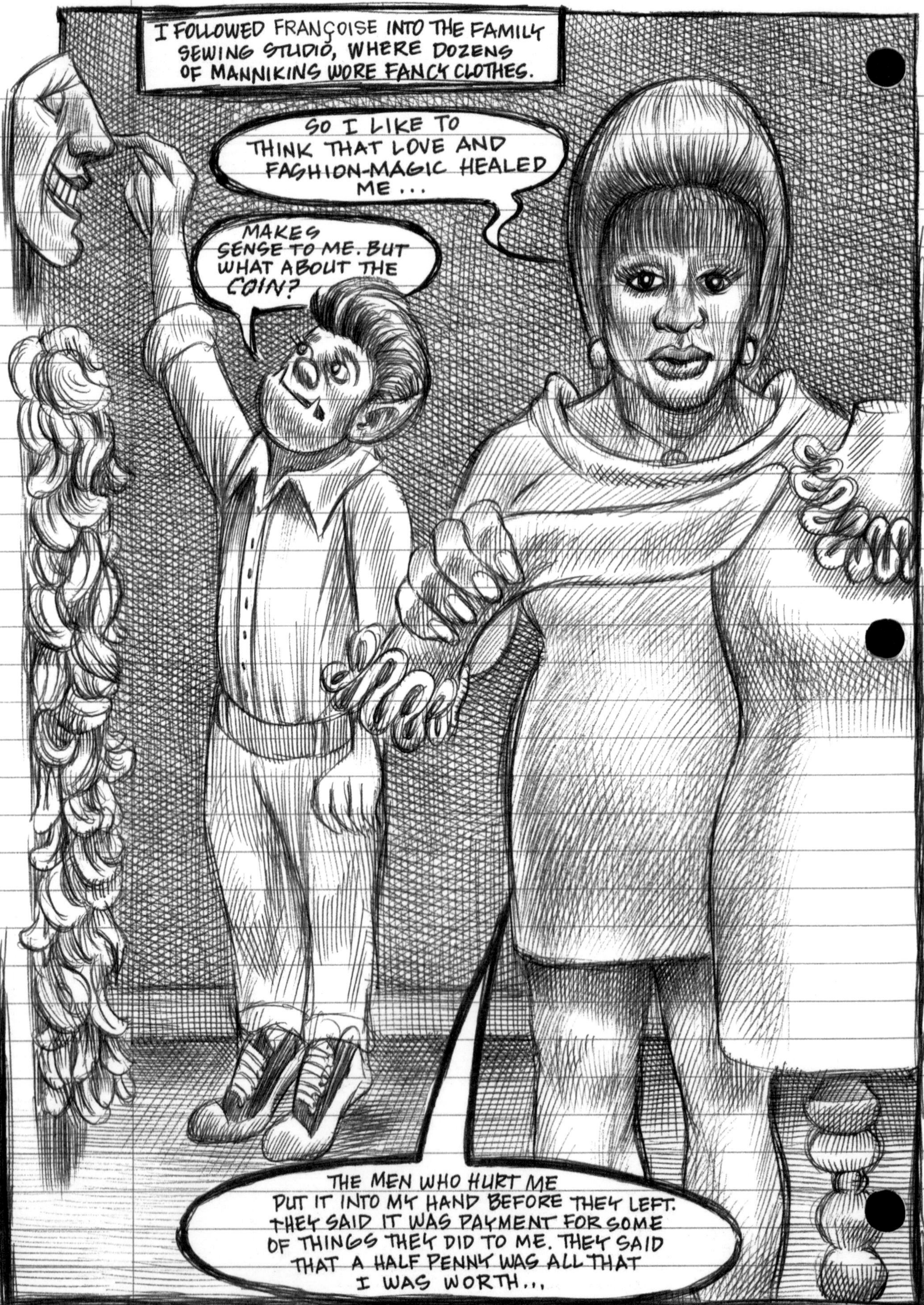
I FOLLOWED FRANÇOISE INTO THE FAMILY SEWING STUDIO, WHERE DOZENS OF MANNIKINS WORE FANCY CLOTHES.
SO I LIKE TO THINK THAT LOVE AND FASHION-MAGIC HEALED ME...
MAKES SENSE TO ME. BUT WHAT ABOUT THE COIN?
THE MEN WHO HURT ME PUT IT INTO MY HAND BEFORE THEY LEFT. THEY SAID IT WAS PAYMENT FOR SOME OF THINGS THEY DID TO ME. THEY SAID THAT A HALF PENNY WAS ALL THAT I WAS WORTH...

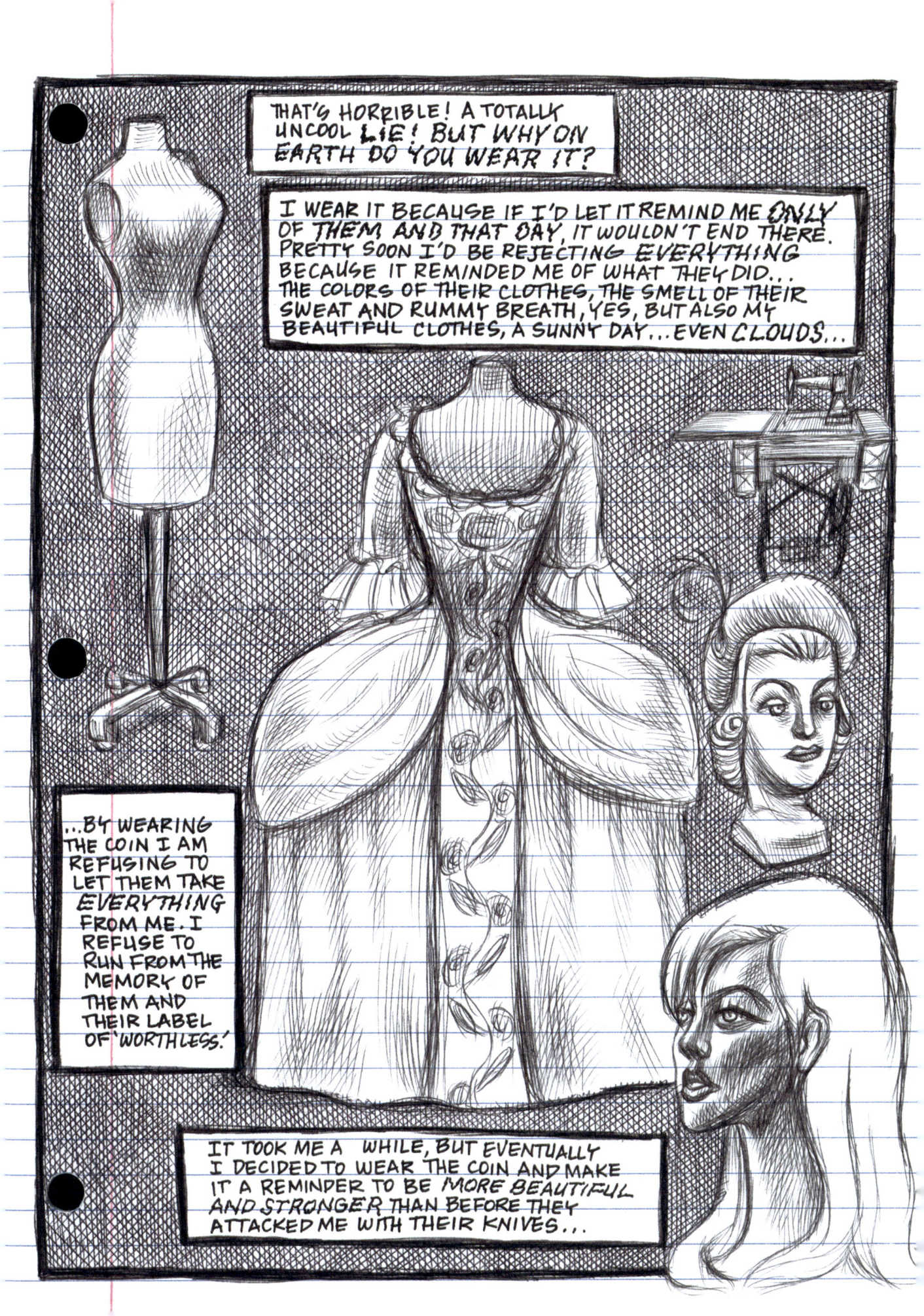

THAT'S HORRIBLE! A TOTALLY UNCOOL *LIE!* BUT WHY ON EARTH DO YOU WEAR IT?

I WEAR IT BECAUSE IF I'D LET IT REMIND ME *ONLY* OF *THEM*, AND THAT *DAY*, IT WOULDN'T END THERE. PRETTY SOON I'D BE REJECTING *EVERYTHING* BECAUSE IT REMINDED ME OF WHAT THEY DID... THE COLORS OF THEIR CLOTHES, THE SMELL OF THEIR SWEAT AND RUMMY BREATH, YES, BUT ALSO MY BEAUTIFUL CLOTHES, A SUNNY DAY... EVEN *CLOUDS*...

...BY WEARING THE COIN I AM REFUSING TO LET THEM TAKE *EVERYTHING* FROM ME. I REFUSE TO RUN FROM THE MEMORY OF THEM AND THEIR LABEL OF 'WORTHLESS.'

IT TOOK ME A WHILE, BUT EVENTUALLY I DECIDED TO WEAR THE COIN AND MAKE IT A REMINDER TO BE *MORE BEAUTIFUL AND STRONGER* THAN BEFORE THEY ATTACKED ME WITH THEIR KNIVES...

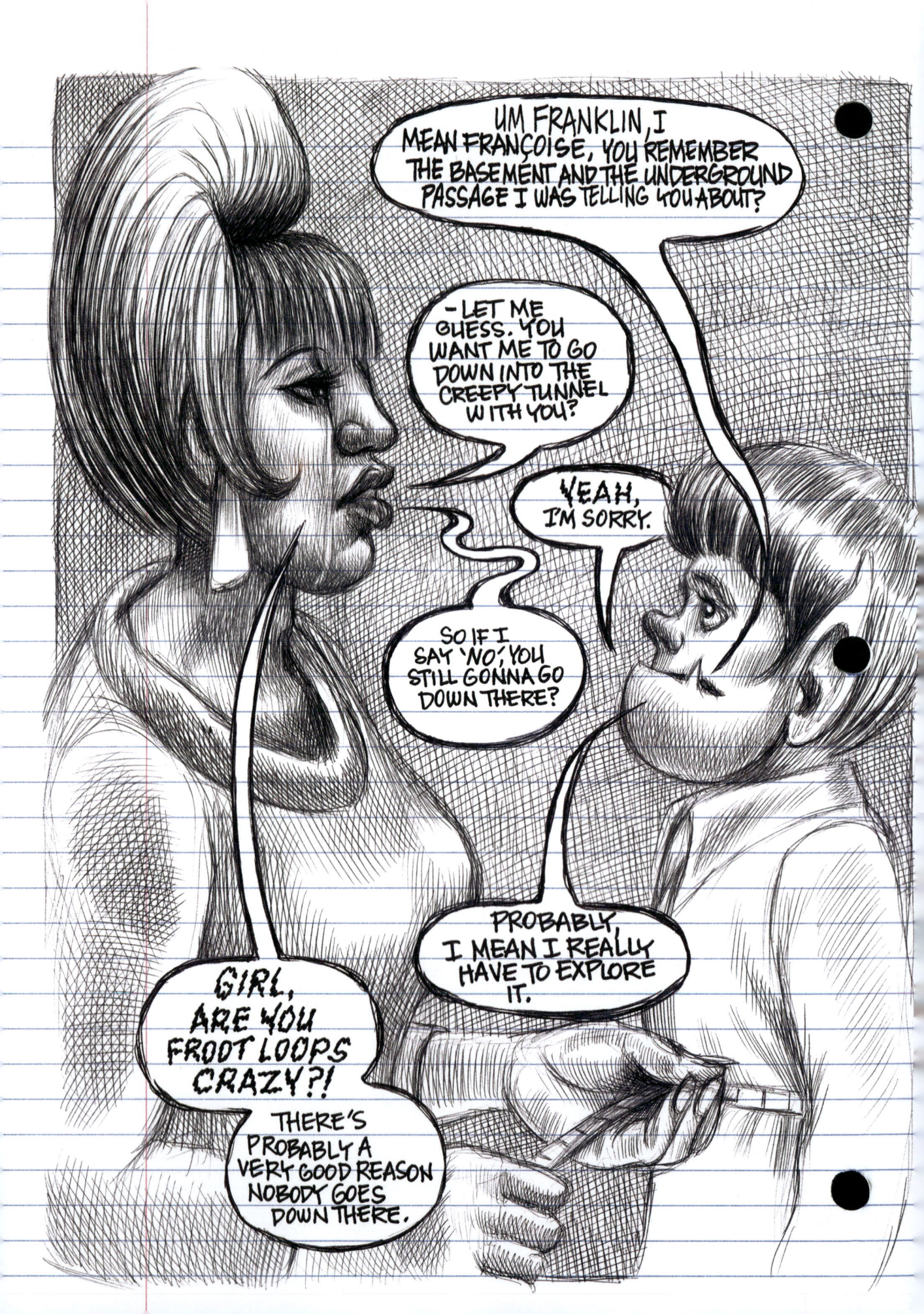

UM FRANKLIN, I MEAN FRANÇOISE, YOU REMEMBER THE BASEMENT AND THE UNDERGROUND PASSAGE I WAS TELLING YOU ABOUT?

- LET ME GUESS. YOU WANT ME TO GO DOWN INTO THE CREEPY TUNNEL WITH YOU?

YEAH, I'M SORRY.

SO IF I SAY 'NO', YOU STILL GONNA GO DOWN THERE?

PROBABLY. I MEAN I REALLY HAVE TO EXPLORE IT.

GIRL, ARE YOU FROOT LOOPS CRAZY?!

THERE'S PROBABLY A VERY GOOD REASON NOBODY GOES DOWN THERE.

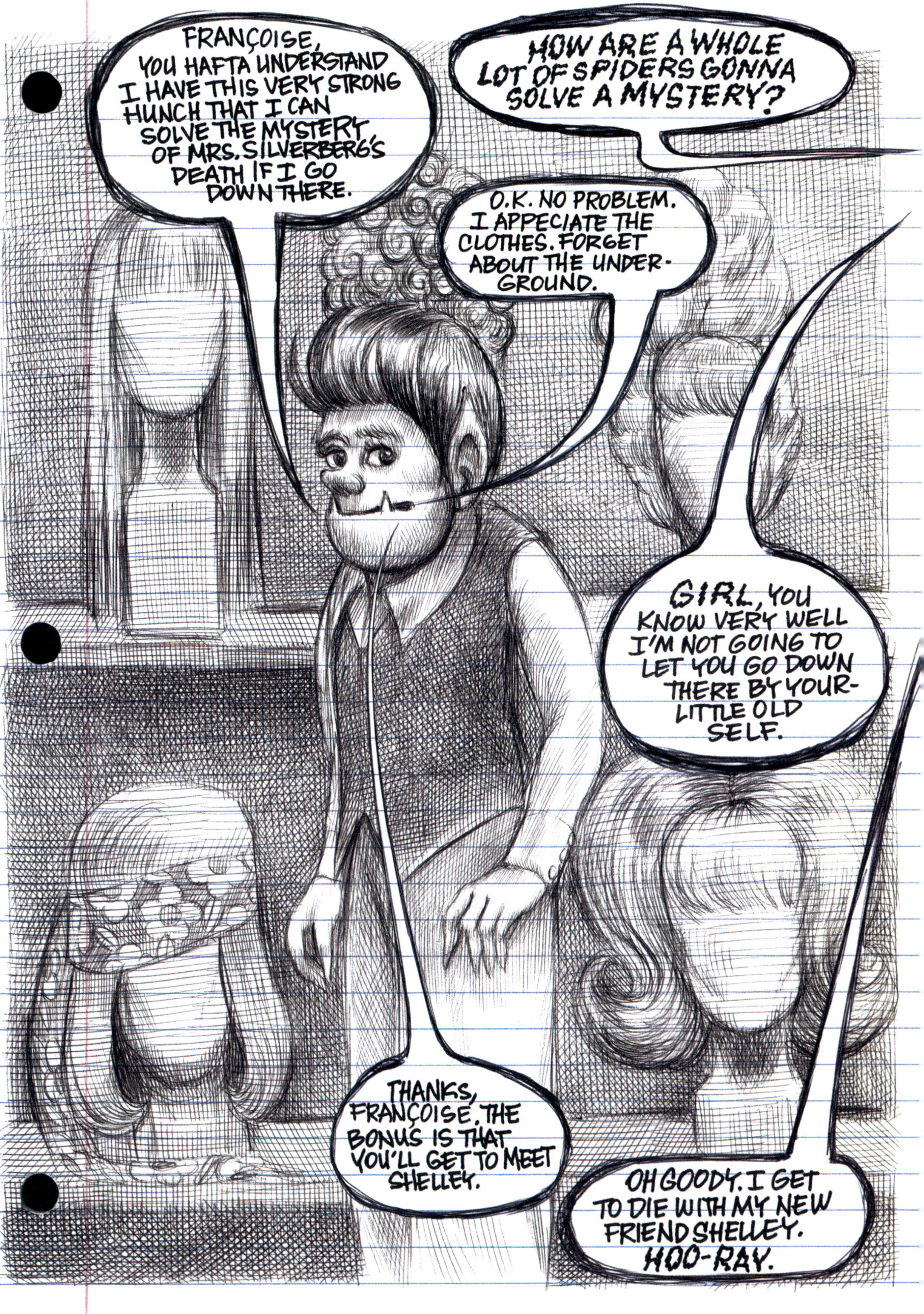
FRANÇOISE, YOU HAFTA UNDERSTAND I HAVE THIS VERY STRONG HUNCH THAT I CAN SOLVE THE MYSTERY OF MRS. SILVERBERG'S DEATH IF I GO DOWN THERE.
HOW ARE A WHOLE LOT OF SPIDERS GONNA SOLVE A MYSTERY?
O.K. NO PROBLEM. I APPECIATE THE CLOTHES. FORGET ABOUT THE UNDER-GROUND.
GIRL, YOU KNOW VERY WELL I'M NOT GOING TO LET YOU GO DOWN THERE BY YOUR-LITTLE OLD SELF.
THANKS, FRANÇOISE. THE BONUS IS THAT YOU'LL GET TO MEET SHELLEY.
OH GOODY. I GET TO DIE WITH MY NEW FRIEND SHELLEY. HOO-RAY.

WHEN I ASKED FRANÇOISE WHY HER MOM WAS WALKING WITH US SHE SAID HER MOM WAS 'PACKING HEAT' AND WOULDN'T HESITATE TO USE IT IF ANYONE TRIES TO HURT US.

"DEEZE SAYS IT'S ILLEGAL TO CARRY A GUN AROUND WITHOUT A PERMIT BUT I'M PRETTY SURE HE DOES IT ANYWAY."

"WELL, FAMOUS PEOPLE ALL HAVE ARMED BODYGUARDS... MY MOM SAYS IT'S BETTER TO BE JUDGED BY TWELVE THAN CARRIED BY SIX."

"KAREN, WHAT I KNOW ABOUT VIOLENCE ISN'T SIMPLE. IT'S DEEP AND COMPLEX."

"BUT I THOUGHT YOU WERE AGAINST VIOLENCE AND STUFF."

"THE WORLD IS VIOLENT, BUT THE MOST DANGEROUS ACTS AREN'T ONLY WHAT PEOPLE DO TO EACH OTHER. IT'S WHAT THIS SYSTEM CONVINCES YOU IS THE TRUTH ABOUT *YOU!* THEY GO AFTER ARTISTS TWICE AS HARD. MOM SAYS IT'S LIKE A BAD HUSBAND. HE WANTS TO EAT YOUR PEPPER POT SOUP SO HE MAKES YOU BELIEVE YOU ARE WORTH SO LITTLE THAT NO ONE ELSE WOULD HAVE YOU."

"I MYSELF AM HEAVEN AND HELL." MAYBE THE POET WROTE THAT TO CONVINCE US THAT WE ARE BOTH.

THAT'S WHEN FRANÇOISE TURNED HER HEAD AND LOCKED HER BEAUTIFUL EYES ONTO MINE.

"FRANÇOISE, MY DARLING, PUT THAT HAT BACK ON YOUR HEAD."

"MOM, I TOOK THE HAT OFF SO THAT KAREN WOULD UNDERSTAND HOW SERIOUS I AM RIGHT NOW."

"IT FREAKS MOM OUT CUZ I STILL HAVE MY GORGEOUS FALSE EYELASHES ON."

"THIS IS A TIME WHEN YOU MIGHT BE TEMPTED TO CLOSE YOUR HEART. YOU MIGHT BELIEVE THAT YOU'D BE CRAZY TO CONTINUE LOVING A WORLD WHERE MOTHERS CAN DIE. IN THAT KIND OF A STATE OF GRIEF AND LOSS I... I TOOK REVENGE... BUT INSTEAD OF RELIEF, I FELT A HELLISH *DESPAIR*. I STOLE THE SPARK OF LIFE THAT MY ENEMY HELD IN HIS CRUEL HANDS AND I EXTINGUISHED IT. IN THAT MOMENT I SAW THAT I WAS STRONG ENOUGH TO TAKE A LIFE BUT I WOULD NEVER BE POWERFUL ENOUGH TO *GIVE IT BACK.*"

"GIRLFRIEND, I SENSE THAT SOMEONE OR SOME*THING* IS FOLLOWING YOU."

"UM, WAIT. WHAT? UH OH."

I TOLD FRANÇOISE I UNDERSTOOD WHY SHE'D GOTTEN ANGRY ENOUGH TO HURT SOMEONE AND WHEN WE REACHED MY BUILDING FRANÇOISE HUGGED ME AND WHISPERED IN MY EAR THAT I SHOULD STAY IN MY APARTMENT.

DREAD

50¢

I SPENT THE WHOLE SCHOOL WEEK (HELL WEEK) WAITING FOR SATURDAY NIGHT WHEN I'D INTRODUCE SHELLEY AND FRANÇOISE AND WE'D GO INTO THE UNDERGROUND...

CHARON THE FERRYMAN

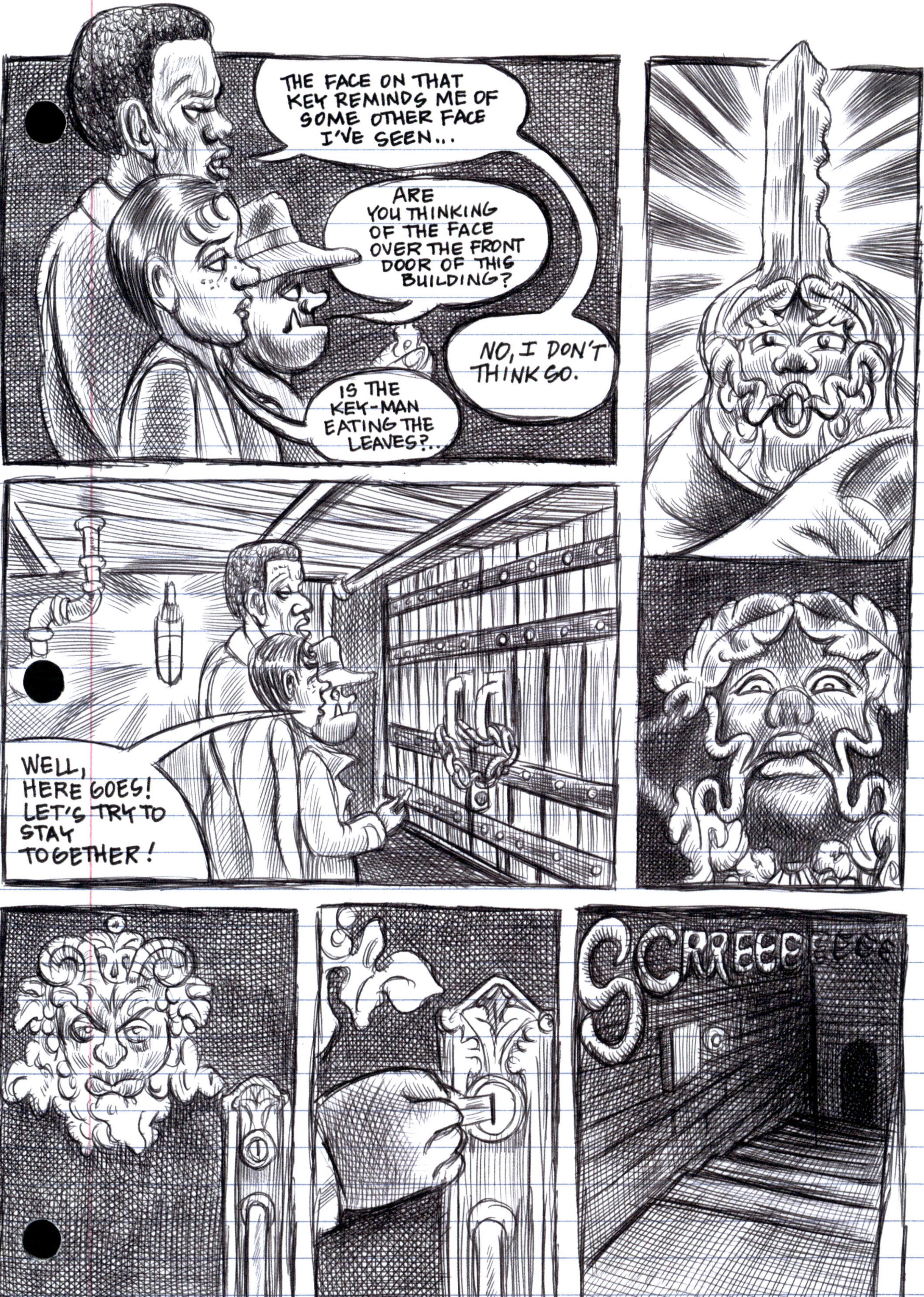
THE FACE ON THAT KEY REMINDS ME OF SOME OTHER FACE I'VE SEEN...
ARE YOU THINKING OF THE FACE OVER THE FRONT DOOR OF THIS BUILDING?
NO, I DON'T THINK SO.
IS THE KEY-MAN EATING THE LEAVES?...
WELL, HERE GOES! LET'S TRY TO STAY TOGETHER!
SCRREEEEEEE

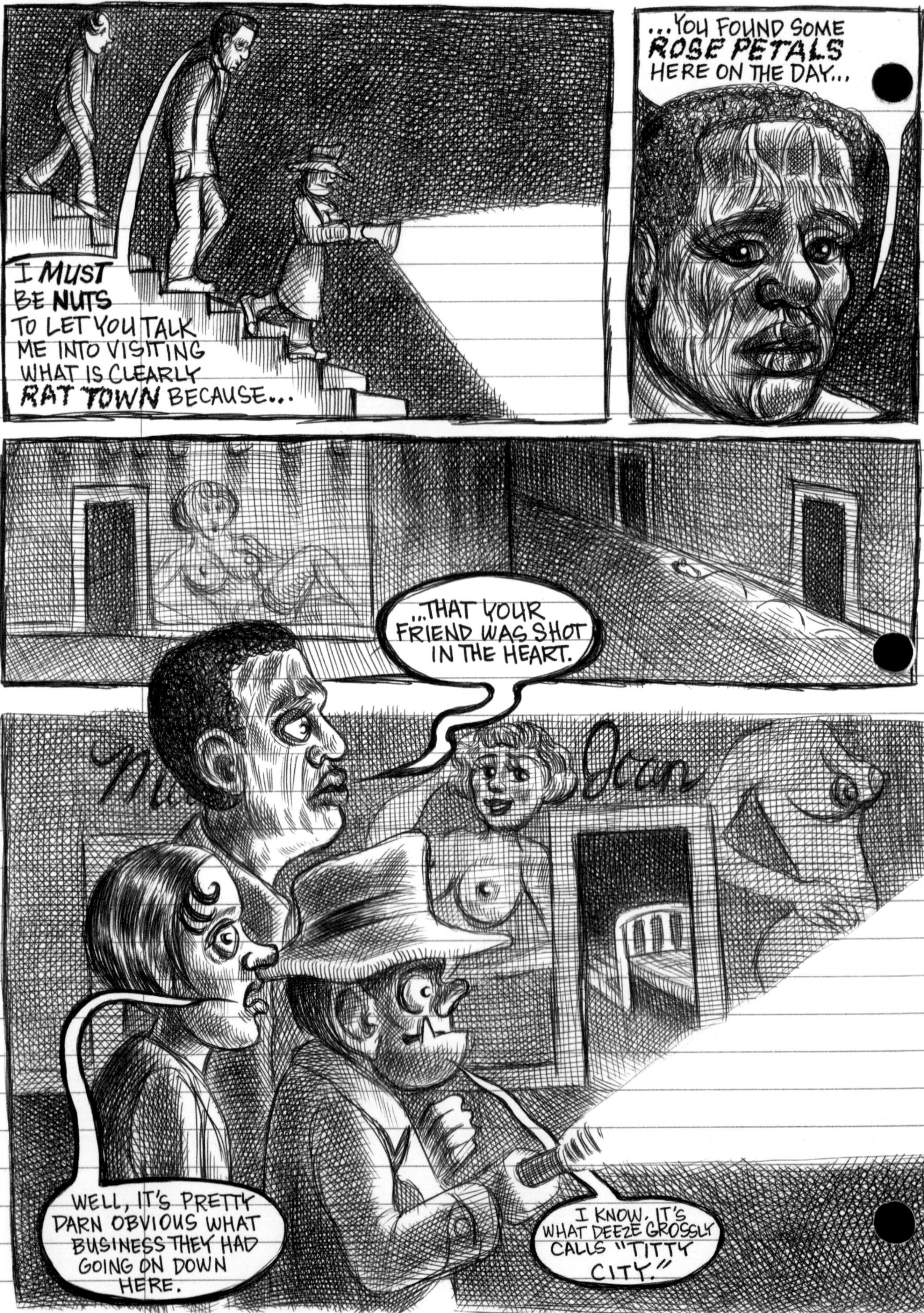
I MUST BE NUTS TO LET YOU TALK ME INTO VISITING WHAT IS CLEARLY RAT TOWN BECAUSE...
...YOU FOUND SOME ROSE PETALS HERE ON THE DAY...
...THAT YOUR FRIEND WAS SHOT IN THE HEART.
WELL, IT'S PRETTY DARN OBVIOUS WHAT BUSINESS THEY HAD GOING ON DOWN HERE.
I KNOW. IT'S WHAT DEEZE GROSSLY CALLS "TITTY CITY."

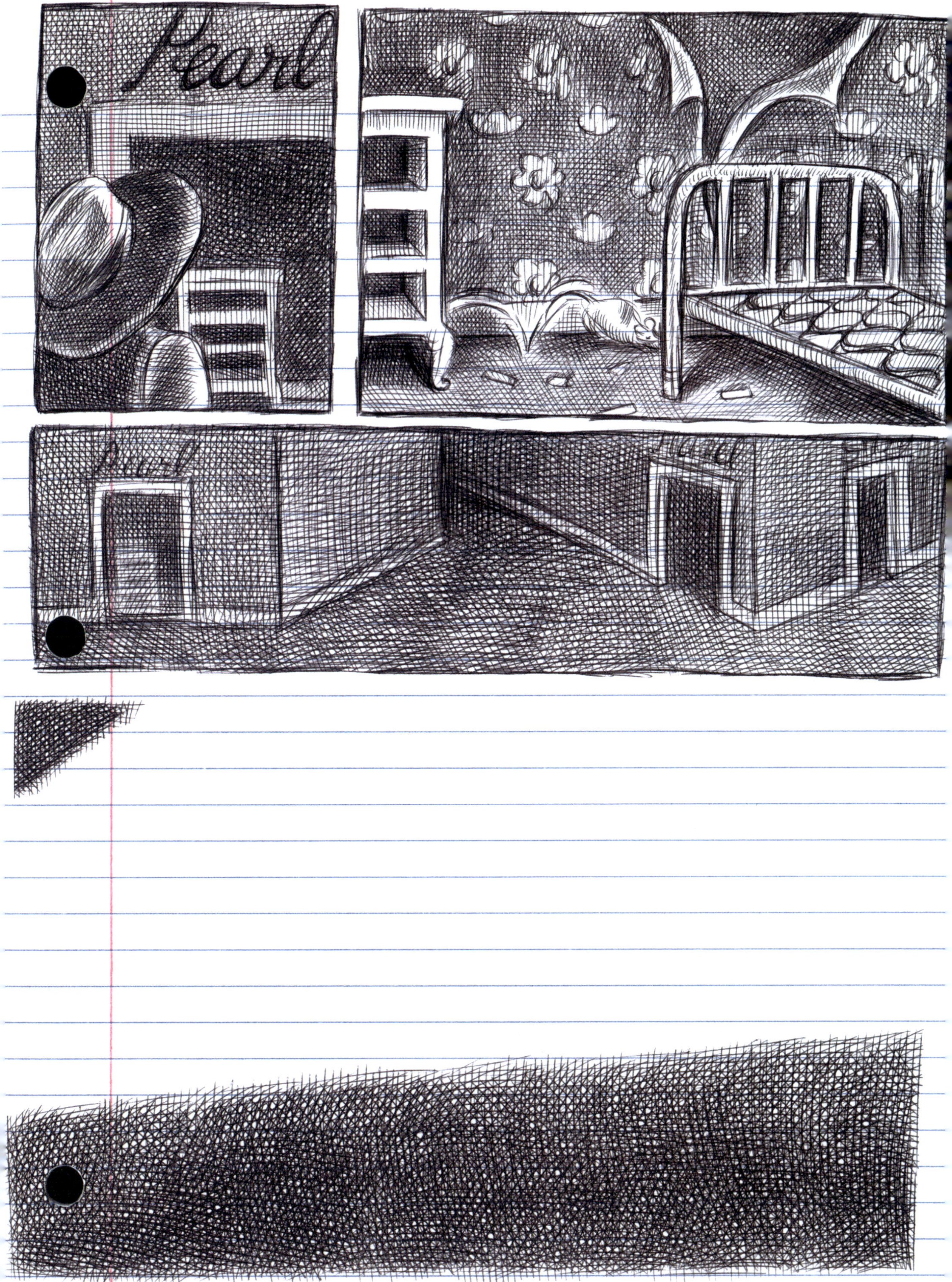
Pearl

"HEY, WAIT A SECOND. WHERE'S SHELLEY?"

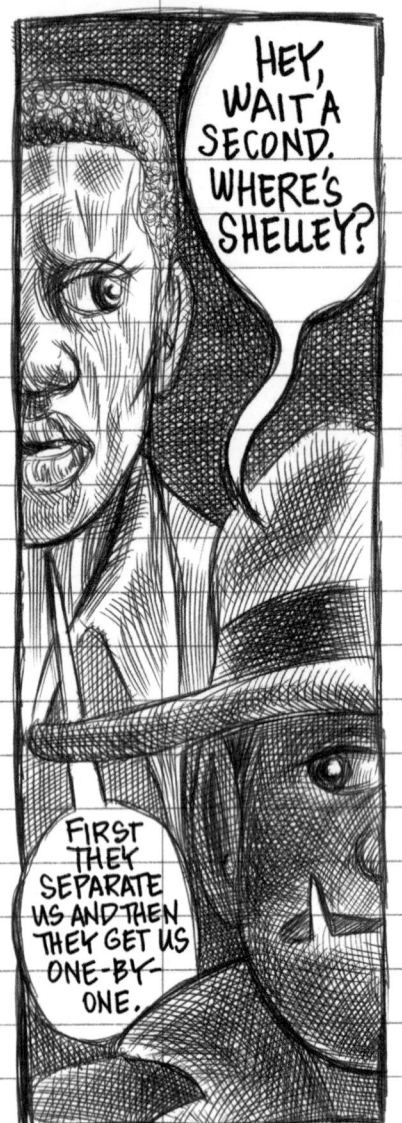

LUCKILY RIGHT THEN I HEARD SHELLEY CALLING TO ME FROM SOMEWHERE DEEP IN A DARK HALL.

"KAREN... KAAAARRRENN... THERE'S A LITTLE MAN HERE BUT HE ISN'T ALIVE."

"FIRST THEY SEPARATE US AND THEN THEY GET US ONE-BY-ONE."

WHEN WE FOUND HER SHE WAS KIND OF SAD AND FREAKED OUT...

"HE'S A CLUE... BUT... ...I'M NOT SURE WHAT THE CRIME WAS..."

THE THOUGHT OCCURRED TO ME THAT THE SMALL PERSON MIGHT BE MY MISSING NEIGHBOR — THE VENTRILOQUIST MR. SEAMUS CHUGG.

"HIS NAME IS C.J. CHUGG."

C.J. WAS LIKE MR. CHUGG'S FIRST BORN SON AND HE *NEVER* WENT ANYWHERE WITHOUT HIM.

"WE NEED TO VAMOOSE! BUT AS WE GO WE NEED TO KEEP AN EYE OUT FOR MR. CHUGG'S BODY."

"IT WORRIES ME THAT MR. CHUGG LEFT C.J. HERE... I PACKED HIM INTO HIS CASE..."

AS WE HIGHTAILED IT OUT OF THERE, WE PASSED STILLS...

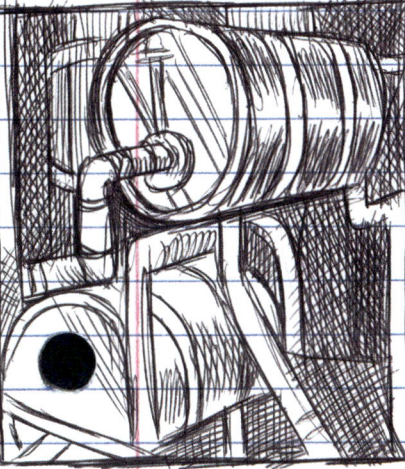

...AND WE PASSED PLACES TO DRINK WHAT THE SIGNS DESCRIBED AS 'GIGGLE WATER.'

"HOLD IT RIGHT THERE!"

MY BLOOD RAN COLD.

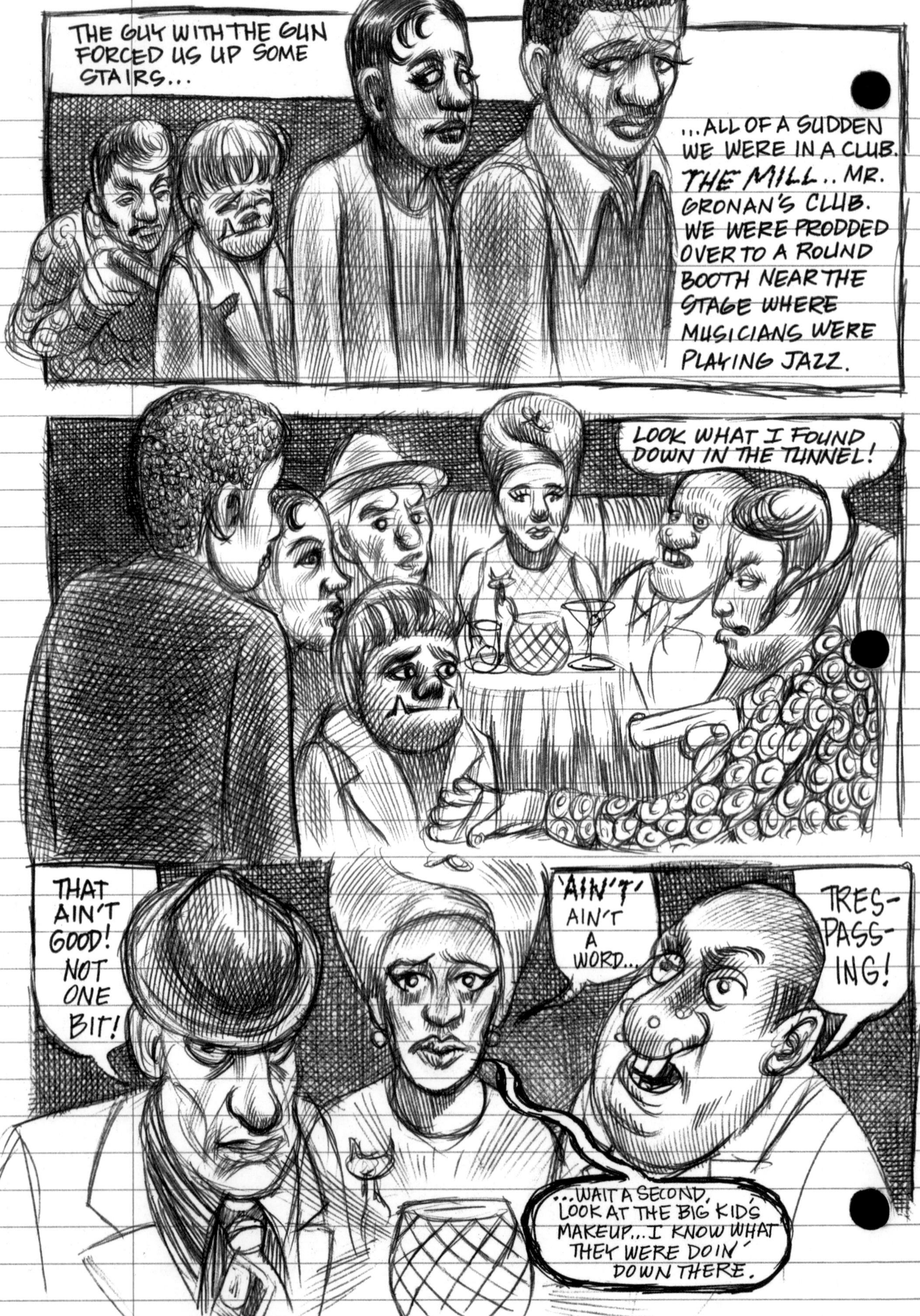
THE GUY WITH THE GUN FORCED US UP SOME STAIRS...
...ALL OF A SUDDEN WE WERE IN A CLUB. THE MILL.. MR. GRONAN'S CLUB. WE WERE PRODDED OVER TO A ROUND BOOTH NEAR THE STAGE WHERE MUSICIANS WERE PLAYING JAZZ.
LOOK WHAT I FOUND DOWN IN THE TUNNEL!
THAT AIN'T GOOD! NOT ONE BIT!
'AIN'T' AIN'T A WORD...
TRES-PASS-ING!
...WAIT A SECOND, LOOK AT THE BIG KID'S MAKEUP... I KNOW WHAT THEY WERE DOIN' DOWN THERE.

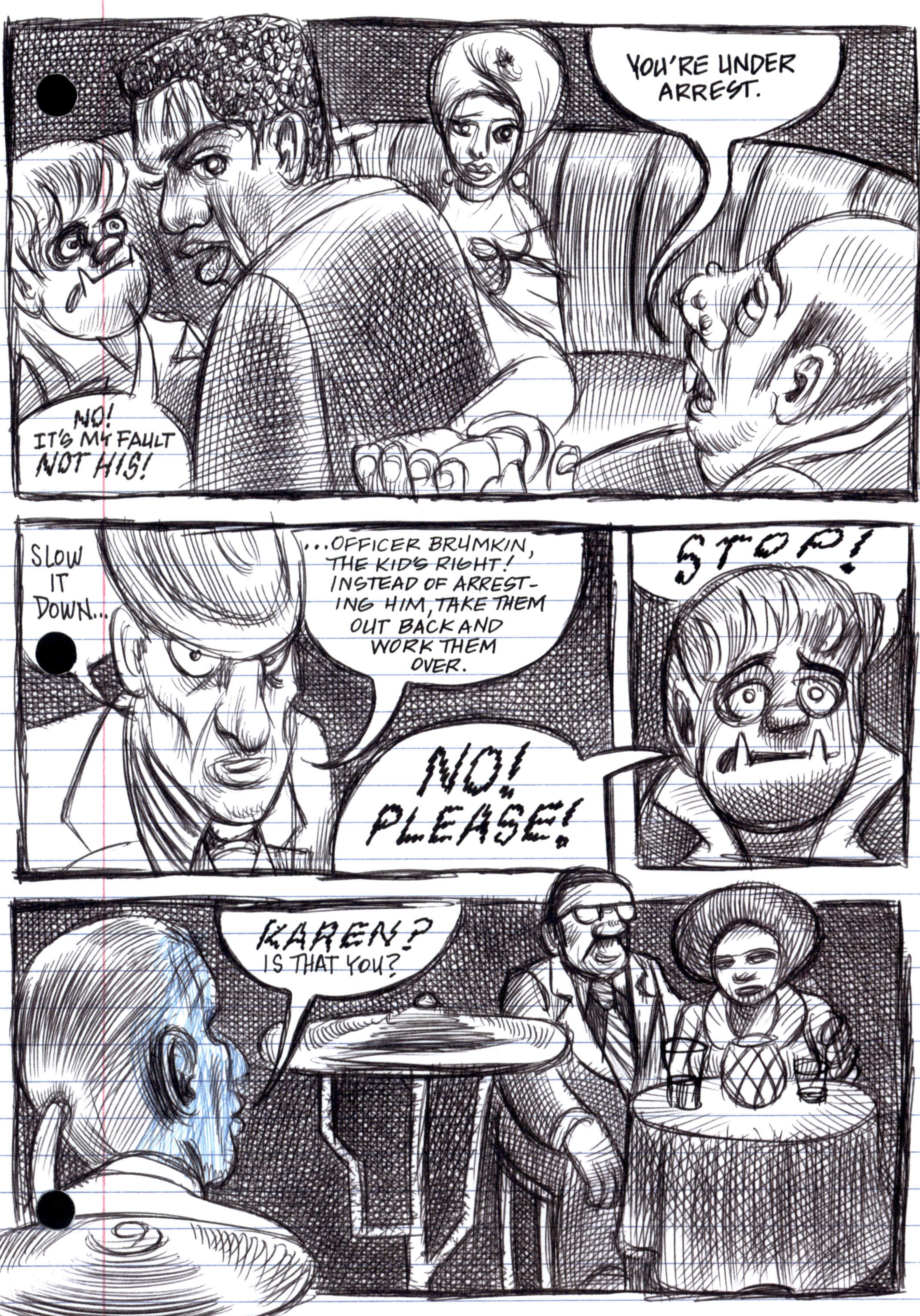
YOU'RE UNDER ARREST.
NO! IT'S MY FAULT NOT HIS!
SLOW IT DOWN...
...OFFICER BRUMKIN, THE KID'S RIGHT! INSTEAD OF ARRESTING HIM, TAKE THEM OUT BACK AND WORK THEM OVER.
STOP!
NO! PLEASE!
KAREN? IS THAT YOU?

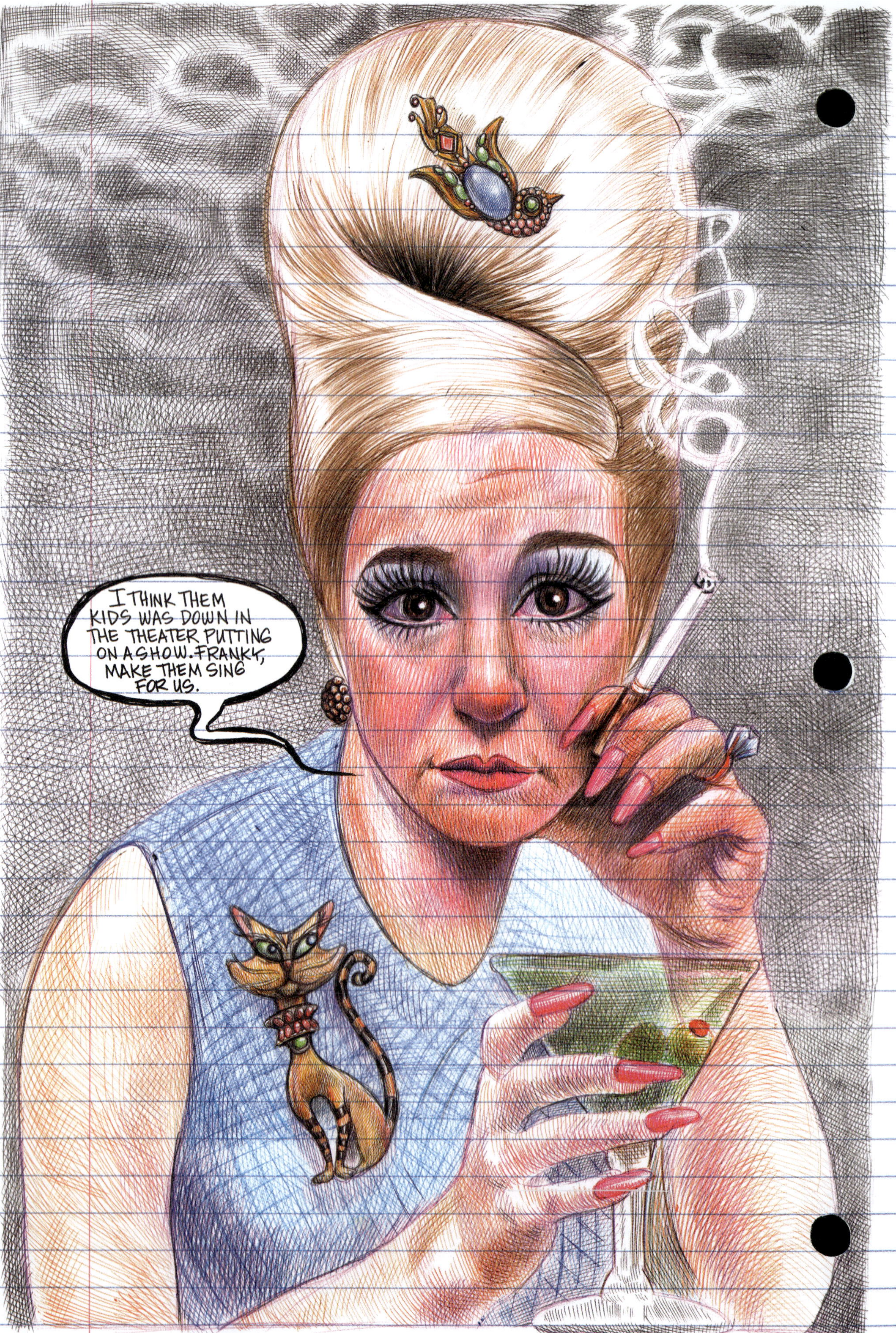
I THINK THEM KIDS WAS DOWN IN THE THEATER PUTTING ON A SHOW. FRANKY, MAKE THEM SING FOR US.

"YOU HEARD THE LADY... GIVE US A SONG *NOW!*"

WHEN THE GUY DEMANDED A SONG, FRANÇOISE JUMPED INTO ACTION BUT WITH SO MUCH EXCITEMENT AND HAPPINESS THAT IT KIND OF CONFUSED EVEN OFFICER PUMPKIN. FRANÇOISE WHISPERED TO SAM SILVERBERG AND EACH MEMBER OF HIS BAND. THEY ALL NODDED AND GAVE HIM AND EACH OTHER HALF-SMILES.
    THEN FRANÇOISE PICKED UP A MICROPHONE. SHE DID THIS SWIRLY MOTION WITH HER HANDS. THE CROWD WENT STRANGELY QUIET AND THEN...

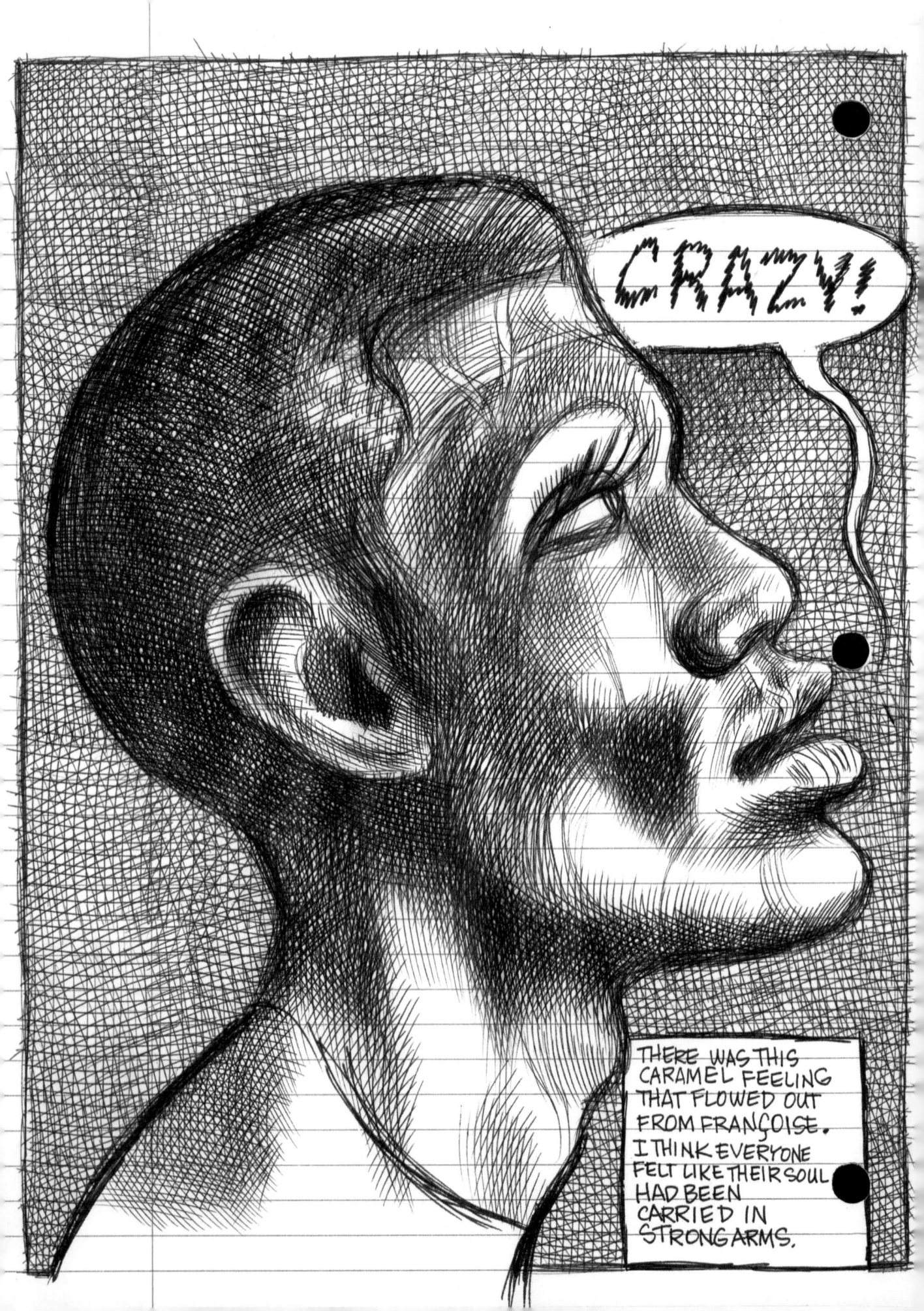

CRAZY!

There was this caramel feeling that flowed out from Françoise. I think everyone felt like their soul had been carried in strong arms.

BRAVO! BRAVO!

WHEN THE SONG ENDED THE CLUB KIND OF EXPLODED INTO APPLAUSE AND HOOTING. THE MOBSTER WAS SMILING AND HIS LADY FRIEND WINKED AT ME. SHE KIND OF SAVED US FROM TROUBLE, BUT HOW DID SHE KNOW THAT ANY OF US COULD SING?

LATER ON WHEN WE GOT TO OUR HOMES, WE BOTH GOT ON THE PHONE...

"FRANÇOISE PERFORMED THAT PATSY CLINE SONG EXACTLY AS PATSY HERSELF WOULD HAVE. IT WAS LIKE FRANÇOISE WAS CALLING **HERSELF** 'CRAZY' FOR LOVING A WORLD THAT WOULD HURT HER SO BAD, BUT SHE CAN'T STOP LOVING IT."

"YEAH. SHE TOLD ME IT WAS 'AN ARTIST THING.' AS ARTISTS WE WANT TO GIVE THE WORLD THE GIFTS WE WERE SENT HERE TO GIVE, BUT WE KNOW THE WORLD WON'T ALWAYS RESPECT THE GIFT... AND SOMETIMES EVEN HURT US... IT'S KIND OF CRAZY."

"YEAH, IT'S TOTALLY WEIRD AND MESSED UP, BUT FRANÇOISE CHARMED EVERYONE."

"TONIGHT I THINK I FORGAVE MONSTERS FOR NOT BITING MY MOM."

EGOTBU.   EGOTBU.

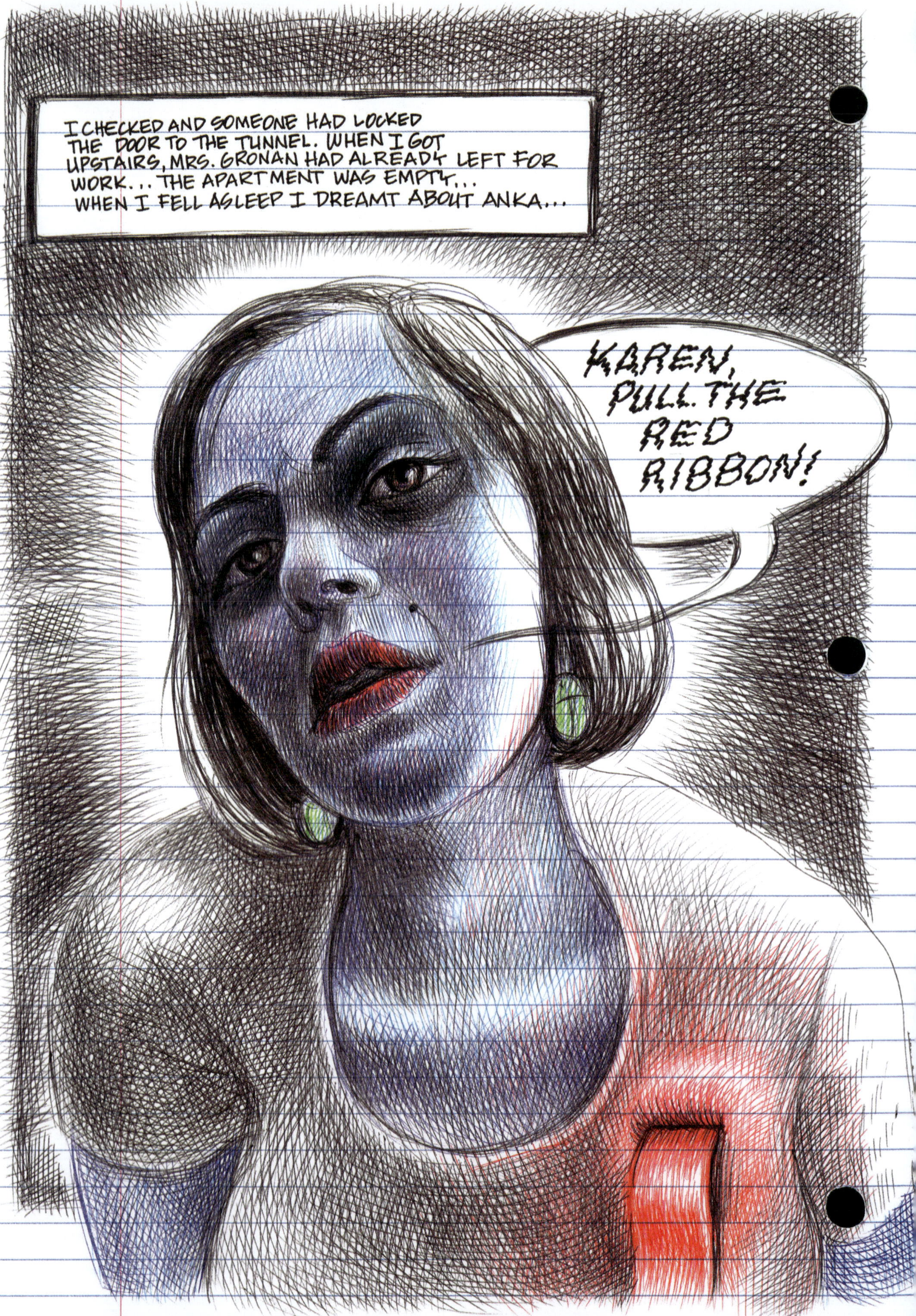
I CHECKED AND SOMEONE HAD LOCKED THE DOOR TO THE TUNNEL. WHEN I GOT UPSTAIRS, MRS. GRONAN HAD ALREADY LEFT FOR WORK... THE APARTMENT WAS EMPTY... WHEN I FELL ASLEEP I DREAMT ABOUT ANKA...
KAREN, PULL THE RED RIBBON!

I PULLED AND AS I PULLED, MY HANDS GOT RED...

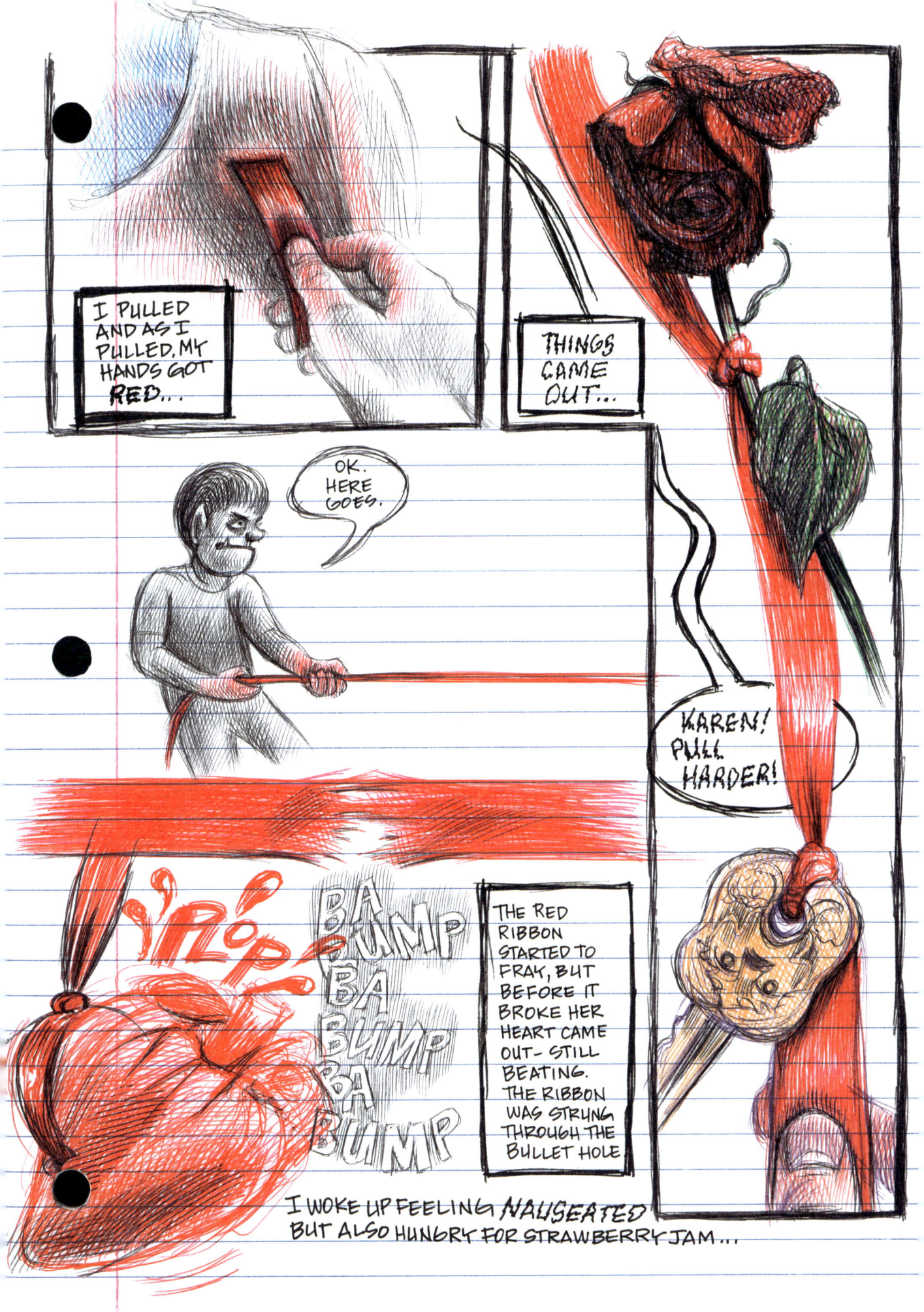

THINGS CAME OUT...

OK. HERE GOES.

KAREN! PULL HARDER!

BA BUMP BA BUMP BA BUMP

PLOP!

THE RED RIBBON STARTED TO FRAY, BUT BEFORE IT BROKE HER HEART CAME OUT- STILL BEATING. THE RIBBON WAS STRUNG THROUGH THE BULLET HOLE

I WOKE UP FEELING NAUSEATED BUT ALSO HUNGRY FOR STRAWBERRY JAM...

AFTER THE WEIRD DREAM I WOKE UP IN MRS. GRONAN'S SUPER CLOWNY GUEST ROOM THINKING ABOUT THE DAY THAT ANKA SILVERBERG *DIED.*
A VERY UPSET MR. CHUGG HAD BEEN IN THE DINER. HE HAD BEEN DOING WHAT HE ALWAYS DID, BUT WHY UNTIL NOW DID I NOT RECALL THAT HE WAS...

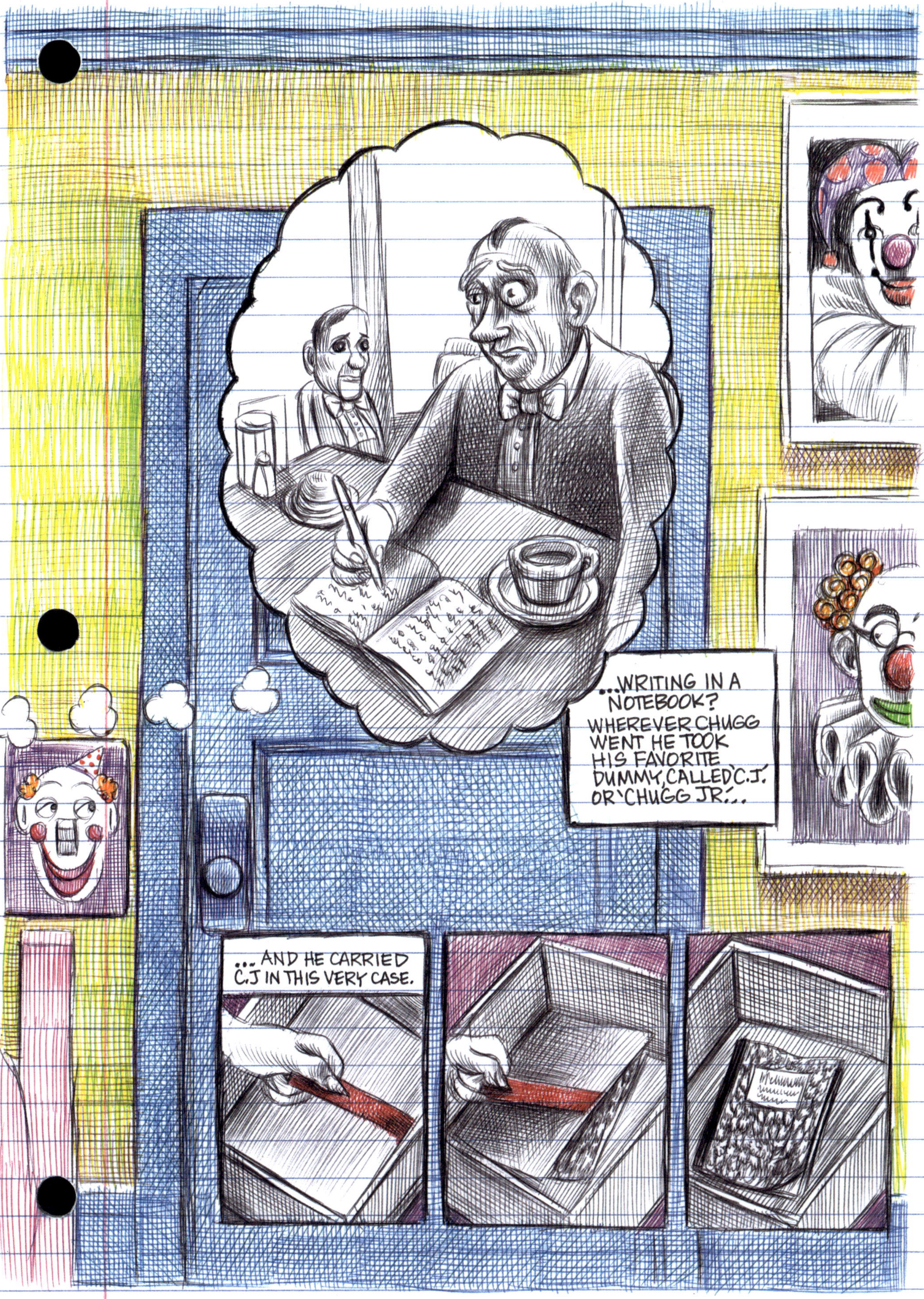
...WRITING IN A NOTEBOOK? WHEREVER CHUGG WENT HE TOOK HIS FAVORITE DUMMY, CALLED "C.J." OR "CHUGG JR."...
... AND HE CARRIED C.J IN THIS VERY CASE.

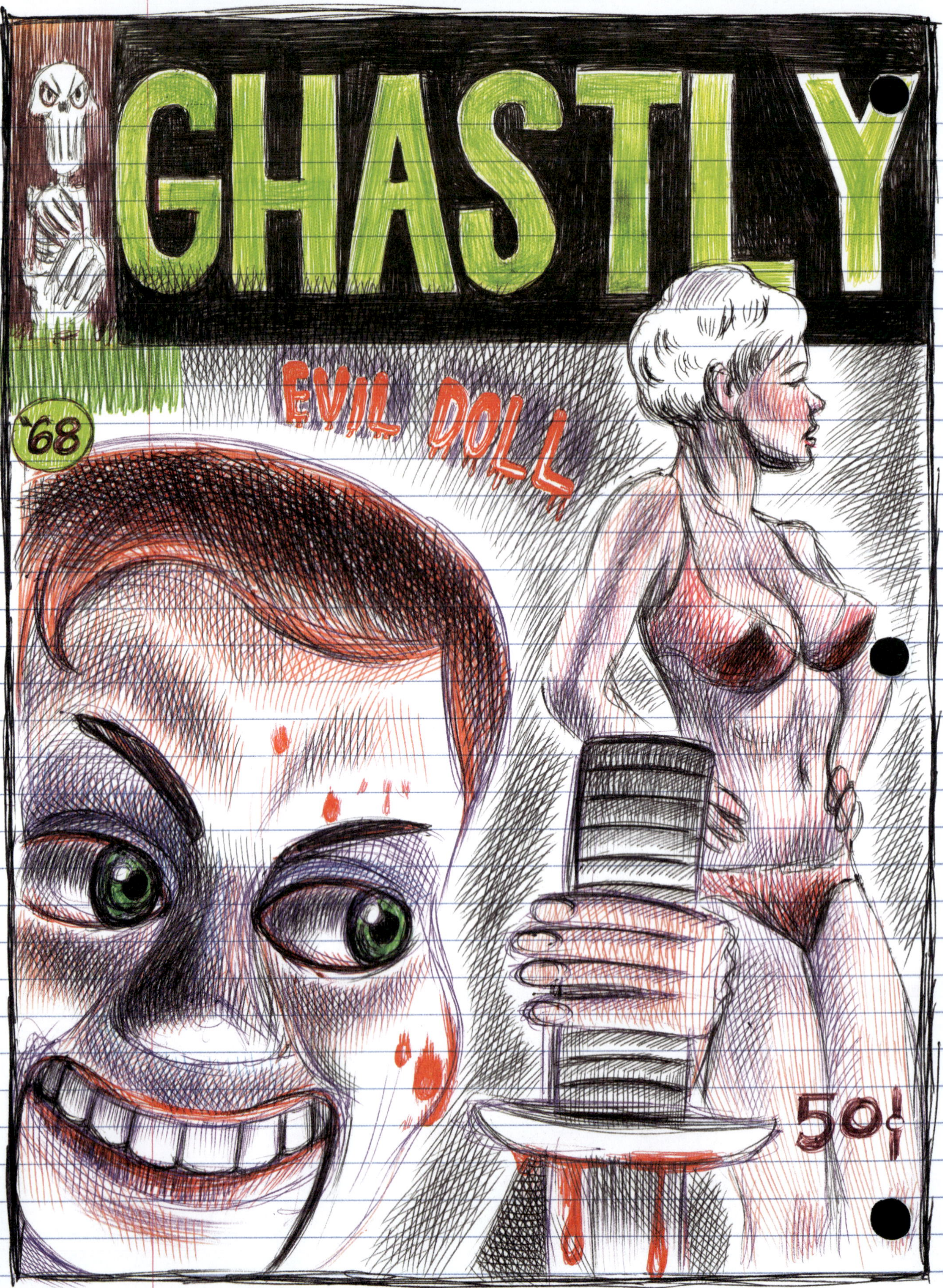
GHASTLY
'68
EVIL DOLL
50¢

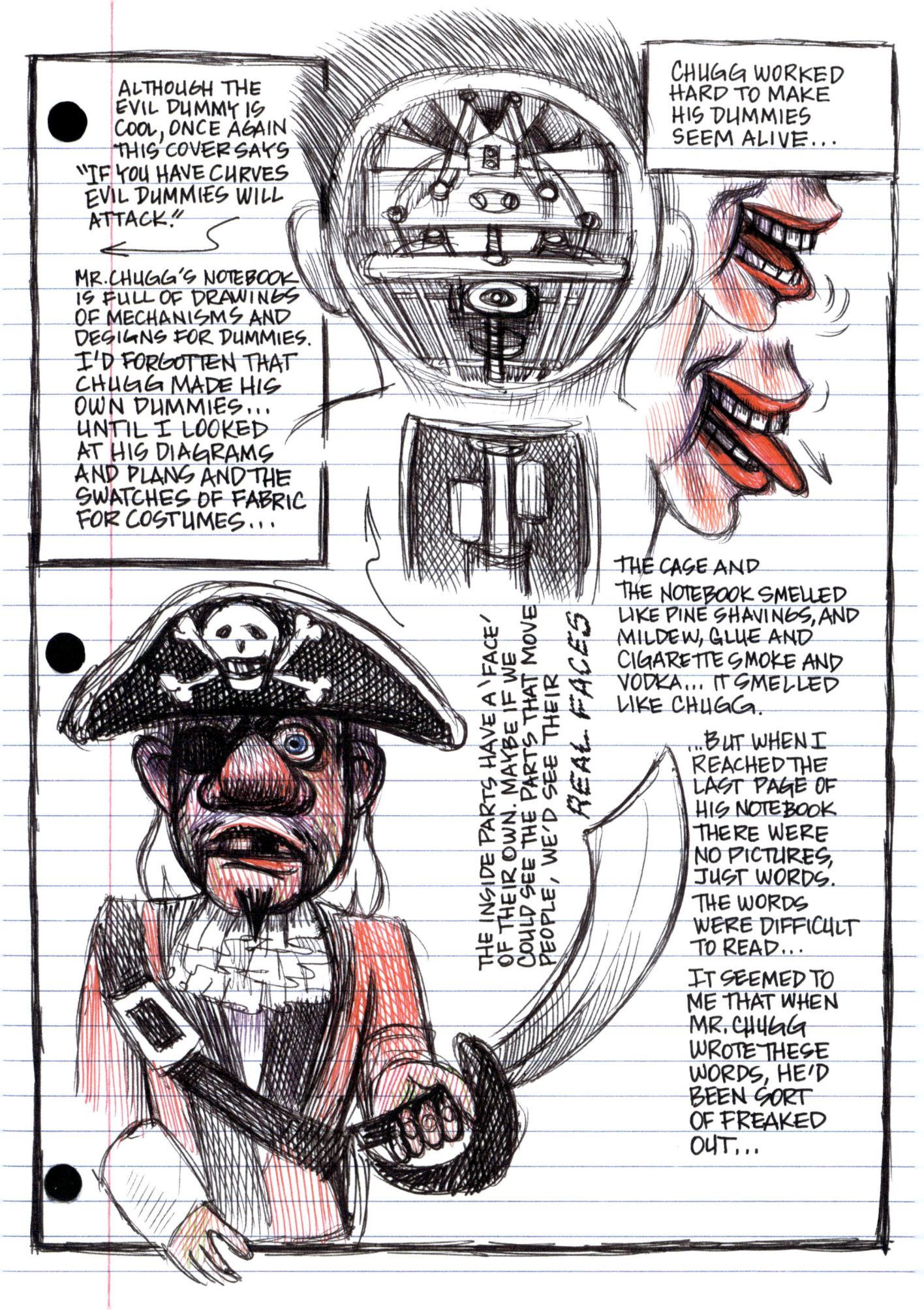

ALTHOUGH THE EVIL DUMMY IS COOL, ONCE AGAIN THIS COVER SAYS "IF YOU HAVE CURVES EVIL DUMMIES WILL ATTACK."

MR. CHUGG'S NOTEBOOK IS FULL OF DRAWINGS OF MECHANISMS AND DESIGNS FOR DUMMIES. I'D FORGOTTEN THAT CHUGG MADE HIS OWN DUMMIES... UNTIL I LOOKED AT HIS DIAGRAMS AND PLANS AND THE SWATCHES OF FABRIC FOR COSTUMES...

CHUGG WORKED HARD TO MAKE HIS DUMMIES SEEM ALIVE...

THE INSIDE PARTS HAVE A 'FACE' OF THEIR OWN. MAYBE IF WE COULD SEE THE PARTS THAT MOVE PEOPLE, WE'D SEE THEIR REAL FACES

THE CASE AND THE NOTEBOOK SMELLED LIKE PINE SHAVINGS, AND MILDEW, GLUE AND CIGARETTE SMOKE AND VODKA... IT SMELLED LIKE CHUGG.

...BUT WHEN I REACHED THE LAST PAGE OF HIS NOTEBOOK THERE WERE NO PICTURES, JUST WORDS. THE WORDS WERE DIFFICULT TO READ...

IT SEEMED TO ME THAT WHEN MR. CHUGG WROTE THESE WORDS, HE'D BEEN SORT OF FREAKED OUT...

THE DRAWINGS IN CHUGG'S NOTEBOOK ARE MADE WITH COLORED PENCILS AND A LOT OF THEM SHOW PLANS FOR THE MAKING OF A DUMMY WITH...

ANKA'S FACE!

I DON'T KNOW IF HE MADE THE 'ANKA' DUMMY, BUT IF HE DID MAKE HER, THERE'S A CHANCE THAT *SHE'S THE ONLY ONE HE TOOK WITH HIM.*

AGAIN AND AGAIN CHUGG REFERS TO 'HIS QUEEN.' CHUGG'S NOTEBOOK WAS FULL OF LITTLE NOTES SUCH AS "SAW MY QUEEN EATING IN THE DINER" OR "TODAY MY QUEEN WEEDED HER GARDEN." IS IT *CREEPY?* IS IT *SWEET?* OR IS IT... *CREEPY SWEET?*

SINCE I'VE HEARD CHUGG TALKING WITH HIS DUMMIES I KNOW WHAT HE MEANS BY 'EVERYONE'!

"A GUN-SHOT?"

MR. CHUGG WROTE THAT AT AROUND MID-MORNING ON VALENTINE'S DAY 'EVERYONE' WAS WOKEN BY A LOUD SOUND...

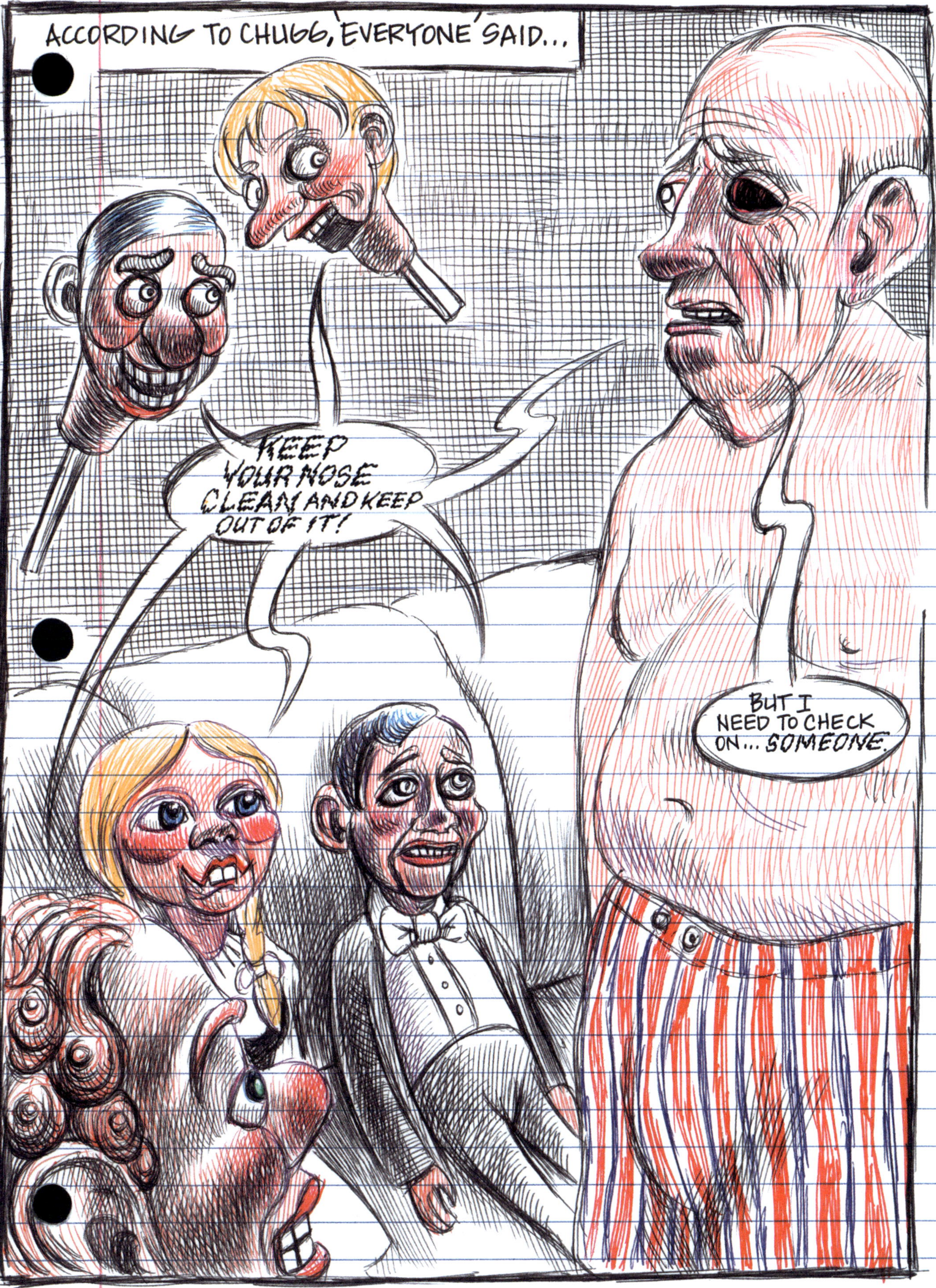
ACCORDING TO CHUGG, 'EVERYONE' SAID...
KEEP YOUR NOSE CLEAN AND KEEP OUT OF IT!
BUT I NEED TO CHECK ON... SOMEONE.

HE DRESSED QUICKLY AND WHILE HE WAS PUTTING IN HIS GLASS EYE, HE HEARD SOMEONE RATTLING THE CHAINS OF THE UNDERGROUND PASSAGE...

SLAM

SOMEONE HAD GONE DOWN THE STAIRS...

CHUGG LOOKED BEYOND THE DOOR OF HIS BASEMENT APARTMENT...

THAT'S WHEN CHUGG SAID HE SAW SOMEONE HE RECOGNIZED. A PERSON WHO ALSO SAW HIM — A FACT THAT SCARED CHUGG.

CHUGG SAID HE FELT IT MADE SENSE TO BE SCARED OF THE PERSON HE SAW BECAUSE "*THE PERSON HAD KILLED A MEMBER OF THEIR OWN FAMILY!*" MR. CHUGG WAS SO AFRAID THAT HE DIDN'T FOLLOW THE PERSON BUT INSTEAD...

MR. CHUGG WROTE THAT HE FOLLOWED TO WHAT HE THOUGHT WAS THE SOURCE OF THE GUNSHOT... THE SILVERBERG APARTMENT. WHEN I READ THIS I GOT A CHILL. I HAD A FEELING THAT CHUGG HAD ALREADY BEEN IN THE HABIT OF LOOKING INTO ANKA'S WINDOWS...

HUH?

CHUGG SAID HE HADN'T CALLED THE COPS BUT...

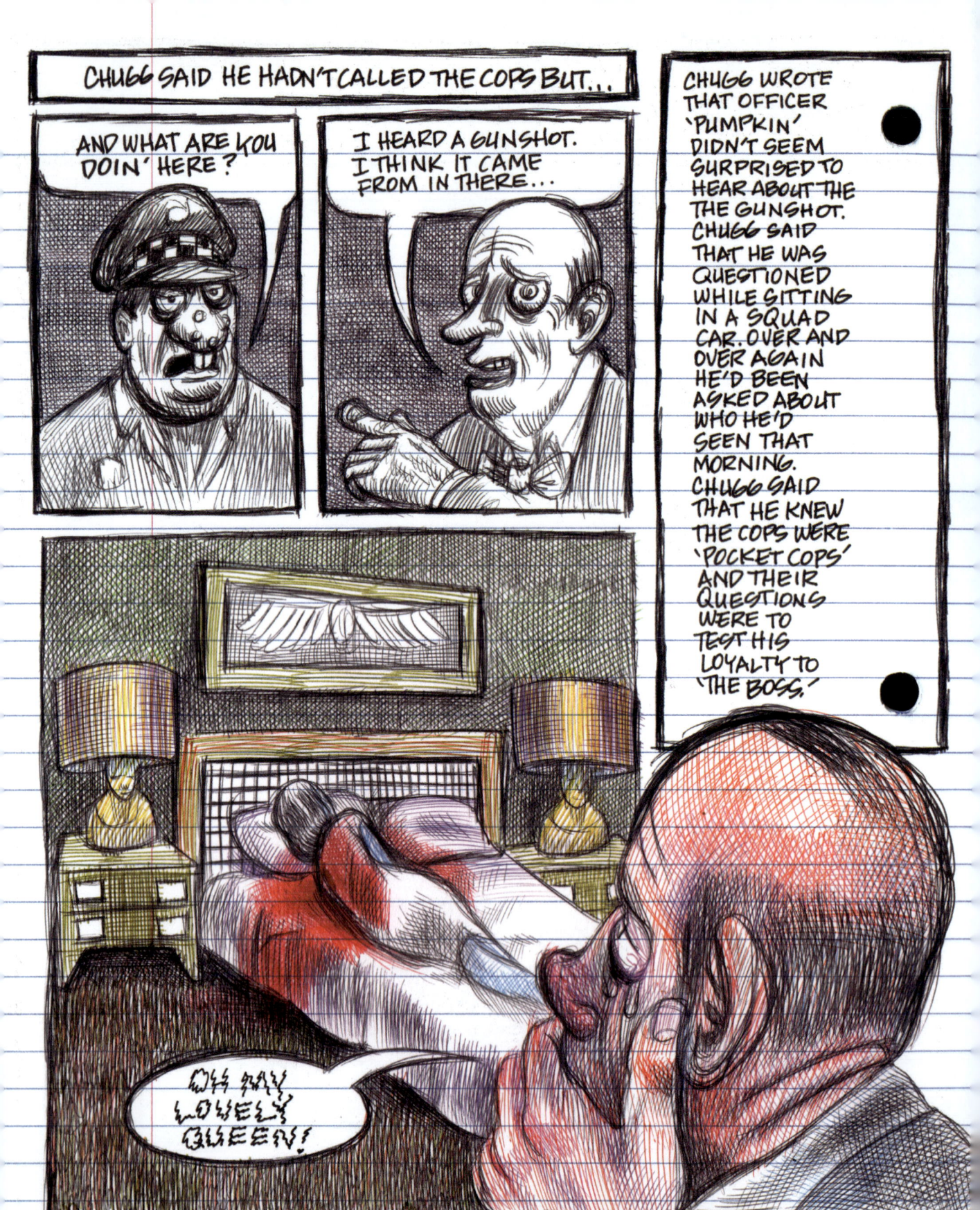

AND WHAT ARE YOU DOIN' HERE?

I HEARD A GUNSHOT. I THINK IT CAME FROM IN THERE...

CHUGG WROTE THAT OFFICER 'PUMPKIN' DIDN'T SEEM SURPRISED TO HEAR ABOUT THE GUNSHOT. CHUGG SAID THAT HE WAS QUESTIONED WHILE SITTING IN A SQUAD CAR. OVER AND OVER AGAIN HE'D BEEN ASKED ABOUT WHO HE'D SEEN THAT MORNING. CHUGG SAID THAT HE KNEW THE COPS WERE 'POCKET COPS' AND THEIR QUESTIONS WERE TO TEST HIS LOYALTY TO 'THE BOSS.'

OH MY LOVELY QUEEN!

ON A TEAR-STAINED PAGE CHUGG DESCRIBED SEEING ANKA'S BODY.

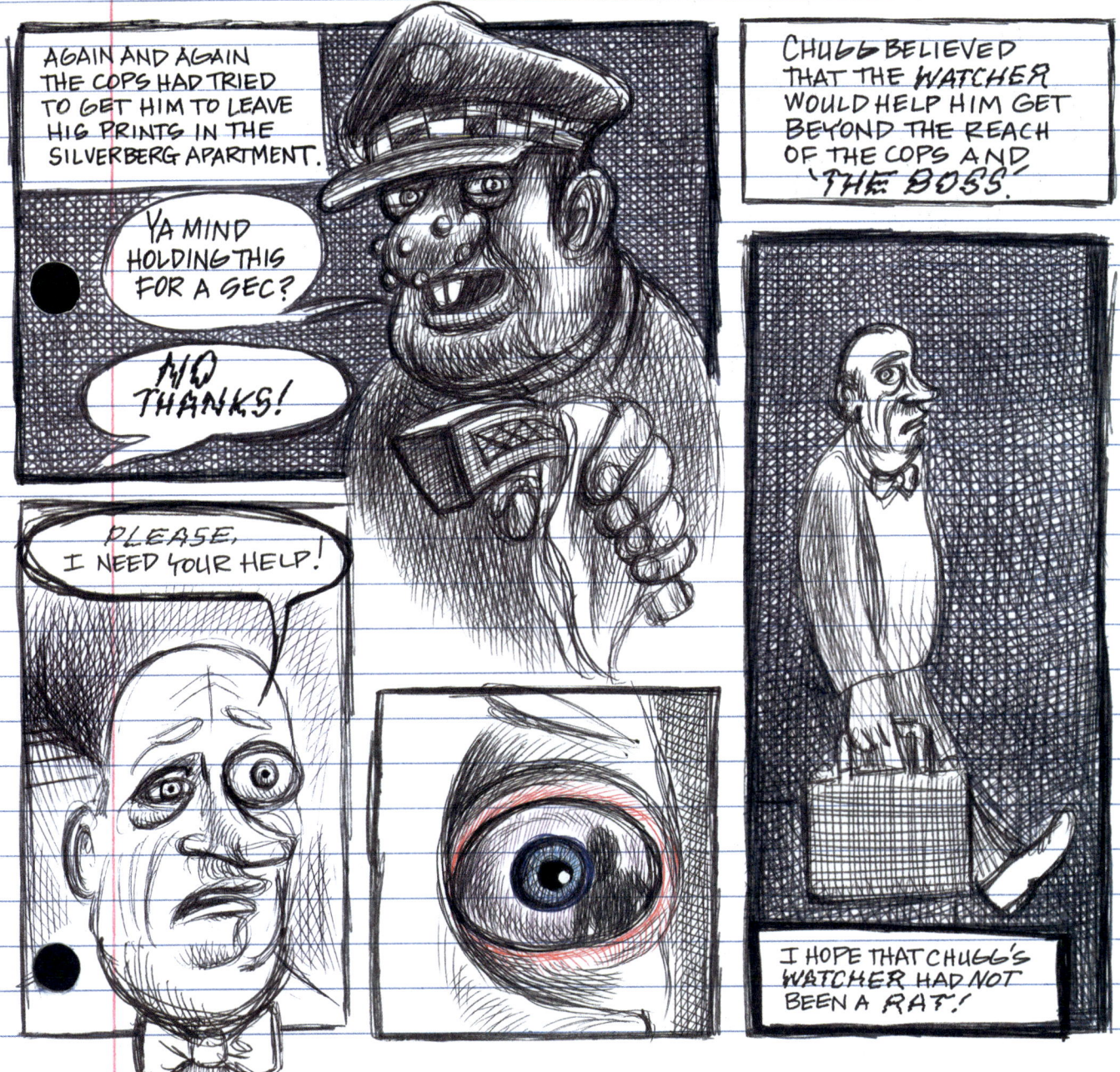

Panel 1: CHUGG RECALLED HOW HE'D SPENT YEARS NOTING THE TIME THAT ANKA WOULD NORMALLY DO THINGS LIKE RETRIEVE HER MAIL AND GROCERY SHOP. HE MANAGED TO BE ON HAND — HOPING FOR A SINGLE WORD OR A GLANCE OR A PRECIOUS SMILE...

"...AND HOW IS MY FRIEND YOUNG C.J.?"

"I'D BE BETTER IF I WERE IN *YOUR* ARMS AND NOT WITH *THIS* DUMMY."

Panel 2: AGAIN AND AGAIN THE COPS HAD TRIED TO GET HIM TO LEAVE HIS PRINTS IN THE SILVERBERG APARTMENT.

"YA MIND HOLDING THIS FOR A SEC?"

"NO THANKS!"

Panel 3: CHUGG BELIEVED THAT THE *WATCHER* WOULD HELP HIM GET BEYOND THE REACH OF THE COPS AND '*THE BOSS*'.

Panel 4: "PLEASE, I NEED YOUR HELP!"

Panel 5: I HOPE THAT CHUGG'S *WATCHER* HAD *NOT* BEEN A *RAT*!

MR. CHUGG'S NOTEBOOK HAD TWO DRAWINGS OF ANKA – **DEAD.** I DIDN'T TEAR THE PAGE OUT OF THE NOTEBOOK BUT I COPIED THE LARGER DRAWING INTO MY NOTEBOOK. MR. CHUGG WROTE THAT THERE WAS A LOT OF BLOOD BUT IT SEEMED LIKE CHUGG WAS REALLY FREAKED OUT BY HOW ANKA'S TONGUE WAS STICKING OUT. HE WROTE ABOUT HOW IT HURT HIM TO SEE HER THAT WAY. AFTER I FINISHED COPYING THE DRAWING *MY BLOOD RAN COLD!* A FEW MONTHS AGO I'D BEEN RUMMAGING IN THE WASTE BASKET NEXT TO DEEZE'S DRAFTING TABLE AND I FOUND THIS...

DEEZE THROWS AWAY DRAWINGS WHEN HE DOESN'T LIKE THEM. IT IS MY OPINION THAT THE REASON HE TOSSES CERTAIN DRAWINGS IS BECAUSE THOSE DRAWINGS — THE ARTWORK HE *HATES* — ARE THE ***TRUEST CLUES TO WHAT IS REALLY GOING ON IN DEEZY'S HEAD!*** WHAT THIS DRAWING TELLS ME IS THAT AT SOME POINT DEEZE PROBABLY SAW ANKA'S ***DEAD BODY!***

AFTER SEEING THAT PICTURE OF ANKA IT WAS HARD FOR ME TO KEEP MY MIND ON MY FIRST DATE BUT THEN...

...I REMEMBERED SOMETHING THAT ANKA ALWAYS SAID. IT WAS A GOETHE QUOTE. "NOTHING IS WORTH MORE THAN THIS DAY. YOU CANNOT RELIVE YESTERDAY. TOMORROW IS STILL BEYOND YOUR REACH."

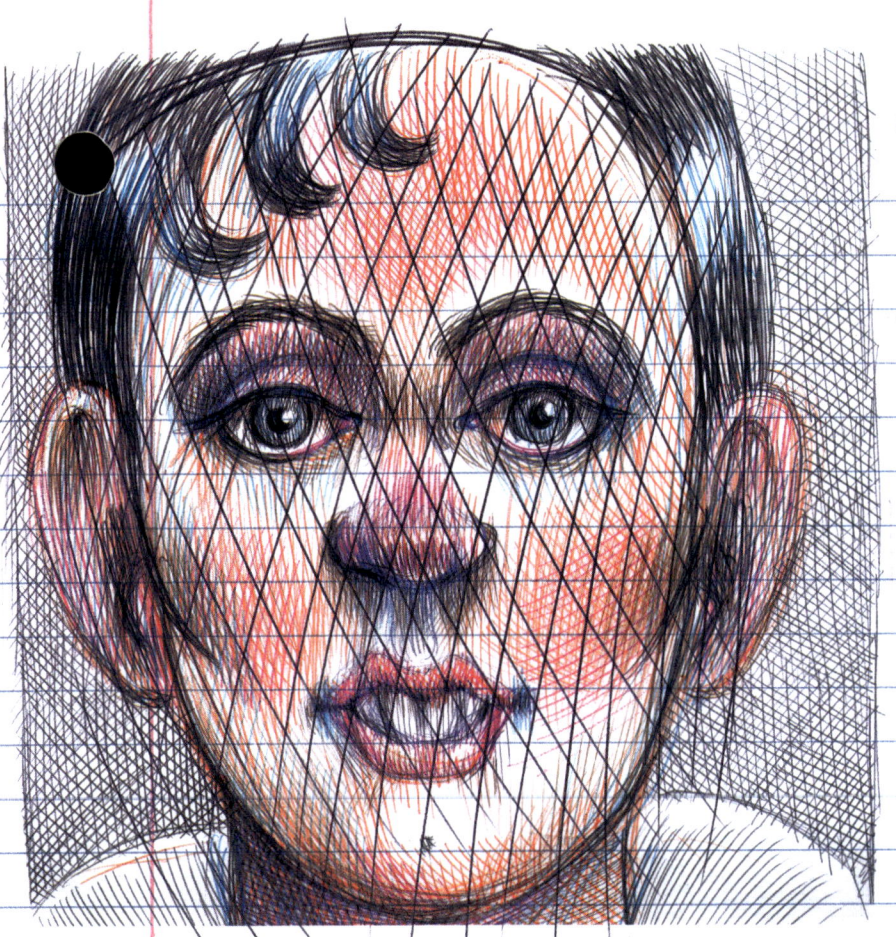

EVEN THOUGH DEEZE TOLD ME NOT TO BRING FLOWERS OR CANDY (BECAUSE ONLY CHUMPS DO THAT). I BROUGHT HER FLOWERS AND IT SEEMED LIKE SHE LIKED THEM.

ALL MY WORDS HAD BACKED UP. I COULDN'T SAY ANYTHING AND SHELLEY TOOK THE FLOWERS AND PUT THEM IN A VASE. SHE SNAPPED OFF ONE BLOSSOM AND PUT IT IN MY LAPEL. WHEN SHE TOUCHED MY SUIT I JUMPED AND SHELLEY LAUGHED BUT NOT IN A MEAN WAY.

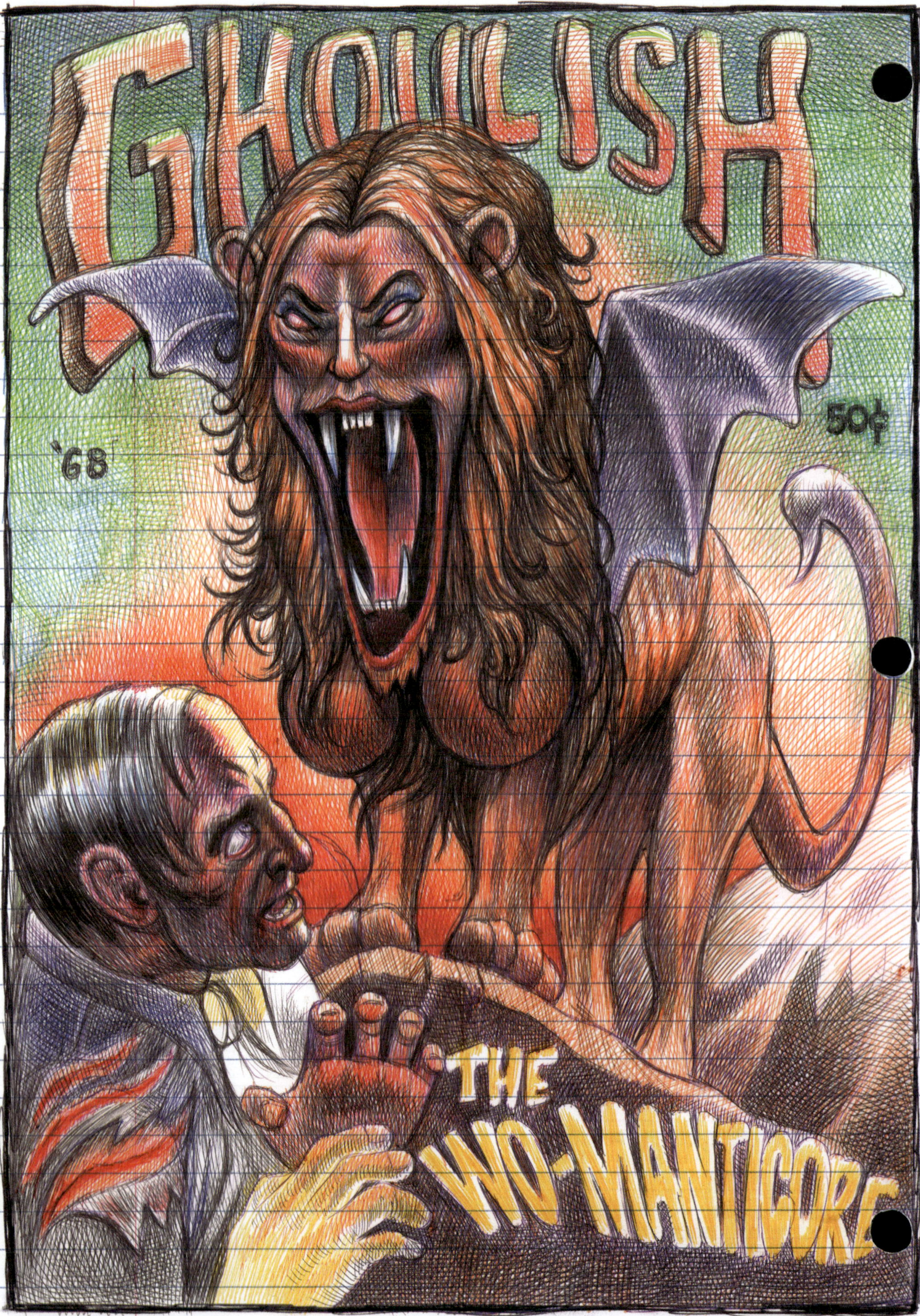
GHOULISH
'68
50¢
THE
WO-MANTICORE

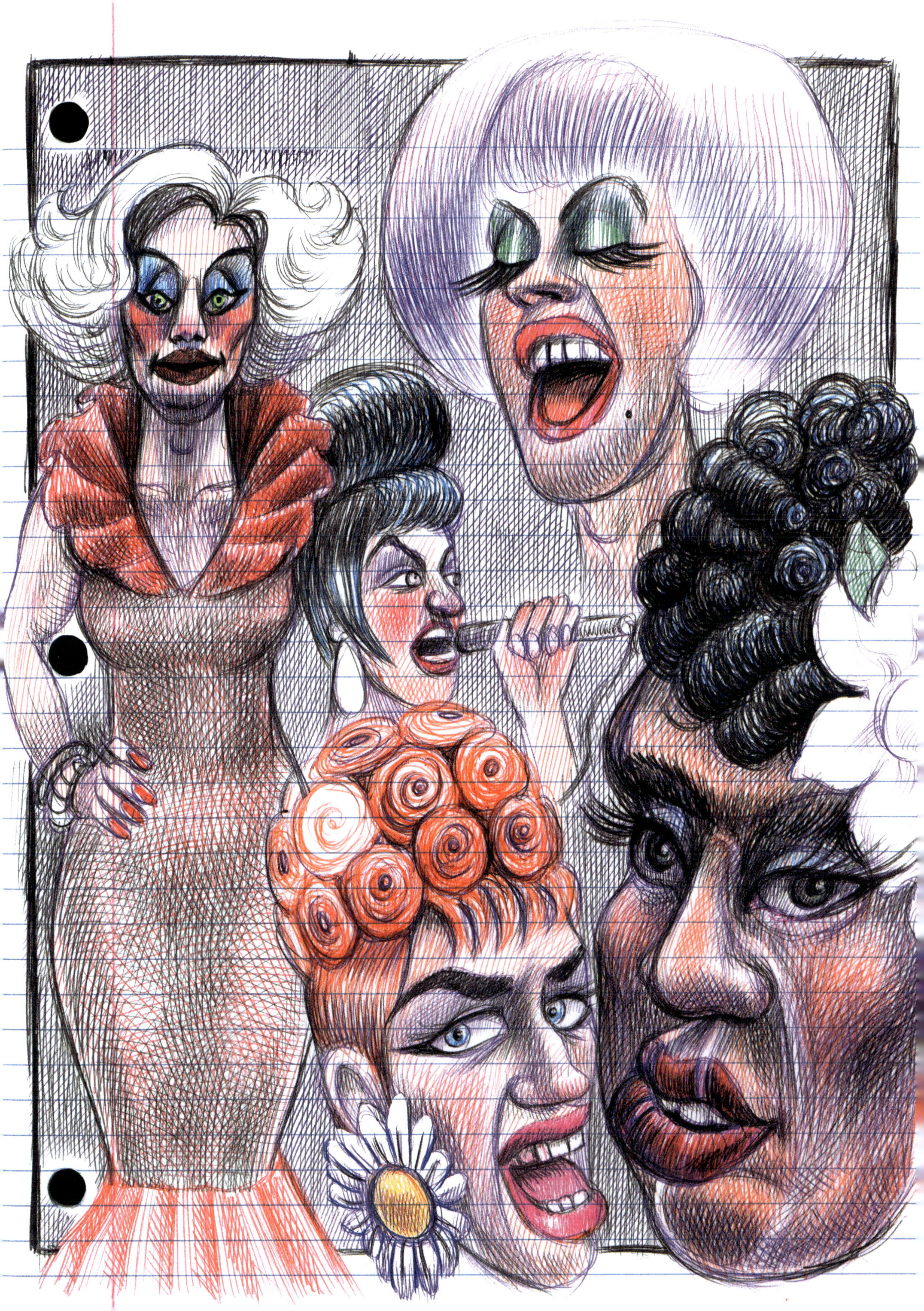

FRANÇOISE BROUGHT US SHIRLEY TEMPLE DRINKS. UNDER THE TABLE WE HELD HANDS FOR A FEW MINUTES. FRANÇOISE SANG A SONG THAT SHELLEY SAID BILLIE HOLIDAY HAD MADE FAMOUS. EVERYTHING WAS PERFECT UNTIL FRANÇOISE AND HER MOM WALKED US HOME...

...AS WE WERE WALKING DOWN BROADWAY...

...I SAW THIS GUY BOTHERING ONE OF THE LADIES WHO STAND IN FRONT OF GOLDBLATTS. SHE WAS MINDING HER OWN BIZ, BUT HE YELLED OUT *GROSS* AND *MEAN* STUFF THAT MADE ME ANGRY. WHAT SURPRISED ME WAS THAT I RECOGNIZED HIM. HE WAS THE SAME GUY WHO PEED ON THE WINDOW NEXT TO ME AT THE DINER A WHILE AGO!

"HEY THERE ZELDA, YOU CAN SUCK MY COCK BUT YOU'RE SO *UGLY* THAT I'M GOING TO CHARGE *YOU* TO DO IT! HA HA HA HA HA!"

BUT AFTER THAT, THE REALLY AMAZING THING HAPPENED...

"SHUT UP, FRANK REYES! YOU PISS-SOAKED MOTHERFUCKING *LOSER!*"

SUPPOSEDLY *FRANK REYES* IS MY FATHER'S NAME! I SPRINTED DOWN RACINE. I WAS FOLLOWING THE DRUNKEN GUY. I WATCHED HIM...

...AS HE WALKED INTO THE DARLINGTON HOTEL. IT WAS LIKE A WHOLE LOT OF PIECES OF THE PUZZLE FELL INTO PLACE — DEEZE NOT WANTING ME TO GO TO THE DINER ALONE, DEEZE NOT WANTING US TO SIT IN THE WINDOW OF THE DINER, MAMA NEVER WANTING TO GET ON OR OFF THE EL AT THE LAWRENCE STOP.

"HE WAS PROBABLY IN THE NEIGHBORHOOD MY WHOLE LIFE BUT NOBODY TOLD ME."

"WHY ARE YOU OVER HERE? SOMETHING WRONG?"

"NAW. I'M COOL."

I DIDN'T ADMIT THAT THE DIRTY DRUNKEN MESS WAS *MY ACTUAL FATHER!* I WAS ASHAMED OF WHO MY FATHER IS, AND I KNOW THAT IF I GO AND TALK TO HIM ABOUT *NOT* HURTING DEEZE, I WILL HAVE TO TAKE SOME PROTECTION WITH ME. SO WHEN I GOT BACK TO OUR APARTMENT I STARTED HUNTING FOR DEEZE'S GUN...

WHERE IS THAT GUN?

I FOUND THE GUN IN AN OLD ELECTRICAL BOX ATTACHED TO THE WALL IN DEEZE'S BEDROOM CLOSET. HOLDING IT MADE ME SICK TO MY STOMACH. MAYBE BECAUSE THE LAST TIME I SAW IT IT WAS IN AL'S MOUTH. THE NEXT DAY I WALKED ALL THE WAY DOWN CLARK STREET TO TALK TO MAMA AT HER GRAVE. I SENSED THAT MAMA DIDN'T WANT ME TO GO AND TALK TO MY FATHER, BUT IF JUDITH HAD CHICKENED OUT ALL HER PEOPLE WOULD HAVE DIED.

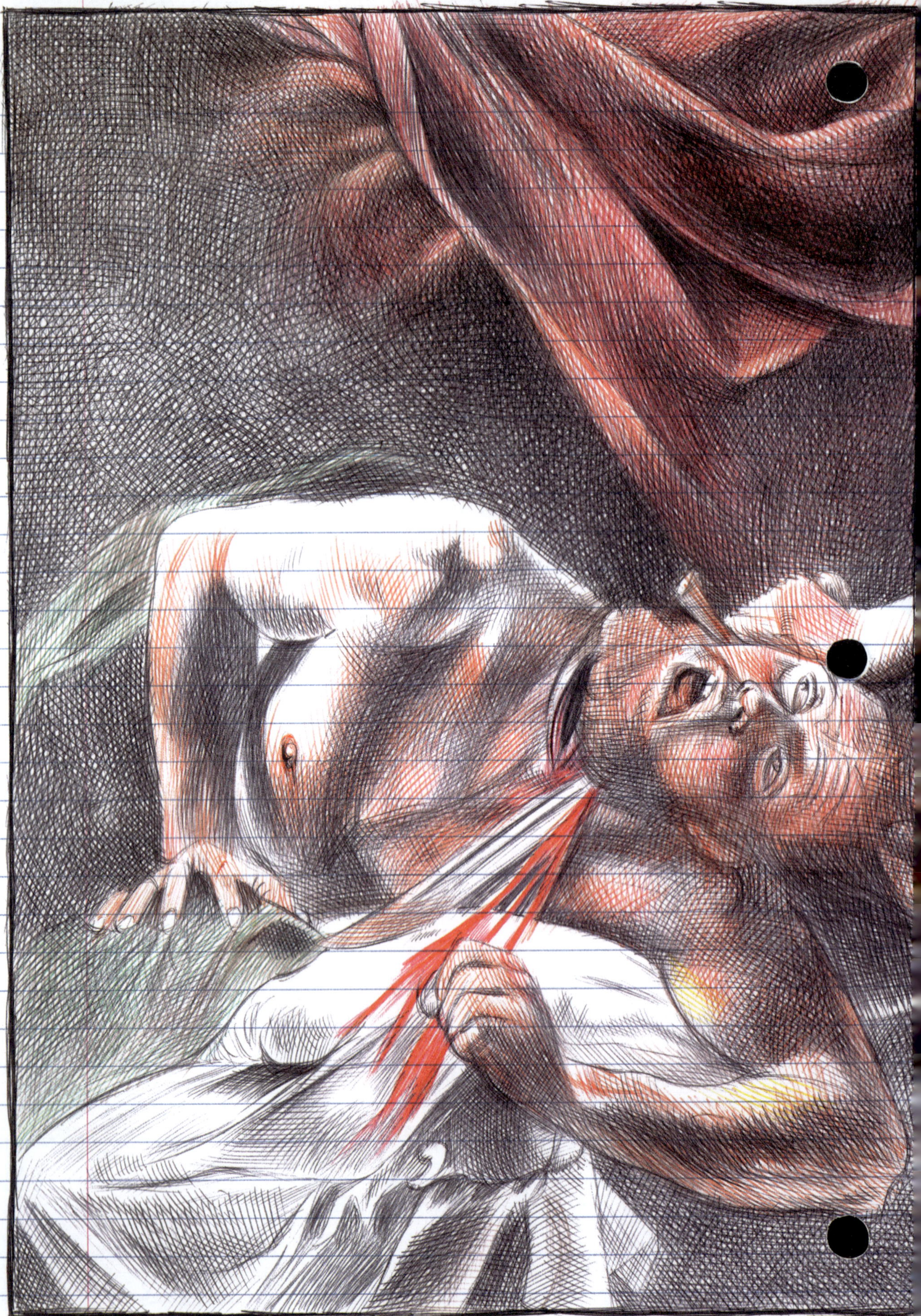

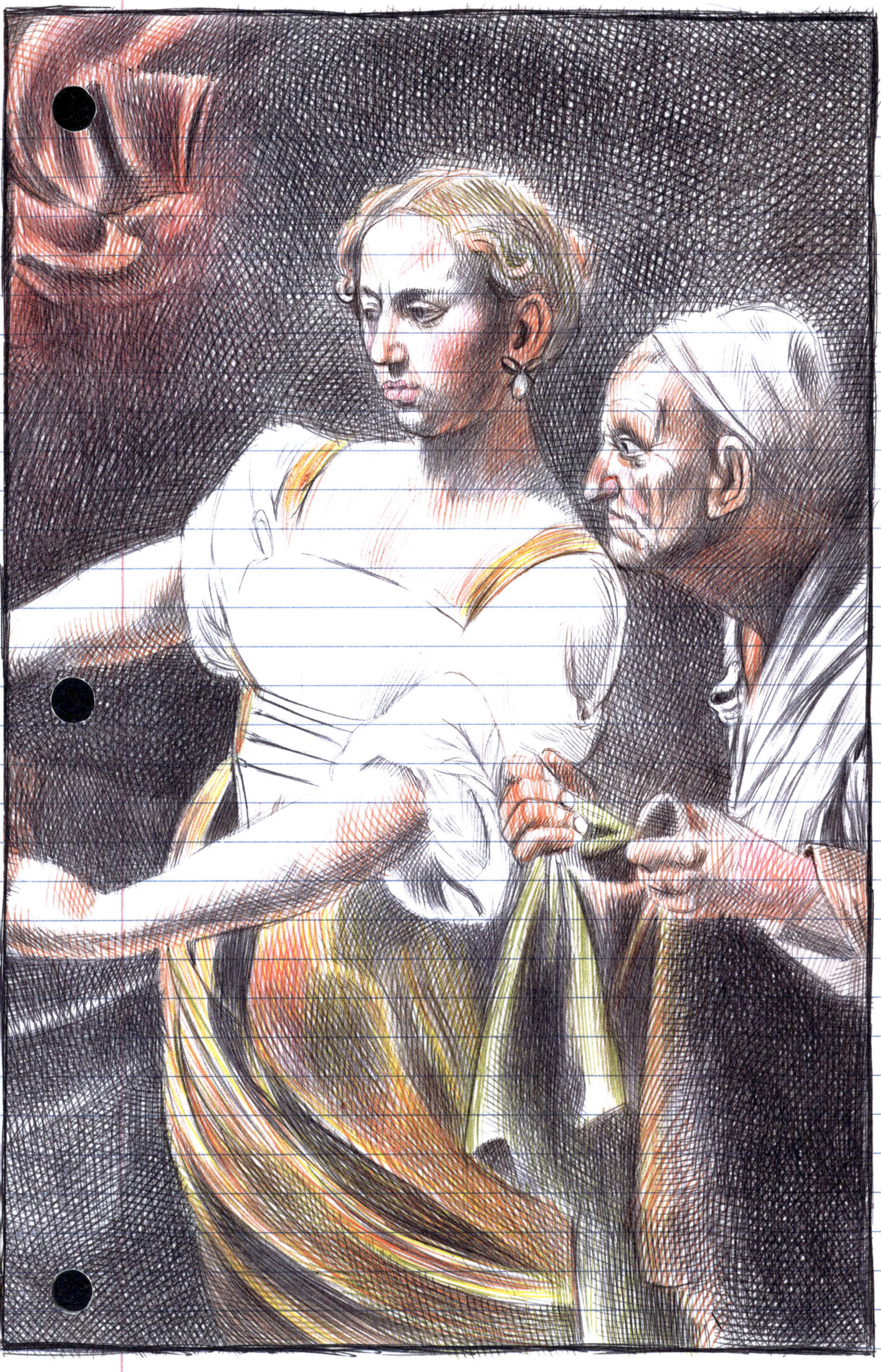

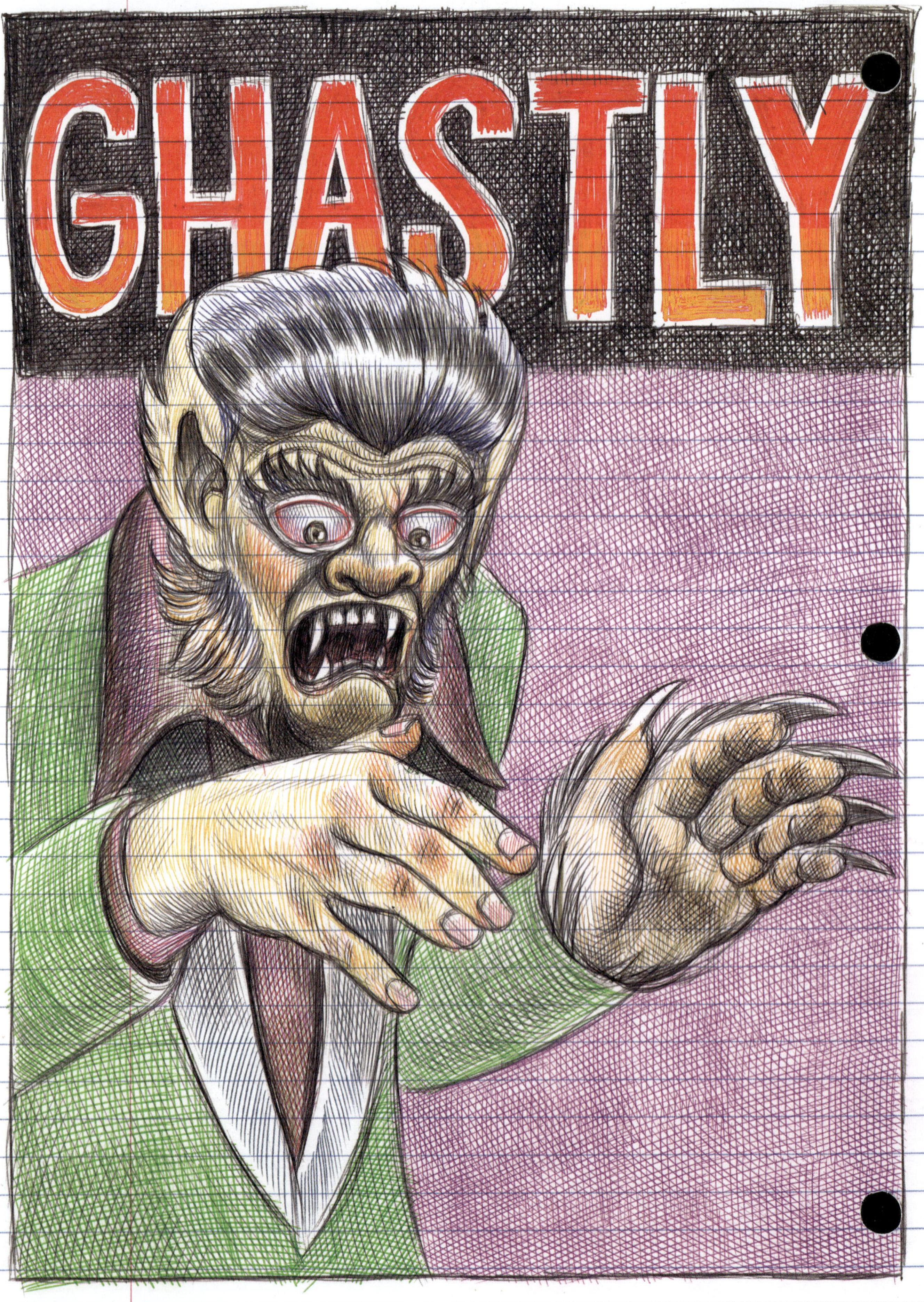
GHASTLY

IN THE WOLF MAN MOVIE WHEN LARRY TALBOT IS LYING IN THE FOREST INJURED AND CHANGING BETWEEN WEREWOLF AND HUMAN, A FEARLESS FORTUNE TELLER COMES TO HIS RESCUE. IT WAS A LOT LIKE THAT WHEN...

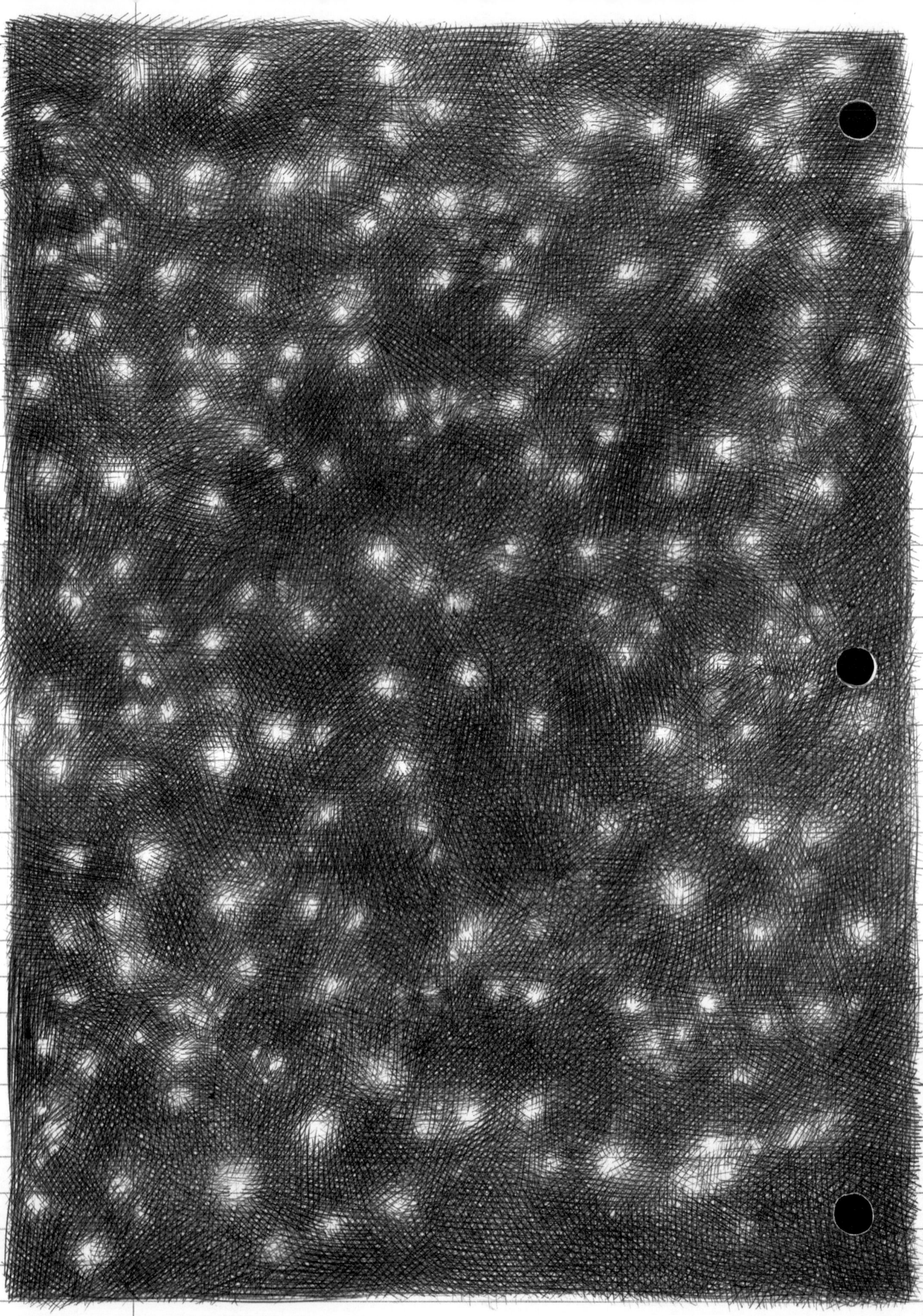

...I WOKE UP AND FOUND THAT I WAS **SICK AND BLOODY AND LAYING IN AN ALLEY**...

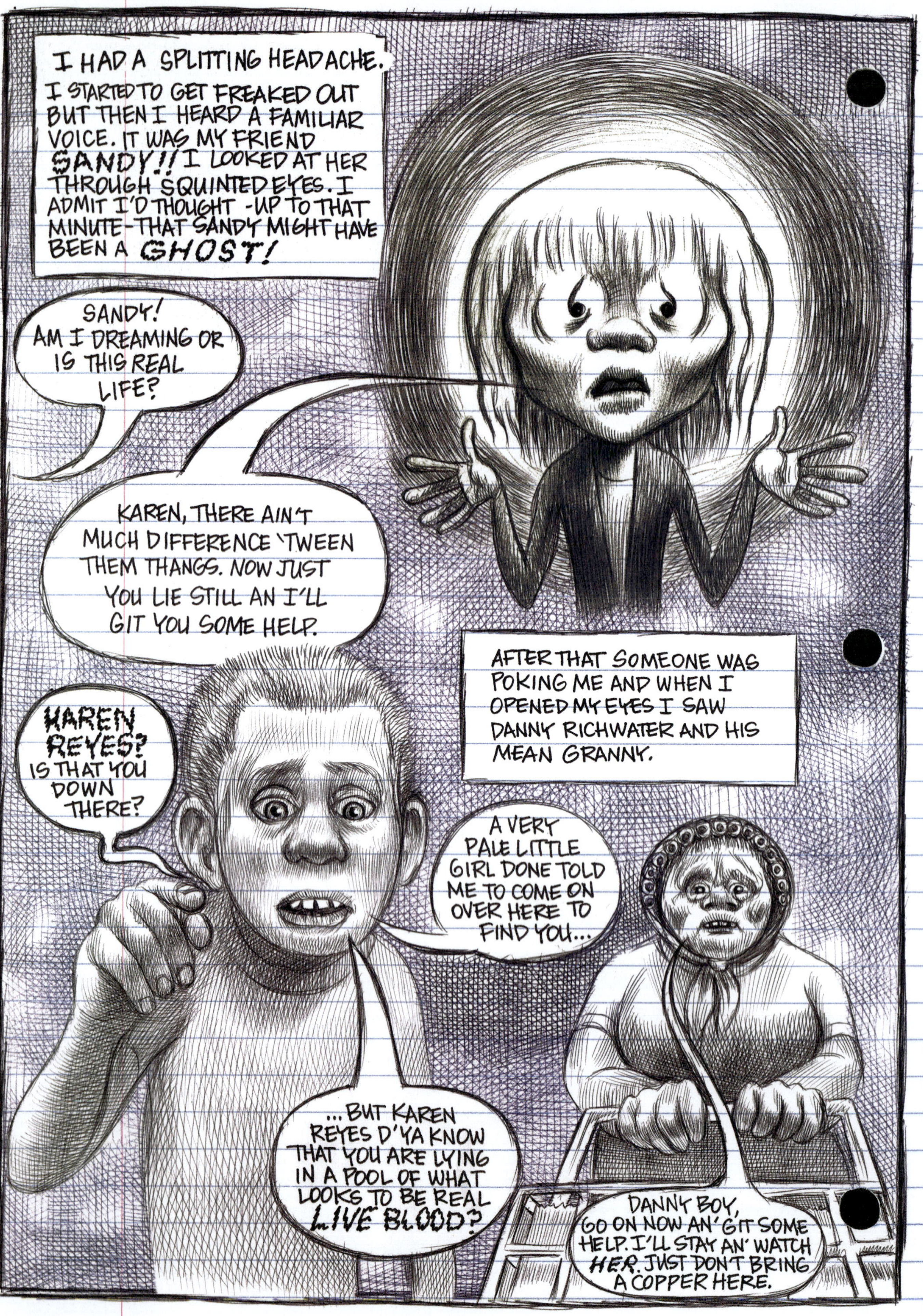

I HAD A SPLITTING HEADACHE. I STARTED TO GET FREAKED OUT BUT THEN I HEARD A FAMILIAR VOICE. IT WAS MY FRIEND SANDY!! I LOOKED AT HER THROUGH SQUINTED EYES. I ADMIT I'D THOUGHT -UP TO THAT MINUTE- THAT SANDY MIGHT HAVE BEEN A GHOST!
SANDY! AM I DREAMING OR IS THIS REAL LIFE?
KAREN, THERE AIN'T MUCH DIFFERENCE 'TWEEN THEM THANGS. NOW JUST YOU LIE STILL AN I'LL GIT YOU SOME HELP.
AFTER THAT SOMEONE WAS POKING ME AND WHEN I OPENED MY EYES I SAW DANNY RICHWATER AND HIS MEAN GRANNY.
KAREN REYES? IS THAT YOU DOWN THERE?
A VERY PALE LITTLE GIRL DONE TOLD ME TO COME ON OVER HERE TO FIND YOU...
...BUT KAREN REYES D'YA KNOW THAT YOU ARE LYING IN A POOL OF WHAT LOOKS TO BE REAL LIVE BLOOD?
DANNY BOY, GO ON NOW AN' GIT SOME HELP. I'LL STAY AN' WATCH HER. JUST DON'T BRING A COPPER HERE.

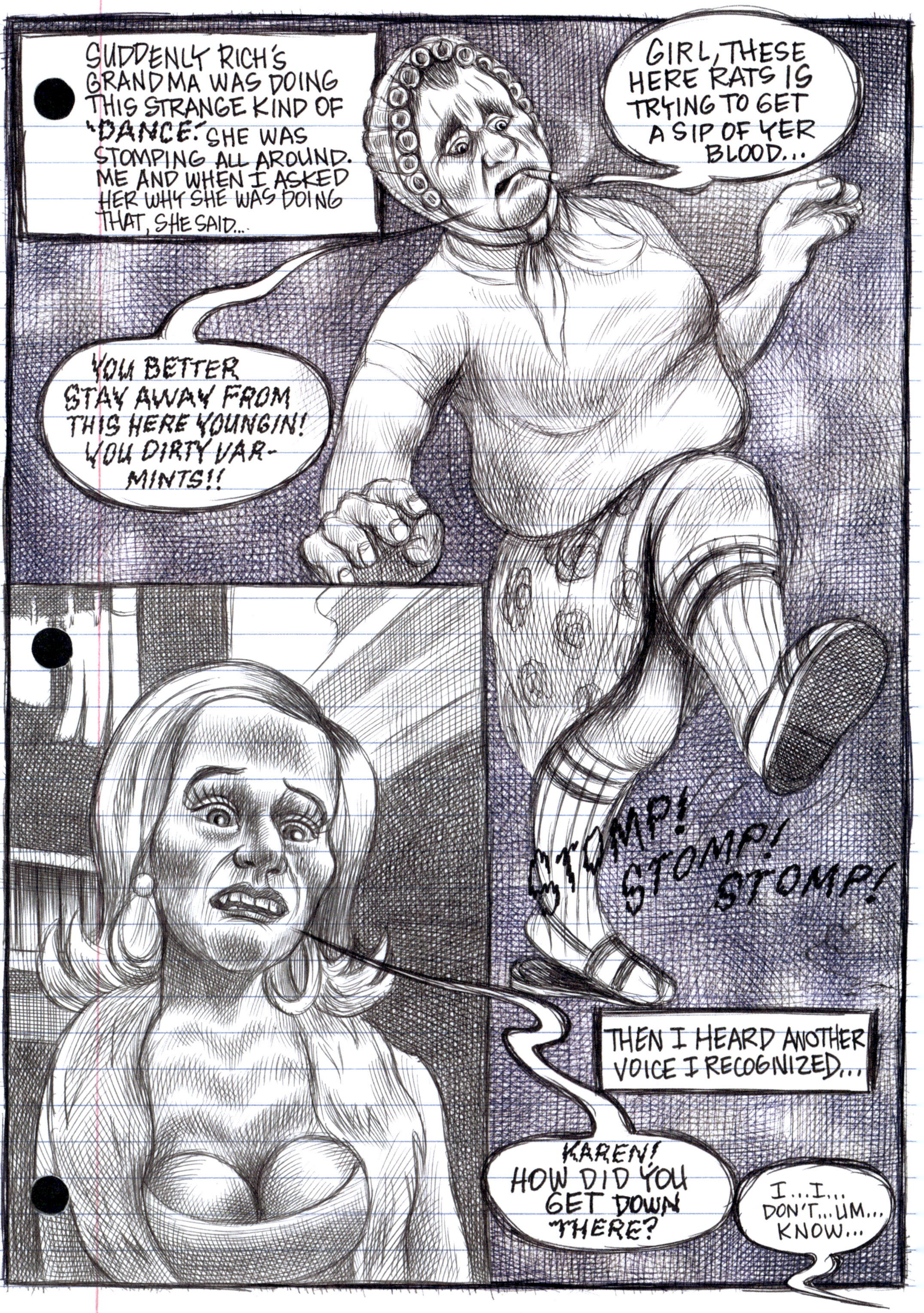
SUDDENLY RICH'S GRANDMA WAS DOING THIS STRANGE KIND OF "DANCE." SHE WAS STOMPING ALL AROUND. ME AND WHEN I ASKED HER WHY SHE WAS DOING THAT, SHE SAID...
GIRL, THESE HERE RATS IS TRYING TO GET A SIP OF YER BLOOD...
YOU BETTER STAY AWAY FROM THIS HERE YOUNGIN! YOU DIRTY VAR-MINTS!!
STOMP! STOMP! STOMP!
THEN I HEARD ANOTHER VOICE I RECOGNIZED...
KAREN! HOW DID YOU GET DOWN THERE?
I...I... DON'T...UM... KNOW...

"KID?!"

I HAD TROUBLE OPENING MY EYES BUT WHEN I DID I SAW THAT IT WAS DEEZE'S FRIENDS — DORINE AND CARMEL.

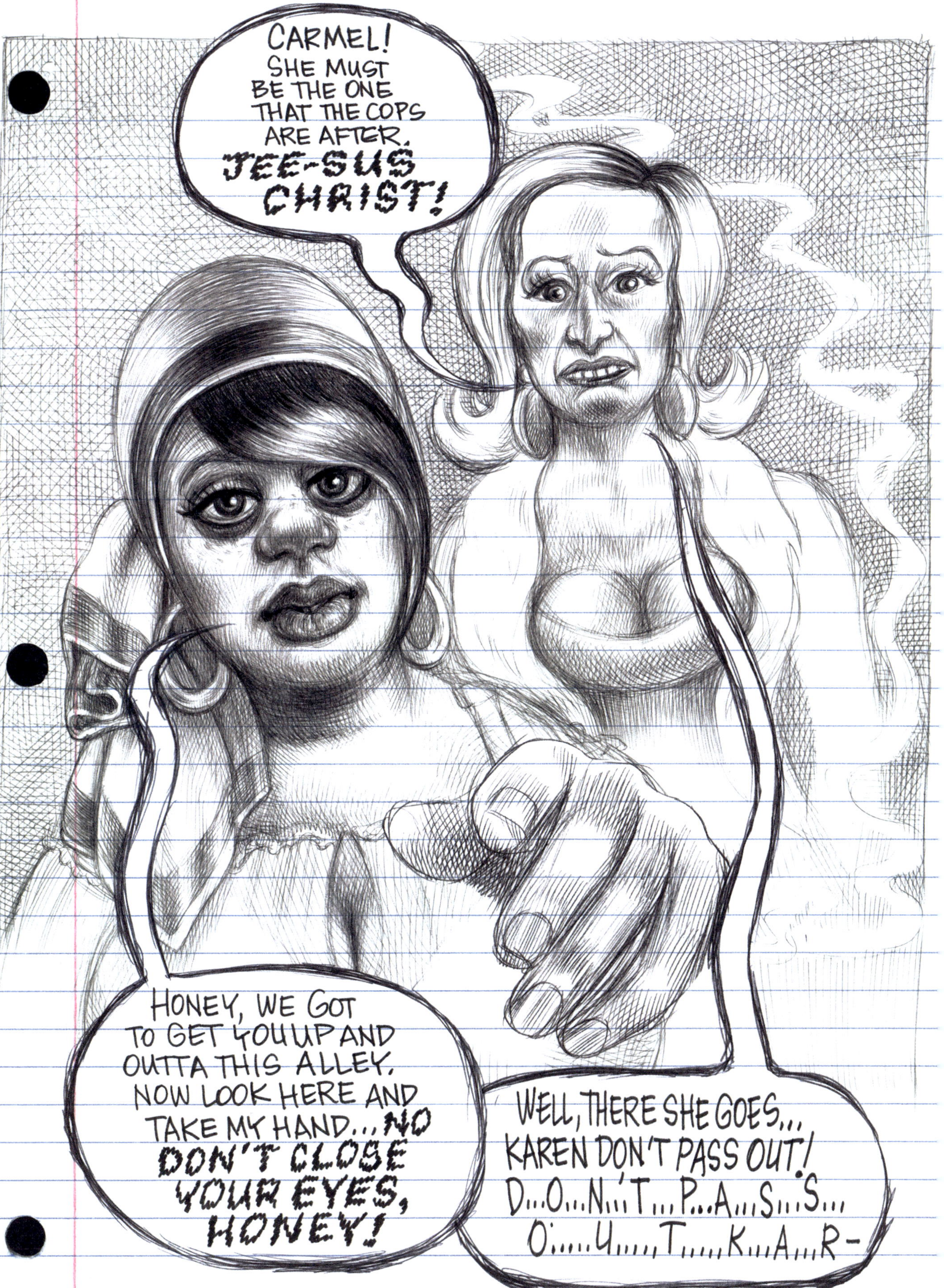
CARMEL! SHE MUST BE THE ONE THAT THE COPS ARE AFTER. JEE-SUS CHRIST!
HONEY, WE GOT TO GET YOU UP AND OUTTA THIS ALLEY. NOW LOOK HERE AND TAKE MY HAND... NO DON'T CLOSE YOUR EYES, HONEY!
WELL, THERE SHE GOES... KAREN DON'T PASS OUT! D...O...N...'T...P...A...S...S... O.....U.....T.....K...A...R-

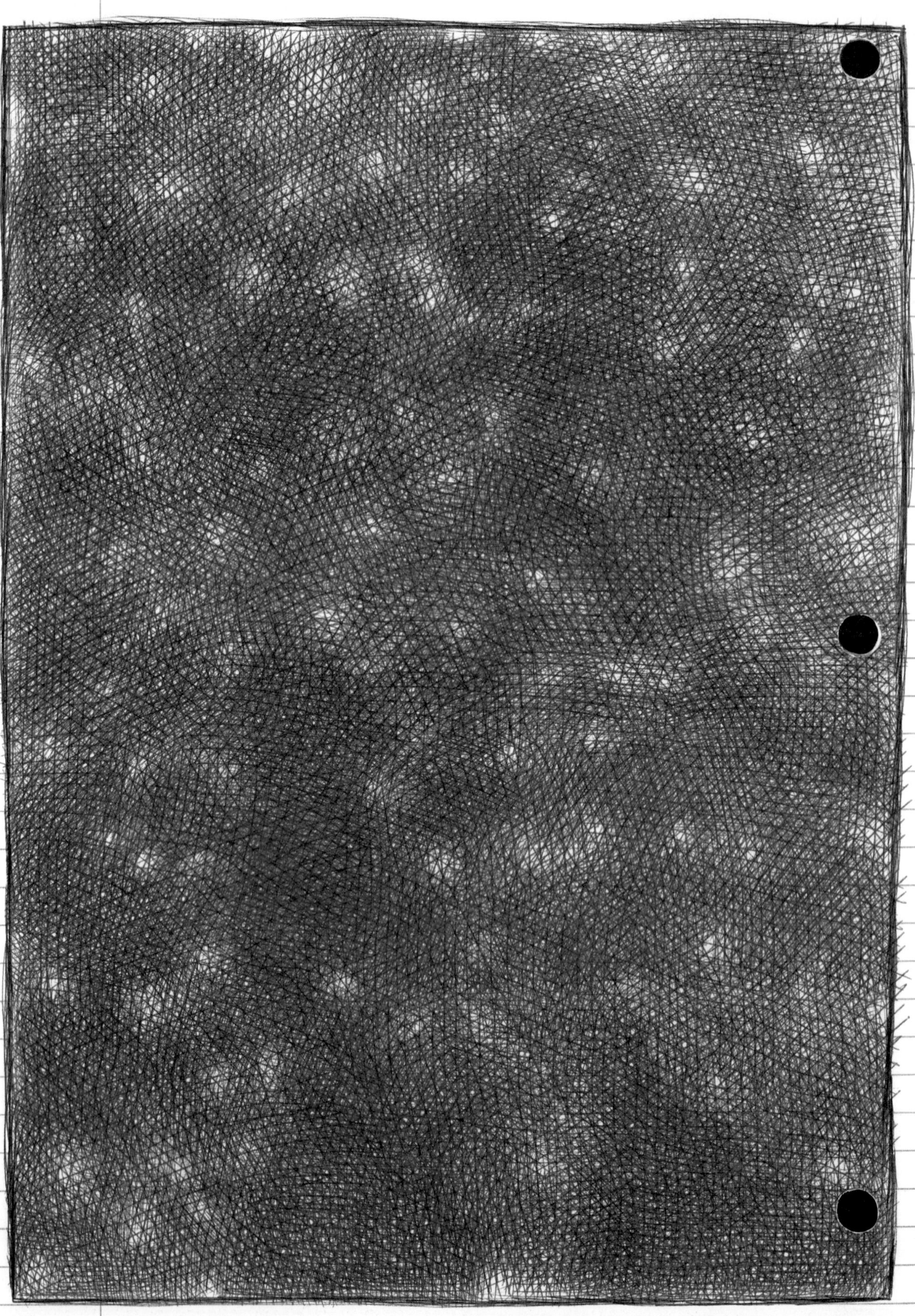

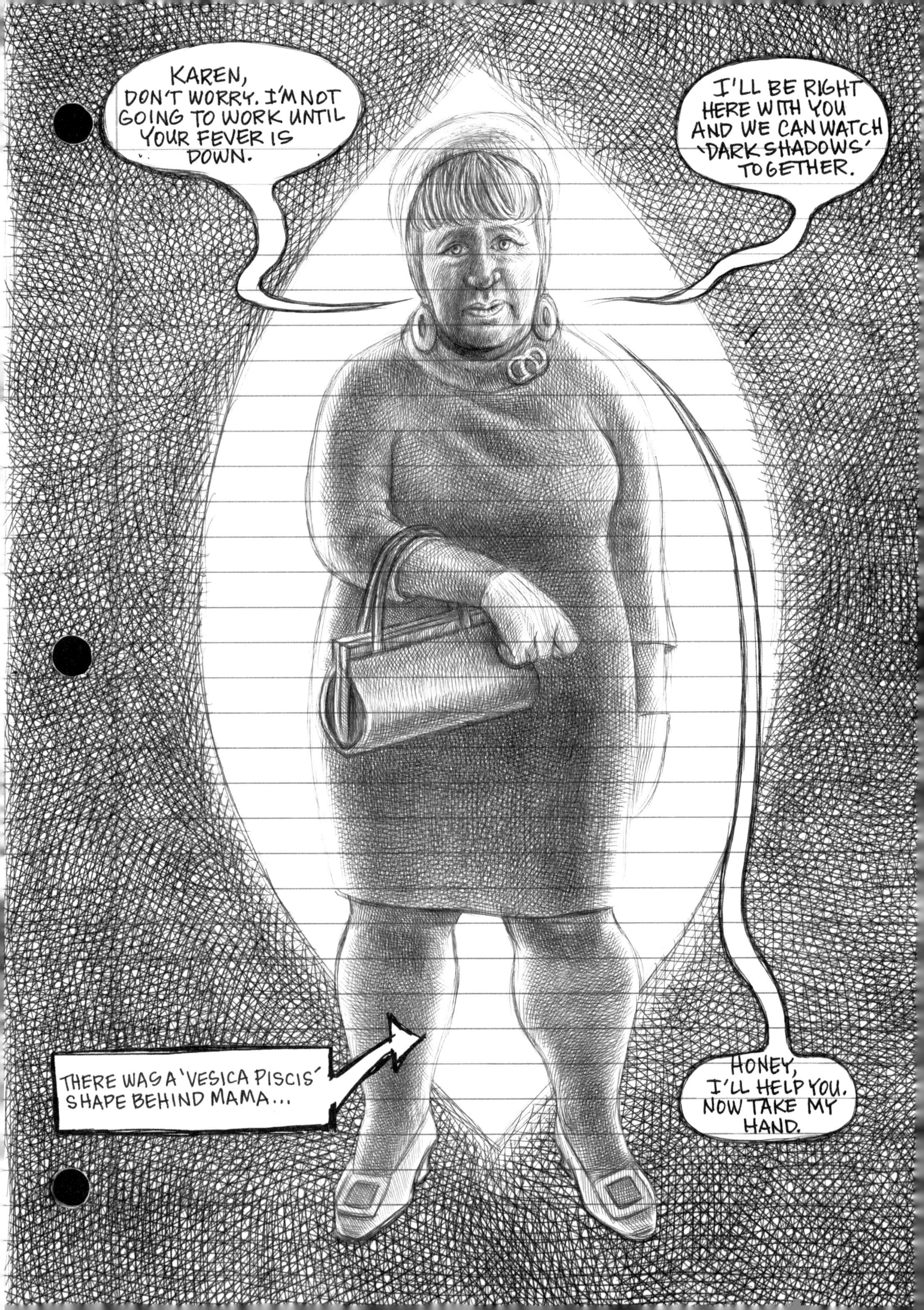
KAREN, DON'T WORRY. I'M NOT GOING TO WORK UNTIL YOUR FEVER IS DOWN.
I'LL BE RIGHT HERE WITH YOU AND WE CAN WATCH 'DARK SHADOWS' TOGETHER.
THERE WAS A 'VESICA PISCIS' SHAPE BEHIND MAMA...
HONEY, I'LL HELP YOU. NOW TAKE MY HAND.

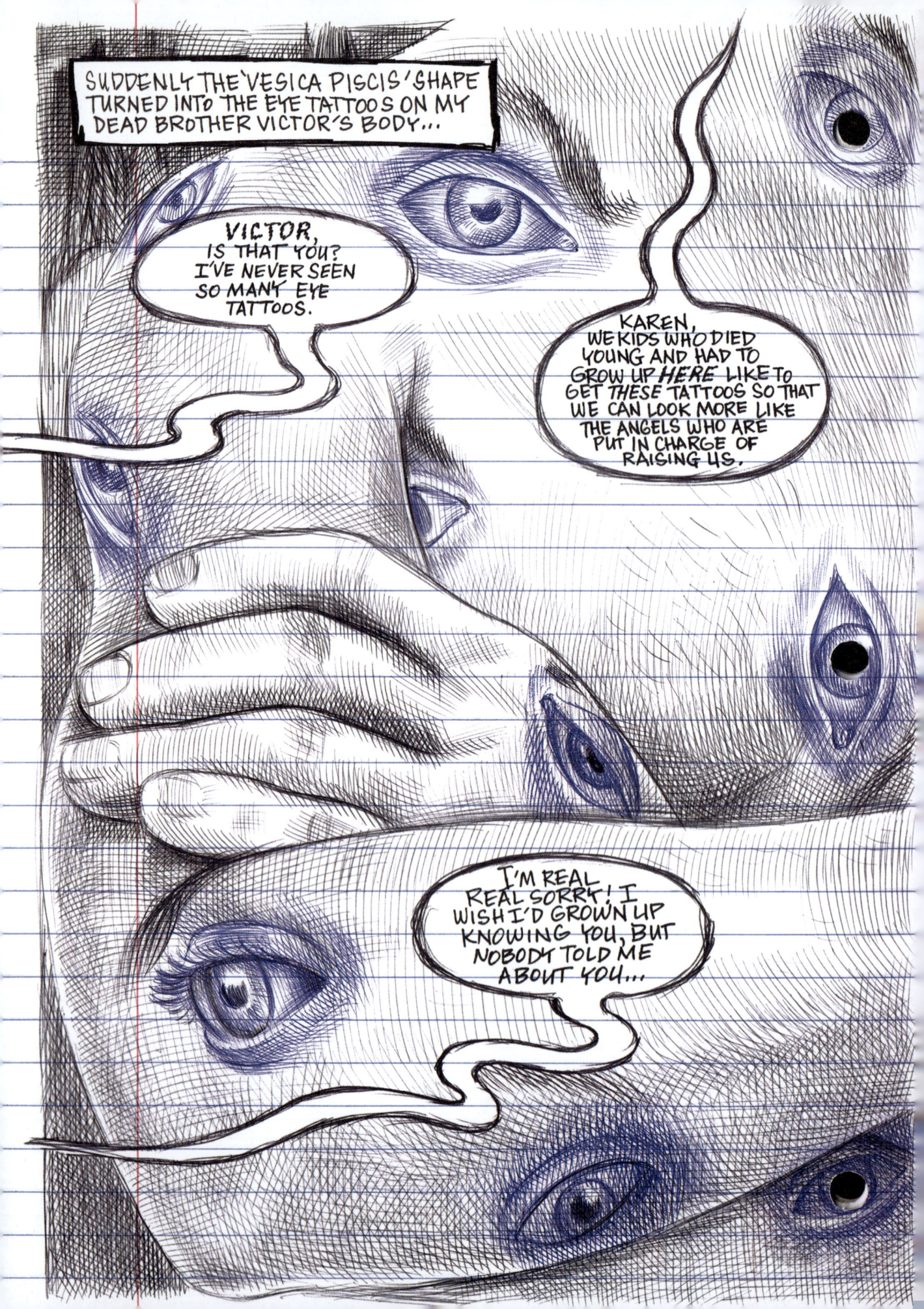

SUDDENLY THE 'VESICA PISCIS' SHAPE TURNED INTO THE EYE TATTOOS ON MY DEAD BROTHER VICTOR'S BODY...

VICTOR, IS THAT YOU? I'VE NEVER SEEN SO MANY EYE TATTOOS.

KAREN, WE KIDS WHO DIED YOUNG AND HAD TO GROW UP HERE LIKE TO GET THESE TATTOOS SO THAT WE CAN LOOK MORE LIKE THE ANGELS WHO ARE PUT IN CHARGE OF RAISING US.

I'M REAL REAL SORRY! I WISH I'D GROWN UP KNOWING YOU, BUT NOBODY TOLD ME ABOUT YOU...

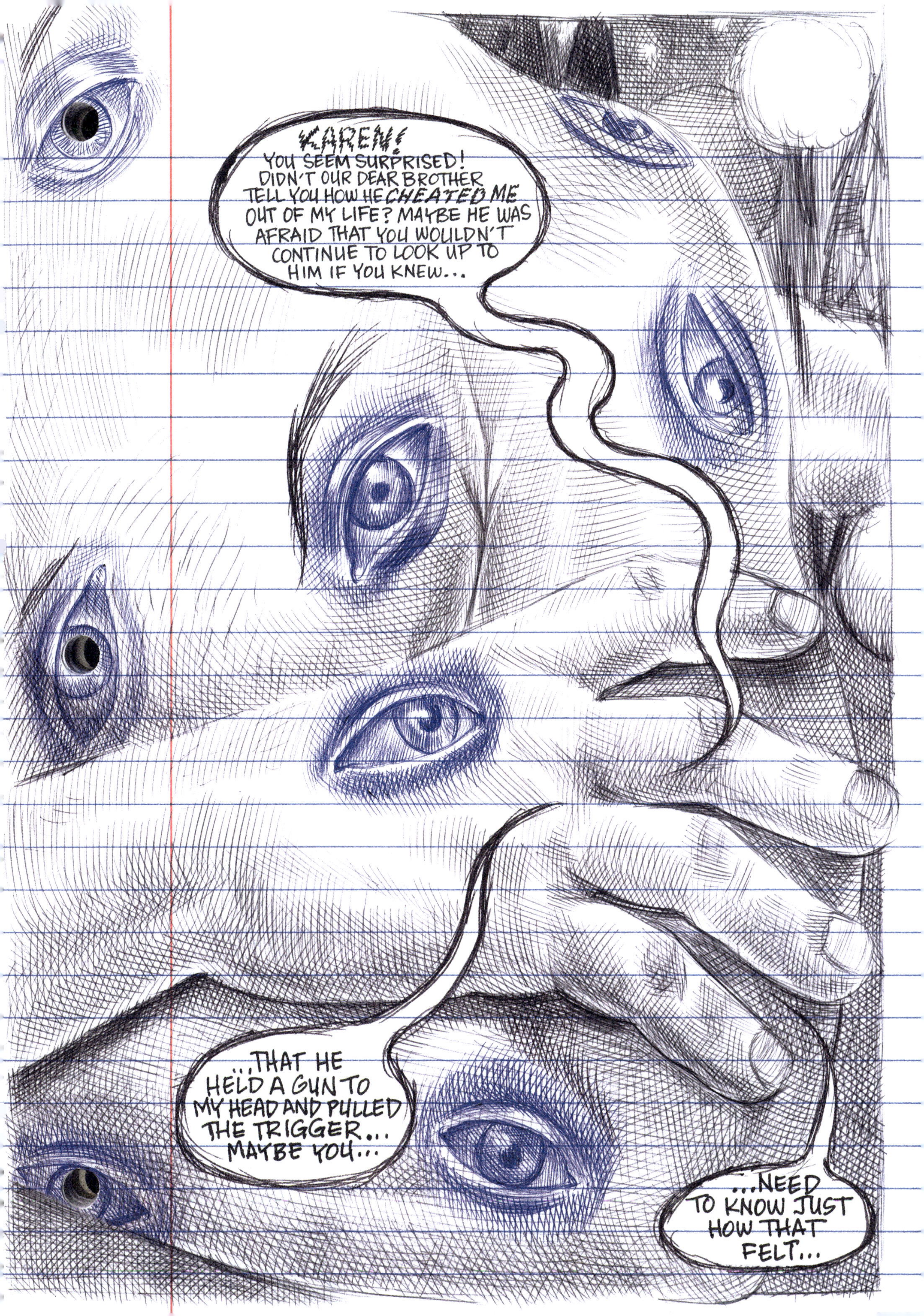
KAREN! YOU SEEM SURPRISED! DIDN'T OUR DEAR BROTHER TELL YOU HOW HE CHEATED ME OUT OF MY LIFE? MAYBE HE WAS AFRAID THAT YOU WOULDN'T CONTINUE TO LOOK UP TO HIM IF YOU KNEW...
...THAT HE HELD A GUN TO MY HEAD AND PULLED THE TRIGGER... MAYBE YOU...
...NEED TO KNOW JUST HOW THAT FELT...

SUDDENLY IT WAS LIKE A BULLET WAS IN MY HEAD... IT WAS A TERRIBLE FEELING! I FELT REALLY BAD FOR VICTOR BUT MY BRAIN WAS SO WEIRD THAT I COULN'T TELL HIM THAT I HATED WHAT HE'D GONE THROUGH... AND THEN...

I THINK IT'S TIME FOR ME TO HURT DIEGO THE WAY HE HURT ME... SO I WILL DESTROY THE ONLY THING THAT OUR BROTHER LOVES... AND THAT THING... **IS YOU!!!**

...ALL OF A SUDDEN IN THE DREAM VICTOR WAS A BIG SCARY GIANT...

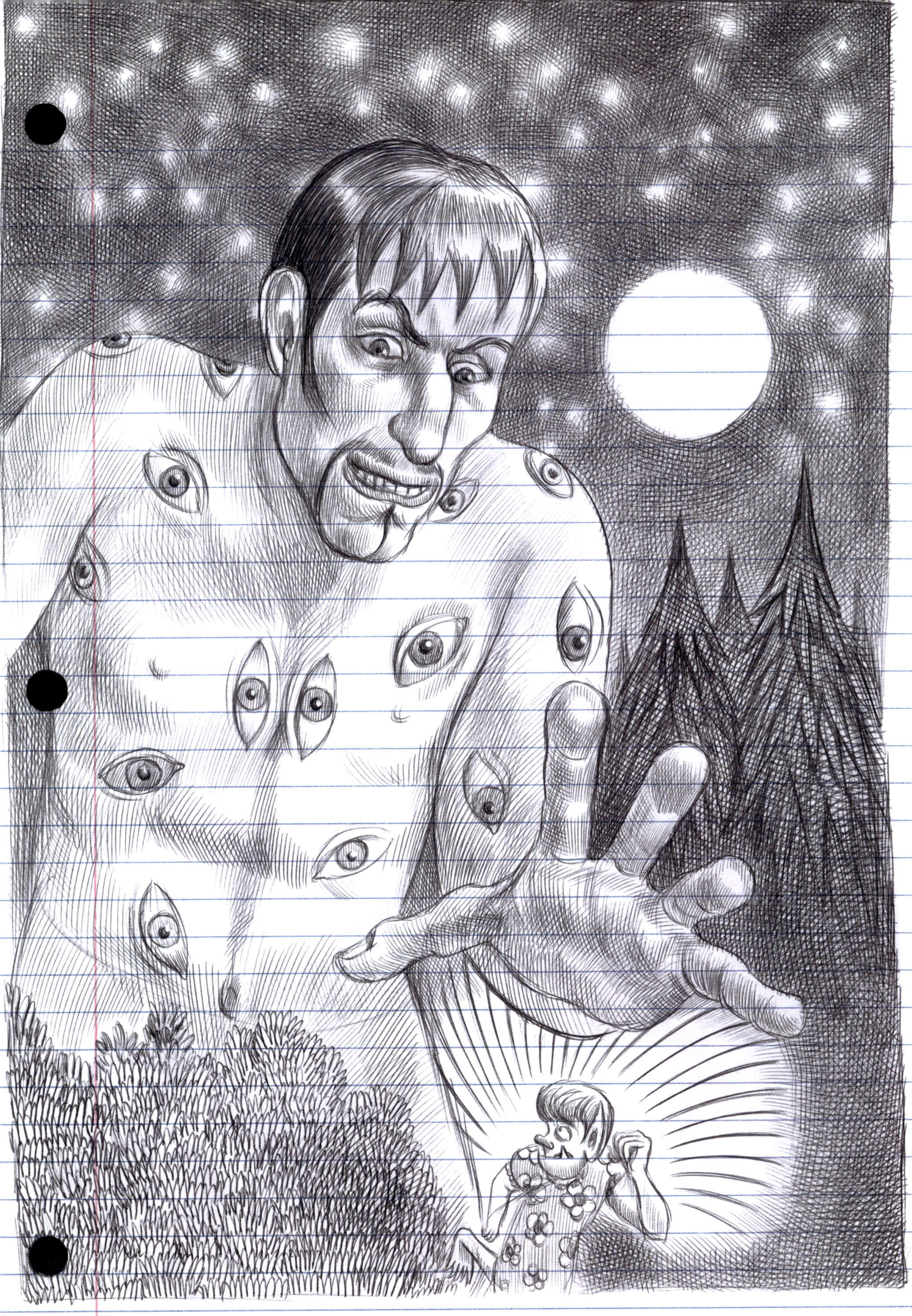

MY FEET ARE AS HEAVY AS LEAD!!!

SLAM!

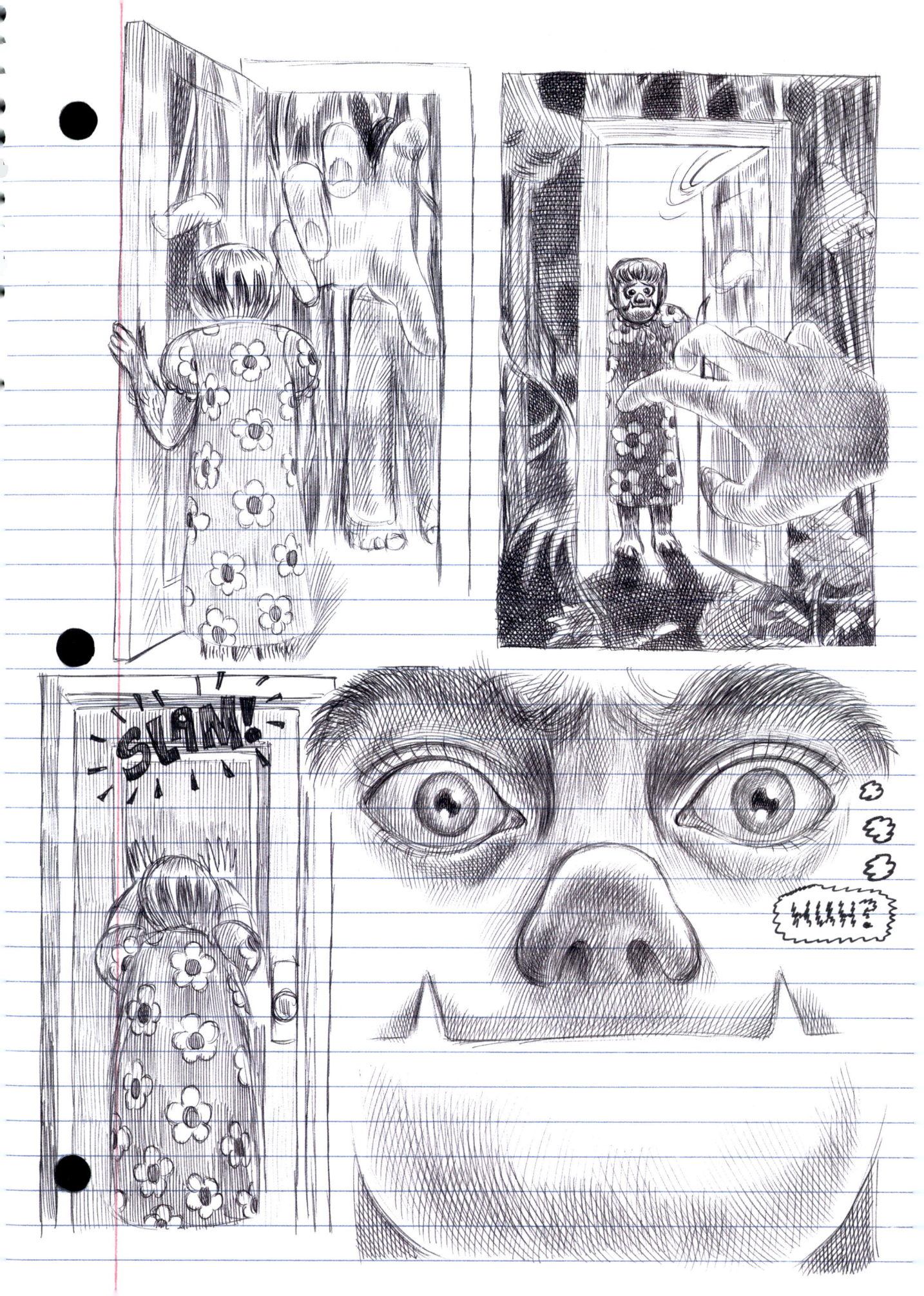

HUH?

"YES, KAREN, I'M A WOLF BUT REALLY MORE TO THE POINT I'M HERE TO SAVE YOU FROM YOUR BROTHER AS I'VE DONE SO MANY TIMES BEFORE."

THAT WAS WHEN I SAW THE BLOODY SCREW EYES THAT SOMEONE HAD DRILLED INTO THE WOLF'S CHEST.

"WOLF, YOU'RE HURT! WHY ARE YOU SMILING WHEN YOU'RE INJURED?"

"WE WOLVES ALWAYS SMILE WHEN WE'RE LOOKING AT OUR PACK."

AT THAT MINUTE IN THE DREAM I ALMOST CRIED AT THE THOUGHT THAT I HAD A PACK.

"BUT WOLF, WHO DID THIS TO YOU?"

"KAREN, WE HAVE TO GET AWAY FROM YOUR BROTHER RIGHT *NOW*. THERE ISN'T TIME TO TELL YOU HOW I GOT HURT. *THE ONLY SAFE PLACE IS...*"

...THE UNKNOWN

WOLF, I CAN'T. I CAN'T DO IT!

RIGHT THEN THE SOUND OF VICTOR'S MEAN LAUGH GOT EVEN LOUDER

EVERY SECOND OF LIFE IS A STEP INTO THE UNKNOWN, BUT THIS TIME...WE MUST... LEAP!

...AND SUDDENLY ME AND THE WOLF WERE IN A TOTAL FREEFALL...

"...WE WERE FALLING INTO DARKNESS BUT I DIDN'T CARE AS LONG AS MY PAW AND THE WOLF'S PAW WERE TOUCHING..."

WHEN I REMOVED THE BANDAGE I SAW THAT I WAS IN A STRANGE APARTMENT. THE BIGGEST THING IN THE ROOM WAS A FANCY OLD HAND-PAINTED SIGN. I HEARD DISTANT VOICES. MY HEAD ACHED AND I WAS WOBBLY ON MY FEET BUT...

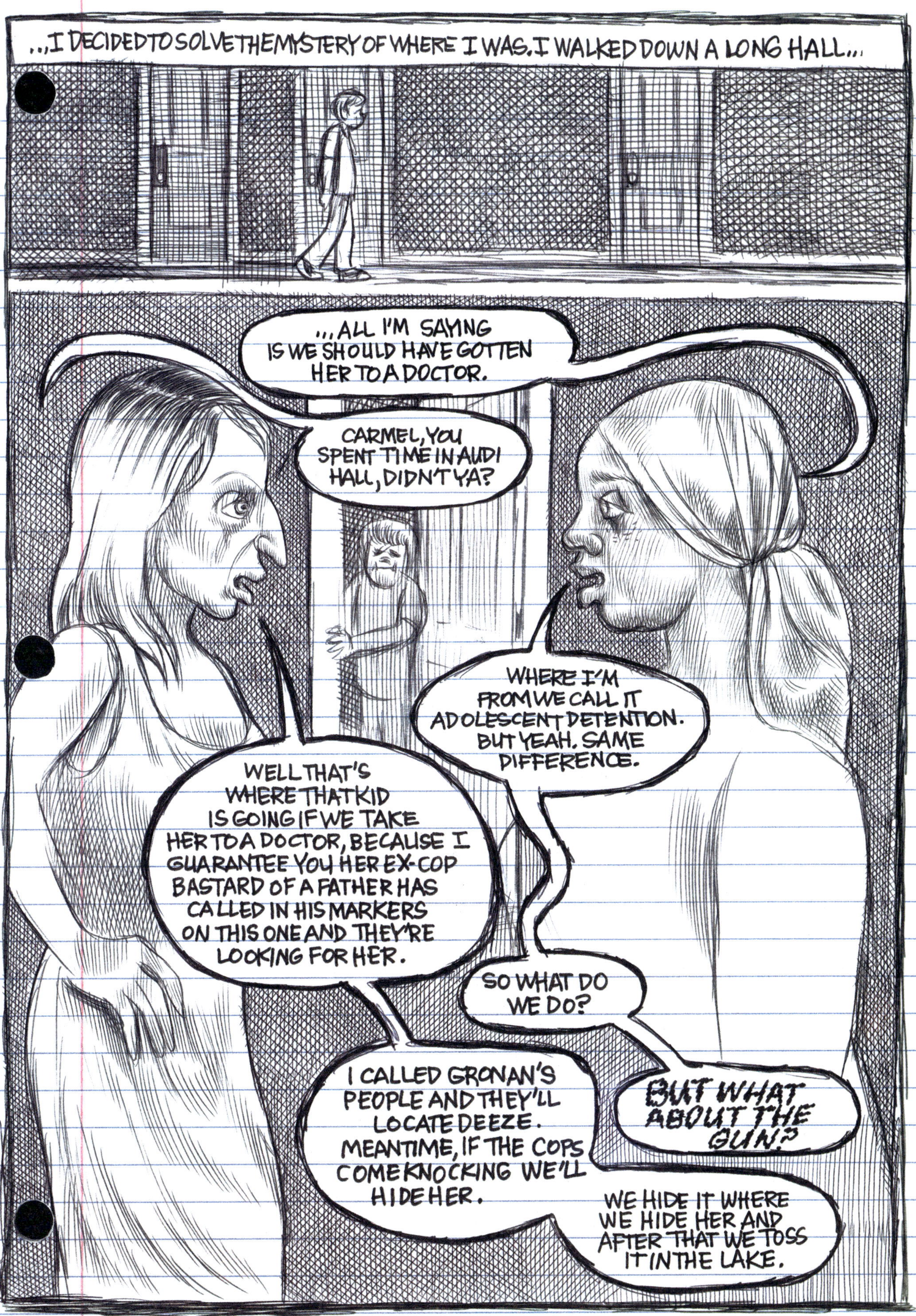
...I DECIDED TO SOLVE THE MYSTERY OF WHERE I WAS. I WALKED DOWN A LONG HALL...
...ALL I'M SAYING IS WE SHOULD HAVE GOTTEN HER TO A DOCTOR.
CARMEL, YOU SPENT TIME IN AUDI HALL, DIDN'T YA?
WHERE I'M FROM WE CALL IT ADOLESCENT DETENTION. BUT YEAH. SAME DIFFERENCE.
WELL THAT'S WHERE THAT KID IS GOING IF WE TAKE HER TO A DOCTOR, BECAUSE I GUARANTEE YOU HER EX-COP BASTARD OF A FATHER HAS CALLED IN HIS MARKERS ON THIS ONE AND THEY'RE LOOKING FOR HER.
SO WHAT DO WE DO?
I CALLED GRONAN'S PEOPLE AND THEY'LL LOCATE DEEZE. MEANTIME, IF THE COPS COME KNOCKING WE'LL HIDE HER.
BUT WHAT ABOUT THE GUN?
WE HIDE IT WHERE WE HIDE HER AND AFTER THAT WE TOSS IT IN THE LAKE.

RIGHT THAT MINUTE WE HEARD THE FRONT DOOR BUZZER GO OFF LIKE THE PERSON PRESSING IT **MEANT BUSINESS!**

BBBZZUUUZZZZZZZZZZZZ

IT'S THE COPS!

IT'S THE COPS! WE'VE GOT TO GET HER INTO THE SPIRITUALIST CLOSET **PRONTO!**

THAT WAS WHEN DORINE TURNED AND SAW ME IN THE DOORWAY...

KID, FOLLOW ME AND KEEP YER TRAP SHUT!

WHEN WE REACHED THE LIVING ROOM, DORINE PRESSED A SECRET BUTTON ON THE WOOD-PANELED WALL AND ONE OF THE WOODEN PANELS POPPED OUT REVEALING A TINY ROOM. DORINE SLID IT OPEN FURTHER AND HISSED...

"IN YOU GO, KID!"

"WHAT'S THAT?"

"FOR YEARS THIS BUILDING WAS OWNED BY A PSYCHIC MEDIUM. THE CLOSET WAS HOW THEY TRICKED PEOPLE INTO BELIEVING THAT THEY WERE TALKING TO DEAD FAMILY MEMBERS."

"BE VERY CAREFUL NOT TO TOUCH ANYTHING! IF YOU DO THERE WILL BE KNOCKS ON THE WALLS."

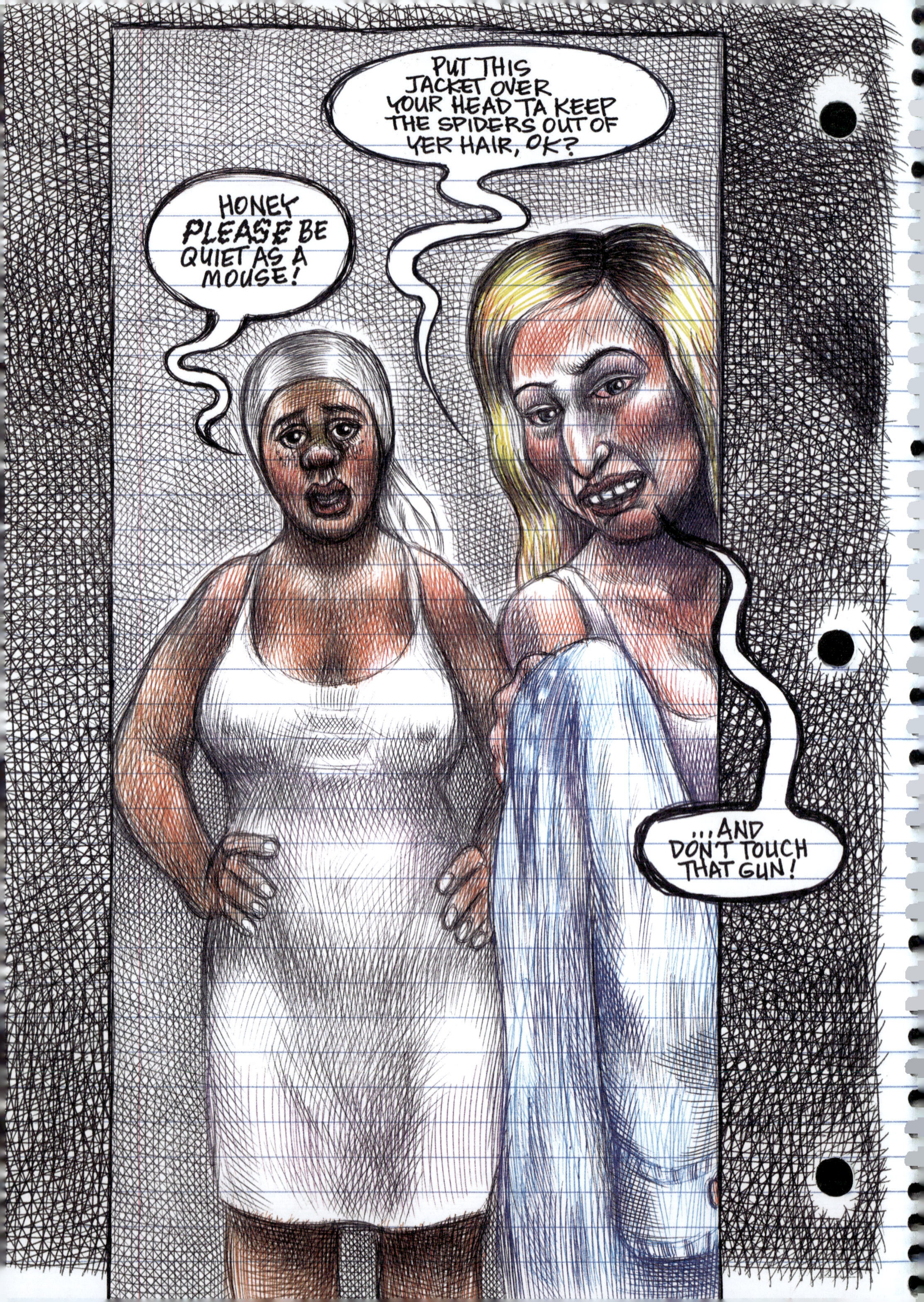
PUT THIS JACKET OVER YOUR HEAD TA KEEP THE SPIDERS OUT OF YER HAIR, OK?
HONEY PLEASE BE QUIET AS A MOUSE!
...AND DON'T TOUCH THAT GUN!

FROM INSIDE THE DARK CLOSET I COULD HEAR THE APARTMENT DOOR OPENING AND TWO DEEP COP VOICES WERE SPEAKING TO DORINE AND CARMEL...

SO GIRLS, WE NEED SOME ANSWERS. YOU WERE SEEN WITH A KID... UM... YESTERDAY—

—YEAH, SO IS THIS REYES KID HERE? WE NEED TO TAKE A LOOK AROUND, OKAY?

YEAH, OFFICER, SHE *WAS* HERE BUT SHE TOOK OFF AND WE HAVEN'T SEEN HER SINCE.

IT'S FINE IF YOU WANNA LOOK AROUND. NO PROBLEM.

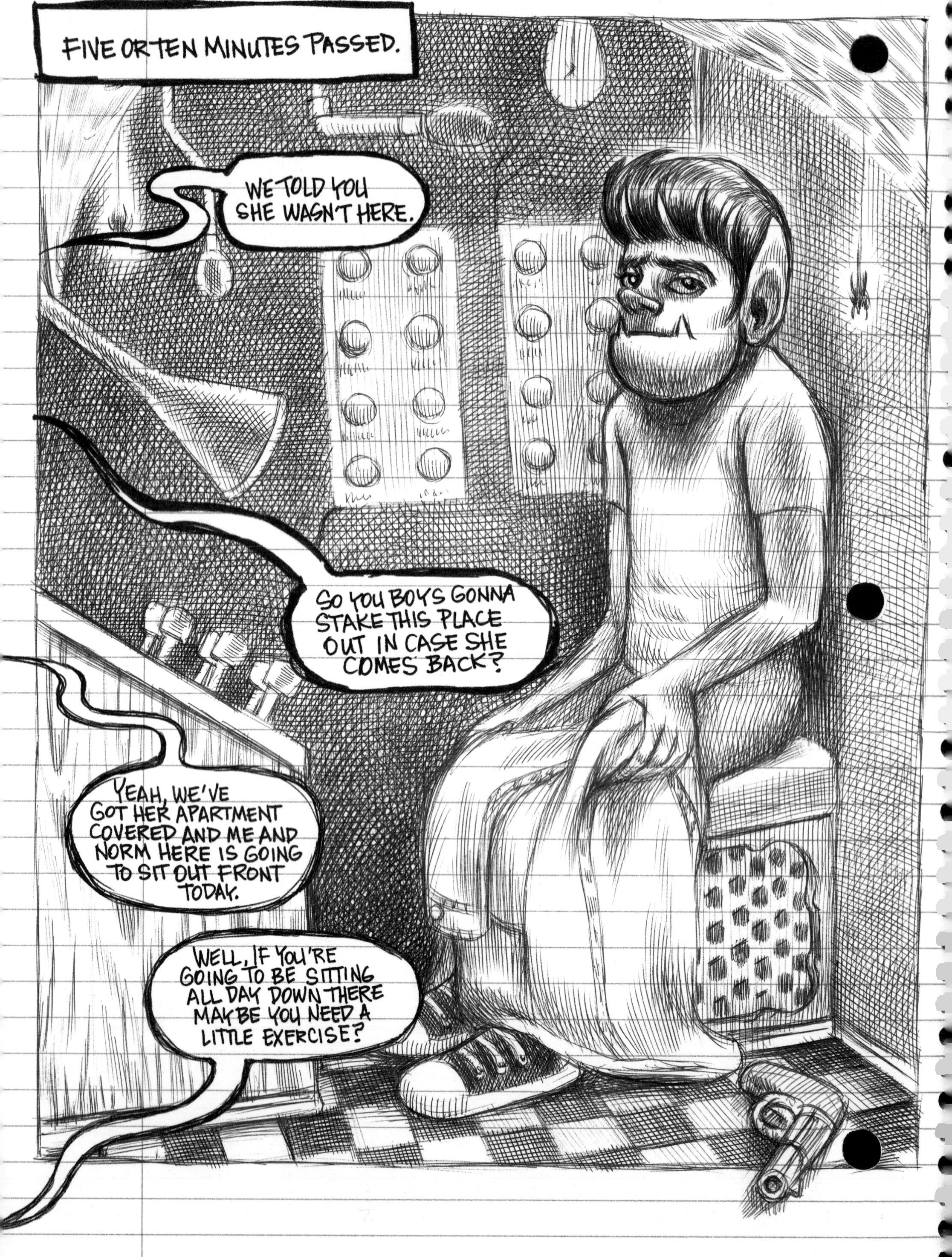
FIVE OR TEN MINUTES PASSED.
WE TOLD YOU SHE WASN'T HERE.
SO YOU BOYS GONNA STAKE THIS PLACE OUT IN CASE SHE COMES BACK?
YEAH, WE'VE GOT HER APARTMENT COVERED AND ME AND NORM HERE IS GOING TO SIT OUT FRONT TODAY.
WELL, IF YOU'RE GOING TO BE SITTING ALL DAY DOWN THERE MAYBE YOU NEED A LITTLE EXERCISE?

"GRATIS?"

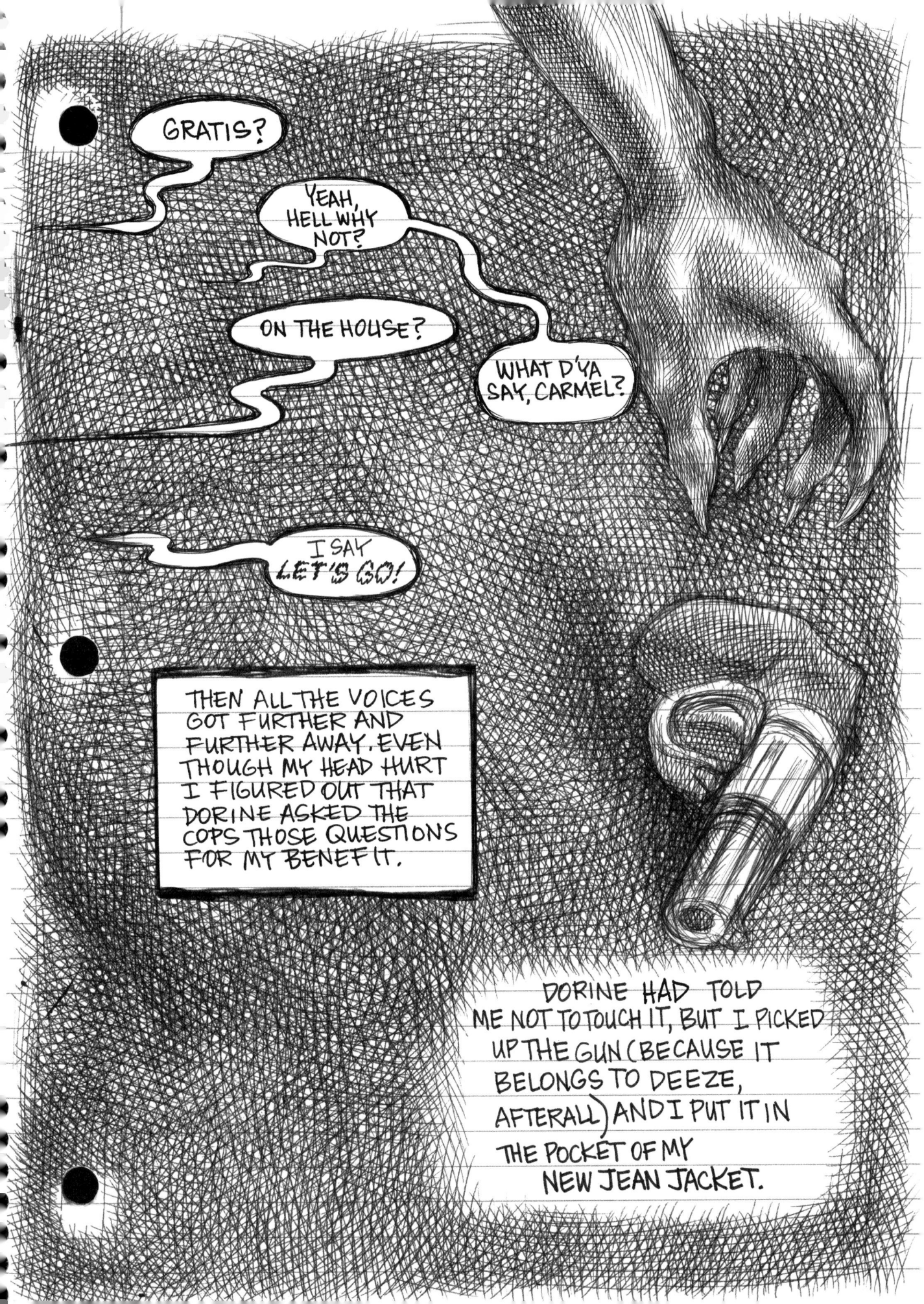

"YEAH, HELL WHY NOT?"

"ON THE HOUSE?"

"WHAT D'YA SAY, CARMEL?"

"I SAY LET'S GO!"

THEN ALL THE VOICES GOT FURTHER AND FURTHER AWAY. EVEN THOUGH MY HEAD HURT I FIGURED OUT THAT DORINE ASKED THE COPS THOSE QUESTIONS FOR MY BENEFIT.

DORINE HAD TOLD ME NOT TO TOUCH IT, BUT I PICKED UP THE GUN (BECAUSE IT BELONGS TO DEEZE, AFTER ALL) AND I PUT IT IN THE POCKET OF MY NEW JEAN JACKET.

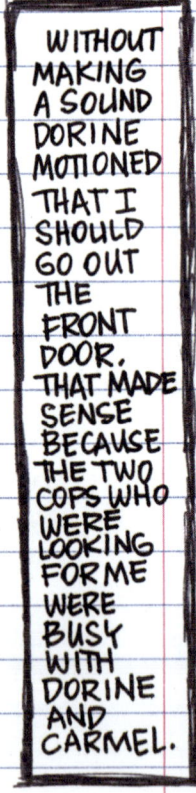

AFTER I LEFT THE SPIRITUALIST CLOSET, I VERY QUIETLY WALKED DOWN THE HALL. I LOOKED INTO A ROOM AND I SAW DORINE AND A COP DOING THE WHOLE 'NIGHT MACHINE' THING (SO GROSS!) LUCKILY THE COP HAD HIS EYES CLOSED BUT DORINE SAW ME. SHE LOOKED TOTALLY FREAKED OUT.

WITHOUT MAKING A SOUND DORINE MOTIONED THAT I SHOULD GO OUT THE FRONT DOOR. THAT MADE SENSE BECAUSE THE TWO COPS WHO WERE LOOKING FOR ME WERE BUSY WITH DORINE AND CARMEL.

GO OUT THE FRONT DOOR.

FIND DEEZE.

DON'T GO HOME!

I CREEPED OUT OF DORINE AND CARMEL'S APARTMENT. WHEN I GOT TO THE STAIRS THAT LED TO THE STREET, A WAVE OF...

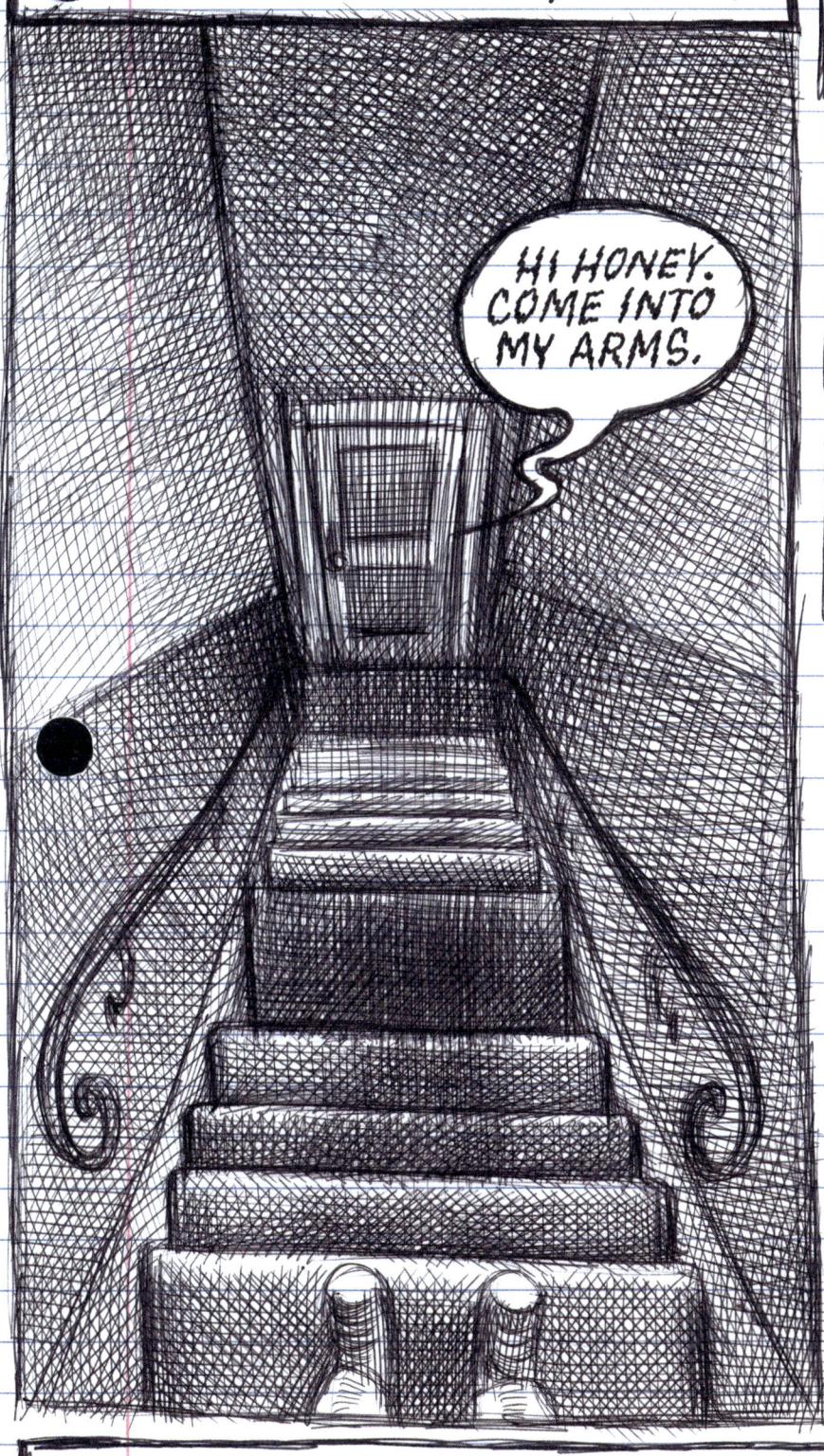

"HI HONEY. COME INTO MY ARMS."

...CRAZY FEELINGS SWEPT OVER ME. FOR A MINUTE IT SEEMED LIKE THE STAIRCASE WAS A KIND OF MOM WHO WANTED ME TO CRAWL UP ON HER LAP AND ALL I HAD TO DO TO GET UP THERE WAS JUST GIVE IN TO MY DIZZIENESS... **AND FALL.** FOR A SECOND I WAS ALMOST SURE THAT **DEATH** IS JUST THE EXPERIENCE OF BEING HUGGED BY THE **UNKNOWN.** I RESISTED THE IMPULSE BECAUSE I KNOW THAT **DEEZE NEEDS ME.** WITHOUT ME DEEZE WOULD BE ALL ALONE IN THE WORLD...

DORINE TOLD ME TO FIND DEEZE AND ALL OF A SUDDEN I FELT SORT OF DESPERATE AND *REALLY FREAKED*, AND LIKE NOTHING WOULD BE O.K. UNTIL I FOUND MY BROTHER...

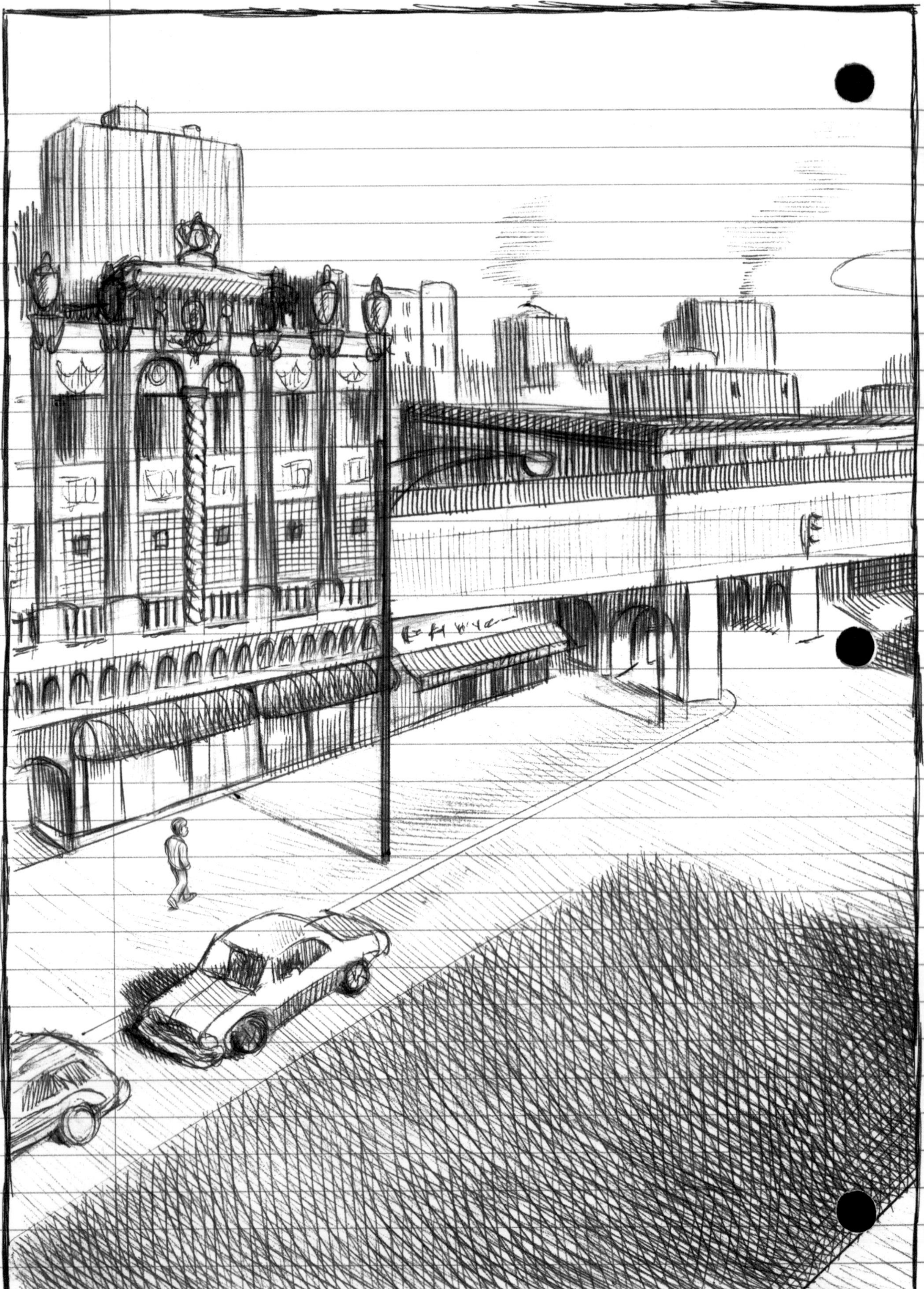

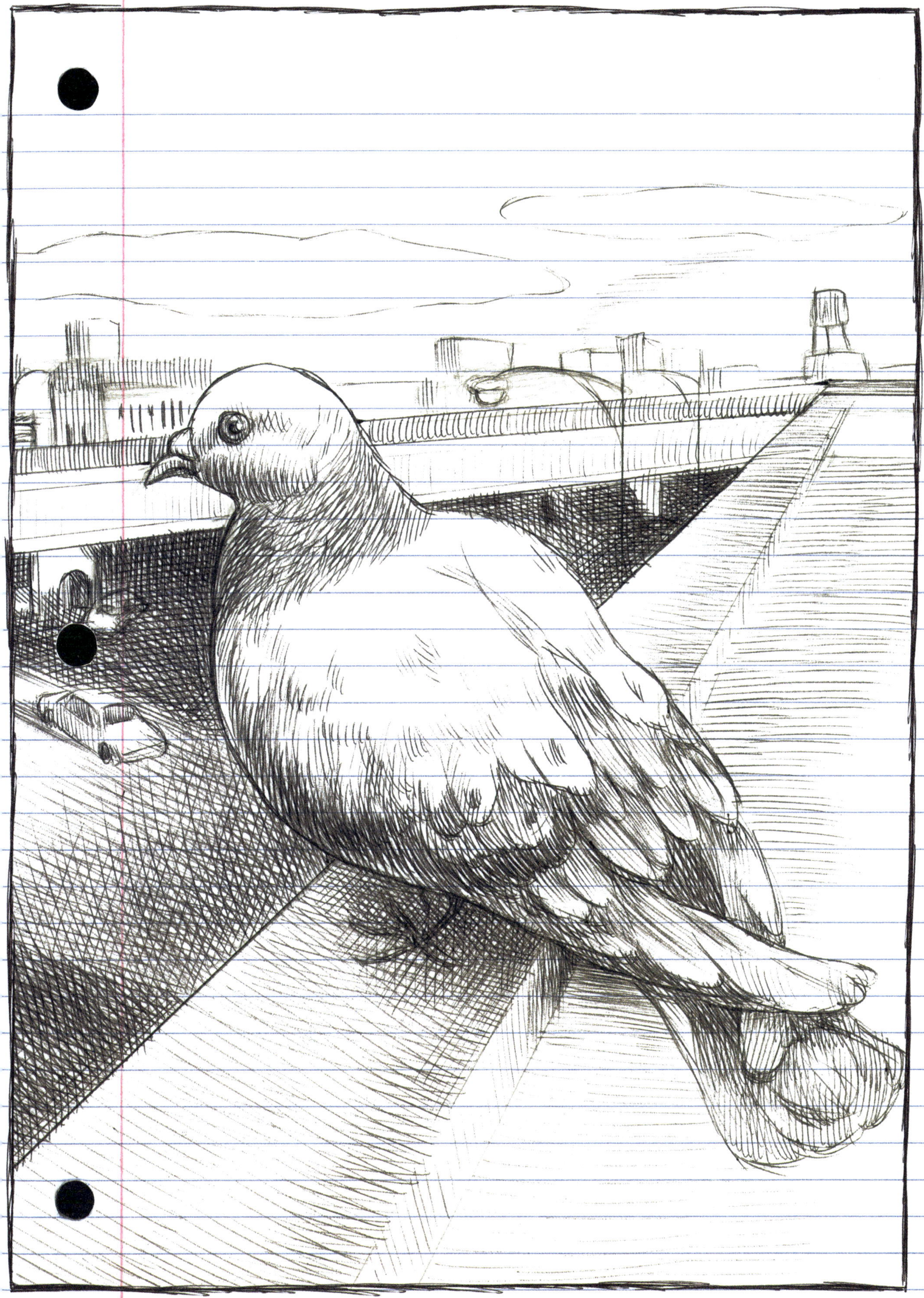

WHEN I SNEAKED OUT OF DORINE AND CARMEL'S APARTMENT I SUPPOSE I THOUGHT I WAS GOING HOME EVEN THOUGH DEEZE WAS ON HIS BUSINESS TRIP. MY HEAD STILL ACHED REALLY BAD AND I WAS DIZZY. I WAS SO LOST AND CONFUSED BUT THEN I HEARD THE BEST, MOST WONDERFUL SOUND I COULD EVER HEAR.

"KARE!"

"DEEZY?"

FOR A SECOND I THOUGHT I WOULD FAINT FROM RELIEF BUT ALSO I WAS AFRAID THAT I WAS IMAGINING HIM. I STARTED TO CRY (EMBARRASSING).

Panel 1:

"KARE, IT'S OK. C'MON, MIJA GET IN THE CAR QUICK, OK?"

"DEEZE ;SOB; I THINK SOMETHING BAD MIGHT HAVE HAPPENED. BUT I CAN'T REMEMBER."

"WE'LL FIGURE IT ALL OUT ONCE WE GET ON THE ROAD BUT FIRST WE'LL GO TO A DOCTOR WHO IS A PAL OF MR. GRONAN'S. AND WE'LL GET YOU ALL FIXED UP."

"MY HEAD HURTS AND IT WAS BLOODY."

Panel 2:

THEN WE WERE ON LAKE SHORE DRIVE AND DEEZE HAD ME NEXT TO HIM AND HIS ARM AROUND ME AND I FELT THE PAIN OF HOW MUCH I MISSED HIM. HIS SMELLS OF CIGARETTE SMOKE AND COLOGNE AND SPRAY STARCH ARE THE BEST SMELLS IN THE WORLD TO ME.

WHEN DEEZE PARKED THE CAR I NOTICED THAT THERE WAS A BUNCH OF MY STUFF IN THE BACKSEAT — CLOTHES AND THE FAMILY PHOTO ALBUM AND EVEN BLEMMY (WHO WAS ANGRY WITH ME AND ACTING LIKE HE COULDN'T SAY A WORD).

WHAT'S THE DEAL WITH ALL MY STUFF IN THE BACKSEAT?

=COF COF=
YEAH KARE, CAMPING TRIP.

DEEZE SAID, "CAMPING TRIP" JUST LIKE WE'D BEEN ON A MILLION OF THEM — INSTEAD OF EXACTLY *NOT EVEN ONE OF THEM*.

THE DOCTOR'S OFFICE WAS IN A FANCY BUILDING ON MICHIGAN AVENUE.

KARE, DON'T BE **FREAKED**. MR. GRONAN, **HIMSELF**, RECOMMENDED THIS DOCTOR TO ME, SO I'M SURE HE'S COOL.

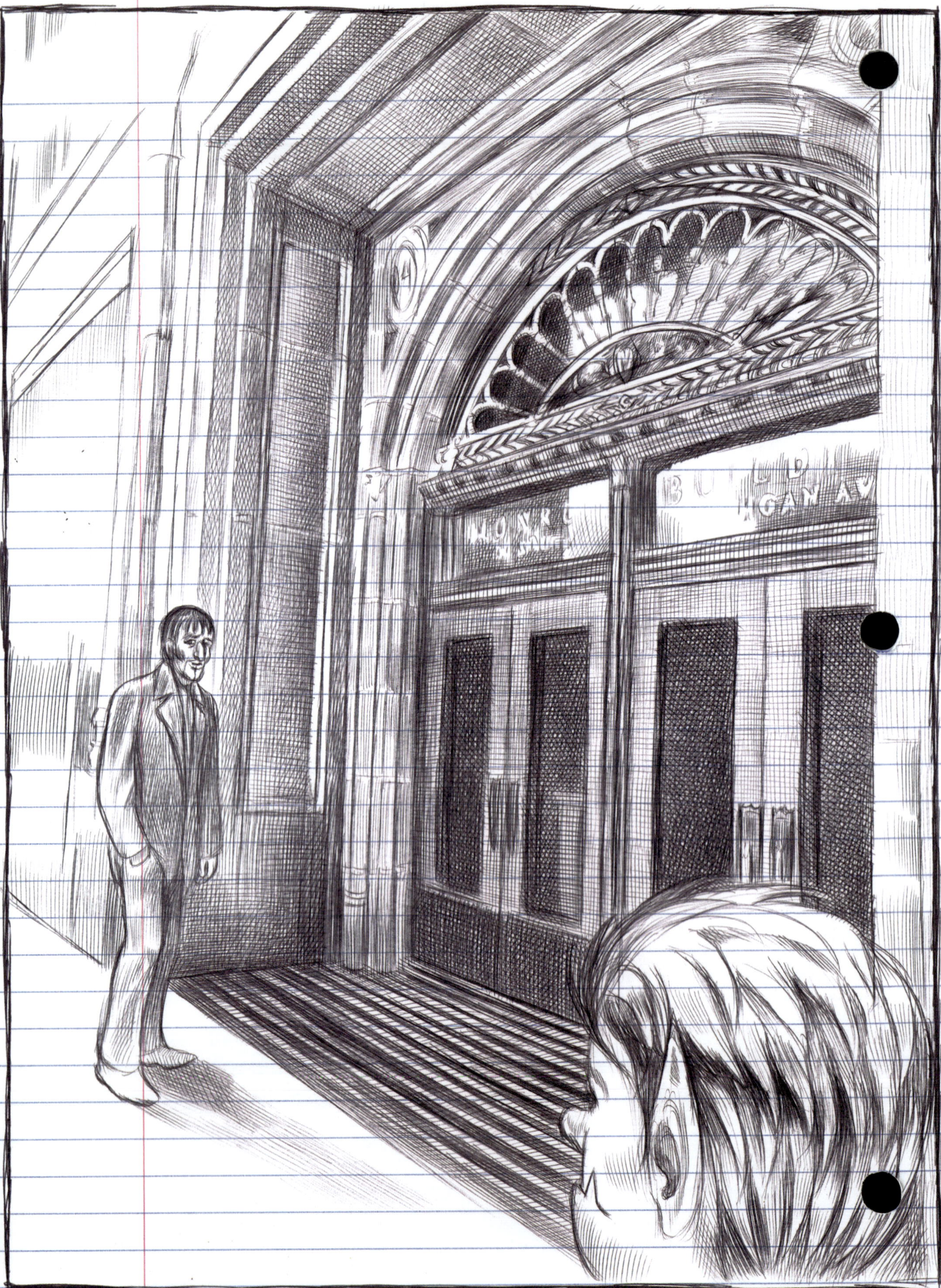

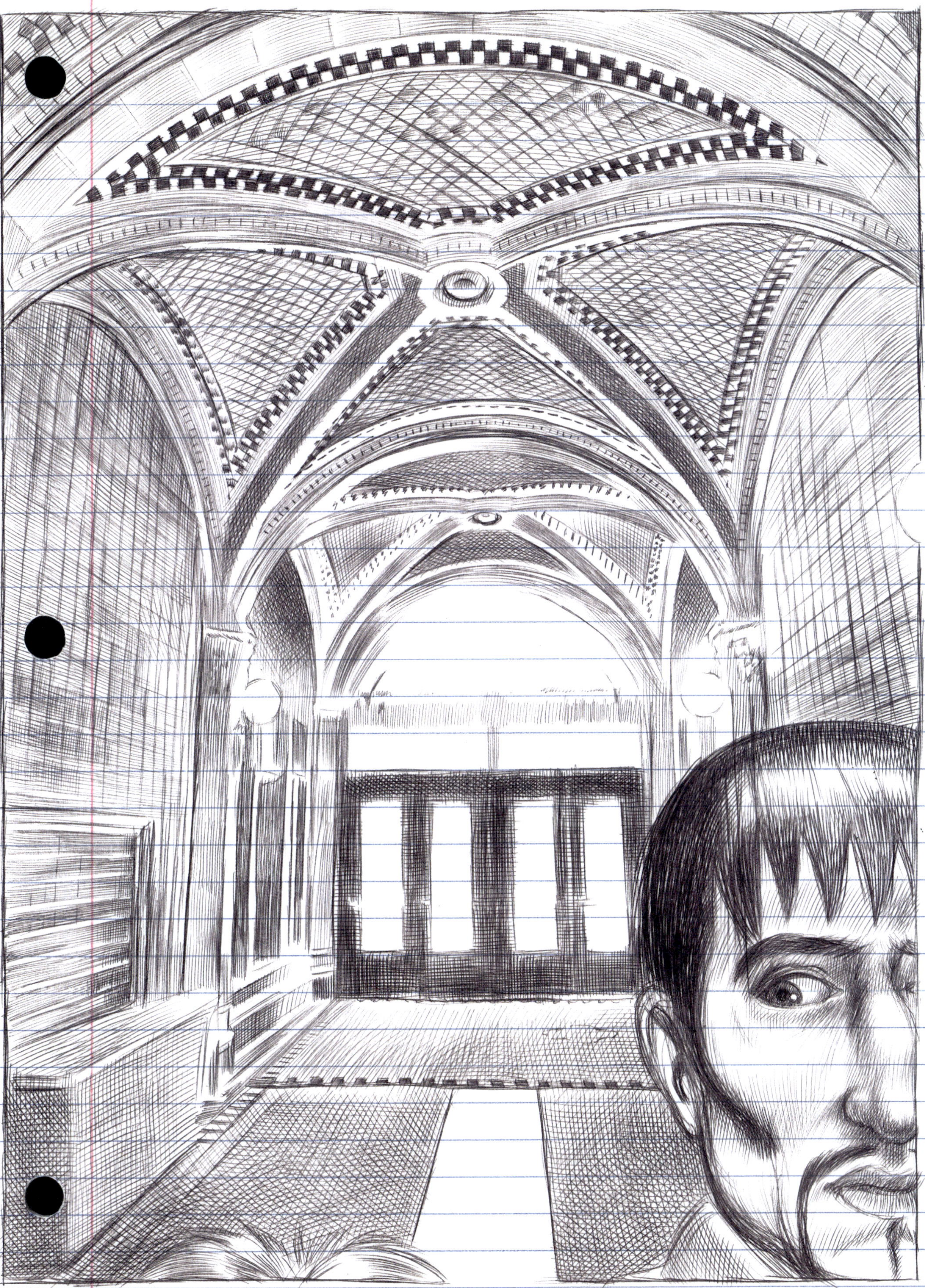

THE DOCTOR WHO ANSWERED THE DOOR DEMANDED THAT DEEZE GIVE HIM 20 BUCKS JUST FOR HIM TO LOOK AT THE CUT ON MY HEAD. AFTER THAT HE MADE BOTH ME AND DEEZE RAISE OUR RIGHT HANDS AND REPEAT AFTER HIM THAT...

"...NO MATTER WHAT I GIVE MY WORD THAT THIS VISIT TO DOCTOR DOCTOROV WILL NEVER BE SPOKEN ABOUT UNDER PENALTY OF DEATH!"

"WHATEVER IT COSTS, DOC. NO PROBLEM."

"WELL, IT'S GOING TO COST 75 CASH FOR ME TO SEW THIS GASH UP."

"GASH!?"

"KARE, IT'S COOL. RELAX, OKAY?"

"NO PROBLEM. I'M GOING TO GIVE YOU SOMETHING SO THAT I CAN CLEAN THIS WOUND UP..."

THEN THE DOCTOR MADE ME LIE FACE DOWN ON THE TABLE. HE HAD DEEZE HOLD MY HEAD STILL. AFTER THAT THE DOC GAVE ME A SHOT INTO THE BACK OF MY HEAD.

"PAIN KILLER IS GONNA COST EXTRA, TOO."

AFTERWARDS WHEN WE WERE ON THE ELEVATOR...

"DR. DOCTORON SMELLED LIKE HAIRSPRAY. DEEZE, SINCE WE'RE HERE LETS GO TO THE MUSEUM? PLLEEASSSE!?"

"YEAH KAREN, I REALLY WISH WE COULD BUT WE JUST... CAN'T."

"THAT'S NOT FAIR!"

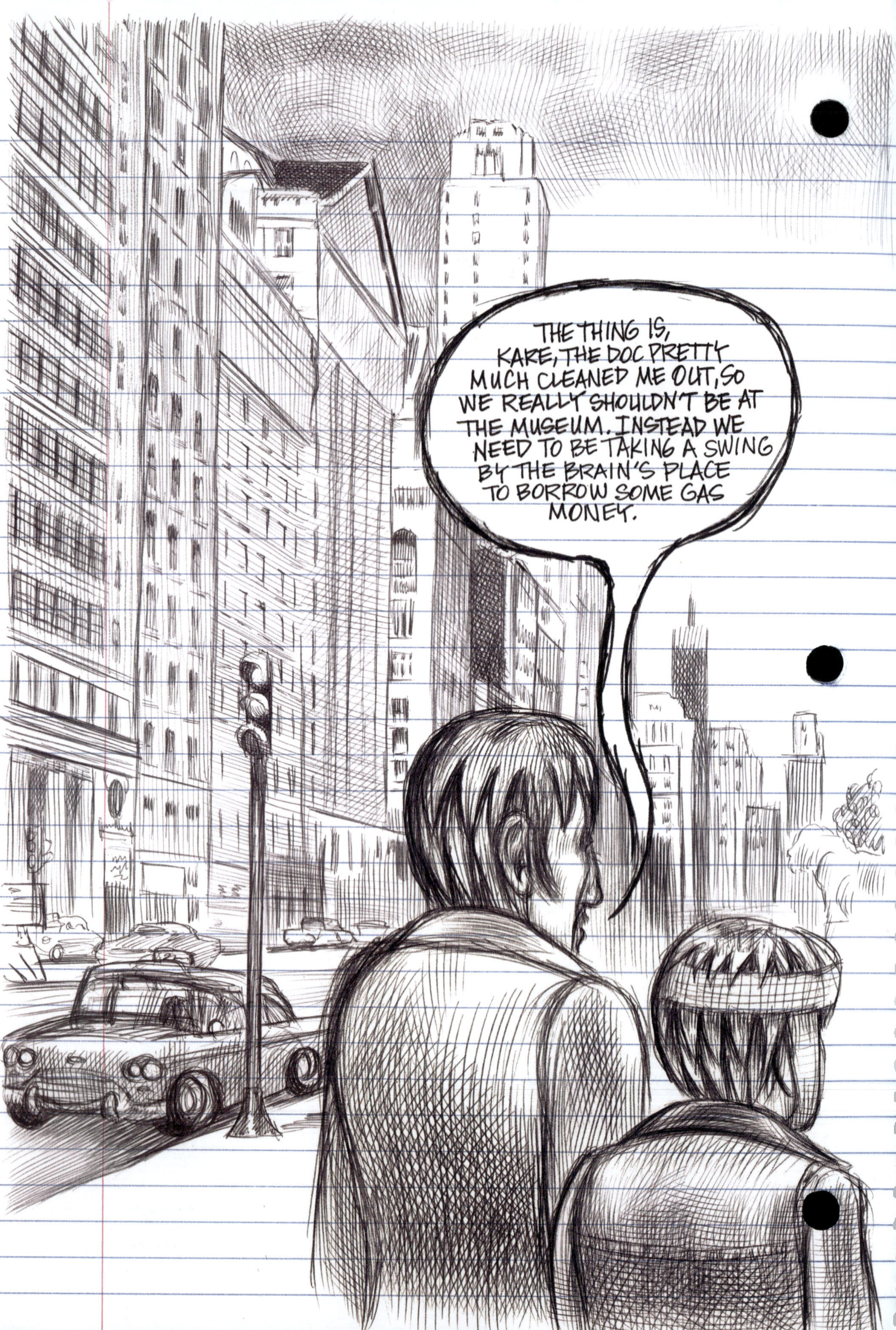
THE THING IS, KARE, THE DOC PRETTY MUCH CLEANED ME OUT, SO WE REALLY SHOULDN'T BE AT THE MUSEUM. INSTEAD WE NEED TO BE TAKING A SWING BY THE BRAIN'S PLACE TO BORROW SOME GAS MONEY.

DEEZE, DO YOU SEE THIS KEY? THIS IS THE KEY TO **EVERY** PAY TOILET LOCKBOX IN THE MUSEUM AND WITH IT I CAN GET US ENOUGH MONEY TO HIT THE ROAD, AND - WHO KNOWS - MAYBE EVEN ENOUGH MONEY FOR A HOTEL ROOM. SO I'M GOING TO NEED YOU TO BE MY LOOKOUT. CAN YOU DO THAT?

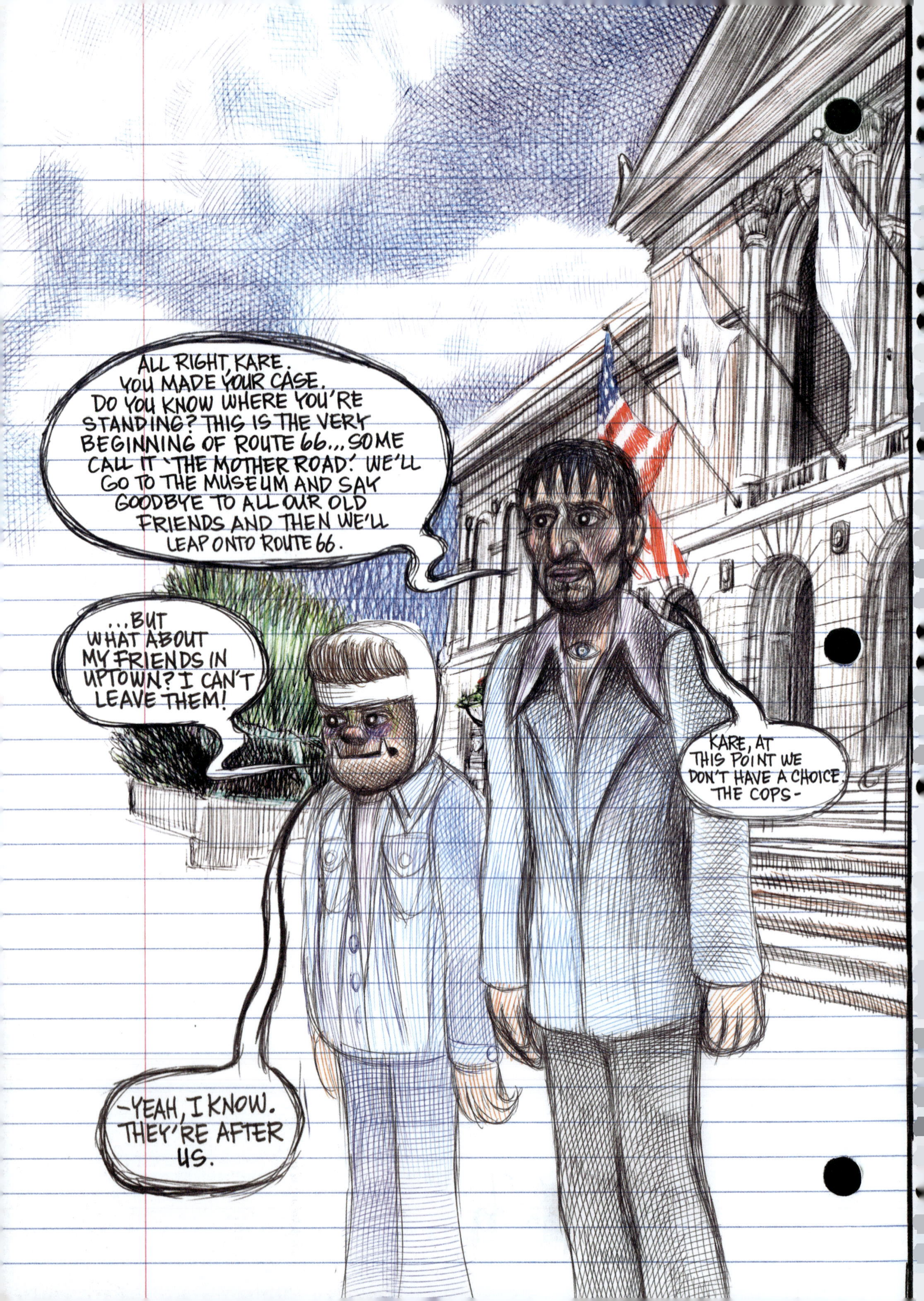
ALL RIGHT, KARE. YOU MADE YOUR CASE. DO YOU KNOW WHERE YOU'RE STANDING? THIS IS THE VERY BEGINNING OF ROUTE 66... SOME CALL IT 'THE MOTHER ROAD.' WE'LL GO TO THE MUSEUM AND SAY GOODBYE TO ALL OUR OLD FRIENDS AND THEN WE'LL LEAP ONTO ROUTE 66.
...BUT WHAT ABOUT MY FRIENDS IN UPTOWN? I CAN'T LEAVE THEM!
KARE, AT THIS POINT WE DON'T HAVE A CHOICE. THE COPS-
-YEAH, I KNOW. THEY'RE AFTER US.

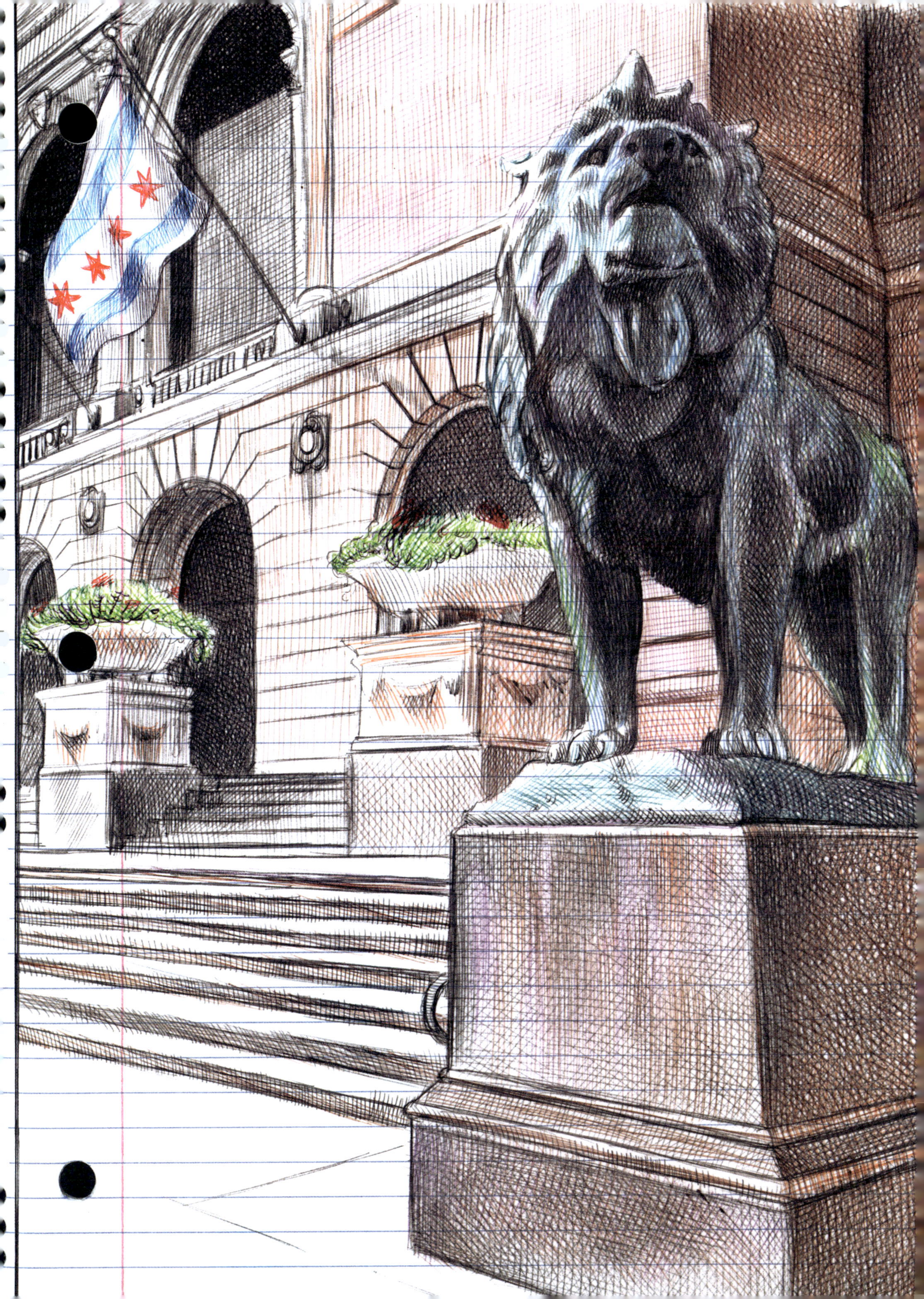

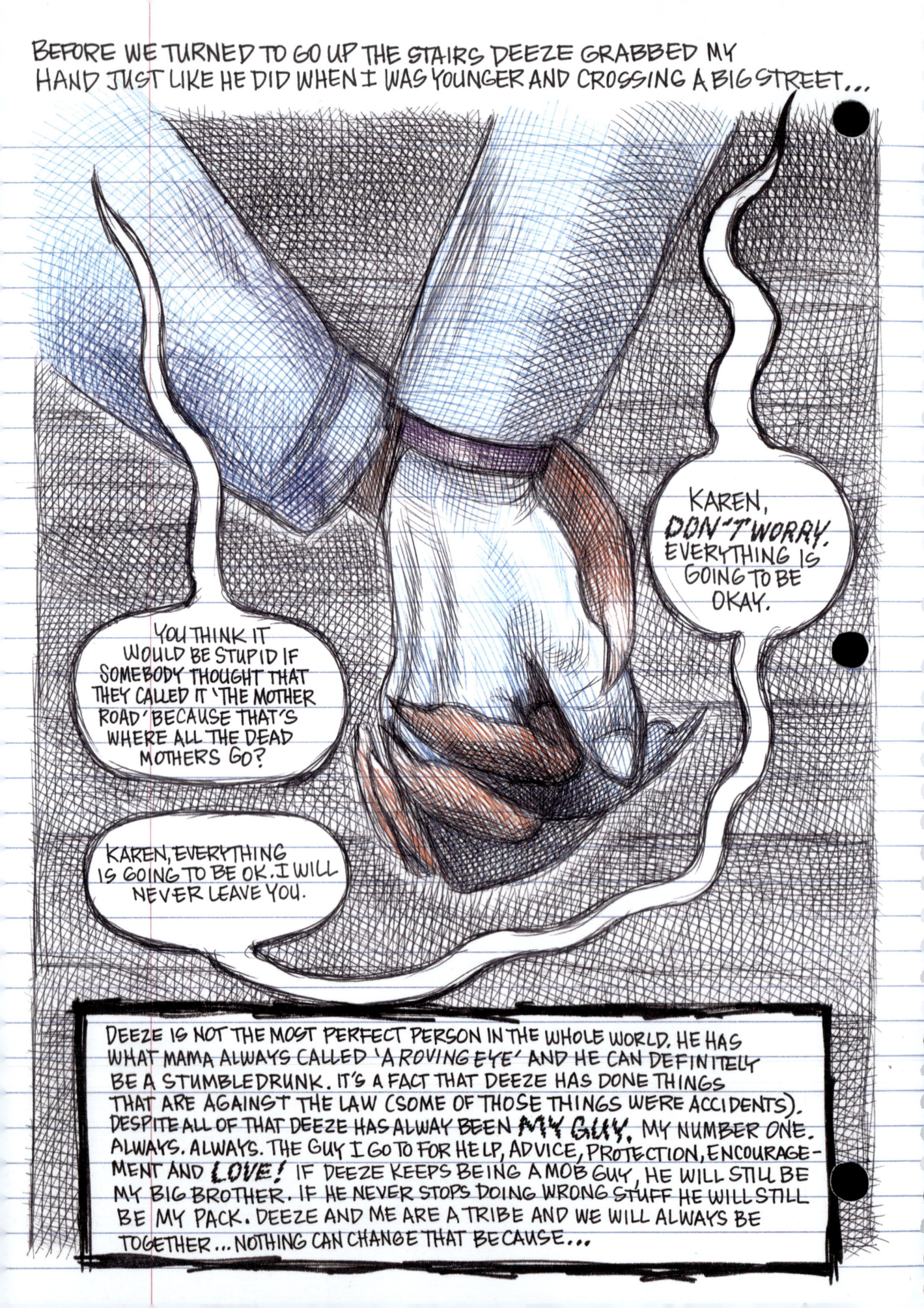

BEFORE WE TURNED TO GO UP THE STAIRS DEEZE GRABBED MY HAND JUST LIKE HE DID WHEN I WAS YOUNGER AND CROSSING A BIG STREET...

> KAREN, **DON'T** WORRY. EVERYTHING IS GOING TO BE OKAY.

> YOU THINK IT WOULD BE STUPID IF SOMEBODY THOUGHT THAT THEY CALLED IT 'THE MOTHER ROAD' BECAUSE THAT'S WHERE ALL THE DEAD MOTHERS GO?

> KAREN, EVERYTHING IS GOING TO BE OK. I WILL NEVER LEAVE YOU.

DEEZE IS NOT THE MOST PERFECT PERSON IN THE WHOLE WORLD. HE HAS WHAT MAMA ALWAYS CALLED 'A ROVING EYE' AND HE CAN DEFINITELY BE A STUMBLEDRUNK. IT'S A FACT THAT DEEZE HAS DONE THINGS THAT ARE AGAINST THE LAW (SOME OF THOSE THINGS WERE ACCIDENTS). DESPITE ALL OF THAT DEEZE HAS ALWAYS BEEN **MY GUY**. MY NUMBER ONE. ALWAYS. ALWAYS. THE GUY I GO TO FOR HELP, ADVICE, PROTECTION, ENCOURAGEMENT AND **LOVE!** IF DEEZE KEEPS BEING A MOB GUY, HE WILL STILL BE MY BIG BROTHER. IF HE NEVER STOPS DOING WRONG STUFF HE WILL STILL BE MY PACK. DEEZE AND ME ARE A TRIBE AND WE WILL ALWAYS BE TOGETHER... NOTHING CAN CHANGE THAT BECAUSE...

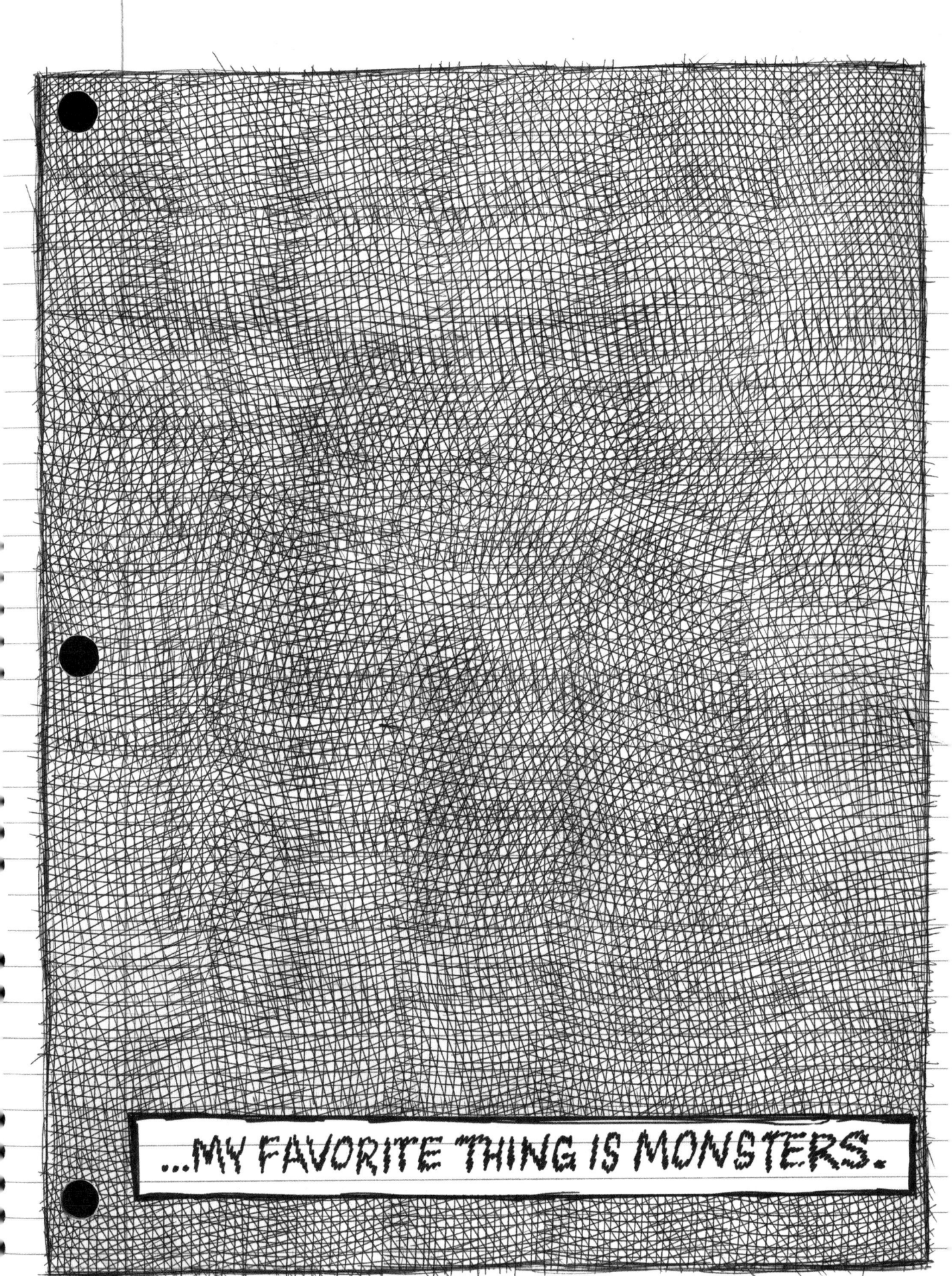

...MY FAVORITE THING IS MONSTERS.

ALSO AVAILABLE:
MY FAVORITE THING IS MONSTERS
BOOK ONE

FANTAGRAPHICS BOOKS INC.
7563 LAKE CITY WAY NE
SEATTLE, WASHINGTON, 98115
www.FANTAGRAPHICS.COM

EDITOR: ERIC REYNOLDS
DESIGNER OF FRONT COVER,
ALL INNER PAGES,
AND INSIDE FRONT COVER: EMIL FERRIS
DESIGNER OF BACK COVER, INSIDE BACK
COVER, AND FLAPS: KAYLA E.
DESIGNER OF SPINE AND FRONT COVER TYPE: JACOB COVEY

PROMOTION: JACQUELENE COHEN

VP / ASSOCIATE PUBLISHER: ERIC REYNOLDS

PRESIDENT / PUBLISHER: GARY GROTH

MY FAVORITE THING IS MONSTERS BOOK TWO IS COPYRIGHT
©2024 EMIL FERRIS

ALL PERMISSION TO EXCERPT MATERIAL FROM THIS BOOK OR THE
PRECEDING BOOK FOR THE PURPOSE OF LIMITED
PRINTED PUBLICATION WILL REQUIRE THE PERMISSION OF BOTH THE
AUTHOR AND THE PUBLISHER. ALL RIGHTS RESERVED.
FANTAGRAPHICS AND THE FANTAGRAPHICS LOGO ARE
TRADEMARKS OF FANTAGRAPHICS BOOKS INC.
ISBN 978-1-68396-927-3
LIBRARY OF CONGRESS CONTROL NUMBER 2023946016
FIRST FANTAGRAPHICS BOOKS EDITION: APRIL 2024
PRINTED IN HONG KONG